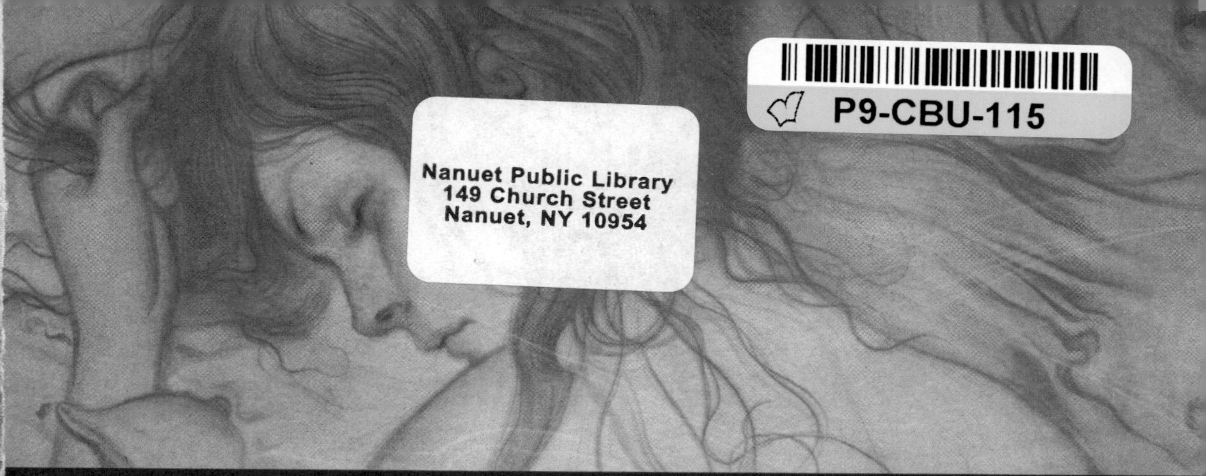

FABLES: ROSE RED

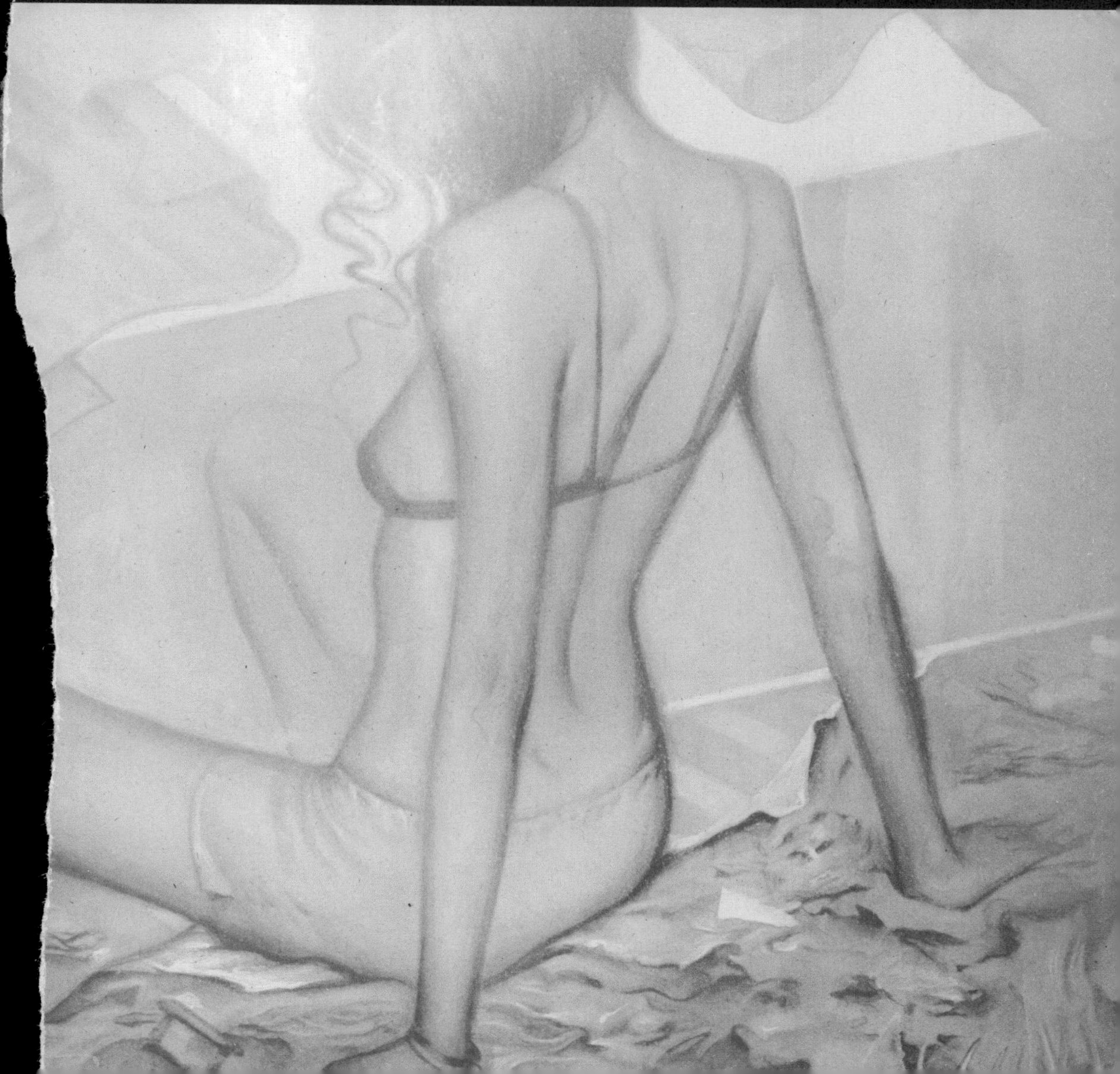

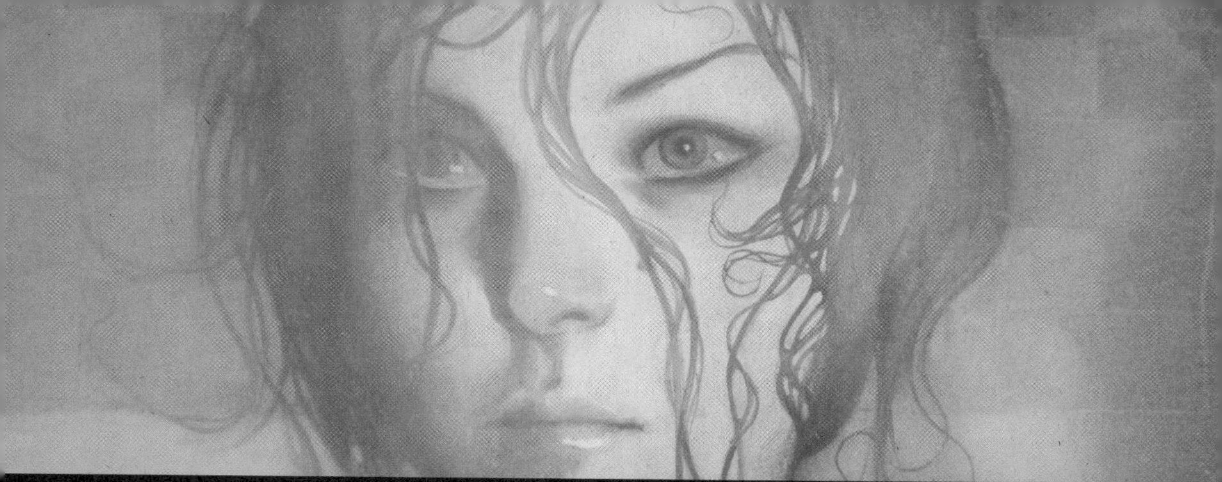

FABLES: ROSE RED

FABLES CREATED BY BILL WILLINGHAM

Bill Willingham
Writer

Mark Buckingham
Steve Leialoha
Inaki Miranda
Andrew Pepoy
Dan Green
Chrissie Zullo
Dave Johnson
Kate McElroy
J.H. Williams III
Joao Ruas
Adam Hughes
Artists

Lee Loughridge
Eva de la Cruz
Dave Stewart
Colorists

Todd Klein
Letterer

Joao Ruas
Cover Art and Original Series Covers

KAREN BERGER
Senior VP – Executive Editor

SHELLY BOND
Editor – Original Series

ANGELA RUFINO
Associate Editor – Original Series

GREGORY LOCKARD
Assistant Editor – Original Series

BOB HARRAS
Group Editor – Collected Editions

SCOTT NYBAKKEN
Editor

ROBBIN BROSTERMAN
Design Director – Books

DC COMICS

DIANE NELSON
President

DAN DIDIO AND **JIM LEE**
Co-Publishers

GEOFF JOHNS
Chief Creative Officer

PATRICK CALDON
EVP – Finance and Administration

JOHN ROOD
EVP – Sales, Marketing and
Business Development

AMY GENKINS
SVP – Business and Legal Affairs

STEVE ROTTERDAM
SVP – Sales and Marketing

JOHN CUNNINGHAM
VP – Marketing

TERRI CUNNINGHAM
VP – Managing Editor

ALISON GILL
VP – Manufacturing

DAVID HYDE
VP – Publicity

SUE POHJA
VP – Book Trade Sales

ALYSSE SOLL
VP – Advertising and Custom Publishing

BOB WAYNE
VP – Sales

MARK CHIARELLO
Art Director

*To Mark B and Ken L, two men,
experts in their respective fields, who've
kept me in the Fables game, alive, well,
and with undiminished enthusiasm to
keep telling "What happens next?"*
— Bill Willingham

*With a whole arc named after Rose Red,
who else could I dedicate this book
to other than my model for her,
my wonderful wife Irma.*
— Mark Buckingham

FABLES: ROSE RED

Published by DC Comics. Cover and compilation
Copyright © 2011 Bill Willingham and DC Comics.
All Rights Reserved.

Originally published in single magazine form
as FABLES 94-100. Copyright © 2010, 2011 Bill
Willingham and DC Comics. All Rights Reserved.
All characters, their distinctive likenesses and
related elements featured in this publication are
trademarks of Bill Willingham. VERTIGO is a
trademark of DC Comics. The stories, characters
and incidents featured in this publication are
entirely fictional. DC Comics does not read or
accept unsolicited submissions of ideas, stories
or artwork.

DC Comics, 1700 Broadway, New York, NY 10019
A Warner Bros. Entertainment Company.
Printed in the USA. First Printing.
ISBN: 978-1-4012-3000-5

SUSTAINABLE
FORESTRY
INITIATIVE

Certified Fiber Sourcing

www.sfiprogram.org

Fiber used in this product line meets the
sourcing requirements of the SFI program.
www.sfiprogram.org SGS-SFICOC-0130

Table of Contents

WHO'S WHO IN FABLETOWN

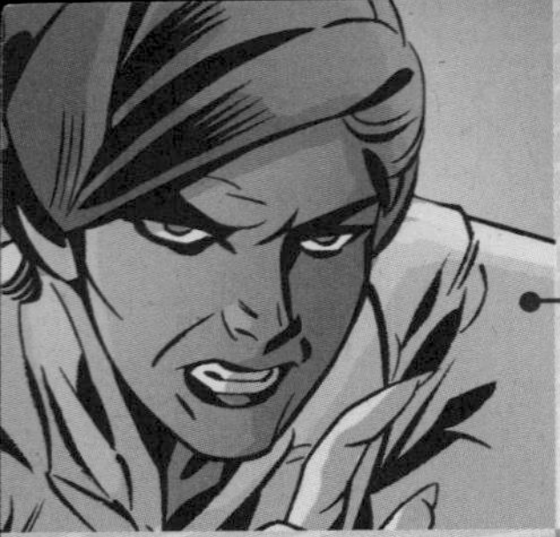

THE BLUE FAIRY

A powerfully magical being with an equally powerful grudge against her longtime tormentor, Geppetto.

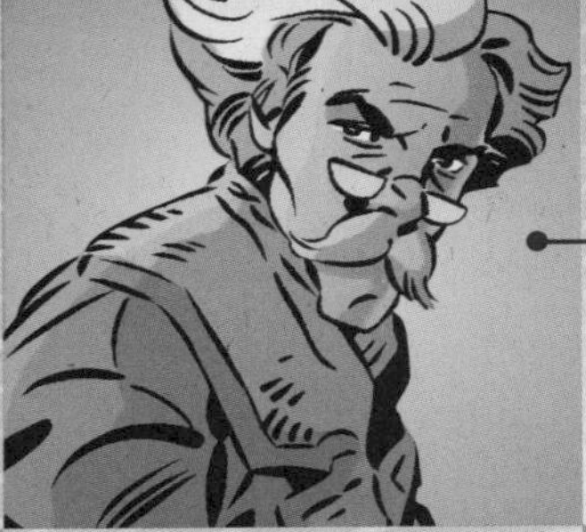

GEPPETTO

Once the ruler of countless worlds, Fabletown's former adversary continues to scheme as its newest citizen.

BEAST

Husband to Beauty and sheriff to Fabletown.

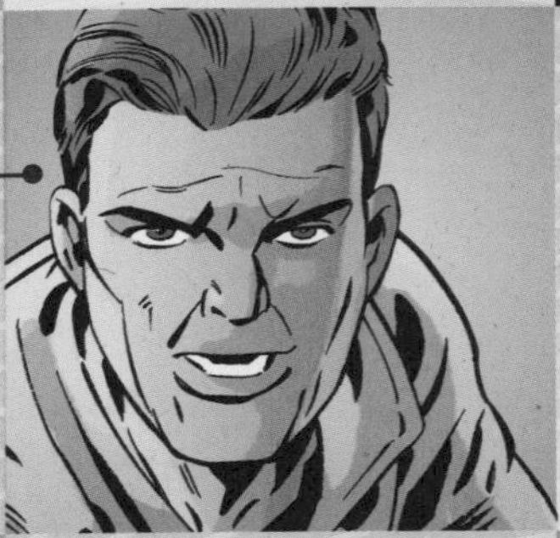

BEAUTY

Fabletown's deputy mayor and Beast's very pregnant wife.

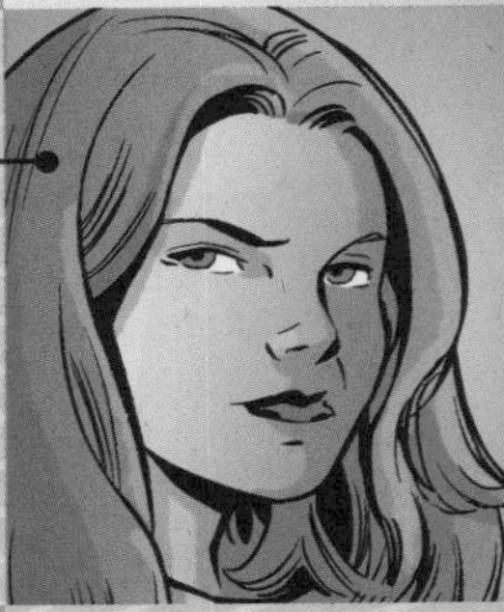

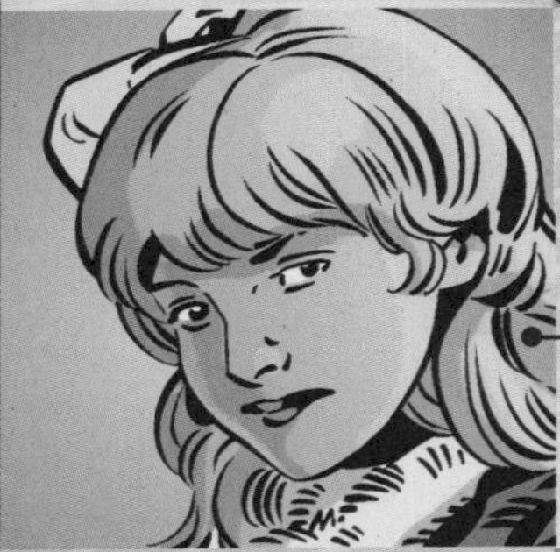

OZMA

The newly elected leader of Fabletown's cohort of witches, wizards and other magical types.

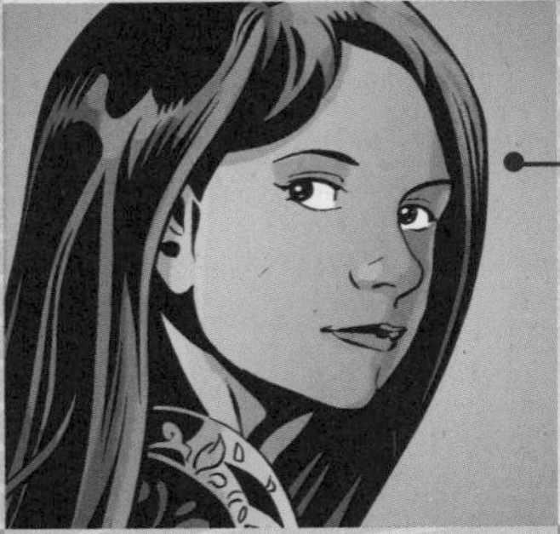

FRAU TOTENKINDER

Fabletown's oldest and most powerful witch, now returned to her original form and claiming the name Bellflower.

BIGBY

The celebrated Big Bad Wolf and former sheriff of Fabletown.

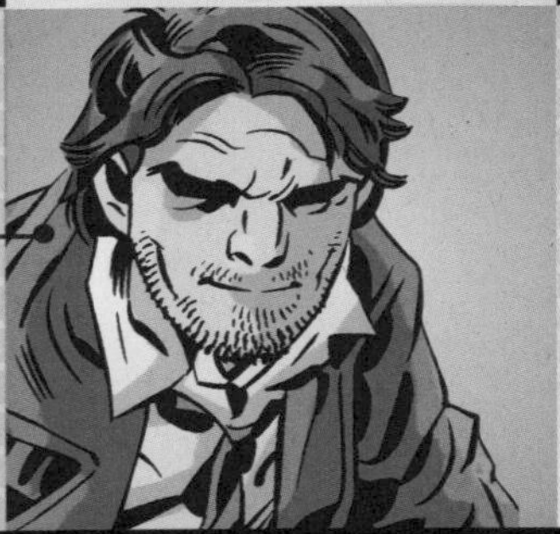

SNOW WHITE

Fabletown's former deputy mayor, wife of Bigby, and mother to their seven cubs.

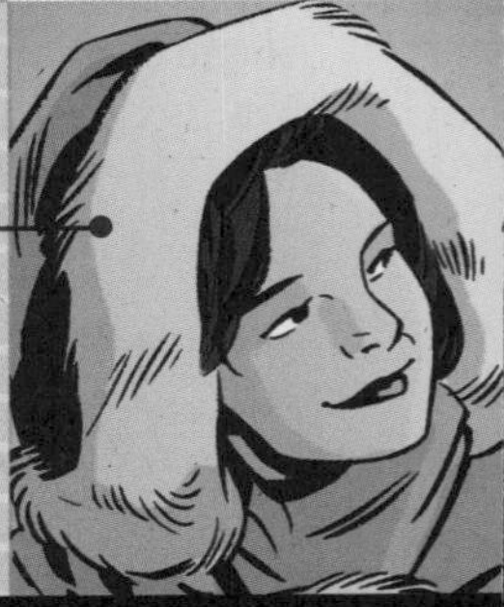

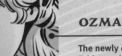

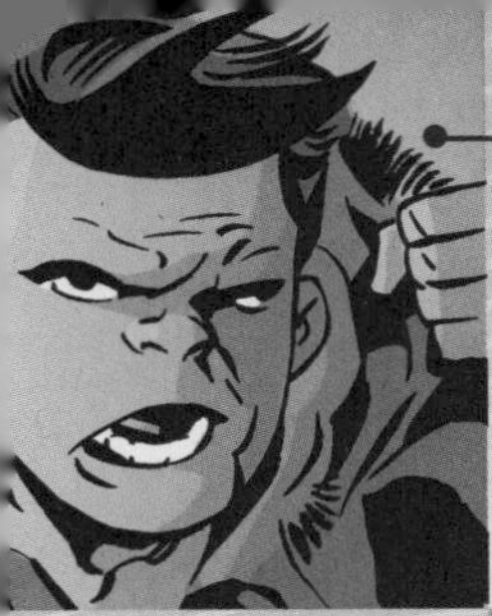

PINOCCHIO

Geppetto's first-carved son, poorly served by his centuries-old transformation into a real — but unchanging — boy.

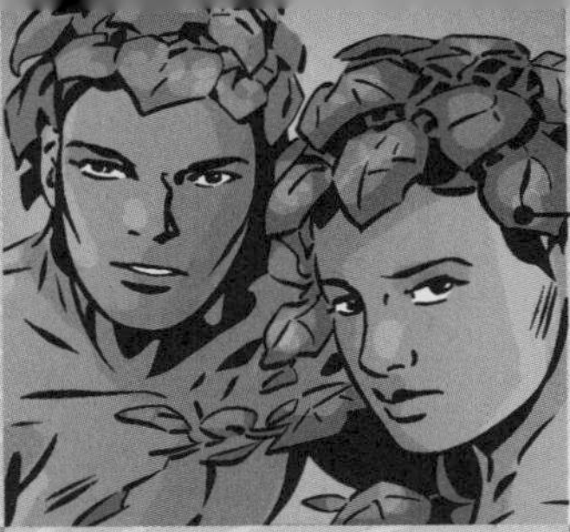

ASPEN AND ALDER

Brother and sister dryads, grown by the primeval forest's Grandfather Oak to serve as Geppetto's bodyguards.

OSE RED

now White's sister and
ne leader of the non-human
able community known as
ne Farm, she has been
edridden since the death
f Boy Blue.

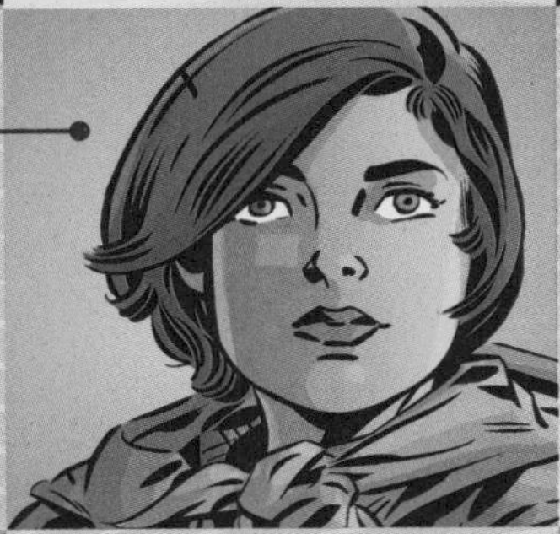

KING COLE

A canny politician and the mayor-in-exile of Fabletown.

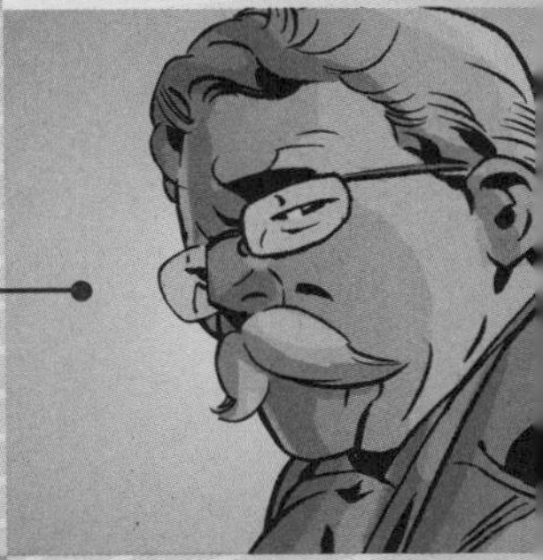

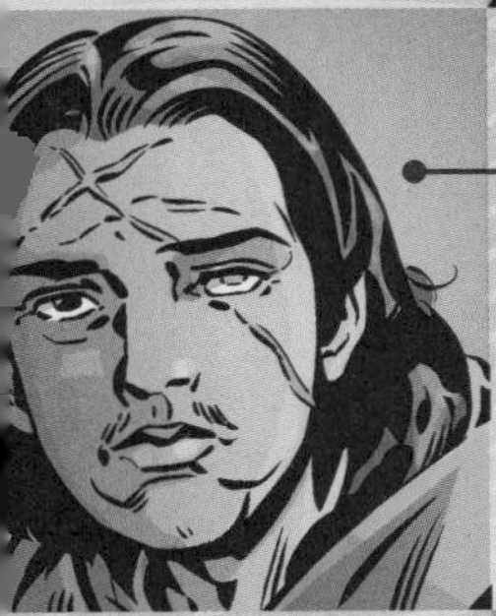

DUNSTER HAPP

A former commander of the Imperial Warlock Corps' élite Boxing League.

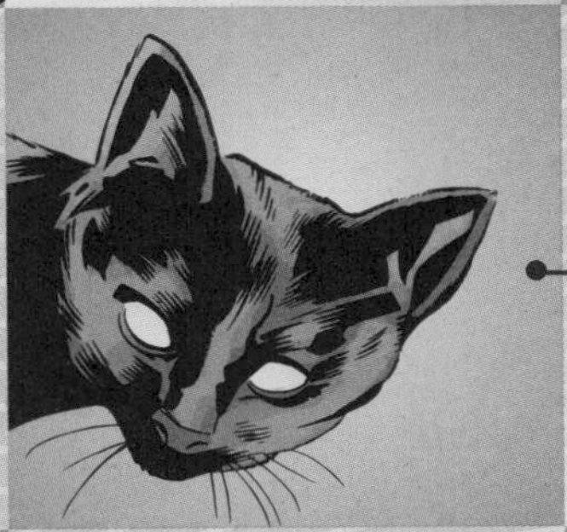

MADDY

Also known as the Invisible Walker, this Fable's stealth would shame an entire clan's worth of ninjas.

STINKY

low renamed Brock
lueheart in honor of Boy
lue, who will, he believes,
eturn from the dead to lead
he Fables to ultimate victory.

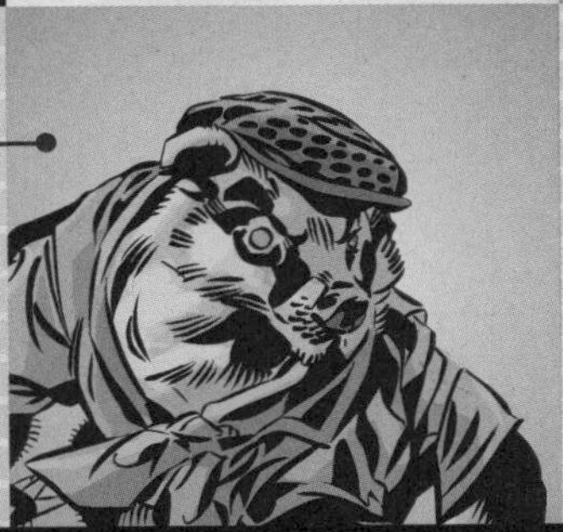

CLARA

A loyal retainer of Rose Red, with a surprising trick or two up her beak.

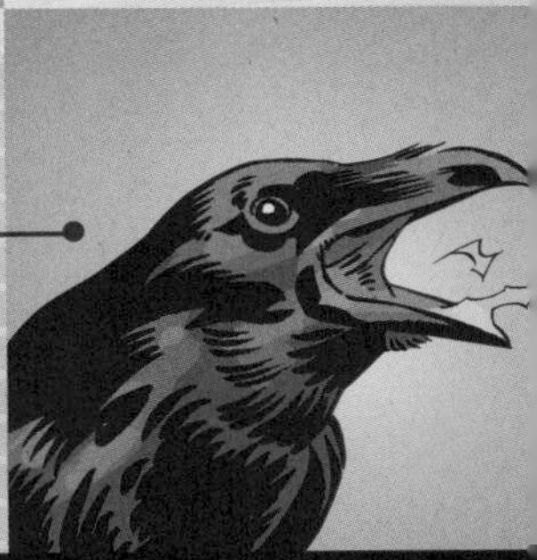

THE STORY SO FAR

Using his ever-growing army of undead witherlings, Mister Dark has begun transforming the ruins of Fabletown into the seat of his new kingdom of shadows. The surviving Free Fables, meanwhile, have retreated to the Farm to regroup and consider their options — none of which are especially good. But with the survival of the entire Mundane World hanging in the balance, drastic action is called for — and responsibility can no longer be shirked.

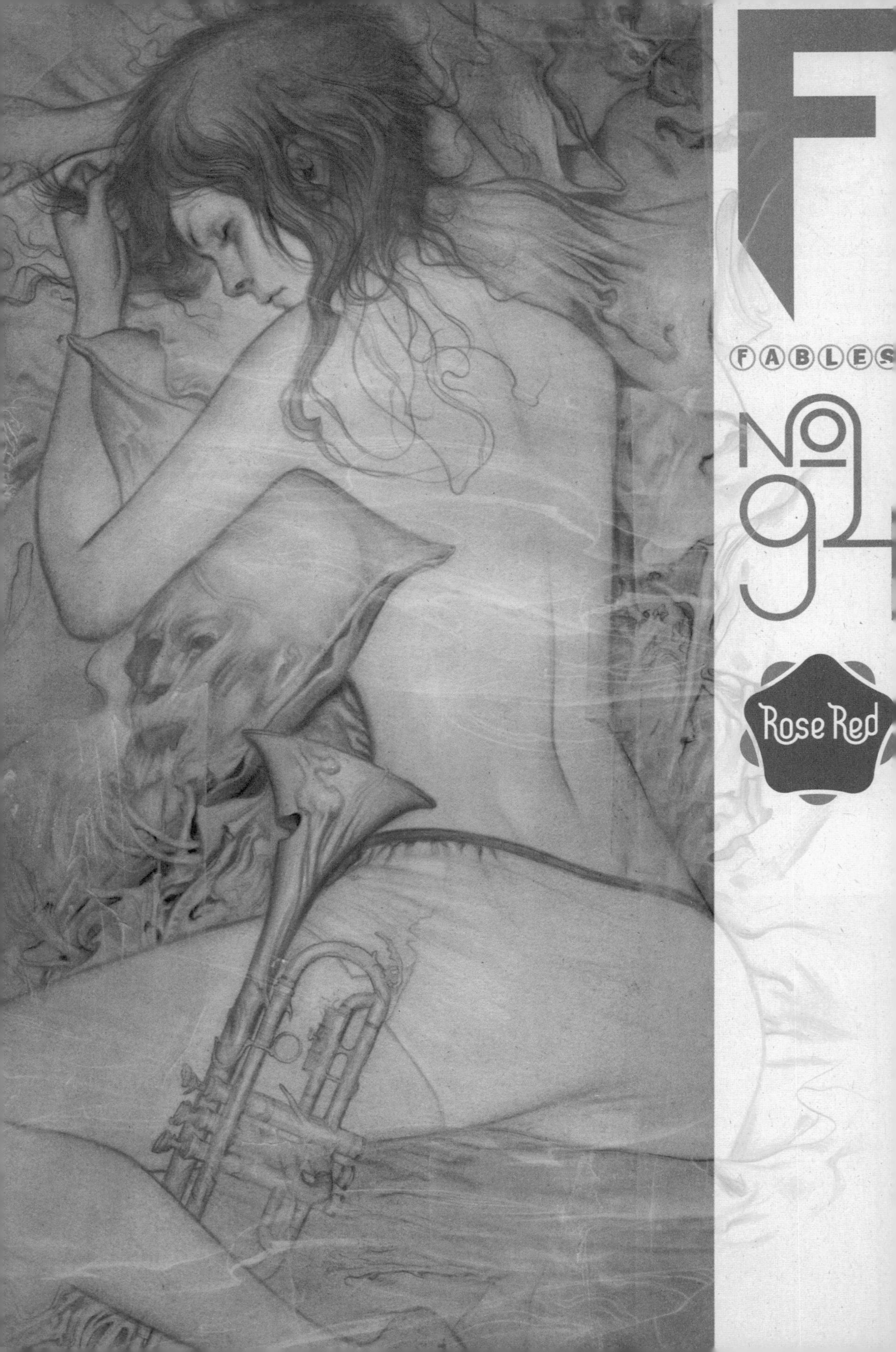
F
FABLES
No 94
Rose Red

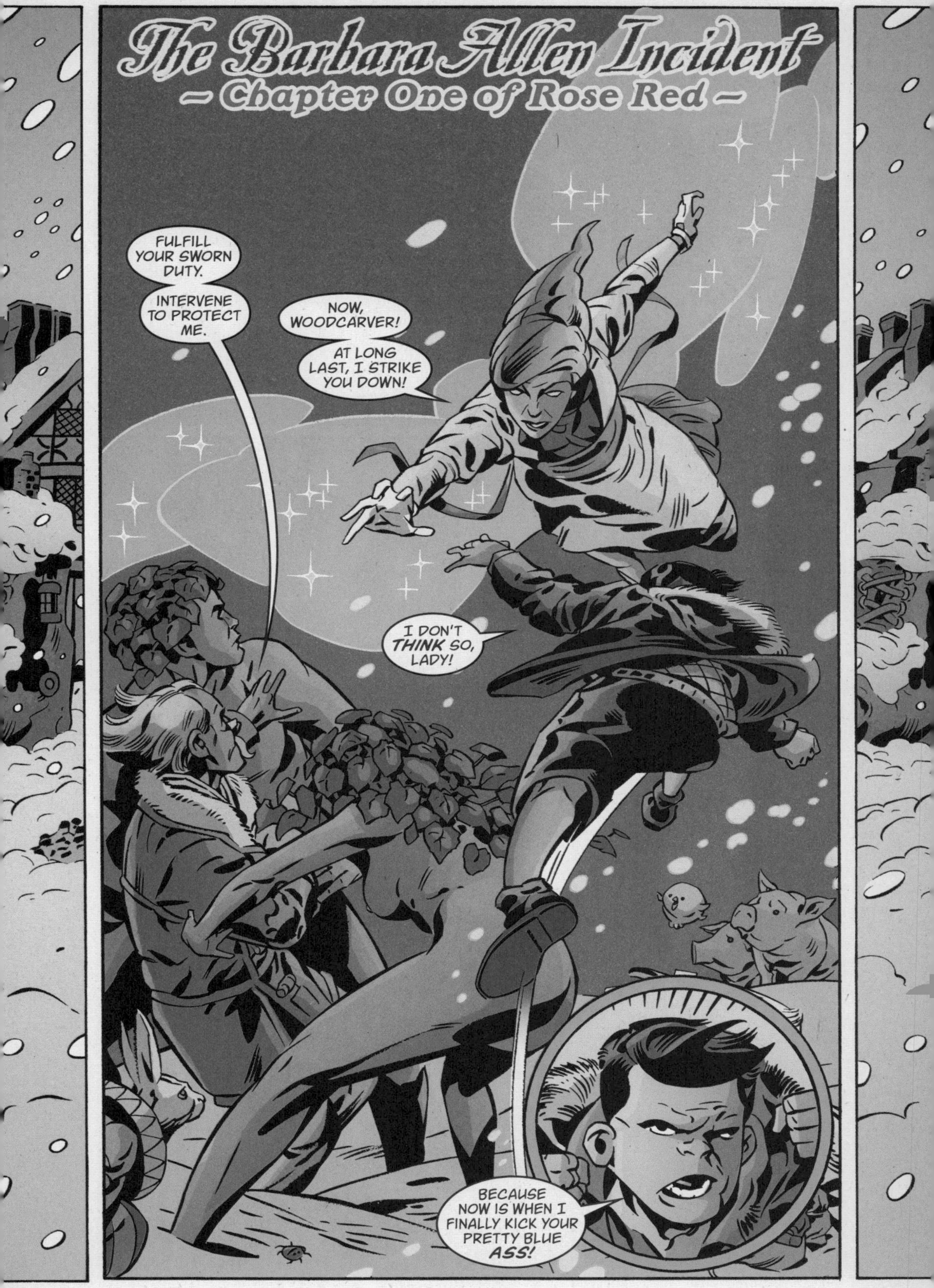
The Barbara Allen Incident
~ Chapter One of Rose Red ~
FULFILL YOUR SWORN DUTY.
INTERVENE TO PROTECT ME.
NOW, WOODCARVER!
AT LONG LAST, I STRIKE YOU DOWN!
I DON'T THINK SO, LADY!
BECAUSE NOW IS WHEN I FINALLY KICK YOUR PRETTY BLUE ASS!

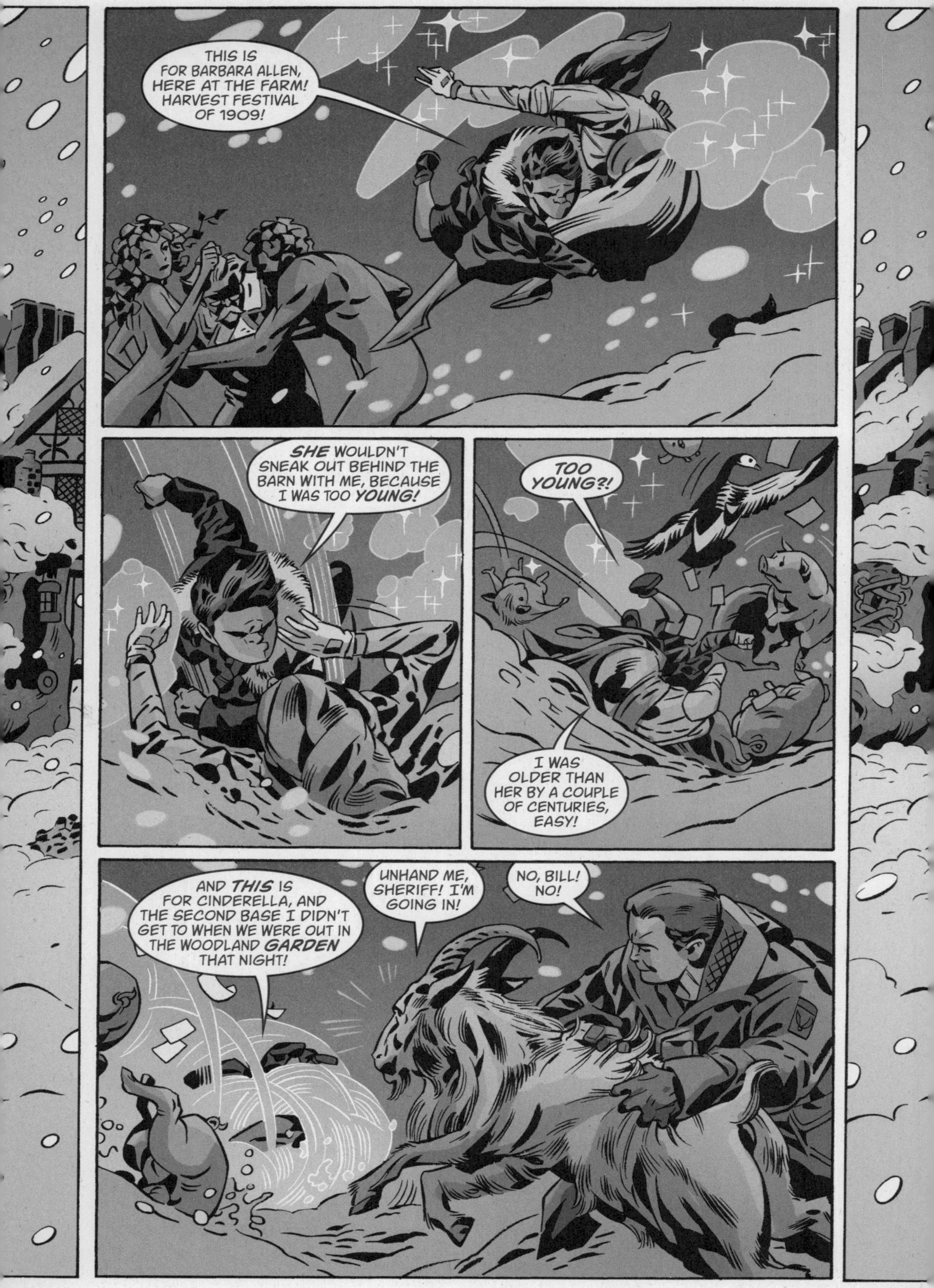
THIS IS FOR BARBARA ALLEN, HERE AT THE FARM! HARVEST FESTIVAL OF 1909!
SHE WOULDN'T SNEAK OUT BEHIND THE BARN WITH ME, BECAUSE I WAS TOO YOUNG!
TOO YOUNG?!
I WAS OLDER THAN HER BY A COUPLE OF CENTURIES, EASY!
AND THIS IS FOR CINDERELLA, AND THE SECOND BASE I DIDN'T GET TO WHEN WE WERE OUT IN THE WOODLAND GARDEN THAT NIGHT!
UNHAND ME, SHERIFF! I'M GOING IN!
NO, BILL! NO!

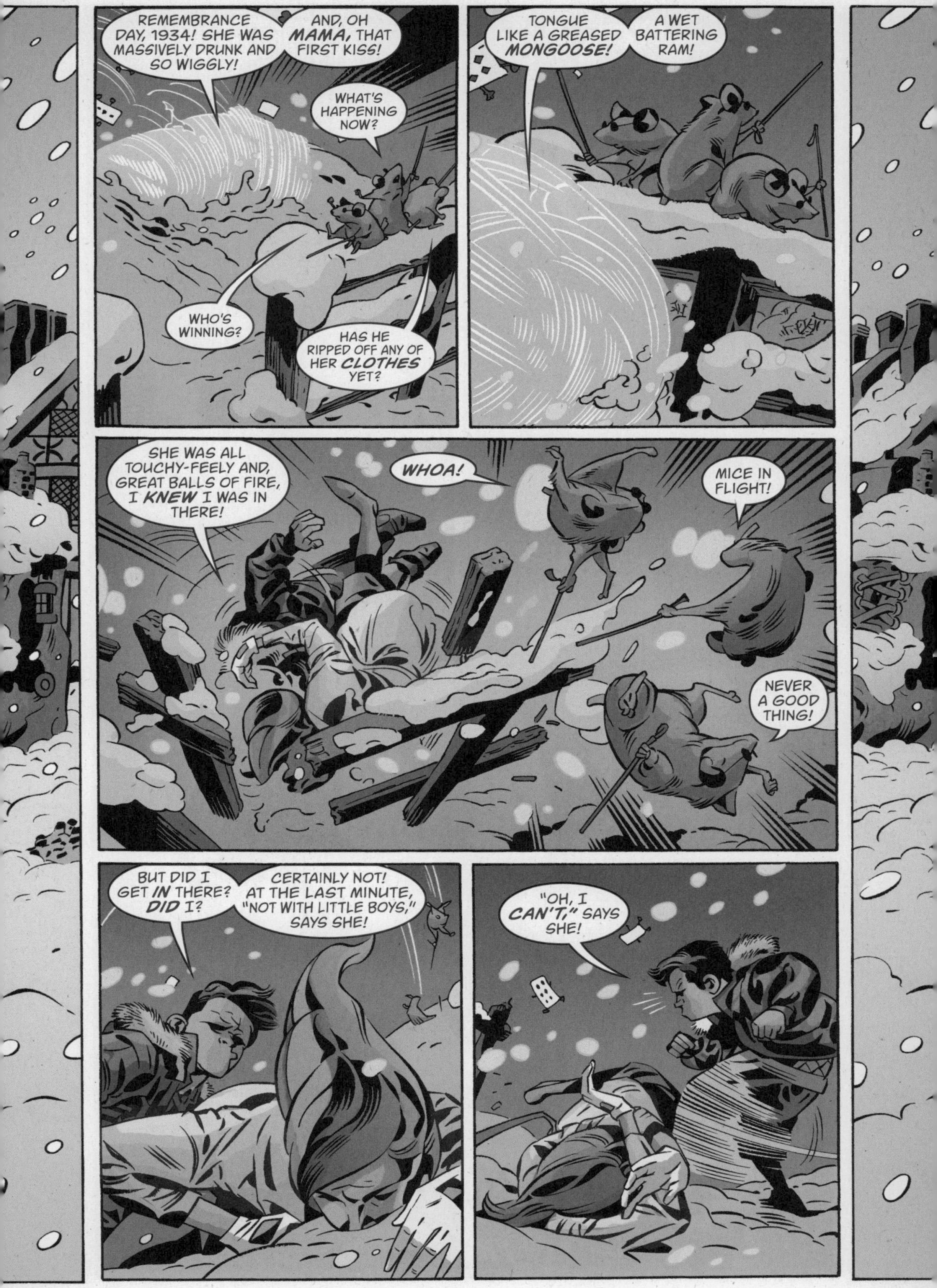
REMEMBRANCE DAY, 1934! SHE WAS MASSIVELY DRUNK AND SO WIGGLY!
AND, OH MAMA, THAT FIRST KISS!
WHAT'S HAPPENING NOW?
WHO'S WINNING?
HAS HE RIPPED OFF ANY OF HER CLOTHES YET?
TONGUE LIKE A GREASED MONGOOSE!
A WET BATTERING RAM!
SHE WAS ALL TOUCHY-FEELY AND, GREAT BALLS OF FIRE, I KNEW I WAS IN THERE!
WHOA!
MICE IN FLIGHT!
NEVER A GOOD THING!
BUT DID I GET IN THERE? DID I?
CERTAINLY NOT! AT THE LAST MINUTE, "NOT WITH LITTLE BOYS," SAYS SHE!
"OH, I CAN'T," SAYS SHE!

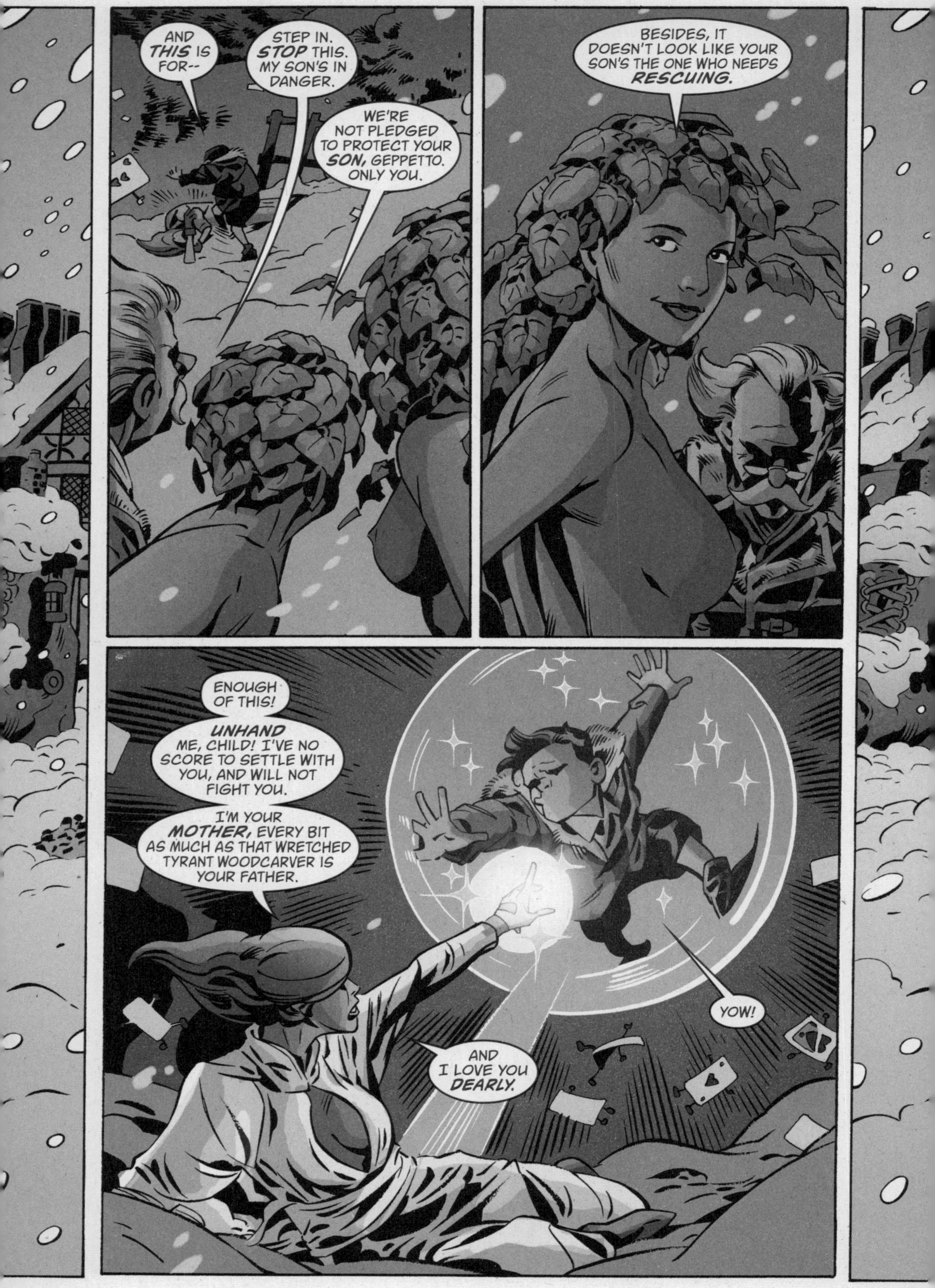
AND THIS IS FOR--
STEP IN. STOP THIS. MY SON'S IN DANGER.
WE'RE NOT PLEDGED TO PROTECT YOUR SON, GEPPETTO. ONLY YOU.
BESIDES, IT DOESN'T LOOK LIKE YOUR SON'S THE ONE WHO NEEDS RESCUING.
ENOUGH OF THIS!
UNHAND ME, CHILD! I'VE NO SCORE TO SETTLE WITH YOU, AND WILL NOT FIGHT YOU.
I'M YOUR MOTHER, EVERY BIT AS MUCH AS THAT WRETCHED TYRANT WOODCARVER IS YOUR FATHER.
YOW!
AND I LOVE YOU DEARLY.

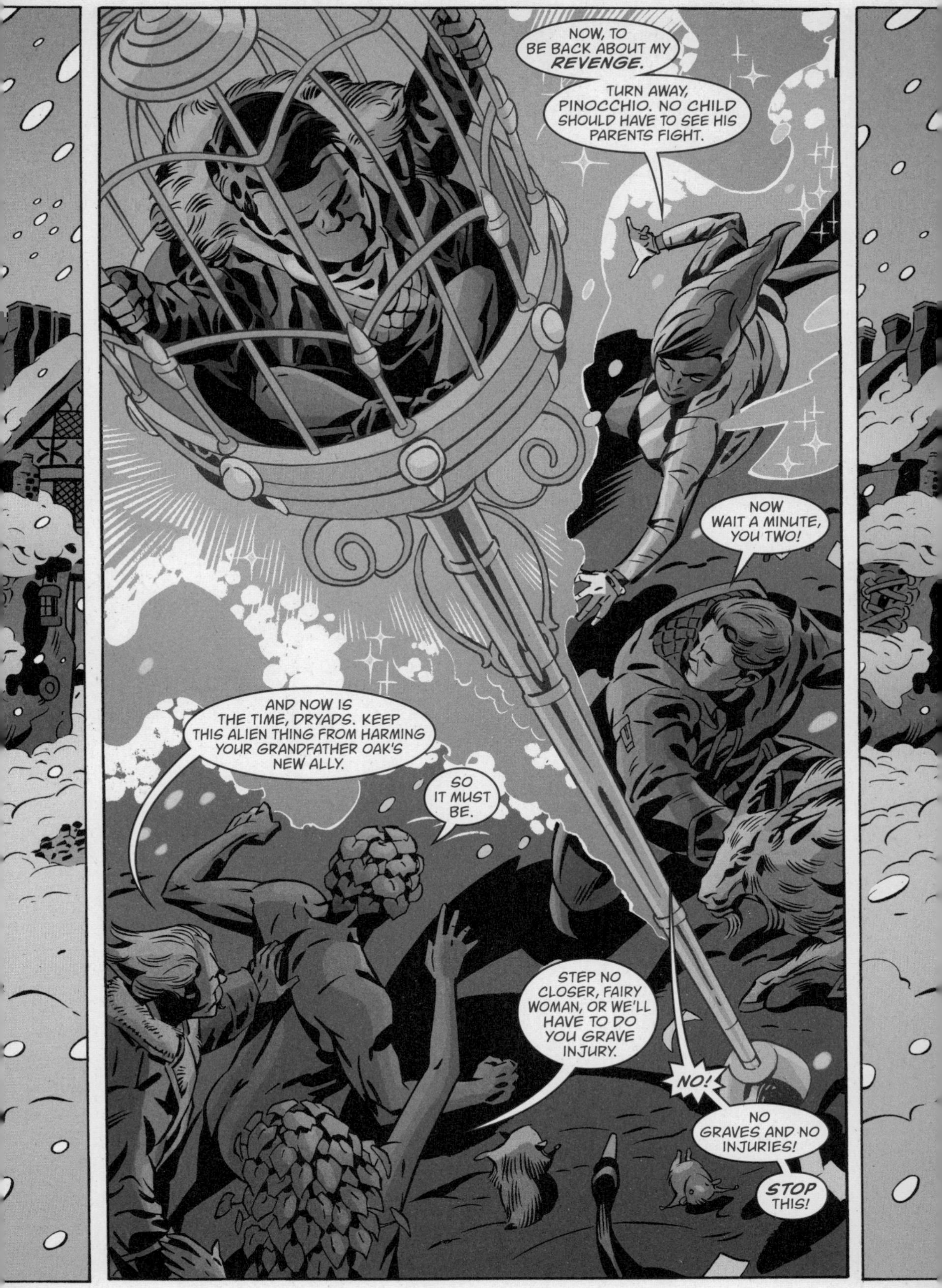
NOW, TO BE BACK ABOUT MY *REVENGE.*
TURN AWAY, PINOCCHIO. NO CHILD SHOULD HAVE TO SEE HIS PARENTS FIGHT.
NOW WAIT A MINUTE, YOU TWO!
AND NOW IS THE TIME, DRYADS. KEEP THIS ALIEN THING FROM HARMING YOUR GRANDFATHER OAK'S NEW ALLY.
SO IT MUST BE.
STEP NO CLOSER, FAIRY WOMAN, OR WE'LL HAVE TO DO YOU GRAVE INJURY.
NO!
NO GRAVES AND NO INJURIES!
STOP THIS!

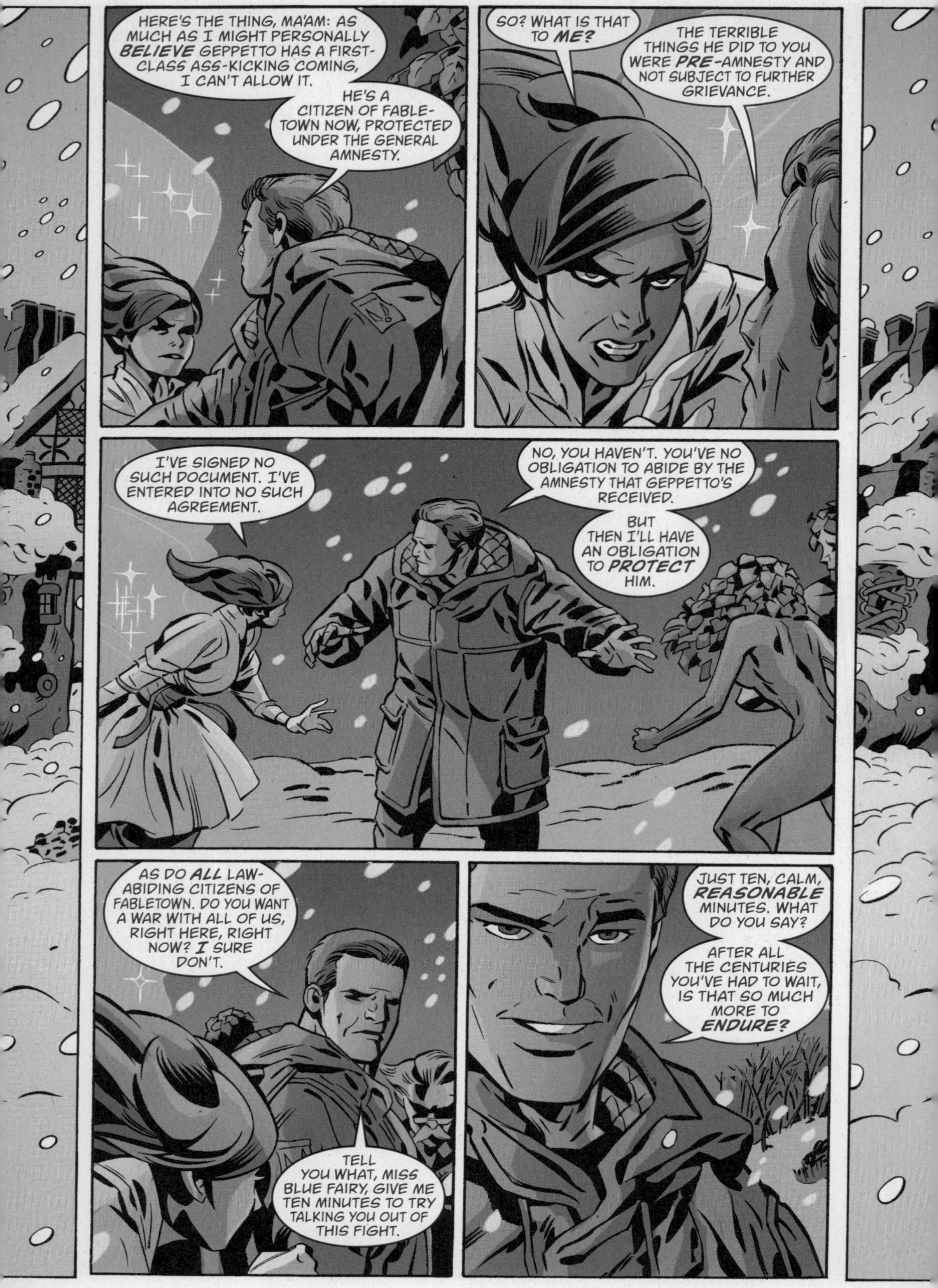
HERE'S THE THING, MA'AM: AS MUCH AS I MIGHT PERSONALLY BELIEVE GEPPETTO HAS A FIRST-CLASS ASS-KICKING COMING, I CAN'T ALLOW IT.
HE'S A CITIZEN OF FABLE-TOWN NOW, PROTECTED UNDER THE GENERAL AMNESTY.
SO? WHAT IS THAT TO ME?
THE TERRIBLE THINGS HE DID TO YOU WERE PRE-AMNESTY AND NOT SUBJECT TO FURTHER GRIEVANCE.
I'VE SIGNED NO SUCH DOCUMENT. I'VE ENTERED INTO NO SUCH AGREEMENT.
NO, YOU HAVEN'T. YOU'VE NO OBLIGATION TO ABIDE BY THE AMNESTY THAT GEPPETTO'S RECEIVED.
BUT THEN I'LL HAVE AN OBLIGATION TO PROTECT HIM.
AS DO ALL LAW-ABIDING CITIZENS OF FABLETOWN. DO YOU WANT A WAR WITH ALL OF US, RIGHT HERE, RIGHT NOW? I SURE DON'T.
TELL YOU WHAT, MISS BLUE FAIRY, GIVE ME TEN MINUTES TO TRY TALKING YOU OUT OF THIS FIGHT.
JUST TEN, CALM, REASONABLE MINUTES. WHAT DO YOU SAY?
AFTER ALL THE CENTURIES YOU'VE HAD TO WAIT, IS THAT SO MUCH MORE TO ENDURE?

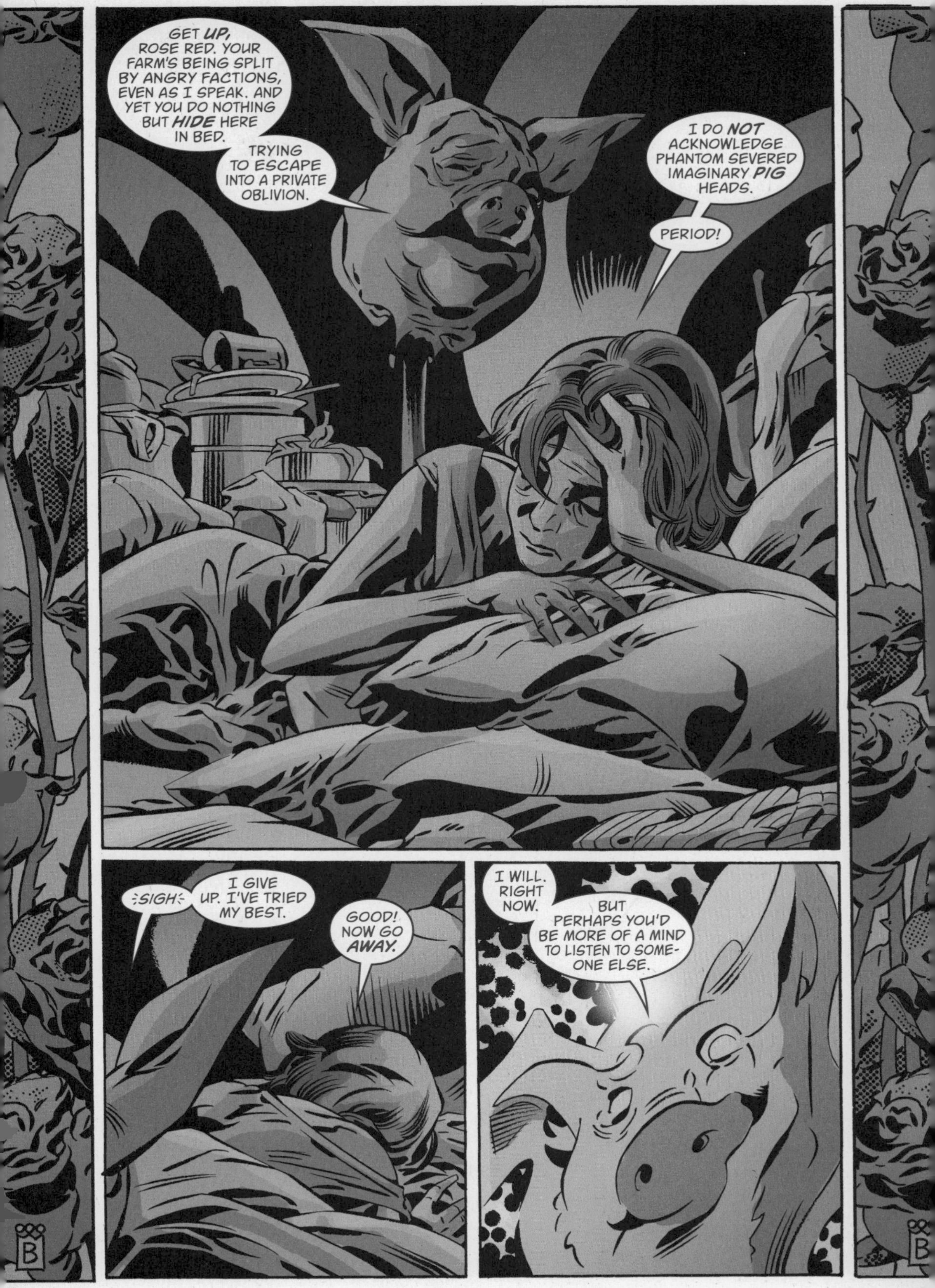
GET *UP*, ROSE RED. YOUR FARM'S BEING SPLIT BY ANGRY FACTIONS, EVEN AS I SPEAK. AND YET YOU DO NOTHING BUT *HIDE* HERE IN BED.
TRYING TO ESCAPE INTO A PRIVATE OBLIVION.
I DO *NOT* ACKNOWLEDGE PHANTOM SEVERED IMAGINARY *PIG* HEADS.
PERIOD!
SIGH
I GIVE UP. I'VE TRIED MY BEST.
GOOD! NOW GO *AWAY.*
I WILL. RIGHT NOW.
BUT PERHAPS YOU'D BE MORE OF A MIND TO LISTEN TO SOME-ONE ELSE.

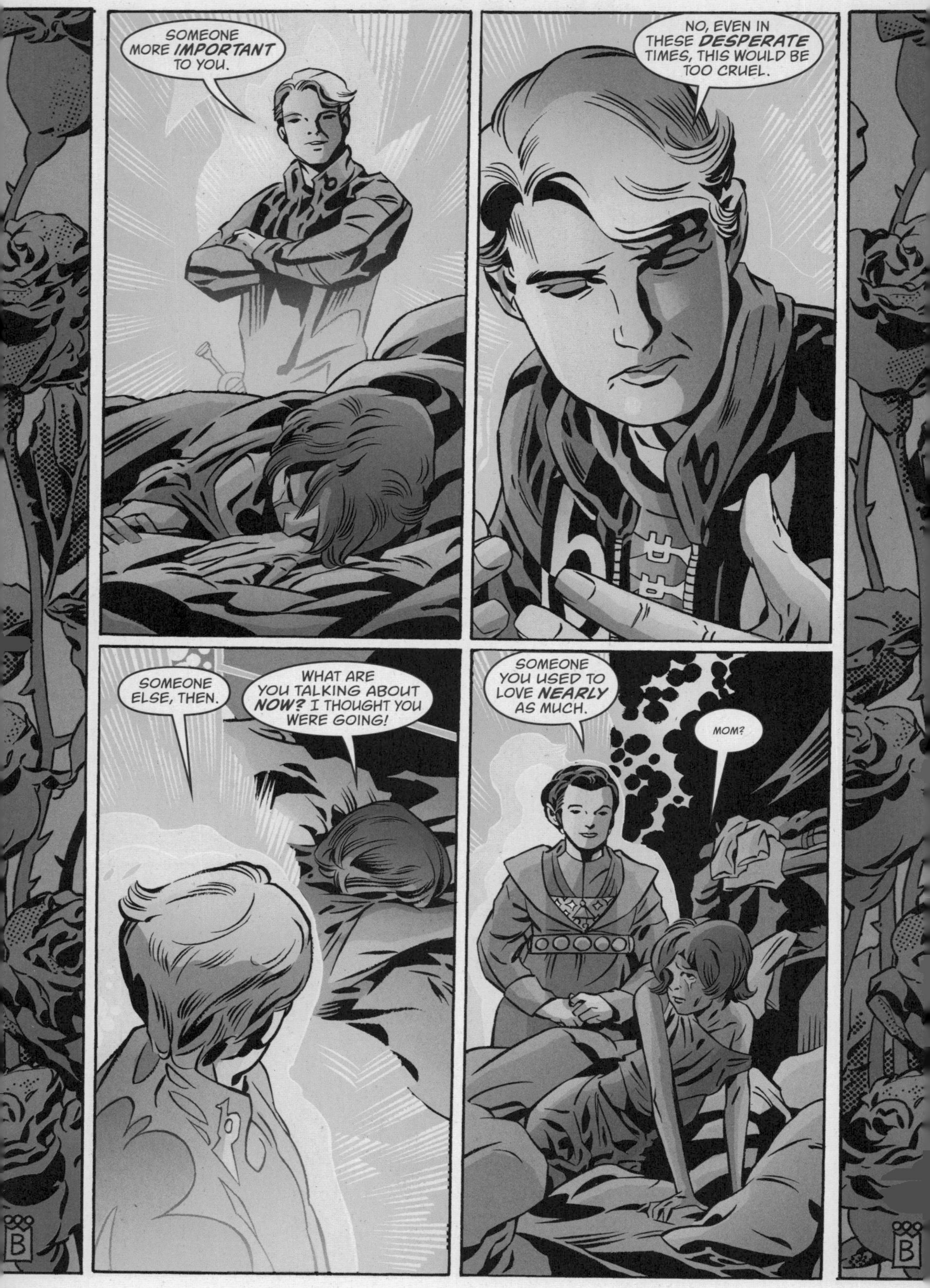
SOMEONE MORE IMPORTANT TO YOU.
NO, EVEN IN THESE DESPERATE TIMES, THIS WOULD BE TOO CRUEL.
SOMEONE ELSE, THEN.
WHAT ARE YOU TALKING ABOUT NOW? I THOUGHT YOU WERE GOING!
SOMEONE YOU USED TO LOVE NEARLY AS MUCH.
MOM?

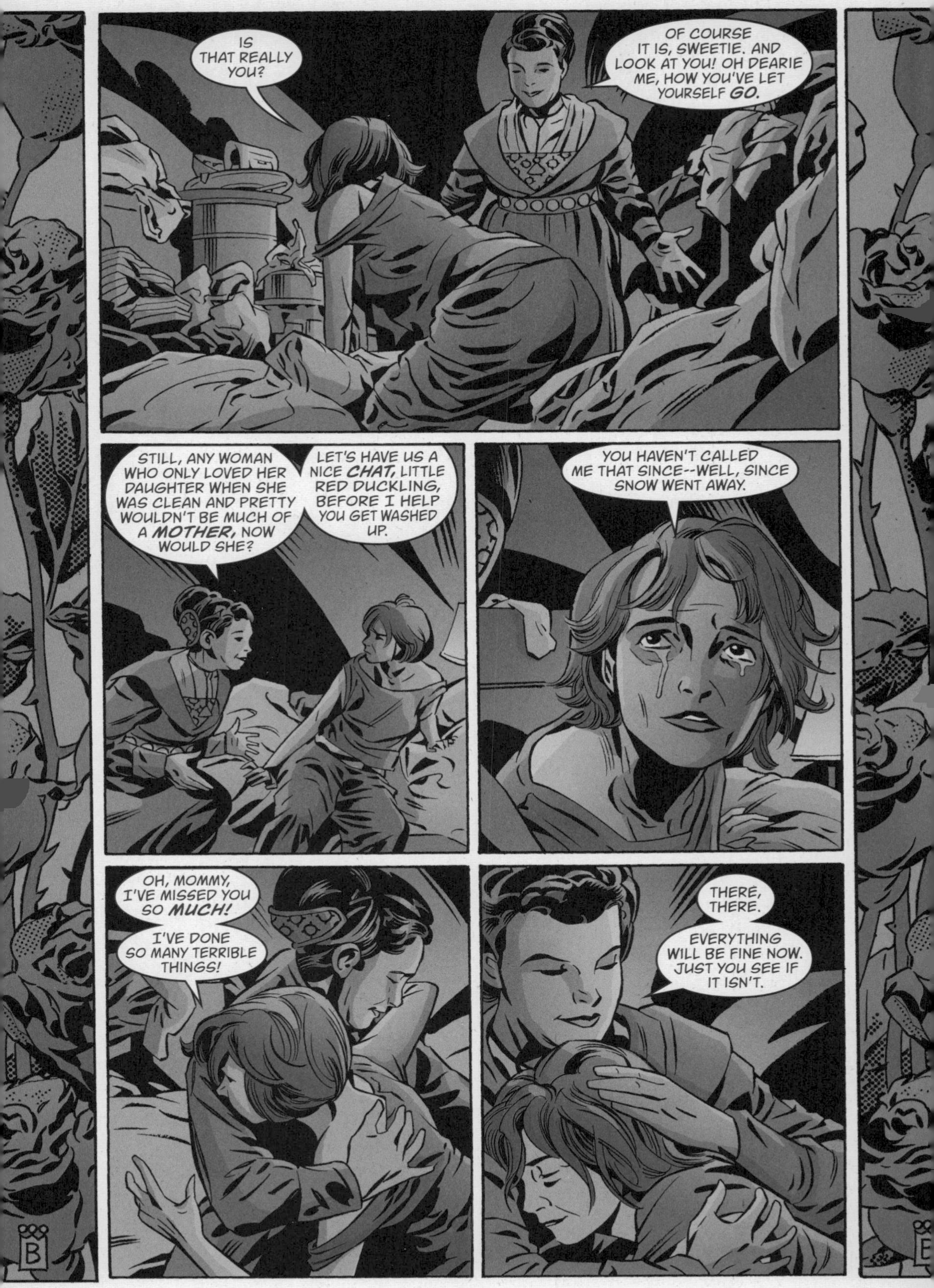
IS THAT REALLY YOU?
OF COURSE IT IS, SWEETIE. AND LOOK AT YOU! OH DEARIE ME, HOW YOU'VE LET YOURSELF GO.
STILL, ANY WOMAN WHO ONLY LOVED HER DAUGHTER WHEN SHE WAS CLEAN AND PRETTY WOULDN'T BE MUCH OF A MOTHER, NOW WOULD SHE?
LET'S HAVE US A NICE CHAT, LITTLE RED DUCKLING, BEFORE I HELP YOU GET WASHED UP.
YOU HAVEN'T CALLED ME THAT SINCE--WELL, SINCE SNOW WENT AWAY.
OH, MOMMY, I'VE MISSED YOU SO MUCH!
I'VE DONE SO MANY TERRIBLE THINGS!
THERE, THERE.
EVERYTHING WILL BE FINE NOW. JUST YOU SEE IF IT ISN'T.

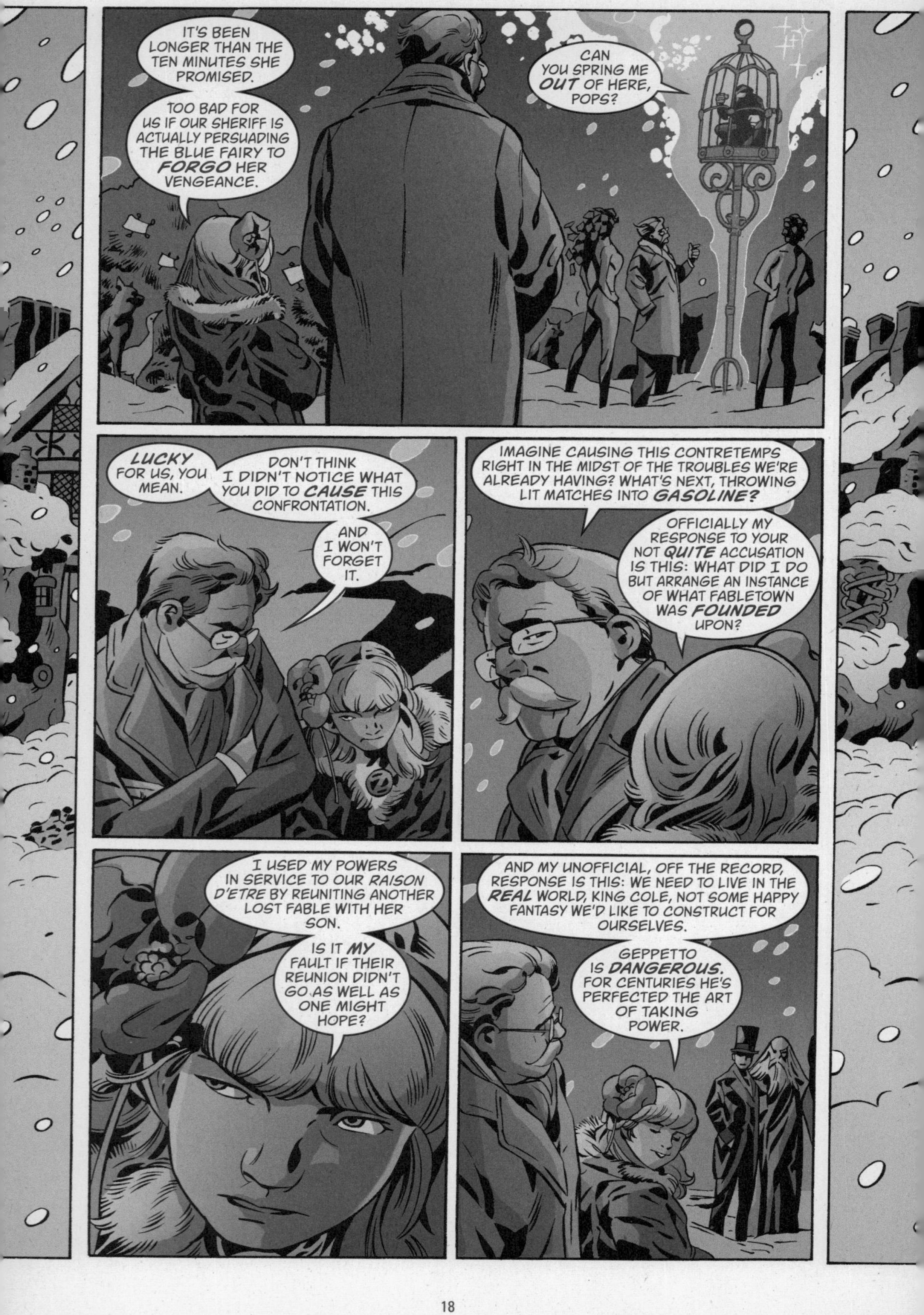
IT'S BEEN LONGER THAN THE TEN MINUTES SHE PROMISED.
TOO BAD FOR US IF OUR SHERIFF IS ACTUALLY PERSUADING THE BLUE FAIRY TO FORGO HER VENGEANCE.
CAN YOU SPRING ME OUT OF HERE, POPS?
LUCKY FOR US, YOU MEAN.
DON'T THINK I DIDN'T NOTICE WHAT YOU DID TO CAUSE THIS CONFRONTATION.
AND I WON'T FORGET IT.
IMAGINE CAUSING THIS CONTRETEMPS RIGHT IN THE MIDST OF THE TROUBLES WE'RE ALREADY HAVING? WHAT'S NEXT, THROWING LIT MATCHES INTO GASOLINE?
OFFICIALLY MY RESPONSE TO YOUR NOT QUITE ACCUSATION IS THIS: WHAT DID I DO BUT ARRANGE AN INSTANCE OF WHAT FABLETOWN WAS FOUNDED UPON?
I USED MY POWERS IN SERVICE TO OUR RAISON D'ETRE BY REUNITING ANOTHER LOST FABLE WITH HER SON.
IS IT MY FAULT IF THEIR REUNION DIDN'T GO AS WELL AS ONE MIGHT HOPE?
AND MY UNOFFICIAL, OFF THE RECORD, RESPONSE IS THIS: WE NEED TO LIVE IN THE REAL WORLD, KING COLE, NOT SOME HAPPY FANTASY WE'D LIKE TO CONSTRUCT FOR OURSELVES.
GEPPETTO IS DANGEROUS. FOR CENTURIES HE'S PERFECTED THE ART OF TAKING POWER.

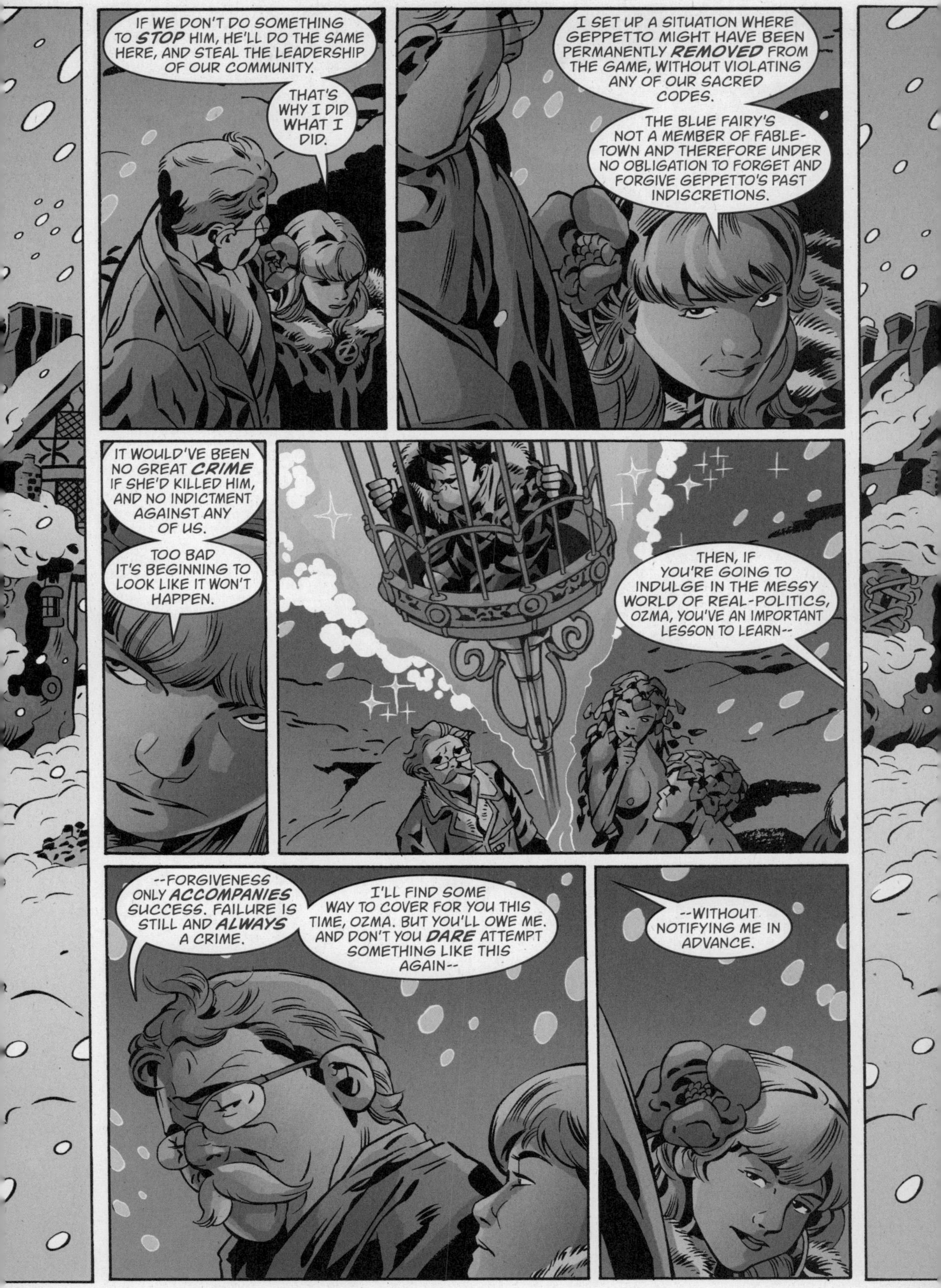
IF WE DON'T DO SOMETHING TO STOP HIM, HE'LL DO THE SAME HERE, AND STEAL THE LEADERSHIP OF OUR COMMUNITY.
THAT'S WHY I DID WHAT I DID.
I SET UP A SITUATION WHERE GEPPETTO MIGHT HAVE BEEN PERMANENTLY REMOVED FROM THE GAME, WITHOUT VIOLATING ANY OF OUR SACRED CODES.
THE BLUE FAIRY'S NOT A MEMBER OF FABLE-TOWN AND THEREFORE UNDER NO OBLIGATION TO FORGET AND FORGIVE GEPPETTO'S PAST INDISCRETIONS.
IT WOULD'VE BEEN NO GREAT CRIME IF SHE'D KILLED HIM, AND NO INDICTMENT AGAINST ANY OF US.
TOO BAD IT'S BEGINNING TO LOOK LIKE IT WON'T HAPPEN.
THEN, IF YOU'RE GOING TO INDULGE IN THE MESSY WORLD OF REAL-POLITICS, OZMA, YOU'VE AN IMPORTANT LESSON TO LEARN--
--FORGIVENESS ONLY ACCOMPANIES SUCCESS. FAILURE IS STILL AND ALWAYS A CRIME.
I'LL FIND SOME WAY TO COVER FOR YOU THIS TIME, OZMA. BUT YOU'LL OWE ME. AND DON'T YOU DARE ATTEMPT SOMETHING LIKE THIS AGAIN--
--WITHOUT NOTIFYING ME IN ADVANCE.

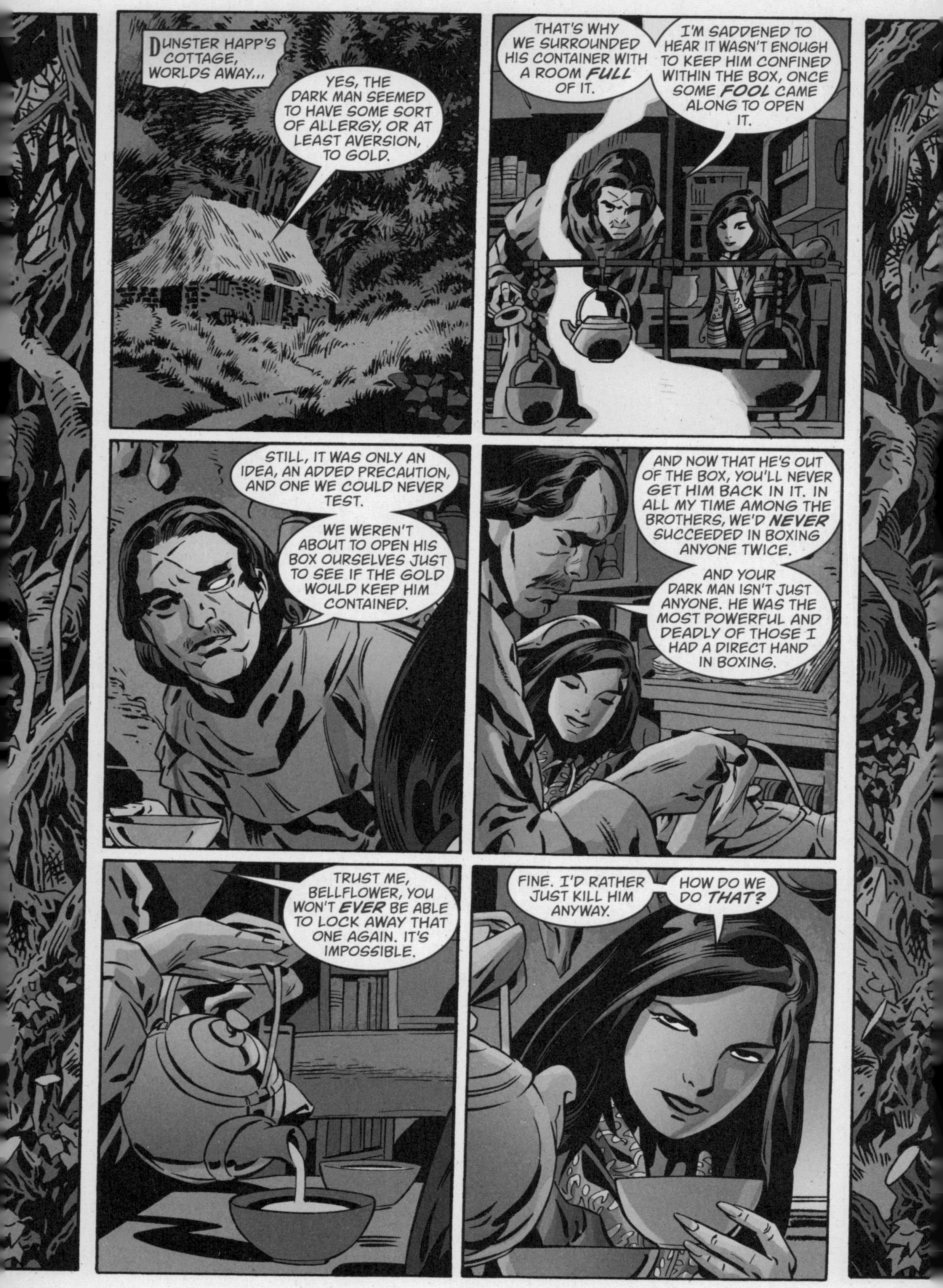
DUNSTER HAPP'S COTTAGE, WORLDS AWAY...
YES, THE DARK MAN SEEMED TO HAVE SOME SORT OF ALLERGY, OR AT LEAST AVERSION, TO GOLD.
THAT'S WHY WE SURROUNDED HIS CONTAINER WITH A ROOM FULL OF IT.
I'M SADDENED TO HEAR IT WASN'T ENOUGH TO KEEP HIM CONFINED WITHIN THE BOX, ONCE SOME FOOL CAME ALONG TO OPEN IT.
STILL, IT WAS ONLY AN IDEA, AN ADDED PRECAUTION, AND ONE WE COULD NEVER TEST.
WE WEREN'T ABOUT TO OPEN HIS BOX OURSELVES JUST TO SEE IF THE GOLD WOULD KEEP HIM CONTAINED.
AND NOW THAT HE'S OUT OF THE BOX, YOU'LL NEVER GET HIM BACK IN IT. IN ALL MY TIME AMONG THE BROTHERS, WE'D NEVER SUCCEEDED IN BOXING ANYONE TWICE.
AND YOUR DARK MAN ISN'T JUST ANYONE. HE WAS THE MOST POWERFUL AND DEADLY OF THOSE I HAD A DIRECT HAND IN BOXING.
TRUST ME, BELLFLOWER, YOU WON'T EVER BE ABLE TO LOCK AWAY THAT ONE AGAIN. IT'S IMPOSSIBLE.
FINE. I'D RATHER JUST KILL HIM ANYWAY.
HOW DO WE DO THAT?

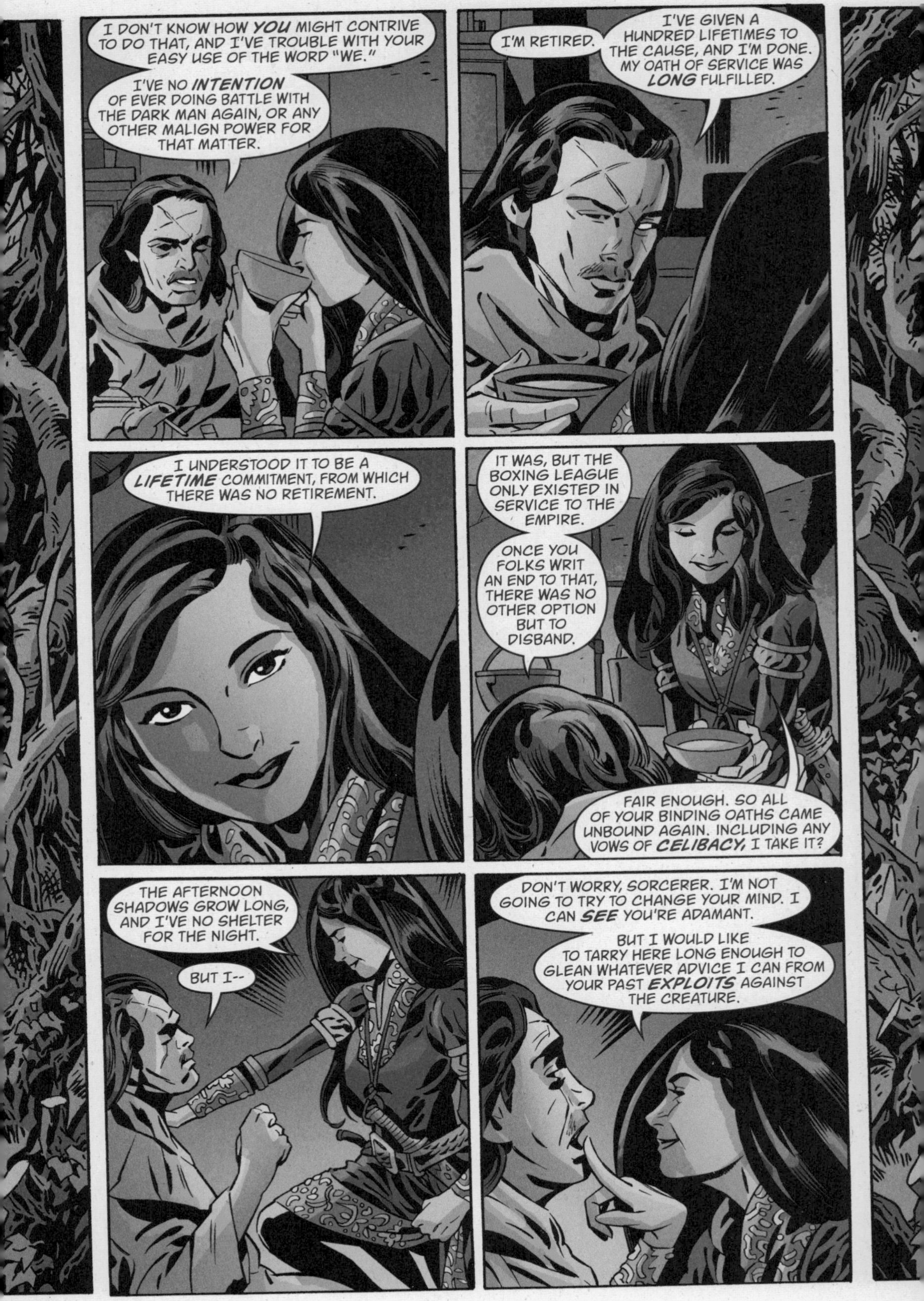
I DON'T KNOW HOW *YOU* MIGHT CONTRIVE TO DO THAT, AND I'VE TROUBLE WITH YOUR EASY USE OF THE WORD "WE."
I'VE NO *INTENTION* OF EVER DOING BATTLE WITH THE DARK MAN AGAIN, OR ANY OTHER MALIGN POWER FOR THAT MATTER.
I'M RETIRED.
I'VE GIVEN A HUNDRED LIFETIMES TO THE CAUSE, AND I'M DONE. MY OATH OF SERVICE WAS *LONG* FULFILLED.
I UNDERSTOOD IT TO BE A *LIFETIME* COMMITMENT, FROM WHICH THERE WAS NO RETIREMENT.
IT WAS, BUT THE BOXING LEAGUE ONLY EXISTED IN SERVICE TO THE EMPIRE.
ONCE YOU FOLKS WRIT AN END TO THAT, THERE WAS NO OTHER OPTION BUT TO DISBAND.
FAIR ENOUGH. SO ALL OF YOUR BINDING OATHS CAME UNBOUND AGAIN. INCLUDING ANY VOWS OF *CELIBACY,* I TAKE IT?
THE AFTERNOON SHADOWS GROW LONG, AND I'VE NO SHELTER FOR THE NIGHT.
BUT I--
DON'T WORRY, SORCERER. I'M NOT GOING TO TRY TO CHANGE YOUR MIND. I CAN *SEE* YOU'RE ADAMANT.
BUT I WOULD LIKE TO TARRY HERE LONG ENOUGH TO GLEAN WHATEVER ADVICE I CAN FROM YOUR PAST *EXPLOITS* AGAINST THE CREATURE.

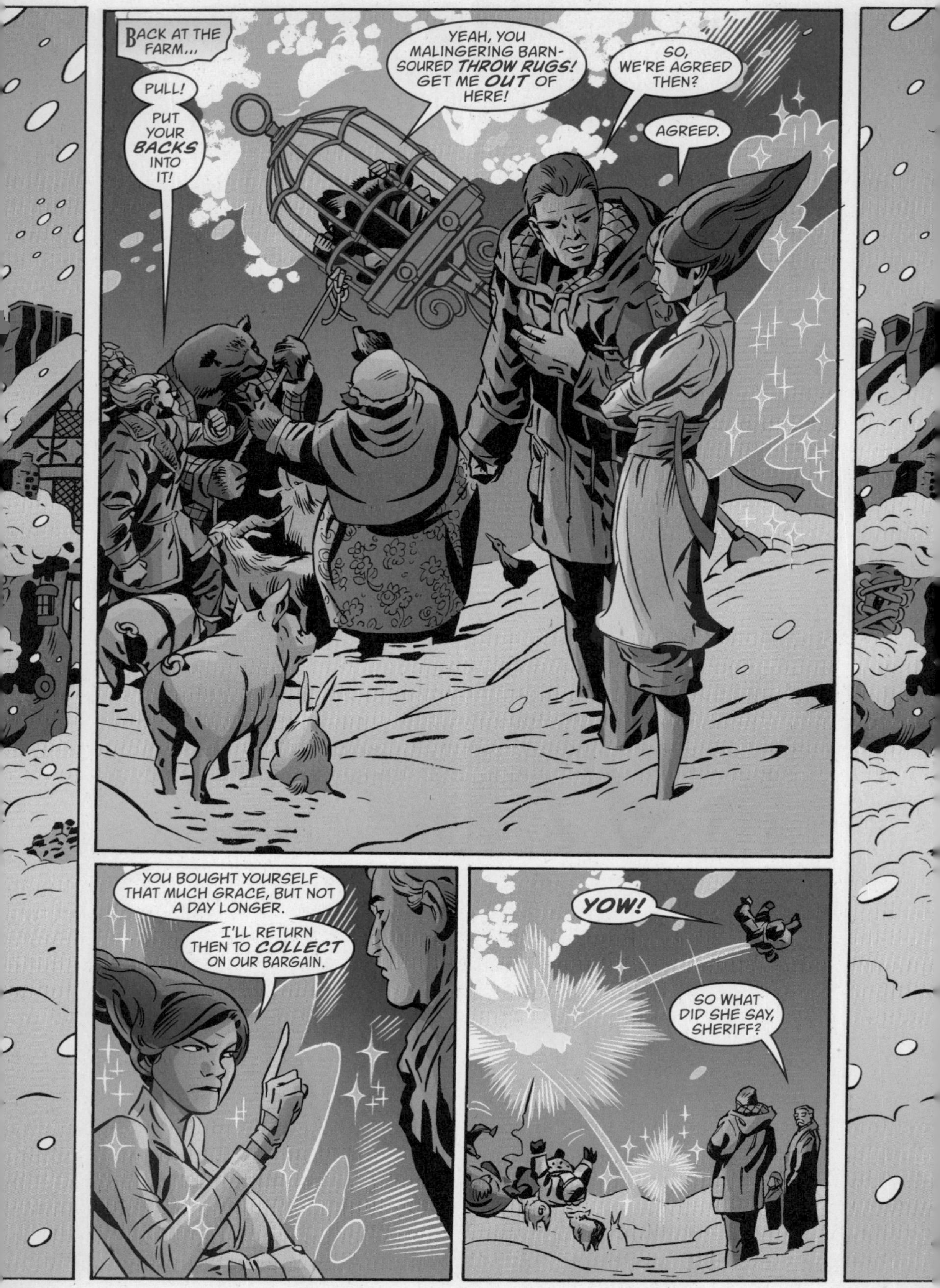

BACK AT THE FARM...
PULL!
PUT YOUR BACKS INTO IT!
YEAH, YOU MALINGERING BARN-SOURED THROW RUGS! GET ME OUT OF HERE!
SO, WE'RE AGREED THEN?
AGREED.
YOU BOUGHT YOURSELF THAT MUCH GRACE, BUT NOT A DAY LONGER.
I'LL RETURN THEN TO COLLECT ON OUR BARGAIN.
YOW!
SO WHAT DID SHE SAY, SHERIFF?

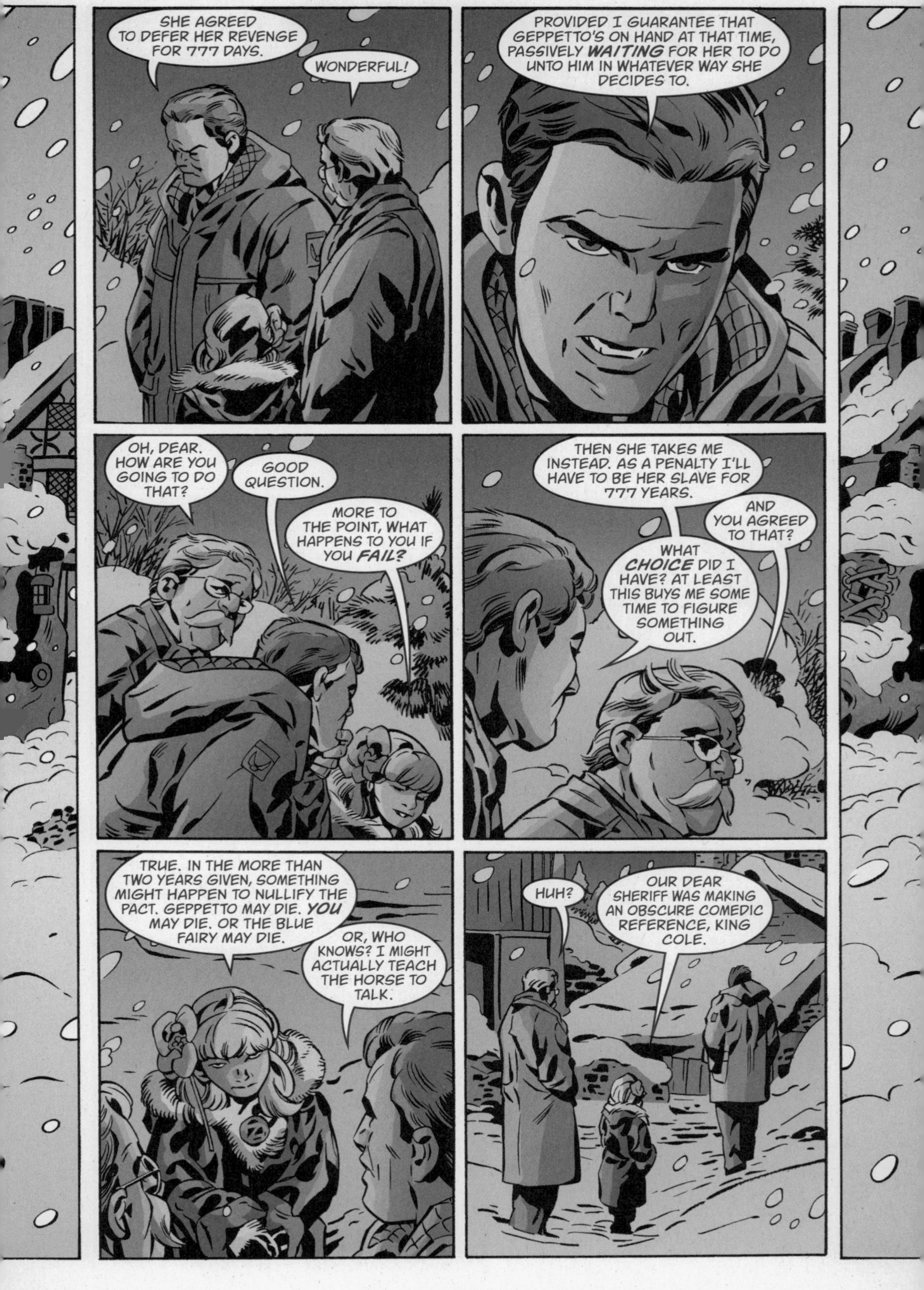
SHE AGREED TO DEFER HER REVENGE FOR 777 DAYS.
WONDERFUL!
PROVIDED I GUARANTEE THAT GEPPETTO'S ON HAND AT THAT TIME, PASSIVELY WAITING FOR HER TO DO UNTO HIM IN WHATEVER WAY SHE DECIDES TO.
OH, DEAR. HOW ARE YOU GOING TO DO THAT?
GOOD QUESTION.
MORE TO THE POINT, WHAT HAPPENS TO YOU IF YOU FAIL?
THEN SHE TAKES ME INSTEAD. AS A PENALTY I'LL HAVE TO BE HER SLAVE FOR 777 YEARS.
AND YOU AGREED TO THAT?
WHAT CHOICE DID I HAVE? AT LEAST THIS BUYS ME SOME TIME TO FIGURE SOMETHING OUT.
TRUE. IN THE MORE THAN TWO YEARS GIVEN, SOMETHING MIGHT HAPPEN TO NULLIFY THE PACT. GEPPETTO MAY DIE. YOU MAY DIE. OR THE BLUE FAIRY MAY DIE.
OR, WHO KNOWS? I MIGHT ACTUALLY TEACH THE HORSE TO TALK.
HUH?
OUR DEAR SHERIFF WAS MAKING AN OBSCURE COMEDIC REFERENCE, KING COLE.

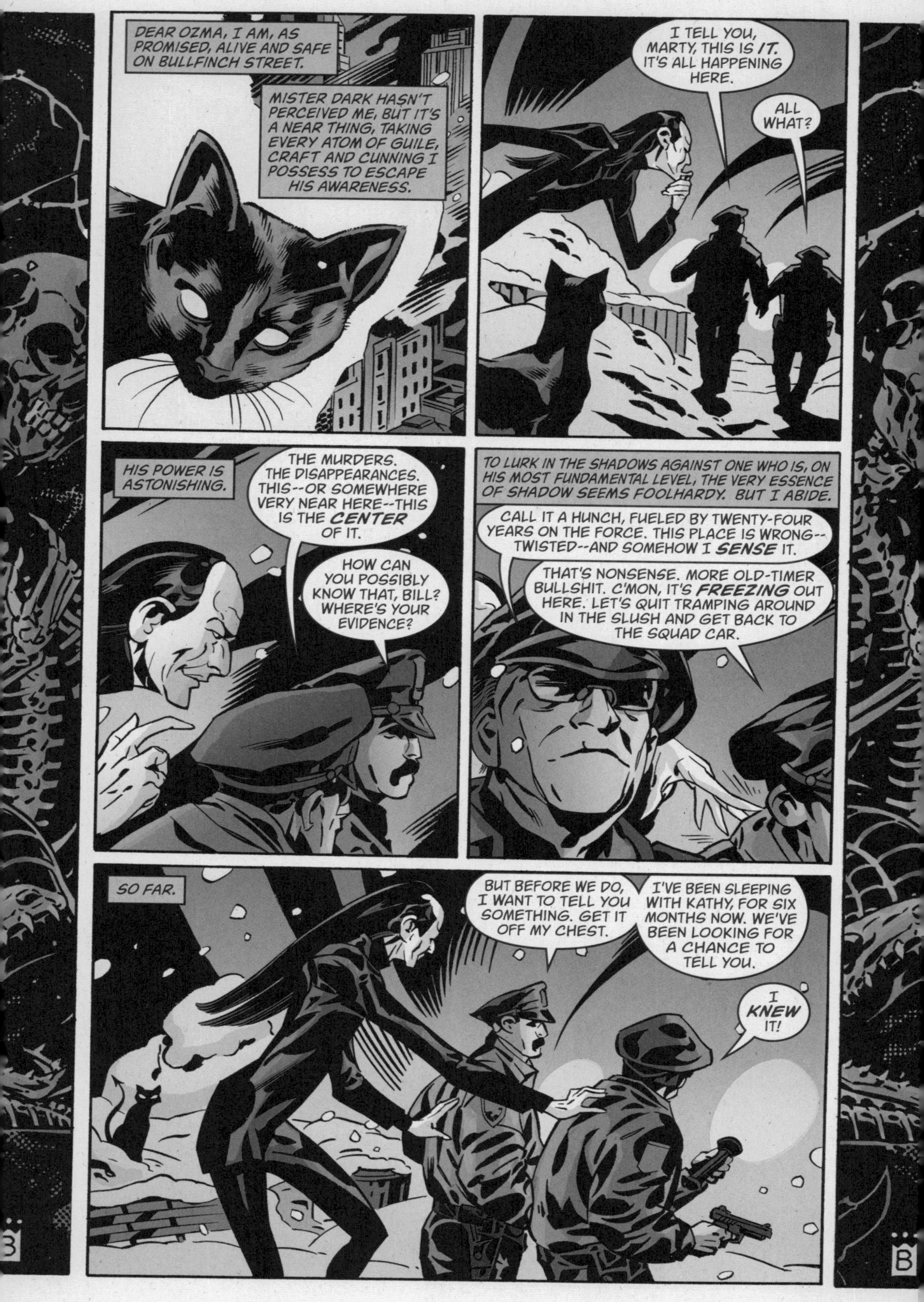
DEAR OZMA, I AM, AS PROMISED, ALIVE AND SAFE ON BULLFINCH STREET.
MISTER DARK HASN'T PERCEIVED ME, BUT IT'S A NEAR THING, TAKING EVERY ATOM OF GUILE, CRAFT AND CUNNING I POSSESS TO ESCAPE HIS AWARENESS.
I TELL YOU, MARTY, THIS IS IT. IT'S ALL HAPPENING HERE.
ALL WHAT?
HIS POWER IS ASTONISHING.
THE MURDERS. THE DISAPPEARANCES. THIS--OR SOMEWHERE VERY NEAR HERE--THIS IS THE CENTER OF IT.
HOW CAN YOU POSSIBLY KNOW THAT, BILL? WHERE'S YOUR EVIDENCE?
TO LURK IN THE SHADOWS AGAINST ONE WHO IS, ON HIS MOST FUNDAMENTAL LEVEL, THE VERY ESSENCE OF SHADOW SEEMS FOOLHARDY. BUT I ABIDE.
CALL IT A HUNCH, FUELED BY TWENTY-FOUR YEARS ON THE FORCE. THIS PLACE IS WRONG-- TWISTED--AND SOMEHOW I SENSE IT.
THAT'S NONSENSE. MORE OLD-TIMER BULLSHIT. C'MON, IT'S FREEZING OUT HERE. LET'S QUIT TRAMPING AROUND IN THE SLUSH AND GET BACK TO THE SQUAD CAR.
SO FAR.
BUT BEFORE WE DO, I WANT TO TELL YOU SOMETHING. GET IT OFF MY CHEST.
I'VE BEEN SLEEPING WITH KATHY, FOR SIX MONTHS NOW. WE'VE BEEN LOOKING FOR A CHANCE TO TELL YOU.
I KNEW IT!

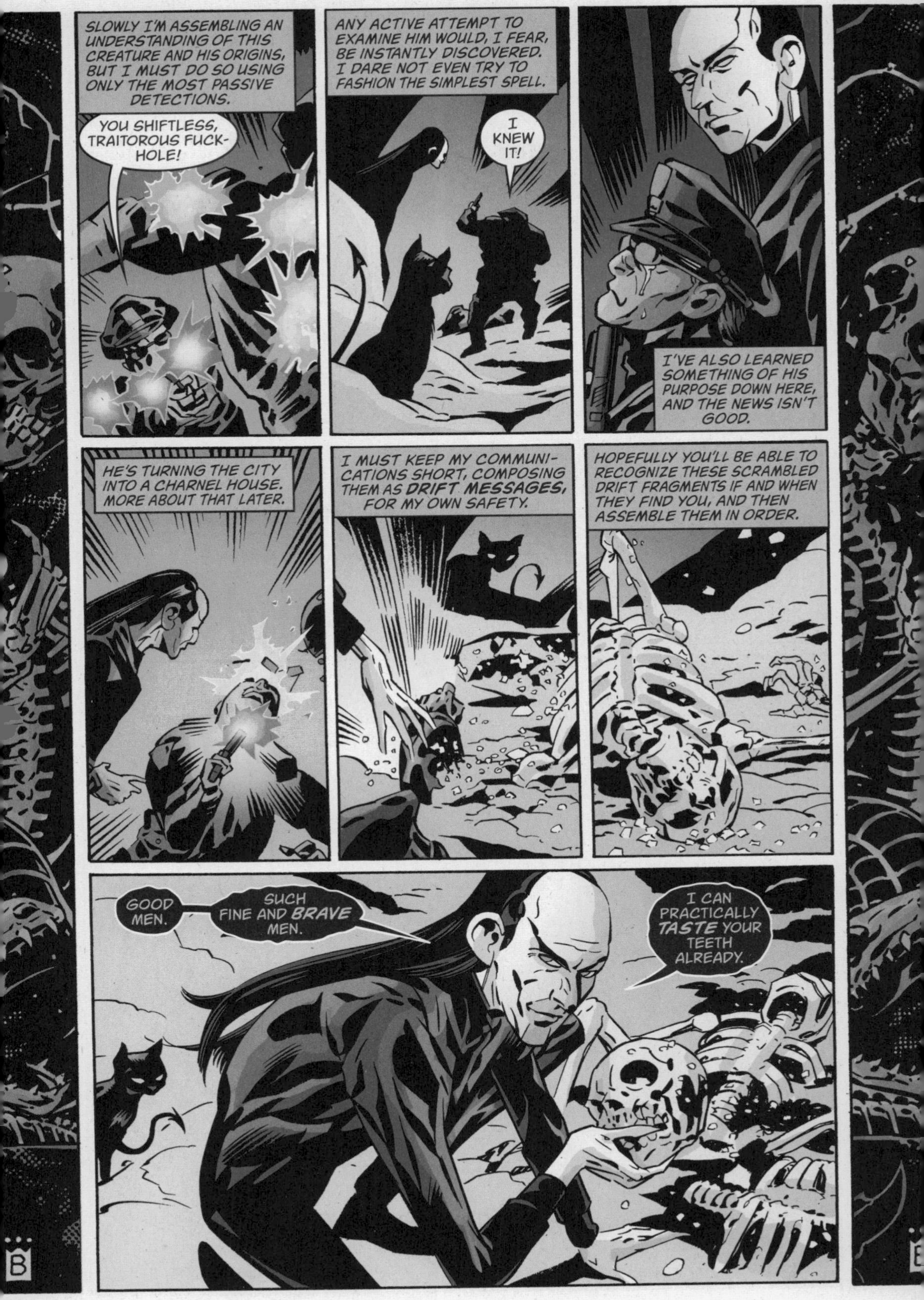
SLOWLY I'M ASSEMBLING AN UNDERSTANDING OF THIS CREATURE AND HIS ORIGINS, BUT I MUST DO SO USING ONLY THE MOST PASSIVE DETECTIONS.
YOU SHIFTLESS, TRAITOROUS FUCK-HOLE!
ANY ACTIVE ATTEMPT TO EXAMINE HIM WOULD, I FEAR, BE INSTANTLY DISCOVERED. I DARE NOT EVEN TRY TO FASHION THE SIMPLEST SPELL.
I KNEW IT!
I'VE ALSO LEARNED SOMETHING OF HIS PURPOSE DOWN HERE, AND THE NEWS ISN'T GOOD.
HE'S TURNING THE CITY INTO A CHARNEL HOUSE. MORE ABOUT THAT LATER.
I MUST KEEP MY COMMUNICATIONS SHORT, COMPOSING THEM AS DRIFT MESSAGES, FOR MY OWN SAFETY.
HOPEFULLY YOU'LL BE ABLE TO RECOGNIZE THESE SCRAMBLED DRIFT FRAGMENTS IF AND WHEN THEY FIND YOU, AND THEN ASSEMBLE THEM IN ORDER.
GOOD MEN.
SUCH FINE AND BRAVE MEN.
I CAN PRACTICALLY TASTE YOUR TEETH ALREADY.

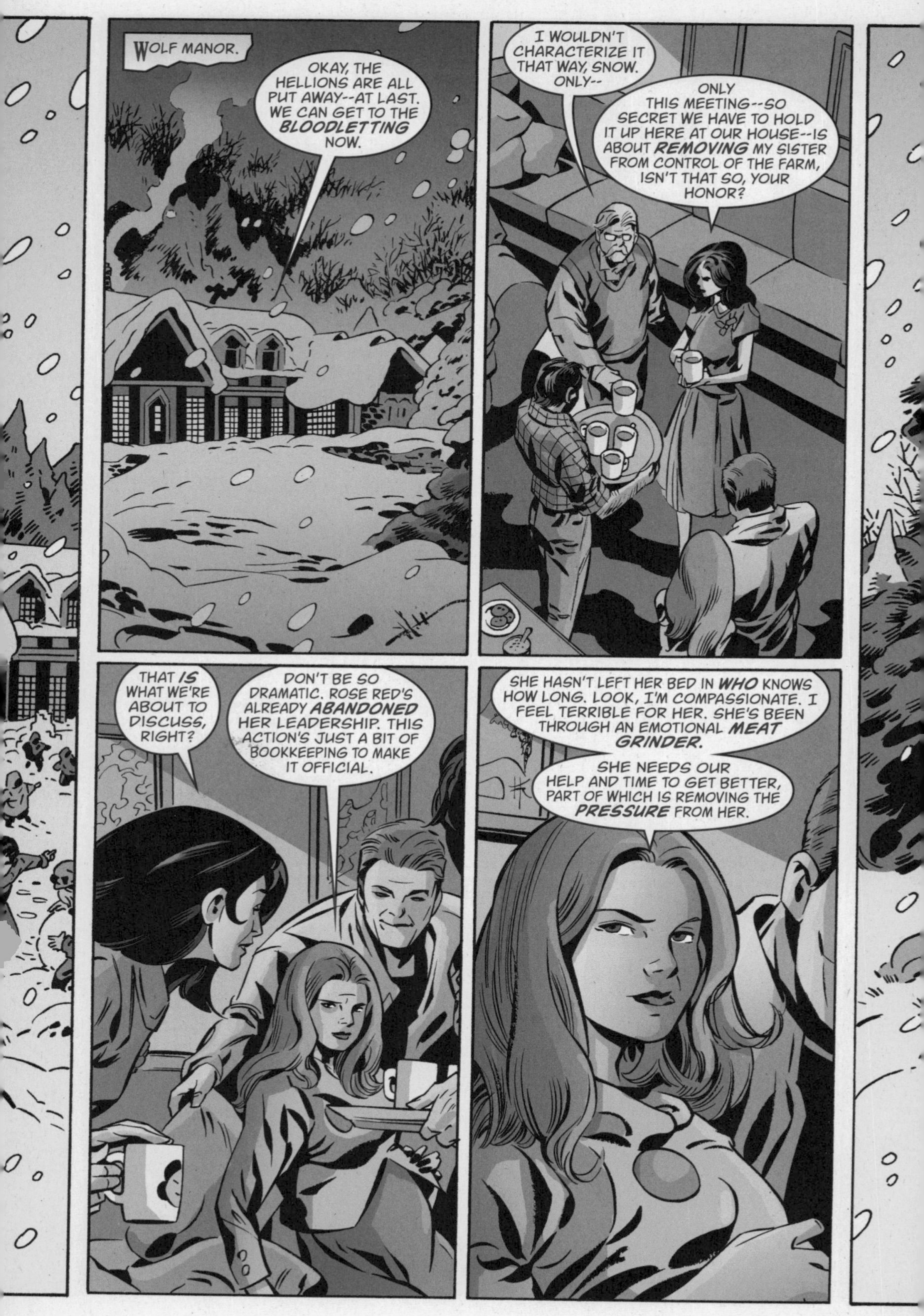
WOLF MANOR.
OKAY, THE HELLIONS ARE ALL PUT AWAY--AT LAST. WE CAN GET TO THE BLOODLETTING NOW.
I WOULDN'T CHARACTERIZE IT THAT WAY, SNOW. ONLY--
ONLY THIS MEETING--SO SECRET WE HAVE TO HOLD IT UP HERE AT OUR HOUSE--IS ABOUT REMOVING MY SISTER FROM CONTROL OF THE FARM, ISN'T THAT SO, YOUR HONOR?
THAT IS WHAT WE'RE ABOUT TO DISCUSS, RIGHT?
DON'T BE SO DRAMATIC. ROSE RED'S ALREADY ABANDONED HER LEADERSHIP. THIS ACTION'S JUST A BIT OF BOOKKEEPING TO MAKE IT OFFICIAL.
SHE HASN'T LEFT HER BED IN WHO KNOWS HOW LONG. LOOK, I'M COMPASSIONATE. I FEEL TERRIBLE FOR HER. SHE'S BEEN THROUGH AN EMOTIONAL MEAT GRINDER.
SHE NEEDS OUR HELP AND TIME TO GET BETTER, PART OF WHICH IS REMOVING THE PRESSURE FROM HER.

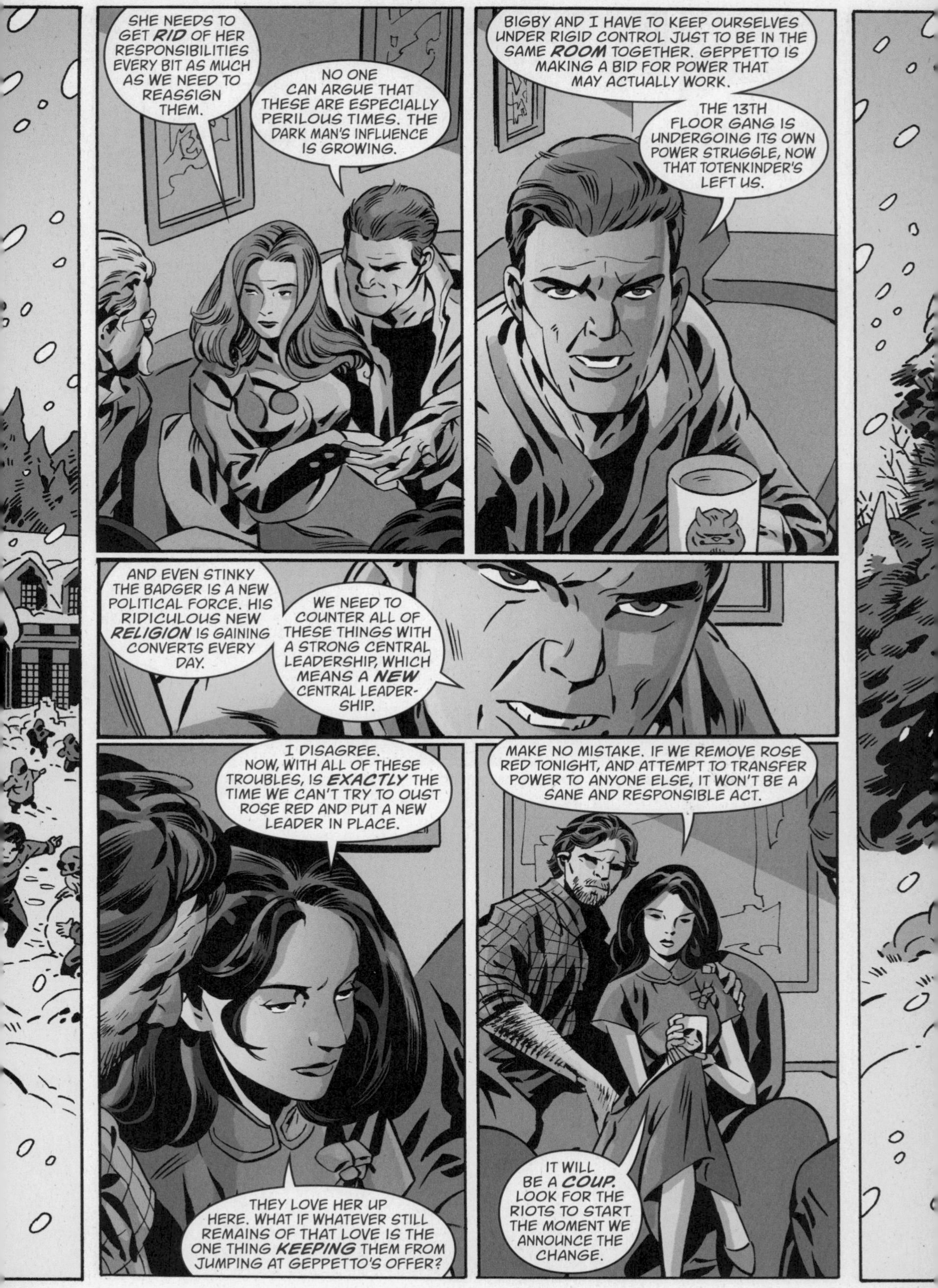

SHE NEEDS TO GET RID OF HER RESPONSIBILITIES EVERY BIT AS MUCH AS WE NEED TO REASSIGN THEM.
NO ONE CAN ARGUE THAT THESE ARE ESPECIALLY PERILOUS TIMES. THE DARK MAN'S INFLUENCE IS GROWING.
BIGBY AND I HAVE TO KEEP OURSELVES UNDER RIGID CONTROL JUST TO BE IN THE SAME ROOM TOGETHER. GEPPETTO IS MAKING A BID FOR POWER THAT MAY ACTUALLY WORK.
THE 13TH FLOOR GANG IS UNDERGOING ITS OWN POWER STRUGGLE, NOW THAT TOTENKINDER'S LEFT US.
AND EVEN STINKY THE BADGER IS A NEW POLITICAL FORCE. HIS RIDICULOUS NEW RELIGION IS GAINING CONVERTS EVERY DAY.
WE NEED TO COUNTER ALL OF THESE THINGS WITH A STRONG CENTRAL LEADERSHIP, WHICH MEANS A NEW CENTRAL LEADER-SHIP.
I DISAGREE. NOW, WITH ALL OF THESE TROUBLES, IS EXACTLY THE TIME WE CAN'T TRY TO OUST ROSE RED AND PUT A NEW LEADER IN PLACE.
THEY LOVE HER UP HERE. WHAT IF WHATEVER STILL REMAINS OF THAT LOVE IS THE ONE THING KEEPING THEM FROM JUMPING AT GEPPETTO'S OFFER?
MAKE NO MISTAKE. IF WE REMOVE ROSE RED TONIGHT, AND ATTEMPT TO TRANSFER POWER TO ANYONE ELSE, IT WON'T BE A SANE AND RESPONSIBLE ACT.
IT WILL BE A COUP. LOOK FOR THE RIOTS TO START THE MOMENT WE ANNOUNCE THE CHANGE.

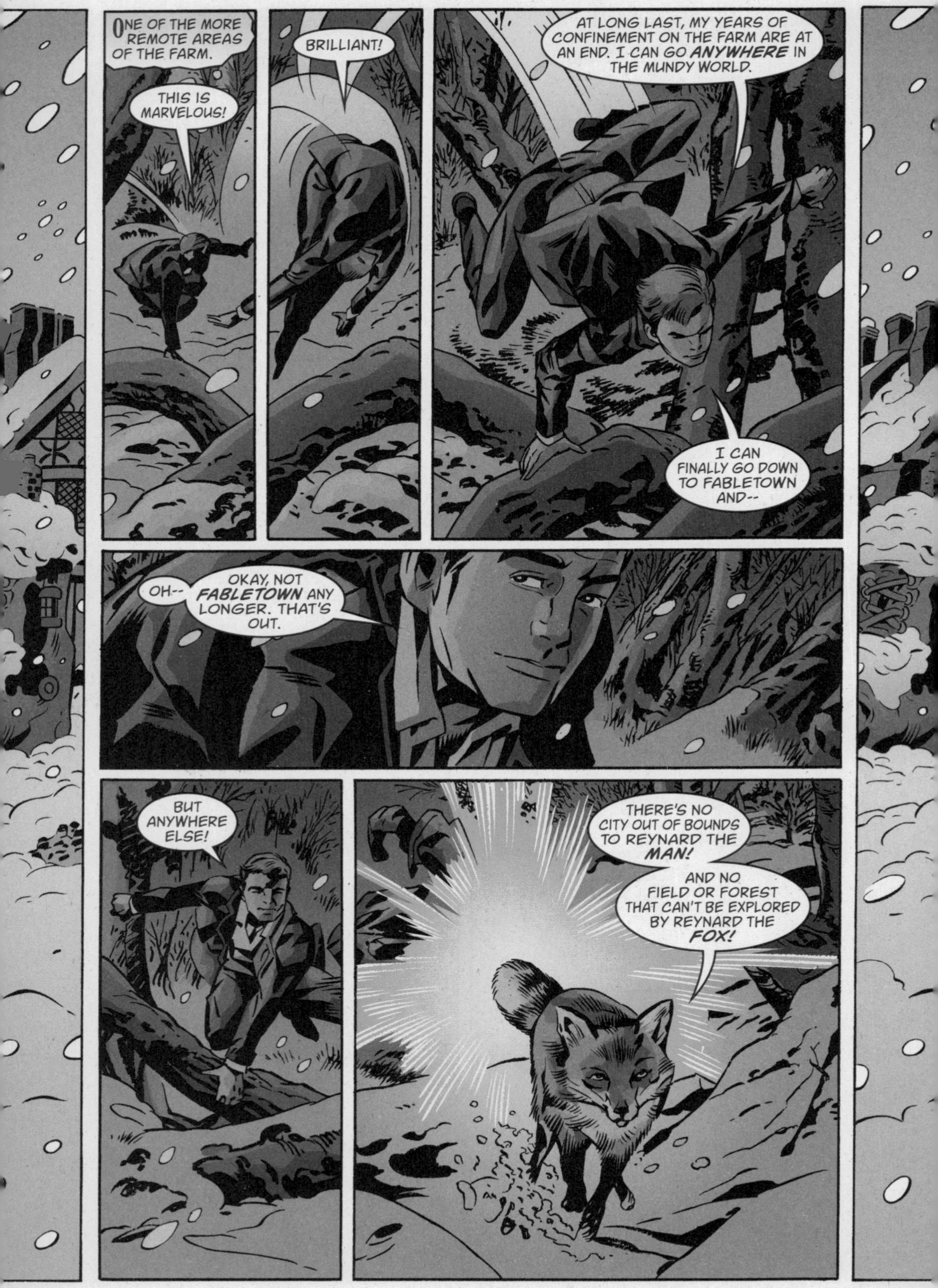

ONE OF THE MORE REMOTE AREAS OF THE FARM.
THIS IS MARVELOUS!
BRILLIANT!
AT LONG LAST, MY YEARS OF CONFINEMENT ON THE FARM ARE AT AN END. I CAN GO ANYWHERE IN THE MUNDY WORLD.
I CAN FINALLY GO DOWN TO FABLETOWN AND--
OH--
OKAY, NOT FABLETOWN ANY LONGER. THAT'S OUT.
BUT ANYWHERE ELSE!
THERE'S NO CITY OUT OF BOUNDS TO REYNARD THE MAN!
AND NO FIELD OR FOREST THAT CAN'T BE EXPLORED BY REYNARD THE FOX!

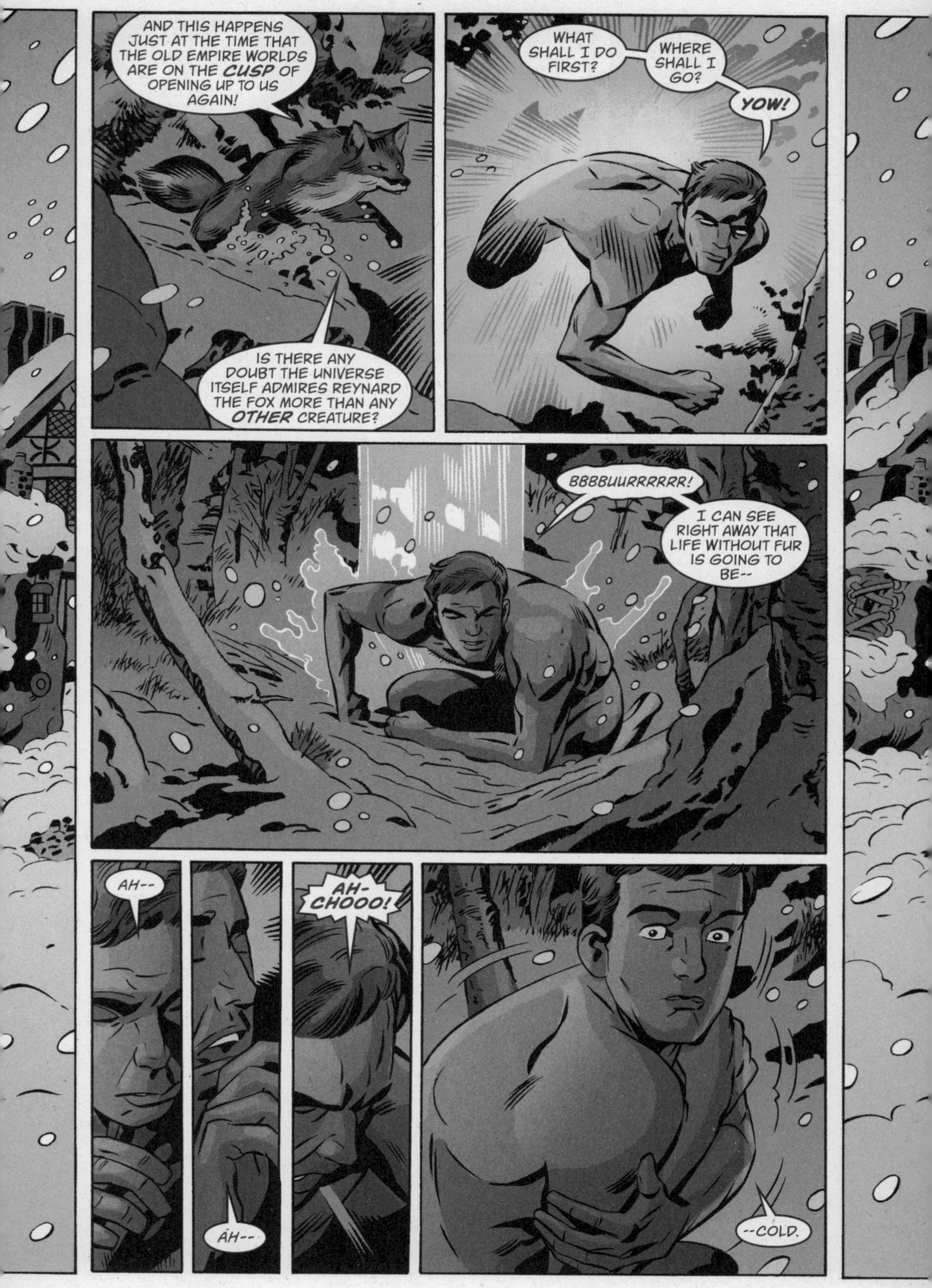
AND THIS HAPPENS JUST AT THE TIME THAT THE OLD EMPIRE WORLDS ARE ON THE CUSP OF OPENING UP TO US AGAIN!
IS THERE ANY DOUBT THE UNIVERSE ITSELF ADMIRES REYNARD THE FOX MORE THAN ANY OTHER CREATURE?
WHAT SHALL I DO FIRST?
WHERE SHALL I GO?
YOW!
BBBBUURRRRRR!
I CAN SEE RIGHT AWAY THAT LIFE WITHOUT FUR IS GOING TO BE--
AH--
AH--
AH-CHOOO!
--COLD.

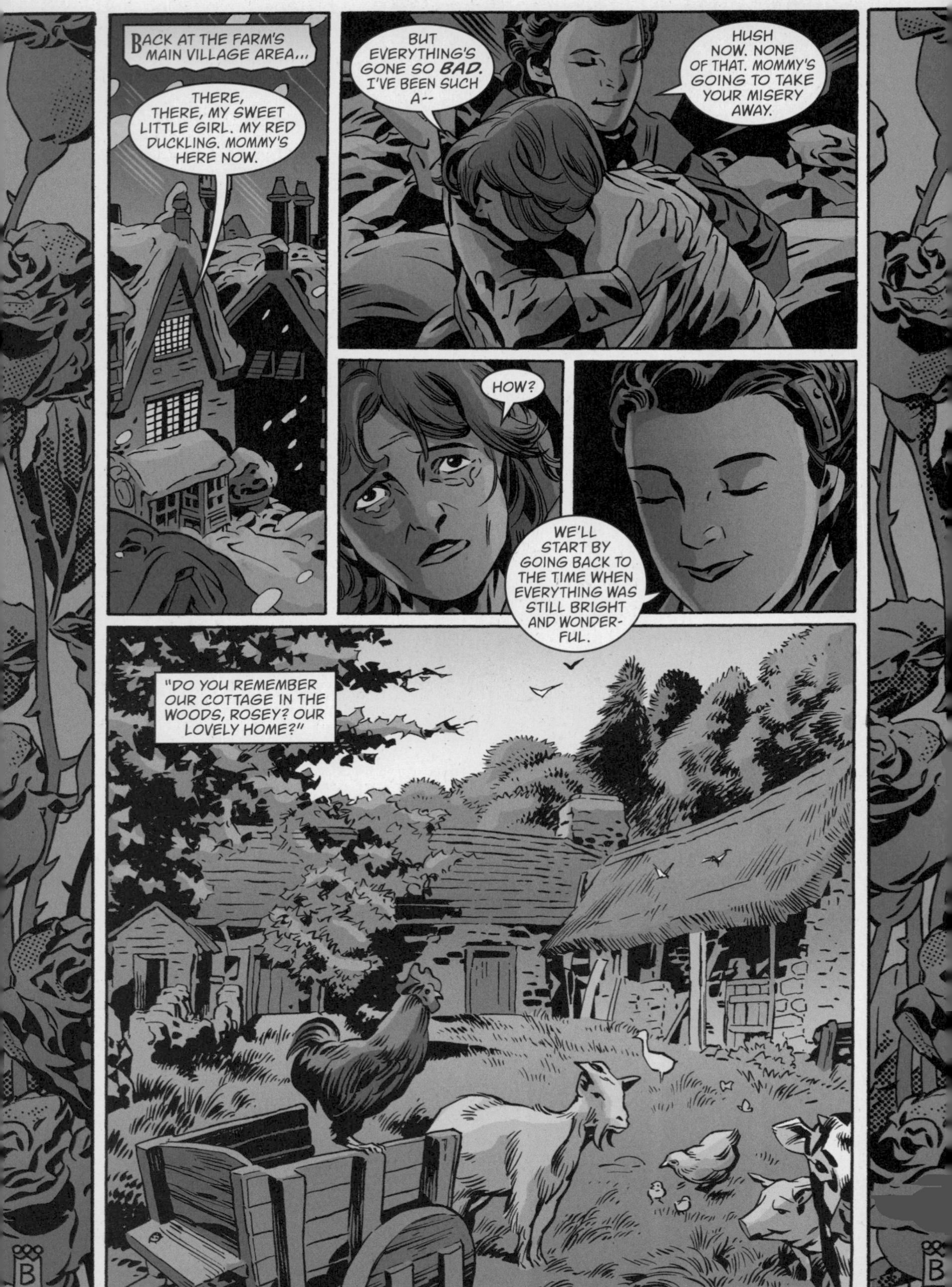
BACK AT THE FARM'S MAIN VILLAGE AREA...
THERE, THERE, MY SWEET LITTLE GIRL. MY RED DUCKLING. MOMMY'S HERE NOW.
BUT EVERYTHING'S GONE SO *BAD*. I'VE BEEN SUCH A--
HUSH NOW. NONE OF THAT. MOMMY'S GOING TO TAKE YOUR MISERY AWAY.
HOW?
WE'LL START BY GOING BACK TO THE TIME WHEN EVERYTHING WAS STILL BRIGHT AND WONDER-FUL.
"DO YOU REMEMBER OUR COTTAGE IN THE WOODS, ROSEY? OUR LOVELY HOME?"

NEXT: THE STORY OF SNOW WHITE AND ROSE RED.

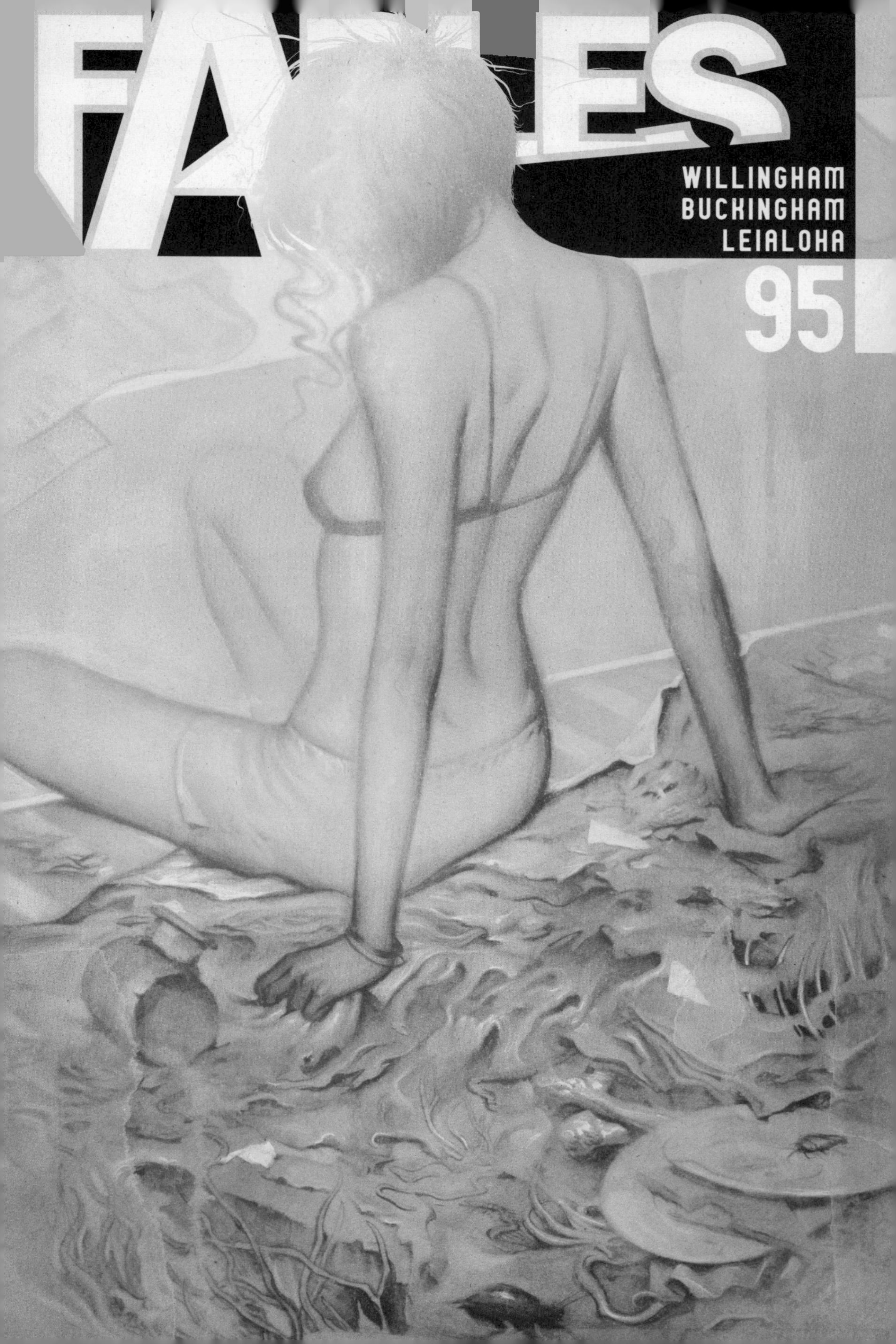
FABLES
WILLINGHAM
BUCKINGHAM
LEIALOHA
95

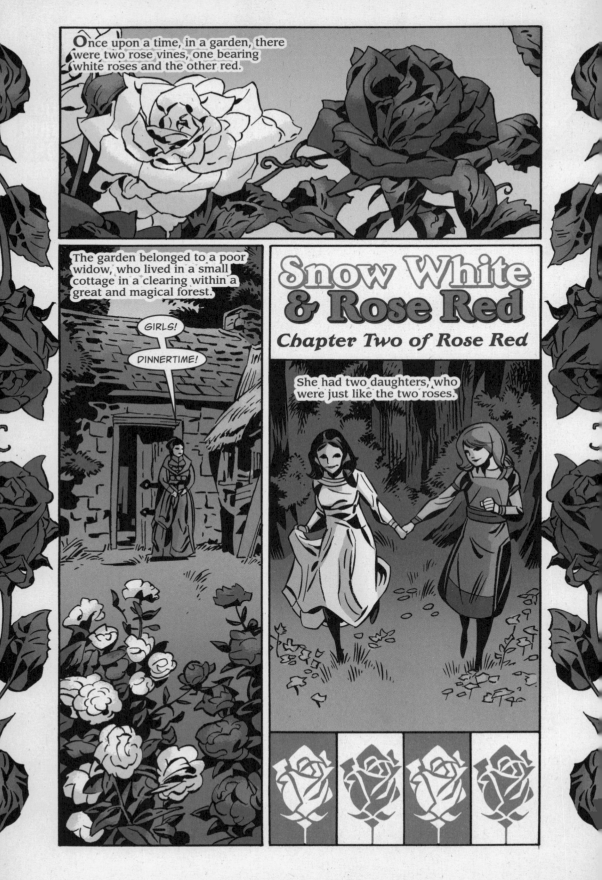

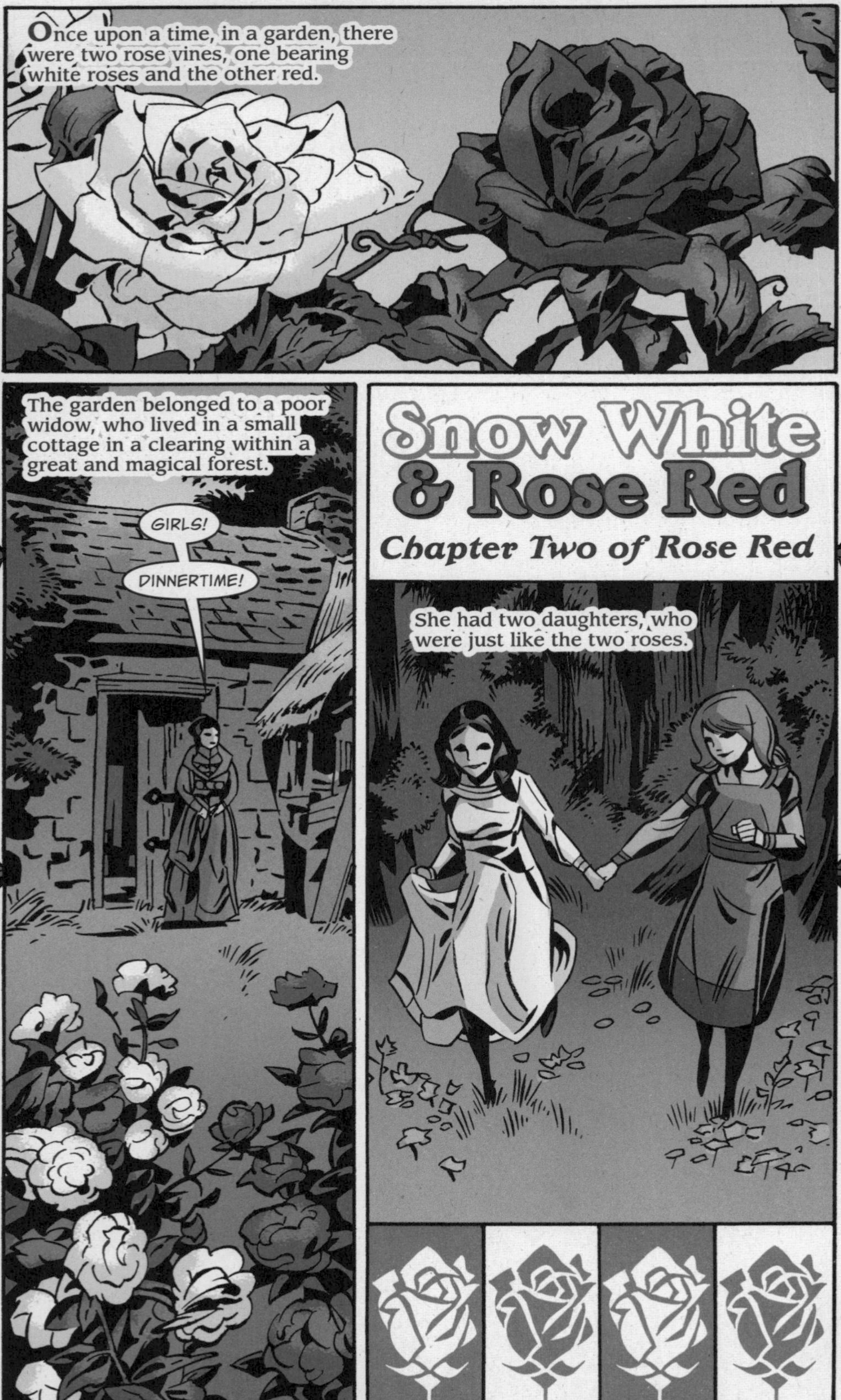
Once upon a time, in a garden, there were two rose vines, one bearing white roses and the other red.
The garden belonged to a poor widow, who lived in a small cottage in a clearing within a great and magical forest.
GIRLS!
DINNERTIME!
Snow White & Rose Red
Chapter Two of Rose Red
She had two daughters, who were just like the two roses.

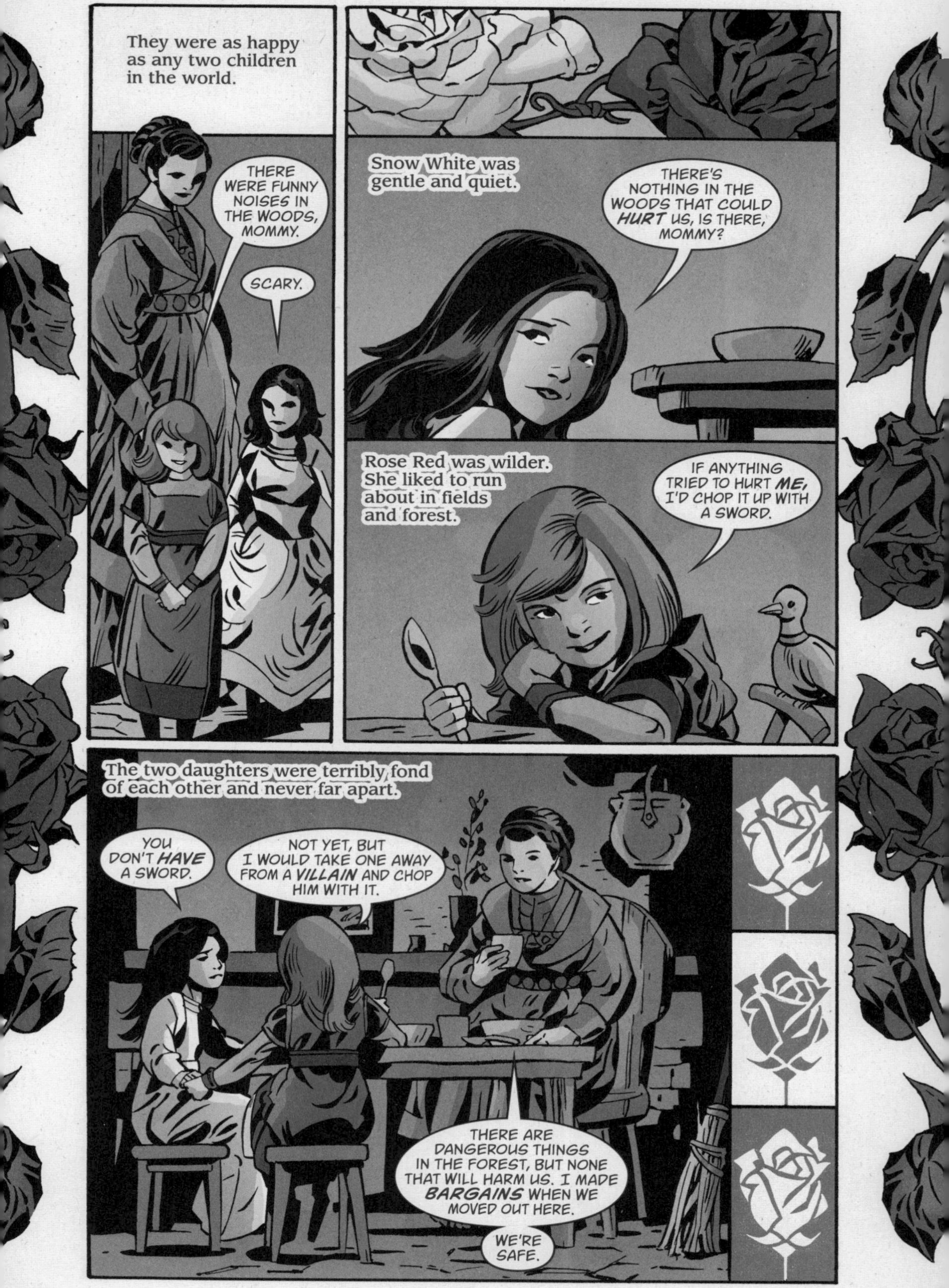
They were as happy as any two children in the world.
THERE WERE FUNNY NOISES IN THE WOODS, MOMMY.
SCARY.
Snow White was gentle and quiet.
THERE'S NOTHING IN THE WOODS THAT COULD HURT US, IS THERE, MOMMY?
Rose Red was wilder. She liked to run about in fields and forest.
IF ANYTHING TRIED TO HURT ME, I'D CHOP IT UP WITH A SWORD.
The two daughters were terribly fond of each other and never far apart.
YOU DON'T HAVE A SWORD.
NOT YET, BUT I WOULD TAKE ONE AWAY FROM A VILLAIN AND CHOP HIM WITH IT.
THERE ARE DANGEROUS THINGS IN THE FOREST, BUT NONE THAT WILL HARM US. I MADE BARGAINS WHEN WE MOVED OUT HERE.
WE'RE SAFE.

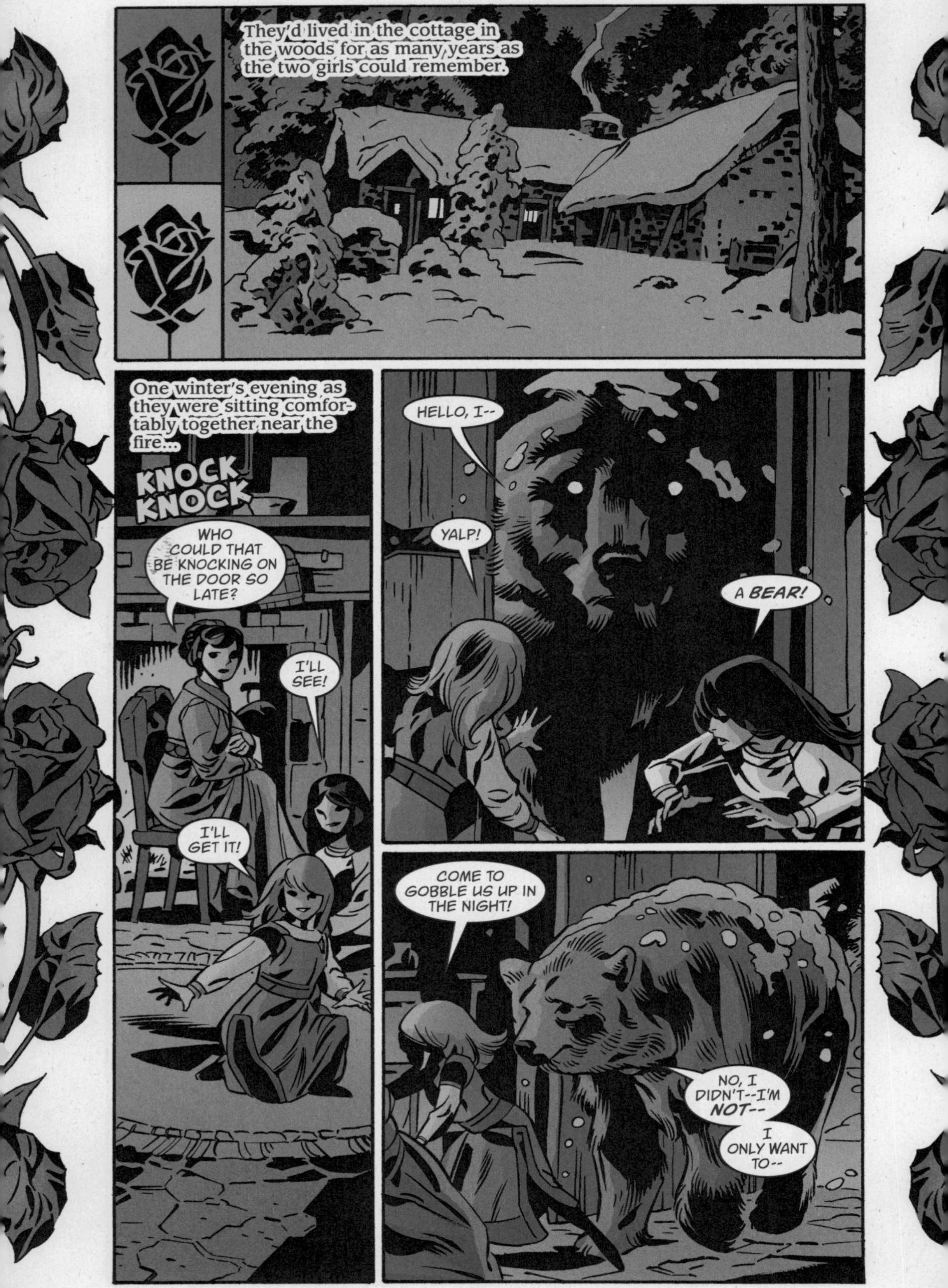
They'd lived in the cottage in the woods for as many years as the two girls could remember.
One winter's evening as they were sitting comfortably together near the fire...
KNOCK KNOCK
WHO COULD THAT BE KNOCKING ON THE DOOR SO LATE?
I'LL SEE!
I'LL GET IT!
HELLO, I--
YALP!
A BEAR!
COME TO GOBBLE US UP IN THE NIGHT!
NO, I DIDN'T--I'M NOT--
I ONLY WANT TO--

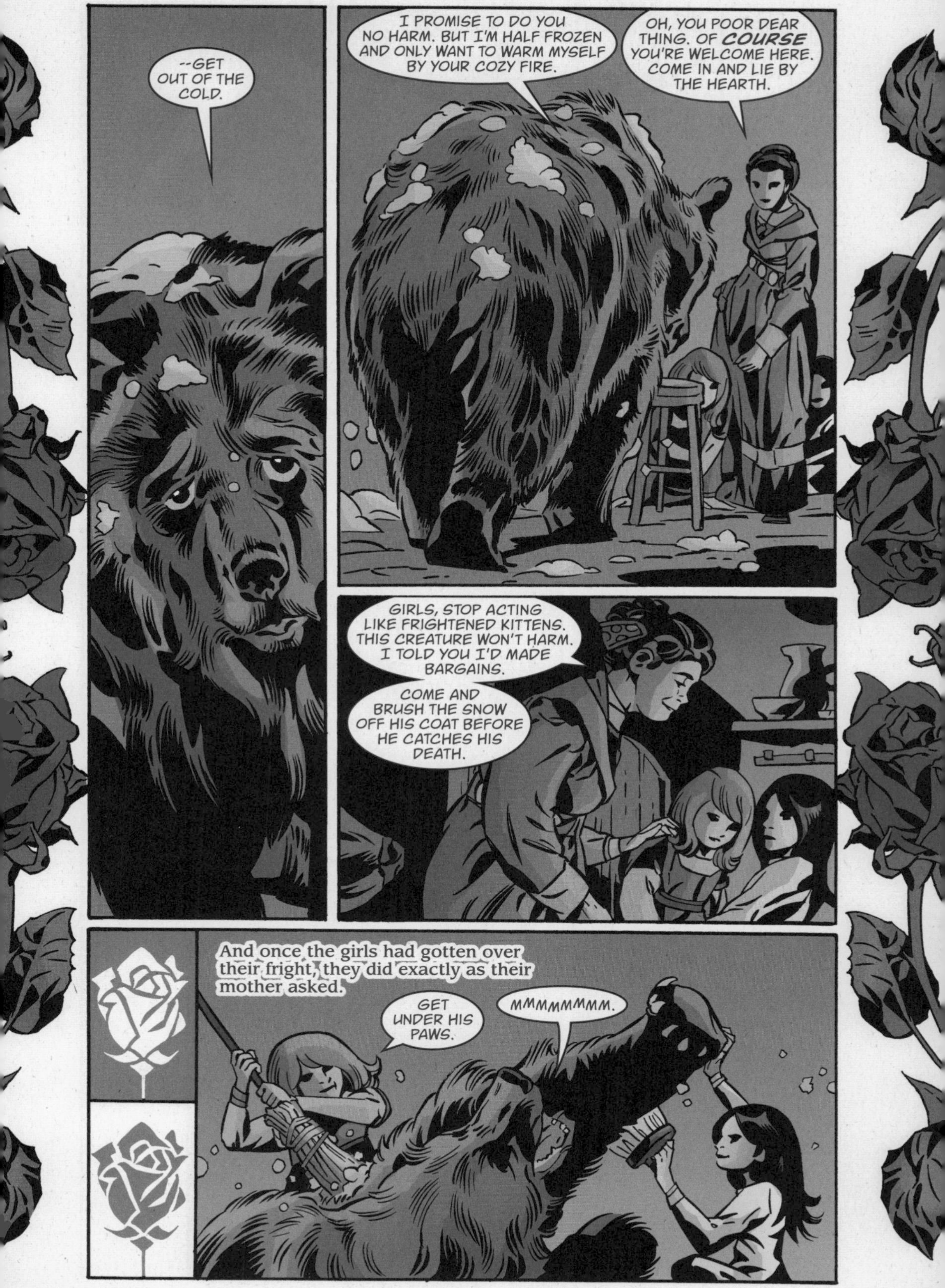
--GET OUT OF THE COLD.
I PROMISE TO DO YOU NO HARM. BUT I'M HALF FROZEN AND ONLY WANT TO WARM MYSELF BY YOUR COZY FIRE.
OH, YOU POOR DEAR THING. OF COURSE YOU'RE WELCOME HERE. COME IN AND LIE BY THE HEARTH.
GIRLS, STOP ACTING LIKE FRIGHTENED KITTENS. THIS CREATURE WON'T HARM. I TOLD YOU I'D MADE BARGAINS.
COME AND BRUSH THE SNOW OFF HIS COAT BEFORE HE CATCHES HIS DEATH.
And once the girls had gotten over their fright, they did exactly as their mother asked.
GET UNDER HIS PAWS.
MMMMMMMM.

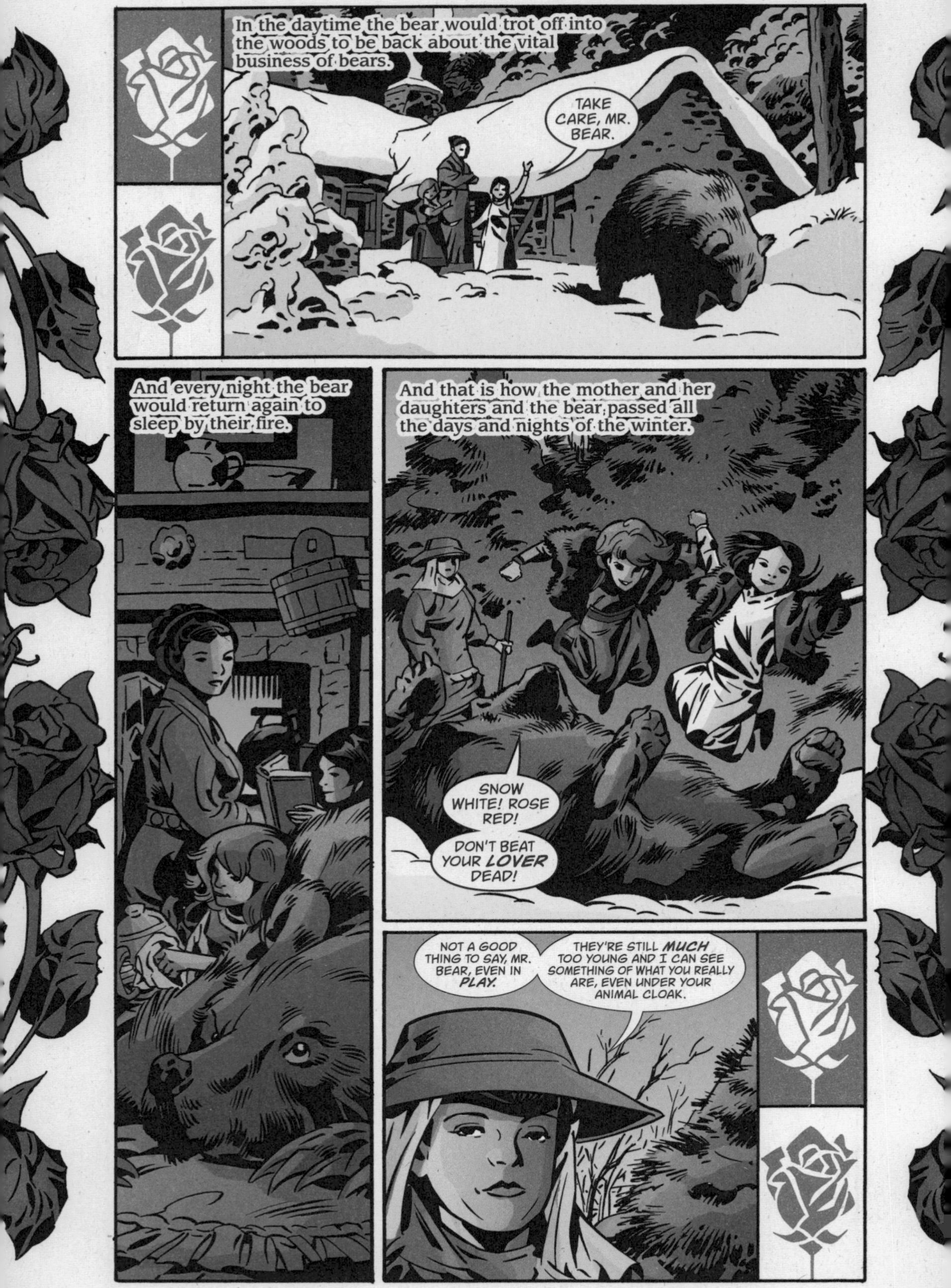
In the daytime the bear would trot off into the woods to be back about the vital business of bears.
TAKE CARE, MR. BEAR.
And every night the bear would return again to sleep by their fire.
And that is how the mother and her daughters and the bear passed all the days and nights of the winter.
SNOW WHITE! ROSE RED!
DON'T BEAT YOUR LOVER DEAD!
NOT A GOOD THING TO SAY, MR. BEAR, EVEN IN PLAY.
THEY'RE STILL MUCH TOO YOUNG AND I CAN SEE SOMETHING OF WHAT YOU REALLY ARE, EVEN UNDER YOUR ANIMAL CLOAK.

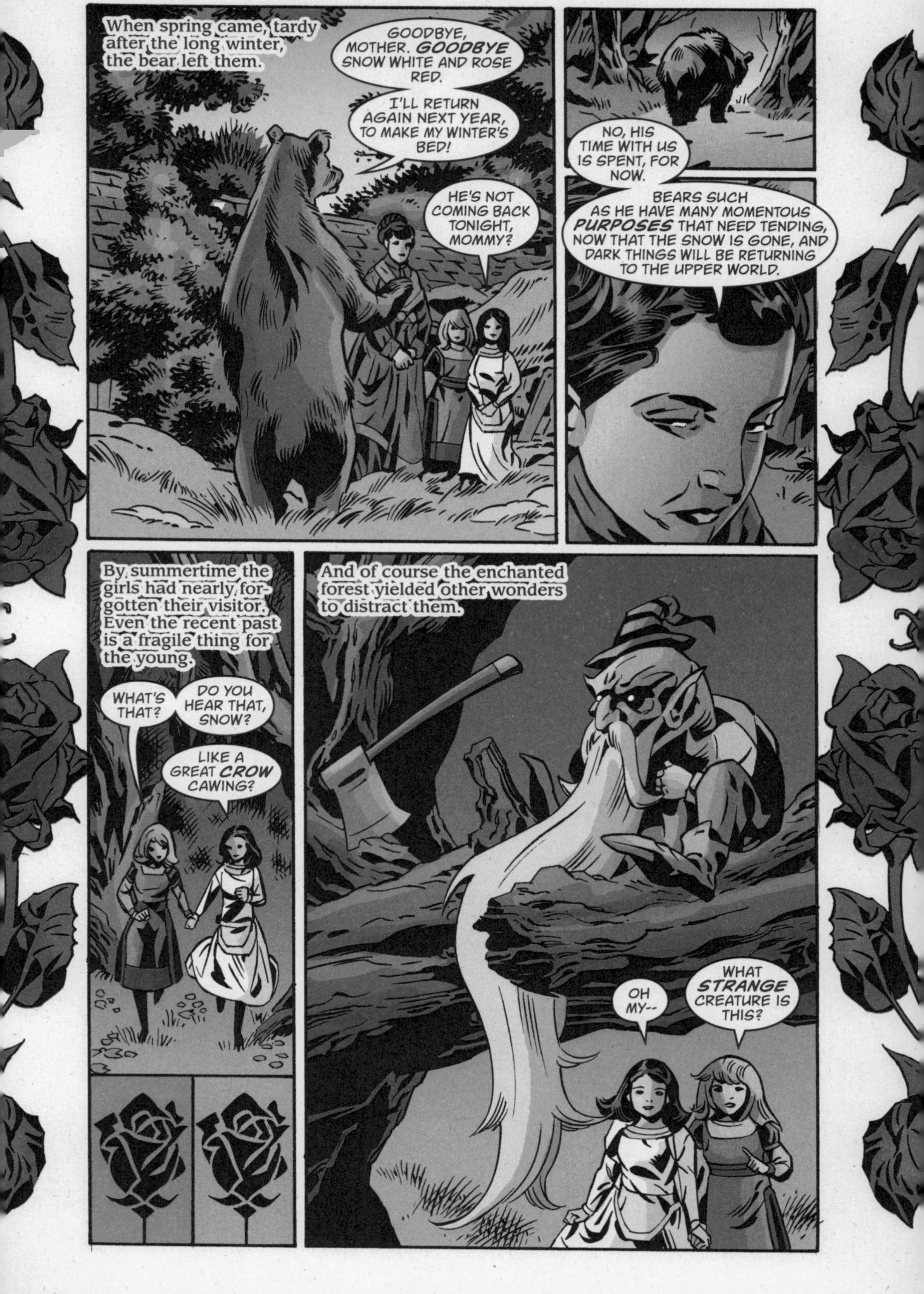
When spring came, tardy after the long winter, the bear left them.
GOODBYE, MOTHER. GOODBYE SNOW WHITE AND ROSE RED.
I'LL RETURN AGAIN NEXT YEAR, TO MAKE MY WINTER'S BED!
HE'S NOT COMING BACK TONIGHT, MOMMY?
NO, HIS TIME WITH US IS SPENT, FOR NOW.
BEARS SUCH AS HE HAVE MANY MOMENTOUS PURPOSES THAT NEED TENDING, NOW THAT THE SNOW IS GONE, AND DARK THINGS WILL BE RETURNING TO THE UPPER WORLD.
By summertime the girls had nearly forgotten their visitor. Even the recent past is a fragile thing for the young.
DO YOU HEAR THAT, SNOW?
WHAT'S THAT?
LIKE A GREAT CROW CAWING?
And of course the enchanted forest yielded other wonders to distract them.
OH MY--
WHAT STRANGE CREATURE IS THIS?

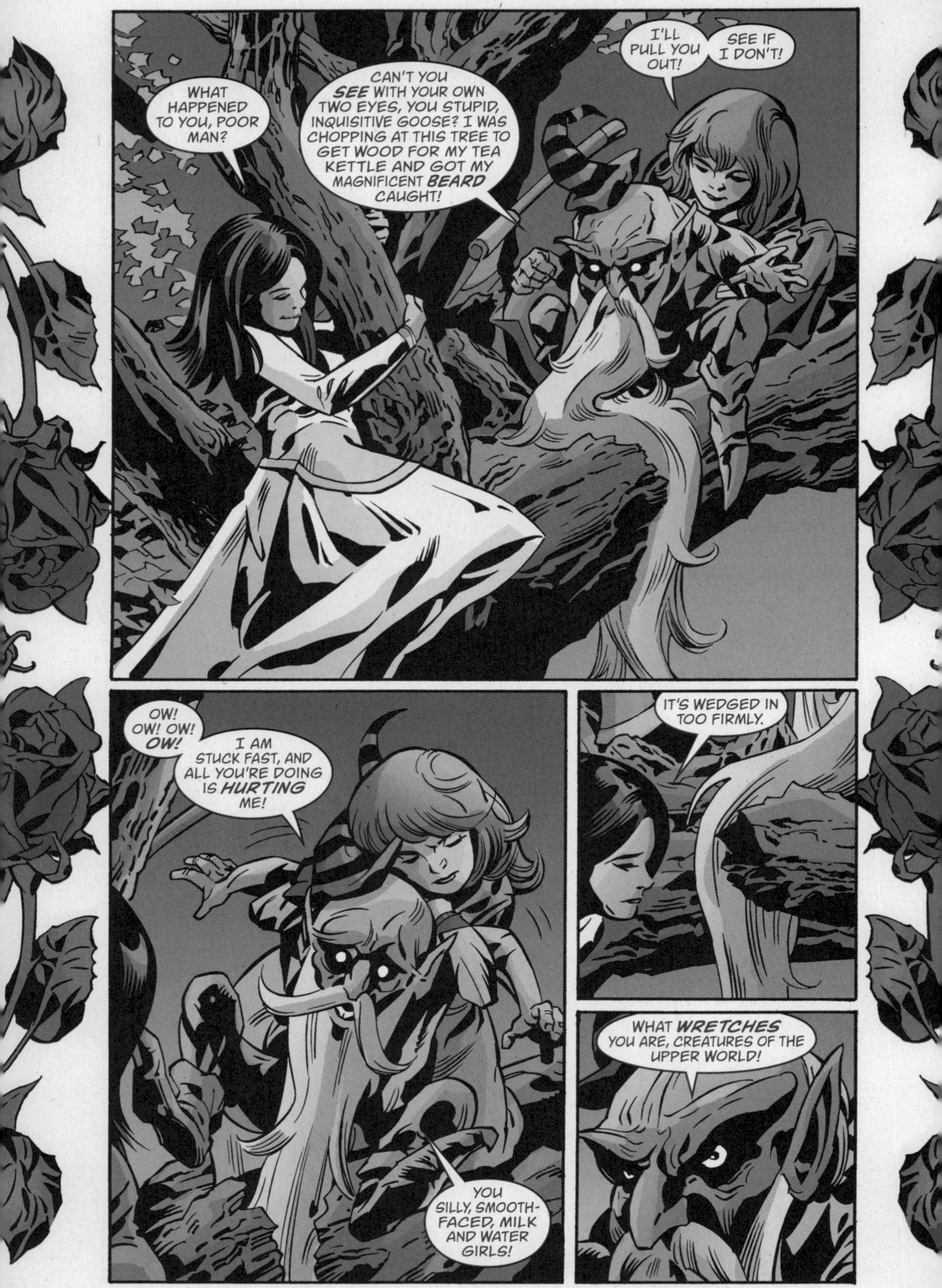
WHAT HAPPENED TO YOU, POOR MAN?
CAN'T YOU SEE WITH YOUR OWN TWO EYES, YOU STUPID, INQUISITIVE GOOSE? I WAS CHOPPING AT THIS TREE TO GET WOOD FOR MY TEA KETTLE AND GOT MY MAGNIFICENT BEARD CAUGHT!
I'LL PULL YOU OUT!
SEE IF I DON'T!
OW! OW! OW! OW!
I AM STUCK FAST, AND ALL YOU'RE DOING IS HURTING ME!
YOU SILLY, SMOOTH-FACED, MILK AND WATER GIRLS!
IT'S WEDGED IN TOO FIRMLY.
WHAT WRETCHES YOU ARE, CREATURES OF THE UPPER WORLD!

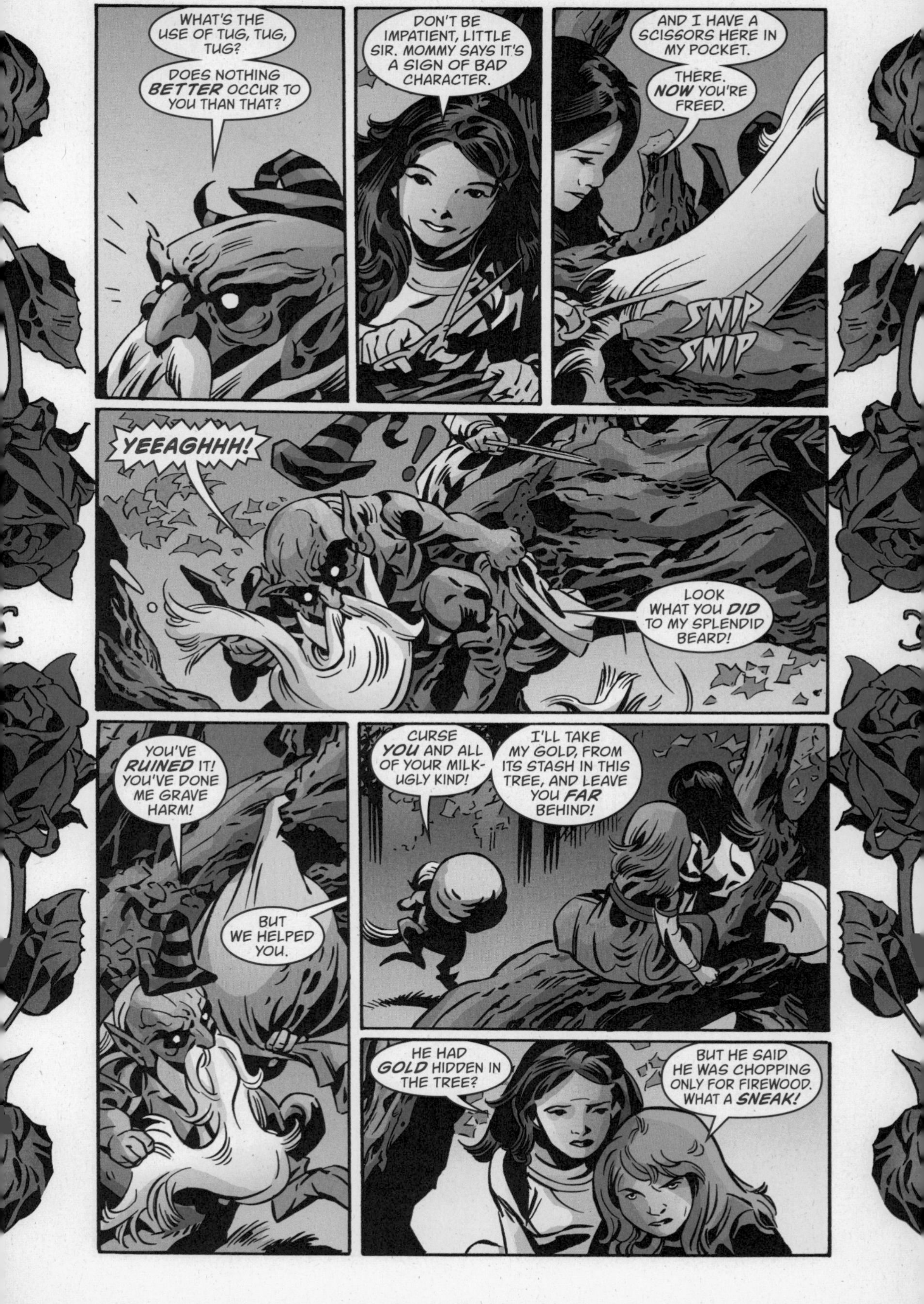
WHAT'S THE USE OF TUG, TUG, TUG?
DOES NOTHING BETTER OCCUR TO YOU THAN THAT?
DON'T BE IMPATIENT, LITTLE SIR. MOMMY SAYS IT'S A SIGN OF BAD CHARACTER.
AND I HAVE A SCISSORS HERE IN MY POCKET.
THERE. NOW YOU'RE FREED.
SNIP SNIP
YEEAGHHH!
LOOK WHAT YOU DID TO MY SPLENDID BEARD!
YOU'VE RUINED IT! YOU'VE DONE ME GRAVE HARM!
BUT WE HELPED YOU.
CURSE YOU AND ALL OF YOUR MILK-UGLY KIND!
I'LL TAKE MY GOLD, FROM ITS STASH IN THIS TREE, AND LEAVE YOU FAR BEHIND!
HE HAD GOLD HIDDEN IN THE TREE?
BUT HE SAID HE WAS CHOPPING ONLY FOR FIREWOOD. WHAT A SNEAK!

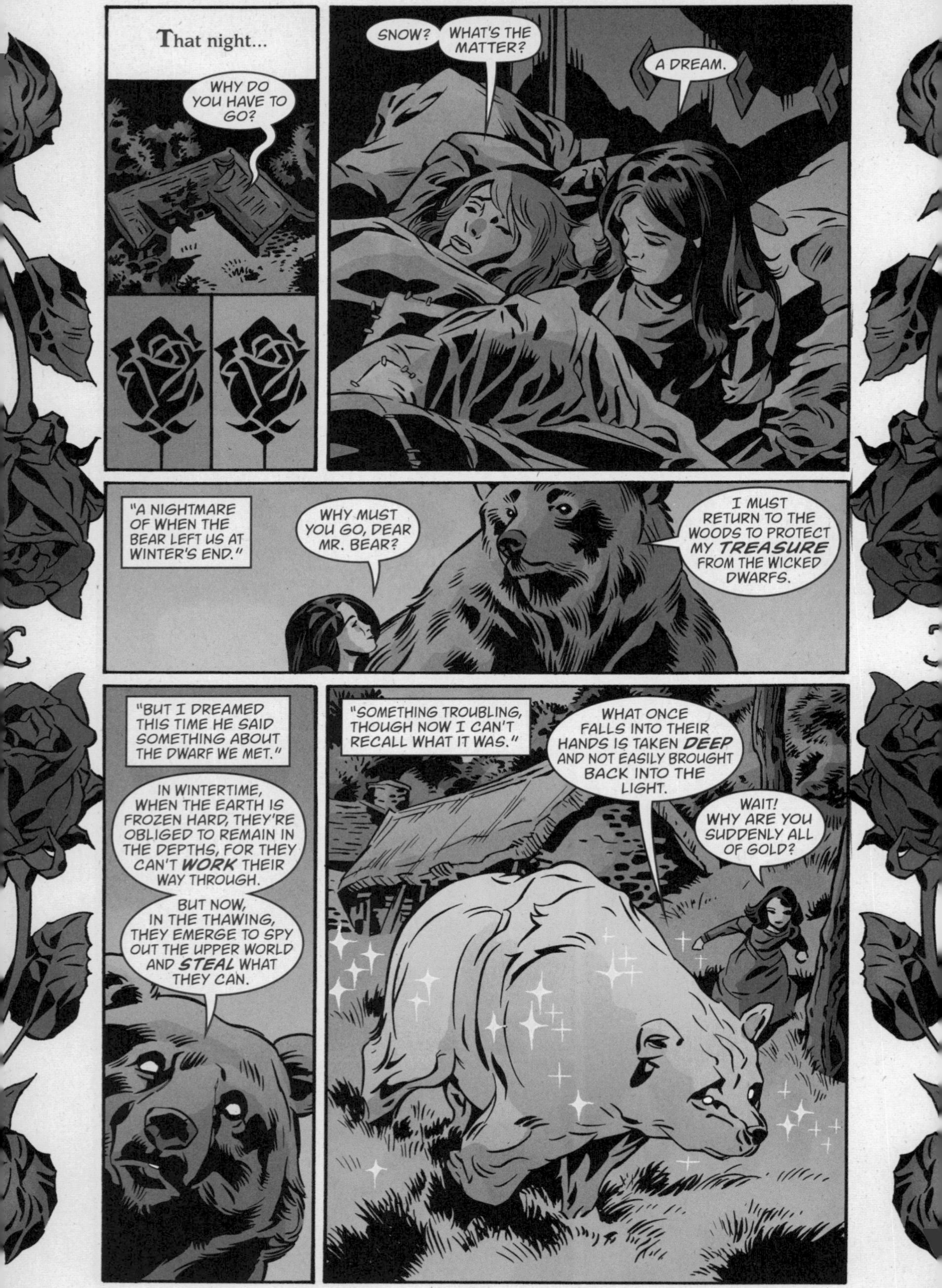
That night...
WHY DO YOU HAVE TO GO?
SNOW? WHAT'S THE MATTER?
A DREAM.
"A NIGHTMARE OF WHEN THE BEAR LEFT US AT WINTER'S END."
WHY MUST YOU GO, DEAR MR. BEAR?
I MUST RETURN TO THE WOODS TO PROTECT MY *TREASURE* FROM THE WICKED DWARFS.
"BUT I DREAMED THIS TIME HE SAID SOMETHING ABOUT THE DWARF WE MET."
IN WINTERTIME, WHEN THE EARTH IS FROZEN HARD, THEY'RE OBLIGED TO REMAIN IN THE DEPTHS, FOR THEY CAN'T *WORK* THEIR WAY THROUGH.
BUT NOW, IN THE THAWING, THEY EMERGE TO SPY OUT THE UPPER WORLD AND *STEAL* WHAT THEY CAN.
"SOMETHING TROUBLING, THOUGH NOW I CAN'T RECALL WHAT IT WAS."
WHAT ONCE FALLS INTO THEIR HANDS IS TAKEN *DEEP* AND NOT EASILY BROUGHT BACK INTO THE LIGHT.
WAIT! WHY ARE YOU SUDDENLY ALL OF GOLD?

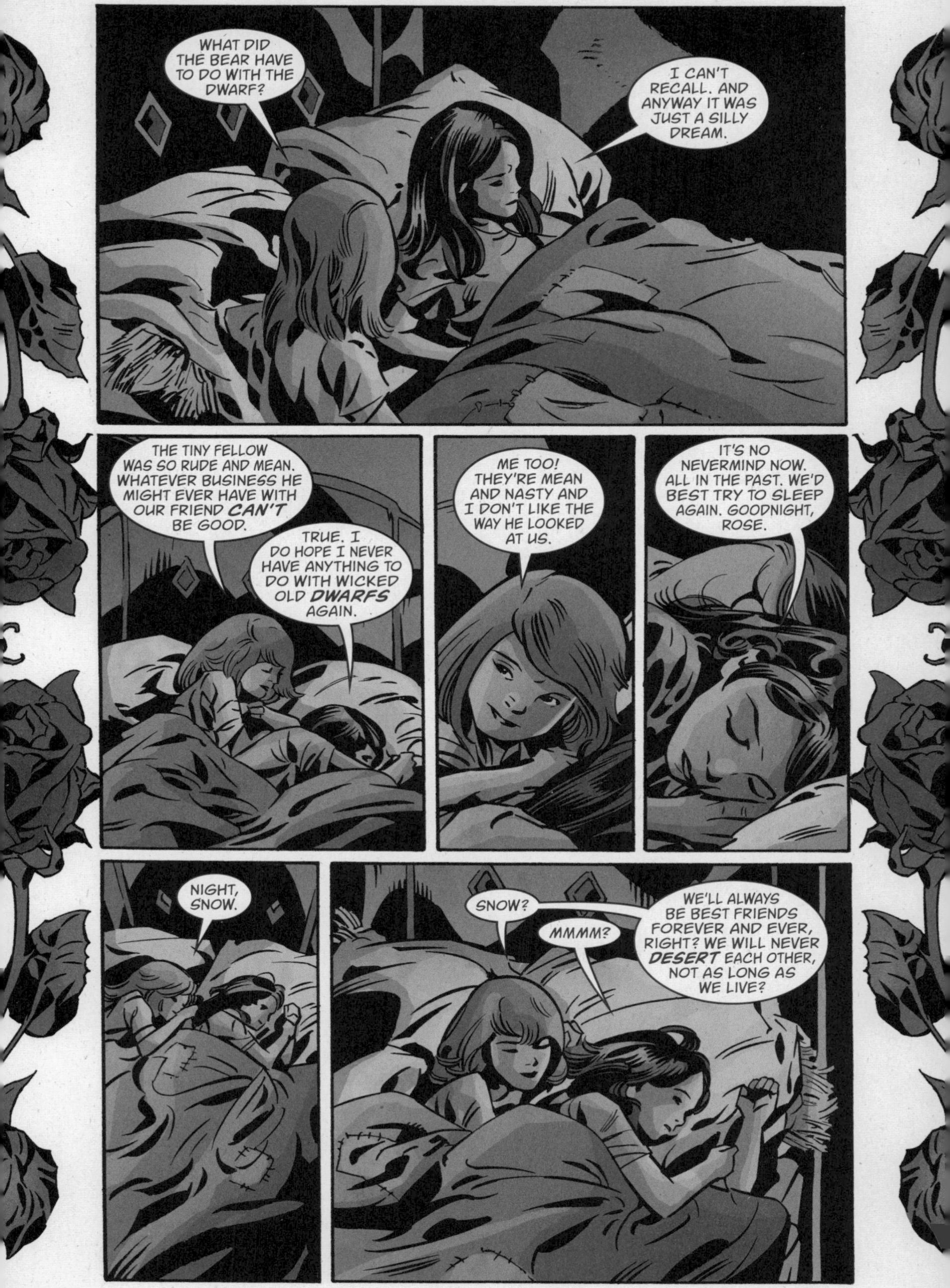
WHAT DID THE BEAR HAVE TO DO WITH THE DWARF?
I CAN'T RECALL. AND ANYWAY IT WAS JUST A SILLY DREAM.
THE TINY FELLOW WAS SO RUDE AND MEAN. WHATEVER BUSINESS HE MIGHT EVER HAVE WITH OUR FRIEND CAN'T BE GOOD.
TRUE. I DO HOPE I NEVER HAVE ANYTHING TO DO WITH WICKED OLD DWARFS AGAIN.
ME TOO! THEY'RE MEAN AND NASTY AND I DON'T LIKE THE WAY HE LOOKED AT US.
IT'S NO NEVERMIND NOW. ALL IN THE PAST. WE'D BEST TRY TO SLEEP AGAIN. GOODNIGHT, ROSE.
NIGHT, SNOW.
SNOW?
MMMM?
WE'LL ALWAYS BE BEST FRIENDS FOREVER AND EVER, RIGHT? WE WILL NEVER DESERT EACH OTHER, NOT AS LONG AS WE LIVE?

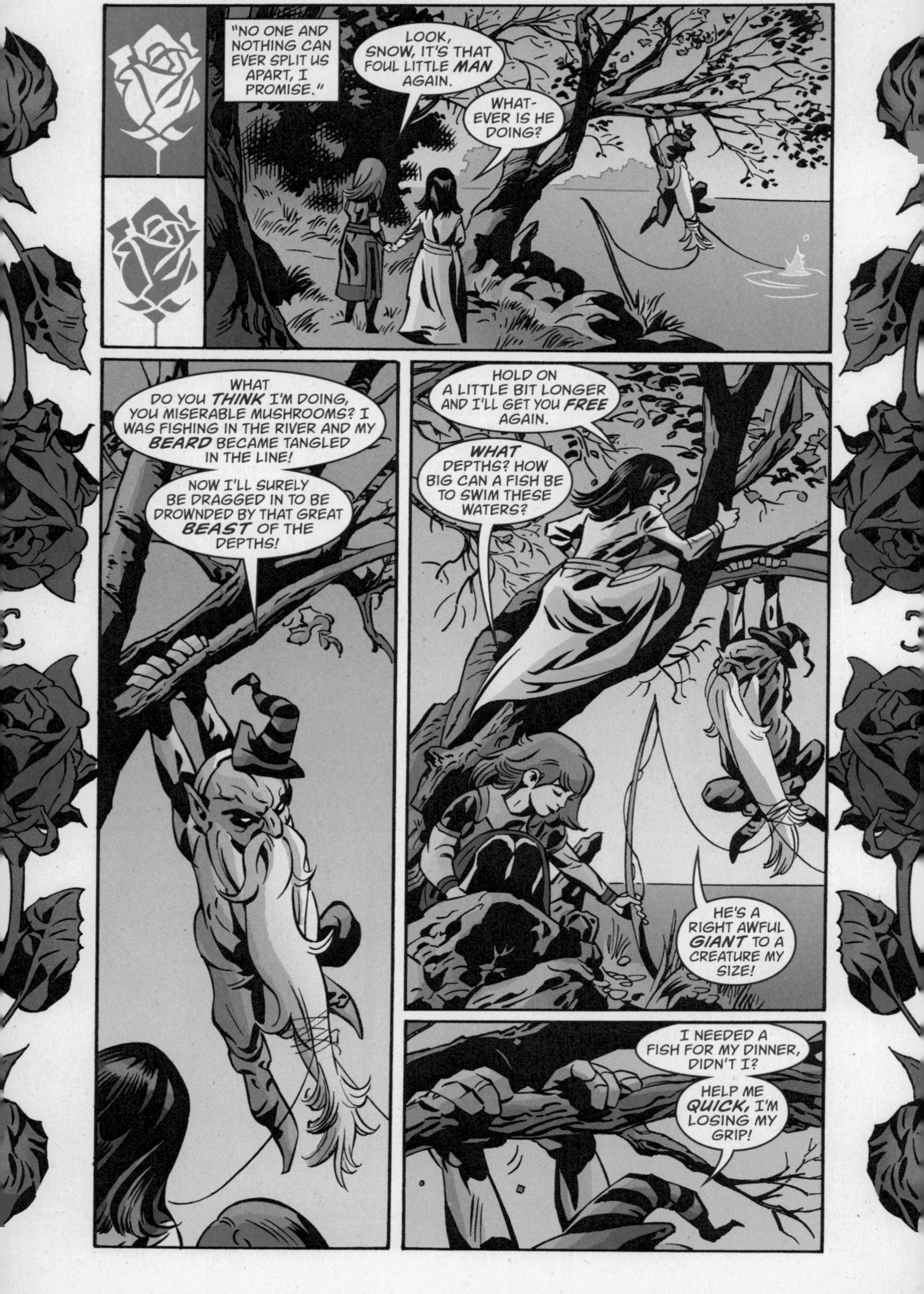
"NO ONE AND NOTHING CAN EVER SPLIT US APART, I PROMISE."
LOOK, SNOW, IT'S THAT FOUL LITTLE MAN AGAIN.
WHAT-EVER IS HE DOING?
WHAT DO YOU THINK I'M DOING, YOU MISERABLE MUSHROOMS? I WAS FISHING IN THE RIVER AND MY BEARD BECAME TANGLED IN THE LINE!
NOW I'LL SURELY BE DRAGGED IN TO BE DROWNDED BY THAT GREAT BEAST OF THE DEPTHS!
HOLD ON A LITTLE BIT LONGER AND I'LL GET YOU FREE AGAIN.
WHAT DEPTHS? HOW BIG CAN A FISH BE TO SWIM THESE WATERS?
HE'S A RIGHT AWFUL GIANT TO A CREATURE MY SIZE!
I NEEDED A FISH FOR MY DINNER, DIDN'T I?
HELP ME QUICK, I'M LOSING MY GRIP!

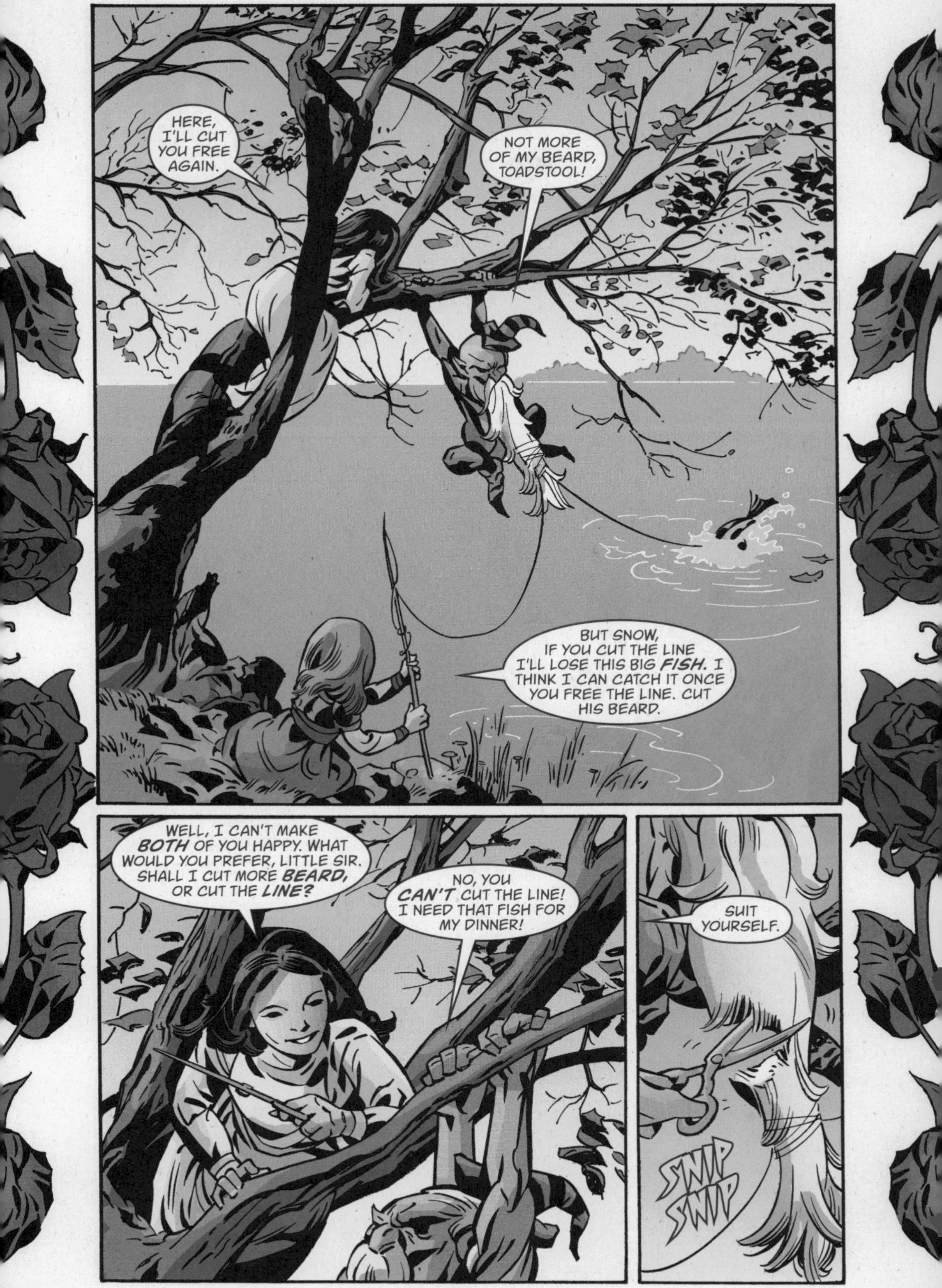
HERE, I'LL CUT YOU FREE AGAIN.
NOT MORE OF MY BEARD, TOADSTOOL!
BUT SNOW, IF YOU CUT THE LINE I'LL LOSE THIS BIG FISH. I THINK I CAN CATCH IT ONCE YOU FREE THE LINE. CUT HIS BEARD.
WELL, I CAN'T MAKE BOTH OF YOU HAPPY. WHAT WOULD YOU PREFER, LITTLE SIR. SHALL I CUT MORE BEARD, OR CUT THE LINE?
NO, YOU CAN'T CUT THE LINE! I NEED THAT FISH FOR MY DINNER!
SUIT YOURSELF.
SNIP SNIP

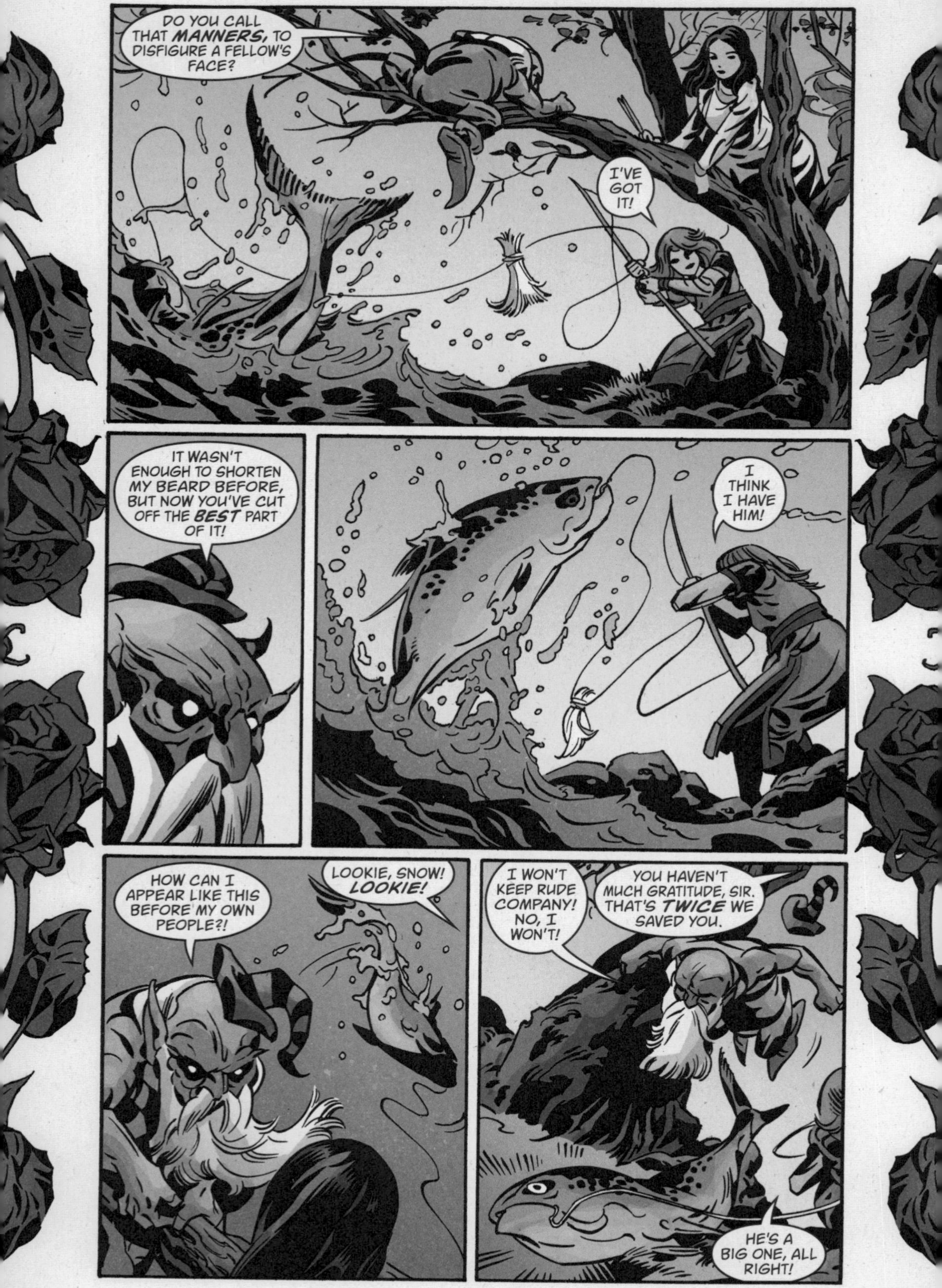
DO YOU CALL THAT MANNERS, TO DISFIGURE A FELLOW'S FACE?
I'VE GOT IT!
IT WASN'T ENOUGH TO SHORTEN MY BEARD BEFORE, BUT NOW YOU'VE CUT OFF THE BEST PART OF IT!
I THINK I HAVE HIM!
HOW CAN I APPEAR LIKE THIS BEFORE MY OWN PEOPLE?!
LOOKIE, SNOW! LOOKIE!
I WON'T KEEP RUDE COMPANY! NO, I WON'T!
YOU HAVEN'T MUCH GRATITUDE, SIR. THAT'S TWICE WE SAVED YOU.
HE'S A BIG ONE, ALL RIGHT!

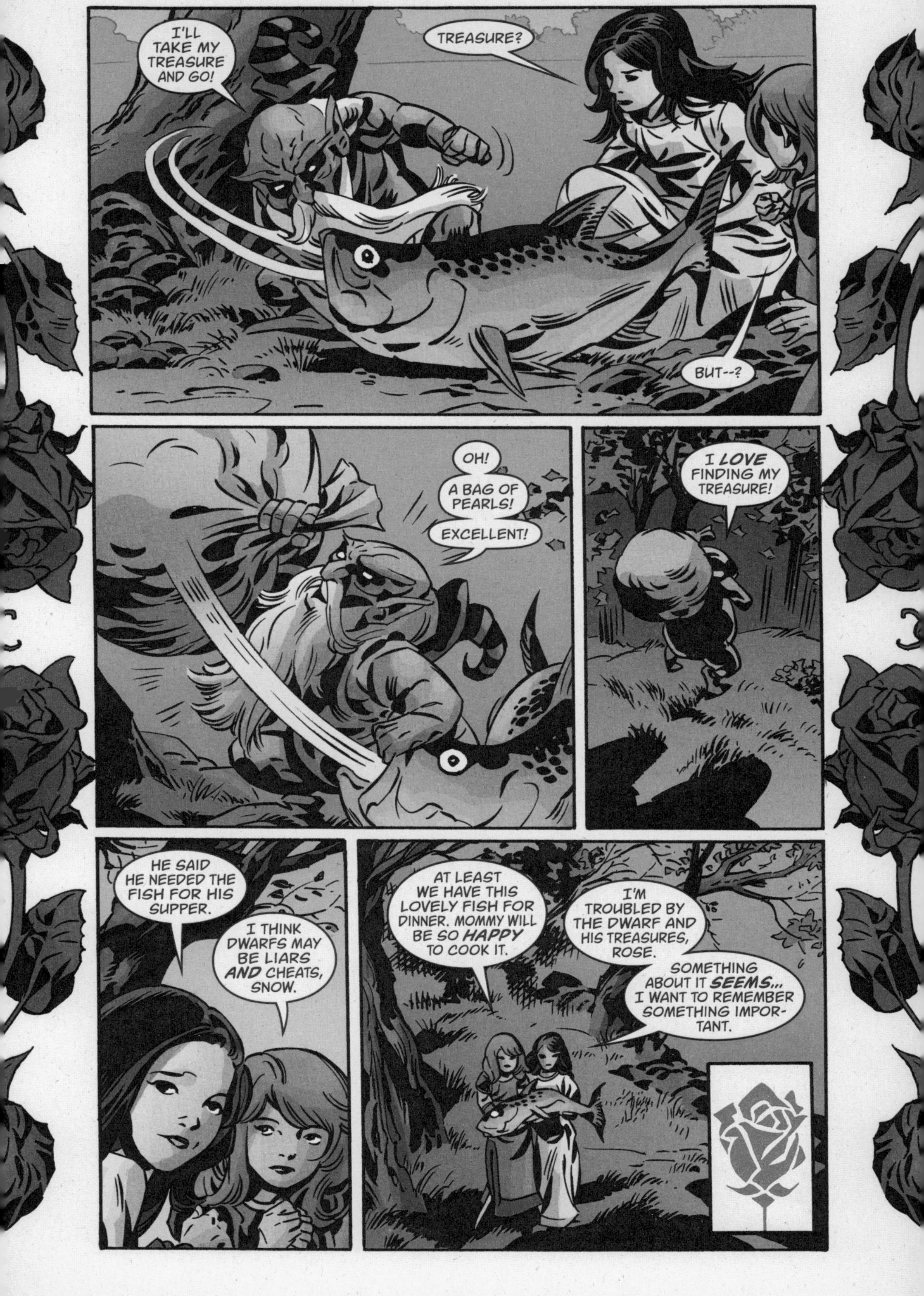
I'LL TAKE MY TREASURE AND GO!
TREASURE?
BUT--?
OH!
A BAG OF PEARLS!
EXCELLENT!
I LOVE FINDING MY TREASURE!
HE SAID HE NEEDED THE FISH FOR HIS SUPPER.
I THINK DWARFS MAY BE LIARS AND CHEATS, SNOW.
AT LEAST WE HAVE THIS LOVELY FISH FOR DINNER. MOMMY WILL BE SO HAPPY TO COOK IT.
I'M TROUBLED BY THE DWARF AND HIS TREASURES, ROSE.
SOMETHING ABOUT IT SEEMS... I WANT TO REMEMBER SOMETHING IMPORTANT.

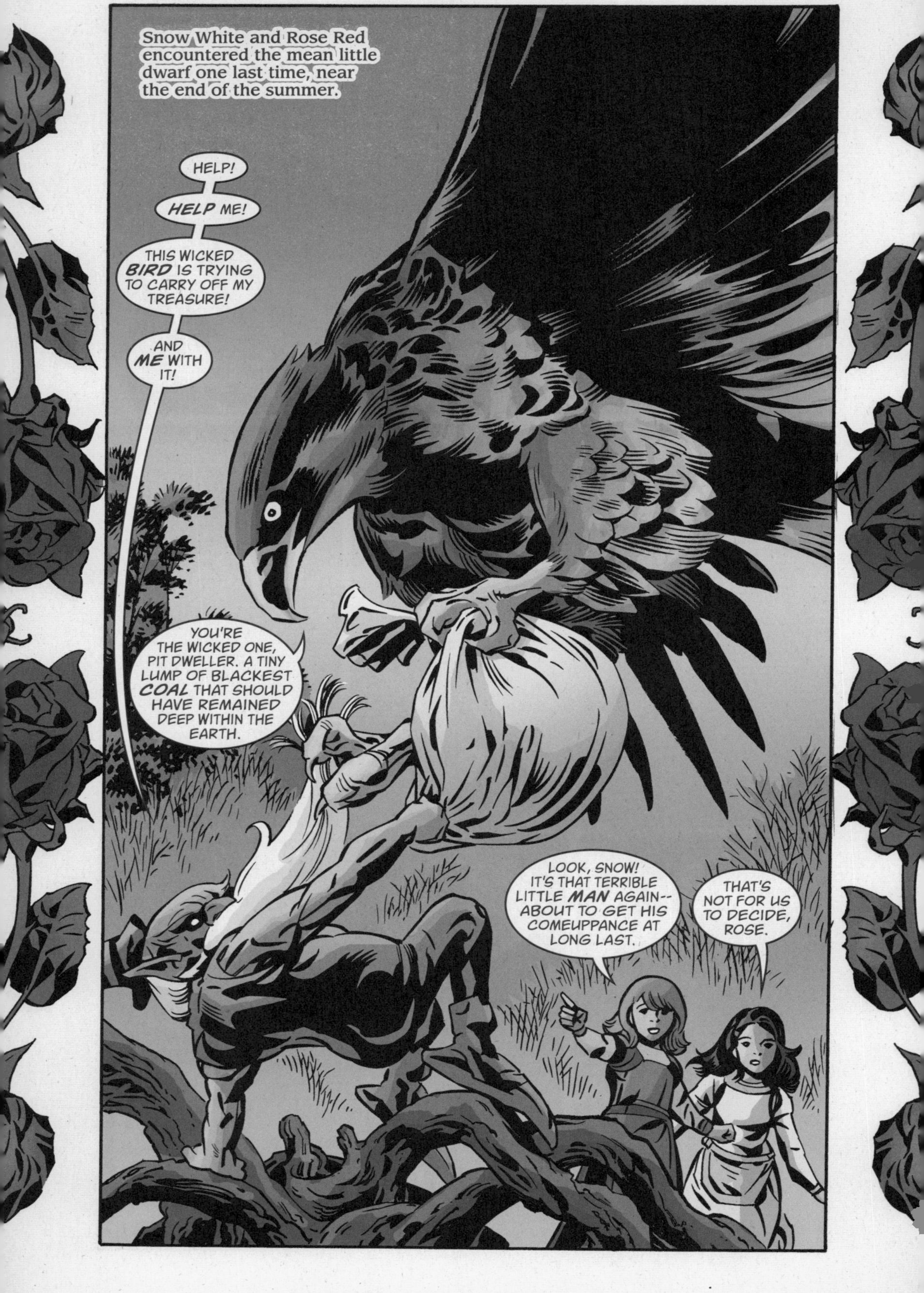
Snow White and Rose Red encountered the mean little dwarf one last time, near the end of the summer.
HELP!
HELP ME!
THIS WICKED BIRD IS TRYING TO CARRY OFF MY TREASURE!
AND ME WITH IT!
YOU'RE THE WICKED ONE, PIT DWELLER. A TINY LUMP OF BLACKEST COAL THAT SHOULD HAVE REMAINED DEEP WITHIN THE EARTH.
LOOK, SNOW! IT'S THAT TERRIBLE LITTLE MAN AGAIN-- ABOUT TO GET HIS COMEUPPANCE AT LONG LAST.
THAT'S NOT FOR US TO DECIDE, ROSE.

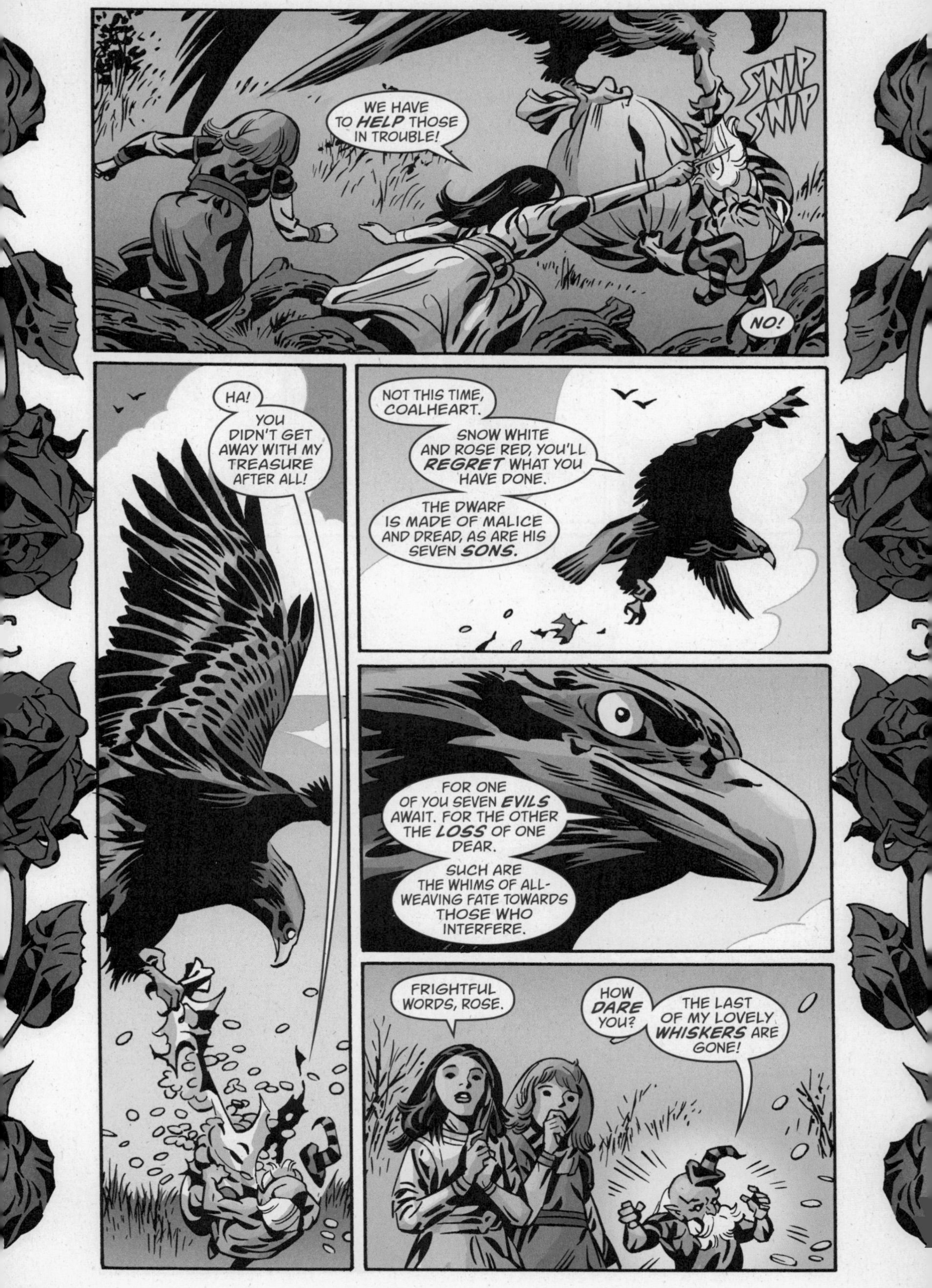
WE HAVE TO HELP THOSE IN TROUBLE!
SNIP SNIP
NO!
HA!
YOU DIDN'T GET AWAY WITH MY TREASURE AFTER ALL!
NOT THIS TIME, COALHEART.
SNOW WHITE AND ROSE RED, YOU'LL REGRET WHAT YOU HAVE DONE.
THE DWARF IS MADE OF MALICE AND DREAD, AS ARE HIS SEVEN SONS.
FOR ONE OF YOU SEVEN EVILS AWAIT. FOR THE OTHER THE LOSS OF ONE DEAR.
SUCH ARE THE WHIMS OF ALL-WEAVING FATE TOWARDS THOSE WHO INTERFERE.
FRIGHTFUL WORDS, ROSE.
HOW DARE YOU?
THE LAST OF MY LOVELY WHISKERS ARE GONE!

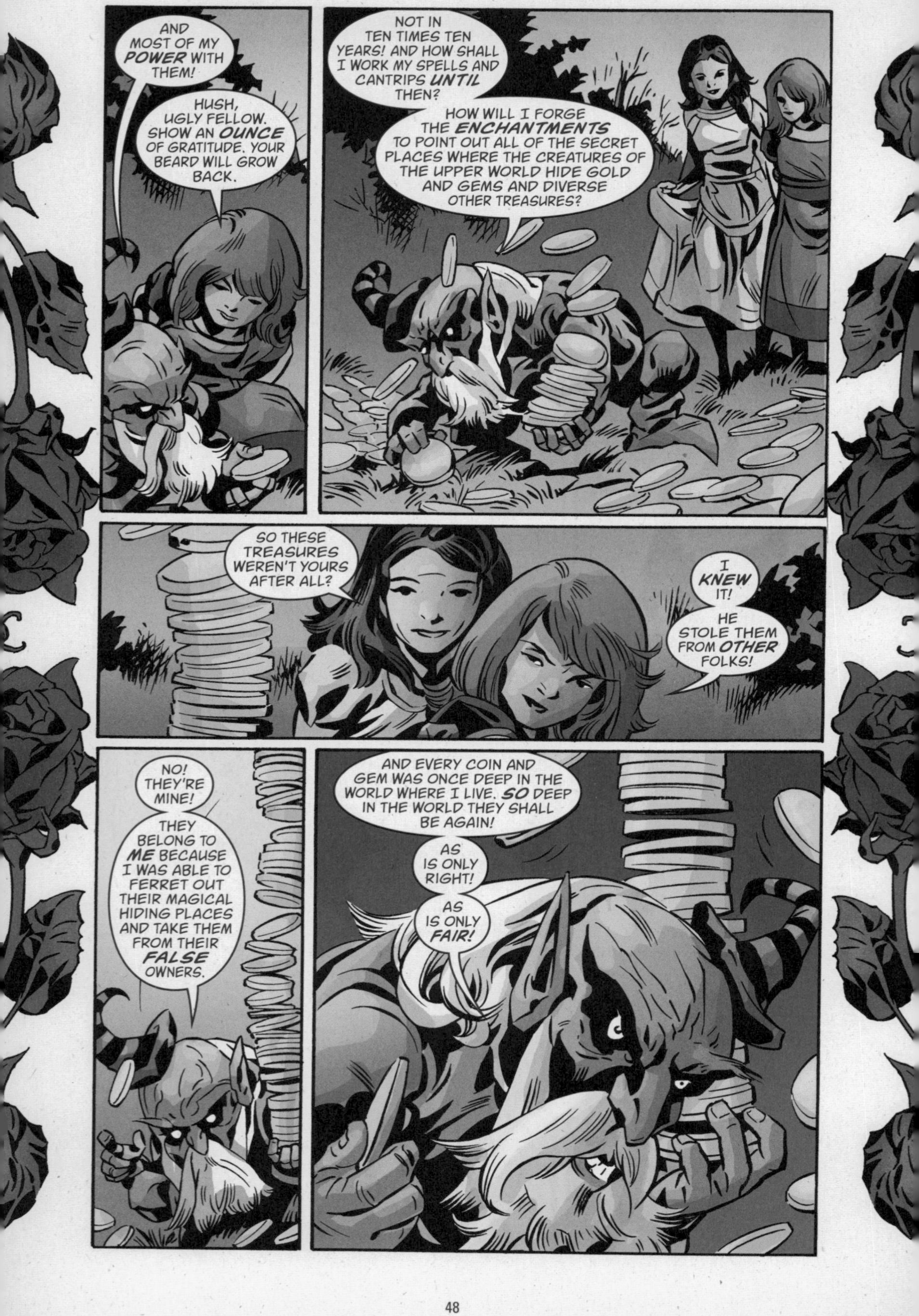
AND MOST OF MY POWER WITH THEM!
HUSH, UGLY FELLOW. SHOW AN OUNCE OF GRATITUDE. YOUR BEARD WILL GROW BACK.
NOT IN TEN TIMES TEN YEARS! AND HOW SHALL I WORK MY SPELLS AND CANTRIPS UNTIL THEN?
HOW WILL I FORGE THE ENCHANTMENTS TO POINT OUT ALL OF THE SECRET PLACES WHERE THE CREATURES OF THE UPPER WORLD HIDE GOLD AND GEMS AND DIVERSE OTHER TREASURES?
SO THESE TREASURES WEREN'T YOURS AFTER ALL?
I KNEW IT!
HE STOLE THEM FROM OTHER FOLKS!
NO! THEY'RE MINE!
THEY BELONG TO ME BECAUSE I WAS ABLE TO FERRET OUT THEIR MAGICAL HIDING PLACES AND TAKE THEM FROM THEIR FALSE OWNERS.
AND EVERY COIN AND GEM WAS ONCE DEEP IN THE WORLD WHERE I LIVE. SO DEEP IN THE WORLD THEY SHALL BE AGAIN!
AS IS ONLY RIGHT!
AS IS ONLY FAIR!

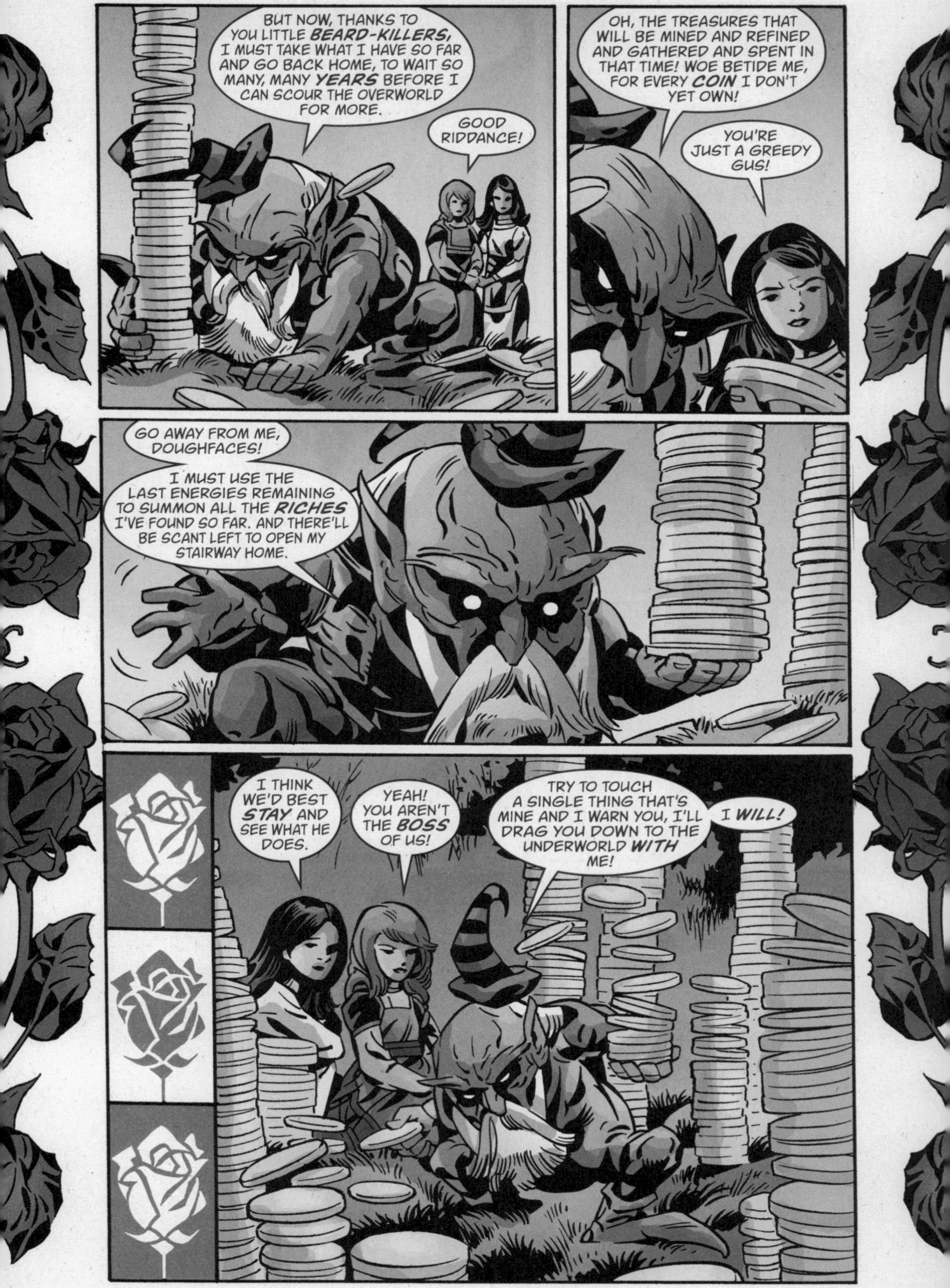
BUT NOW, THANKS TO YOU LITTLE BEARD-KILLERS, I MUST TAKE WHAT I HAVE SO FAR AND GO BACK HOME, TO WAIT SO MANY, MANY YEARS BEFORE I CAN SCOUR THE OVERWORLD FOR MORE.
GOOD RIDDANCE!
OH, THE TREASURES THAT WILL BE MINED AND REFINED AND GATHERED AND SPENT IN THAT TIME! WOE BETIDE ME, FOR EVERY COIN I DON'T YET OWN!
YOU'RE JUST A GREEDY GUS!
GO AWAY FROM ME, DOUGHFACES!
I MUST USE THE LAST ENERGIES REMAINING TO SUMMON ALL THE RICHES I'VE FOUND SO FAR. AND THERE'LL BE SCANT LEFT TO OPEN MY STAIRWAY HOME.
I THINK WE'D BEST STAY AND SEE WHAT HE DOES.
YEAH! YOU AREN'T THE BOSS OF US!
TRY TO TOUCH A SINGLE THING THAT'S MINE AND I WARN YOU, I'LL DRAG YOU DOWN TO THE UNDERWORLD WITH ME!
I WILL!

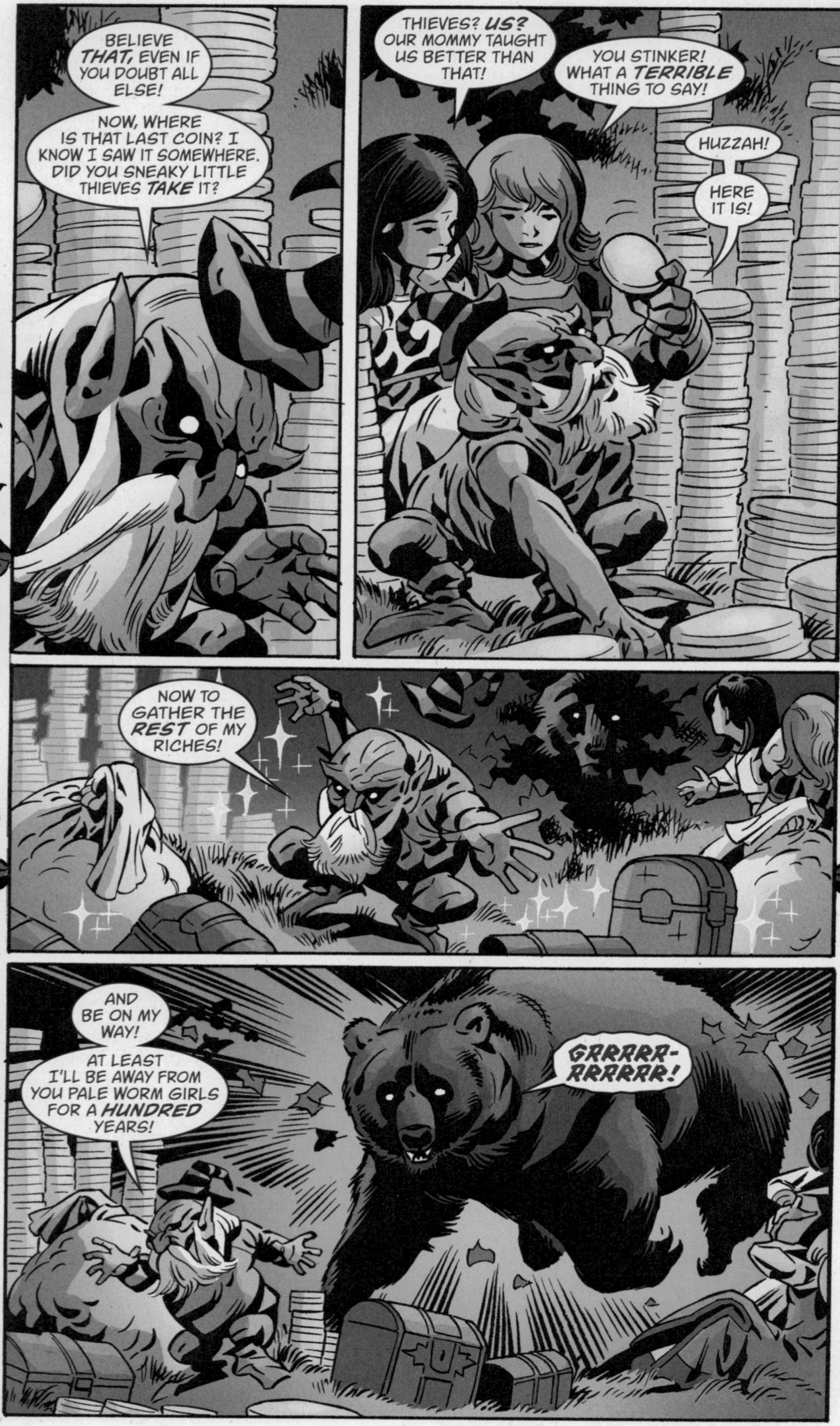
BELIEVE THAT, EVEN IF YOU DOUBT ALL ELSE!
NOW, WHERE IS THAT LAST COIN? I KNOW I SAW IT SOMEWHERE. DID YOU SNEAKY LITTLE THIEVES TAKE IT?
THIEVES? US? OUR MOMMY TAUGHT US BETTER THAN THAT!
YOU STINKER! WHAT A TERRIBLE THING TO SAY!
HUZZAH!
HERE IT IS!
NOW TO GATHER THE REST OF MY RICHES!
AND BE ON MY WAY!
AT LEAST I'LL BE AWAY FROM YOU PALE WORM GIRLS FOR A HUNDRED YEARS!
GRRRRR-RRRRRR!

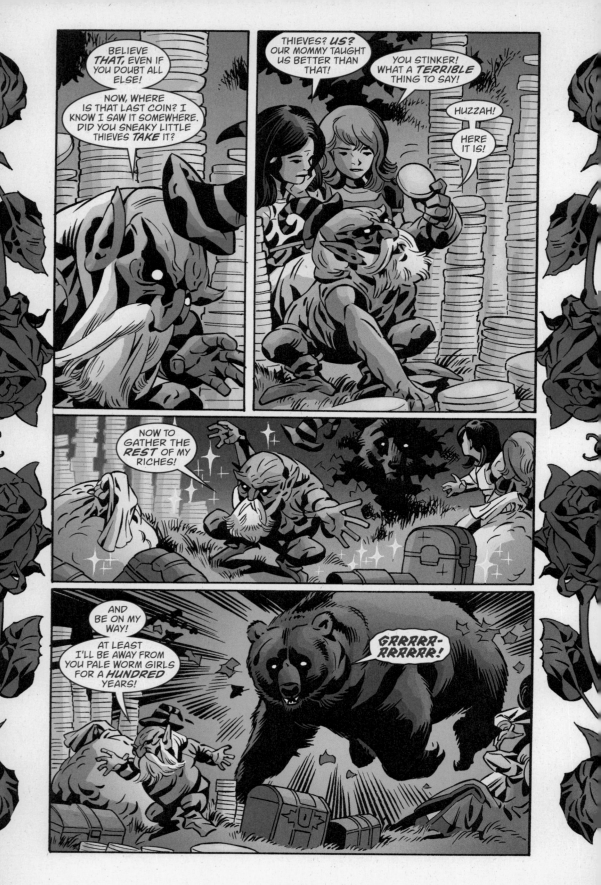

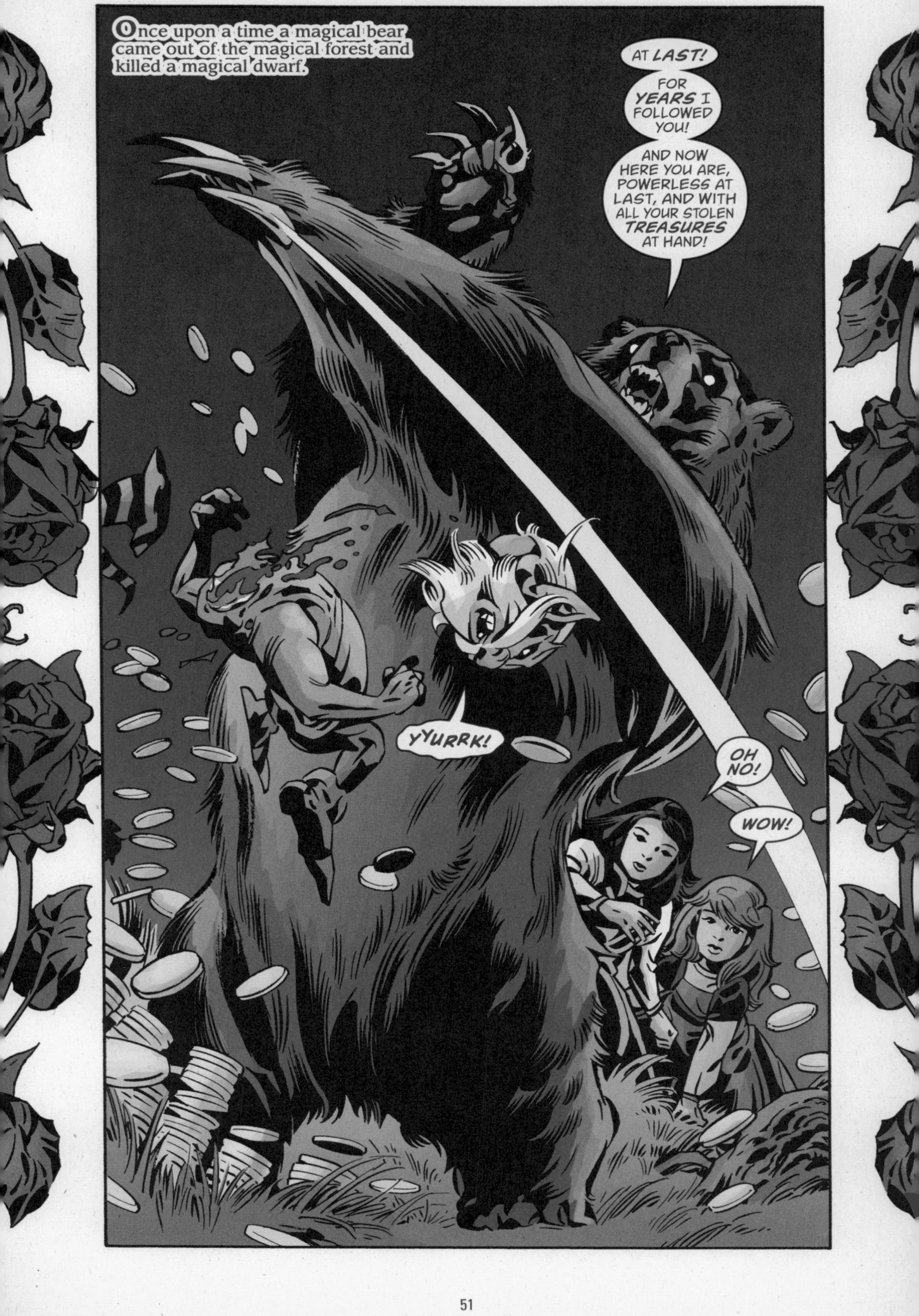
Once upon a time a magical bear came out of the magical forest and killed a magical dwarf.
AT LAST!
FOR YEARS I FOLLOWED YOU!
AND NOW HERE YOU ARE, POWERLESS AT LAST, AND WITH ALL YOUR STOLEN TREASURES AT HAND!
YYURRK!
OH NO!
WOW!

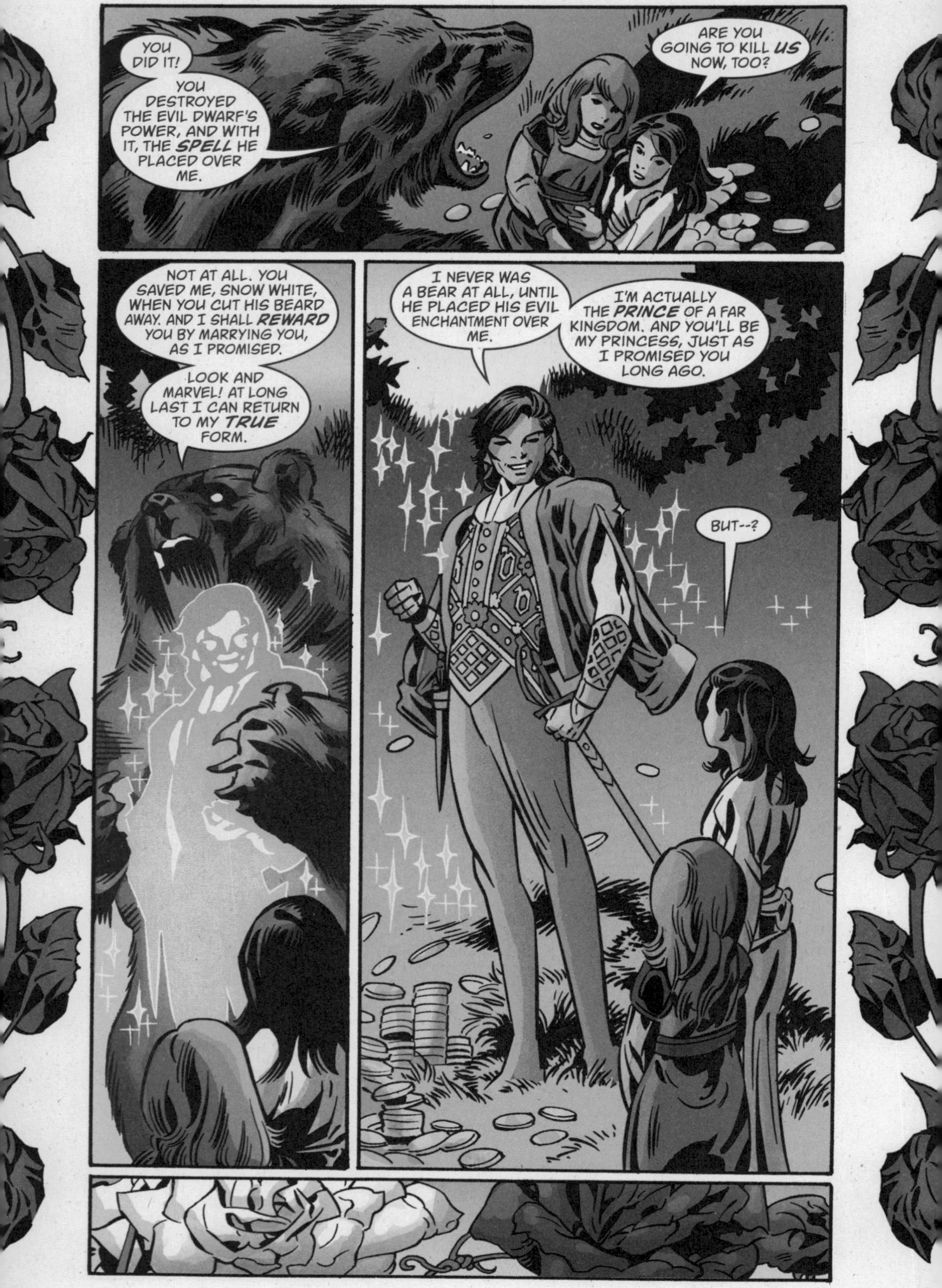
YOU DID IT!
YOU DESTROYED THE EVIL DWARF'S POWER, AND WITH IT, THE *SPELL* HE PLACED OVER ME.
ARE YOU GOING TO KILL *US* NOW, TOO?
NOT AT ALL. YOU SAVED ME, SNOW WHITE, WHEN YOU CUT HIS BEARD AWAY. AND I SHALL *REWARD* YOU BY MARRYING YOU, AS I PROMISED.
LOOK AND MARVEL! AT LONG LAST I CAN RETURN TO MY *TRUE* FORM.
I NEVER WAS A BEAR AT ALL, UNTIL HE PLACED HIS EVIL ENCHANTMENT OVER ME.
I'M ACTUALLY THE *PRINCE* OF A FAR KINGDOM. AND YOU'LL BE MY PRINCESS, JUST AS I PROMISED YOU LONG AGO.
BUT--?

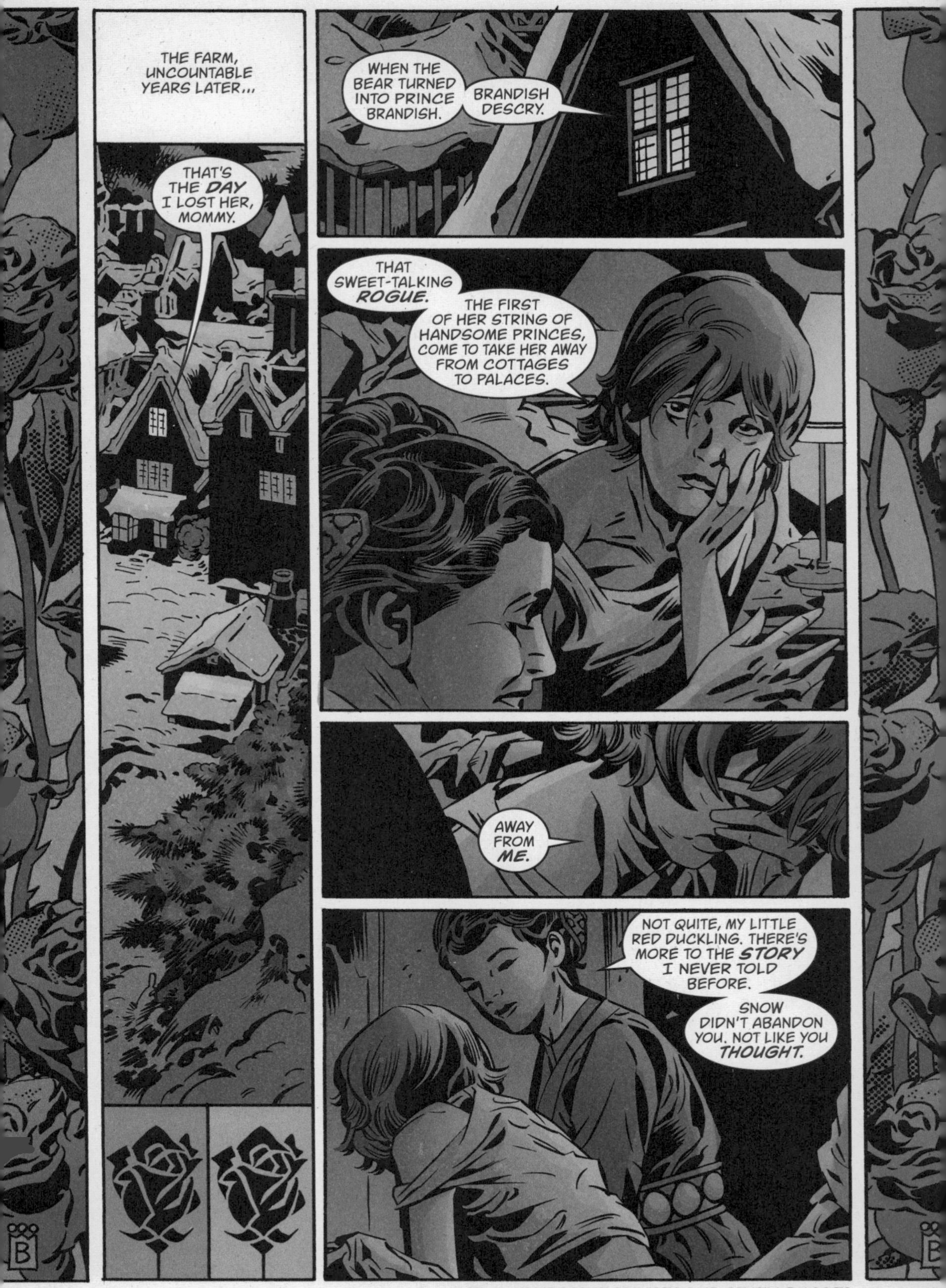
THE FARM, UNCOUNTABLE YEARS LATER...
THAT'S THE DAY I LOST HER, MOMMY.
WHEN THE BEAR TURNED INTO PRINCE BRANDISH.
BRANDISH DESCRY.
THAT SWEET-TALKING ROGUE.
THE FIRST OF HER STRING OF HANDSOME PRINCES, COME TO TAKE HER AWAY FROM COTTAGES TO PALACES.
AWAY FROM ME.
NOT QUITE, MY LITTLE RED DUCKLING. THERE'S MORE TO THE STORY I NEVER TOLD BEFORE.
SNOW DIDN'T ABANDON YOU. NOT LIKE YOU THOUGHT.

NEXT: HANDSOME PRINCES AND SEVEN DWARFS

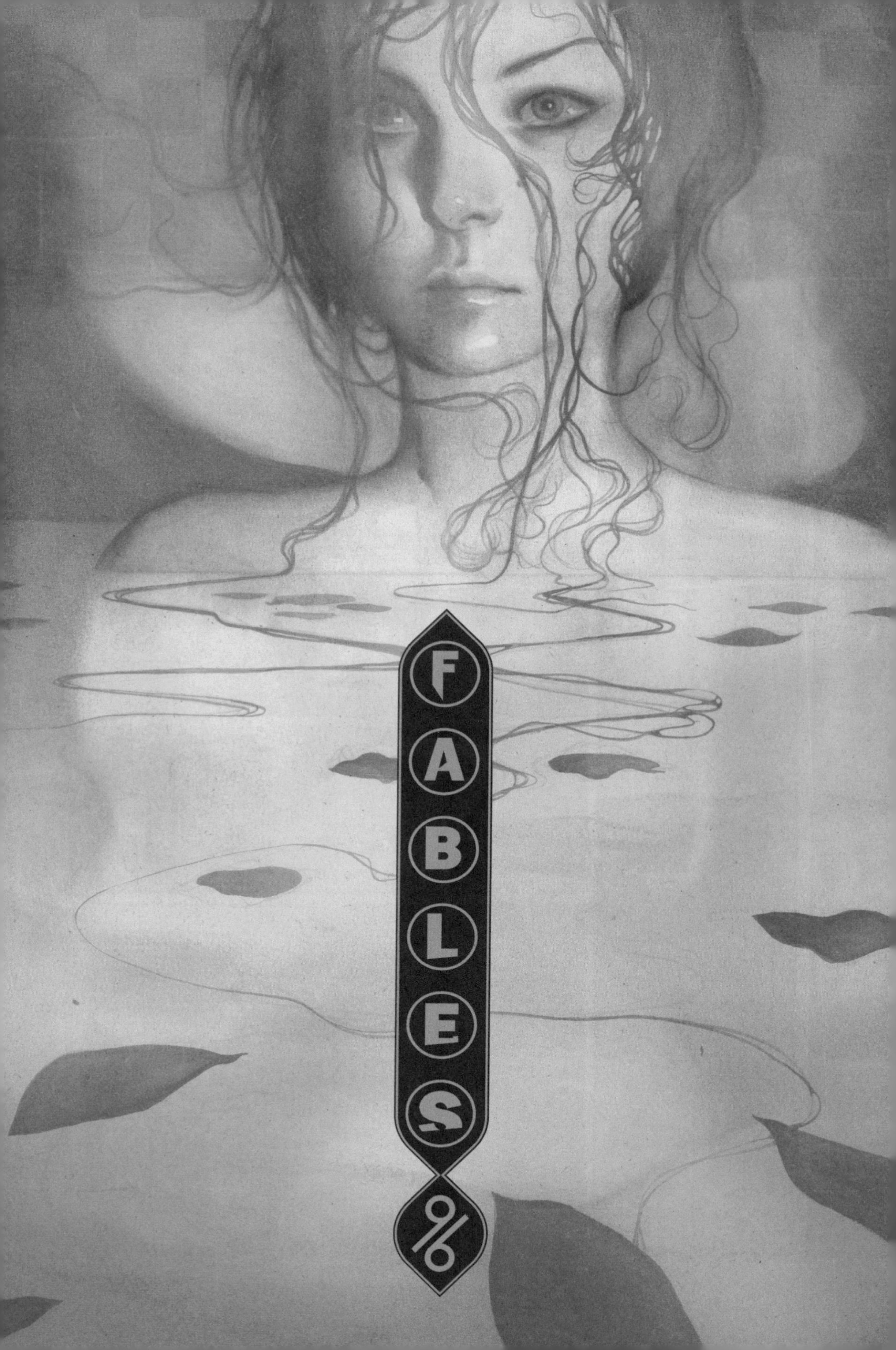
FABLES
96

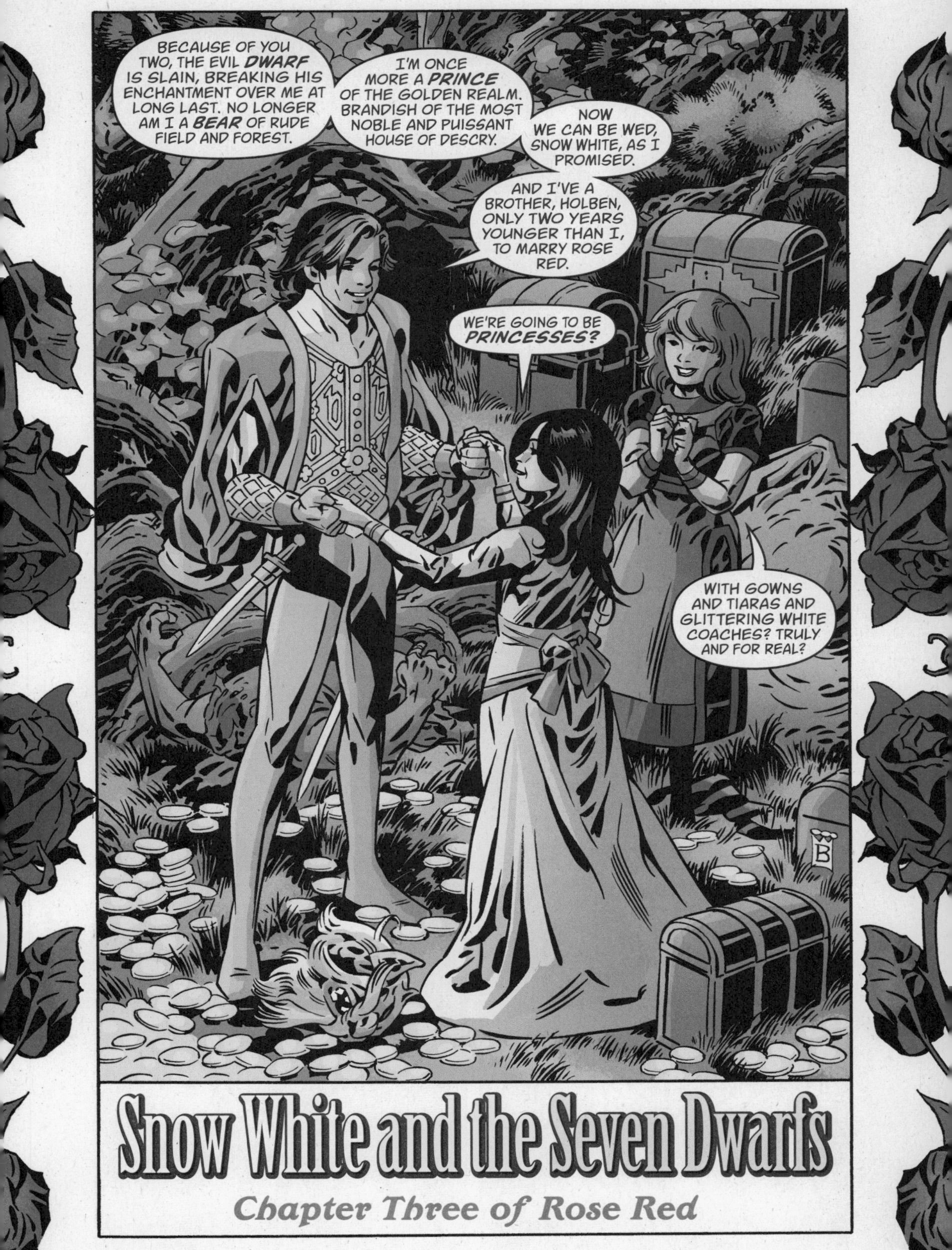
BECAUSE OF YOU TWO, THE EVIL DWARF IS SLAIN, BREAKING HIS ENCHANTMENT OVER ME AT LONG LAST. NO LONGER AM I A BEAR OF RUDE FIELD AND FOREST.
I'M ONCE MORE A PRINCE OF THE GOLDEN REALM. BRANDISH OF THE MOST NOBLE AND PUISSANT HOUSE OF DESCRY.
NOW WE CAN BE WED, SNOW WHITE, AS I PROMISED.
AND I'VE A BROTHER, HOLBEN, ONLY TWO YEARS YOUNGER THAN I, TO MARRY ROSE RED.
WE'RE GOING TO BE PRINCESSES?
WITH GOWNS AND TIARAS AND GLITTERING WHITE COACHES? TRULY AND FOR REAL?

Snow White and the Seven Dwarfs

Chapter Three of Rose Red

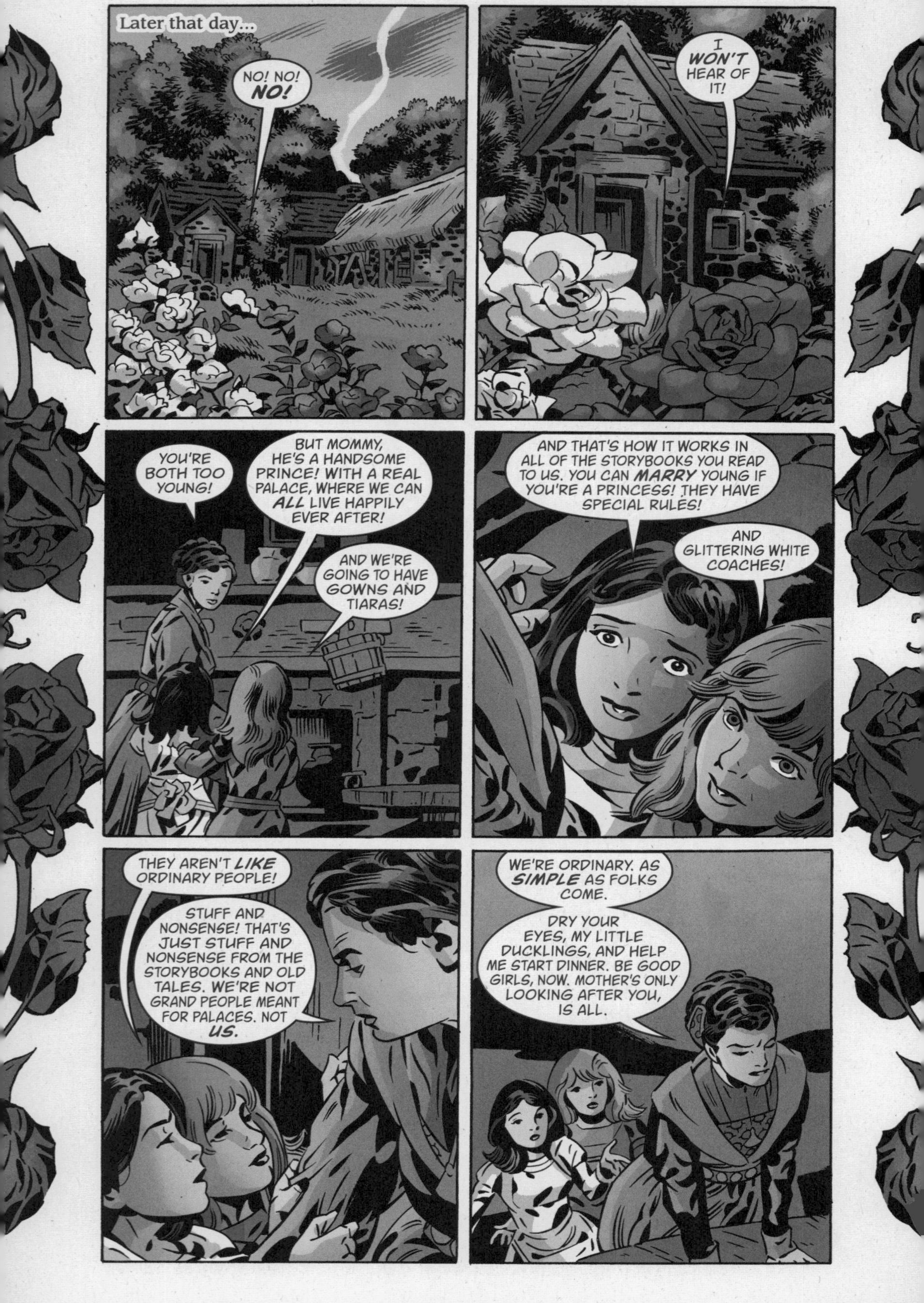
Later that day...
NO! NO! NO!
I WON'T HEAR OF IT!
YOU'RE BOTH TOO YOUNG!
BUT MOMMY, HE'S A HANDSOME PRINCE! WITH A REAL PALACE, WHERE WE CAN ALL LIVE HAPPILY EVER AFTER!
AND WE'RE GOING TO HAVE GOWNS AND TIARAS!
AND THAT'S HOW IT WORKS IN ALL OF THE STORYBOOKS YOU READ TO US. YOU CAN MARRY YOUNG IF YOU'RE A PRINCESS! THEY HAVE SPECIAL RULES!
AND GLITTERING WHITE COACHES!
THEY AREN'T LIKE ORDINARY PEOPLE!
STUFF AND NONSENSE! THAT'S JUST STUFF AND NONSENSE FROM THE STORYBOOKS AND OLD TALES. WE'RE NOT GRAND PEOPLE MEANT FOR PALACES. NOT US.
WE'RE ORDINARY. AS SIMPLE AS FOLKS COME.
DRY YOUR EYES, MY LITTLE DUCKLINGS, AND HELP ME START DINNER. BE GOOD GIRLS, NOW. MOTHER'S ONLY LOOKING AFTER YOU, IS ALL.

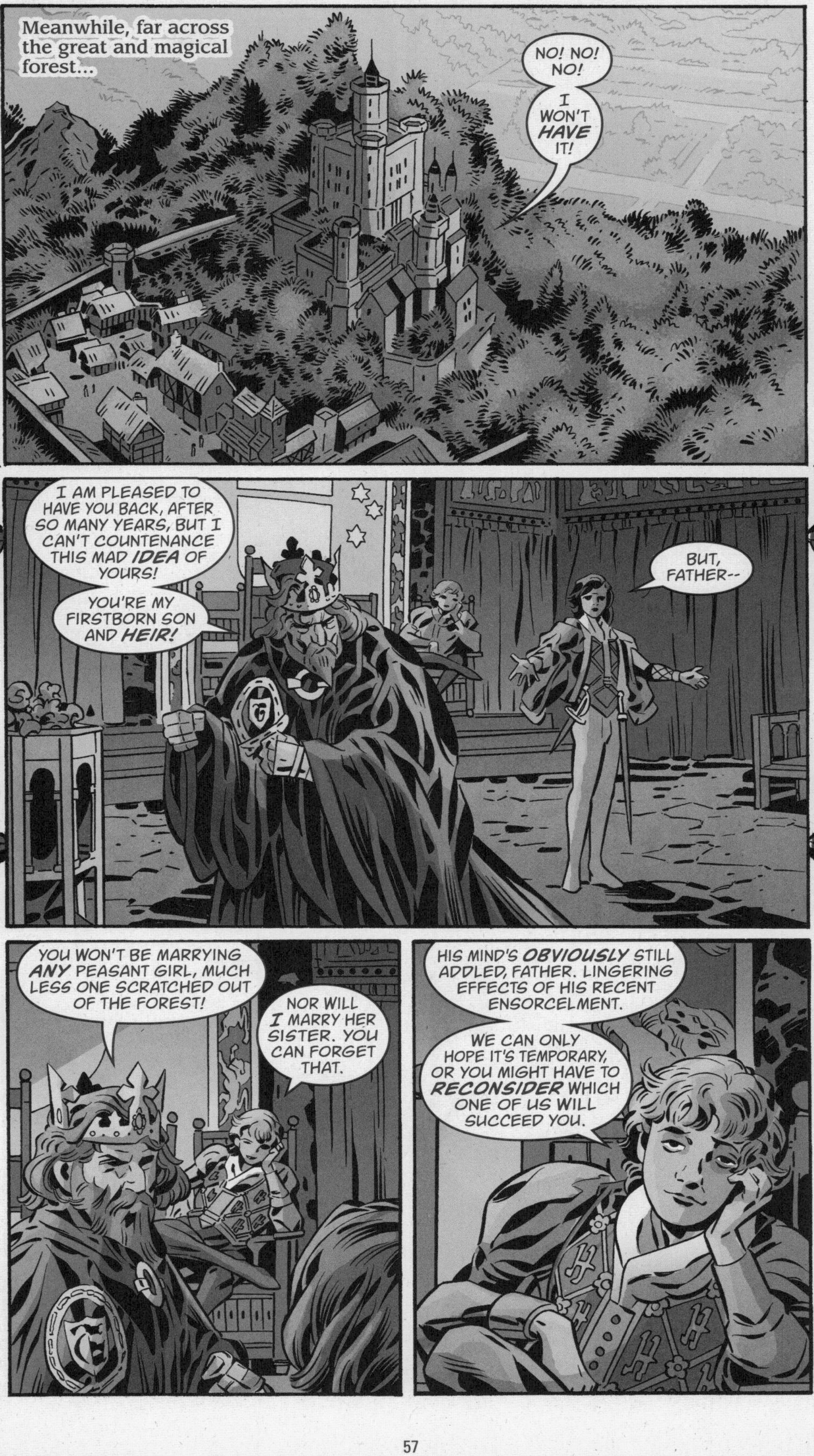

Meanwhile, far across the great and magical forest...
NO! NO! NO!
I WON'T HAVE IT!
I AM PLEASED TO HAVE YOU BACK, AFTER SO MANY YEARS, BUT I CAN'T COUNTENANCE THIS MAD IDEA OF YOURS!
YOU'RE MY FIRSTBORN SON AND HEIR!
BUT, FATHER--
YOU WON'T BE MARRYING ANY PEASANT GIRL, MUCH LESS ONE SCRATCHED OUT OF THE FOREST!
NOR WILL I MARRY HER SISTER. YOU CAN FORGET THAT.
HIS MIND'S OBVIOUSLY STILL ADDLED, FATHER. LINGERING EFFECTS OF HIS RECENT ENSORCELMENT.
WE CAN ONLY HOPE IT'S TEMPORARY, OR YOU MIGHT HAVE TO RECONSIDER WHICH ONE OF US WILL SUCCEED YOU.

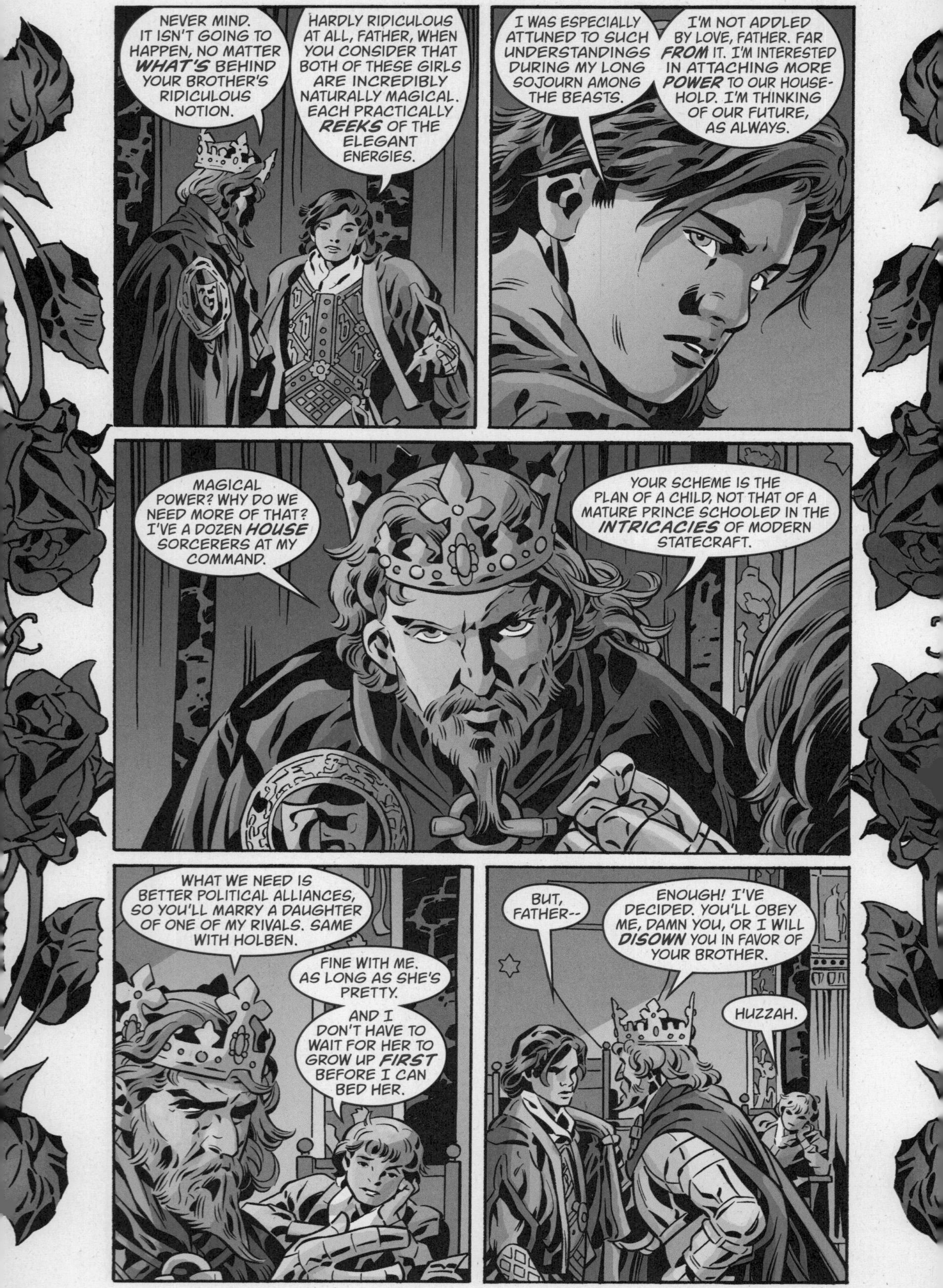
NEVER MIND. IT ISN'T GOING TO HAPPEN, NO MATTER WHAT'S BEHIND YOUR BROTHER'S RIDICULOUS NOTION.
HARDLY RIDICULOUS AT ALL, FATHER, WHEN YOU CONSIDER THAT BOTH OF THESE GIRLS ARE INCREDIBLY NATURALLY MAGICAL. EACH PRACTICALLY REEKS OF THE ELEGANT ENERGIES.
I WAS ESPECIALLY ATTUNED TO SUCH UNDERSTANDINGS DURING MY LONG SOJOURN AMONG THE BEASTS.
I'M NOT ADDLED BY LOVE, FATHER. FAR FROM IT. I'M INTERESTED IN ATTACHING MORE POWER TO OUR HOUSE-HOLD. I'M THINKING OF OUR FUTURE, AS ALWAYS.
MAGICAL POWER? WHY DO WE NEED MORE OF THAT? I'VE A DOZEN HOUSE SORCERERS AT MY COMMAND.
YOUR SCHEME IS THE PLAN OF A CHILD, NOT THAT OF A MATURE PRINCE SCHOOLED IN THE INTRICACIES OF MODERN STATECRAFT.
WHAT WE NEED IS BETTER POLITICAL ALLIANCES, SO YOU'LL MARRY A DAUGHTER OF ONE OF MY RIVALS. SAME WITH HOLBEN.
FINE WITH ME. AS LONG AS SHE'S PRETTY.
AND I DON'T HAVE TO WAIT FOR HER TO GROW UP FIRST BEFORE I CAN BED HER.
BUT, FATHER--
ENOUGH! I'VE DECIDED. YOU'LL OBEY ME, DAMN YOU, OR I WILL DISOWN YOU IN FAVOR OF YOUR BROTHER.
HUZZAH.

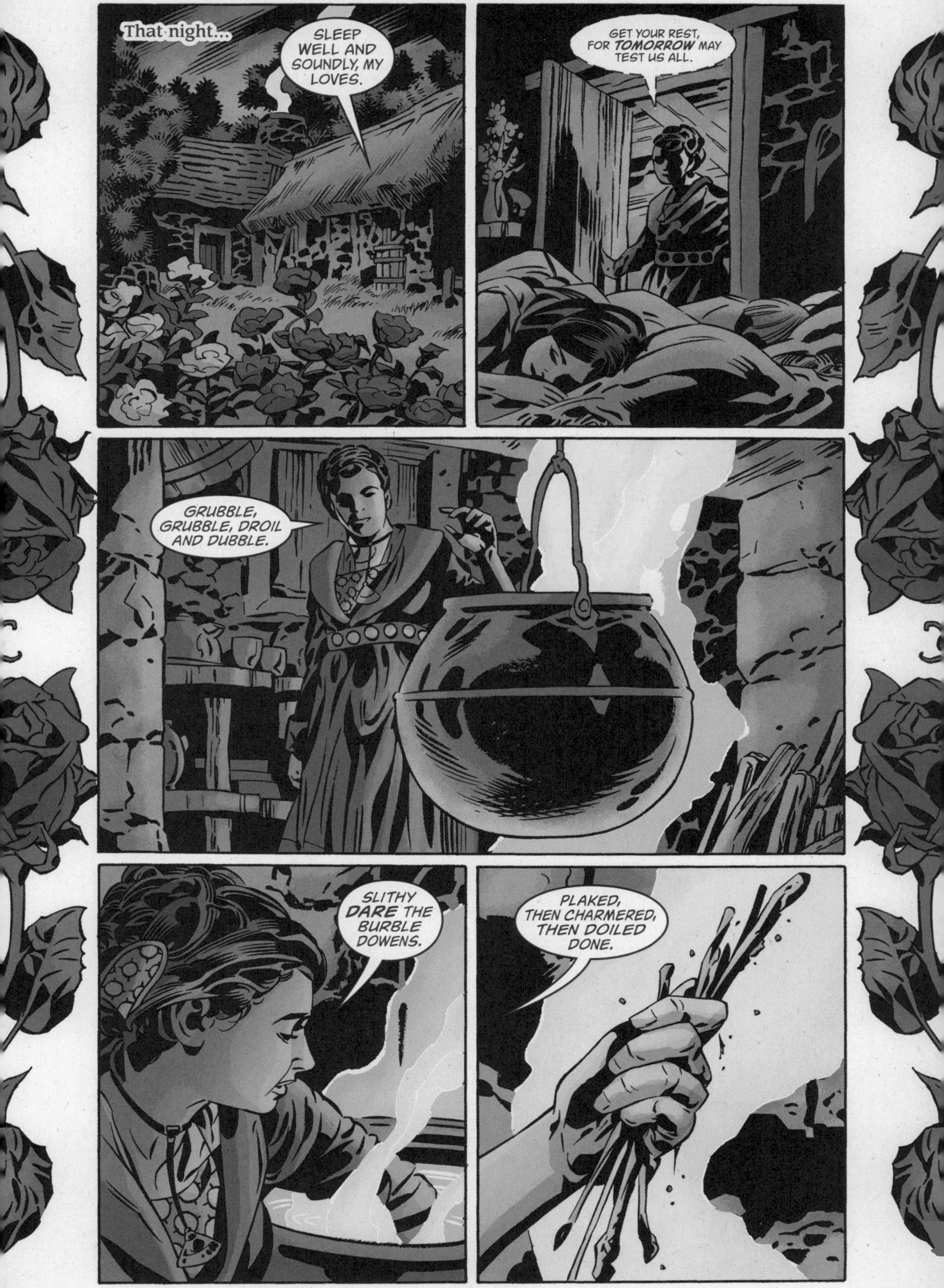

That night...
SLEEP WELL AND SOUNDLY, MY LOVES.
GET YOUR REST, FOR TOMORROW MAY TEST US ALL.
GRUBBLE, GRUBBLE, DROIL AND DUBBLE.
SLITHY DARE THE BURBLE DOWENS.
PLAKED, THEN CHARMERED, THEN DOILED DONE.

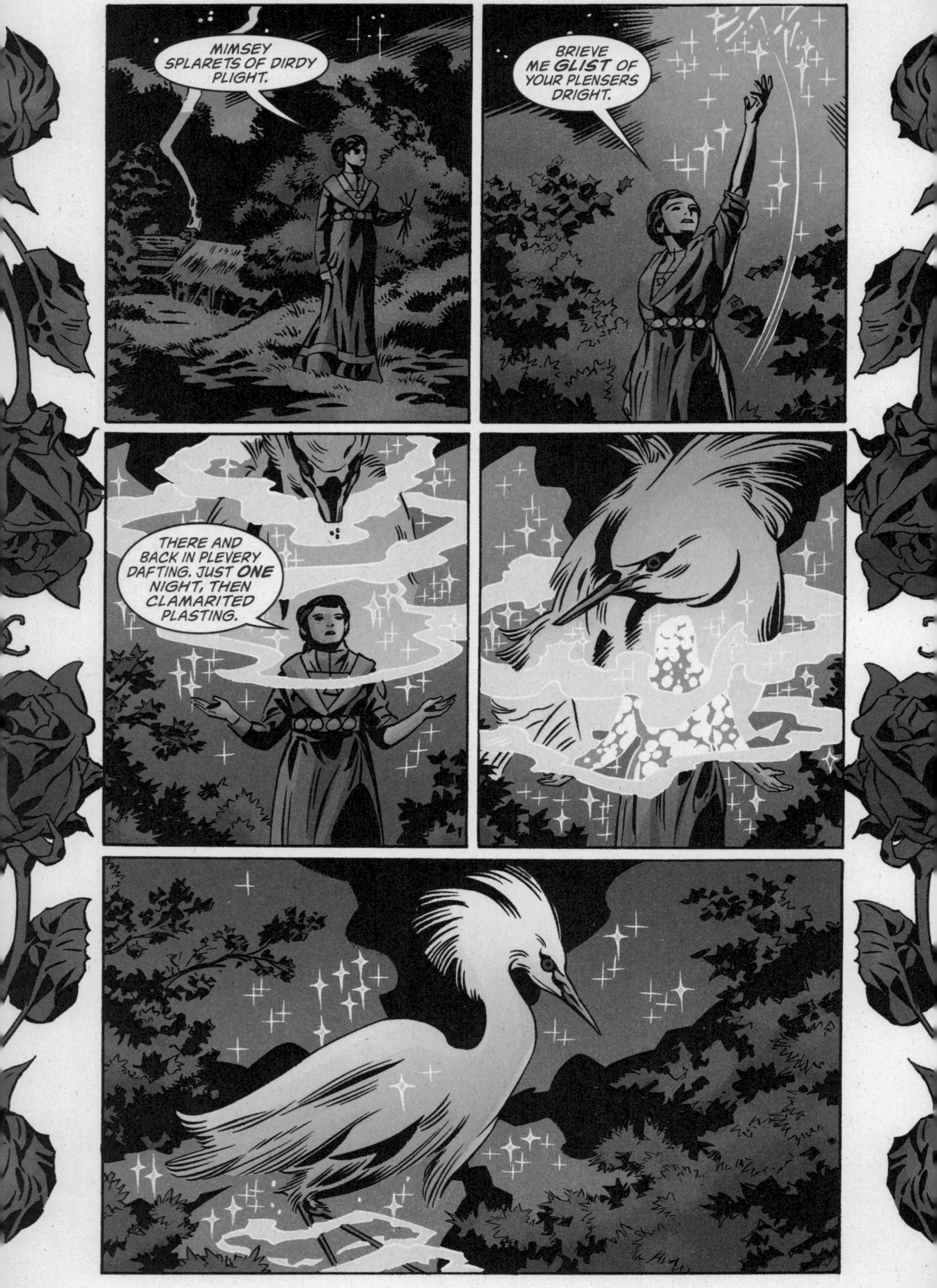
MIMSEY SPLARETS OF DIRDY PLIGHT.
BRIEVE ME GLIST OF YOUR PLENSERS DRIGHT.
THERE AND BACK IN PLEVERY DAFTING. JUST ONE NIGHT, THEN CLAMARITED PLASTING.

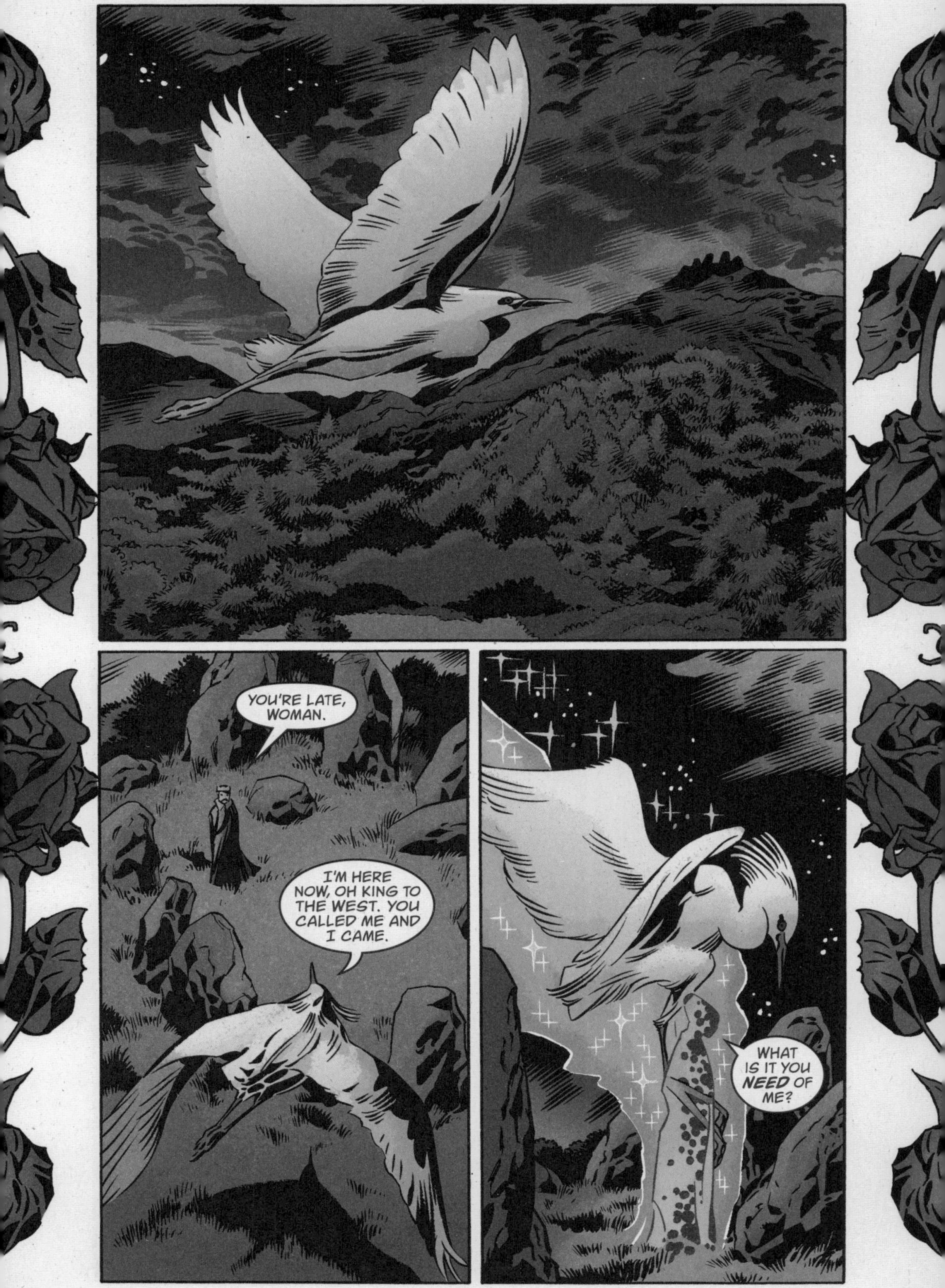
YOU'RE LATE, WOMAN.
I'M HERE NOW, OH KING TO THE WEST. YOU CALLED ME AND I CAME.
WHAT IS IT YOU NEED OF ME?

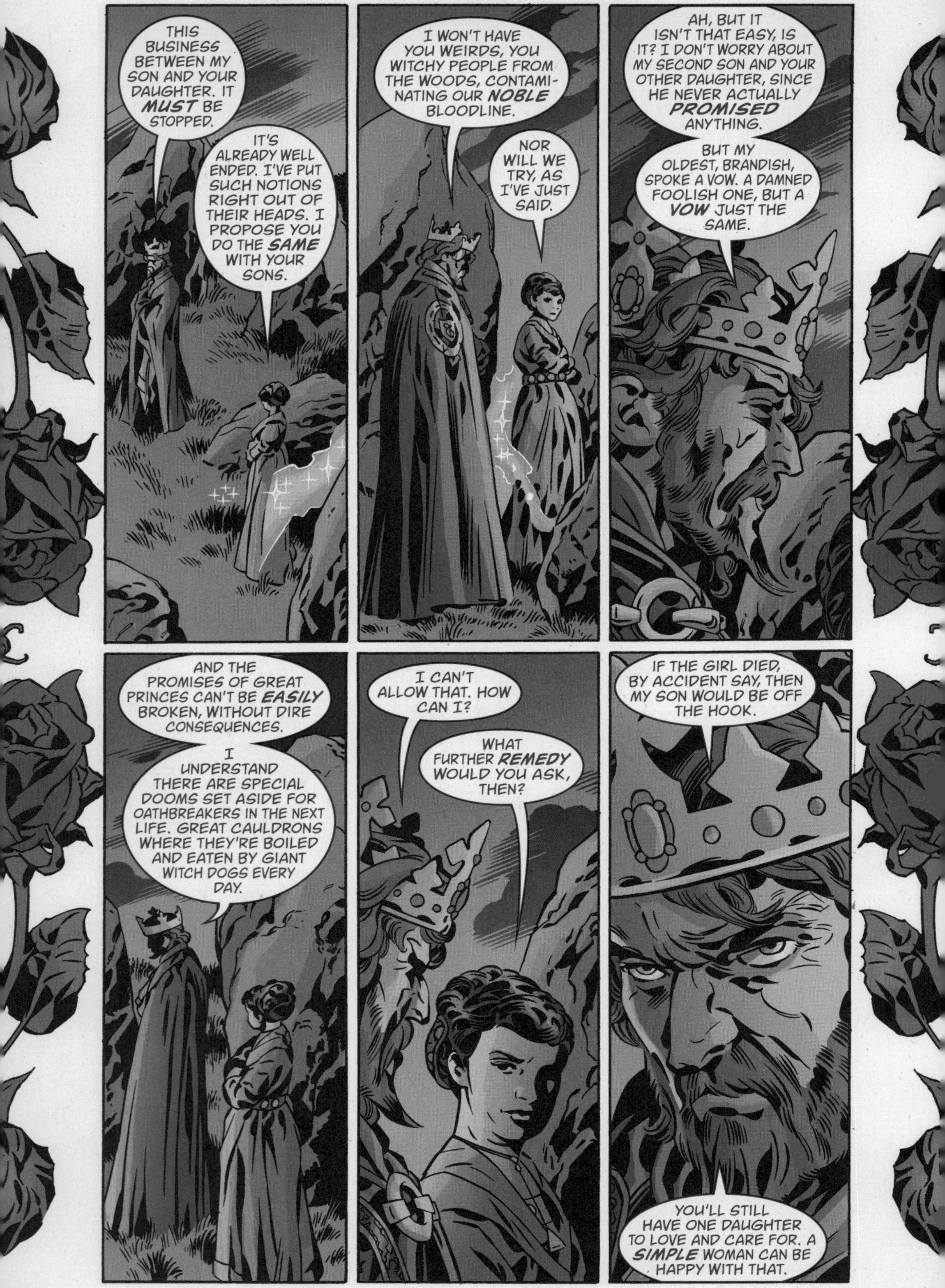
THIS BUSINESS BETWEEN MY SON AND YOUR DAUGHTER. IT MUST BE STOPPED.
IT'S ALREADY WELL ENDED. I'VE PUT SUCH NOTIONS RIGHT OUT OF THEIR HEADS. I PROPOSE YOU DO THE SAME WITH YOUR SONS.
I WON'T HAVE YOU WEIRDS, YOU WITCHY PEOPLE FROM THE WOODS, CONTAMINATING OUR NOBLE BLOODLINE.
NOR WILL WE TRY, AS I'VE JUST SAID.
AH, BUT IT ISN'T THAT EASY, IS IT? I DON'T WORRY ABOUT MY SECOND SON AND YOUR OTHER DAUGHTER, SINCE HE NEVER ACTUALLY PROMISED ANYTHING.
BUT MY OLDEST, BRANDISH, SPOKE A VOW. A DAMNED FOOLISH ONE, BUT A VOW JUST THE SAME.
AND THE PROMISES OF GREAT PRINCES CAN'T BE EASILY BROKEN, WITHOUT DIRE CONSEQUENCES.
I UNDERSTAND THERE ARE SPECIAL DOOMS SET ASIDE FOR OATHBREAKERS IN THE NEXT LIFE. GREAT CAULDRONS WHERE THEY'RE BOILED AND EATEN BY GIANT WITCH DOGS EVERY DAY.
I CAN'T ALLOW THAT. HOW CAN I?
WHAT FURTHER REMEDY WOULD YOU ASK, THEN?
IF THE GIRL DIED, BY ACCIDENT SAY, THEN MY SON WOULD BE OFF THE HOOK.
YOU'LL STILL HAVE ONE DAUGHTER TO LOVE AND CARE FOR. A SIMPLE WOMAN CAN BE HAPPY WITH THAT.

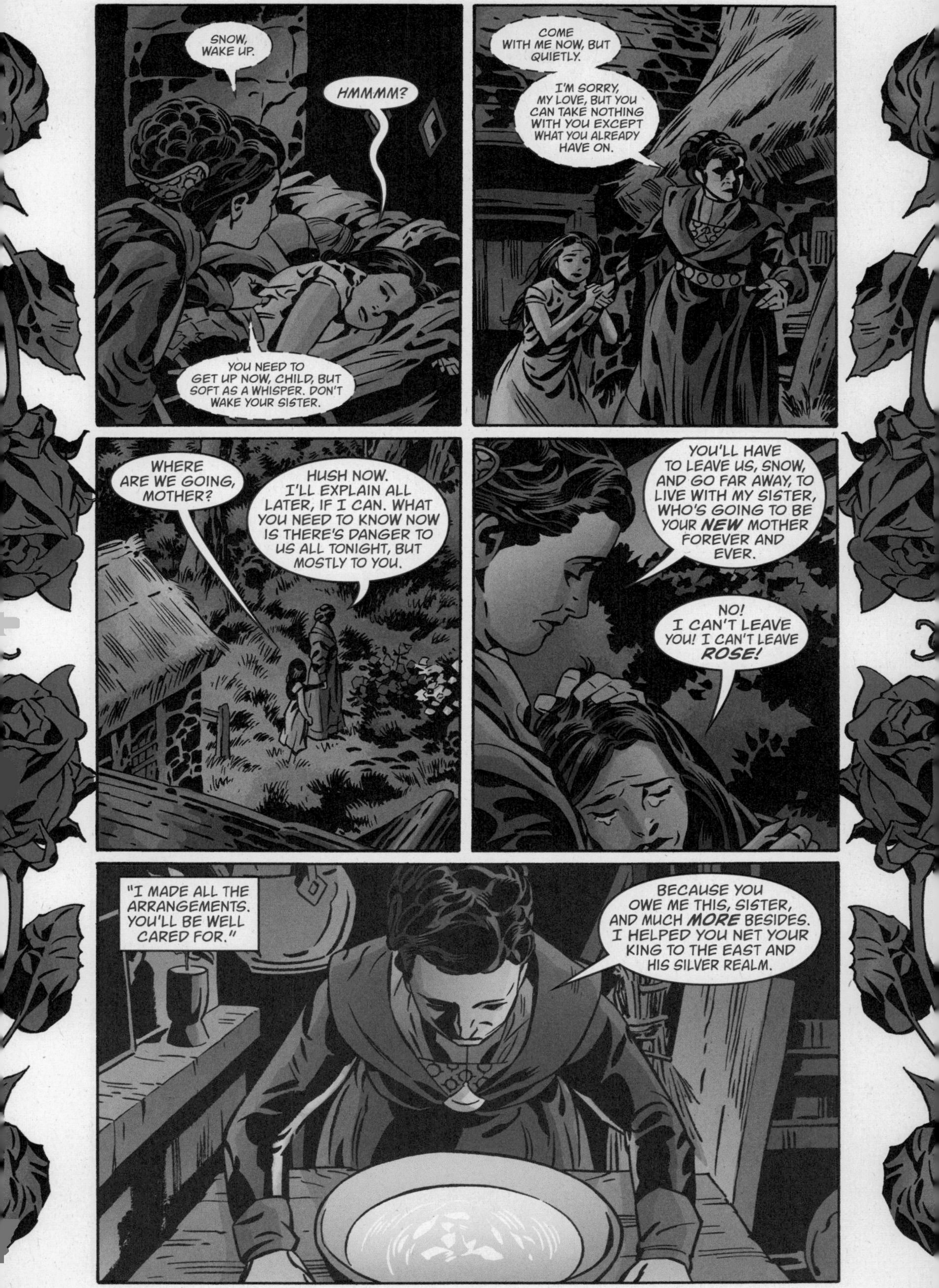
SNOW, WAKE UP.
HMMMM?
YOU NEED TO GET UP NOW, CHILD, BUT SOFT AS A WHISPER. DON'T WAKE YOUR SISTER.
COME WITH ME NOW, BUT QUIETLY.
I'M SORRY, MY LOVE, BUT YOU CAN TAKE NOTHING WITH YOU EXCEPT WHAT YOU ALREADY HAVE ON.
WHERE ARE WE GOING, MOTHER?
HUSH NOW. I'LL EXPLAIN ALL LATER, IF I CAN. WHAT YOU NEED TO KNOW NOW IS THERE'S DANGER TO US ALL TONIGHT, BUT MOSTLY TO YOU.
YOU'LL HAVE TO LEAVE US, SNOW, AND GO FAR AWAY, TO LIVE WITH MY SISTER, WHO'S GOING TO BE YOUR NEW MOTHER FOREVER AND EVER.
NO! I CAN'T LEAVE YOU! I CAN'T LEAVE ROSE!
"I MADE ALL THE ARRANGEMENTS. YOU'LL BE WELL CARED FOR."
BECAUSE YOU OWE ME THIS, SISTER, AND MUCH MORE BESIDES. I HELPED YOU NET YOUR KING TO THE EAST AND HIS SILVER REALM.

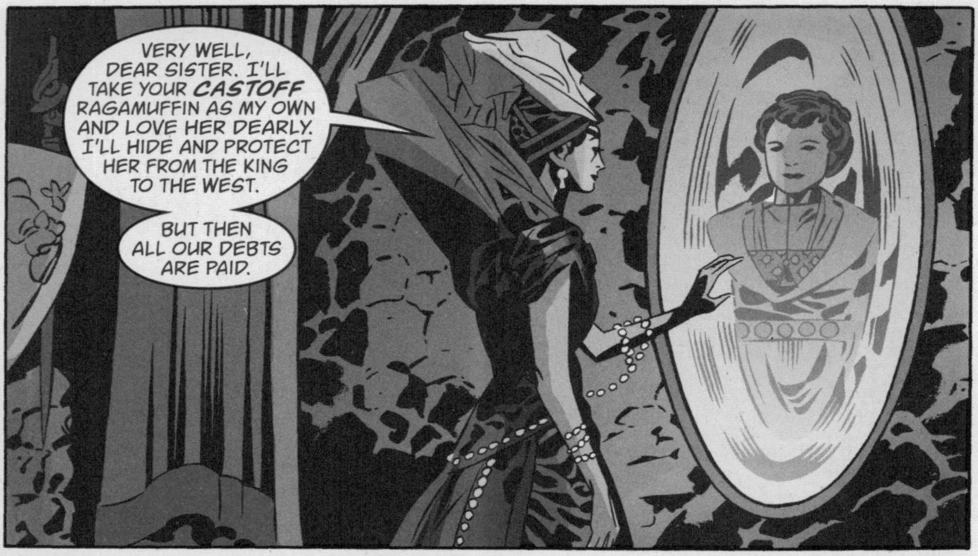
VERY WELL, DEAR SISTER. I'LL TAKE YOUR CASTOFF RAGAMUFFIN AS MY OWN AND LOVE HER DEARLY. I'LL HIDE AND PROTECT HER FROM THE KING TO THE WEST.
BUT THEN ALL OUR DEBTS ARE PAID.

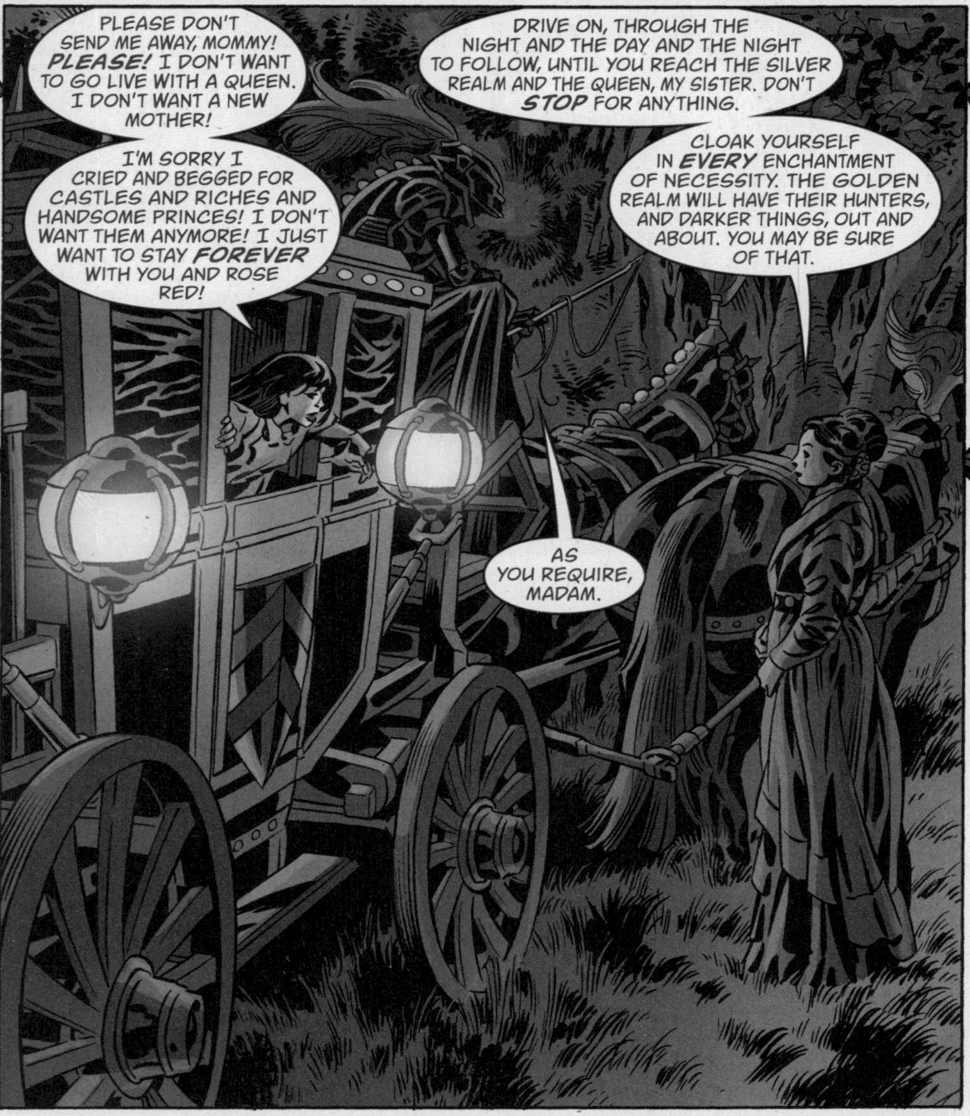
PLEASE DON'T SEND ME AWAY, MOMMY! PLEASE! I DON'T WANT TO GO LIVE WITH A QUEEN. I DON'T WANT A NEW MOTHER!
I'M SORRY I CRIED AND BEGGED FOR CASTLES AND RICHES AND HANDSOME PRINCES! I DON'T WANT THEM ANYMORE! I JUST WANT TO STAY FOREVER WITH YOU AND ROSE RED!
DRIVE ON, THROUGH THE NIGHT AND THE DAY AND THE NIGHT TO FOLLOW, UNTIL YOU REACH THE SILVER REALM AND THE QUEEN, MY SISTER. DON'T STOP FOR ANYTHING.
CLOAK YOURSELF IN EVERY ENCHANTMENT OF NECESSITY. THE GOLDEN REALM WILL HAVE THEIR HUNTERS, AND DARKER THINGS, OUT AND ABOUT. YOU MAY BE SURE OF THAT.
AS YOU REQUIRE, MADAM.

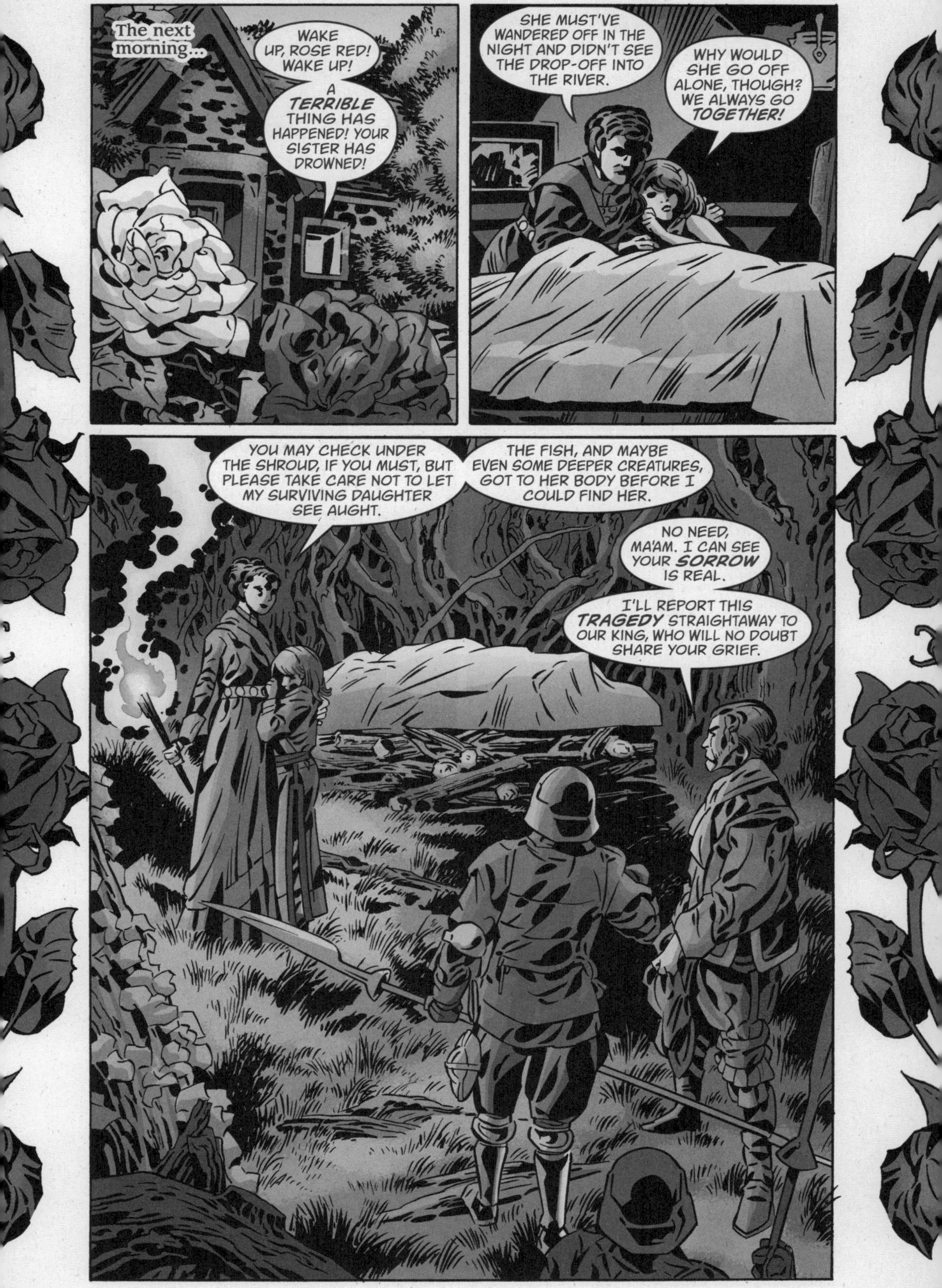
The next morning...
WAKE UP, ROSE RED! WAKE UP!
A TERRIBLE THING HAS HAPPENED! YOUR SISTER HAS DROWNED!
SHE MUST'VE WANDERED OFF IN THE NIGHT AND DIDN'T SEE THE DROP-OFF INTO THE RIVER.
WHY WOULD SHE GO OFF ALONE, THOUGH? WE ALWAYS GO TOGETHER!
YOU MAY CHECK UNDER THE SHROUD, IF YOU MUST, BUT PLEASE TAKE CARE NOT TO LET MY SURVIVING DAUGHTER SEE AUGHT.
THE FISH, AND MAYBE EVEN SOME DEEPER CREATURES, GOT TO HER BODY BEFORE I COULD FIND HER.
NO NEED, MA'AM. I CAN SEE YOUR SORROW IS REAL.
I'LL REPORT THIS TRAGEDY STRAIGHTAWAY TO OUR KING, WHO WILL NO DOUBT SHARE YOUR GRIEF.

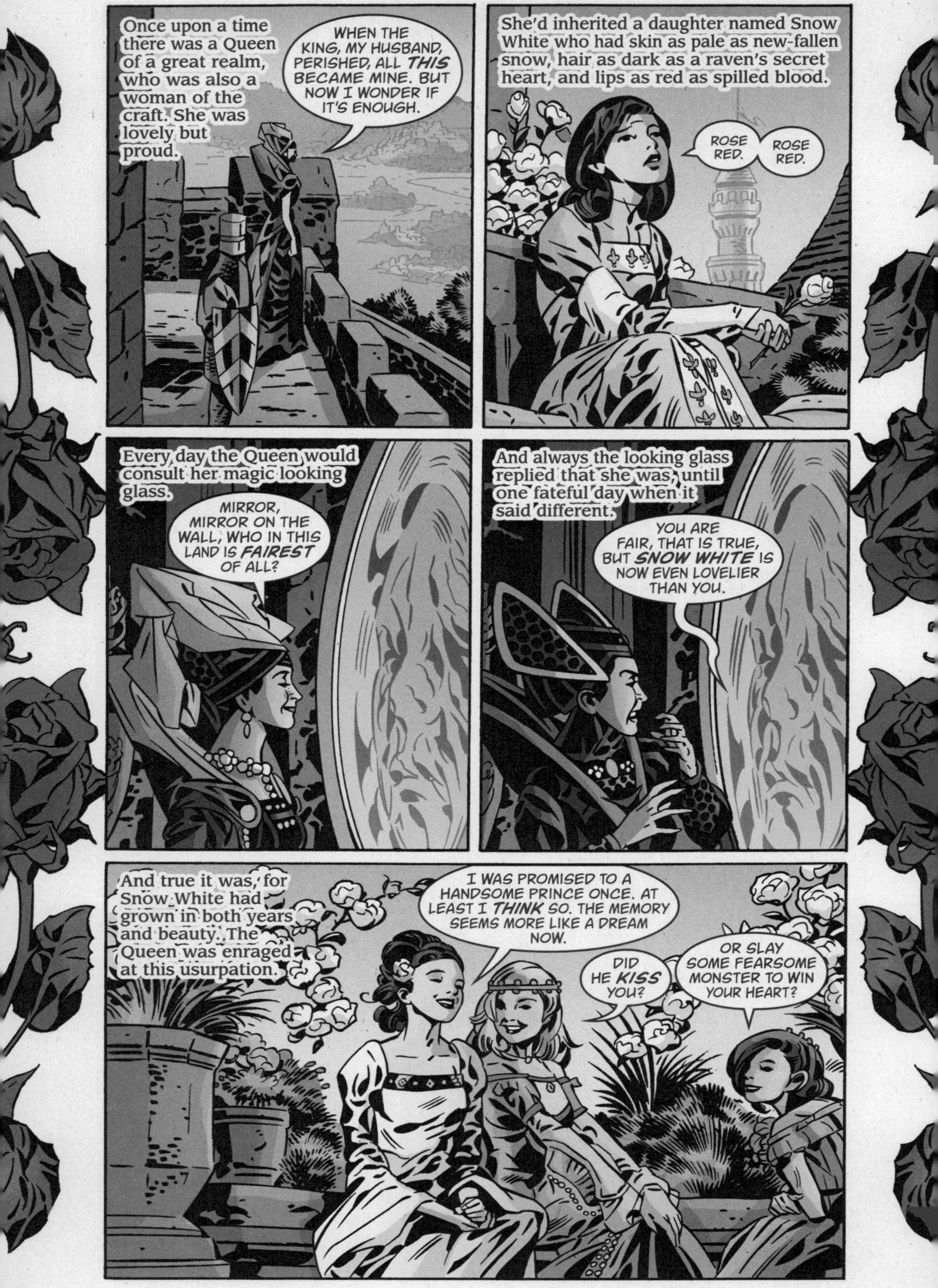
Once upon a time there was a Queen of a great realm, who was also a woman of the craft. She was lovely but proud.
WHEN THE KING, MY HUSBAND, PERISHED, ALL THIS BECAME MINE. BUT NOW I WONDER IF IT'S ENOUGH.
She'd inherited a daughter named Snow White who had skin as pale as new-fallen snow, hair as dark as a raven's secret heart, and lips as red as spilled blood.
ROSE RED.
ROSE RED.
Every day the Queen would consult her magic looking glass.
MIRROR, MIRROR ON THE WALL, WHO IN THIS LAND IS FAIREST OF ALL?
And always the looking glass replied that she was, until one fateful day when it said different.
YOU ARE FAIR, THAT IS TRUE, BUT SNOW WHITE IS NOW EVEN LOVELIER THAN YOU.
And true it was, for Snow White had grown in both years and beauty. The Queen was enraged at this usurpation.
I WAS PROMISED TO A HANDSOME PRINCE ONCE. AT LEAST I THINK SO. THE MEMORY SEEMS MORE LIKE A DREAM NOW.
DID HE KISS YOU?
OR SLAY SOME FEARSOME MONSTER TO WIN YOUR HEART?

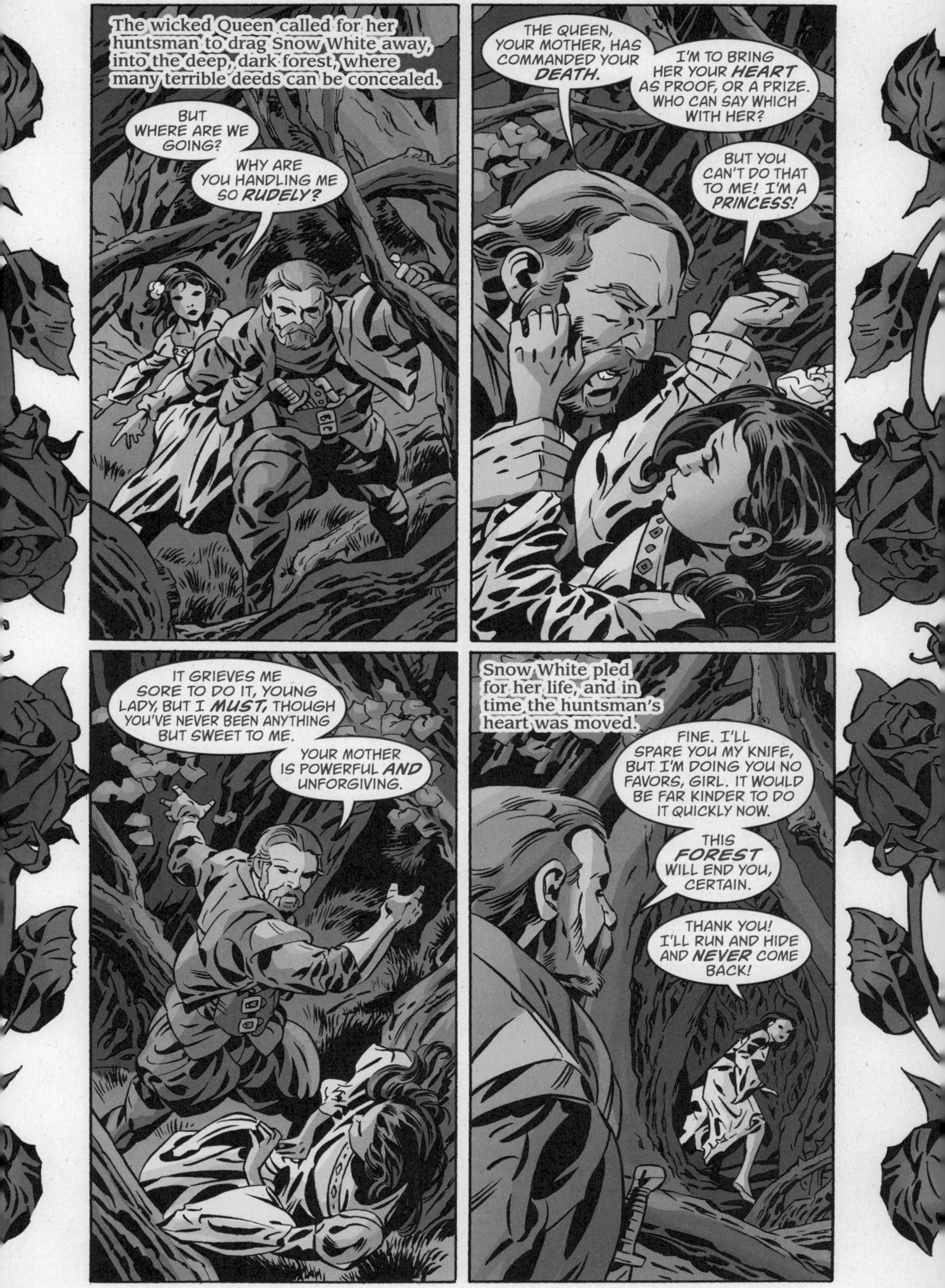
The wicked Queen called for her huntsman to drag Snow White away, into the deep, dark forest, where many terrible deeds can be concealed.
BUT WHERE ARE WE GOING?
WHY ARE YOU HANDLING ME SO RUDELY?
THE QUEEN, YOUR MOTHER, HAS COMMANDED YOUR DEATH.
I'M TO BRING HER YOUR HEART AS PROOF, OR A PRIZE. WHO CAN SAY WHICH WITH HER?
BUT YOU CAN'T DO THAT TO ME! I'M A PRINCESS!
IT GRIEVES ME SORE TO DO IT, YOUNG LADY, BUT I MUST, THOUGH YOU'VE NEVER BEEN ANYTHING BUT SWEET TO ME.
YOUR MOTHER IS POWERFUL AND UNFORGIVING.
Snow White pled for her life, and in time the huntsman's heart was moved.
FINE. I'LL SPARE YOU MY KNIFE, BUT I'M DOING YOU NO FAVORS, GIRL. IT WOULD BE FAR KINDER TO DO IT QUICKLY NOW.
THIS FOREST WILL END YOU, CERTAIN.
THANK YOU! I'LL RUN AND HIDE AND NEVER COME BACK!

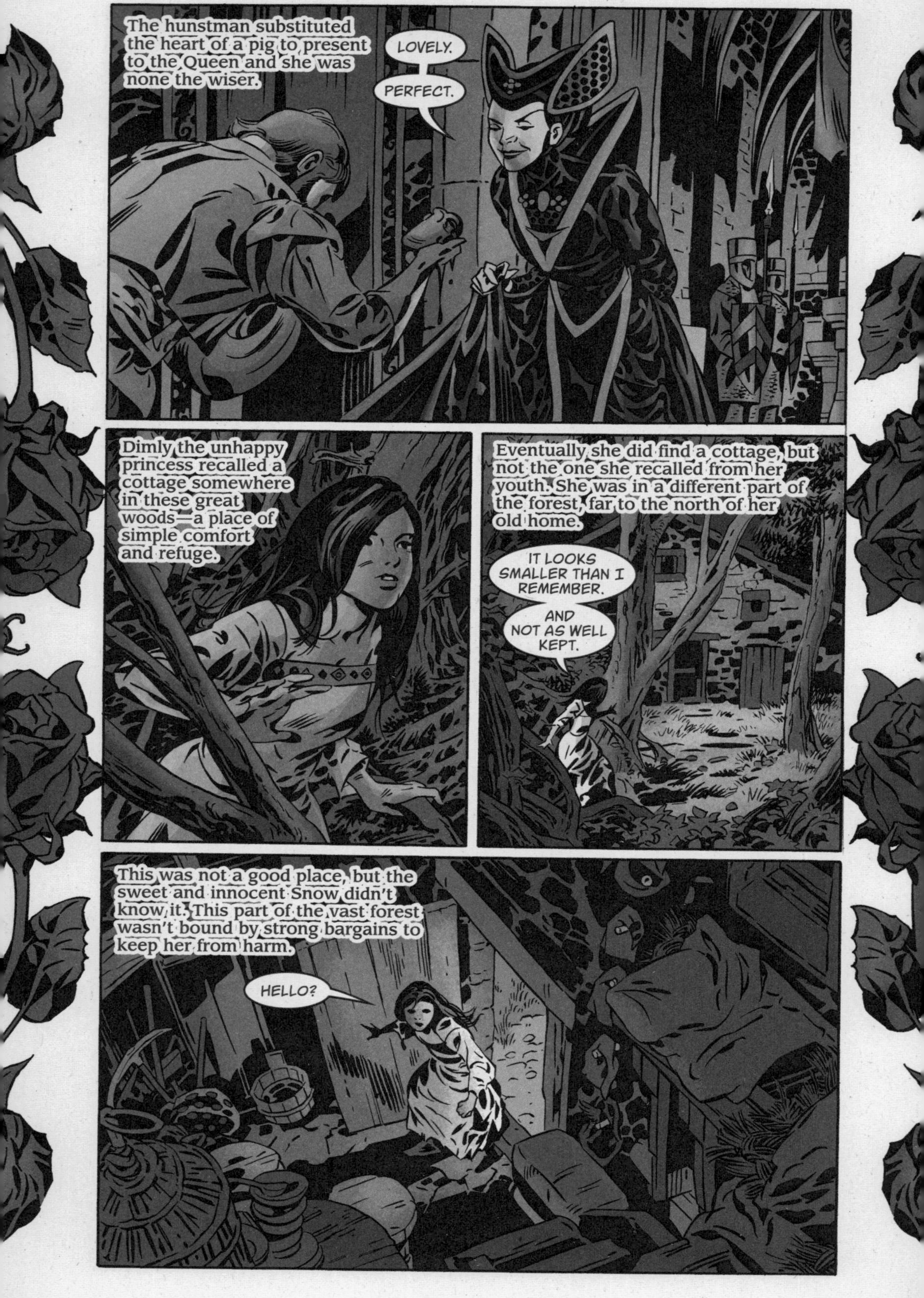
The hunstman substituted the heart of a pig to present to the Queen and she was none the wiser.
LOVELY.
PERFECT.
Dimly the unhappy princess recalled a cottage somewhere in these great woods—a place of simple comfort and refuge.
Eventually she did find a cottage, but not the one she recalled from her youth. She was in a different part of the forest, far to the north of her old home.
IT LOOKS SMALLER THAN I REMEMBER.
AND NOT AS WELL KEPT.
This was not a good place, but the sweet and innocent Snow didn't know it. This part of the vast forest wasn't bound by strong bargains to keep her from harm.
HELLO?

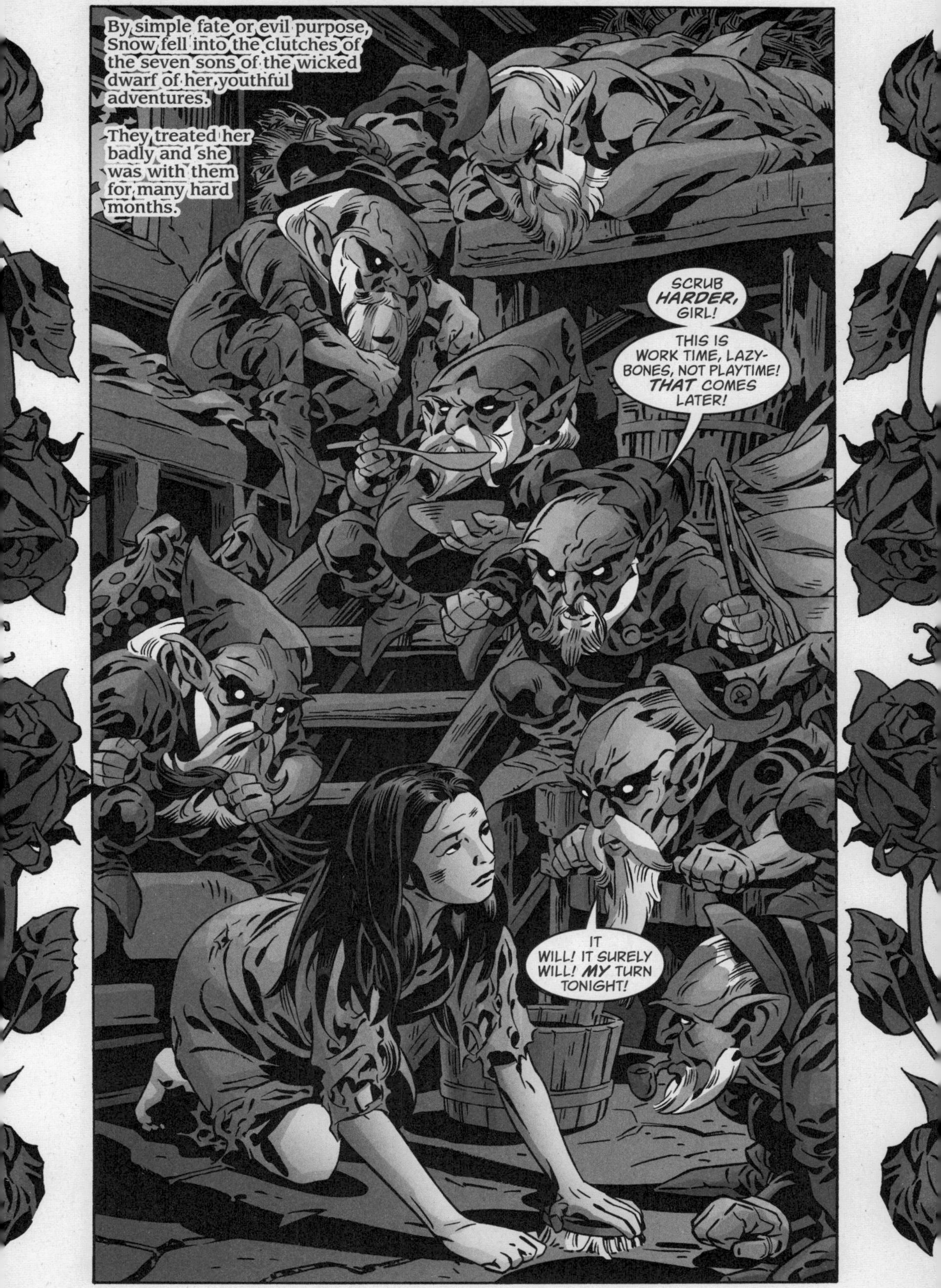
By simple fate or evil purpose, Snow fell into the clutches of the seven sons of the wicked dwarf of her youthful adventures.
They treated her badly and she was with them for many hard months.
SCRUB HARDER, GIRL!
THIS IS WORK TIME, LAZY-BONES, NOT PLAYTIME! THAT COMES LATER!
IT WILL! IT SURELY WILL! MY TURN TONIGHT!

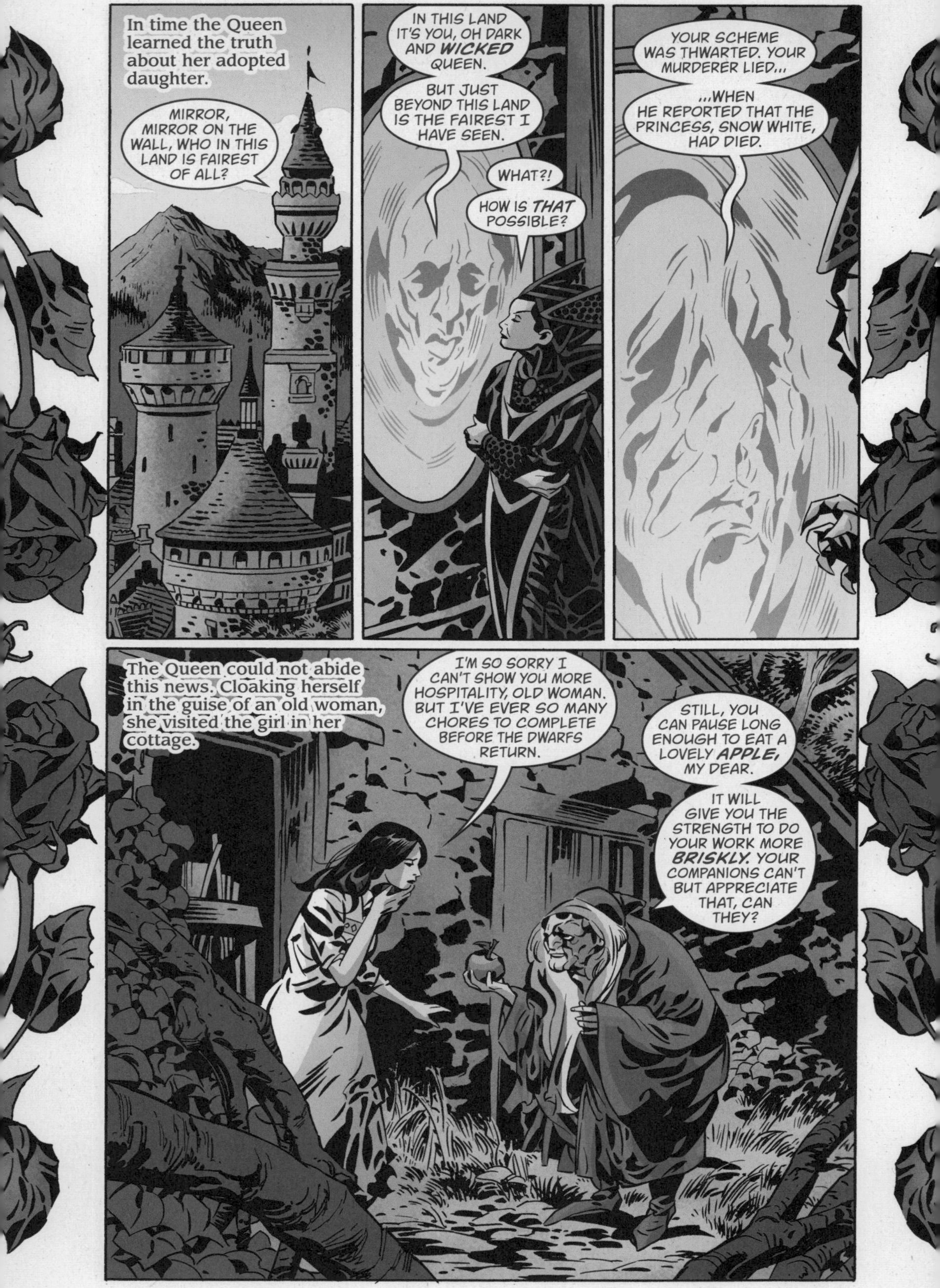
In time the Queen learned the truth about her adopted daughter.
MIRROR, MIRROR ON THE WALL, WHO IN THIS LAND IS FAIREST OF ALL?
IN THIS LAND IT'S YOU, OH DARK AND WICKED QUEEN.
BUT JUST BEYOND THIS LAND IS THE FAIREST I HAVE SEEN.
WHAT?!
HOW IS THAT POSSIBLE?
YOUR SCHEME WAS THWARTED. YOUR MURDERER LIED...
...WHEN HE REPORTED THAT THE PRINCESS, SNOW WHITE, HAD DIED.
The Queen could not abide this news. Cloaking herself in the guise of an old woman, she visited the girl in her cottage.
I'M SO SORRY I CAN'T SHOW YOU MORE HOSPITALITY, OLD WOMAN. BUT I'VE EVER SO MANY CHORES TO COMPLETE BEFORE THE DWARFS RETURN.
STILL, YOU CAN PAUSE LONG ENOUGH TO EAT A LOVELY APPLE, MY DEAR.
IT WILL GIVE YOU THE STRENGTH TO DO YOUR WORK MORE BRISKLY. YOUR COMPANIONS CAN'T BUT APPRECIATE THAT, CAN THEY?

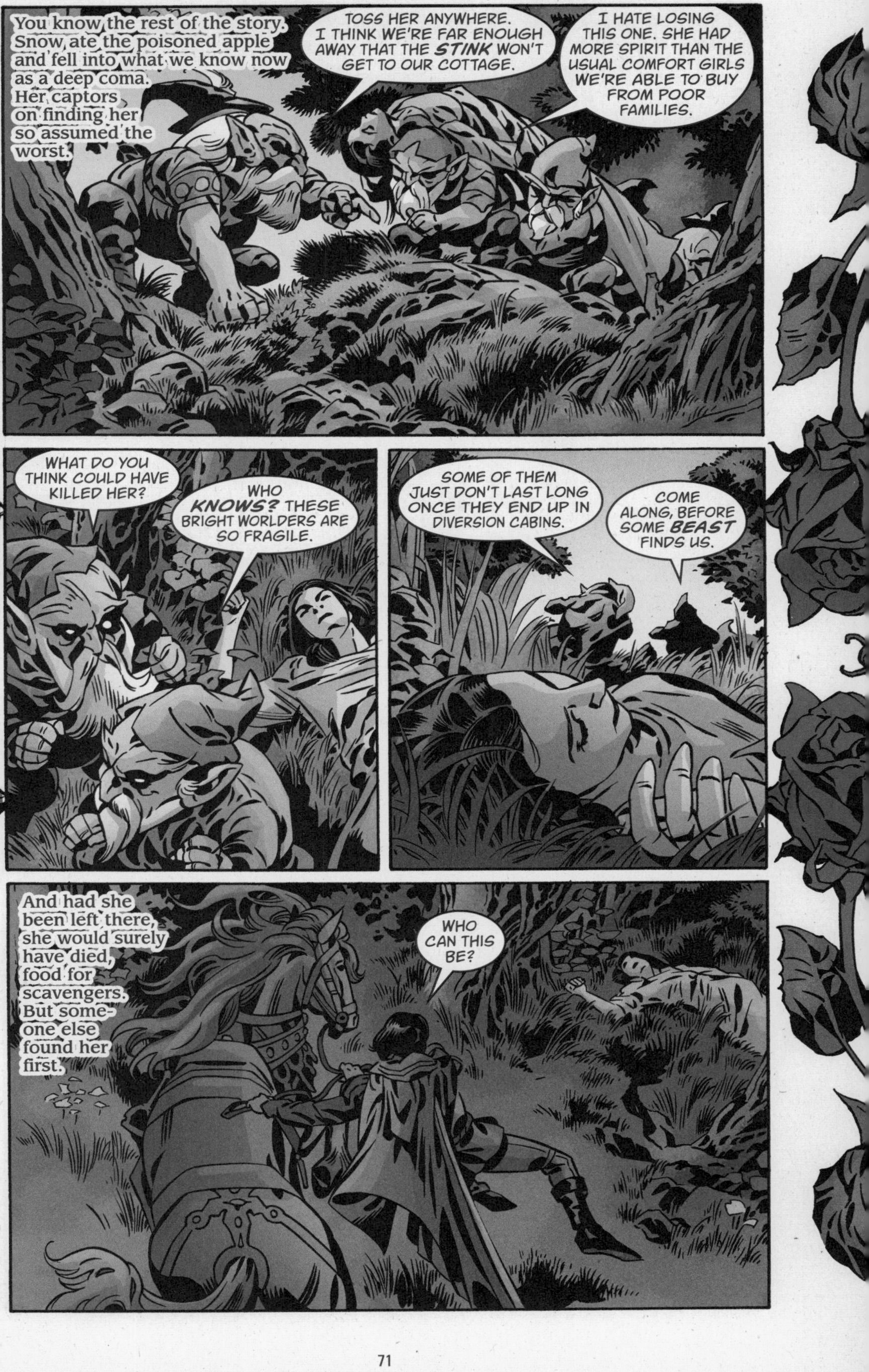
You know the rest of the story. Snow ate the poisoned apple and fell into what we know now as a deep coma. Her captors on finding her so assumed the worst.
TOSS HER ANYWHERE. I THINK WE'RE FAR ENOUGH AWAY THAT THE STINK WON'T GET TO OUR COTTAGE.
I HATE LOSING THIS ONE. SHE HAD MORE SPIRIT THAN THE USUAL COMFORT GIRLS WE'RE ABLE TO BUY FROM POOR FAMILIES.
WHAT DO YOU THINK COULD HAVE KILLED HER?
WHO KNOWS? THESE BRIGHT WORLDERS ARE SO FRAGILE.
SOME OF THEM JUST DON'T LAST LONG ONCE THEY END UP IN DIVERSION CABINS.
COME ALONG, BEFORE SOME BEAST FINDS US.
And had she been left there, she would surely have died, food for scavengers. But some-one else found her first.
WHO CAN THIS BE?

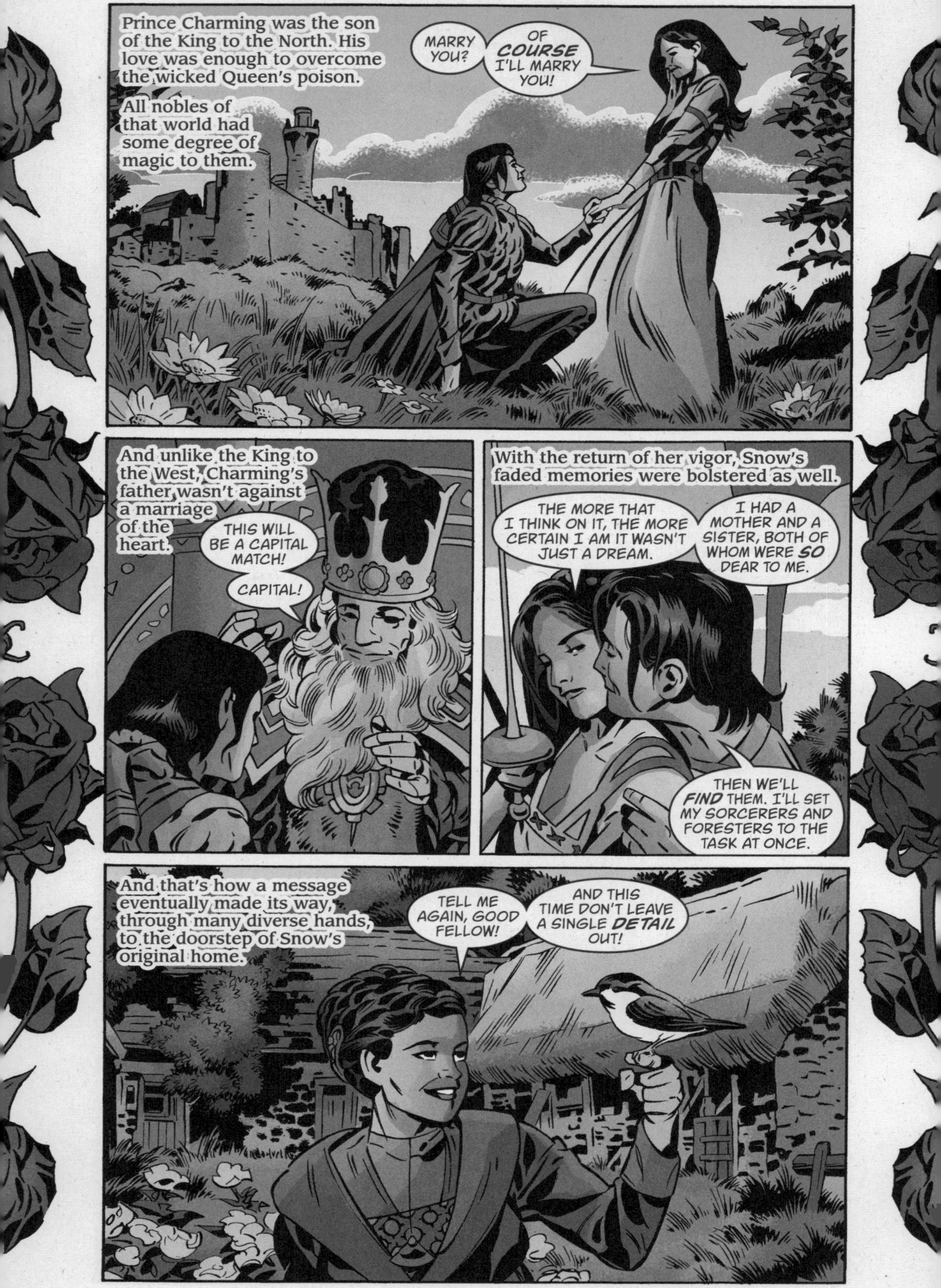
Prince Charming was the son of the King to the North. His love was enough to overcome the wicked Queen's poison.
All nobles of that world had some degree of magic to them.
MARRY YOU?
OF COURSE I'LL MARRY YOU!
And unlike the King to the West, Charming's father wasn't against a marriage of the heart.
THIS WILL BE A CAPITAL MATCH!
CAPITAL!
With the return of her vigor, Snow's faded memories were bolstered as well.
THE MORE THAT I THINK ON IT, THE MORE CERTAIN I AM IT WASN'T JUST A DREAM.
I HAD A MOTHER AND A SISTER, BOTH OF WHOM WERE SO DEAR TO ME.
THEN WE'LL FIND THEM. I'LL SET MY SORCERERS AND FORESTERS TO THE TASK AT ONCE.
And that's how a message eventually made its way, through many diverse hands, to the doorstep of Snow's original home.
TELL ME AGAIN, GOOD FELLOW!
AND THIS TIME DON'T LEAVE A SINGLE DETAIL OUT!

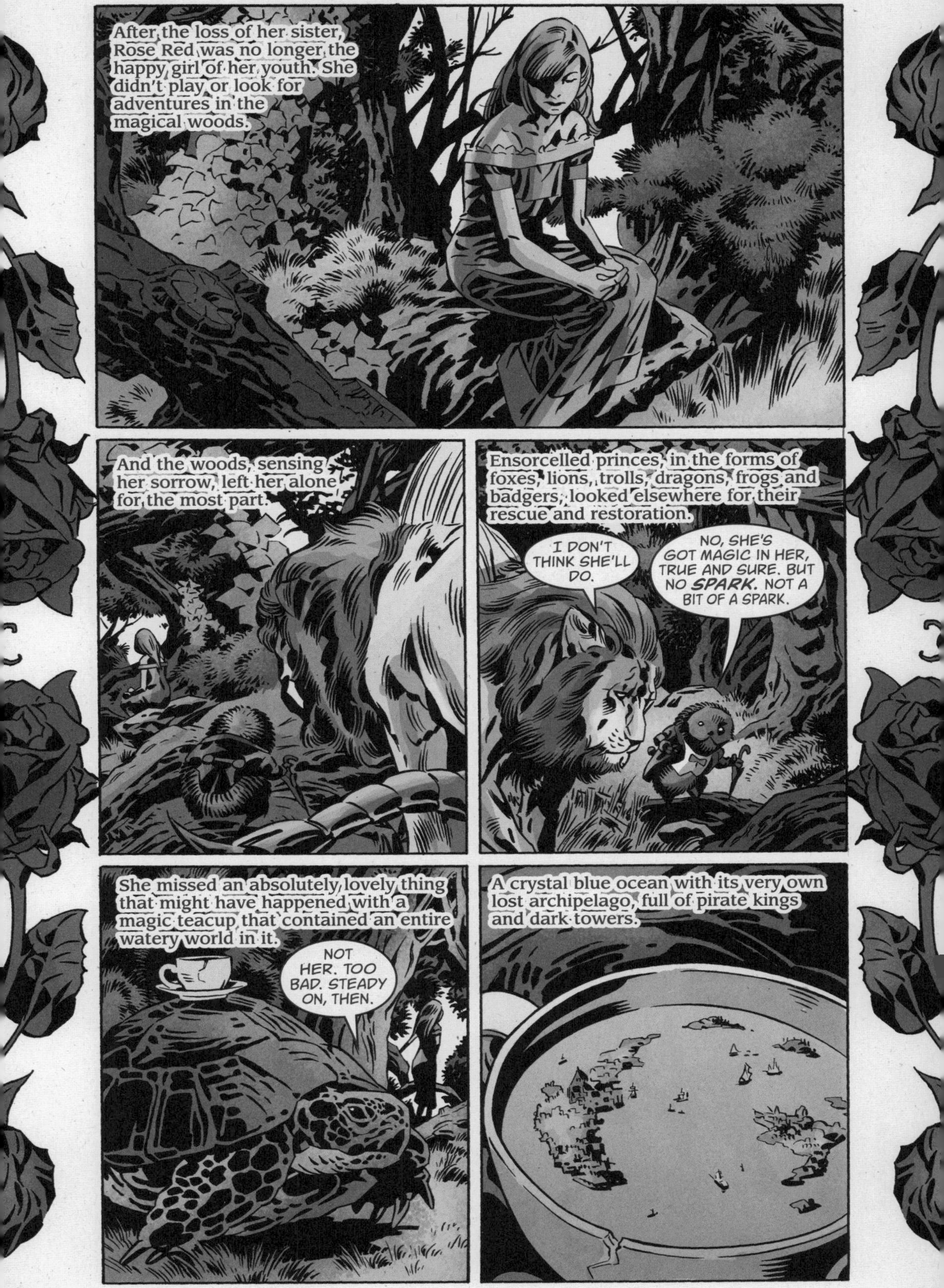
After the loss of her sister, Rose Red was no longer the happy girl of her youth. She didn't play or look for adventures in the magical woods.
And the woods, sensing her sorrow, left her alone for the most part.
Ensorcelled princes, in the forms of foxes, lions, trolls, dragons, frogs and badgers, looked elsewhere for their rescue and restoration.
I DON'T THINK SHE'LL DO.
NO, SHE'S GOT MAGIC IN HER, TRUE AND SURE. BUT NO SPARK. NOT A BIT OF A SPARK.
She missed an absolutely lovely thing that might have happened with a magic teacup that contained an entire watery world in it.
NOT HER. TOO BAD. STEADY ON, THEN.
A crystal blue ocean with its very own lost archipelago, full of pirate kings and dark towers.

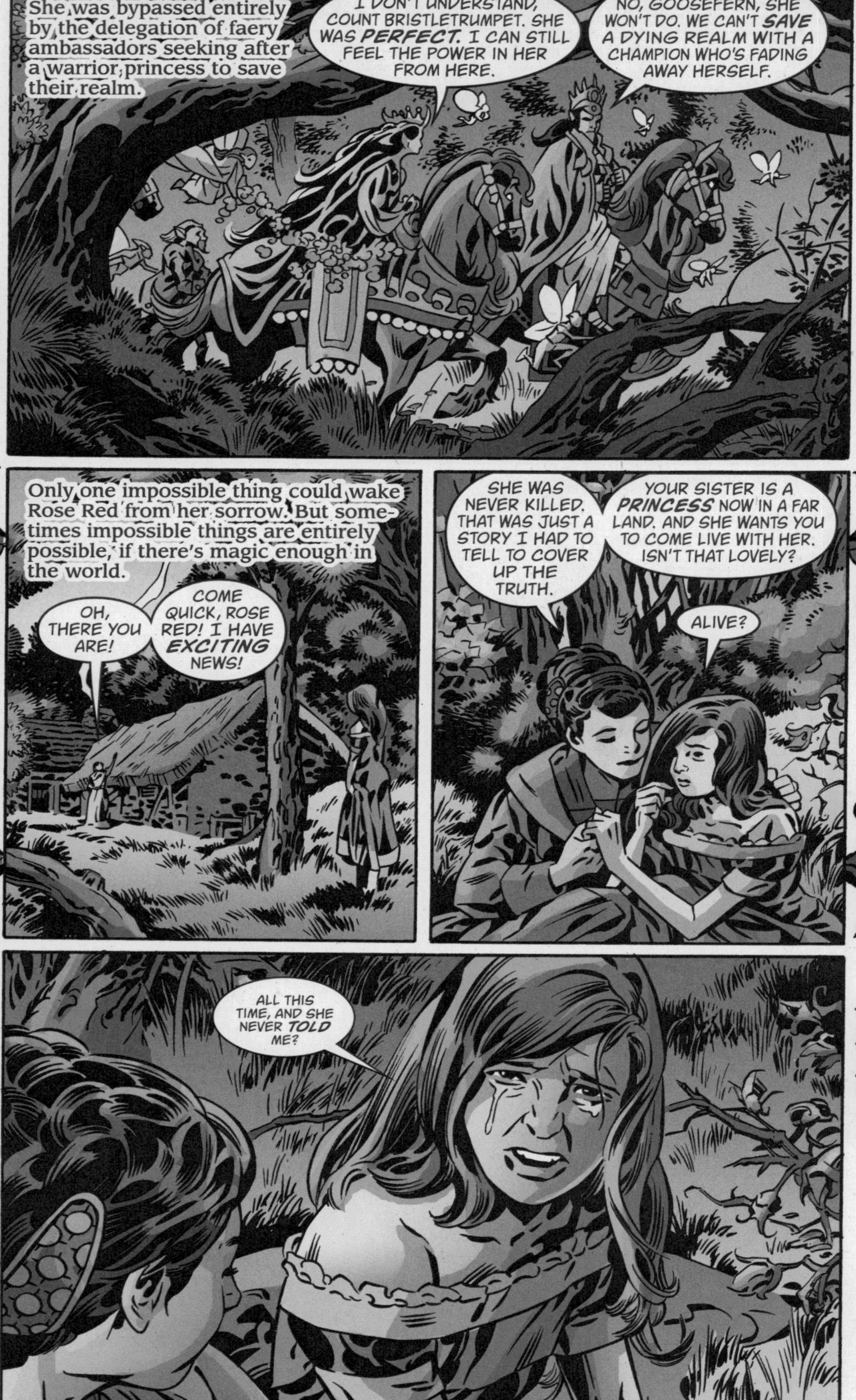

She was bypassed entirely by the delegation of faery ambassadors seeking after a warrior princess to save their realm.
I DON'T UNDERSTAND, COUNT BRISTLETRUMPET. SHE WAS PERFECT. I CAN STILL FEEL THE POWER IN HER FROM HERE.
NO, GOOSEFERN, SHE WON'T DO. WE CAN'T SAVE A DYING REALM WITH A CHAMPION WHO'S FADING AWAY HERSELF.
Only one impossible thing could wake Rose Red from her sorrow. But sometimes impossible things are entirely possible, if there's magic enough in the world.
OH, THERE YOU ARE!
COME QUICK, ROSE RED! I HAVE EXCITING NEWS!
SHE WAS NEVER KILLED. THAT WAS JUST A STORY I HAD TO TELL TO COVER UP THE TRUTH.
YOUR SISTER IS A PRINCESS NOW IN A FAR LAND. AND SHE WANTS YOU TO COME LIVE WITH HER. ISN'T THAT LOVELY?
ALIVE?
ALL THIS TIME, AND SHE NEVER TOLD ME?

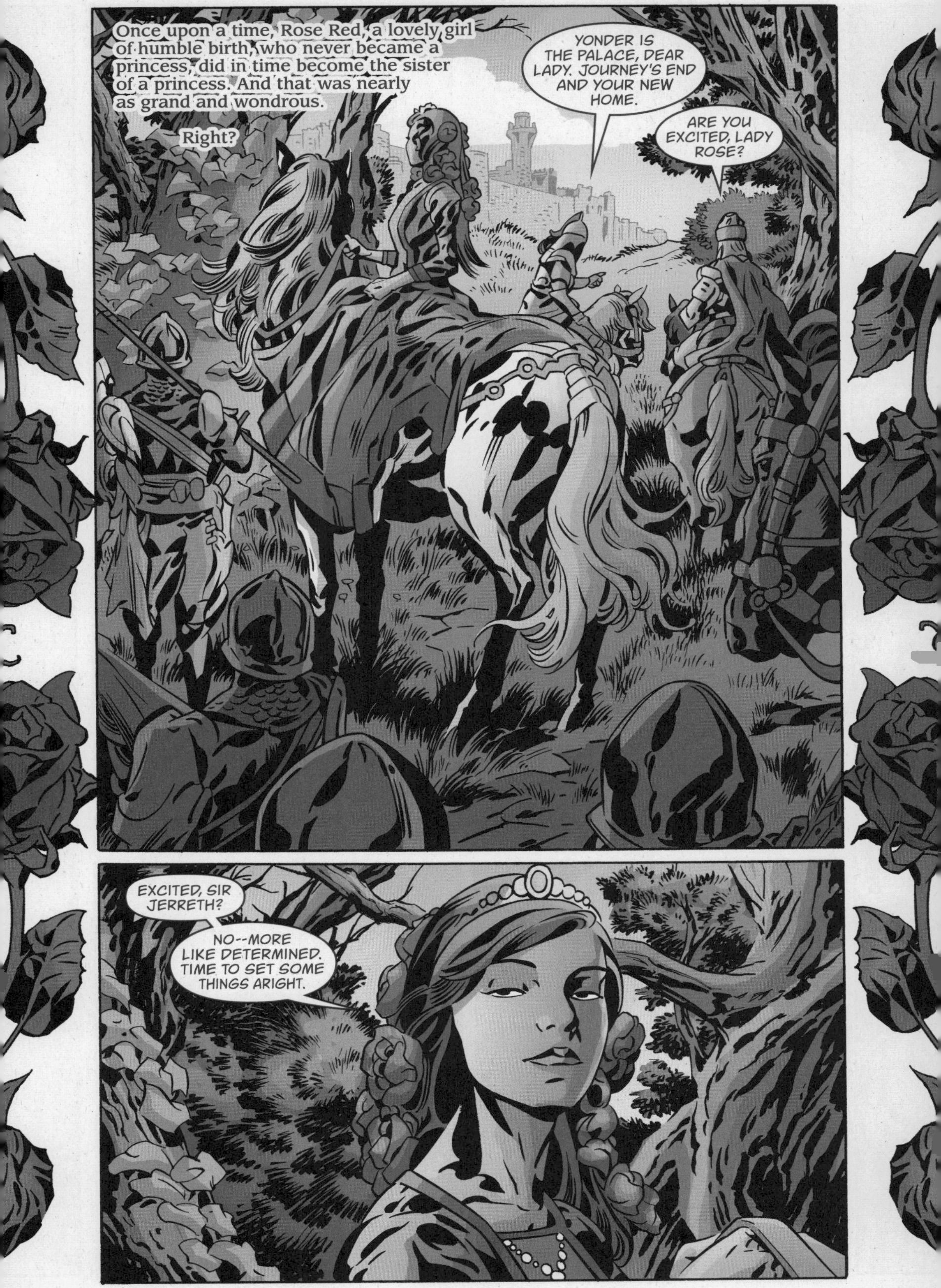
Once upon a time, Rose Red, a lovely girl of humble birth, who never became a princess, did in time become the sister of a princess. And that was nearly as grand and wondrous.
Right?
YONDER IS THE PALACE, DEAR LADY. JOURNEY'S END AND YOUR NEW HOME.
ARE YOU EXCITED, LADY ROSE?
EXCITED, SIR JERRETH?
NO--MORE LIKE DETERMINED. TIME TO SET SOME THINGS ARIGHT.

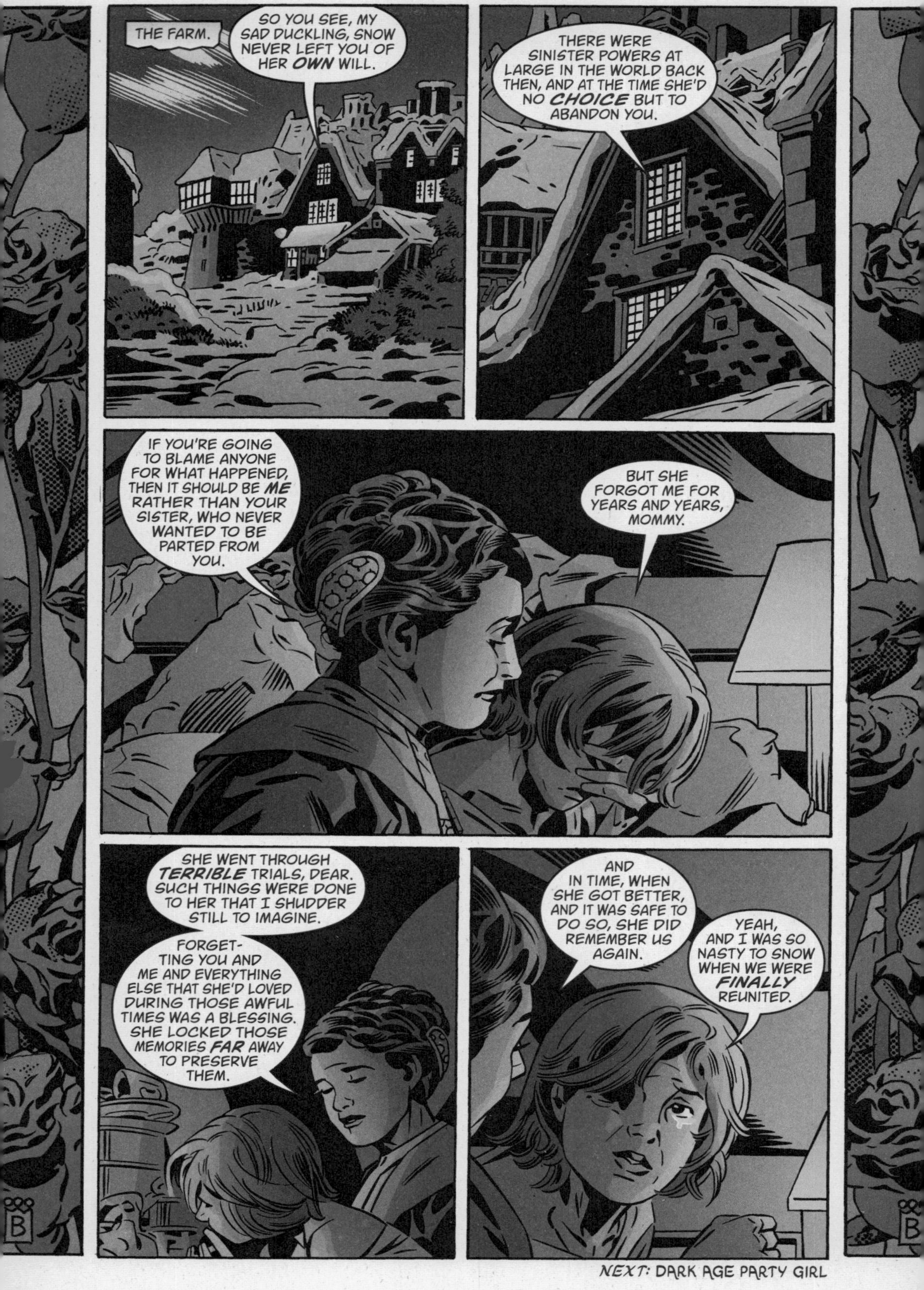
THE FARM.
SO YOU SEE, MY SAD DUCKLING, SNOW NEVER LEFT YOU OF HER OWN WILL.
THERE WERE SINISTER POWERS AT LARGE IN THE WORLD BACK THEN, AND AT THE TIME SHE'D NO CHOICE BUT TO ABANDON YOU.
IF YOU'RE GOING TO BLAME ANYONE FOR WHAT HAPPENED, THEN IT SHOULD BE ME RATHER THAN YOUR SISTER, WHO NEVER WANTED TO BE PARTED FROM YOU.
BUT SHE FORGOT ME FOR YEARS AND YEARS, MOMMY.
SHE WENT THROUGH TERRIBLE TRIALS, DEAR. SUCH THINGS WERE DONE TO HER THAT I SHUDDER STILL TO IMAGINE.
FORGET-TING YOU AND ME AND EVERYTHING ELSE THAT SHE'D LOVED DURING THOSE AWFUL TIMES WAS A BLESSING. SHE LOCKED THOSE MEMORIES FAR AWAY TO PRESERVE THEM.
AND IN TIME, WHEN SHE GOT BETTER, AND IT WAS SAFE TO DO SO, SHE DID REMEMBER US AGAIN.
YEAH, AND I WAS SO NASTY TO SNOW WHEN WE WERE FINALLY REUNITED.

NEXT: DARK AGE PARTY GIRL

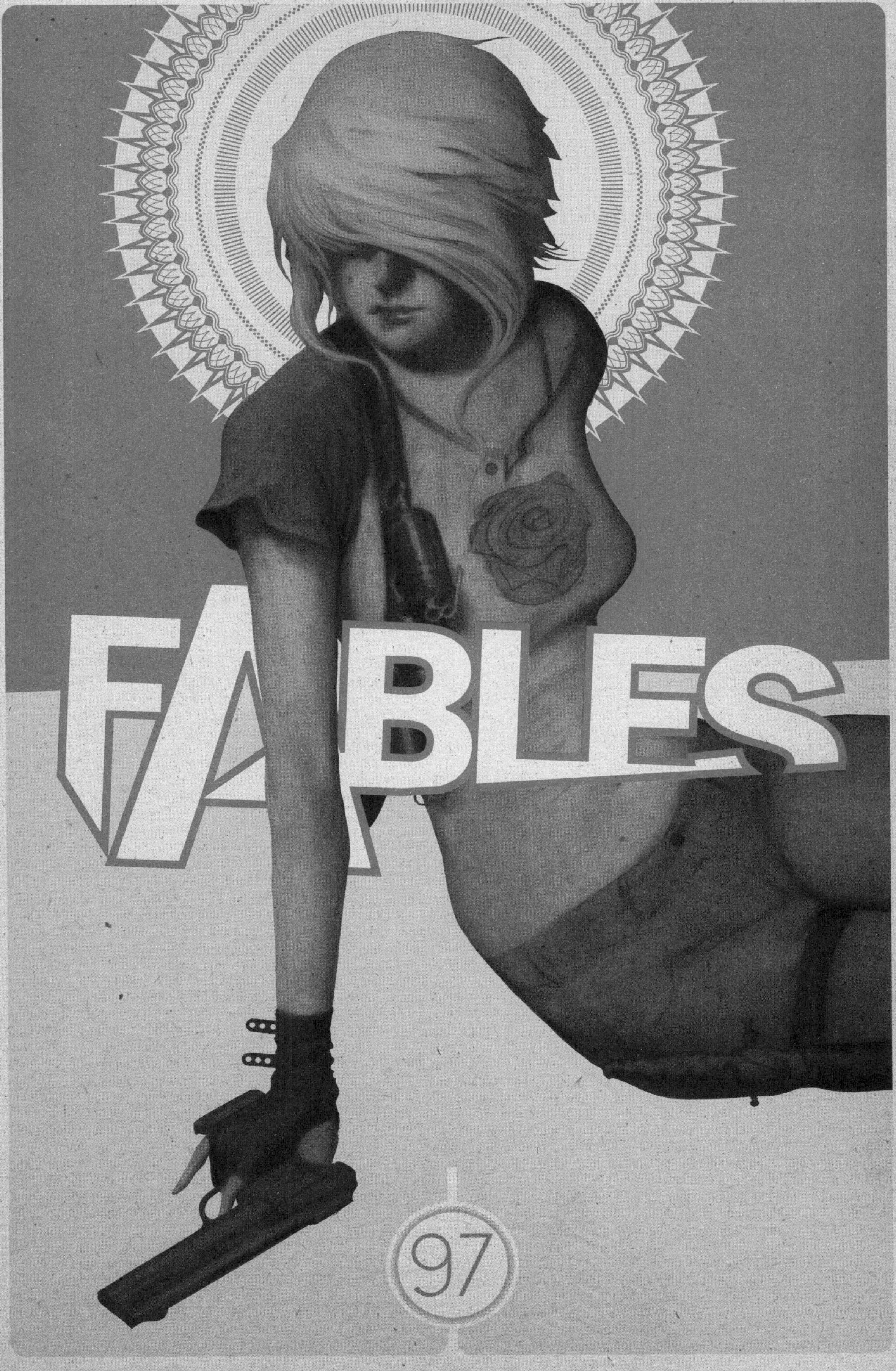
FABLES
97

Once upon a time, a forest-dwelling peasant girl named Rose Red arrived in a distant magical kingdom where her long-lost sister had recently married its crown prince.

She adapted to the courtly and chivalrous life surprisingly, quickly.

YOU'RE EVERY OUNCE AS LOVELY AS YOUR SISTER, LADY RED.

ONLY *AS* LOVELY, SIR ROLAND? NOT MORE THAN?

TO THAT I CAN ONLY ANSWER THAT SNOW WHITE'S BEAUTY CANNOT BE OVERMATCHED BY DICTATES OF MY UNMATCHED *LOYALTY* TO CROWN AND COUNTRY.

SHE *IS* THE ROYAL PRINCESS AFTER ALL, AND SOMEDAY TO BE MY QUEEN.

WELL SAID, SIR ROLAND. WELL *SPOKEN.*

Dark Age Party Girl
Chapter Four of Rose Red

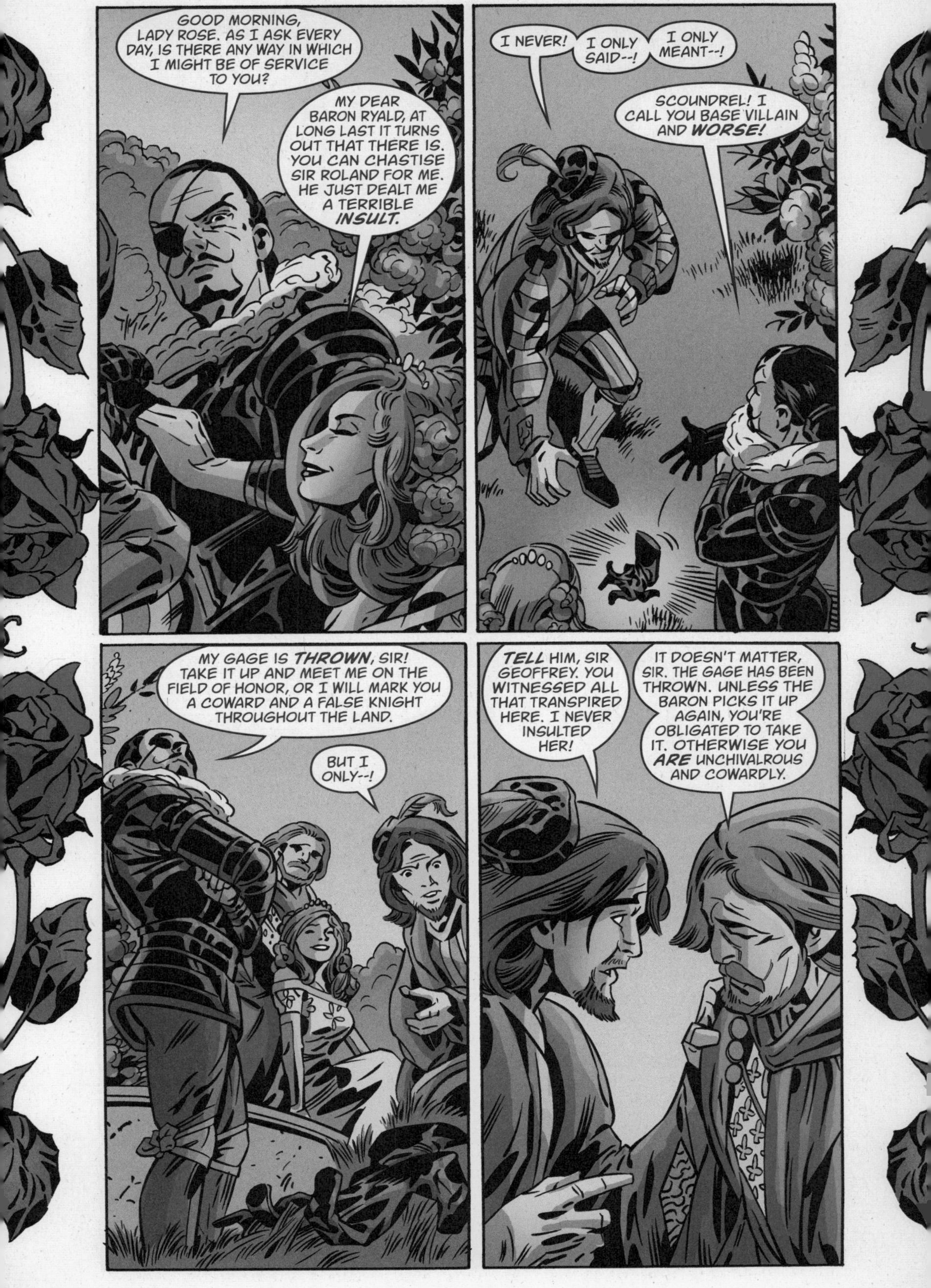
GOOD MORNING, LADY ROSE. AS I ASK EVERY DAY, IS THERE ANY WAY IN WHICH I MIGHT BE OF SERVICE TO YOU?
MY DEAR BARON RYALD, AT LONG LAST IT TURNS OUT THAT THERE IS. YOU CAN CHASTISE SIR ROLAND FOR ME. HE JUST DEALT ME A TERRIBLE INSULT.
I NEVER!
I ONLY SAID--!
I ONLY MEANT--!
SCOUNDREL! I CALL YOU BASE VILLAIN AND WORSE!
MY GAGE IS THROWN, SIR! TAKE IT UP AND MEET ME ON THE FIELD OF HONOR, OR I WILL MARK YOU A COWARD AND A FALSE KNIGHT THROUGHOUT THE LAND.
BUT I ONLY--!
TELL HIM, SIR GEOFFREY. YOU WITNESSED ALL THAT TRANSPIRED HERE. I NEVER INSULTED HER!
IT DOESN'T MATTER, SIR. THE GAGE HAS BEEN THROWN. UNLESS THE BARON PICKS IT UP AGAIN, YOU'RE OBLIGATED TO TAKE IT. OTHERWISE YOU ARE UNCHIVALROUS AND COWARDLY.

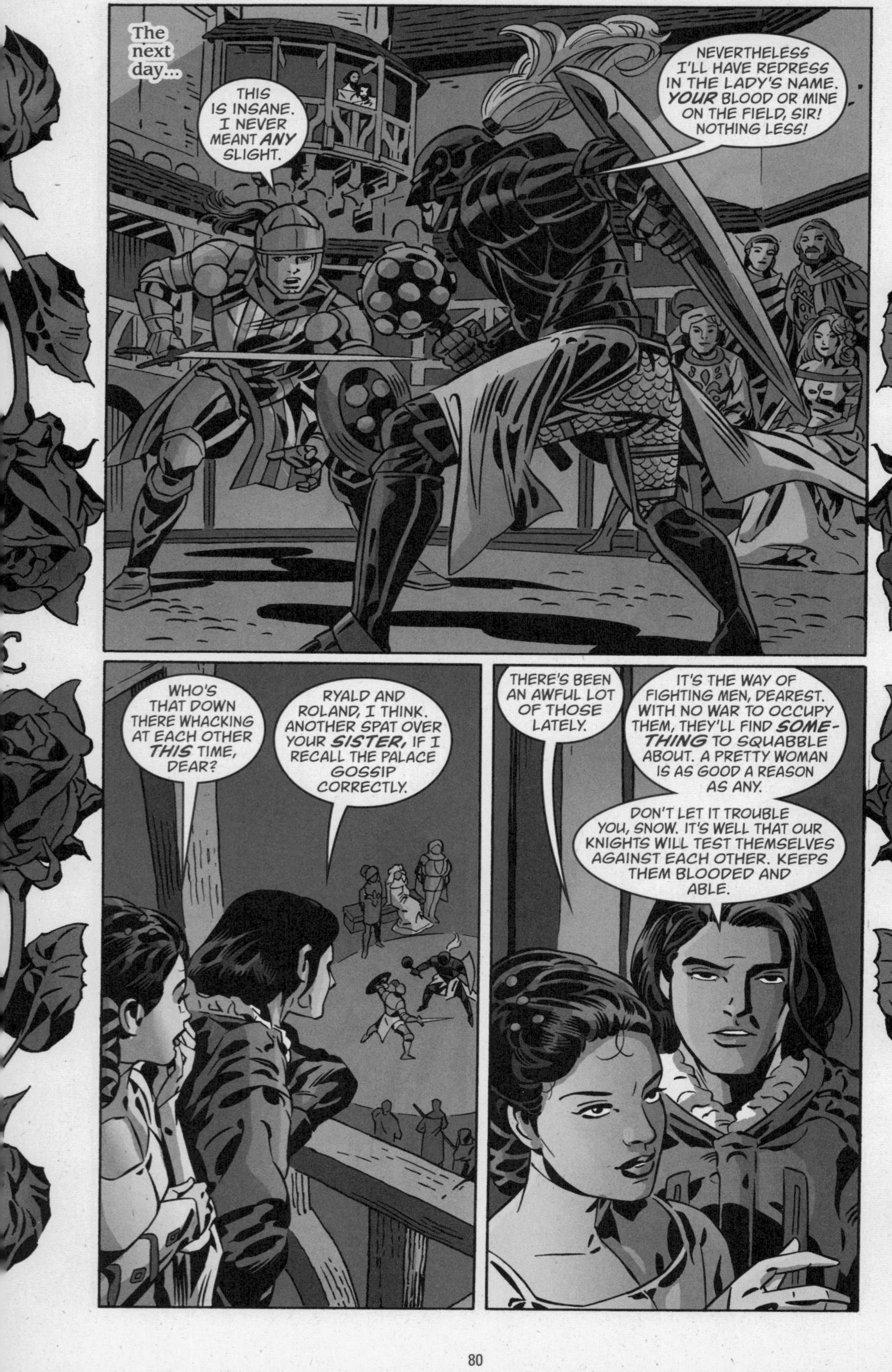
The next day...
THIS IS INSANE. I NEVER MEANT ANY SLIGHT.
NEVERTHELESS I'LL HAVE REDRESS IN THE LADY'S NAME. YOUR BLOOD OR MINE ON THE FIELD, SIR! NOTHING LESS!
WHO'S THAT DOWN THERE WHACKING AT EACH OTHER THIS TIME, DEAR?
RYALD AND ROLAND, I THINK. ANOTHER SPAT OVER YOUR SISTER, IF I RECALL THE PALACE GOSSIP CORRECTLY.
THERE'S BEEN AN AWFUL LOT OF THOSE LATELY.
IT'S THE WAY OF FIGHTING MEN, DEAREST. WITH NO WAR TO OCCUPY THEM, THEY'LL FIND SOMETHING TO SQUABBLE ABOUT. A PRETTY WOMAN IS AS GOOD A REASON AS ANY.
DON'T LET IT TROUBLE YOU, SNOW. IT'S WELL THAT OUR KNIGHTS WILL TEST THEMSELVES AGAINST EACH OTHER. KEEPS THEM BLOODED AND ABLE.

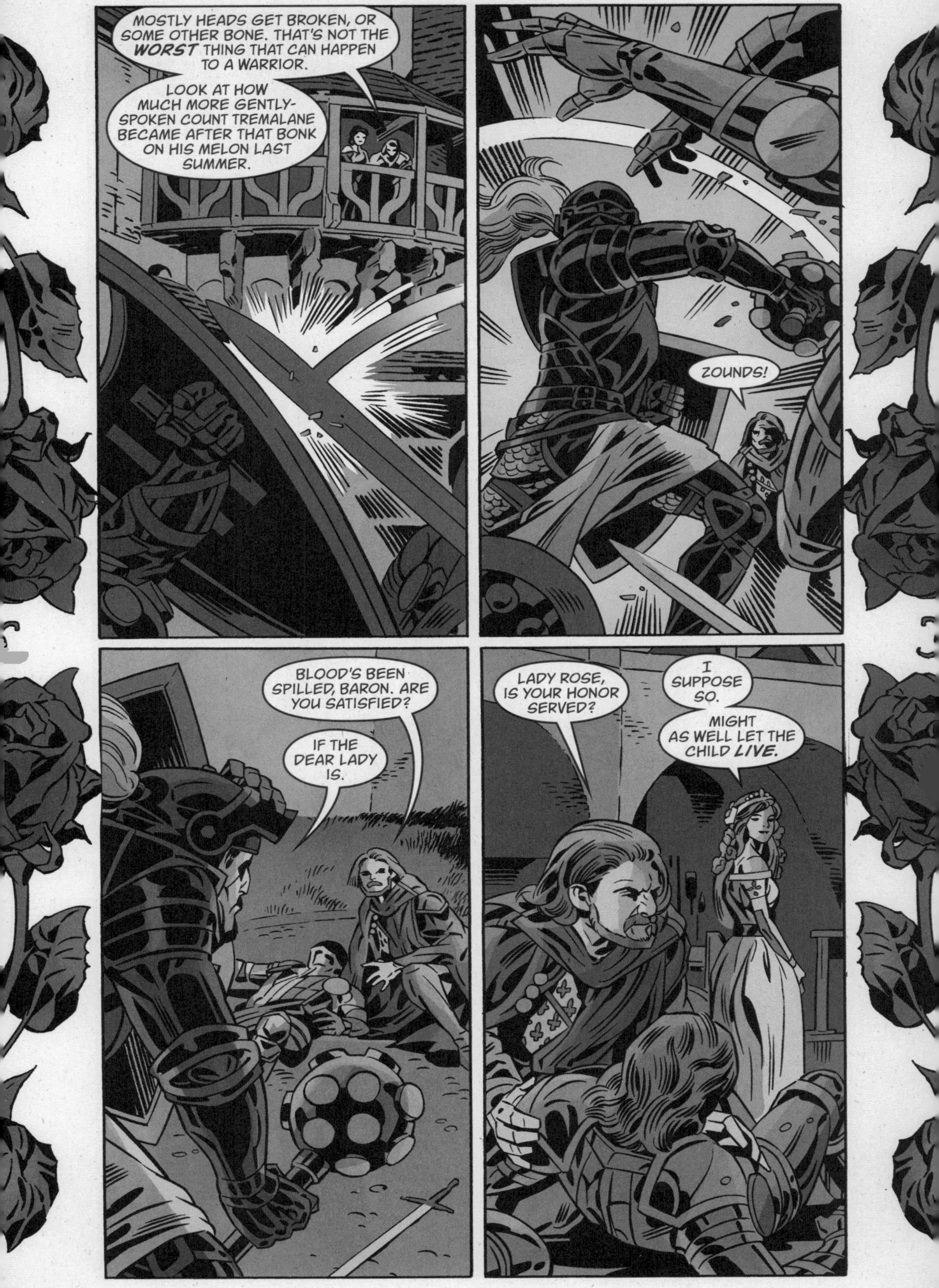
MOSTLY HEADS GET BROKEN, OR SOME OTHER BONE. THAT'S NOT THE **WORST** THING THAT CAN HAPPEN TO A WARRIOR.
LOOK AT HOW MUCH MORE GENTLY-SPOKEN COUNT TREMALANE BECAME AFTER THAT BONK ON HIS MELON LAST SUMMER.
ZOUNDS!
BLOOD'S BEEN SPILLED, BARON. ARE YOU SATISFIED?
IF THE DEAR LADY IS.
LADY ROSE, IS YOUR HONOR SERVED?
I SUPPOSE SO.
MIGHT AS WELL LET THE CHILD ***LIVE.***

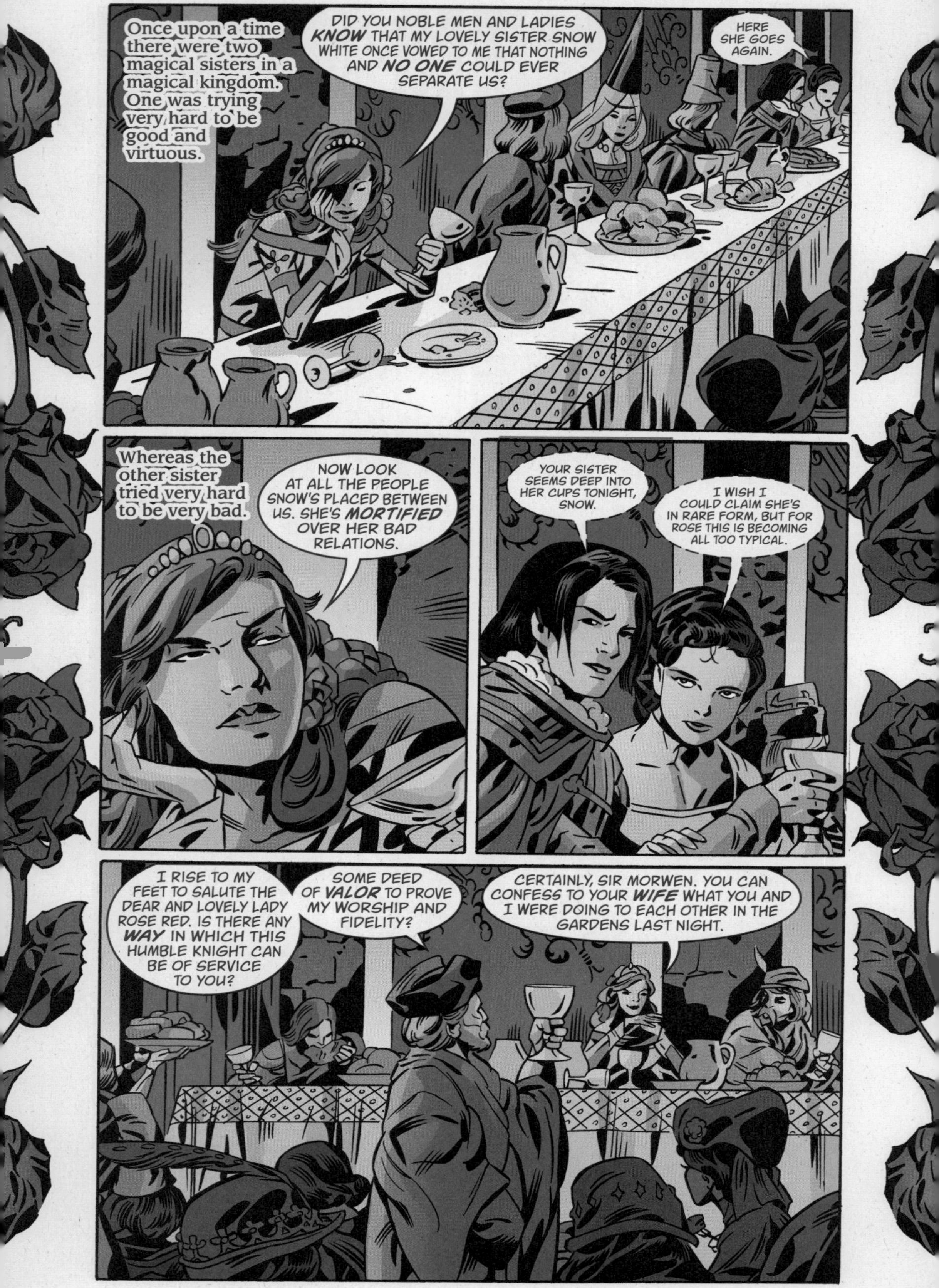
Once upon a time there were two magical sisters in a magical kingdom. One was trying very hard to be good and virtuous.
DID YOU NOBLE MEN AND LADIES KNOW THAT MY LOVELY SISTER SNOW WHITE ONCE VOWED TO ME THAT NOTHING AND NO ONE COULD EVER SEPARATE US?
HERE SHE GOES AGAIN.
Whereas the other sister tried very hard to be very bad.
NOW LOOK AT ALL THE PEOPLE SNOW'S PLACED BETWEEN US. SHE'S MORTIFIED OVER HER BAD RELATIONS.
YOUR SISTER SEEMS DEEP INTO HER CUPS TONIGHT, SNOW.
I WISH I COULD CLAIM SHE'S IN RARE FORM, BUT FOR ROSE THIS IS BECOMING ALL TOO TYPICAL.
I RISE TO MY FEET TO SALUTE THE DEAR AND LOVELY LADY ROSE RED. IS THERE ANY WAY IN WHICH THIS HUMBLE KNIGHT CAN BE OF SERVICE TO YOU?
SOME DEED OF VALOR TO PROVE MY WORSHIP AND FIDELITY?
CERTAINLY, SIR MORWEN. YOU CAN CONFESS TO YOUR WIFE WHAT YOU AND I WERE DOING TO EACH OTHER IN THE GARDENS LAST NIGHT.

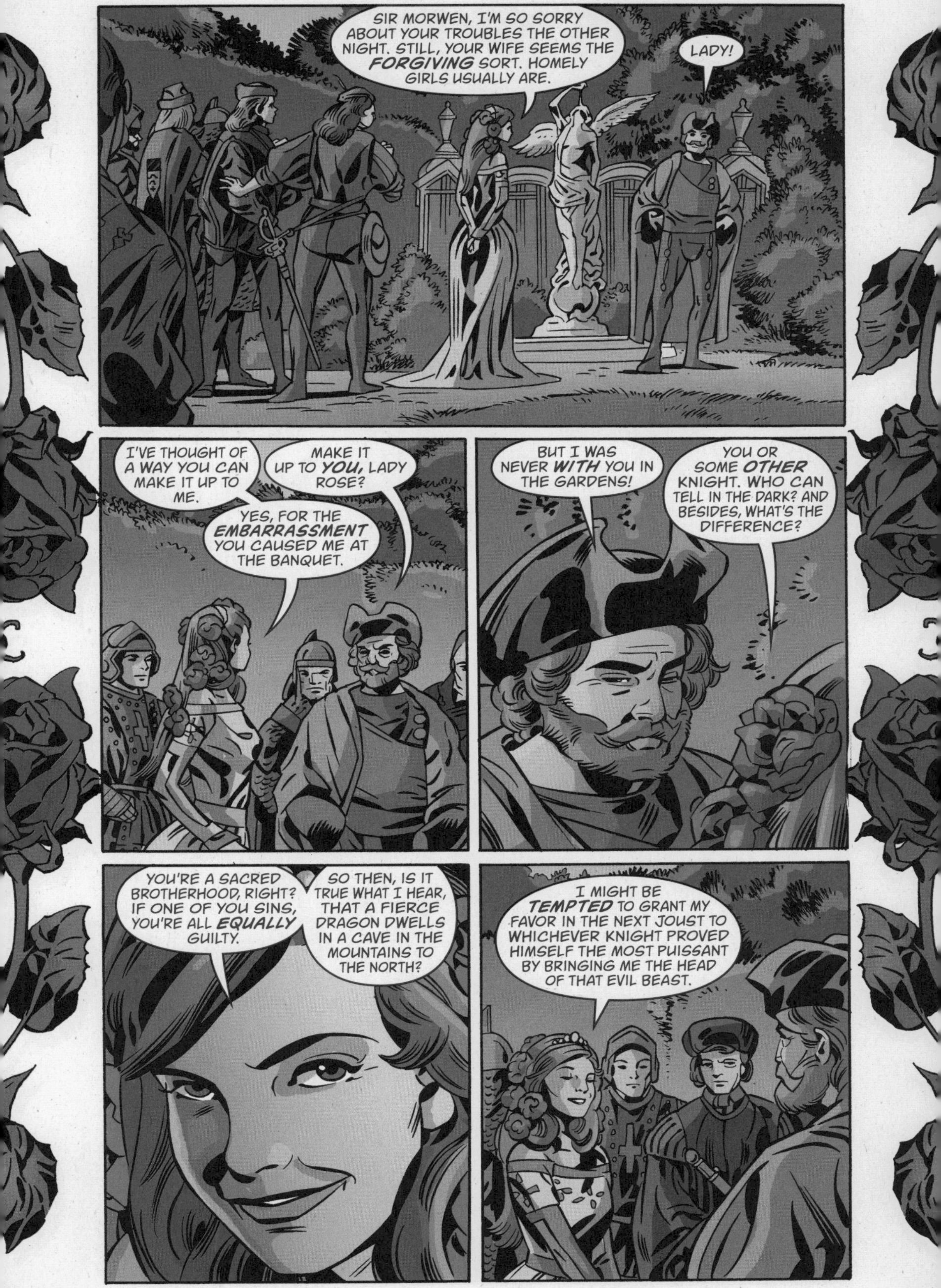
SIR MORWEN, I'M SO SORRY ABOUT YOUR TROUBLES THE OTHER NIGHT. STILL, YOUR WIFE SEEMS THE FORGIVING SORT. HOMELY GIRLS USUALLY ARE.
LADY!
I'VE THOUGHT OF A WAY YOU CAN MAKE IT UP TO ME.
MAKE IT UP TO YOU, LADY ROSE?
YES, FOR THE EMBARRASSMENT YOU CAUSED ME AT THE BANQUET.
BUT I WAS NEVER WITH YOU IN THE GARDENS!
YOU OR SOME OTHER KNIGHT. WHO CAN TELL IN THE DARK? AND BESIDES, WHAT'S THE DIFFERENCE?
YOU'RE A SACRED BROTHERHOOD, RIGHT? IF ONE OF YOU SINS, YOU'RE ALL EQUALLY GUILTY.
SO THEN, IS IT TRUE WHAT I HEAR, THAT A FIERCE DRAGON DWELLS IN A CAVE IN THE MOUNTAINS TO THE NORTH?
I MIGHT BE TEMPTED TO GRANT MY FAVOR IN THE NEXT JOUST TO WHICHEVER KNIGHT PROVED HIMSELF THE MOST PUISSANT BY BRINGING ME THE HEAD OF THAT EVIL BEAST.

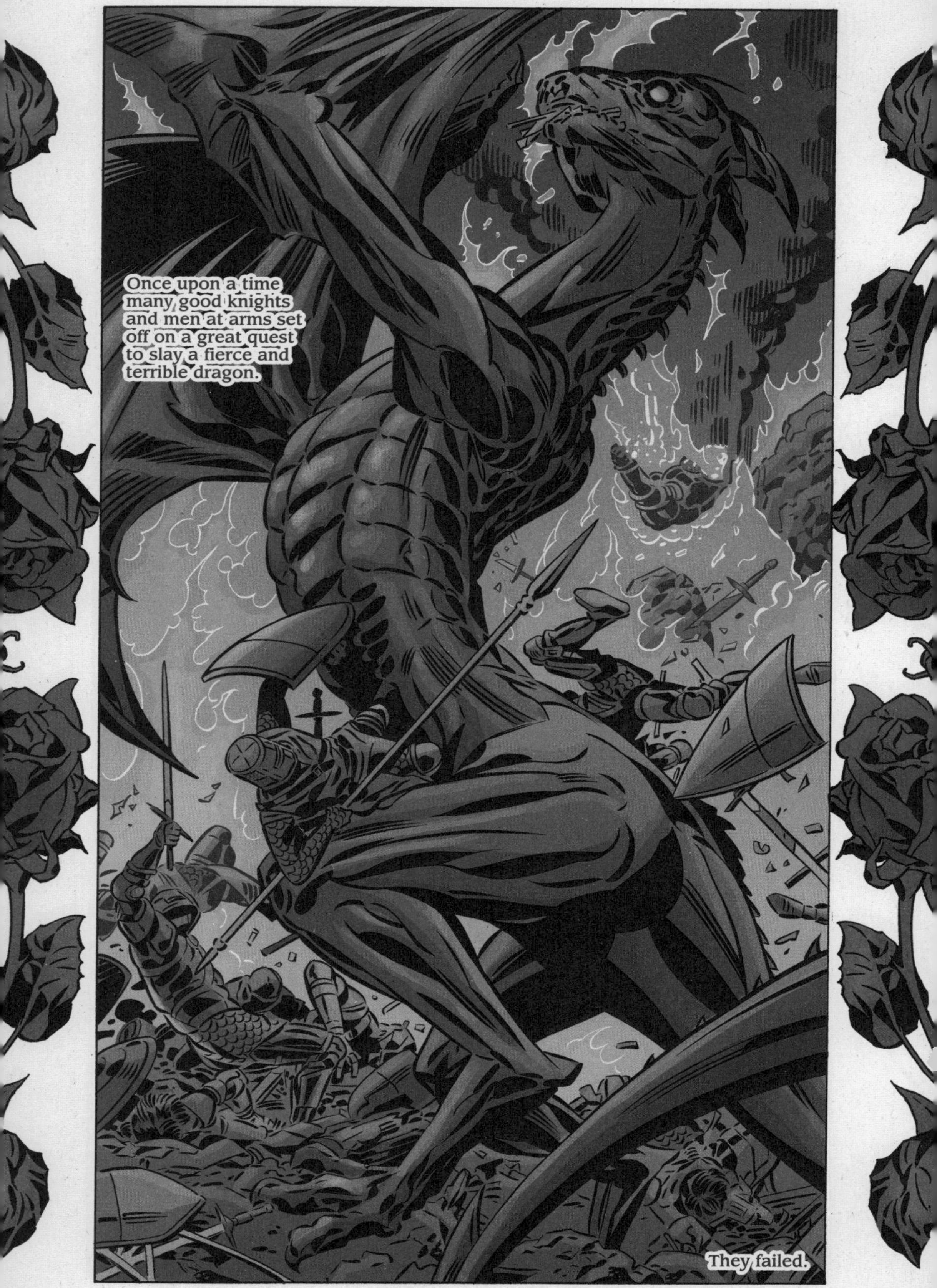
Once upon a time many good knights and men at arms set off on a great quest to slay a fierce and terrible dragon.
They failed.

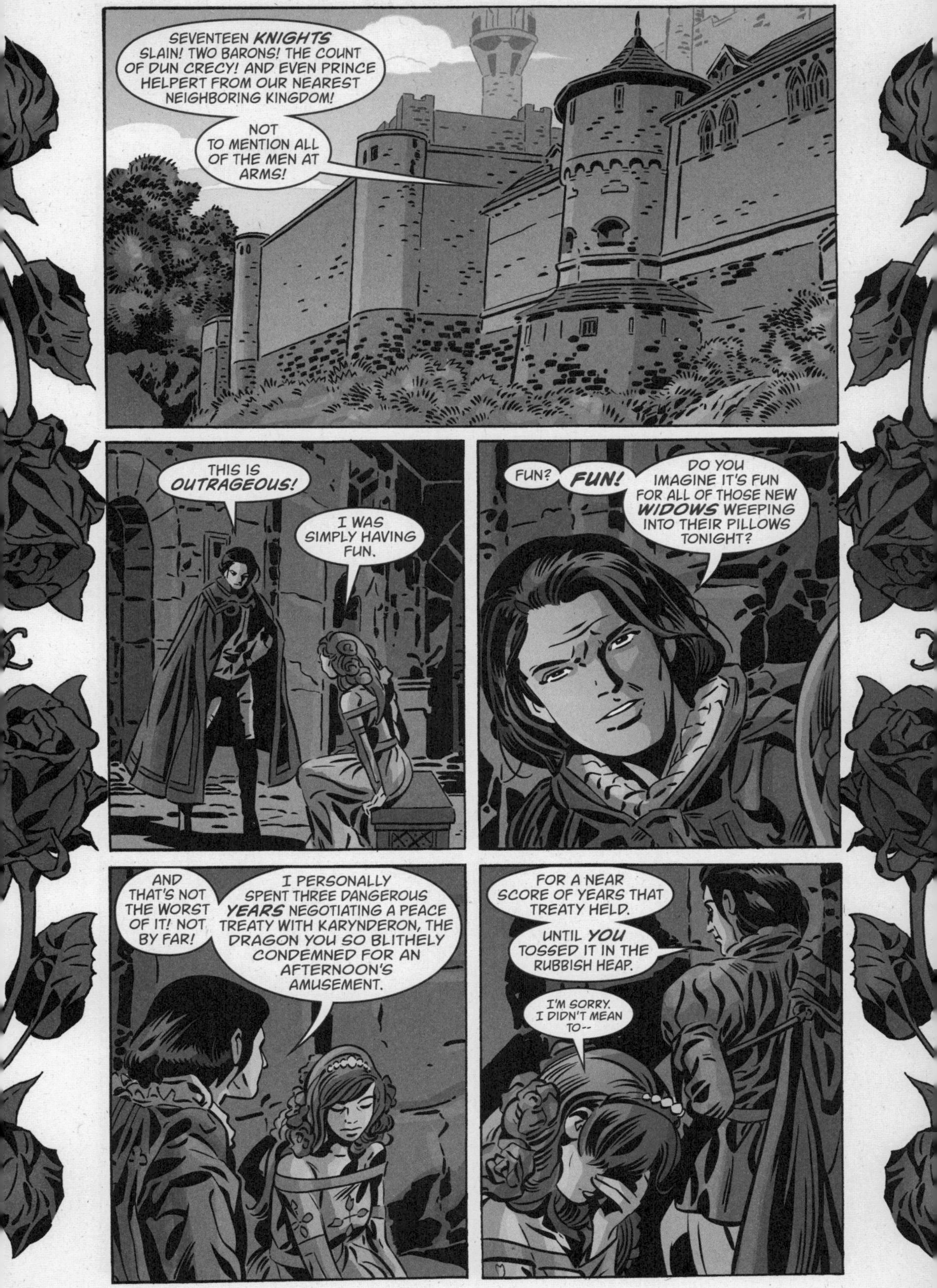
SEVENTEEN KNIGHTS SLAIN! TWO BARONS! THE COUNT OF DUN CRECY! AND EVEN PRINCE HELPERT FROM OUR NEAREST NEIGHBORING KINGDOM!
NOT TO MENTION ALL OF THE MEN AT ARMS!
THIS IS OUTRAGEOUS!
I WAS SIMPLY HAVING FUN.
FUN?
FUN!
DO YOU IMAGINE IT'S FUN FOR ALL OF THOSE NEW WIDOWS WEEPING INTO THEIR PILLOWS TONIGHT?
AND THAT'S NOT THE WORST OF IT! NOT BY FAR!
I PERSONALLY SPENT THREE DANGEROUS YEARS NEGOTIATING A PEACE TREATY WITH KARYNDERON, THE DRAGON YOU SO BLITHELY CONDEMNED FOR AN AFTERNOON'S AMUSEMENT.
FOR A NEAR SCORE OF YEARS THAT TREATY HELD.
UNTIL YOU TOSSED IT IN THE RUBBISH HEAP.
I'M SORRY. I DIDN'T MEAN TO--

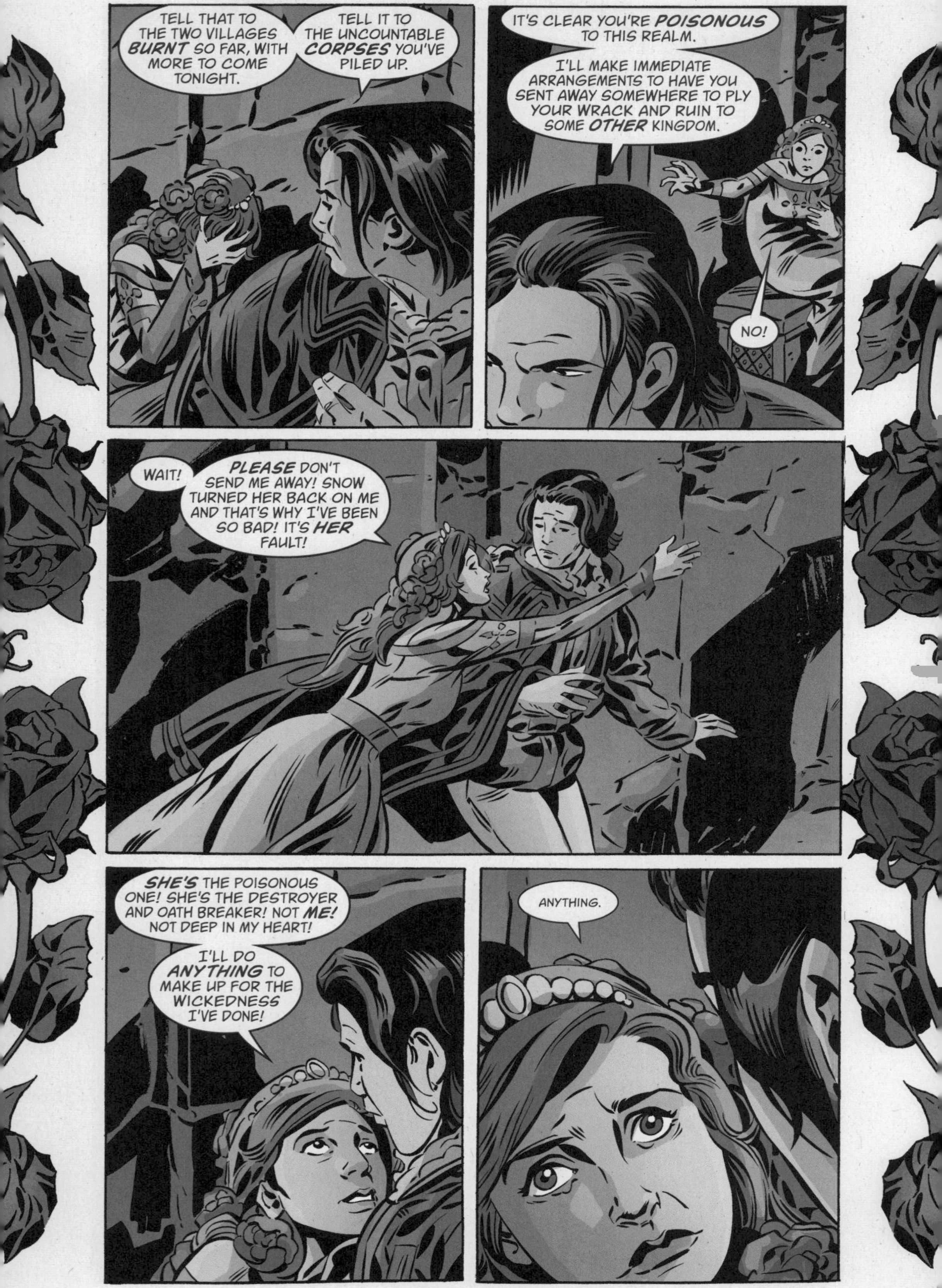
TELL THAT TO THE TWO VILLAGES BURNT SO FAR, WITH MORE TO COME TONIGHT.
TELL IT TO THE UNCOUNTABLE CORPSES YOU'VE PILED UP.
IT'S CLEAR YOU'RE POISONOUS TO THIS REALM.
I'LL MAKE IMMEDIATE ARRANGEMENTS TO HAVE YOU SENT AWAY SOMEWHERE TO PLY YOUR WRACK AND RUIN TO SOME OTHER KINGDOM.
NO!
WAIT!
PLEASE DON'T SEND ME AWAY! SNOW TURNED HER BACK ON ME AND THAT'S WHY I'VE BEEN SO BAD! IT'S HER FAULT!
SHE'S THE POISONOUS ONE! SHE'S THE DESTROYER AND OATH BREAKER! NOT ME! NOT DEEP IN MY HEART!
I'LL DO ANYTHING TO MAKE UP FOR THE WICKEDNESS I'VE DONE!
ANYTHING.

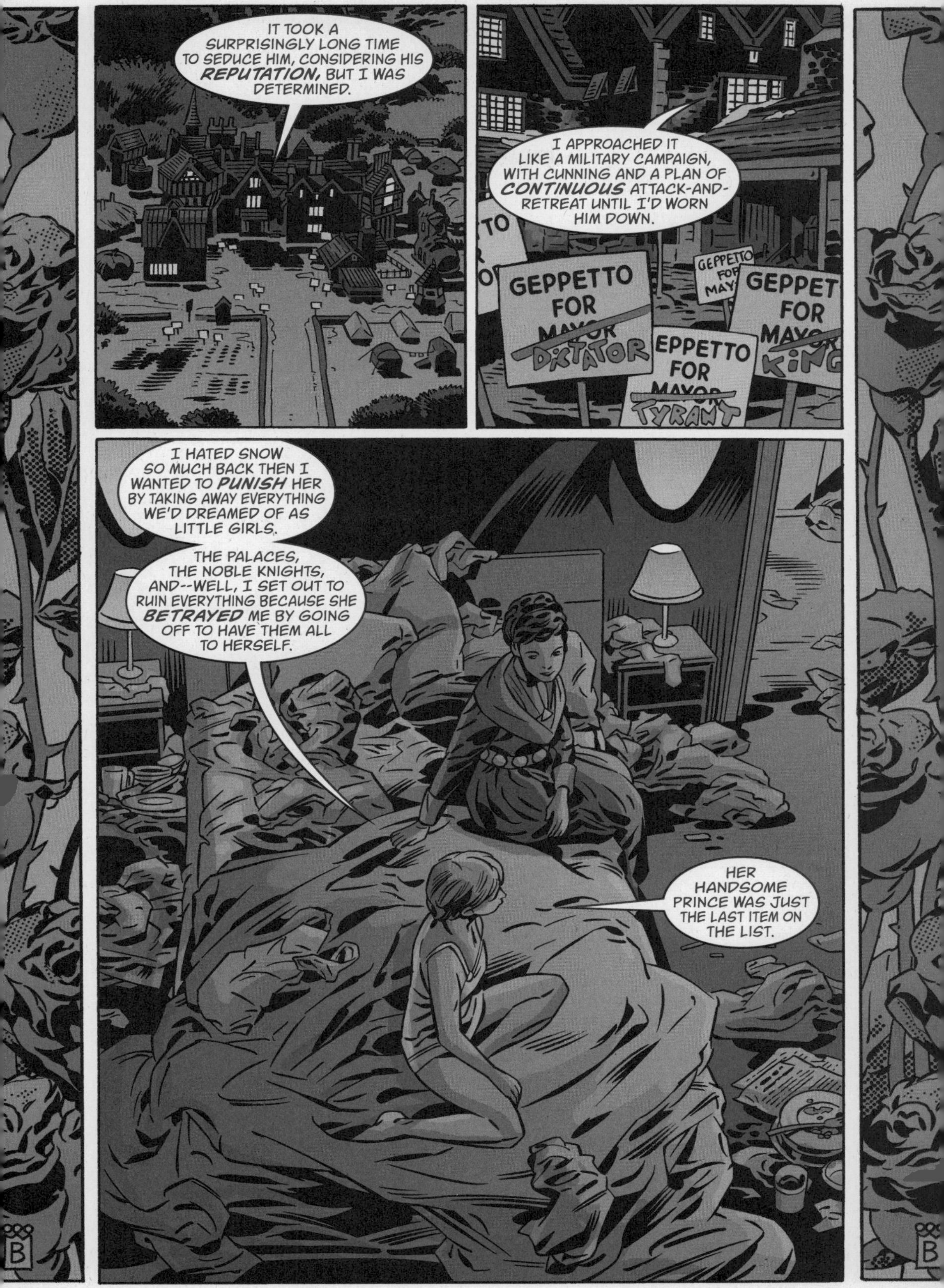
IT TOOK A SURPRISINGLY LONG TIME TO SEDUCE HIM, CONSIDERING HIS *REPUTATION,* BUT I WAS DETERMINED.
I APPROACHED IT LIKE A MILITARY CAMPAIGN, WITH CUNNING AND A PLAN OF *CONTINUOUS* ATTACK-AND-RETREAT UNTIL I'D WORN HIM DOWN.
GEPPETTO FOR ~~MAYOR~~ DICTATOR
EPPETTO FOR ~~MAYOR~~ TYRANT
GEPPETTO FOR MAYOR
GEPPET FOR ~~MAYOR~~ KING
I HATED SNOW SO MUCH BACK THEN I WANTED TO *PUNISH* HER BY TAKING AWAY EVERYTHING WE'D DREAMED OF AS LITTLE GIRLS.
THE PALACES, THE NOBLE KNIGHTS, AND--WELL, I SET OUT TO RUIN EVERYTHING BECAUSE SHE *BETRAYED* ME BY GOING OFF TO HAVE THEM ALL TO HERSELF.
HER HANDSOME PRINCE WAS JUST THE LAST ITEM ON THE LIST.

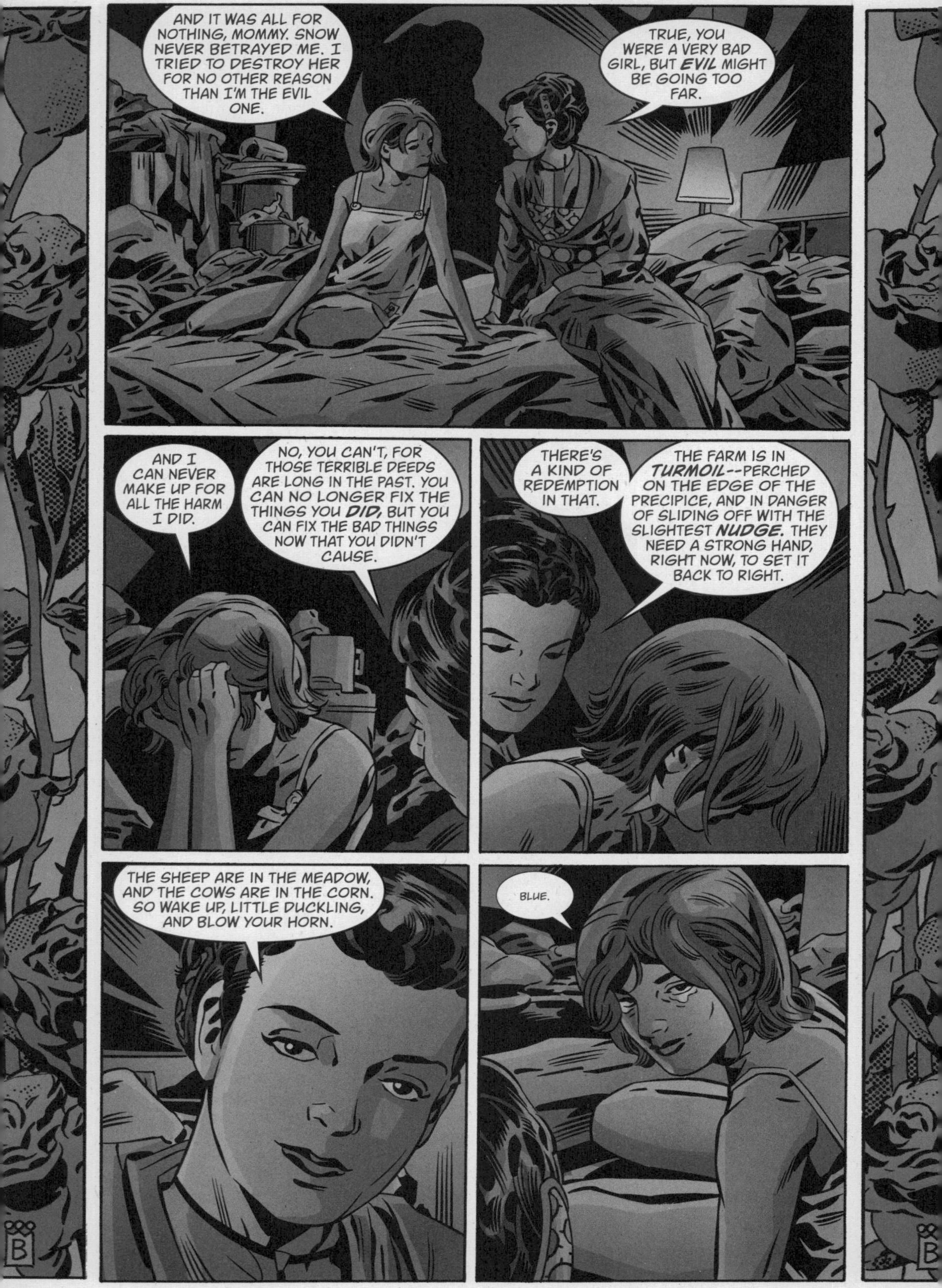
AND IT WAS ALL FOR NOTHING, MOMMY. SNOW NEVER BETRAYED ME. I TRIED TO DESTROY HER FOR NO OTHER REASON THAN I'M THE EVIL ONE.
TRUE, YOU WERE A VERY BAD GIRL, BUT EVIL MIGHT BE GOING TOO FAR.
AND I CAN NEVER MAKE UP FOR ALL THE HARM I DID.
NO, YOU CAN'T, FOR THOSE TERRIBLE DEEDS ARE LONG IN THE PAST. YOU CAN NO LONGER FIX THE THINGS YOU DID, BUT YOU CAN FIX THE BAD THINGS NOW THAT YOU DIDN'T CAUSE.
THERE'S A KIND OF REDEMPTION IN THAT.
THE FARM IS IN TURMOIL--PERCHED ON THE EDGE OF THE PRECIPICE, AND IN DANGER OF SLIDING OFF WITH THE SLIGHTEST NUDGE. THEY NEED A STRONG HAND, RIGHT NOW, TO SET IT BACK TO RIGHT.
THE SHEEP ARE IN THE MEADOW, AND THE COWS ARE IN THE CORN. SO WAKE UP, LITTLE DUCKLING, AND BLOW YOUR HORN.
BLUE.

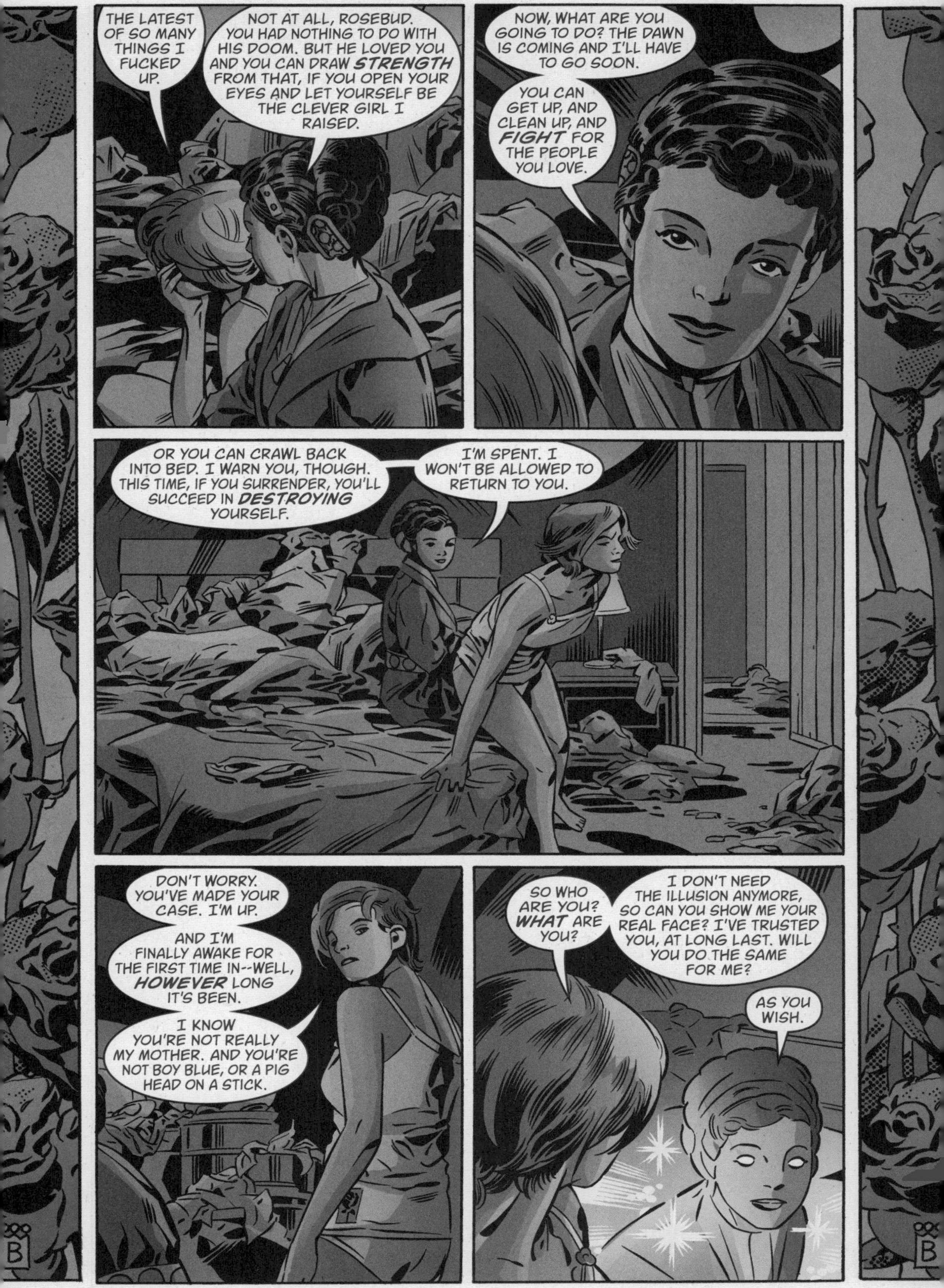
THE LATEST OF SO MANY THINGS I FUCKED UP.
NOT AT ALL, ROSEBUD. YOU HAD NOTHING TO DO WITH HIS DOOM. BUT HE LOVED YOU AND YOU CAN DRAW STRENGTH FROM THAT, IF YOU OPEN YOUR EYES AND LET YOURSELF BE THE CLEVER GIRL I RAISED.
NOW, WHAT ARE YOU GOING TO DO? THE DAWN IS COMING AND I'LL HAVE TO GO SOON.
YOU CAN GET UP, AND CLEAN UP, AND FIGHT FOR THE PEOPLE YOU LOVE.
OR YOU CAN CRAWL BACK INTO BED. I WARN YOU, THOUGH. THIS TIME, IF YOU SURRENDER, YOU'LL SUCCEED IN DESTROYING YOURSELF.
I'M SPENT. I WON'T BE ALLOWED TO RETURN TO YOU.
DON'T WORRY. YOU'VE MADE YOUR CASE. I'M UP.
AND I'M FINALLY AWAKE FOR THE FIRST TIME IN--WELL, HOWEVER LONG IT'S BEEN.
I KNOW YOU'RE NOT REALLY MY MOTHER. AND YOU'RE NOT BOY BLUE, OR A PIG HEAD ON A STICK.
SO WHO ARE YOU? WHAT ARE YOU?
I DON'T NEED THE ILLUSION ANYMORE, SO CAN YOU SHOW ME YOUR REAL FACE? I'VE TRUSTED YOU, AT LONG LAST. WILL YOU DO THE SAME FOR ME?
AS YOU WISH.

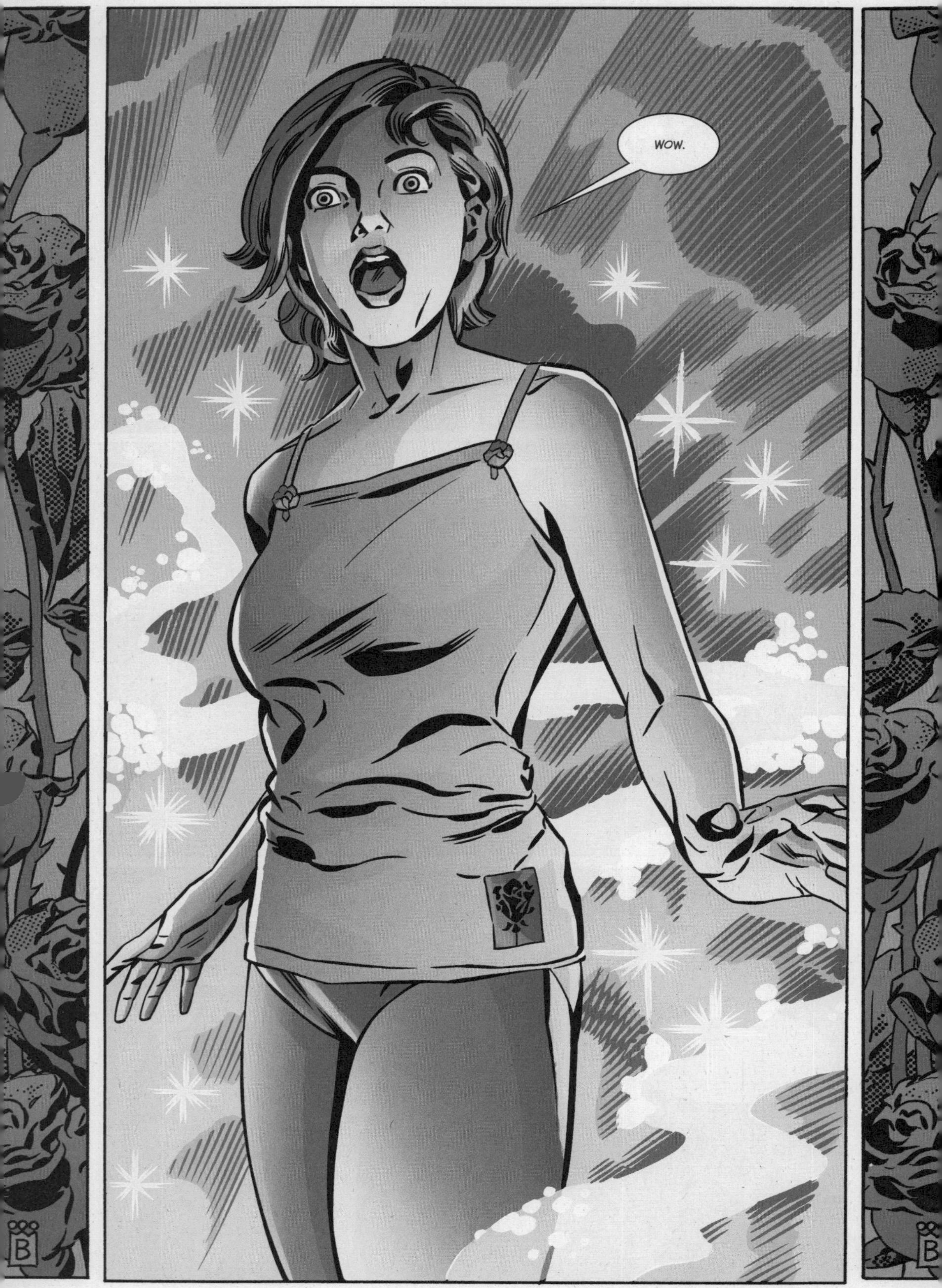
WOW.

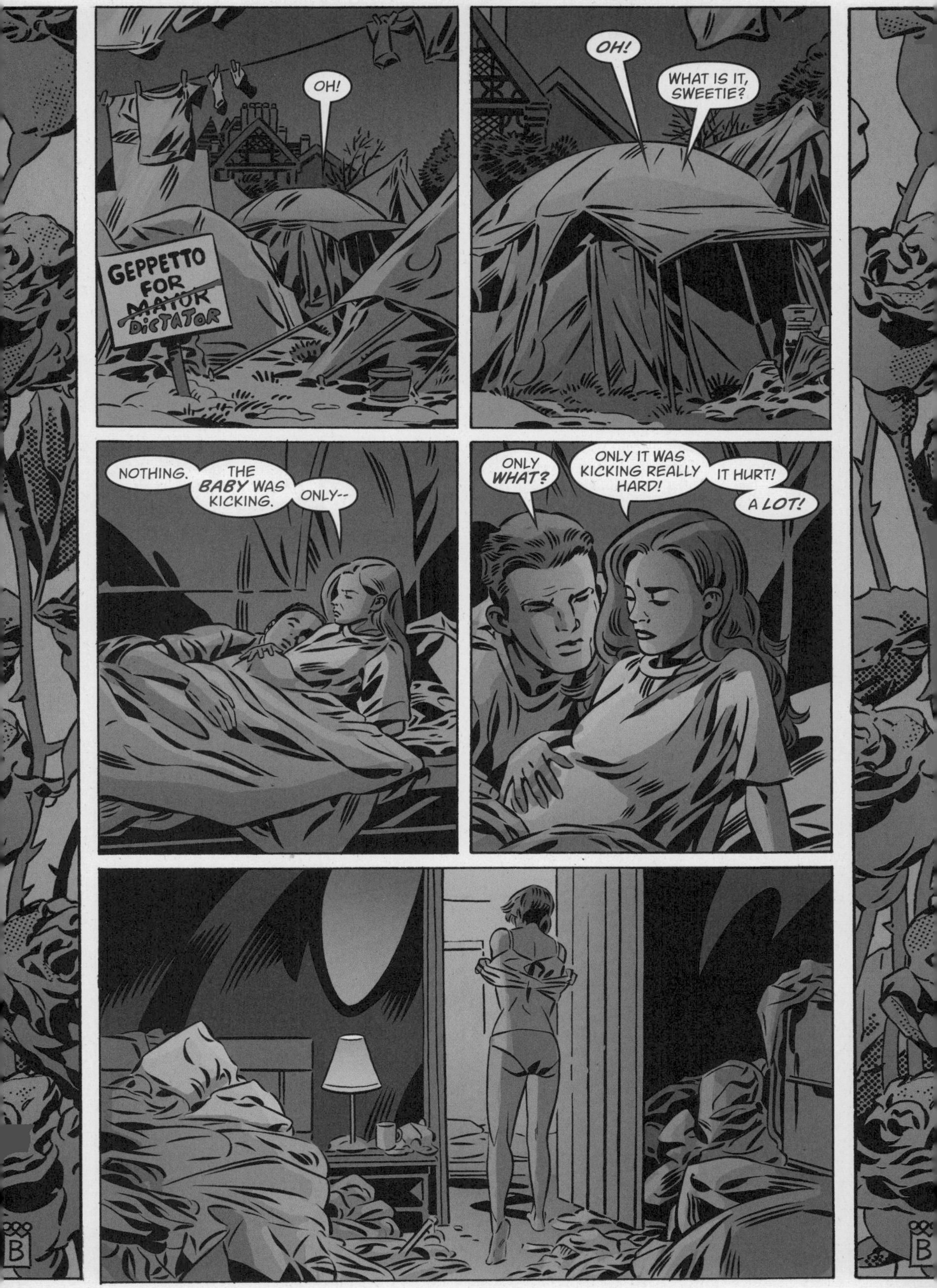

OH!
GEPPETTO FOR MAYOR DICTATOR
OH!
WHAT IS IT, SWEETIE?
NOTHING.
THE BABY WAS KICKING.
ONLY--
ONLY WHAT?
ONLY IT WAS KICKING REALLY HARD!
IT HURT!
A LOT!

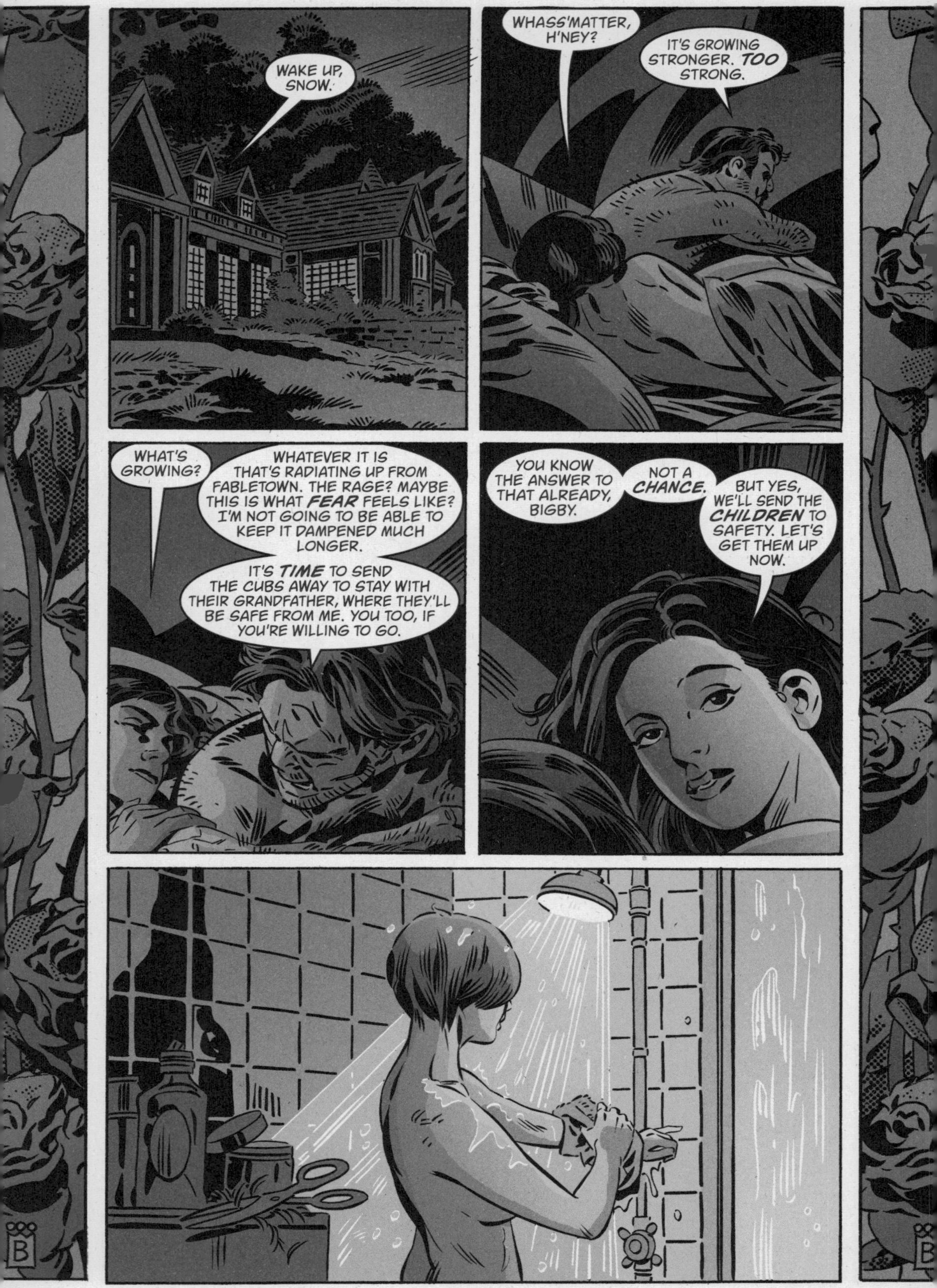
WAKE UP, SNOW.
WHASS'MATTER, H'NEY?
IT'S GROWING STRONGER. TOO STRONG.
WHAT'S GROWING?
WHATEVER IT IS THAT'S RADIATING UP FROM FABLETOWN. THE RAGE? MAYBE THIS IS WHAT FEAR FEELS LIKE? I'M NOT GOING TO BE ABLE TO KEEP IT DAMPENED MUCH LONGER.
IT'S TIME TO SEND THE CUBS AWAY TO STAY WITH THEIR GRANDFATHER, WHERE THEY'LL BE SAFE FROM ME. YOU TOO, IF YOU'RE WILLING TO GO.
YOU KNOW THE ANSWER TO THAT ALREADY, BIGBY.
NOT A CHANCE.
BUT YES, WE'LL SEND THE CHILDREN TO SAFETY. LET'S GET THEM UP NOW.

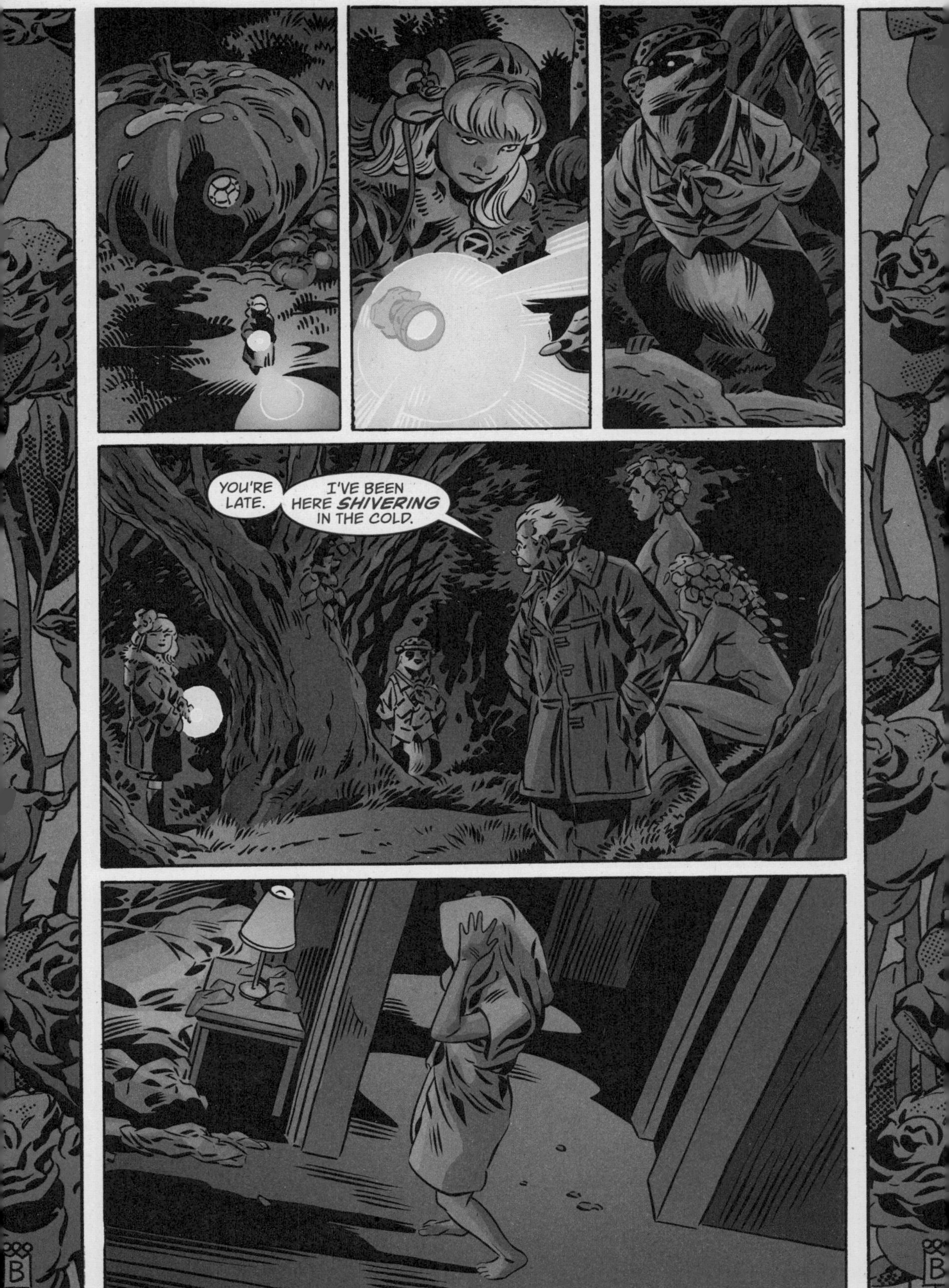
YOU'RE LATE.
I'VE BEEN HERE SHIVERING IN THE COLD.

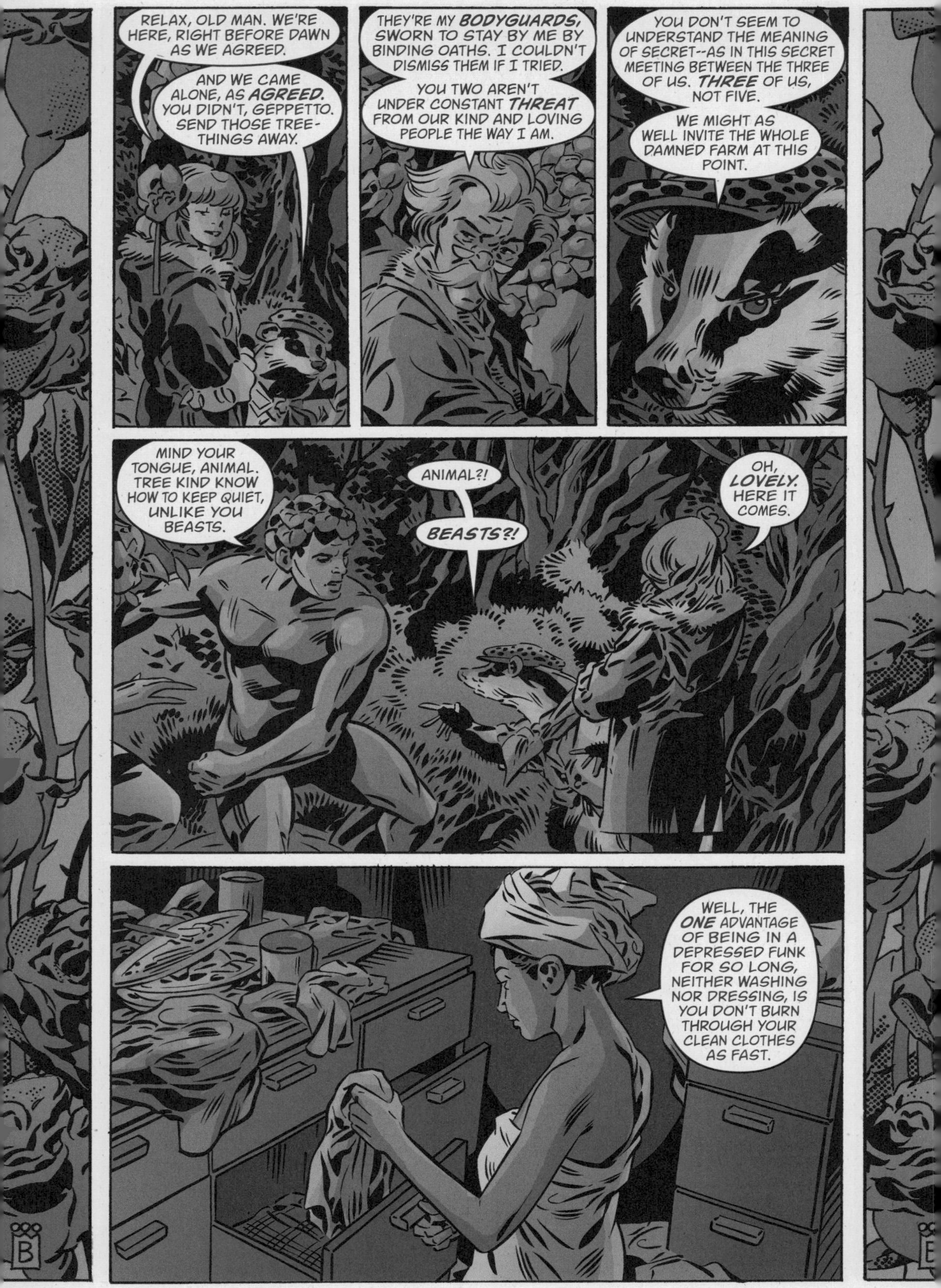
RELAX, OLD MAN. WE'RE HERE, RIGHT BEFORE DAWN AS WE AGREED.
AND WE CAME ALONE, AS **AGREED.** YOU DIDN'T, GEPPETTO. SEND THOSE TREE-THINGS AWAY.
THEY'RE MY **BODYGUARDS,** SWORN TO STAY BY ME BY BINDING OATHS. I COULDN'T DISMISS THEM IF I TRIED.
YOU TWO AREN'T UNDER CONSTANT **THREAT** FROM OUR KIND AND LOVING PEOPLE THE WAY I AM.
YOU DON'T SEEM TO UNDERSTAND THE MEANING OF SECRET--AS IN THIS SECRET MEETING BETWEEN THE THREE OF US. **THREE** OF US, NOT FIVE.
WE MIGHT AS WELL INVITE THE WHOLE DAMNED FARM AT THIS POINT.
MIND YOUR TONGUE, ANIMAL. TREE KIND KNOW HOW TO KEEP QUIET, UNLIKE YOU BEASTS.
ANIMAL?!
BEASTS?!
OH, **LOVELY.** HERE IT COMES.
WELL, THE **ONE** ADVANTAGE OF BEING IN A DEPRESSED FUNK FOR SO LONG, NEITHER WASHING NOR DRESSING, IS YOU DON'T BURN THROUGH YOUR CLEAN CLOTHES AS FAST.

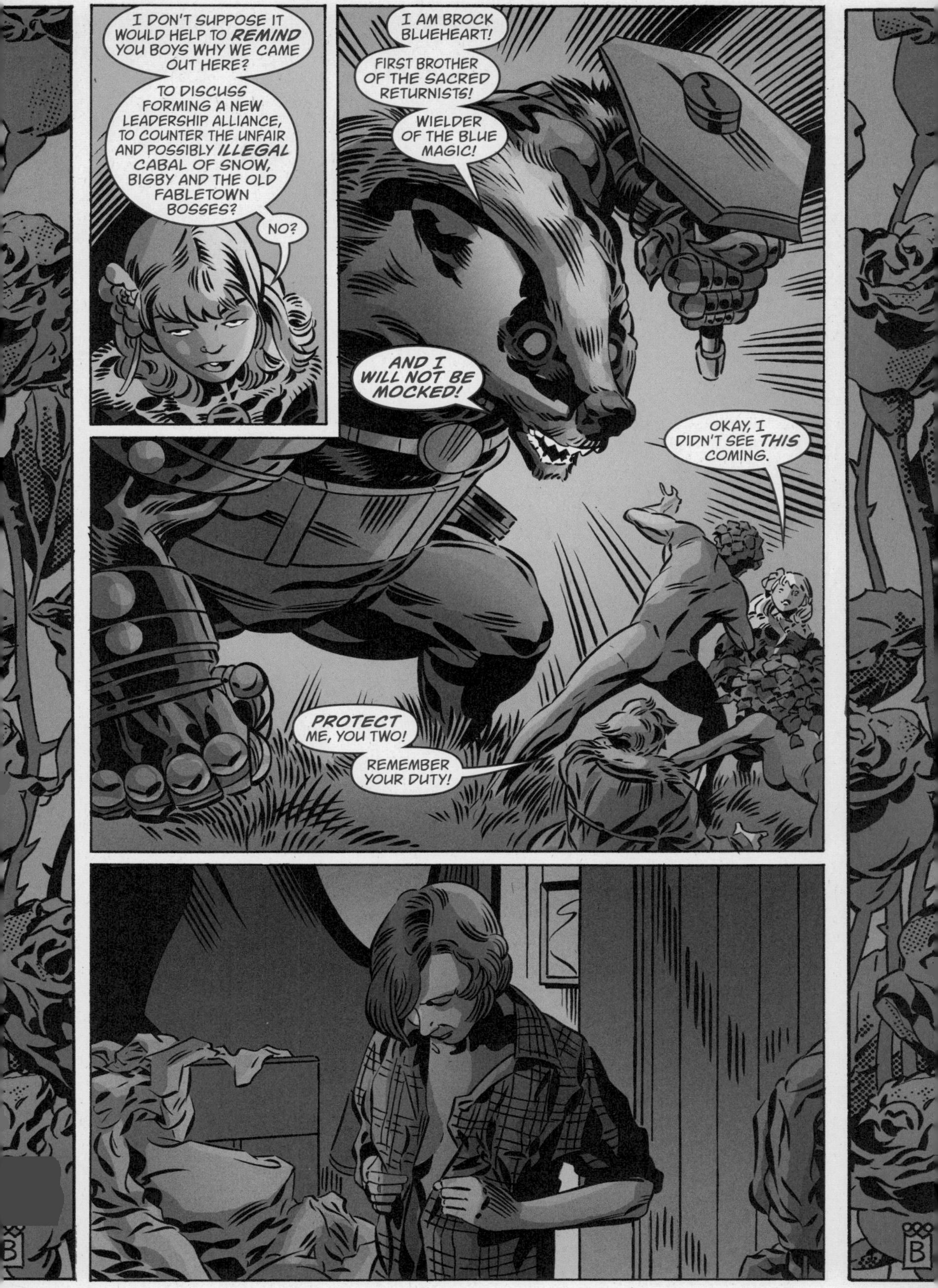
I DON'T SUPPOSE IT WOULD HELP TO REMIND YOU BOYS WHY WE CAME OUT HERE?
TO DISCUSS FORMING A NEW LEADERSHIP ALLIANCE, TO COUNTER THE UNFAIR AND POSSIBLY ILLEGAL CABAL OF SNOW, BIGBY AND THE OLD FABLETOWN BOSSES?
NO?
I AM BROCK BLUEHEART!
FIRST BROTHER OF THE SACRED RETURNISTS!
WIELDER OF THE BLUE MAGIC!
AND I WILL NOT BE MOCKED!
OKAY, I DIDN'T SEE THIS COMING.
PROTECT ME, YOU TWO!
REMEMBER YOUR DUTY!

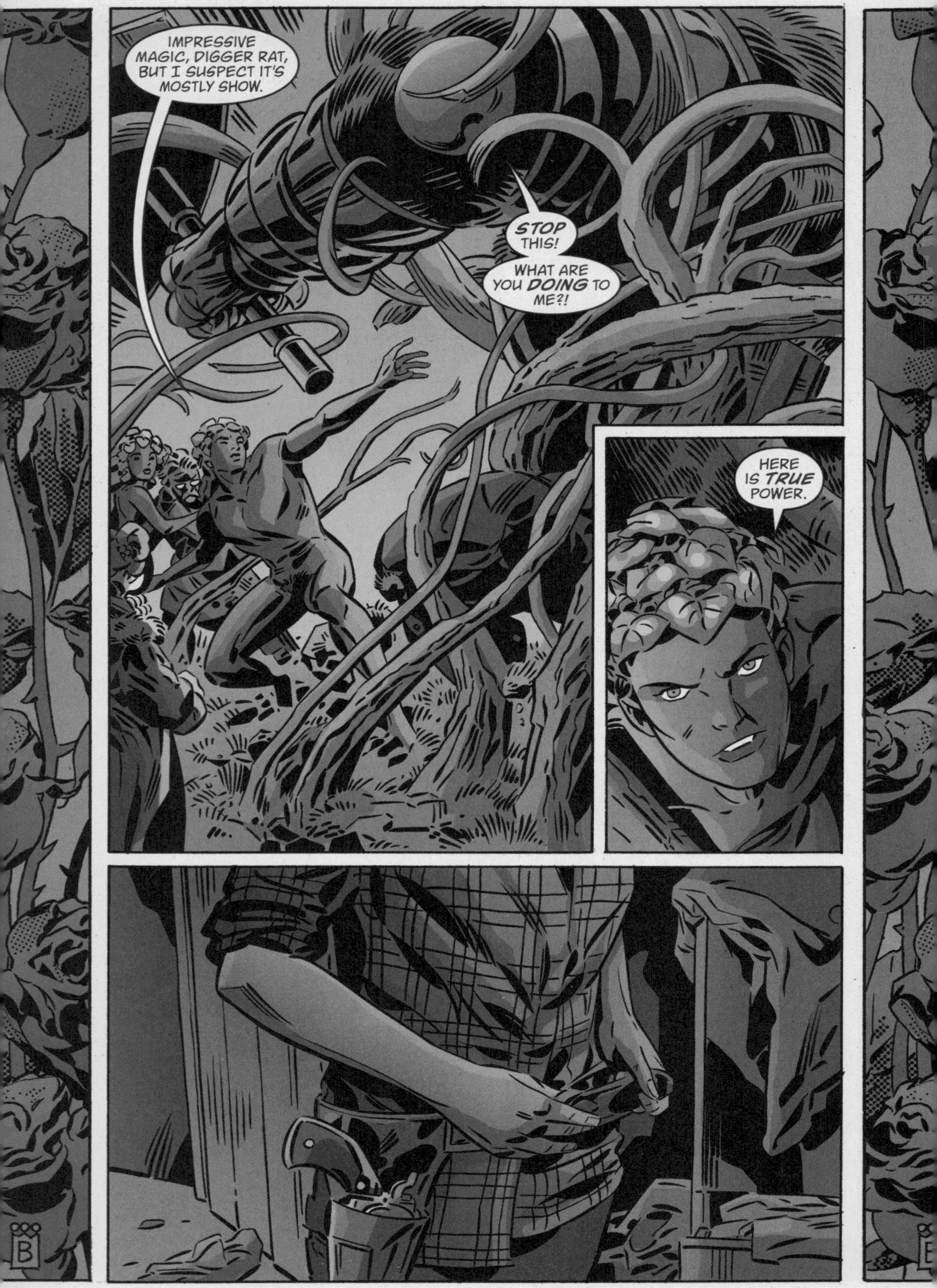
IMPRESSIVE MAGIC, DIGGER RAT, BUT I SUSPECT IT'S MOSTLY SHOW.
STOP THIS!
WHAT ARE YOU DOING TO ME?!
HERE IS TRUE POWER.

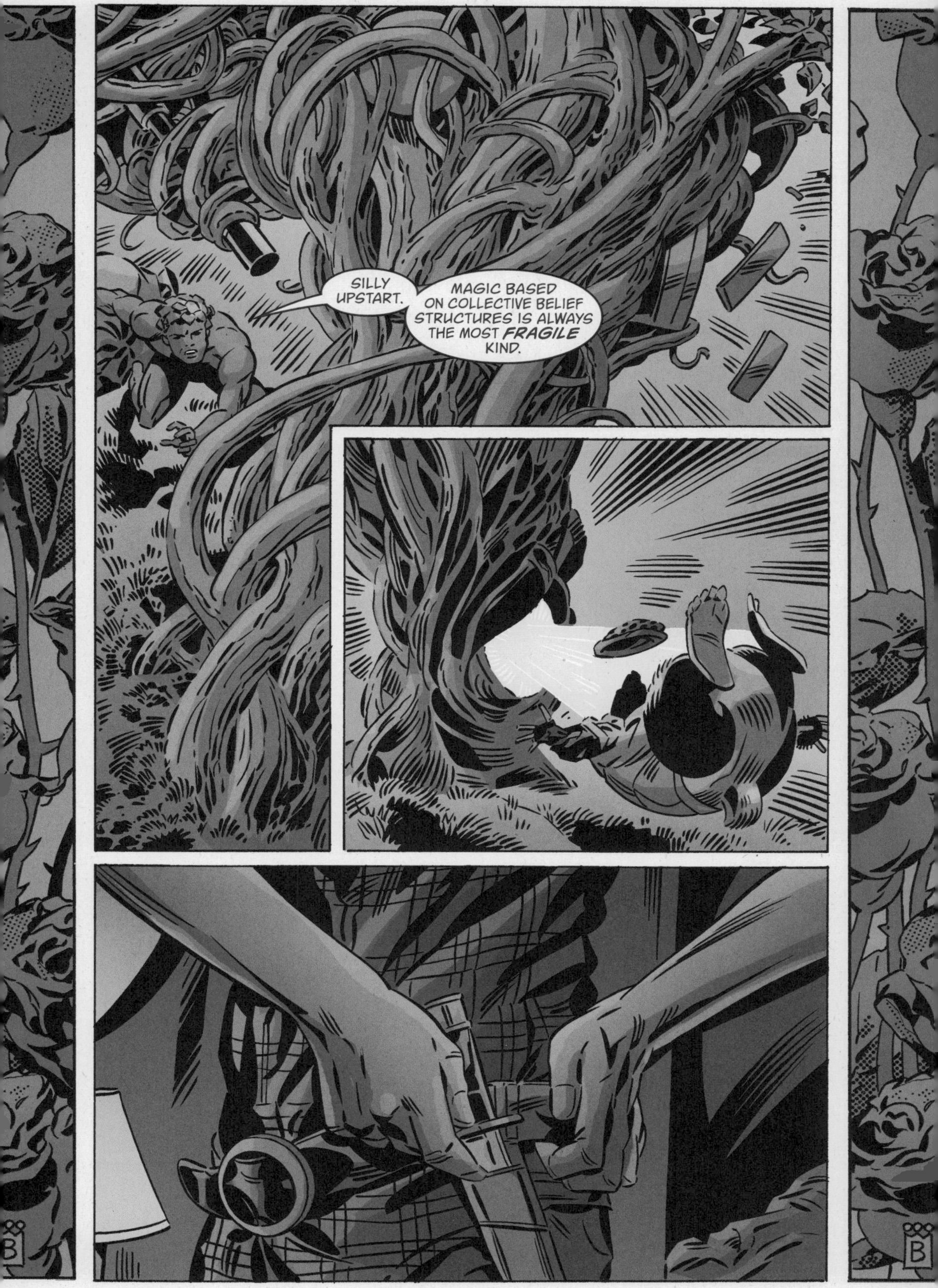

SILLY UPSTART.
MAGIC BASED ON COLLECTIVE BELIEF STRUCTURES IS ALWAYS THE MOST FRAGILE KIND.

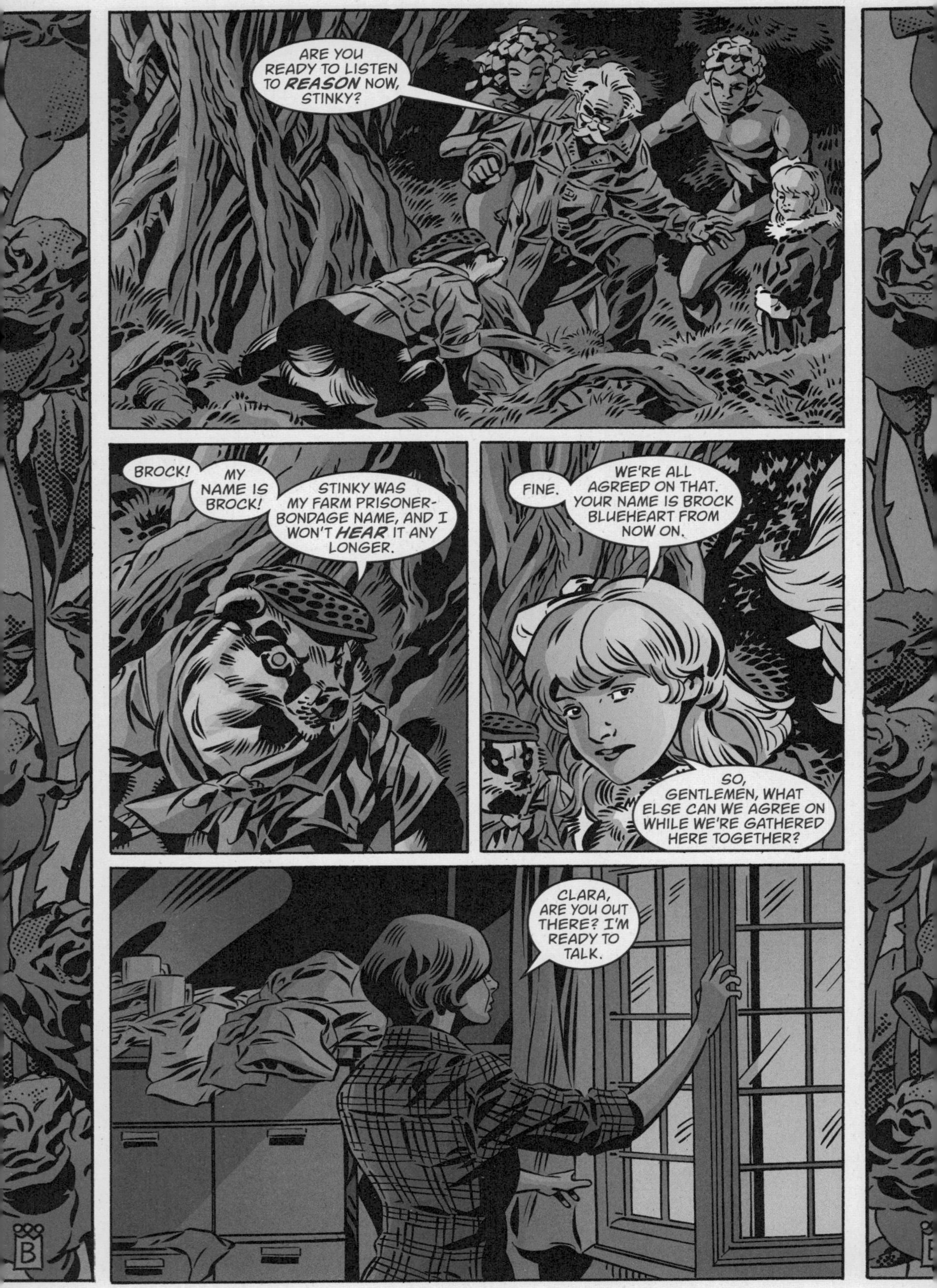

ARE YOU READY TO LISTEN TO REASON NOW, STINKY?
BROCK!
MY NAME IS BROCK!
STINKY WAS MY FARM PRISONER-BONDAGE NAME, AND I WON'T HEAR IT ANY LONGER.
FINE.
WE'RE ALL AGREED ON THAT. YOUR NAME IS BROCK BLUEHEART FROM NOW ON.
SO, GENTLEMEN, WHAT ELSE CAN WE AGREE ON WHILE WE'RE GATHERED HERE TOGETHER?
CLARA, ARE YOU OUT THERE? I'M READY TO TALK.

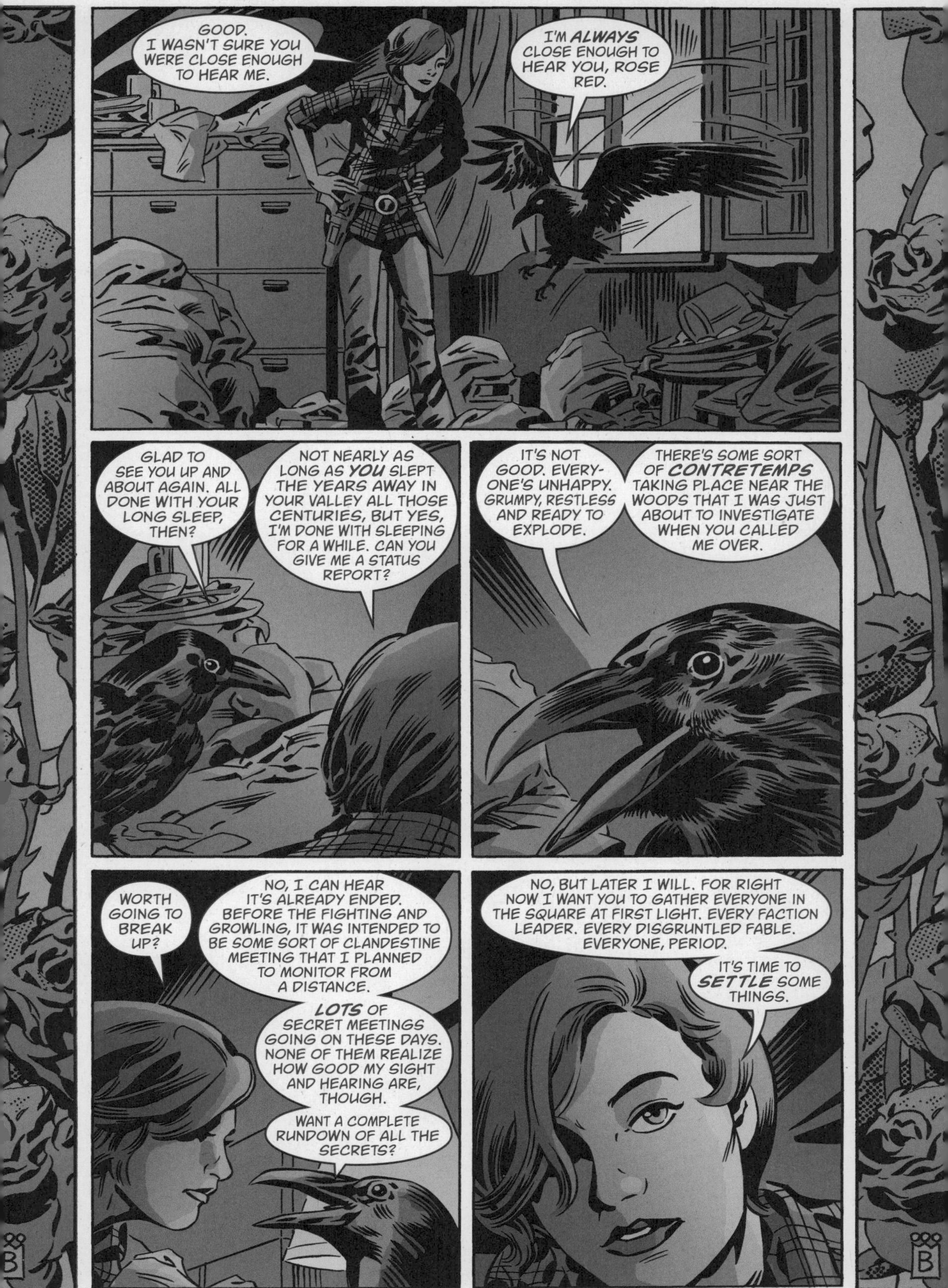

GOOD. I WASN'T SURE YOU WERE CLOSE ENOUGH TO HEAR ME.
I'M ALWAYS CLOSE ENOUGH TO HEAR YOU, ROSE RED.
GLAD TO SEE YOU UP AND ABOUT AGAIN. ALL DONE WITH YOUR LONG SLEEP, THEN?
NOT NEARLY AS LONG AS YOU SLEPT THE YEARS AWAY IN YOUR VALLEY ALL THOSE CENTURIES, BUT YES, I'M DONE WITH SLEEPING FOR A WHILE. CAN YOU GIVE ME A STATUS REPORT?
IT'S NOT GOOD. EVERY-ONE'S UNHAPPY. GRUMPY, RESTLESS AND READY TO EXPLODE.
THERE'S SOME SORT OF CONTRETEMPS TAKING PLACE NEAR THE WOODS THAT I WAS JUST ABOUT TO INVESTIGATE WHEN YOU CALLED ME OVER.
WORTH GOING TO BREAK UP?
NO, I CAN HEAR IT'S ALREADY ENDED. BEFORE THE FIGHTING AND GROWLING, IT WAS INTENDED TO BE SOME SORT OF CLANDESTINE MEETING THAT I PLANNED TO MONITOR FROM A DISTANCE.
LOTS OF SECRET MEETINGS GOING ON THESE DAYS. NONE OF THEM REALIZE HOW GOOD MY SIGHT AND HEARING ARE, THOUGH.
WANT A COMPLETE RUNDOWN OF ALL THE SECRETS?
NO, BUT LATER I WILL. FOR RIGHT NOW I WANT YOU TO GATHER EVERYONE IN THE SQUARE AT FIRST LIGHT. EVERY FACTION LEADER. EVERY DISGRUNTLED FABLE. EVERYONE, PERIOD.
IT'S TIME TO SETTLE SOME THINGS.

NEXT: RED DAWN

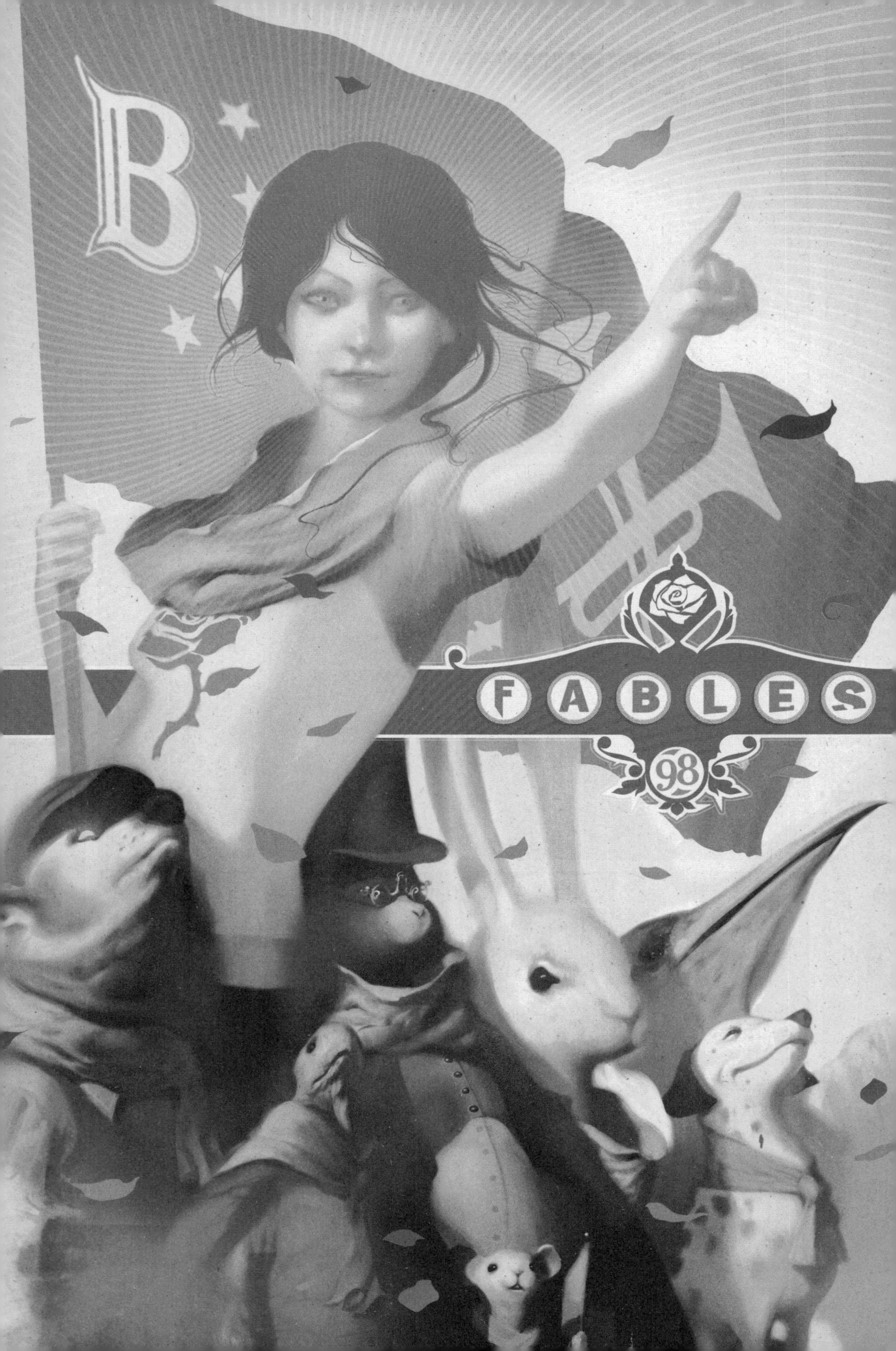
B
FABLES
98

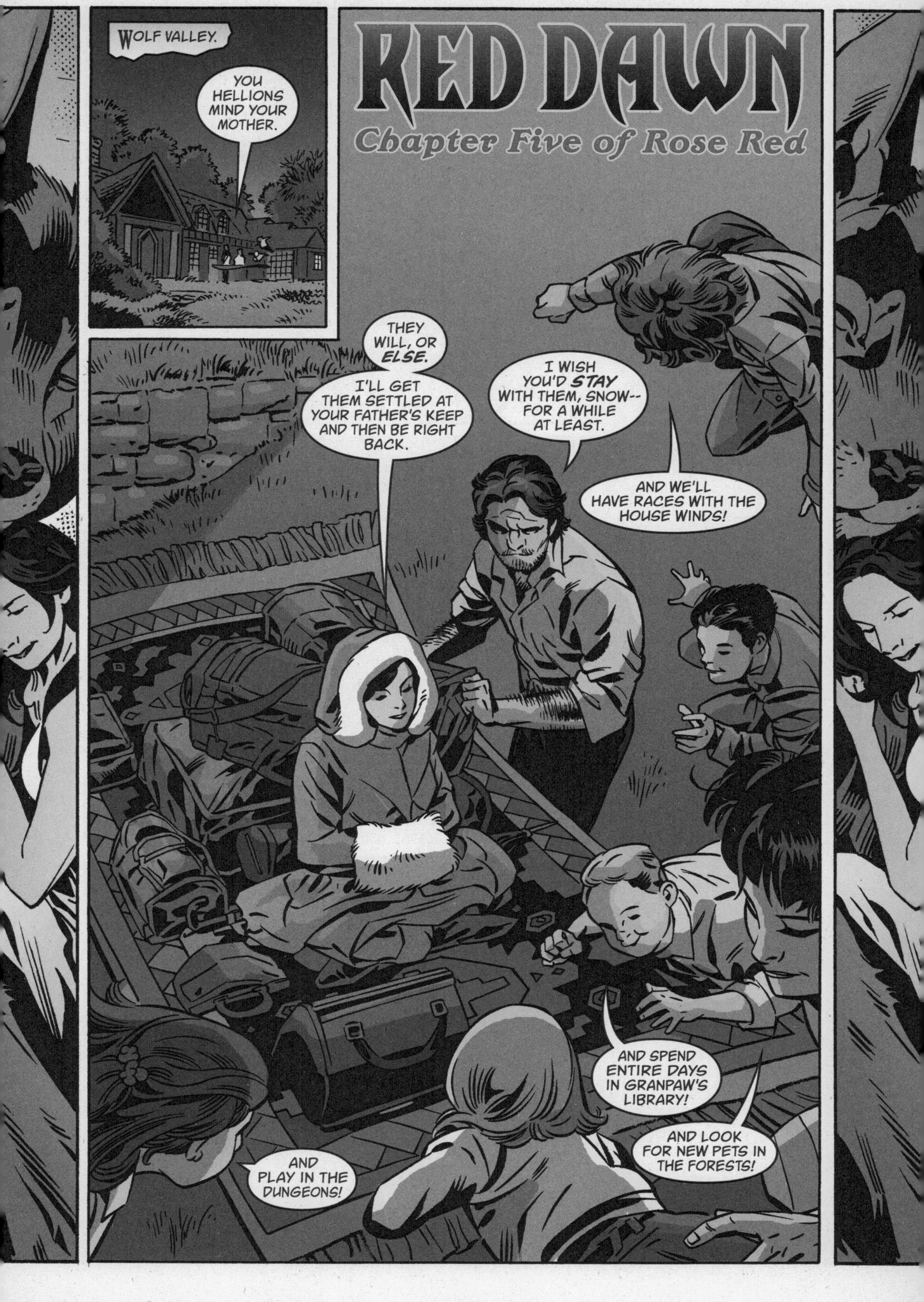
RED DAWN
Chapter Five of Rose Red
WOLF VALLEY.
YOU HELLIONS MIND YOUR MOTHER.
THEY WILL, OR ELSE.
I'LL GET THEM SETTLED AT YOUR FATHER'S KEEP AND THEN BE RIGHT BACK.
I WISH YOU'D STAY WITH THEM, SNOW-- FOR A WHILE AT LEAST.
AND WE'LL HAVE RACES WITH THE HOUSE WINDS!
AND SPEND ENTIRE DAYS IN GRANPAW'S LIBRARY!
AND LOOK FOR NEW PETS IN THE FORESTS!
AND PLAY IN THE DUNGEONS!

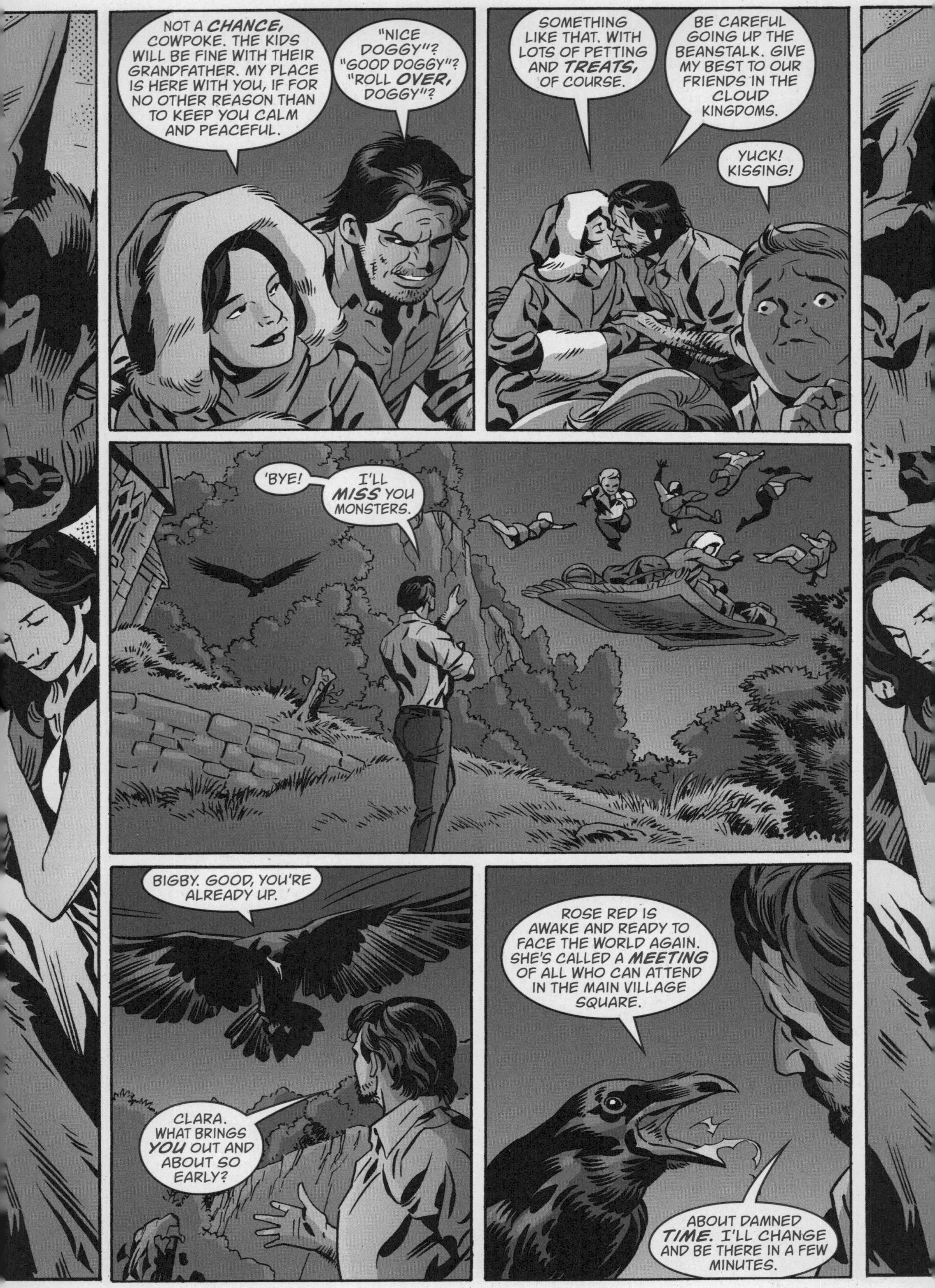
NOT A CHANCE, COWPOKE. THE KIDS WILL BE FINE WITH THEIR GRANDFATHER. MY PLACE IS HERE WITH YOU, IF FOR NO OTHER REASON THAN TO KEEP YOU CALM AND PEACEFUL.
"NICE DOGGY"? "GOOD DOGGY"? "ROLL OVER, DOGGY"?
SOMETHING LIKE THAT. WITH LOTS OF PETTING AND TREATS, OF COURSE.
BE CAREFUL GOING UP THE BEANSTALK. GIVE MY BEST TO OUR FRIENDS IN THE CLOUD KINGDOMS.
YUCK! KISSING!
'BYE!
I'LL MISS YOU MONSTERS.
BIGBY. GOOD, YOU'RE ALREADY UP.
CLARA. WHAT BRINGS YOU OUT AND ABOUT SO EARLY?
ROSE RED IS AWAKE AND READY TO FACE THE WORLD AGAIN. SHE'S CALLED A MEETING OF ALL WHO CAN ATTEND IN THE MAIN VILLAGE SQUARE.
ABOUT DAMNED TIME. I'LL CHANGE AND BE THERE IN A FEW MINUTES.

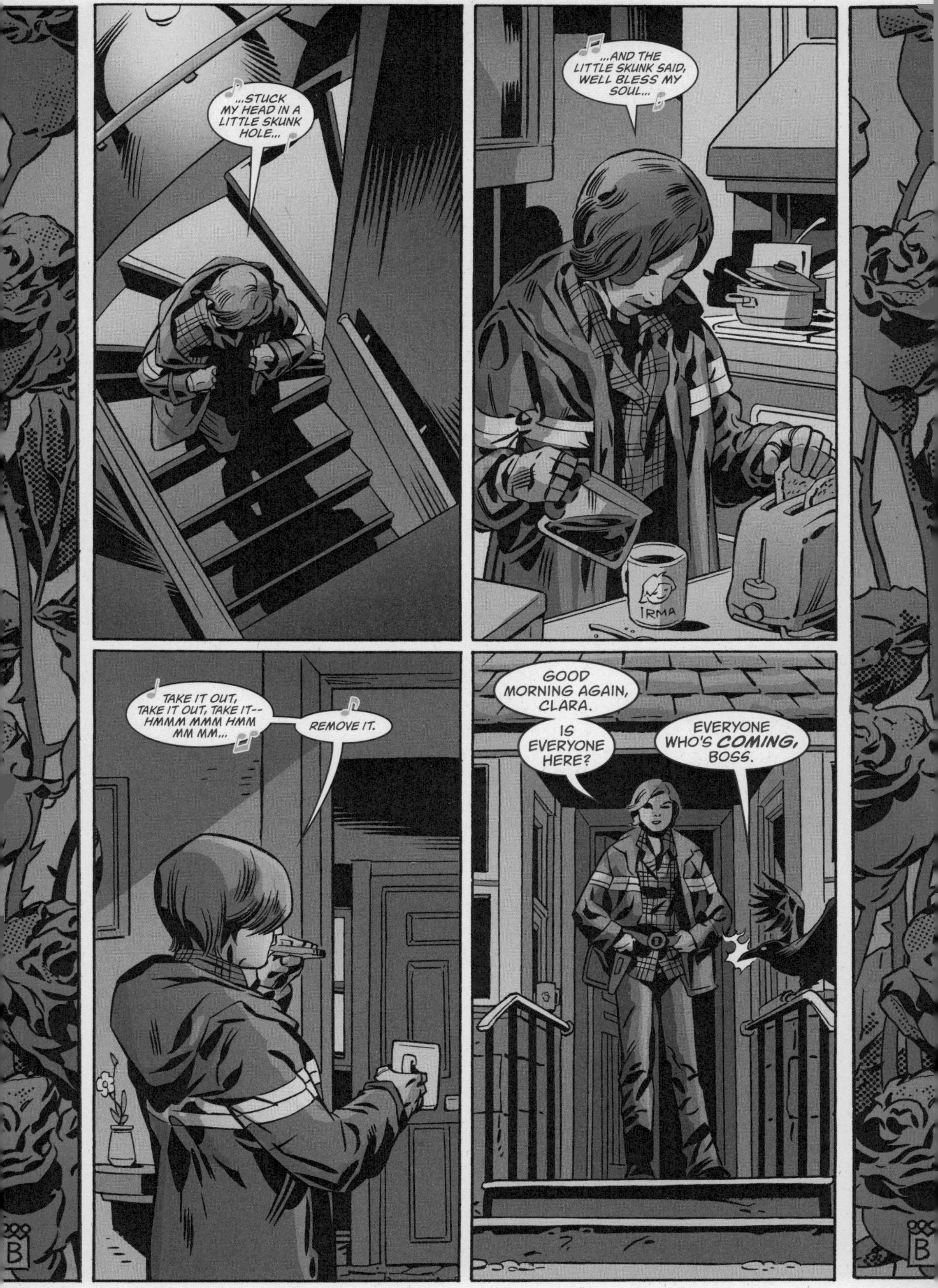
...STUCK MY HEAD IN A LITTLE SKUNK HOLE...
...AND THE LITTLE SKUNK SAID, WELL BLESS MY SOUL...
IRMA
TAKE IT OUT, TAKE IT OUT, TAKE IT-- HMMM MMM HMM MM MM...
REMOVE IT.
GOOD MORNING AGAIN, CLARA.
IS EVERYONE HERE?
EVERYONE WHO'S *COMING,* BOSS.

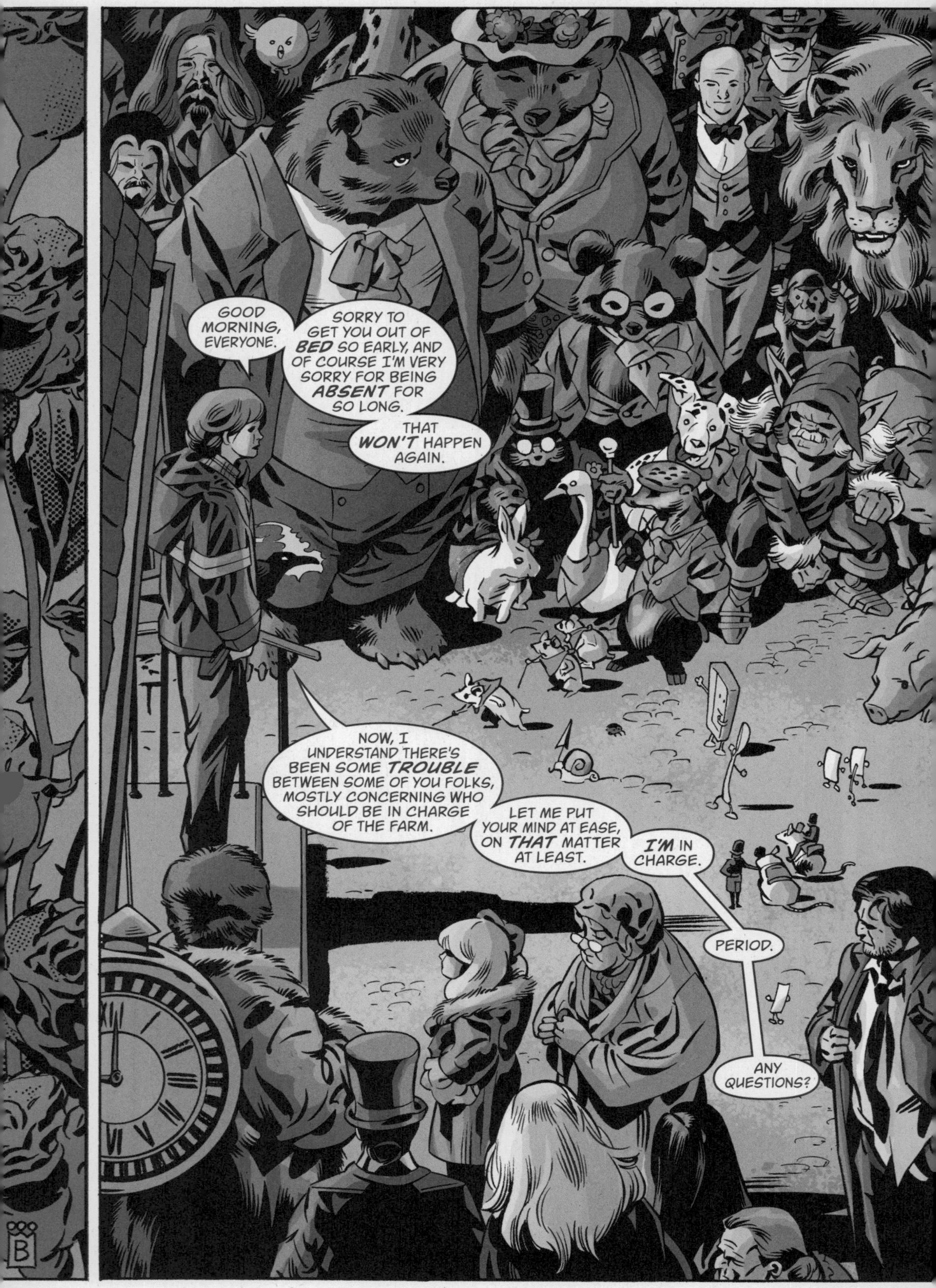
GOOD MORNING, EVERYONE.
SORRY TO GET YOU OUT OF BED SO EARLY, AND OF COURSE I'M VERY SORRY FOR BEING ABSENT FOR SO LONG.
THAT WON'T HAPPEN AGAIN.
NOW, I UNDERSTAND THERE'S BEEN SOME TROUBLE BETWEEN SOME OF YOU FOLKS, MOSTLY CONCERNING WHO SHOULD BE IN CHARGE OF THE FARM.
LET ME PUT YOUR MIND AT EASE, ON THAT MATTER AT LEAST.
I'M IN CHARGE.
PERIOD.
ANY QUESTIONS?

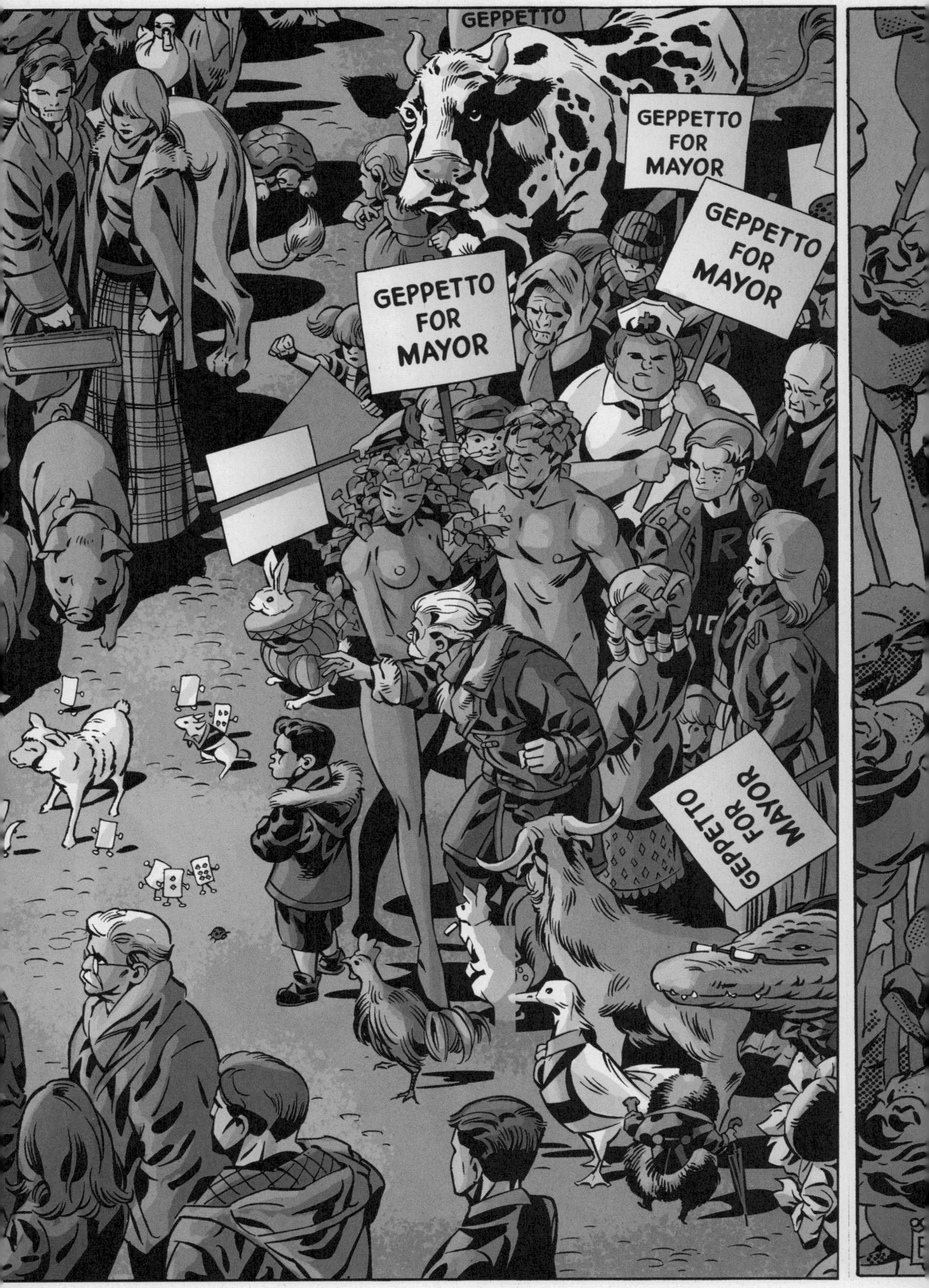
GEPPETTO
GEPPETTO FOR MAYOR
GEPPETTO FOR MAYOR
GEPPETTO FOR MAYOR
GEPPETTO FOR MAYOR

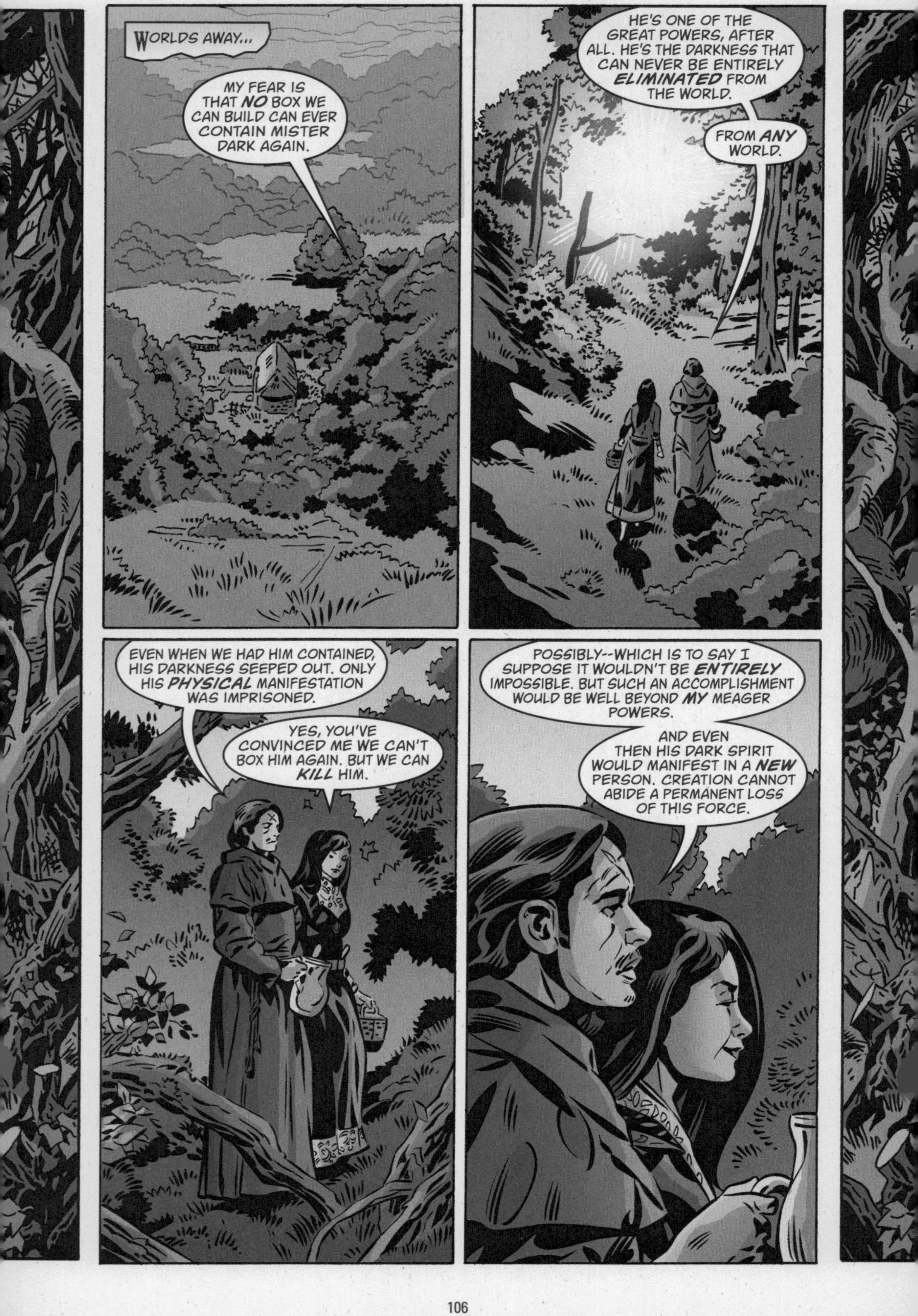
WORLDS AWAY...
MY FEAR IS THAT NO BOX WE CAN BUILD CAN EVER CONTAIN MISTER DARK AGAIN.
HE'S ONE OF THE GREAT POWERS, AFTER ALL. HE'S THE DARKNESS THAT CAN NEVER BE ENTIRELY ELIMINATED FROM THE WORLD.
FROM ANY WORLD.
EVEN WHEN WE HAD HIM CONTAINED, HIS DARKNESS SEEPED OUT. ONLY HIS PHYSICAL MANIFESTATION WAS IMPRISONED.
YES, YOU'VE CONVINCED ME WE CAN'T BOX HIM AGAIN. BUT WE CAN KILL HIM.
POSSIBLY--WHICH IS TO SAY I SUPPOSE IT WOULDN'T BE ENTIRELY IMPOSSIBLE. BUT SUCH AN ACCOMPLISHMENT WOULD BE WELL BEYOND MY MEAGER POWERS.
AND EVEN THEN HIS DARK SPIRIT WOULD MANIFEST IN A NEW PERSON. CREATION CANNOT ABIDE A PERMANENT LOSS OF THIS FORCE.

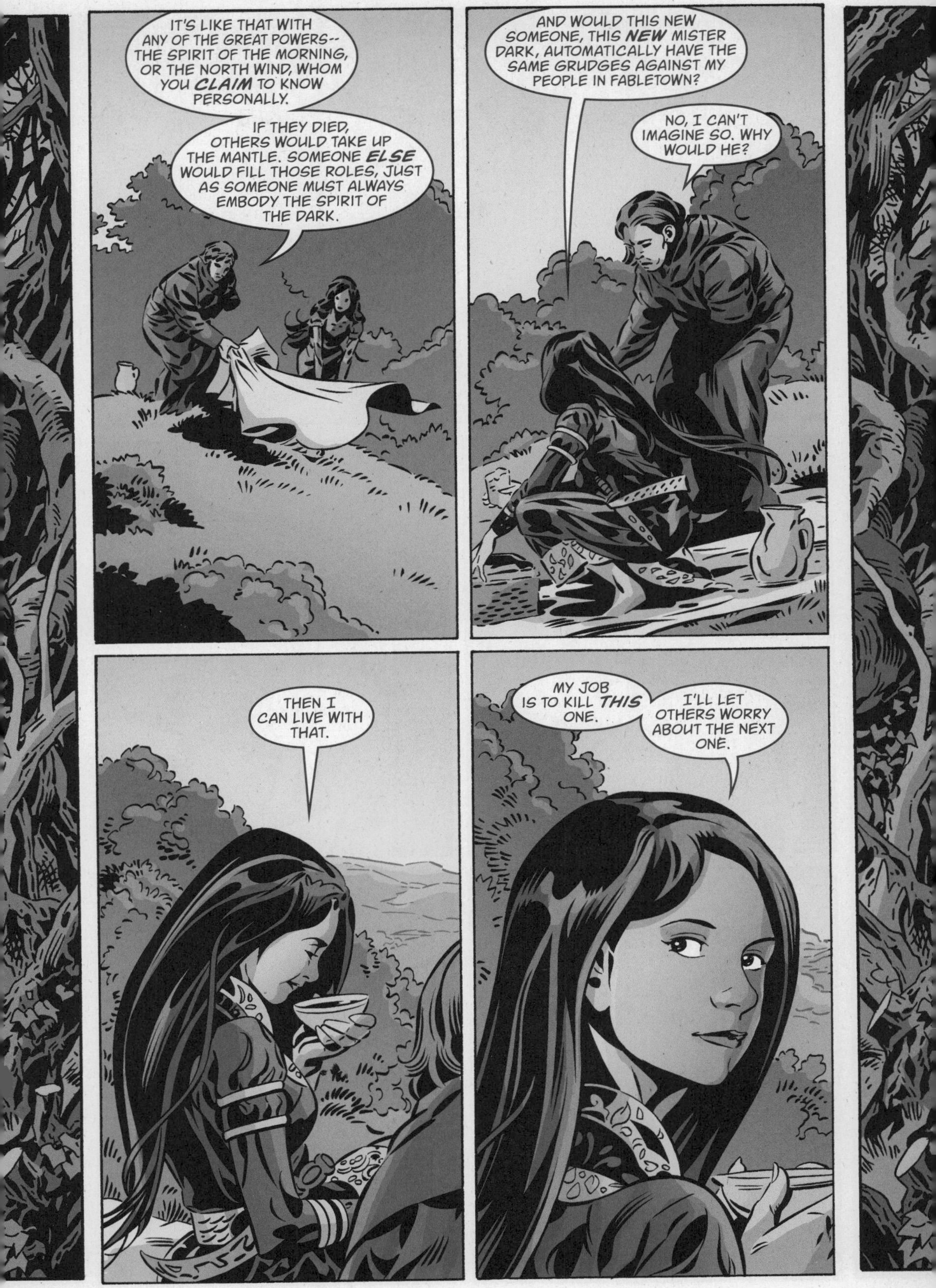
IT'S LIKE THAT WITH ANY OF THE GREAT POWERS-- THE SPIRIT OF THE MORNING, OR THE NORTH WIND, WHOM YOU CLAIM TO KNOW PERSONALLY.
IF THEY DIED, OTHERS WOULD TAKE UP THE MANTLE. SOMEONE ELSE WOULD FILL THOSE ROLES, JUST AS SOMEONE MUST ALWAYS EMBODY THE SPIRIT OF THE DARK.
AND WOULD THIS NEW SOMEONE, THIS NEW MISTER DARK, AUTOMATICALLY HAVE THE SAME GRUDGES AGAINST MY PEOPLE IN FABLETOWN?
NO, I CAN'T IMAGINE SO. WHY WOULD HE?
THEN I CAN LIVE WITH THAT.
MY JOB IS TO KILL THIS ONE.
I'LL LET OTHERS WORRY ABOUT THE NEXT ONE.

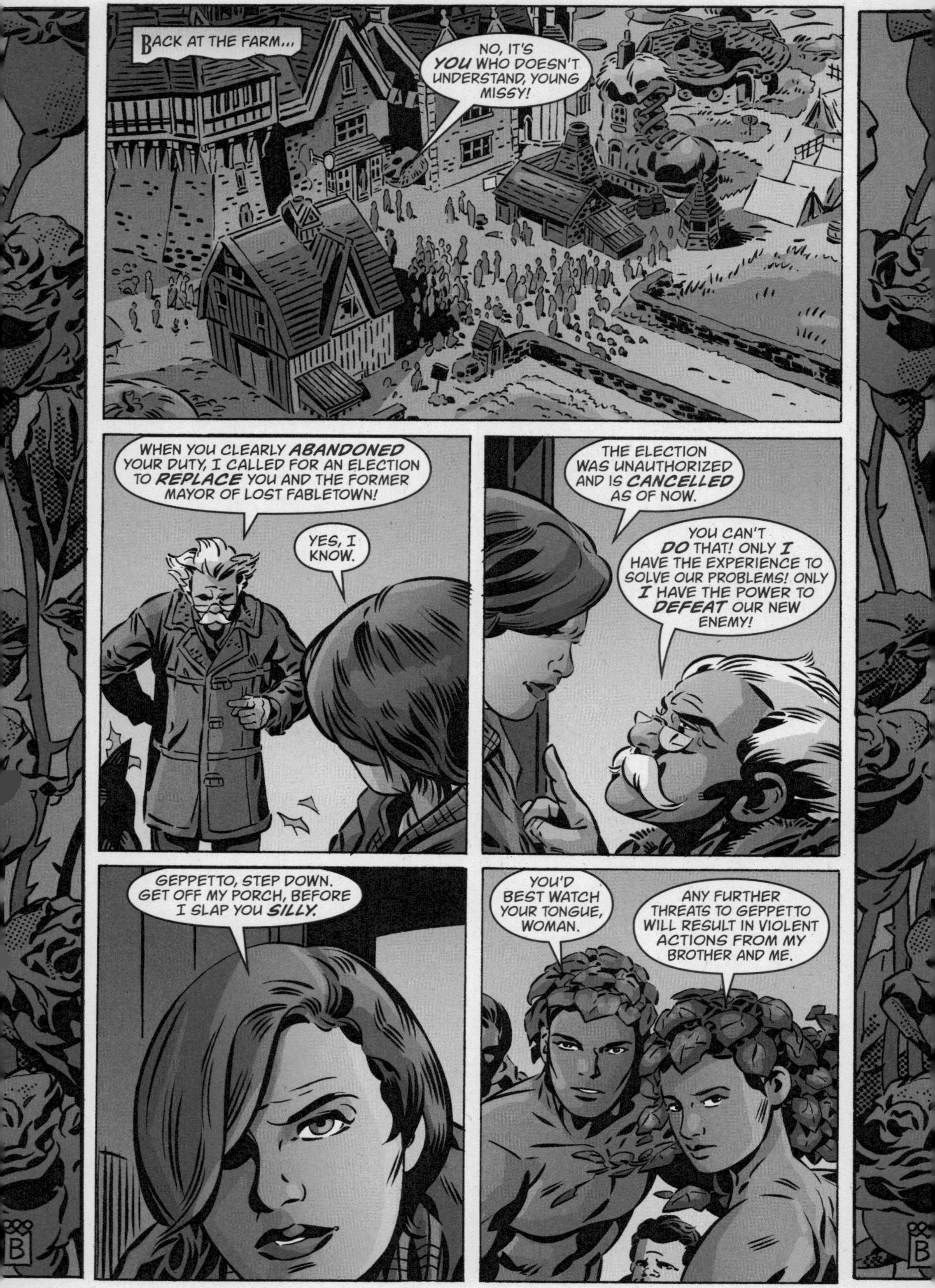
BACK AT THE FARM...
NO, IT'S YOU WHO DOESN'T UNDERSTAND, YOUNG MISSY!
WHEN YOU CLEARLY ABANDONED YOUR DUTY, I CALLED FOR AN ELECTION TO REPLACE YOU AND THE FORMER MAYOR OF LOST FABLETOWN!
YES, I KNOW.
THE ELECTION WAS UNAUTHORIZED AND IS CANCELLED AS OF NOW.
YOU CAN'T DO THAT! ONLY I HAVE THE EXPERIENCE TO SOLVE OUR PROBLEMS! ONLY I HAVE THE POWER TO DEFEAT OUR NEW ENEMY!
GEPPETTO, STEP DOWN. GET OFF MY PORCH, BEFORE I SLAP YOU SILLY.
YOU'D BEST WATCH YOUR TONGUE, WOMAN.
ANY FURTHER THREATS TO GEPPETTO WILL RESULT IN VIOLENT ACTIONS FROM MY BROTHER AND ME.

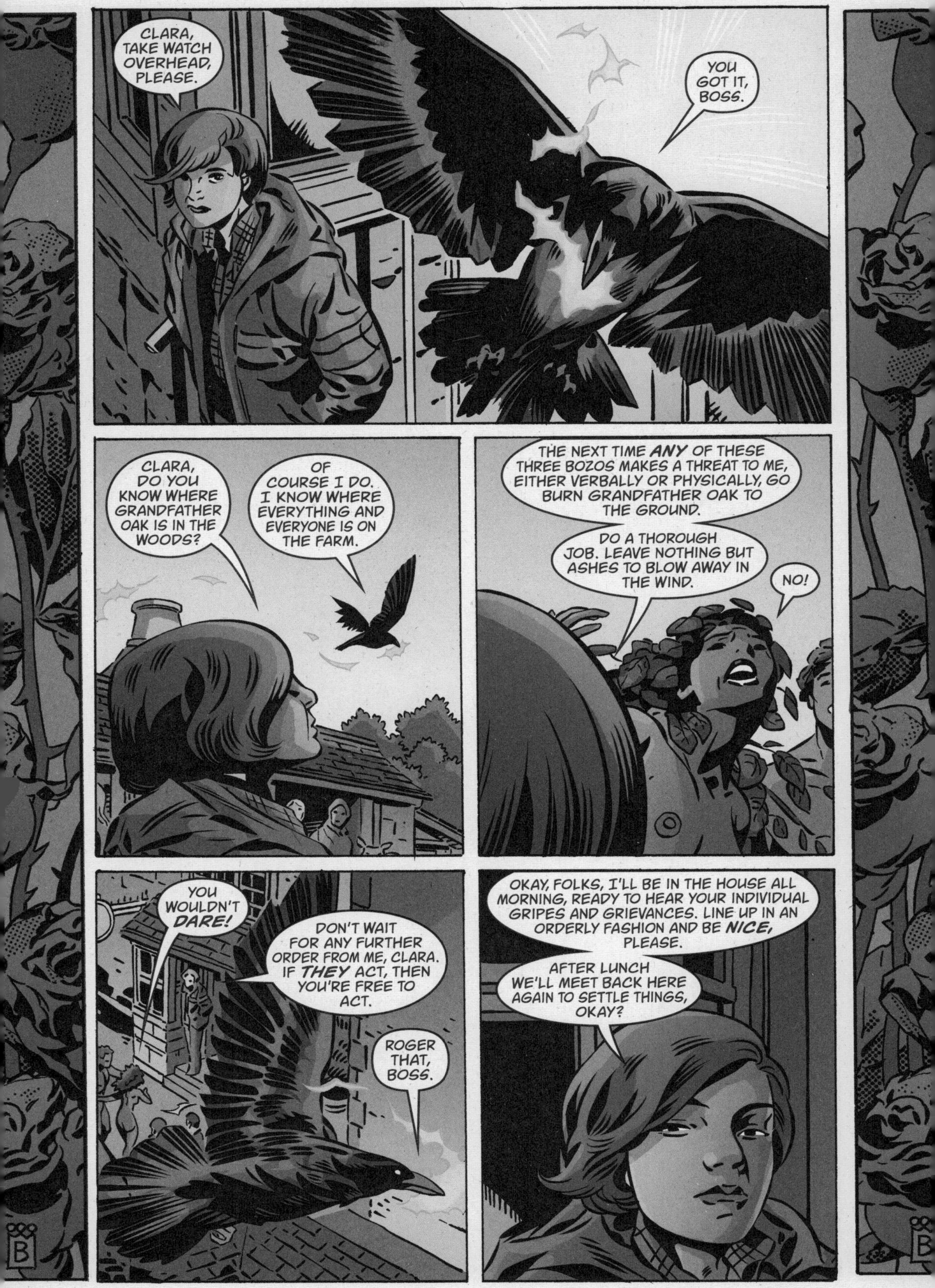
CLARA, TAKE WATCH OVERHEAD, PLEASE.
YOU GOT IT, BOSS.
CLARA, DO YOU KNOW WHERE GRANDFATHER OAK IS IN THE WOODS?
OF COURSE I DO. I KNOW WHERE EVERYTHING AND EVERYONE IS ON THE FARM.
THE NEXT TIME ANY OF THESE THREE BOZOS MAKES A THREAT TO ME, EITHER VERBALLY OR PHYSICALLY, GO BURN GRANDFATHER OAK TO THE GROUND.
DO A THOROUGH JOB. LEAVE NOTHING BUT ASHES TO BLOW AWAY IN THE WIND.
NO!
YOU WOULDN'T DARE!
DON'T WAIT FOR ANY FURTHER ORDER FROM ME, CLARA. IF THEY ACT, THEN YOU'RE FREE TO ACT.
ROGER THAT, BOSS.
OKAY, FOLKS, I'LL BE IN THE HOUSE ALL MORNING, READY TO HEAR YOUR INDIVIDUAL GRIPES AND GRIEVANCES. LINE UP IN AN ORDERLY FASHION AND BE NICE, PLEASE.
AFTER LUNCH WE'LL MEET BACK HERE AGAIN TO SETTLE THINGS, OKAY?

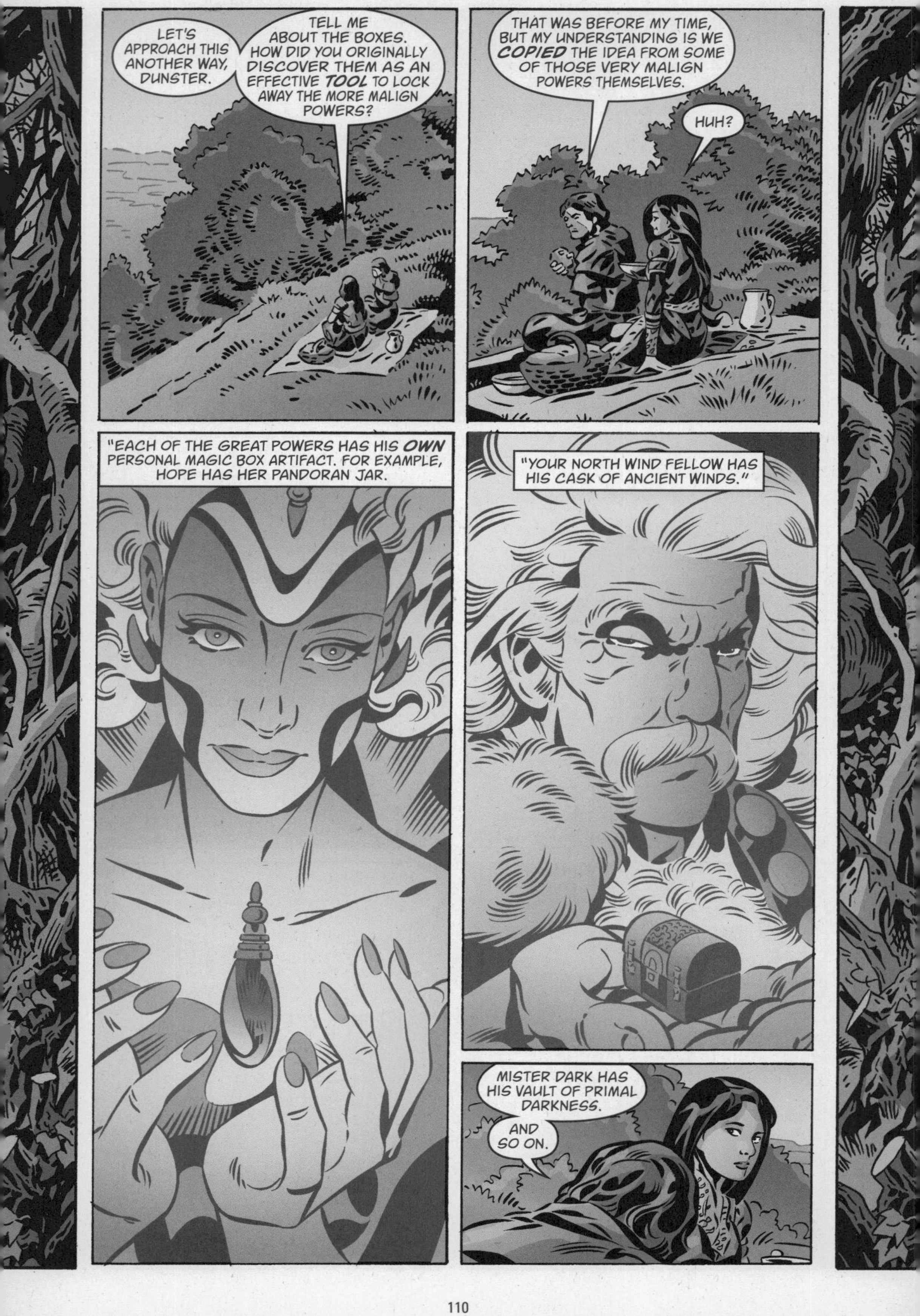
LET'S APPROACH THIS ANOTHER WAY, DUNSTER.
TELL ME ABOUT THE BOXES. HOW DID YOU ORIGINALLY DISCOVER THEM AS AN EFFECTIVE TOOL TO LOCK AWAY THE MORE MALIGN POWERS?
THAT WAS BEFORE MY TIME, BUT MY UNDERSTANDING IS WE COPIED THE IDEA FROM SOME OF THOSE VERY MALIGN POWERS THEMSELVES.
HUH?
"EACH OF THE GREAT POWERS HAS HIS OWN PERSONAL MAGIC BOX ARTIFACT. FOR EXAMPLE, HOPE HAS HER PANDORAN JAR.
"YOUR NORTH WIND FELLOW HAS HIS CASK OF ANCIENT WINDS."
MISTER DARK HAS HIS VAULT OF PRIMAL DARKNESS.
AND SO ON.

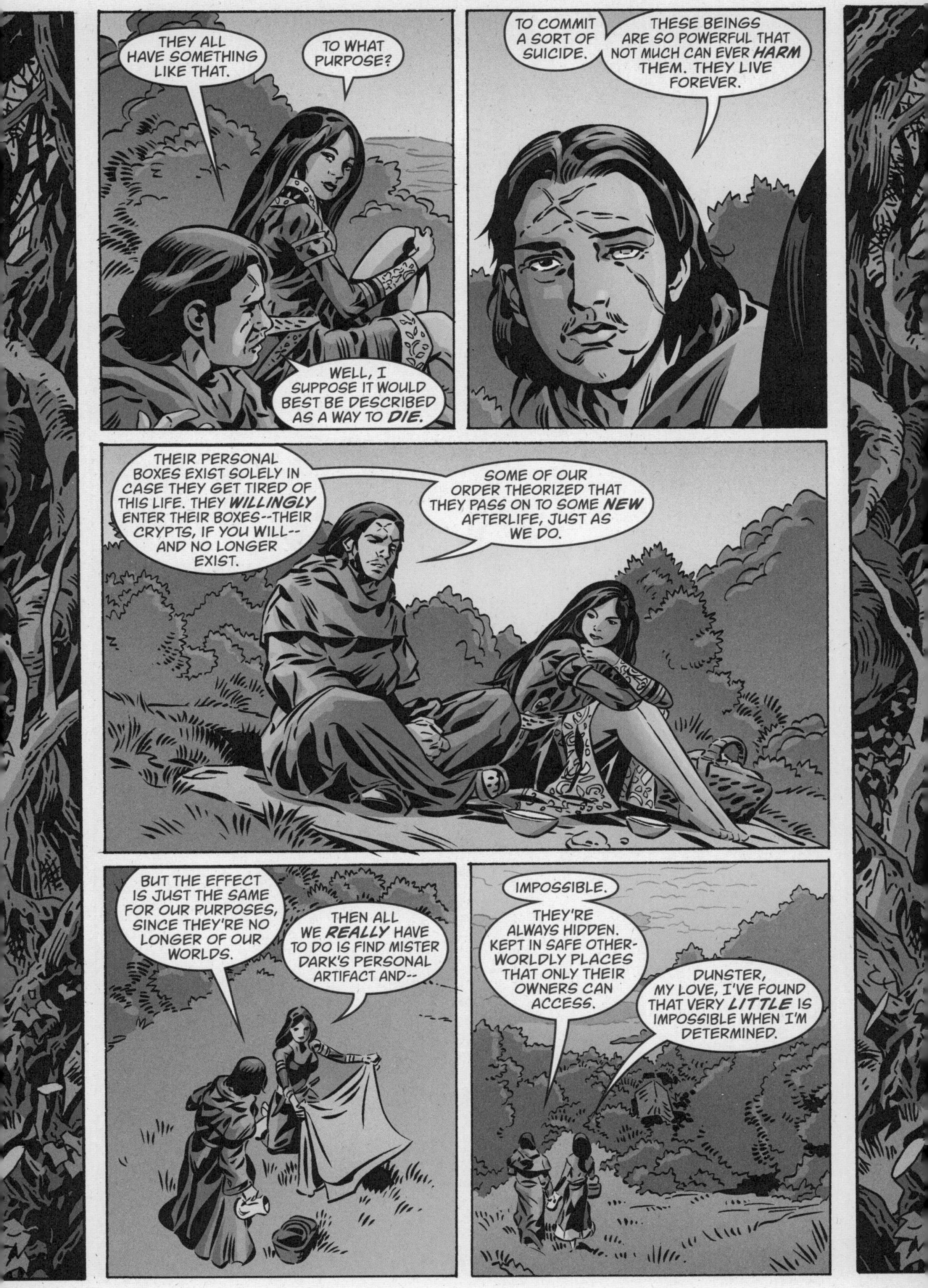
THEY ALL HAVE SOMETHING LIKE THAT.
TO WHAT PURPOSE?
WELL, I SUPPOSE IT WOULD BEST BE DESCRIBED AS A WAY TO DIE.
TO COMMIT A SORT OF SUICIDE.
THESE BEINGS ARE SO POWERFUL THAT NOT MUCH CAN EVER HARM THEM. THEY LIVE FOREVER.
THEIR PERSONAL BOXES EXIST SOLELY IN CASE THEY GET TIRED OF THIS LIFE. THEY WILLINGLY ENTER THEIR BOXES--THEIR CRYPTS, IF YOU WILL--AND NO LONGER EXIST.
SOME OF OUR ORDER THEORIZED THAT THEY PASS ON TO SOME NEW AFTERLIFE, JUST AS WE DO.
BUT THE EFFECT IS JUST THE SAME FOR OUR PURPOSES, SINCE THEY'RE NO LONGER OF OUR WORLDS.
THEN ALL WE REALLY HAVE TO DO IS FIND MISTER DARK'S PERSONAL ARTIFACT AND--
IMPOSSIBLE.
THEY'RE ALWAYS HIDDEN. KEPT IN SAFE OTHER-WORLDLY PLACES THAT ONLY THEIR OWNERS CAN ACCESS.
DUNSTER, MY LOVE, I'VE FOUND THAT VERY LITTLE IS IMPOSSIBLE WHEN I'M DETERMINED.

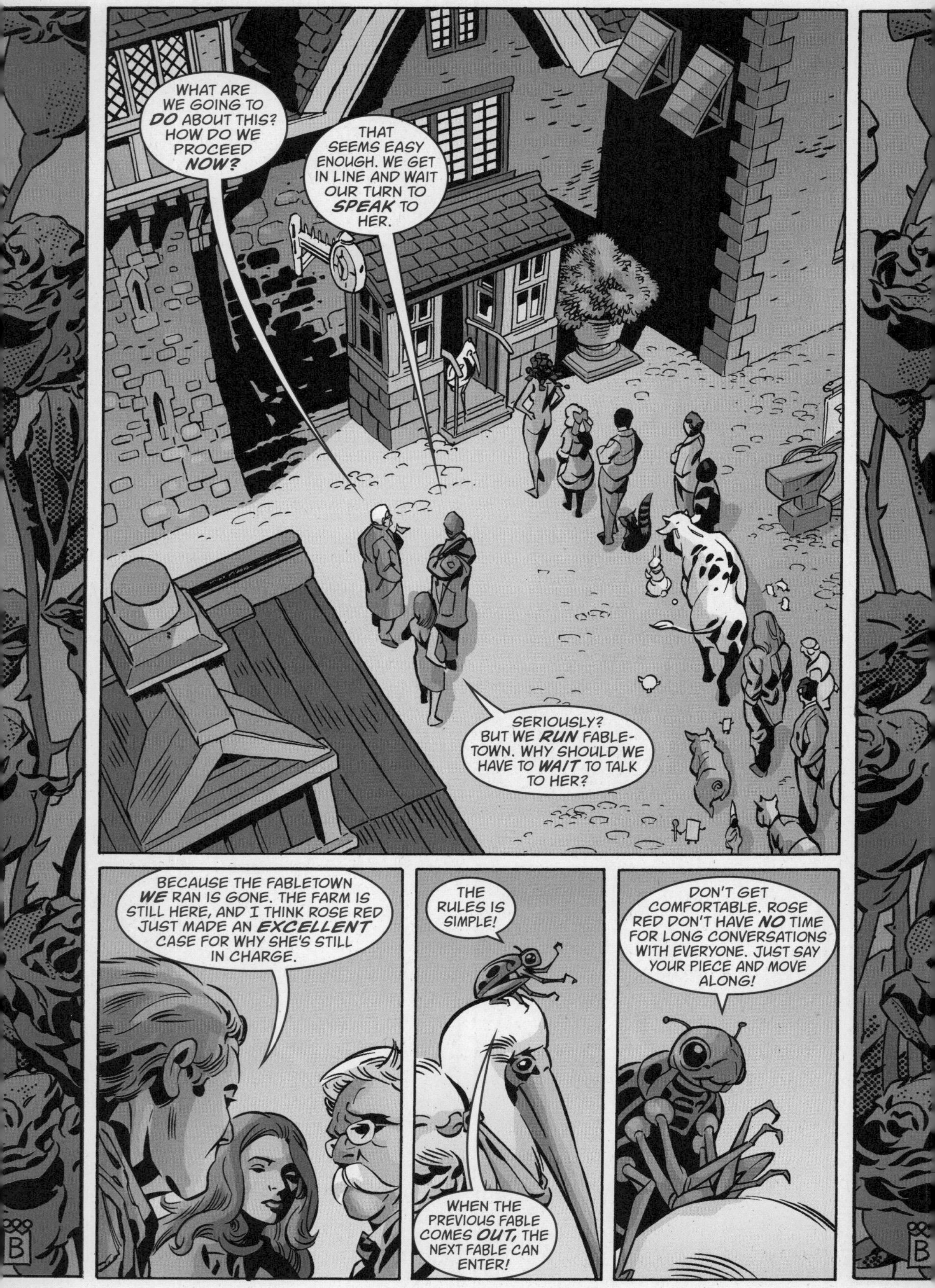
WHAT ARE WE GOING TO DO ABOUT THIS? HOW DO WE PROCEED NOW?
THAT SEEMS EASY ENOUGH. WE GET IN LINE AND WAIT OUR TURN TO SPEAK TO HER.
SERIOUSLY? BUT WE RUN FABLE-TOWN. WHY SHOULD WE HAVE TO WAIT TO TALK TO HER?
BECAUSE THE FABLETOWN WE RAN IS GONE. THE FARM IS STILL HERE, AND I THINK ROSE RED JUST MADE AN EXCELLENT CASE FOR WHY SHE'S STILL IN CHARGE.
THE RULES IS SIMPLE!
WHEN THE PREVIOUS FABLE COMES OUT, THE NEXT FABLE CAN ENTER!
DON'T GET COMFORTABLE. ROSE RED DON'T HAVE NO TIME FOR LONG CONVERSATIONS WITH EVERYONE. JUST SAY YOUR PIECE AND MOVE ALONG!

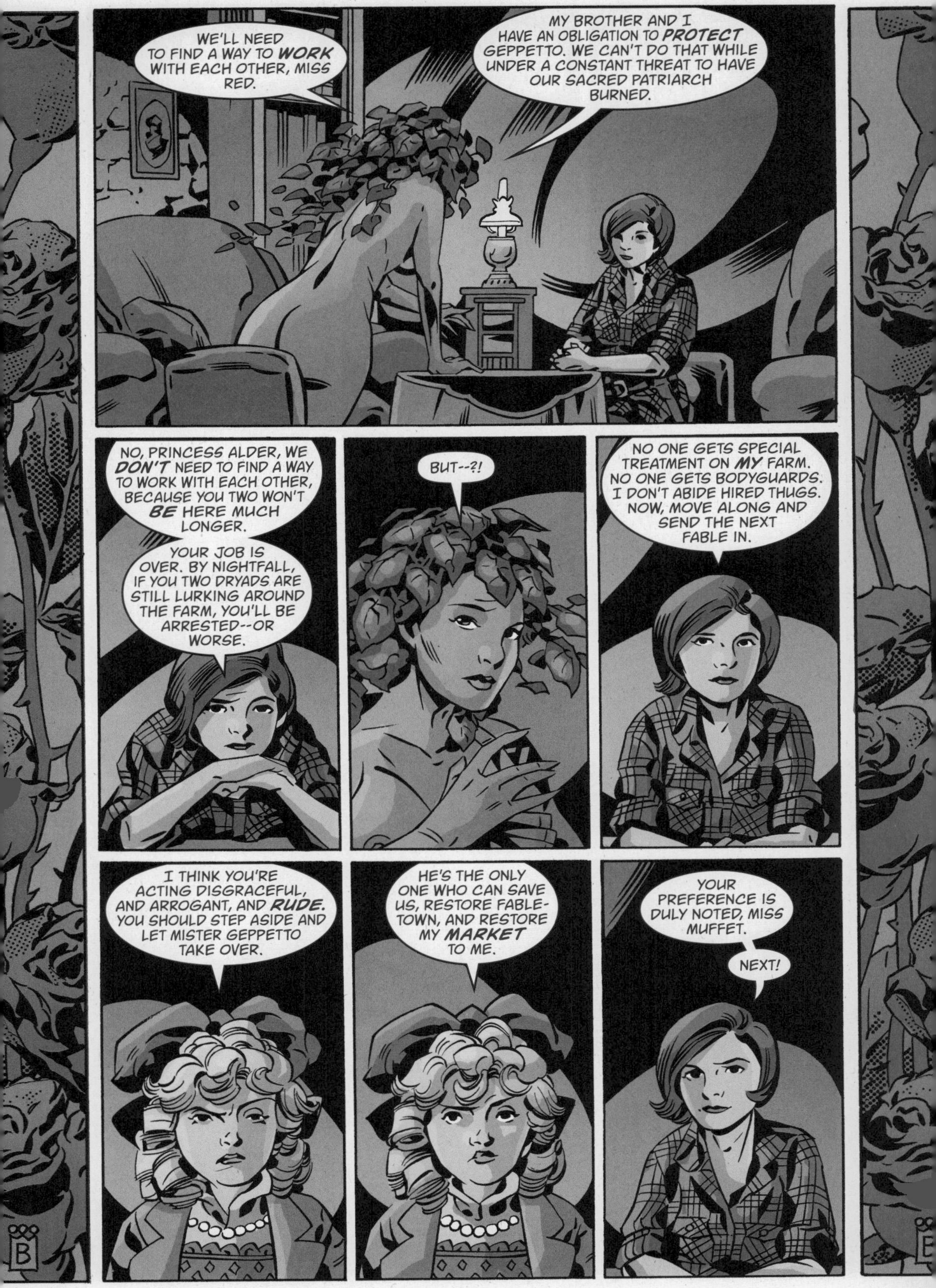
WE'LL NEED TO FIND A WAY TO WORK WITH EACH OTHER, MISS RED.
MY BROTHER AND I HAVE AN OBLIGATION TO PROTECT GEPPETTO. WE CAN'T DO THAT WHILE UNDER A CONSTANT THREAT TO HAVE OUR SACRED PATRIARCH BURNED.
NO, PRINCESS ALDER, WE DON'T NEED TO FIND A WAY TO WORK WITH EACH OTHER, BECAUSE YOU TWO WON'T BE HERE MUCH LONGER.
YOUR JOB IS OVER. BY NIGHTFALL, IF YOU TWO DRYADS ARE STILL LURKING AROUND THE FARM, YOU'LL BE ARRESTED--OR WORSE.
BUT--?!
NO ONE GETS SPECIAL TREATMENT ON MY FARM. NO ONE GETS BODYGUARDS. I DON'T ABIDE HIRED THUGS. NOW, MOVE ALONG AND SEND THE NEXT FABLE IN.
I THINK YOU'RE ACTING DISGRACEFUL, AND ARROGANT, AND RUDE. YOU SHOULD STEP ASIDE AND LET MISTER GEPPETTO TAKE OVER.
HE'S THE ONLY ONE WHO CAN SAVE US, RESTORE FABLE-TOWN, AND RESTORE MY MARKET TO ME.
YOUR PREFERENCE IS DULY NOTED, MISS MUFFET.
NEXT!

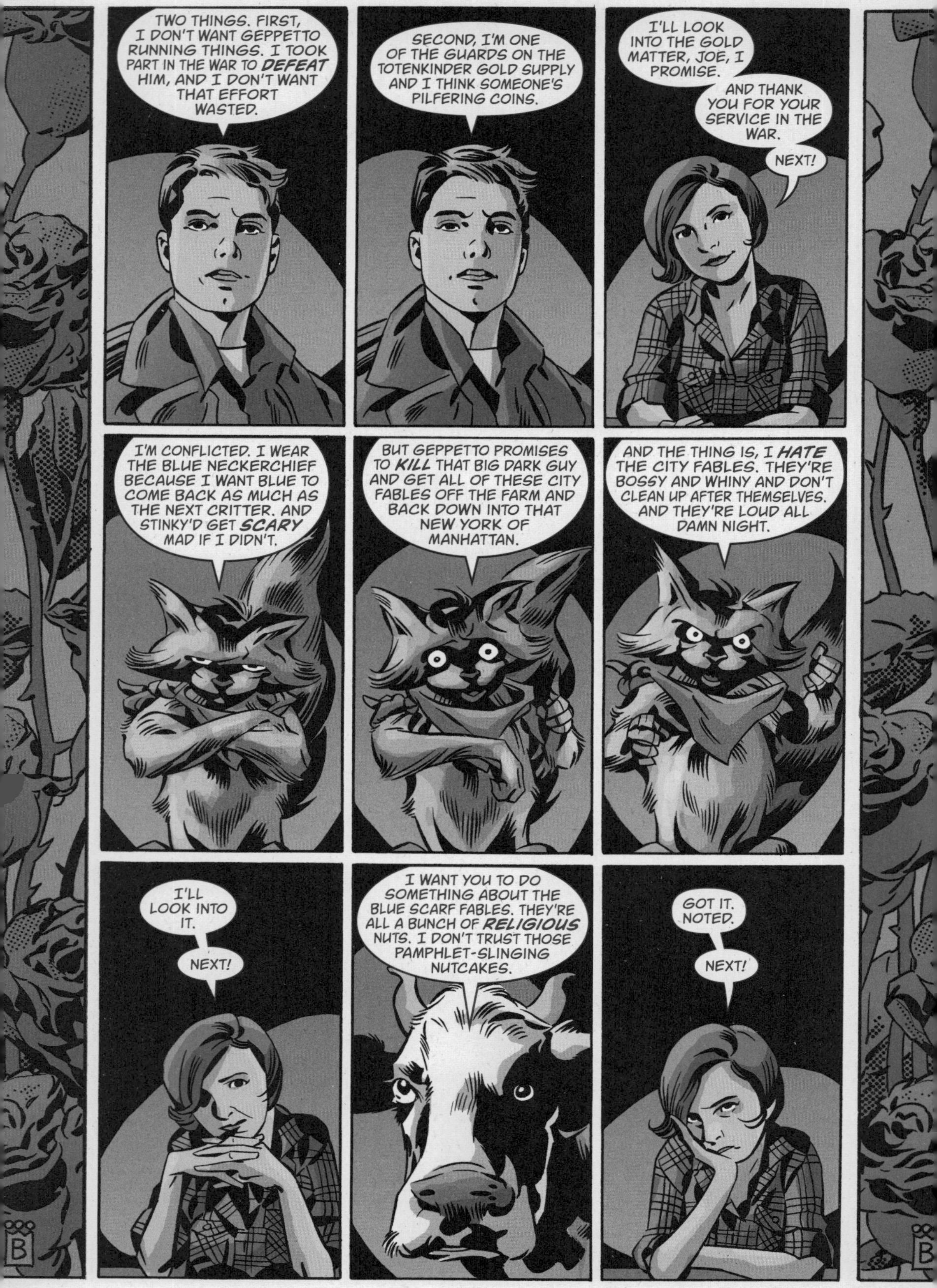
TWO THINGS. FIRST, I DON'T WANT GEPPETTO RUNNING THINGS. I TOOK PART IN THE WAR TO DEFEAT HIM, AND I DON'T WANT THAT EFFORT WASTED.
SECOND, I'M ONE OF THE GUARDS ON THE TOTENKINDER GOLD SUPPLY AND I THINK SOMEONE'S PILFERING COINS.
I'LL LOOK INTO THE GOLD MATTER, JOE, I PROMISE.
AND THANK YOU FOR YOUR SERVICE IN THE WAR.
NEXT!
I'M CONFLICTED. I WEAR THE BLUE NECKERCHIEF BECAUSE I WANT BLUE TO COME BACK AS MUCH AS THE NEXT CRITTER. AND STINKY'D GET SCARY MAD IF I DIDN'T.
BUT GEPPETTO PROMISES TO KILL THAT BIG DARK GUY AND GET ALL OF THESE CITY FABLES OFF THE FARM AND BACK DOWN INTO THAT NEW YORK OF MANHATTAN.
AND THE THING IS, I HATE THE CITY FABLES. THEY'RE BOSSY AND WHINY AND DON'T CLEAN UP AFTER THEMSELVES. AND THEY'RE LOUD ALL DAMN NIGHT.
I'LL LOOK INTO IT.
NEXT!
I WANT YOU TO DO SOMETHING ABOUT THE BLUE SCARF FABLES. THEY'RE ALL A BUNCH OF RELIGIOUS NUTS. I DON'T TRUST THOSE PAMPHLET-SLINGING NUTCAKES.
GOT IT. NOTED.
NEXT!

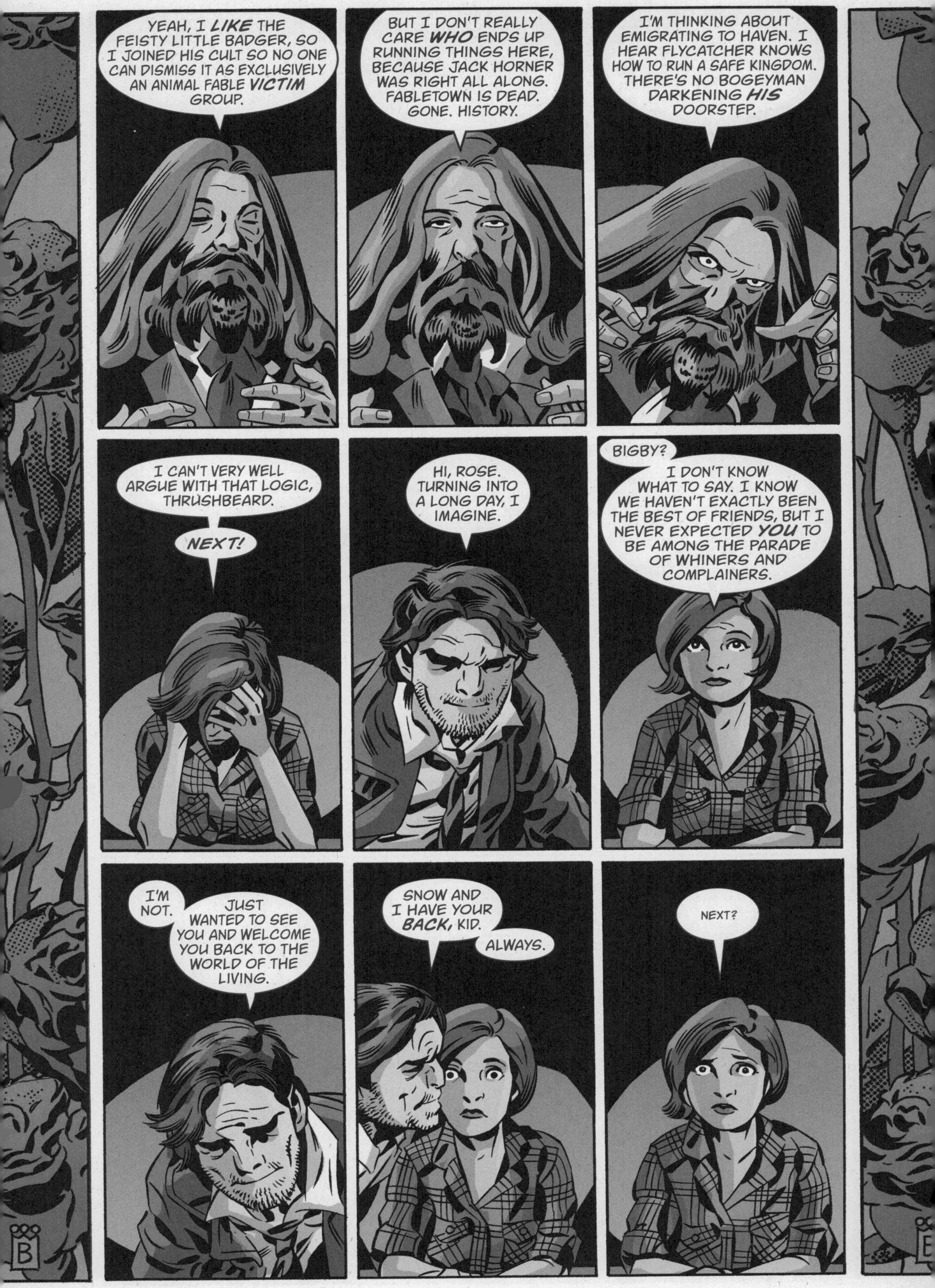
YEAH, I LIKE THE FEISTY LITTLE BADGER, SO I JOINED HIS CULT SO NO ONE CAN DISMISS IT AS EXCLUSIVELY AN ANIMAL FABLE VICTIM GROUP.
BUT I DON'T REALLY CARE WHO ENDS UP RUNNING THINGS HERE, BECAUSE JACK HORNER WAS RIGHT ALL ALONG. FABLETOWN IS DEAD. GONE. HISTORY.
I'M THINKING ABOUT EMIGRATING TO HAVEN. I HEAR FLYCATCHER KNOWS HOW TO RUN A SAFE KINGDOM. THERE'S NO BOGEYMAN DARKENING HIS DOORSTEP.
I CAN'T VERY WELL ARGUE WITH THAT LOGIC, THRUSHBEARD.
NEXT!
HI, ROSE. TURNING INTO A LONG DAY, I IMAGINE.
BIGBY?
I DON'T KNOW WHAT TO SAY. I KNOW WE HAVEN'T EXACTLY BEEN THE BEST OF FRIENDS, BUT I NEVER EXPECTED YOU TO BE AMONG THE PARADE OF WHINERS AND COMPLAINERS.
I'M NOT.
JUST WANTED TO SEE YOU AND WELCOME YOU BACK TO THE WORLD OF THE LIVING.
SNOW AND I HAVE YOUR BACK, KID.
ALWAYS.
NEXT?

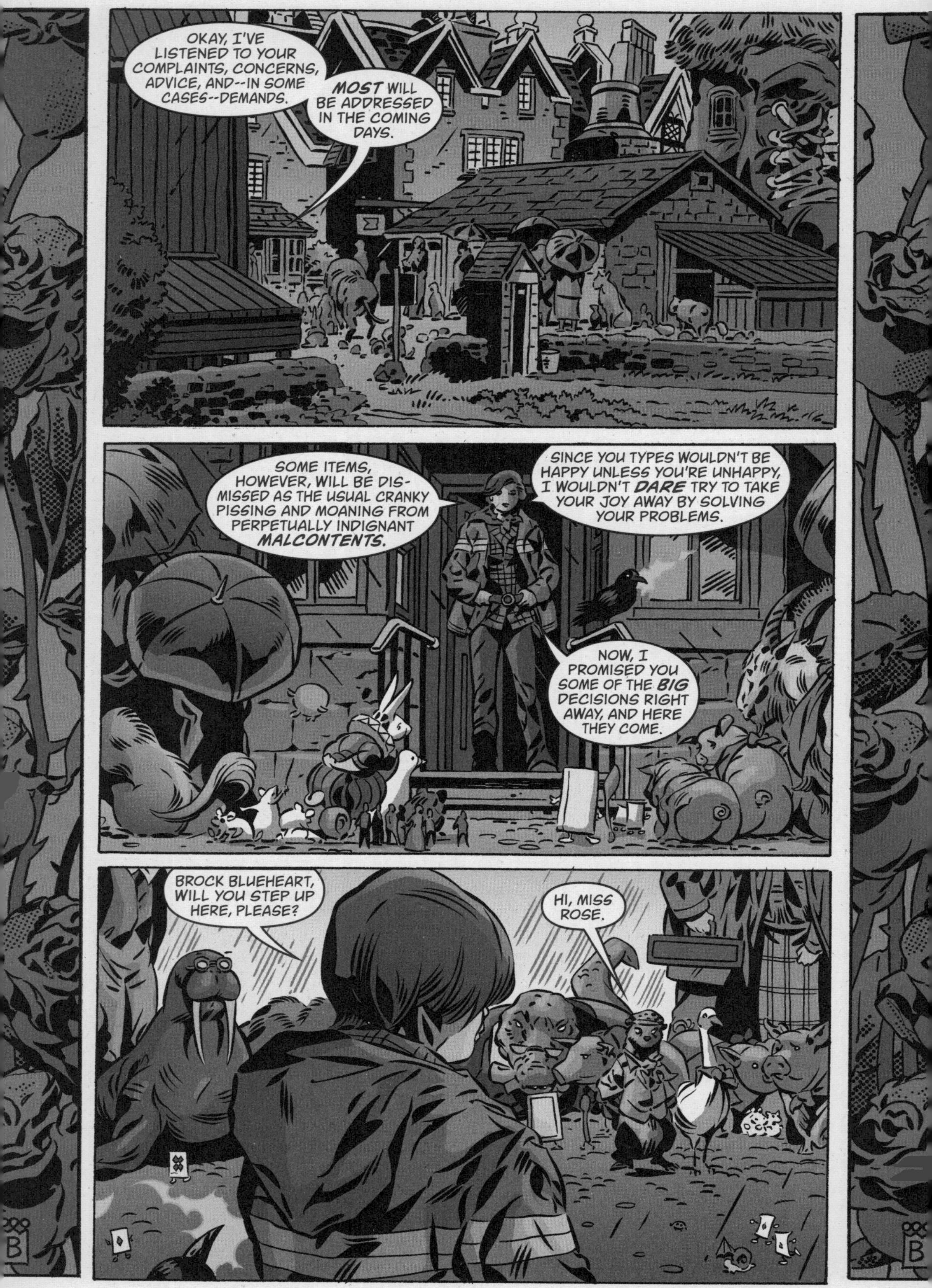
OKAY, I'VE LISTENED TO YOUR COMPLAINTS, CONCERNS, ADVICE, AND--IN SOME CASES--DEMANDS.
MOST WILL BE ADDRESSED IN THE COMING DAYS.
SOME ITEMS, HOWEVER, WILL BE DISMISSED AS THE USUAL CRANKY PISSING AND MOANING FROM PERPETUALLY INDIGNANT MALCONTENTS.
SINCE YOU TYPES WOULDN'T BE HAPPY UNLESS YOU'RE UNHAPPY, I WOULDN'T DARE TRY TO TAKE YOUR JOY AWAY BY SOLVING YOUR PROBLEMS.
NOW, I PROMISED YOU SOME OF THE BIG DECISIONS RIGHT AWAY, AND HERE THEY COME.
BROCK BLUEHEART, WILL YOU STEP UP HERE, PLEASE?
HI, MISS ROSE.

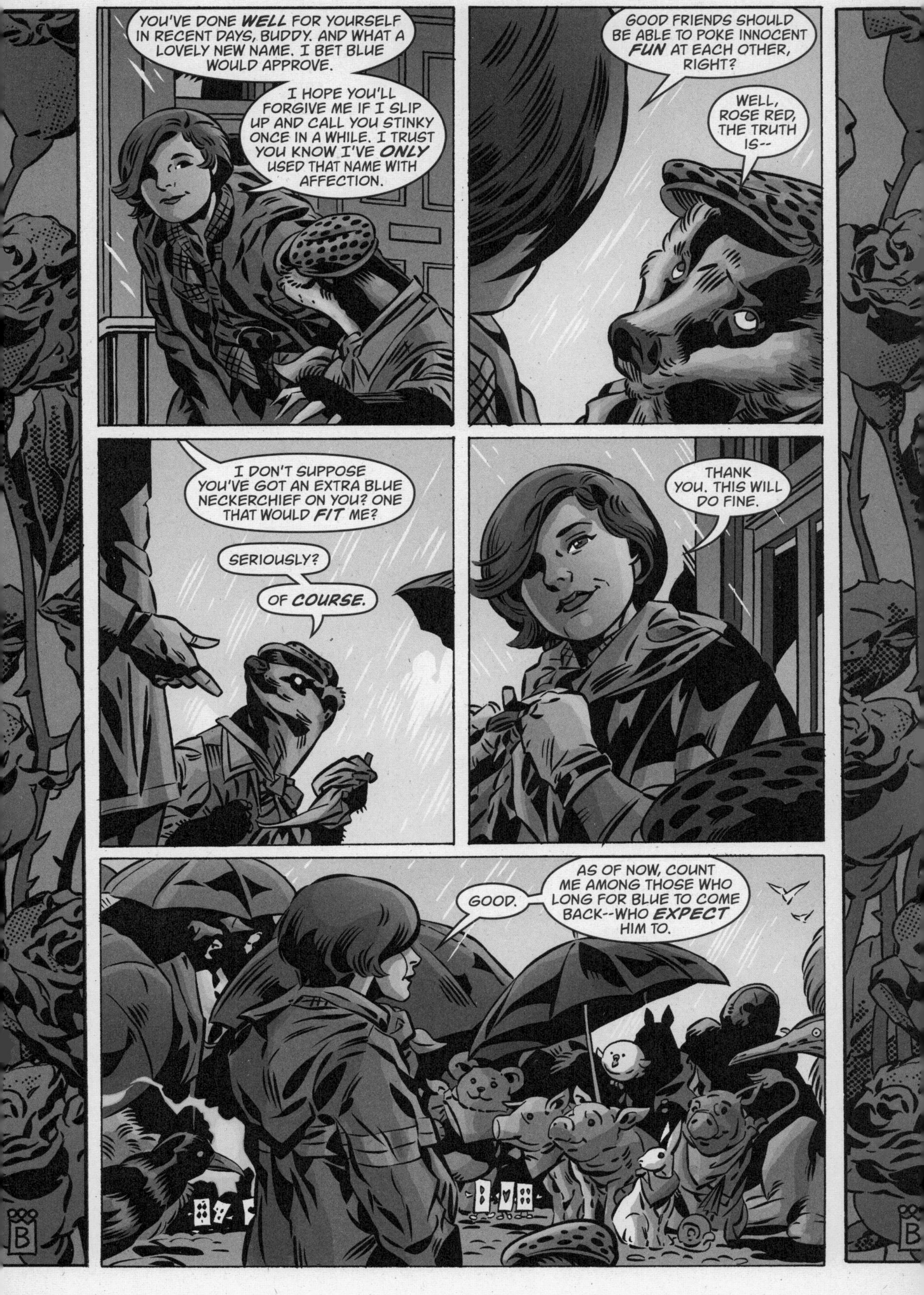

YOU'VE DONE WELL FOR YOURSELF IN RECENT DAYS, BUDDY. AND WHAT A LOVELY NEW NAME. I BET BLUE WOULD APPROVE.
I HOPE YOU'LL FORGIVE ME IF I SLIP UP AND CALL YOU STINKY ONCE IN A WHILE. I TRUST YOU KNOW I'VE ONLY USED THAT NAME WITH AFFECTION.
GOOD FRIENDS SHOULD BE ABLE TO POKE INNOCENT FUN AT EACH OTHER, RIGHT?
WELL, ROSE RED, THE TRUTH IS--
I DON'T SUPPOSE YOU'VE GOT AN EXTRA BLUE NECKERCHIEF ON YOU? ONE THAT WOULD FIT ME?
SERIOUSLY?
OF COURSE.
THANK YOU. THIS WILL DO FINE.
GOOD.
AS OF NOW, COUNT ME AMONG THOSE WHO LONG FOR BLUE TO COME BACK--WHO EXPECT HIM TO.

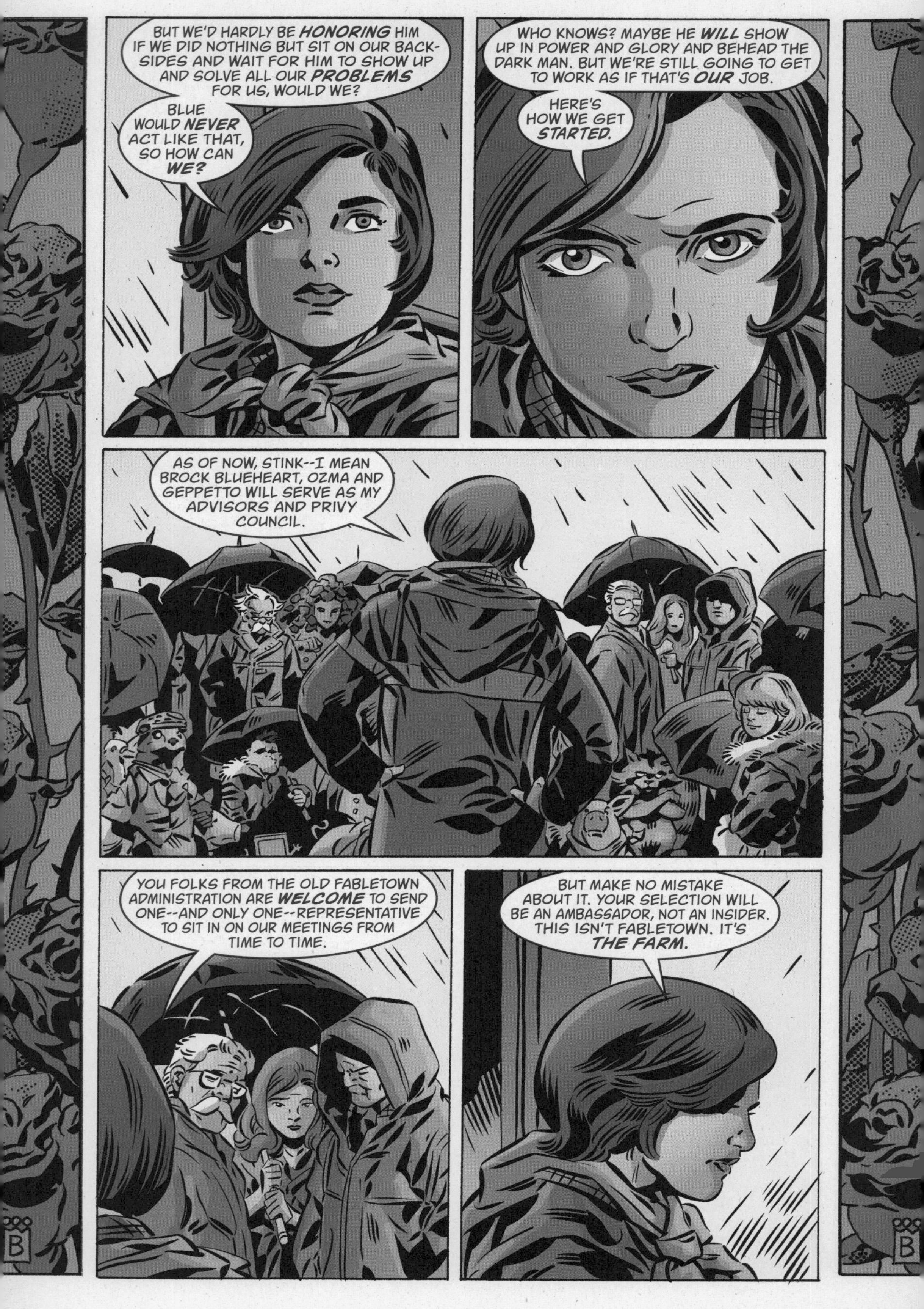
BUT WE'D HARDLY BE HONORING HIM IF WE DID NOTHING BUT SIT ON OUR BACKSIDES AND WAIT FOR HIM TO SHOW UP AND SOLVE ALL OUR PROBLEMS FOR US, WOULD WE?
BLUE WOULD NEVER ACT LIKE THAT, SO HOW CAN WE?
WHO KNOWS? MAYBE HE WILL SHOW UP IN POWER AND GLORY AND BEHEAD THE DARK MAN. BUT WE'RE STILL GOING TO GET TO WORK AS IF THAT'S OUR JOB.
HERE'S HOW WE GET STARTED.
AS OF NOW, STINK--I MEAN BROCK BLUEHEART, OZMA AND GEPPETTO WILL SERVE AS MY ADVISORS AND PRIVY COUNCIL.
YOU FOLKS FROM THE OLD FABLETOWN ADMINISTRATION ARE WELCOME TO SEND ONE--AND ONLY ONE--REPRESENTATIVE TO SIT IN ON OUR MEETINGS FROM TIME TO TIME.
BUT MAKE NO MISTAKE ABOUT IT. YOUR SELECTION WILL BE AN AMBASSADOR, NOT AN INSIDER. THIS ISN'T FABLETOWN. IT'S THE FARM.

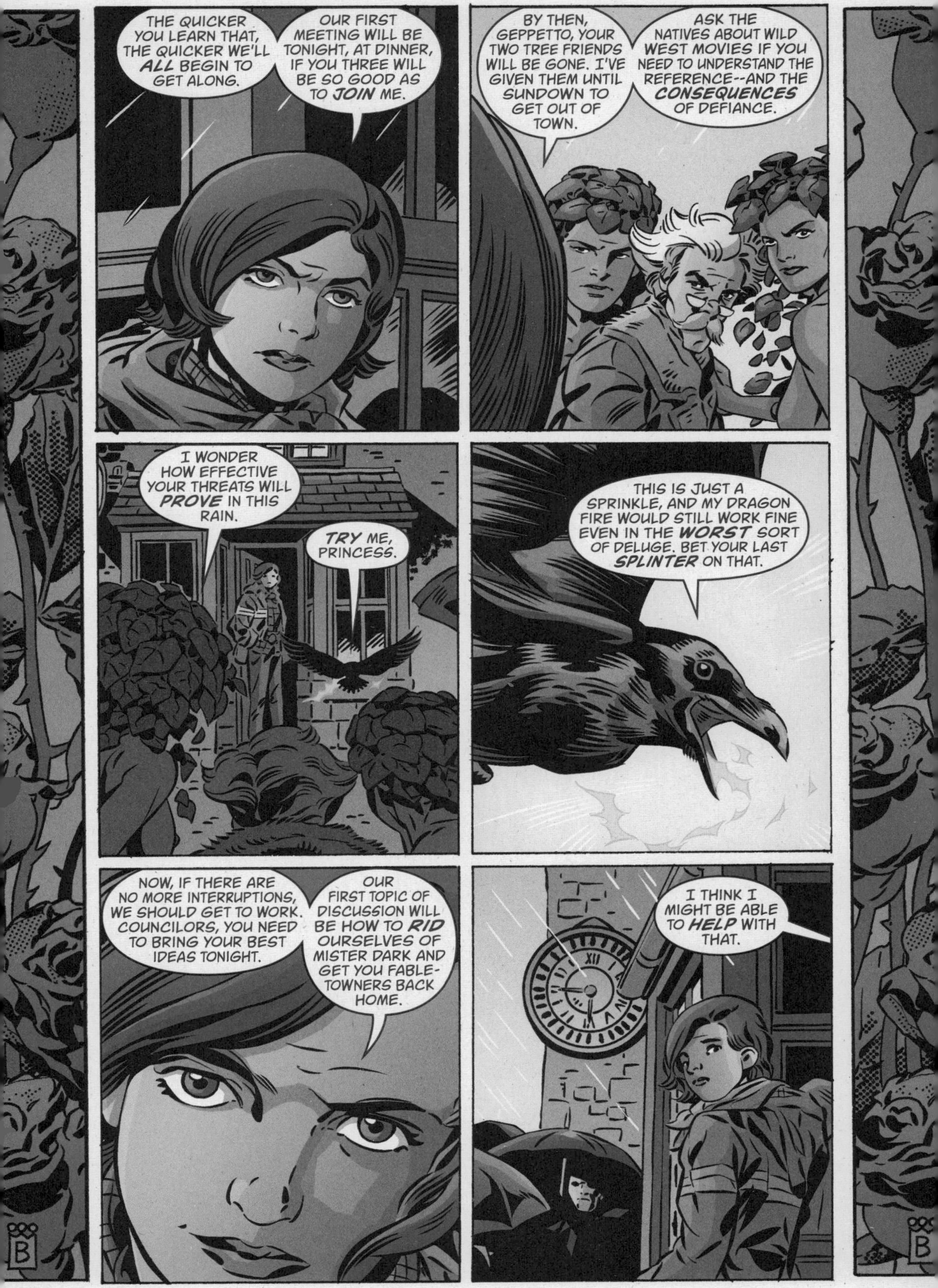
THE QUICKER YOU LEARN THAT, THE QUICKER WE'LL ALL BEGIN TO GET ALONG.
OUR FIRST MEETING WILL BE TONIGHT, AT DINNER, IF YOU THREE WILL BE SO GOOD AS TO JOIN ME.
BY THEN, GEPPETTO, YOUR TWO TREE FRIENDS WILL BE GONE. I'VE GIVEN THEM UNTIL SUNDOWN TO GET OUT OF TOWN.
ASK THE NATIVES ABOUT WILD WEST MOVIES IF YOU NEED TO UNDERSTAND THE REFERENCE--AND THE CONSEQUENCES OF DEFIANCE.
I WONDER HOW EFFECTIVE YOUR THREATS WILL PROVE IN THIS RAIN.
TRY ME, PRINCESS.
THIS IS JUST A SPRINKLE, AND MY DRAGON FIRE WOULD STILL WORK FINE EVEN IN THE WORST SORT OF DELUGE. BET YOUR LAST SPLINTER ON THAT.
NOW, IF THERE ARE NO MORE INTERRUPTIONS, WE SHOULD GET TO WORK. COUNCILORS, YOU NEED TO BRING YOUR BEST IDEAS TONIGHT.
OUR FIRST TOPIC OF DISCUSSION WILL BE HOW TO RID OURSELVES OF MISTER DARK AND GET YOU FABLE-TOWNERS BACK HOME.
I THINK I MIGHT BE ABLE TO HELP WITH THAT.

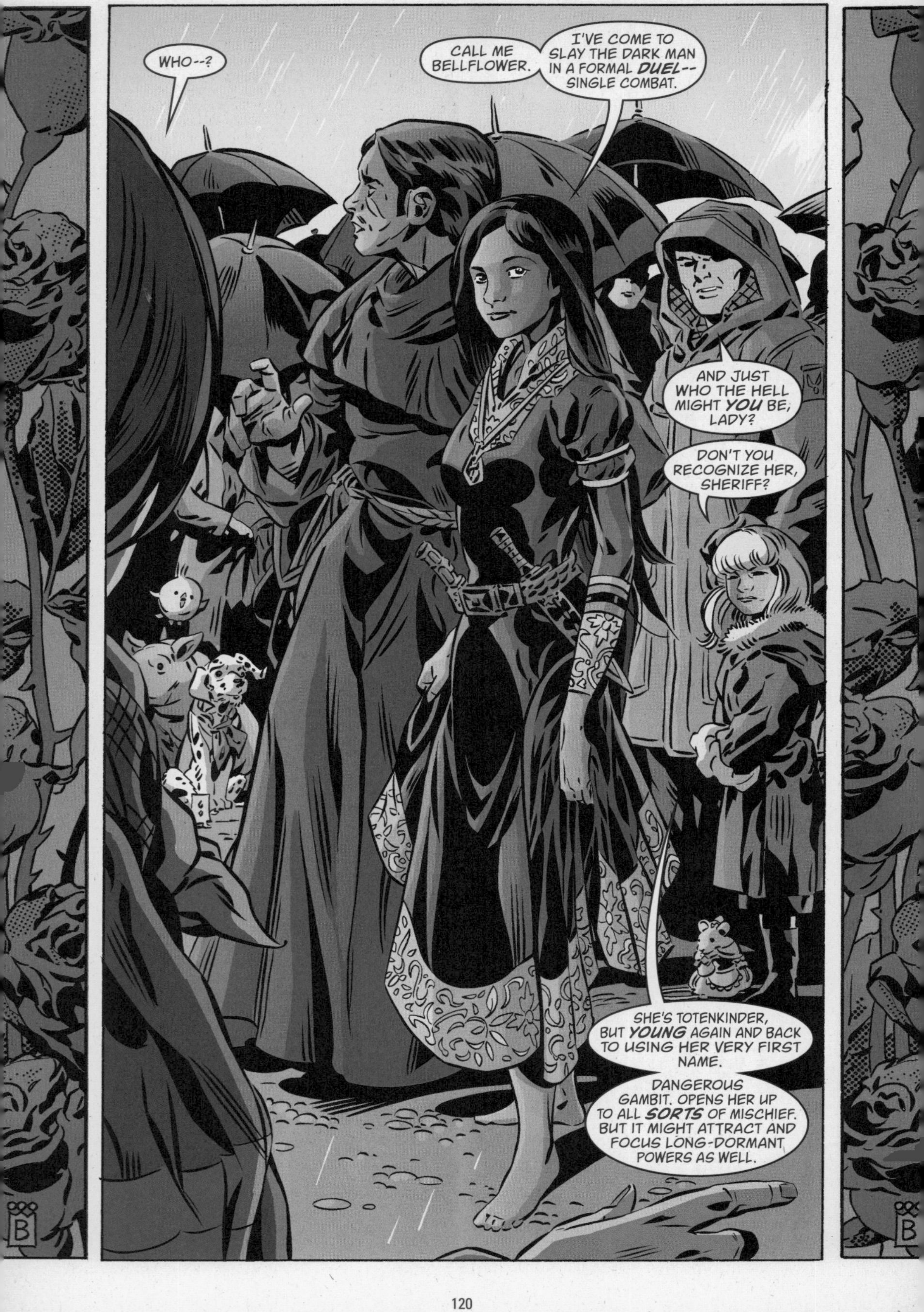

WHO--?
CALL ME BELLFLOWER.
I'VE COME TO SLAY THE DARK MAN IN A FORMAL DUEL-- SINGLE COMBAT.
AND JUST WHO THE HELL MIGHT YOU BE, LADY?
DON'T YOU RECOGNIZE HER, SHERIFF?
SHE'S TOTENKINDER, BUT YOUNG AGAIN AND BACK TO USING HER VERY FIRST NAME.
DANGEROUS GAMBIT. OPENS HER UP TO ALL SORTS OF MISCHIEF. BUT IT MIGHT ATTRACT AND FOCUS LONG-DORMANT POWERS AS WELL.

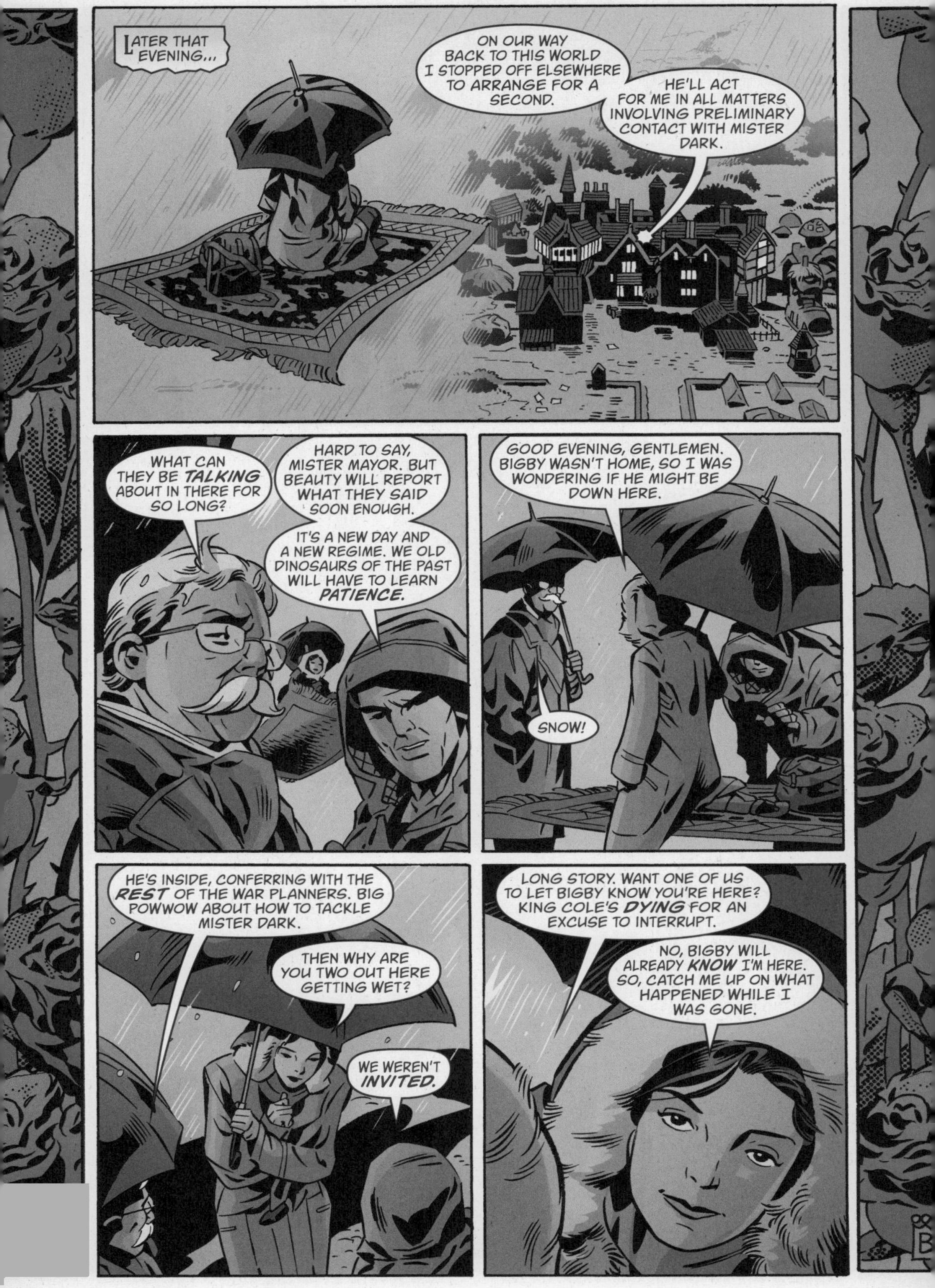
LATER THAT EVENING...
ON OUR WAY BACK TO THIS WORLD I STOPPED OFF ELSEWHERE TO ARRANGE FOR A SECOND.
HE'LL ACT FOR ME IN ALL MATTERS INVOLVING PRELIMINARY CONTACT WITH MISTER DARK.
WHAT CAN THEY BE TALKING ABOUT IN THERE FOR SO LONG?
HARD TO SAY, MISTER MAYOR. BUT BEAUTY WILL REPORT WHAT THEY SAID SOON ENOUGH.
IT'S A NEW DAY AND A NEW REGIME. WE OLD DINOSAURS OF THE PAST WILL HAVE TO LEARN PATIENCE.
GOOD EVENING, GENTLEMEN. BIGBY WASN'T HOME, SO I WAS WONDERING IF HE MIGHT BE DOWN HERE.
SNOW!
HE'S INSIDE, CONFERRING WITH THE REST OF THE WAR PLANNERS. BIG POWWOW ABOUT HOW TO TACKLE MISTER DARK.
THEN WHY ARE YOU TWO OUT HERE GETTING WET?
WE WEREN'T INVITED.
LONG STORY. WANT ONE OF US TO LET BIGBY KNOW YOU'RE HERE? KING COLE'S DYING FOR AN EXCUSE TO INTERRUPT.
NO, BIGBY WILL ALREADY KNOW I'M HERE. SO, CATCH ME UP ON WHAT HAPPENED WHILE I WAS GONE.

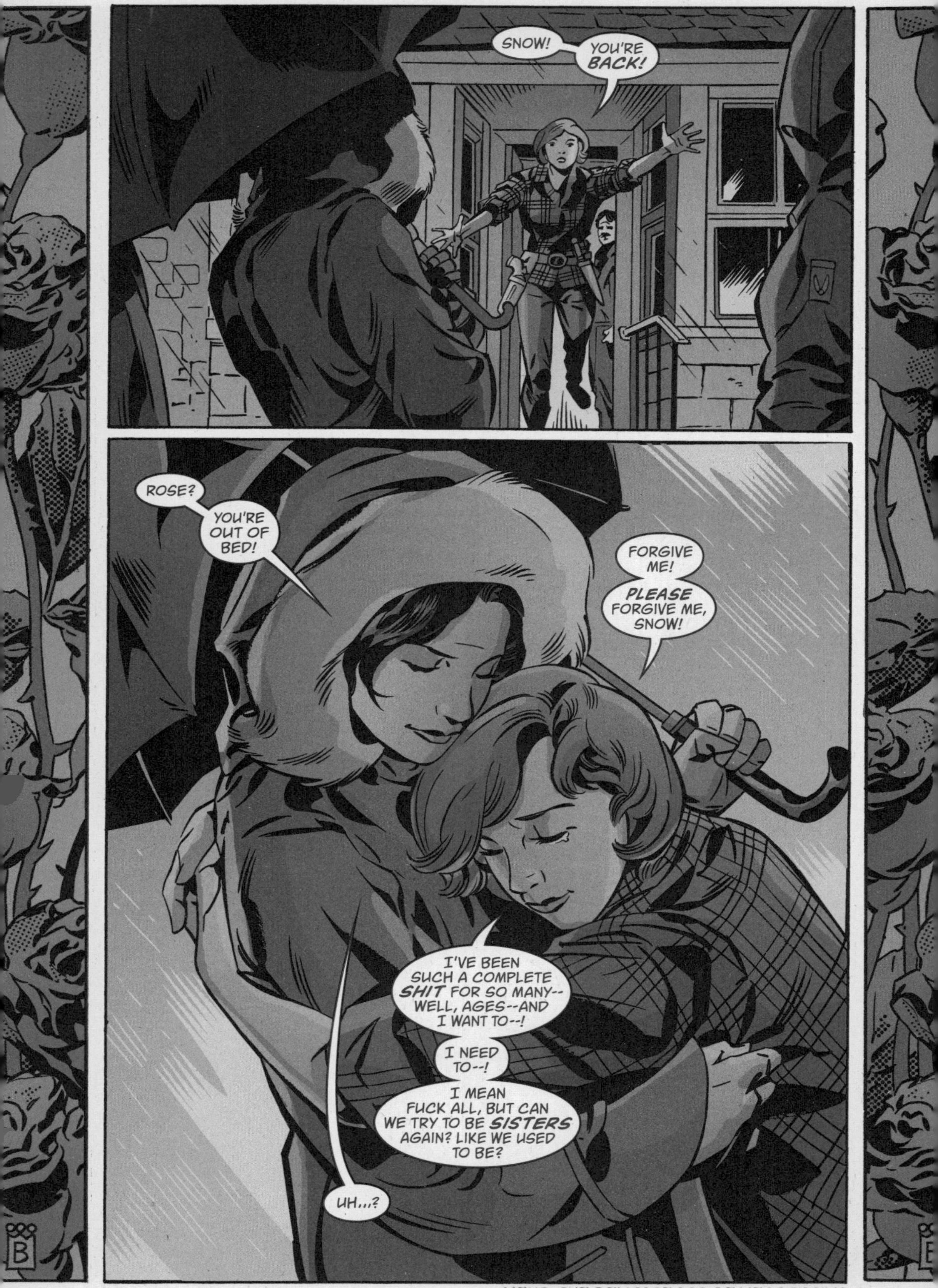
SNOW!
YOU'RE BACK!
ROSE?
YOU'RE OUT OF BED!
FORGIVE ME!
PLEASE FORGIVE ME, SNOW!
I'VE BEEN SUCH A COMPLETE SHIT FOR SO MANY-- WELL, AGES--AND I WANT TO--!
I NEED TO--!
I MEAN FUCK ALL, BUT CAN WE TRY TO BE SISTERS AGAIN? LIKE WE USED TO BE?
UH...?

NEXT: THE DELICATE ART OF NEGOTIATING PRIVATE DUELS WITH GODLIKE MONSTERS!

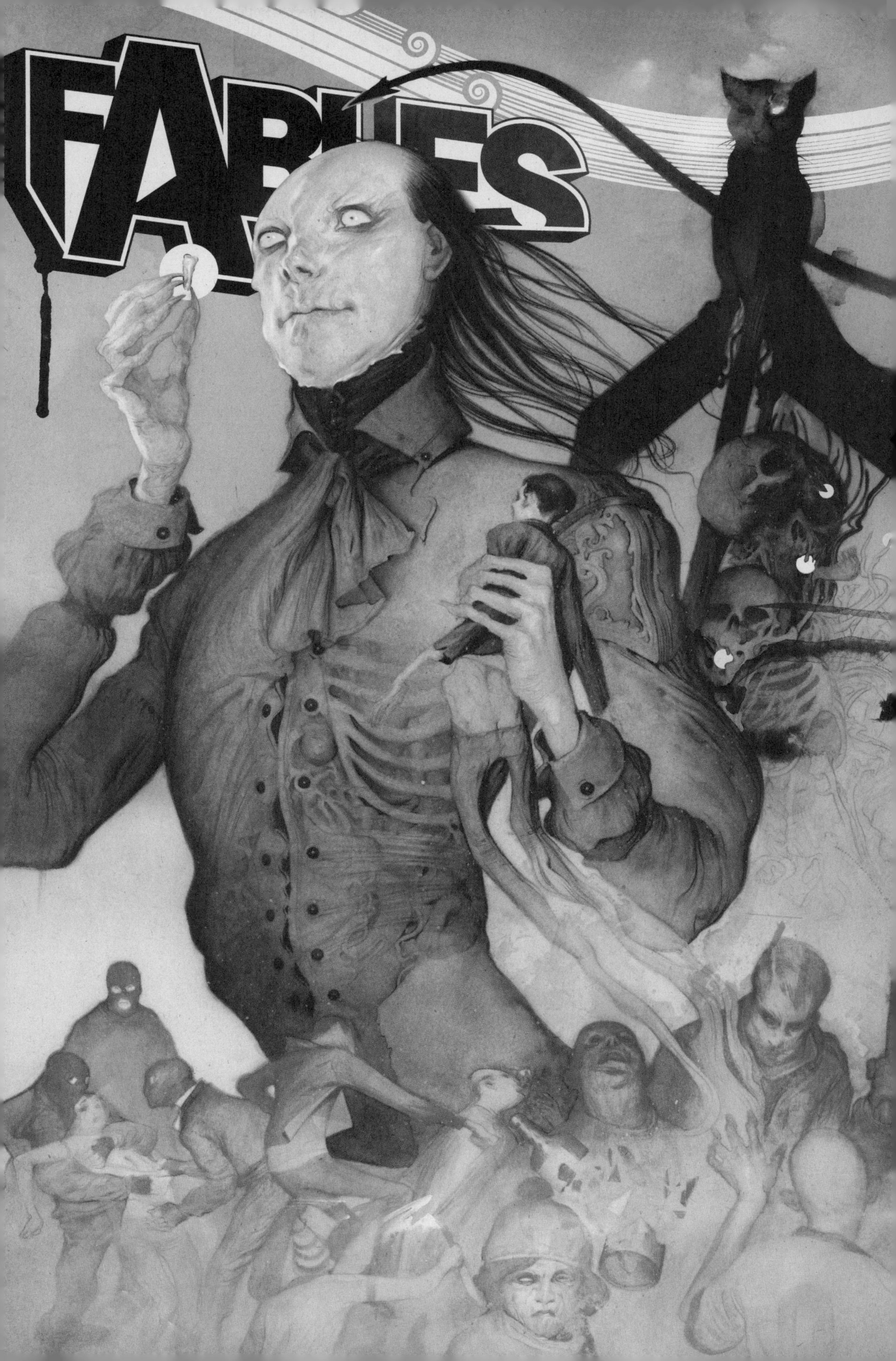
FABLES

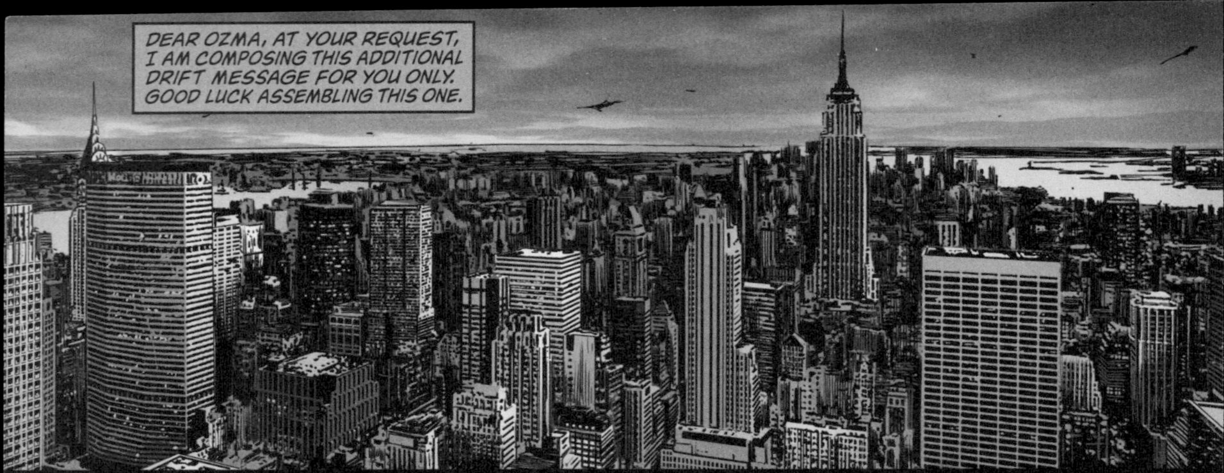
DEAR OZMA, AT YOUR REQUEST, I AM COMPOSING THIS ADDITIONAL DRIFT MESSAGE FOR YOU ONLY. GOOD LUCK ASSEMBLING THIS ONE.

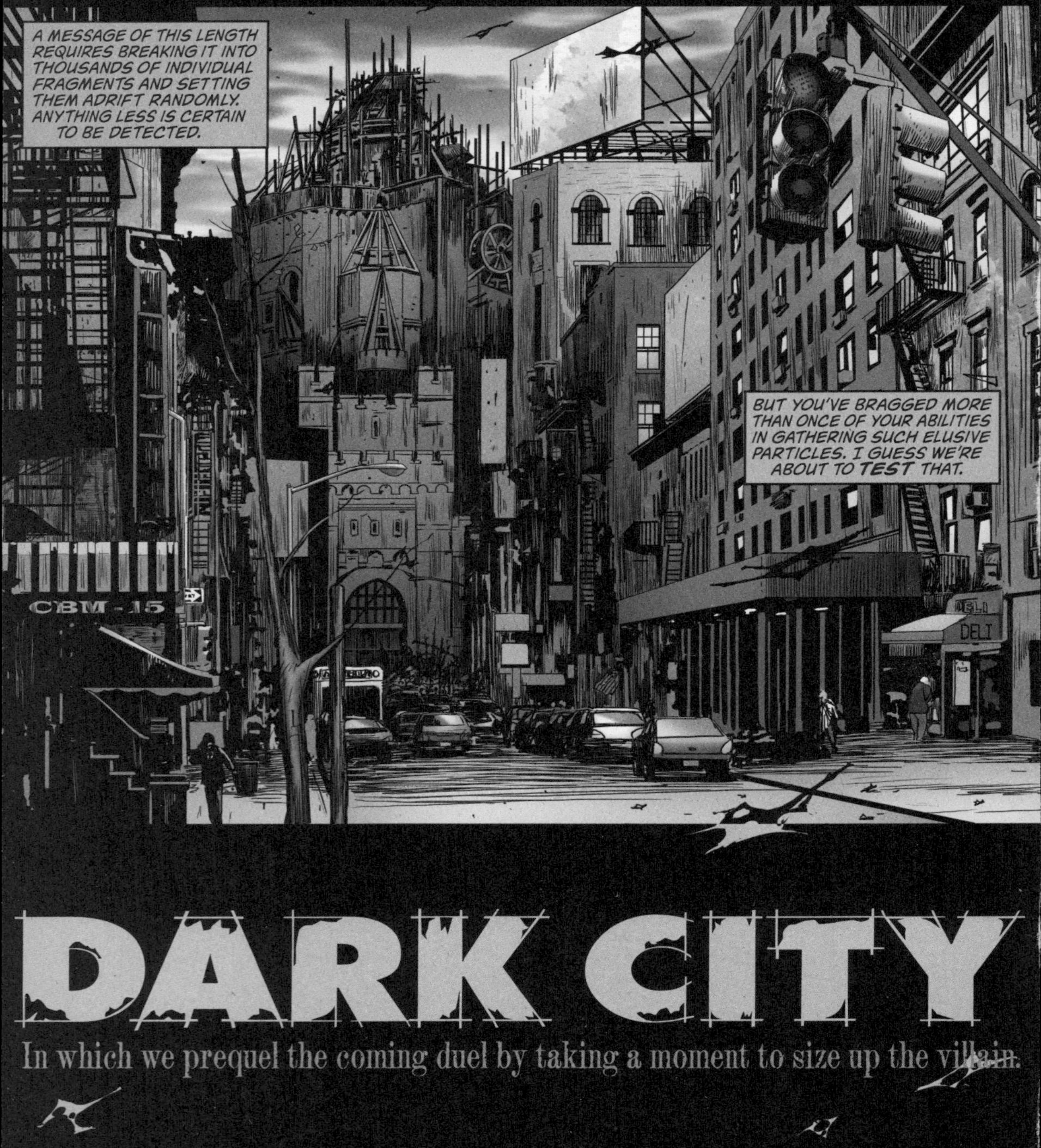
A MESSAGE OF THIS LENGTH REQUIRES BREAKING IT INTO THOUSANDS OF INDIVIDUAL FRAGMENTS AND SETTING THEM ADRIFT RANDOMLY. ANYTHING LESS IS CERTAIN TO BE DETECTED.
BUT YOU'VE BRAGGED MORE THAN ONCE OF YOUR ABILITIES IN GATHERING SUCH ELUSIVE PARTICLES. I GUESS WE'RE ABOUT TO **TEST** THAT.
CBM-15
DELI
DELI

DARK CITY

In which we prequel the coming duel by taking a moment to size up the villain.

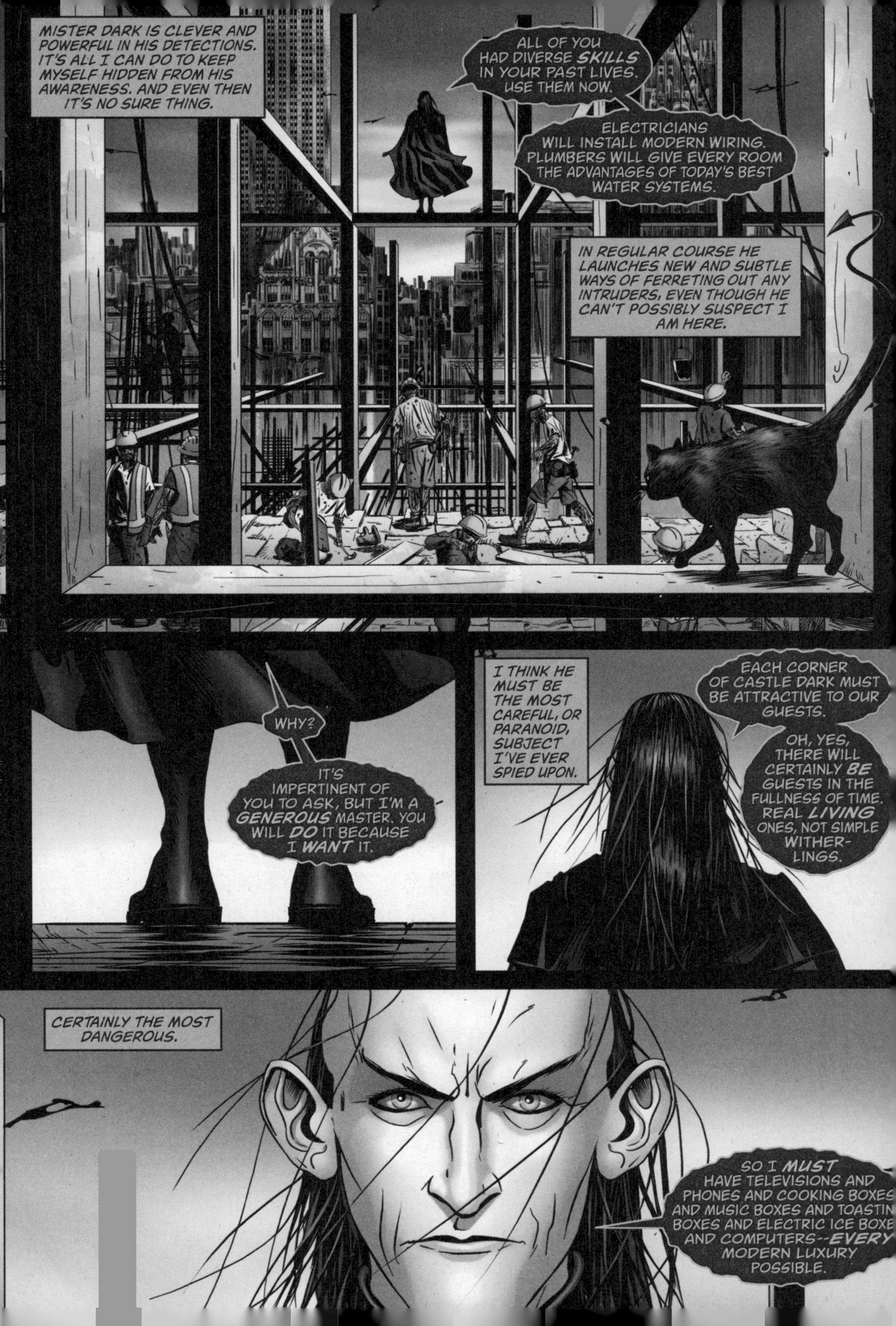
MISTER DARK IS CLEVER AND POWERFUL IN HIS DETECTIONS. IT'S ALL I CAN DO TO KEEP MYSELF HIDDEN FROM HIS AWARENESS. AND EVEN THEN IT'S NO SURE THING.
ALL OF YOU HAD DIVERSE SKILLS IN YOUR PAST LIVES. USE THEM NOW.
ELECTRICIANS WILL INSTALL MODERN WIRING. PLUMBERS WILL GIVE EVERY ROOM THE ADVANTAGES OF TODAY'S BEST WATER SYSTEMS.
IN REGULAR COURSE HE LAUNCHES NEW AND SUBTLE WAYS OF FERRETING OUT ANY INTRUDERS, EVEN THOUGH HE CAN'T POSSIBLY SUSPECT I AM HERE.
WHY?
IT'S IMPERTINENT OF YOU TO ASK, BUT I'M A GENEROUS MASTER. YOU WILL DO IT BECAUSE I WANT IT.
I THINK HE MUST BE THE MOST CAREFUL, OR PARANOID, SUBJECT I'VE EVER SPIED UPON.
EACH CORNER OF CASTLE DARK MUST BE ATTRACTIVE TO OUR GUESTS.
OH, YES, THERE WILL CERTAINLY BE GUESTS IN THE FULLNESS OF TIME. REAL LIVING ONES, NOT SIMPLE WITHER-LINGS.
CERTAINLY THE MOST DANGEROUS.
SO I MUST HAVE TELEVISIONS AND PHONES AND COOKING BOXES AND MUSIC BOXES AND TOASTIN BOXES AND ELECTRIC ICE BOXE AND COMPUTERS--EVERY MODERN LUXURY POSSIBLE.

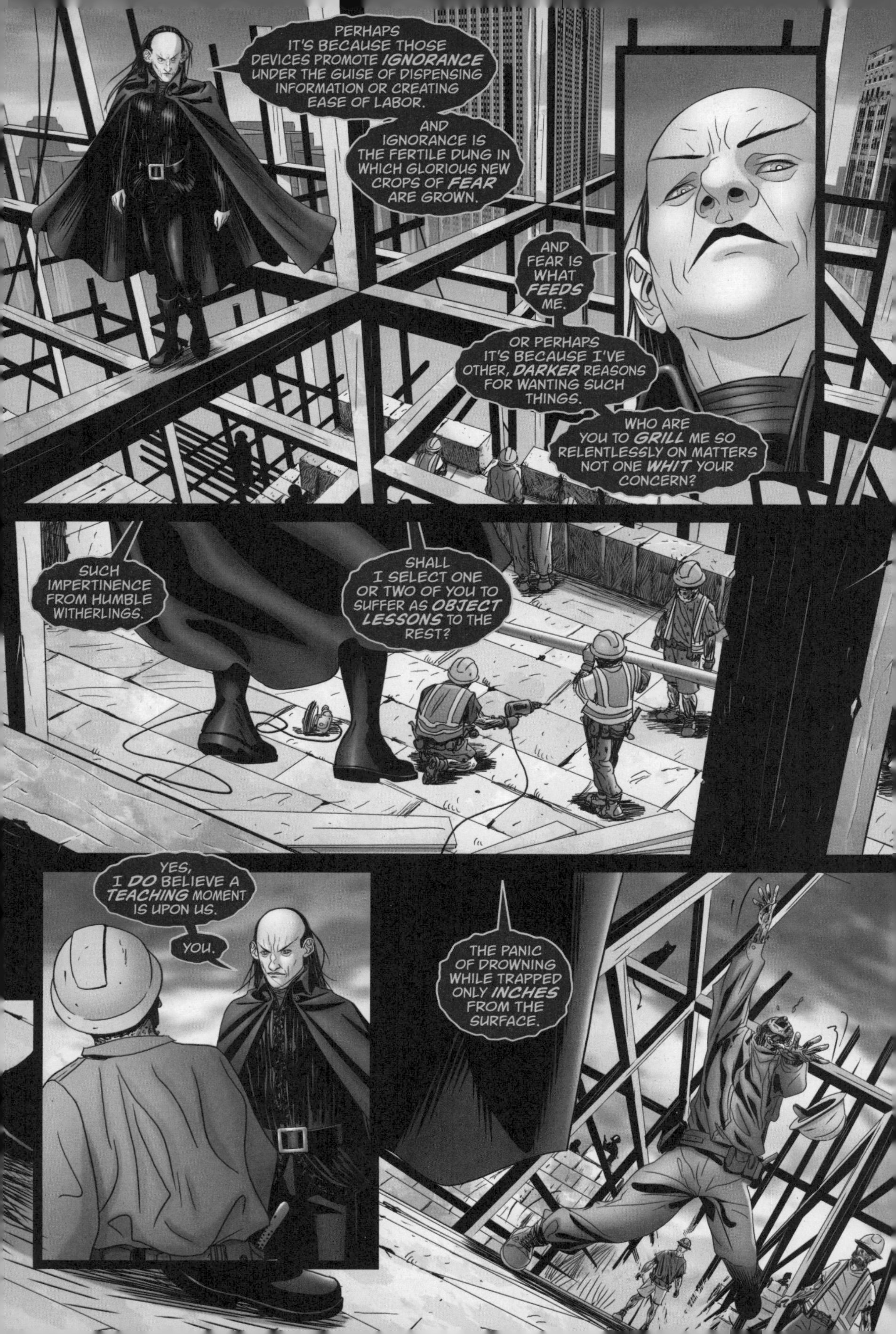
PERHAPS IT'S BECAUSE THOSE DEVICES PROMOTE IGNORANCE UNDER THE GUISE OF DISPENSING INFORMATION OR CREATING EASE OF LABOR.
AND IGNORANCE IS THE FERTILE DUNG IN WHICH GLORIOUS NEW CROPS OF FEAR ARE GROWN.
AND FEAR IS WHAT FEEDS ME.
OR PERHAPS IT'S BECAUSE I'VE OTHER, DARKER REASONS FOR WANTING SUCH THINGS.
WHO ARE YOU TO GRILL ME SO RELENTLESSLY ON MATTERS NOT ONE WHIT YOUR CONCERN?
SUCH IMPERTINENCE FROM HUMBLE WITHERLINGS.
SHALL I SELECT ONE OR TWO OF YOU TO SUFFER AS OBJECT LESSONS TO THE REST?
YES, I DO BELIEVE A TEACHING MOMENT IS UPON US.
YOU.
THE PANIC OF DROWNING WHILE TRAPPED ONLY INCHES FROM THE SURFACE.

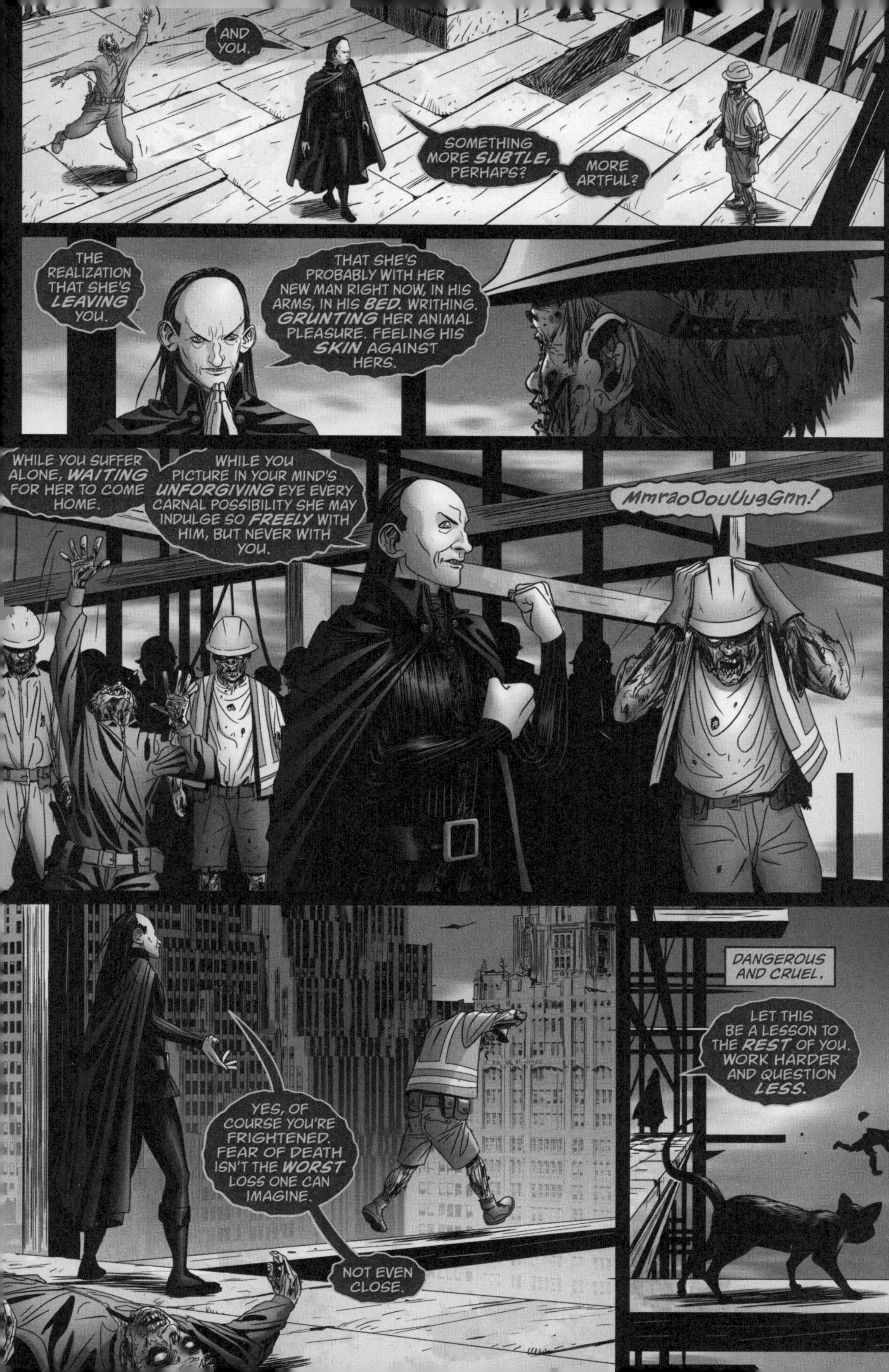
AND YOU.
SOMETHING MORE SUBTLE, PERHAPS?
MORE ARTFUL?
THE REALIZATION THAT SHE'S LEAVING YOU.
THAT SHE'S PROBABLY WITH HER NEW MAN RIGHT NOW, IN HIS ARMS, IN HIS BED. WRITHING. GRUNTING HER ANIMAL PLEASURE. FEELING HIS SKIN AGAINST HERS.
WHILE YOU SUFFER ALONE, WAITING FOR HER TO COME HOME.
WHILE YOU PICTURE IN YOUR MIND'S UNFORGIVING EYE EVERY CARNAL POSSIBILITY SHE MAY INDULGE SO FREELY WITH HIM, BUT NEVER WITH YOU.
MmraoOouUugGnn!
YES, OF COURSE YOU'RE FRIGHTENED. FEAR OF DEATH ISN'T THE WORST LOSS ONE CAN IMAGINE.
NOT EVEN CLOSE.
DANGEROUS AND CRUEL.
LET THIS BE A LESSON TO THE REST OF YOU. WORK HARDER AND QUESTION LESS.

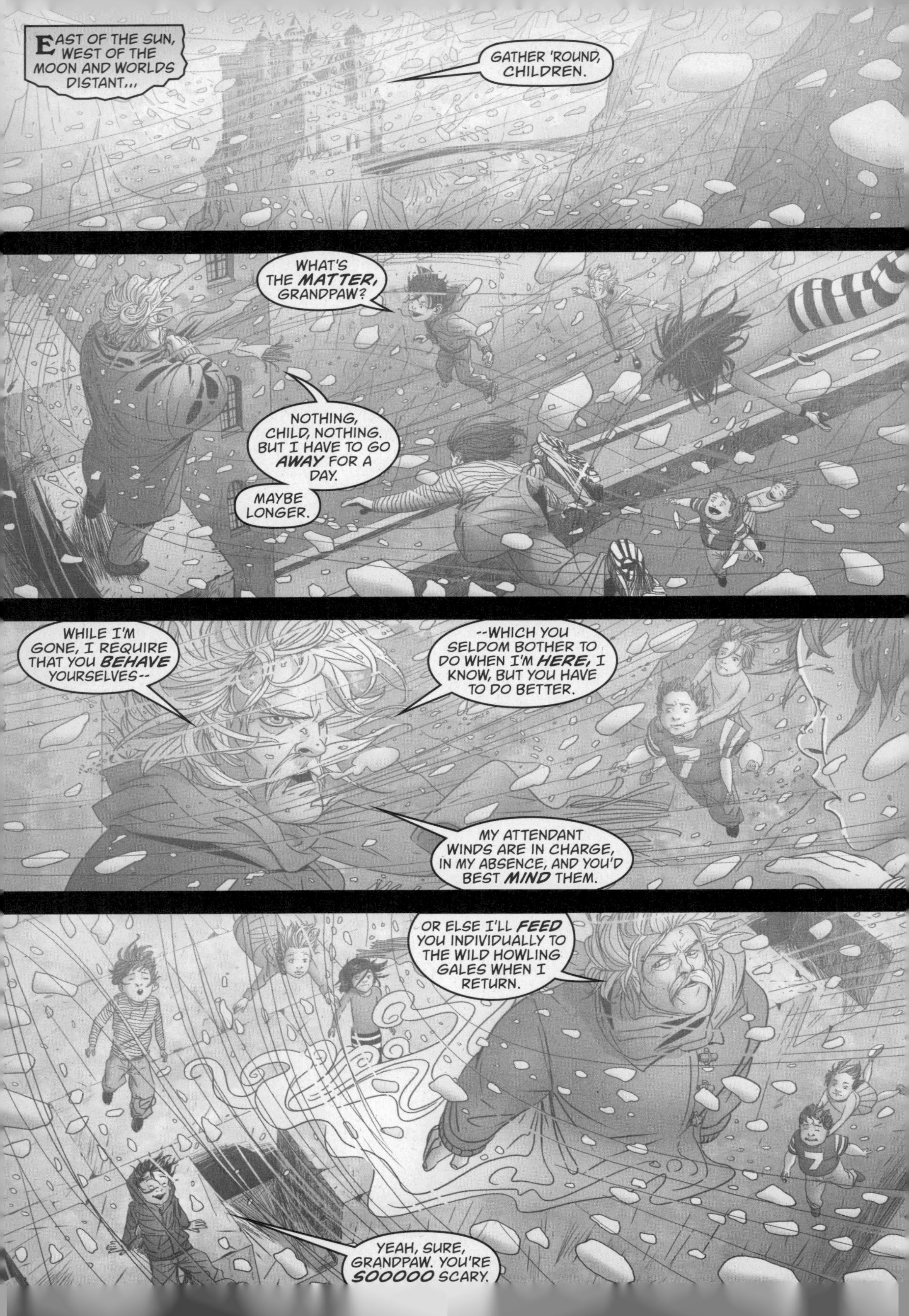
EAST OF THE SUN, WEST OF THE MOON AND WORLDS DISTANT...
GATHER 'ROUND, CHILDREN.
WHAT'S THE MATTER, GRANDPAW?
NOTHING, CHILD, NOTHING. BUT I HAVE TO GO AWAY FOR A DAY.
MAYBE LONGER.
WHILE I'M GONE, I REQUIRE THAT YOU BEHAVE YOURSELVES--
--WHICH YOU SELDOM BOTHER TO DO WHEN I'M HERE, I KNOW, BUT YOU HAVE TO DO BETTER.
MY ATTENDANT WINDS ARE IN CHARGE, IN MY ABSENCE, AND YOU'D BEST MIND THEM.
OR ELSE I'LL FEED YOU INDIVIDUALLY TO THE WILD HOWLING GALES WHEN I RETURN.
YEAH, SURE, GRANDPAW. YOU'RE SOOOOO SCARY.

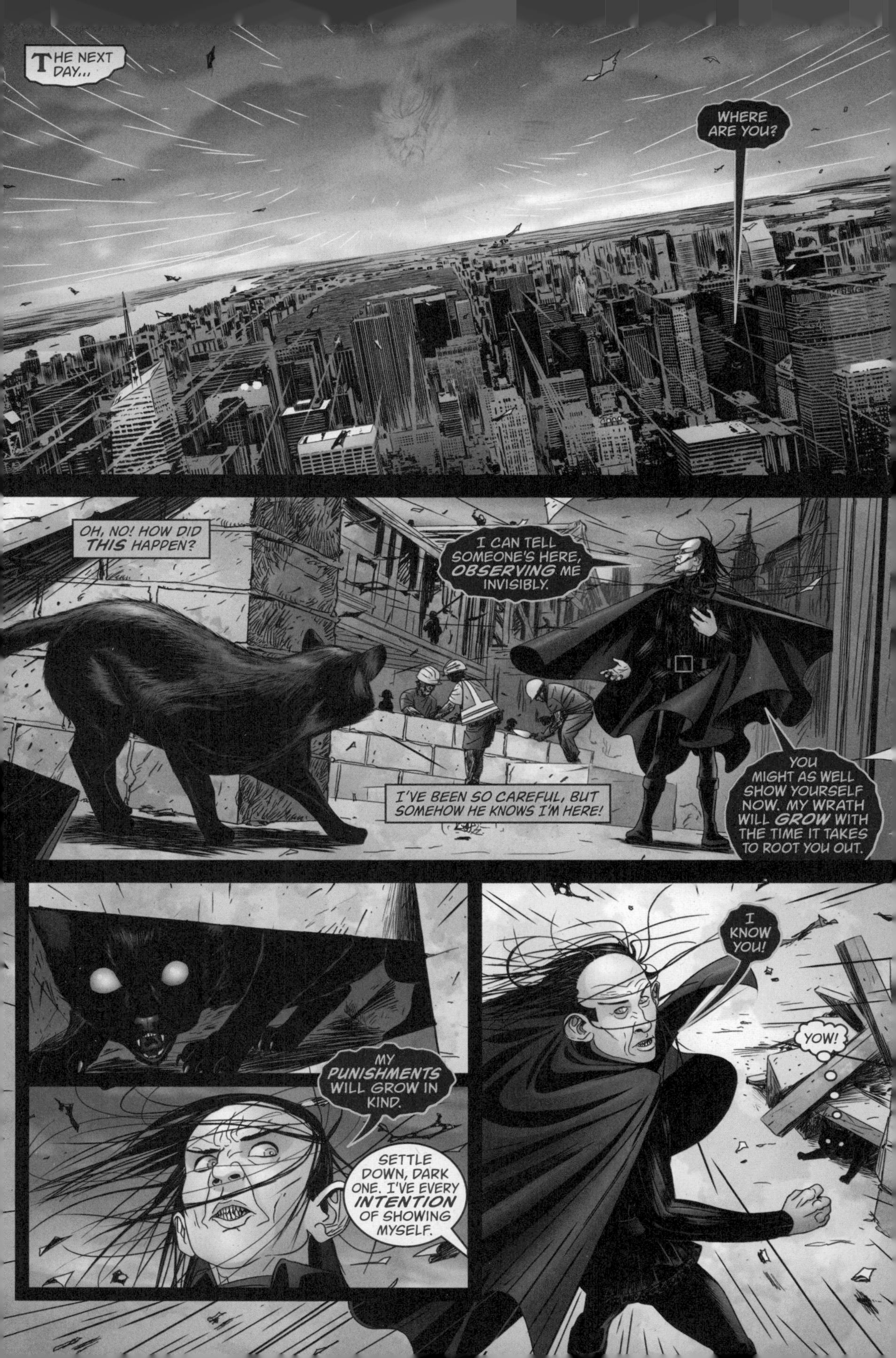
THE NEXT DAY...
WHERE ARE YOU?
OH, NO! HOW DID THIS HAPPEN?
I CAN TELL SOMEONE'S HERE, OBSERVING ME INVISIBLY.
I'VE BEEN SO CAREFUL, BUT SOMEHOW HE KNOWS I'M HERE!
YOU MIGHT AS WELL SHOW YOURSELF NOW. MY WRATH WILL GROW WITH THE TIME IT TAKES TO ROOT YOU OUT.
MY PUNISHMENTS WILL GROW IN KIND.
SETTLE DOWN, DARK ONE. I'VE EVERY INTENTION OF SHOWING MYSELF.
I KNOW YOU!
YOW!

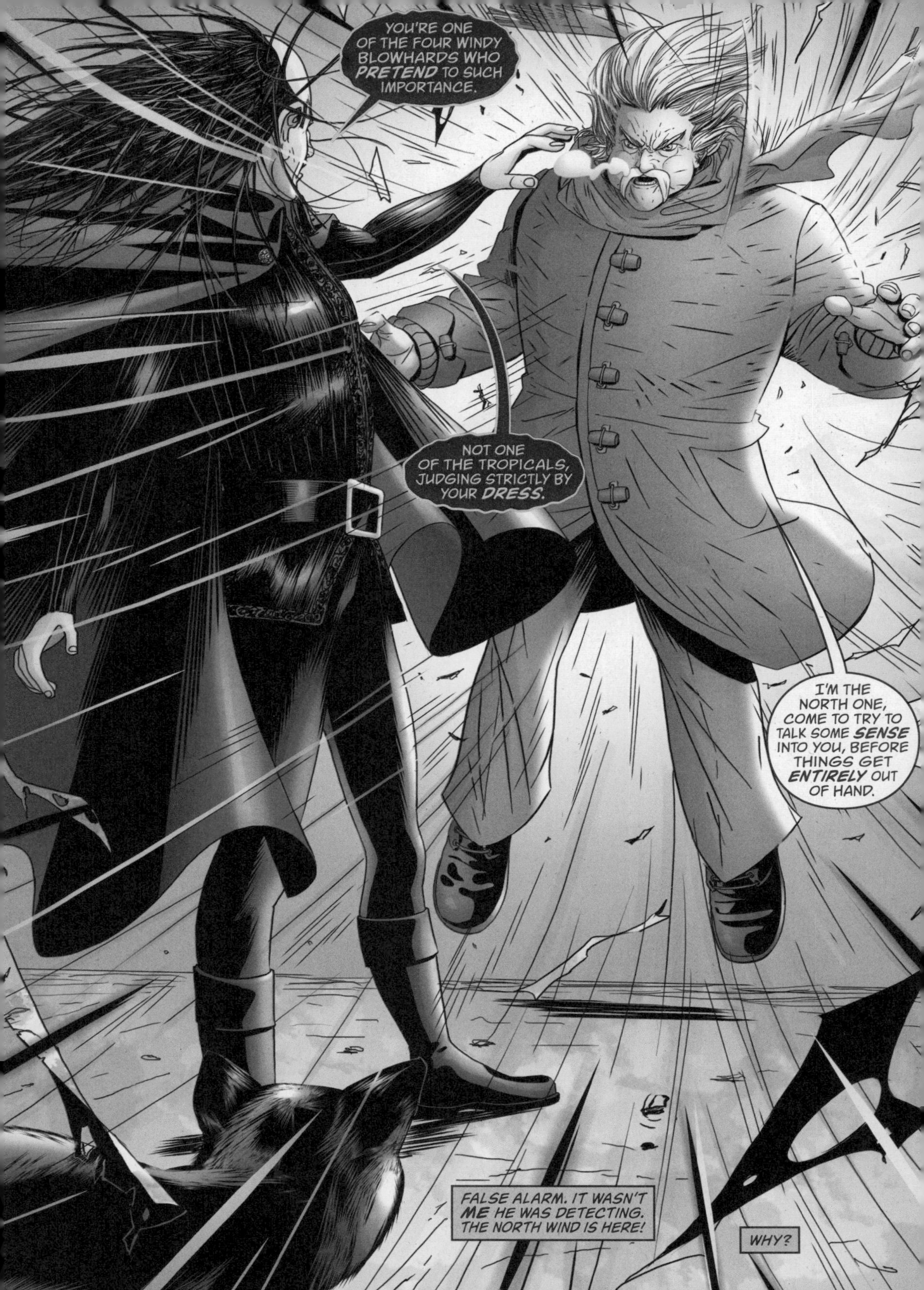
YOU'RE ONE OF THE FOUR WINDY BLOWHARDS WHO PRETEND TO SUCH IMPORTANCE.
NOT ONE OF THE TROPICALS, JUDGING STRICTLY BY YOUR DRESS.
I'M THE NORTH ONE, COME TO TRY TO TALK SOME SENSE INTO YOU, BEFORE THINGS GET ENTIRELY OUT OF HAND.
FALSE ALARM. IT WASN'T ME HE WAS DETECTING. THE NORTH WIND IS HERE!
WHY?

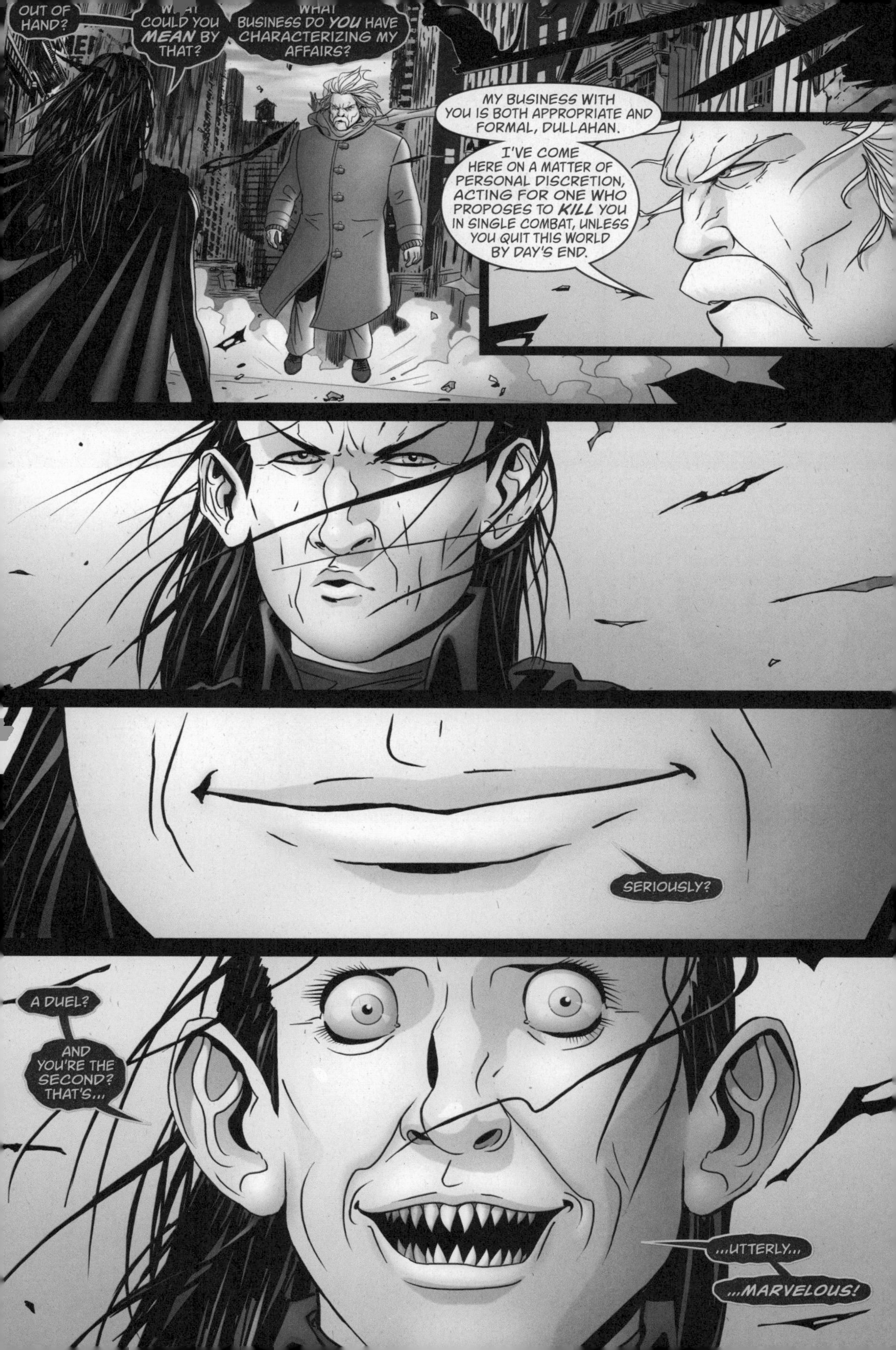
OUT OF HAND?
WHAT COULD YOU MEAN BY THAT?
WHAT BUSINESS DO YOU HAVE CHARACTERIZING MY AFFAIRS?
MY BUSINESS WITH YOU IS BOTH APPROPRIATE AND FORMAL, DULLAHAN.
I'VE COME HERE ON A MATTER OF PERSONAL DISCRETION, ACTING FOR ONE WHO PROPOSES TO KILL YOU IN SINGLE COMBAT, UNLESS YOU QUIT THIS WORLD BY DAY'S END.
SERIOUSLY?
A DUEL?
AND YOU'RE THE SECOND? THAT'S...
...UTTERLY...
...MARVELOUS!

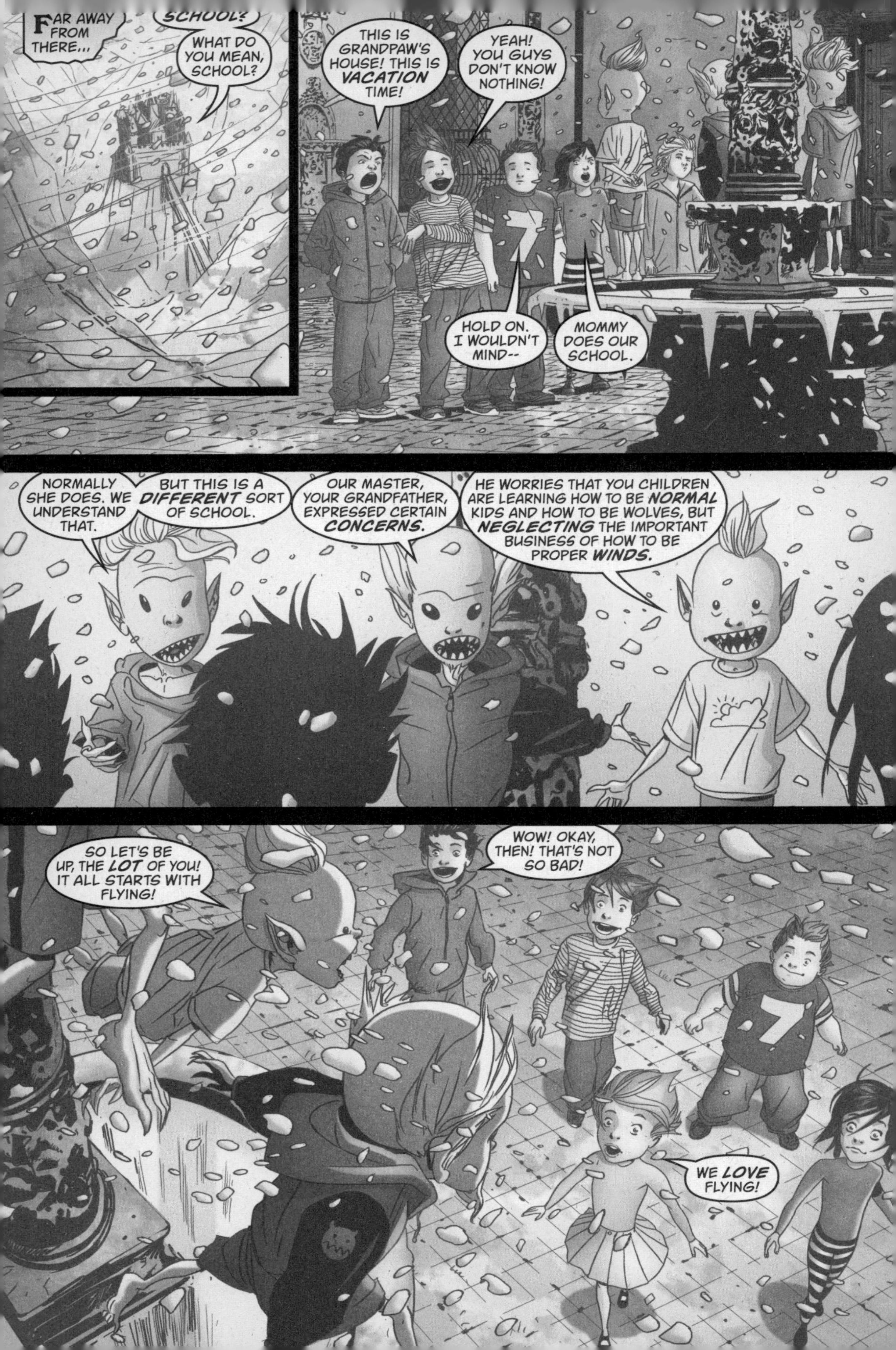
FAR AWAY FROM THERE...
SCHOOL?
WHAT DO YOU MEAN, SCHOOL?
THIS IS GRANDPAW'S HOUSE! THIS IS VACATION TIME!
YEAH! YOU GUYS DON'T KNOW NOTHING!
HOLD ON. I WOULDN'T MIND--
MOMMY DOES OUR SCHOOL.
NORMALLY SHE DOES. WE UNDERSTAND THAT.
BUT THIS IS A DIFFERENT SORT OF SCHOOL.
OUR MASTER, YOUR GRANDFATHER, EXPRESSED CERTAIN CONCERNS.
HE WORRIES THAT YOU CHILDREN ARE LEARNING HOW TO BE NORMAL KIDS AND HOW TO BE WOLVES, BUT NEGLECTING THE IMPORTANT BUSINESS OF HOW TO BE PROPER WINDS.
SO LET'S BE UP, THE LOT OF YOU! IT ALL STARTS WITH FLYING!
WOW! OKAY, THEN! THAT'S NOT SO BAD!
WE LOVE FLYING!

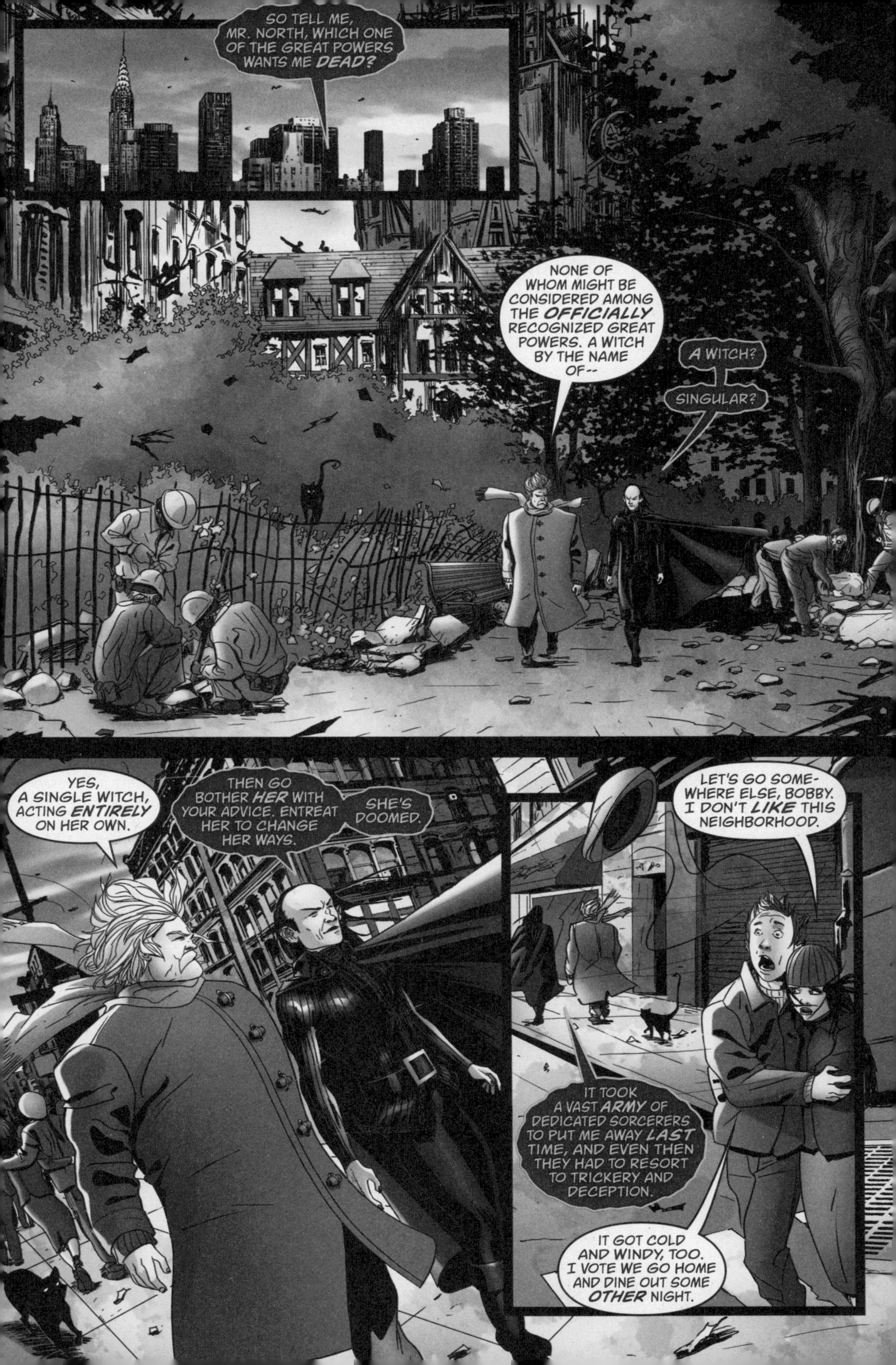
SO TELL ME, MR. NORTH, WHICH ONE OF THE GREAT POWERS WANTS ME DEAD?
NONE OF WHOM MIGHT BE CONSIDERED AMONG THE OFFICIALLY RECOGNIZED GREAT POWERS. A WITCH BY THE NAME OF--
A WITCH?
SINGULAR?
YES, A SINGLE WITCH, ACTING ENTIRELY ON HER OWN.
THEN GO BOTHER HER WITH YOUR ADVICE. ENTREAT HER TO CHANGE HER WAYS.
SHE'S DOOMED.
IT TOOK A VAST ARMY OF DEDICATED SORCERERS TO PUT ME AWAY LAST TIME, AND EVEN THEN THEY HAD TO RESORT TO TRICKERY AND DECEPTION.
LET'S GO SOME-WHERE ELSE, BOBBY. I DON'T LIKE THIS NEIGHBORHOOD.
IT GOT COLD AND WINDY, TOO. I VOTE WE GO HOME AND DINE OUT SOME OTHER NIGHT.

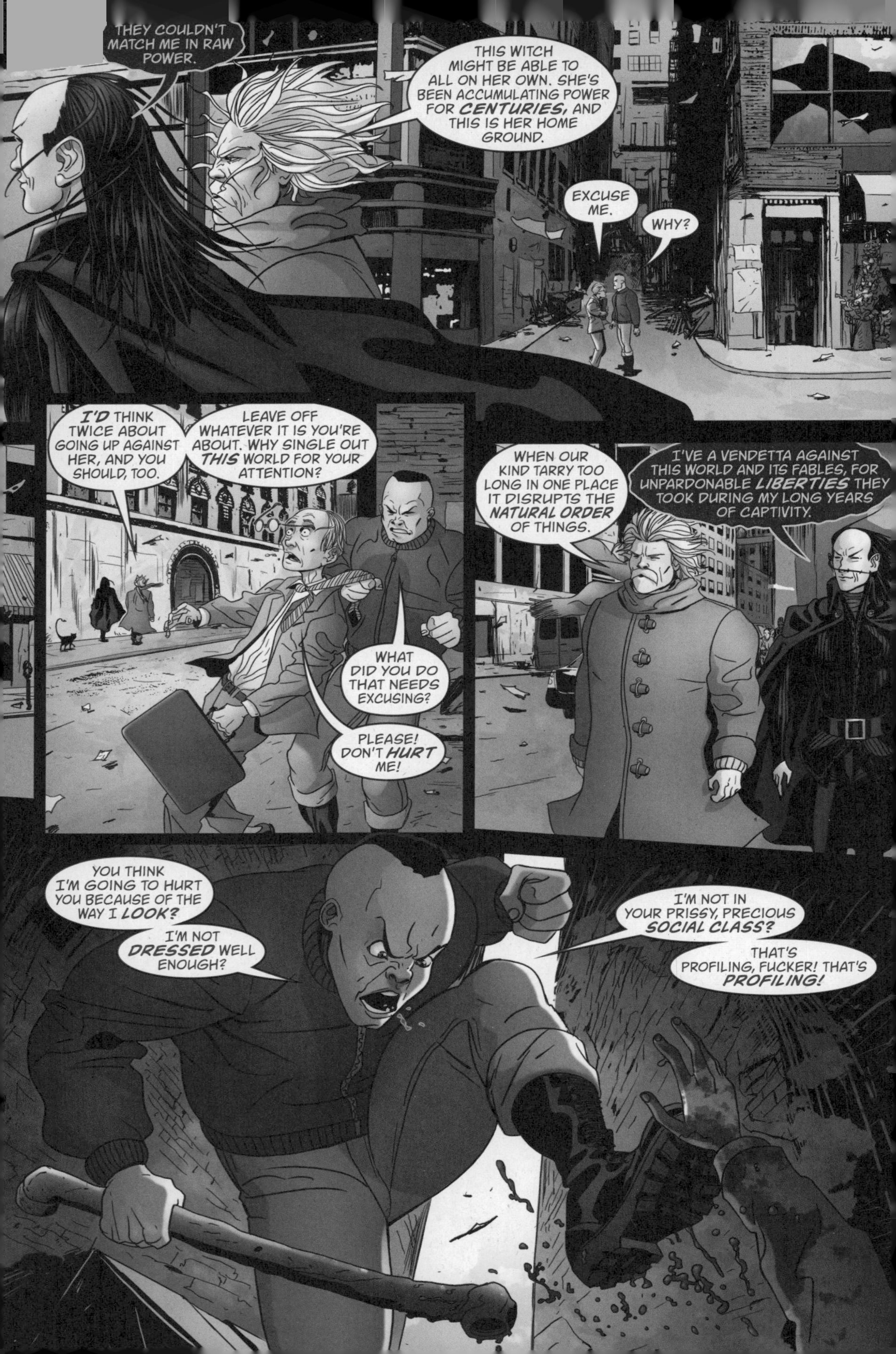
THEY COULDN'T MATCH ME IN RAW POWER.
THIS WITCH MIGHT BE ABLE TO ALL ON HER OWN. SHE'S BEEN ACCUMULATING POWER FOR CENTURIES, AND THIS IS HER HOME GROUND.
EXCUSE ME.
WHY?
I'D THINK TWICE ABOUT GOING UP AGAINST HER, AND YOU SHOULD, TOO.
LEAVE OFF WHATEVER IT IS YOU'RE ABOUT. WHY SINGLE OUT THIS WORLD FOR YOUR ATTENTION?
WHAT DID YOU DO THAT NEEDS EXCUSING?
PLEASE! DON'T HURT ME!
WHEN OUR KIND TARRY TOO LONG IN ONE PLACE IT DISRUPTS THE NATURAL ORDER OF THINGS.
I'VE A VENDETTA AGAINST THIS WORLD AND ITS FABLES, FOR UNPARDONABLE LIBERTIES THEY TOOK DURING MY LONG YEARS OF CAPTIVITY.
YOU THINK I'M GOING TO HURT YOU BECAUSE OF THE WAY I LOOK?
I'M NOT DRESSED WELL ENOUGH?
I'M NOT IN YOUR PRISSY, PRECIOUS SOCIAL CLASS?
THAT'S PROFILING, FUCKER! THAT'S PROFILING!

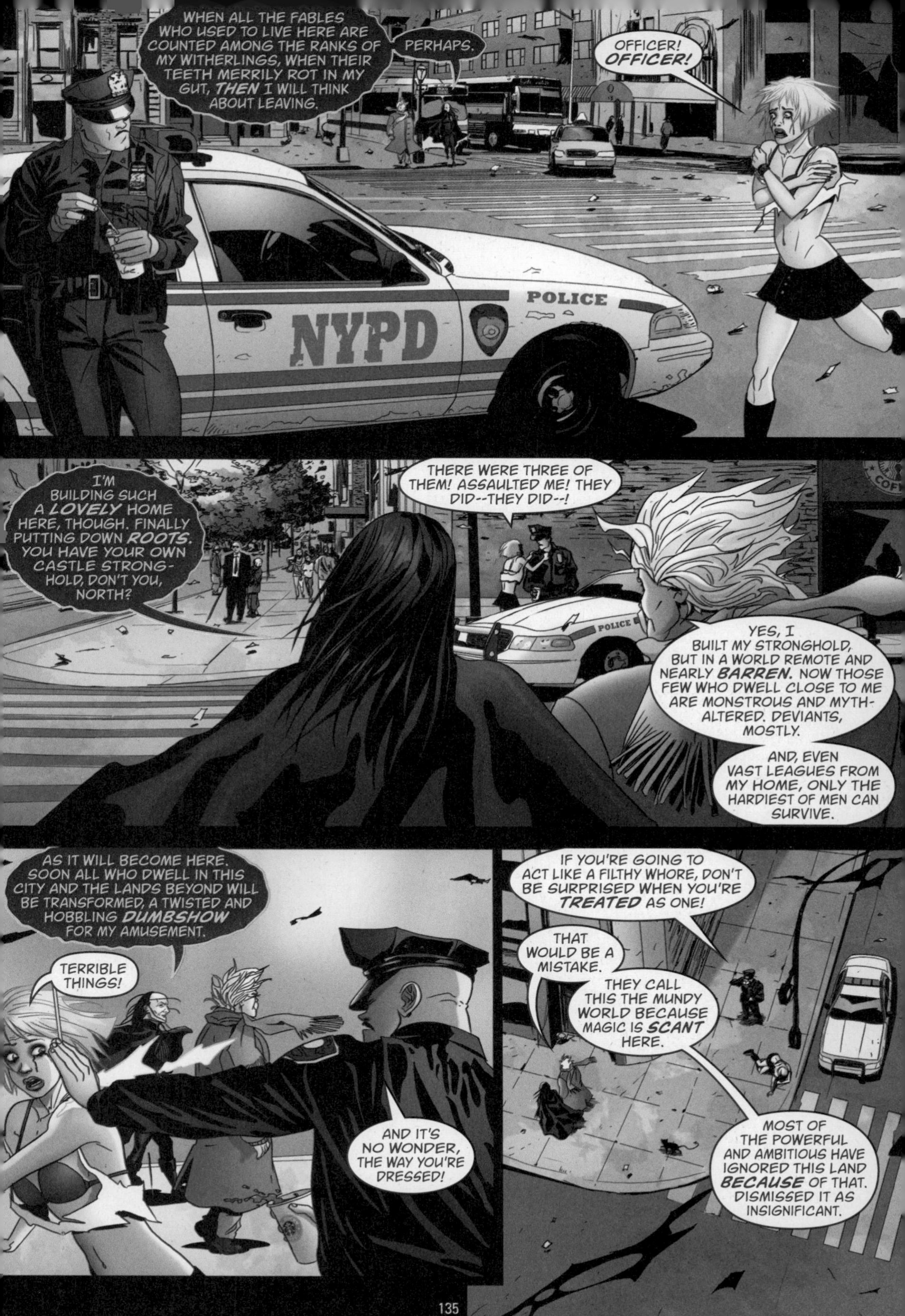
WHEN ALL THE FABLES WHO USED TO LIVE HERE ARE COUNTED AMONG THE RANKS OF MY WITHERLINGS, WHEN THEIR TEETH MERRILY ROT IN MY GUT, THEN I WILL THINK ABOUT LEAVING.
PERHAPS.
OFFICER! OFFICER!
POLICE
NYPD
I'M BUILDING SUCH A LOVELY HOME HERE, THOUGH. FINALLY PUTTING DOWN ROOTS. YOU HAVE YOUR OWN CASTLE STRONGHOLD, DON'T YOU, NORTH?
THERE WERE THREE OF THEM! ASSAULTED ME! THEY DID--THEY DID--!
YES, I BUILT MY STRONGHOLD, BUT IN A WORLD REMOTE AND NEARLY BARREN. NOW THOSE FEW WHO DWELL CLOSE TO ME ARE MONSTROUS AND MYTH-ALTERED. DEVIANTS, MOSTLY.
AND, EVEN VAST LEAGUES FROM MY HOME, ONLY THE HARDIEST OF MEN CAN SURVIVE.
AS IT WILL BECOME HERE. SOON ALL WHO DWELL IN THIS CITY AND THE LANDS BEYOND WILL BE TRANSFORMED, A TWISTED AND HOBBLING DUMBSHOW FOR MY AMUSEMENT.
TERRIBLE THINGS!
AND IT'S NO WONDER, THE WAY YOU'RE DRESSED!
IF YOU'RE GOING TO ACT LIKE A FILTHY WHORE, DON'T BE SURPRISED WHEN YOU'RE TREATED AS ONE!
THAT WOULD BE A MISTAKE.
THEY CALL THIS THE MUNDY WORLD BECAUSE MAGIC IS SCANT HERE.
MOST OF THE POWERFUL AND AMBITIOUS HAVE IGNORED THIS LAND BECAUSE OF THAT. DISMISSED IT AS INSIGNIFICANT.

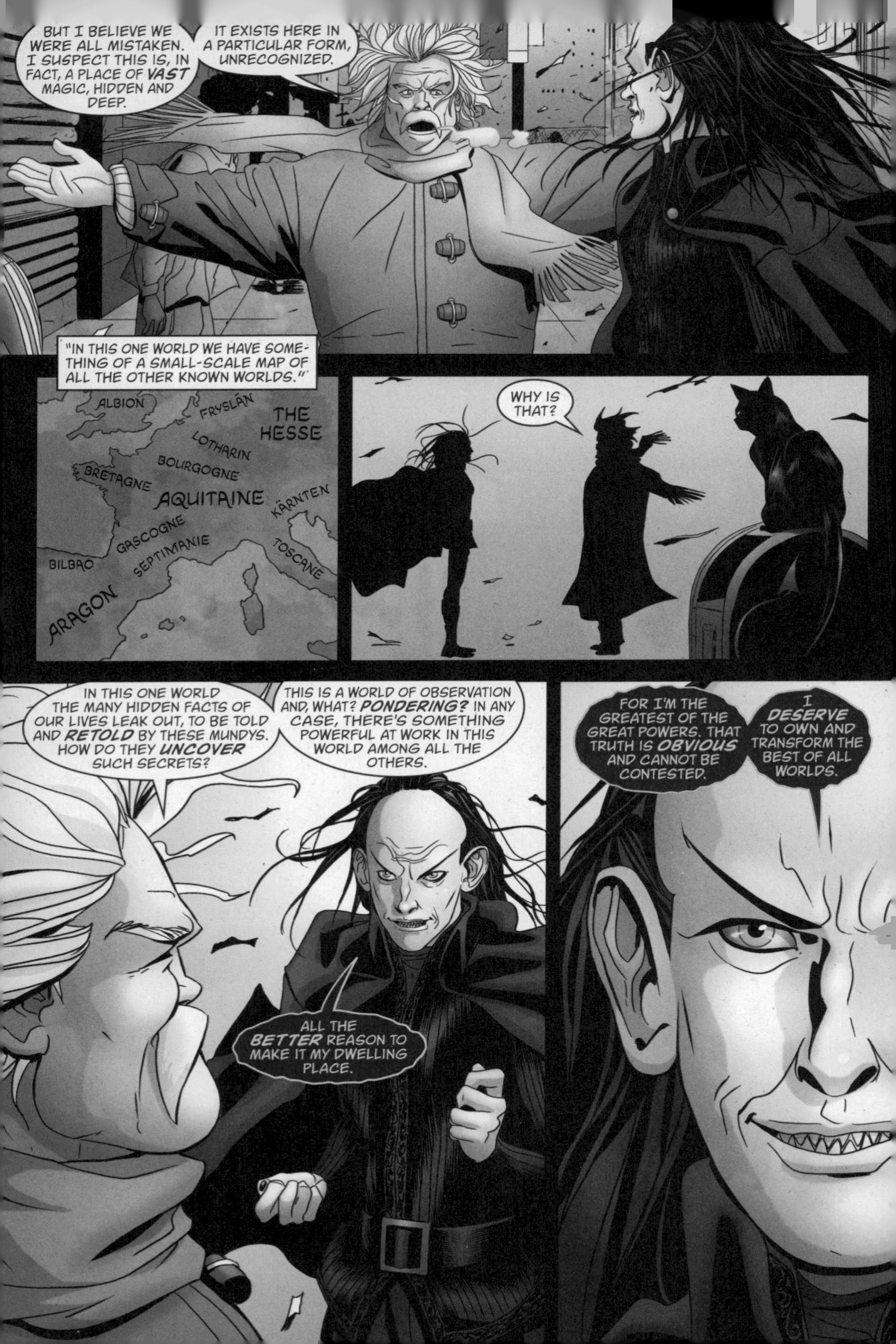
BUT I BELIEVE WE WERE ALL MISTAKEN. I SUSPECT THIS IS, IN FACT, A PLACE OF VAST MAGIC, HIDDEN AND DEEP.
IT EXISTS HERE IN A PARTICULAR FORM, UNRECOGNIZED.
"IN THIS ONE WORLD WE HAVE SOMETHING OF A SMALL-SCALE MAP OF ALL THE OTHER KNOWN WORLDS."
ALBION
FRYSLÂN
THE HESSE
LOTHARIN
BOURGOGNE
BRETAGNE
AQUITAINE
KÄRNTEN
GASCOGNE
SEPTIMANIE
TOSCANE
BILBAO
ARAGON
WHY IS THAT?
IN THIS ONE WORLD THE MANY HIDDEN FACTS OF OUR LIVES LEAK OUT, TO BE TOLD AND RETOLD BY THESE MUNDYS. HOW DO THEY UNCOVER SUCH SECRETS?
THIS IS A WORLD OF OBSERVATION AND, WHAT? PONDERING? IN ANY CASE, THERE'S SOMETHING POWERFUL AT WORK IN THIS WORLD AMONG ALL THE OTHERS.
ALL THE BETTER REASON TO MAKE IT MY DWELLING PLACE.
FOR I'M THE GREATEST OF THE GREAT POWERS. THAT TRUTH IS OBVIOUS AND CANNOT BE CONTESTED.
I DESERVE TO OWN AND TRANSFORM THE BEST OF ALL WORLDS.

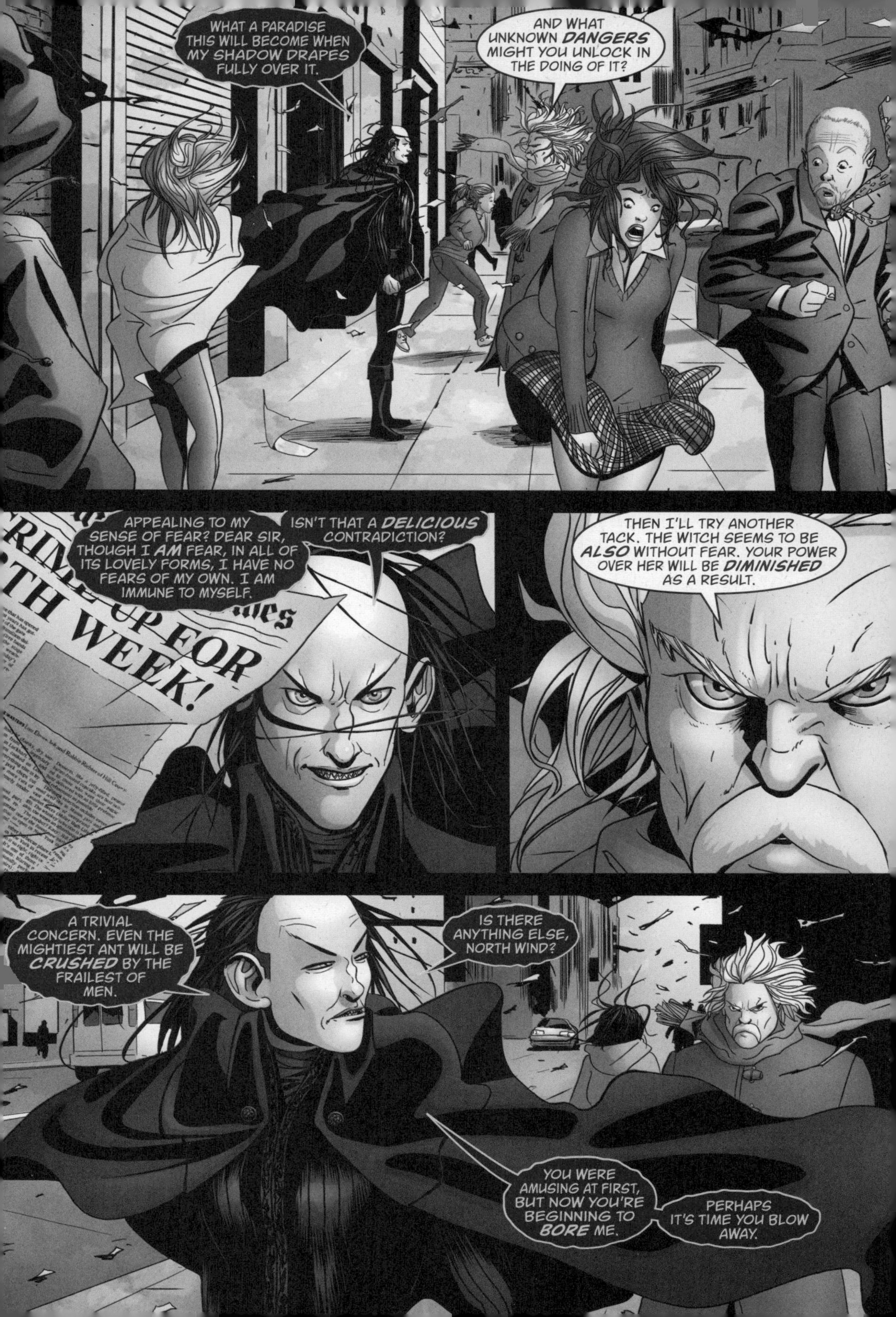
WHAT A PARADISE THIS WILL BECOME WHEN MY SHADOW DRAPES FULLY OVER IT.
AND WHAT UNKNOWN DANGERS MIGHT YOU UNLOCK IN THE DOING OF IT?
APPEALING TO MY SENSE OF FEAR? DEAR SIR, THOUGH I AM FEAR, IN ALL OF ITS LOVELY FORMS, I HAVE NO FEARS OF MY OWN. I AM IMMUNE TO MYSELF.
ISN'T THAT A DELICIOUS CONTRADICTION?
THEN I'LL TRY ANOTHER TACK. THE WITCH SEEMS TO BE ALSO WITHOUT FEAR. YOUR POWER OVER HER WILL BE DIMINISHED AS A RESULT.
A TRIVIAL CONCERN. EVEN THE MIGHTIEST ANT WILL BE CRUSHED BY THE FRAILEST OF MEN.
IS THERE ANYTHING ELSE, NORTH WIND?
YOU WERE AMUSING AT FIRST, BUT NOW YOU'RE BEGINNING TO BORE ME.
PERHAPS IT'S TIME YOU BLOW AWAY.

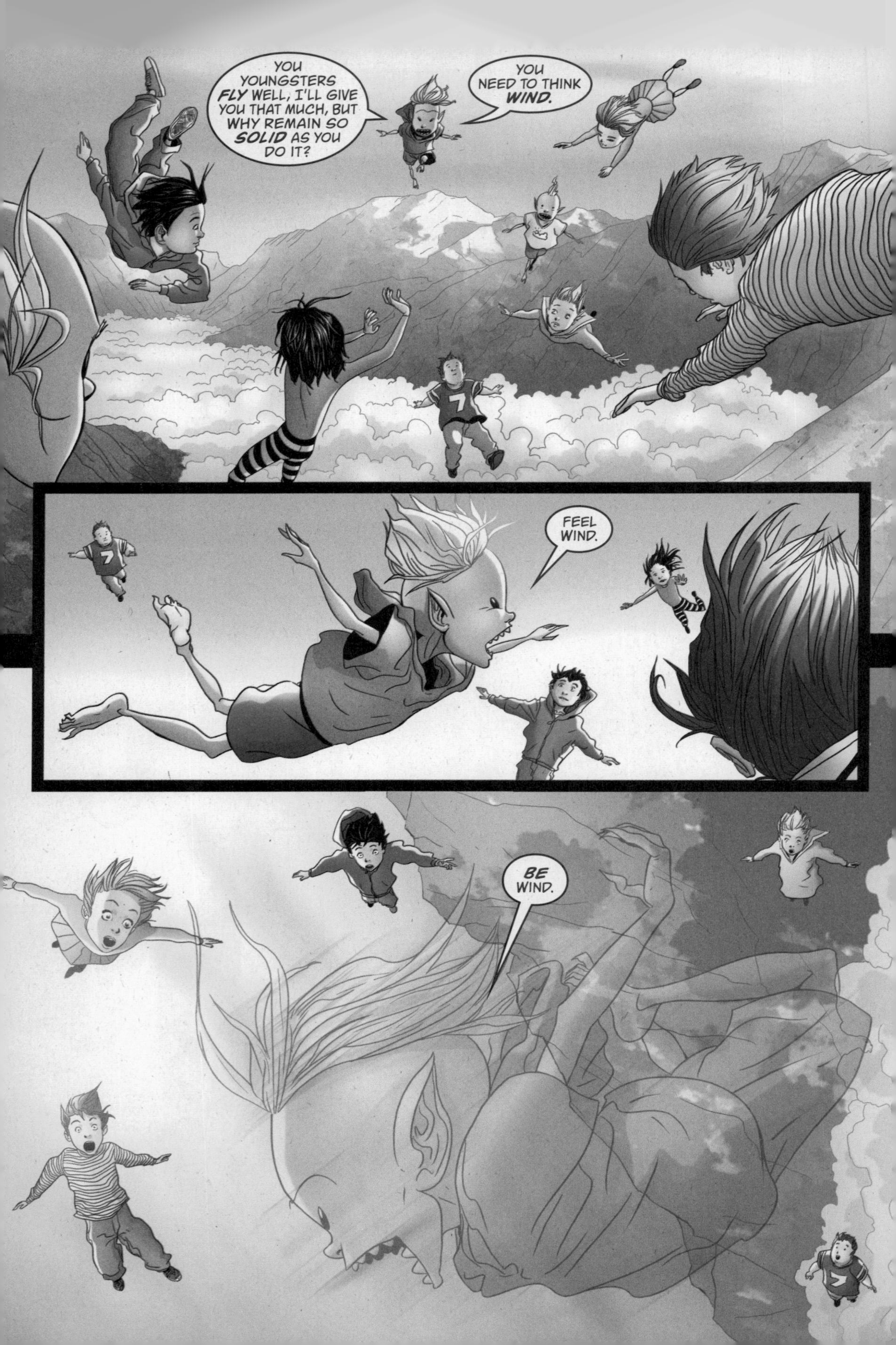
YOU YOUNGSTERS FLY WELL, I'LL GIVE YOU THAT MUCH, BUT WHY REMAIN SO SOLID AS YOU DO IT?
YOU NEED TO THINK WIND.
FEEL WIND.
BE WIND.

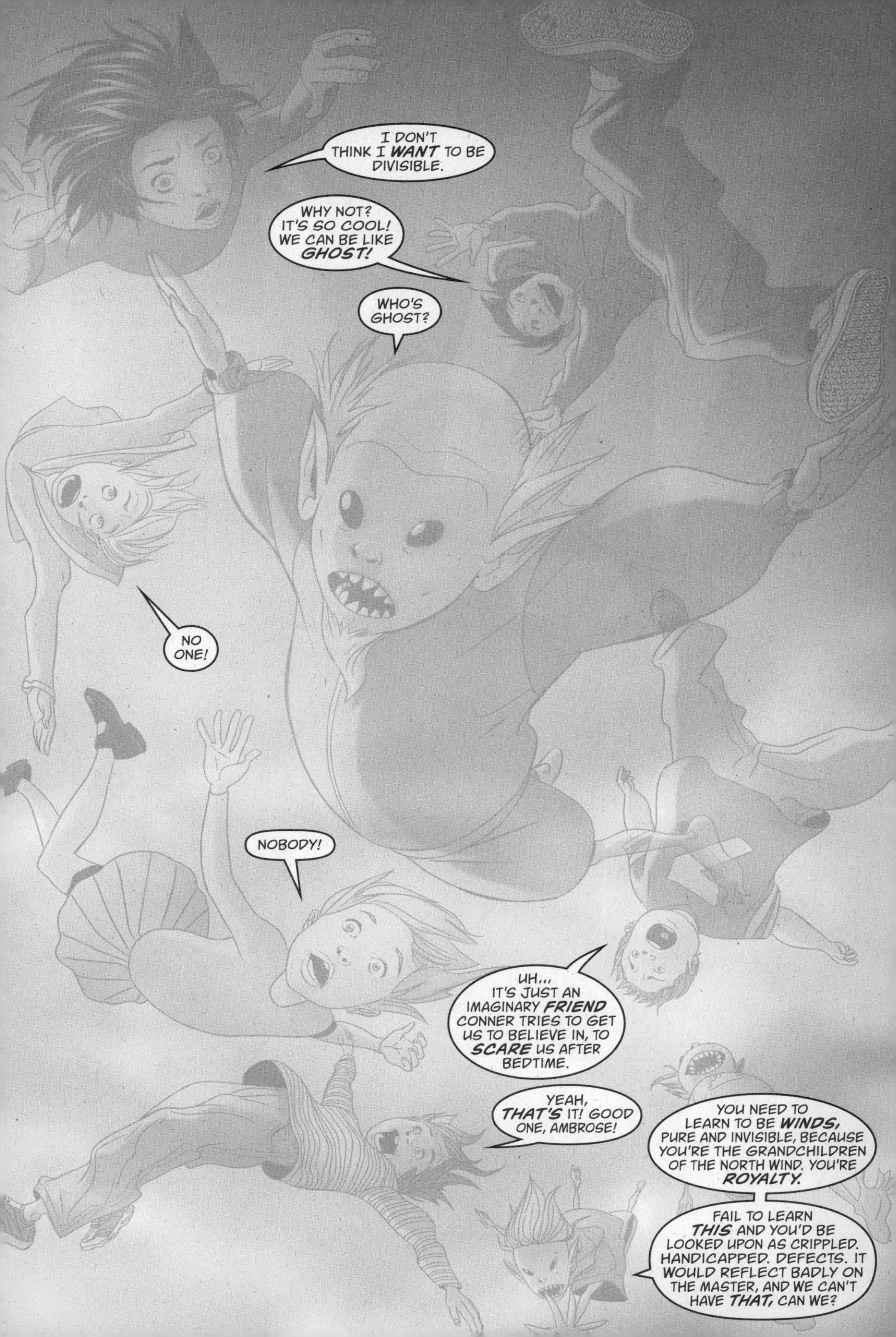
I DON'T THINK I *WANT* TO BE DIVISIBLE.
WHY NOT? IT'S SO COOL! WE CAN BE LIKE *GHOST!*
WHO'S GHOST?
NO ONE!
NOBODY!
UH... IT'S JUST AN IMAGINARY *FRIEND* CONNER TRIES TO GET US TO BELIEVE IN, TO *SCARE* US AFTER BEDTIME.
YEAH, *THAT'S* IT! GOOD ONE, AMBROSE!
YOU NEED TO LEARN TO BE *WINDS,* PURE AND INVISIBLE, BECAUSE YOU'RE THE GRANDCHILDREN OF THE NORTH WIND. YOU'RE *ROYALTY.*
FAIL TO LEARN *THIS* AND YOU'D BE LOOKED UPON AS CRIPPLED. HANDICAPPED. DEFECTS. IT WOULD REFLECT BADLY ON THE MASTER, AND WE CAN'T HAVE *THAT,* CAN WE?

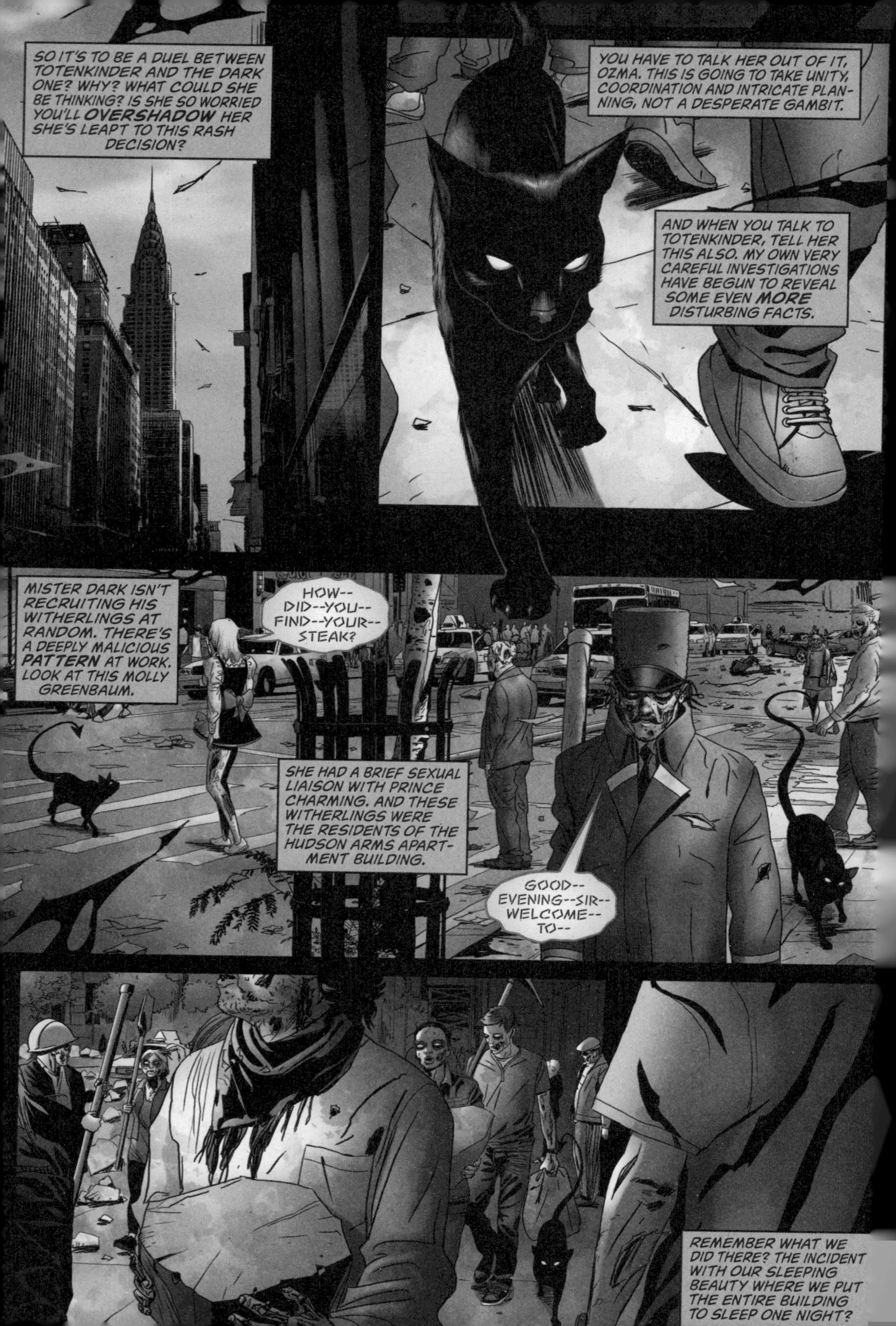
SO IT'S TO BE A DUEL BETWEEN TOTENKINDER AND THE DARK ONE? WHY? WHAT COULD SHE BE THINKING? IS SHE SO WORRIED YOU'LL OVERSHADOW HER SHE'S LEAPT TO THIS RASH DECISION?
YOU HAVE TO TALK HER OUT OF IT, OZMA. THIS IS GOING TO TAKE UNITY, COORDINATION AND INTRICATE PLANNING, NOT A DESPERATE GAMBIT.
AND WHEN YOU TALK TO TOTENKINDER, TELL HER THIS ALSO. MY OWN VERY CAREFUL INVESTIGATIONS HAVE BEGUN TO REVEAL SOME EVEN MORE DISTURBING FACTS.
MISTER DARK ISN'T RECRUITING HIS WITHERLINGS AT RANDOM. THERE'S A DEEPLY MALICIOUS PATTERN AT WORK. LOOK AT THIS MOLLY GREENBAUM.
HOW--DID--YOU--FIND--YOUR--STEAK?
SHE HAD A BRIEF SEXUAL LIAISON WITH PRINCE CHARMING. AND THESE WITHERLINGS WERE THE RESIDENTS OF THE HUDSON ARMS APARTMENT BUILDING.
GOOD--EVENING--SIR--WELCOME--TO--
REMEMBER WHAT WE DID THERE? THE INCIDENT WITH OUR SLEEPING BEAUTY WHERE WE PUT THE ENTIRE BUILDING TO SLEEP ONE NIGHT?

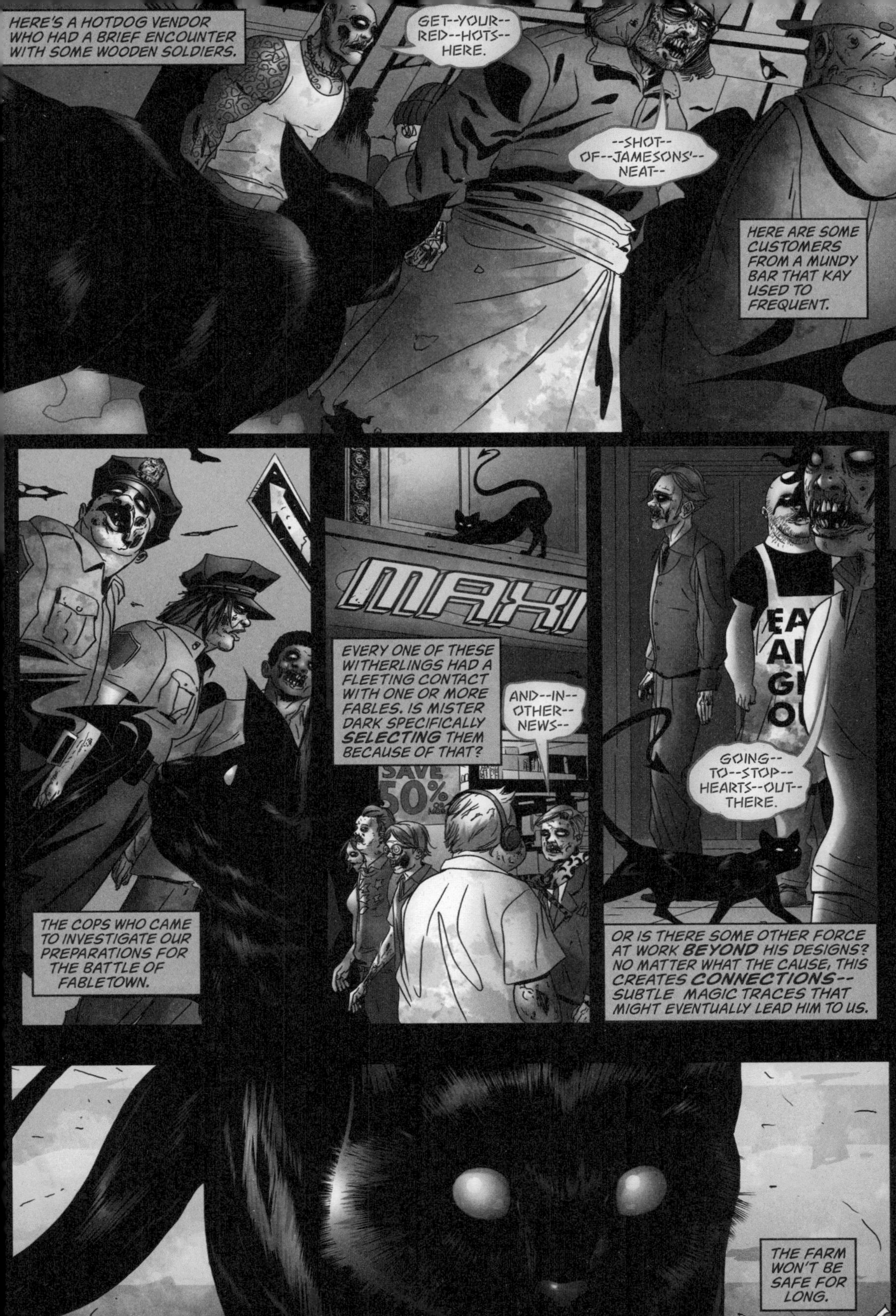
HERE'S A HOTDOG VENDOR WHO HAD A BRIEF ENCOUNTER WITH SOME WOODEN SOLDIERS.
GET--YOUR--RED--HOTS--HERE.
--SHOT--OF--JAMESONS'--NEAT--
HERE ARE SOME CUSTOMERS FROM A MUNDY BAR THAT KAY USED TO FREQUENT.
THE COPS WHO CAME TO INVESTIGATE OUR PREPARATIONS FOR THE BATTLE OF FABLETOWN.
MAXI
EVERY ONE OF THESE WITHERLINGS HAD A FLEETING CONTACT WITH ONE OR MORE FABLES. IS MISTER DARK SPECIFICALLY SELECTING THEM BECAUSE OF THAT?
AND--IN--OTHER--NEWS--
SAVE 50%
GOING--TO--STOP--HEARTS--OUT--THERE.
OR IS THERE SOME OTHER FORCE AT WORK BEYOND HIS DESIGNS? NO MATTER WHAT THE CAUSE, THIS CREATES CONNECTIONS--SUBTLE MAGIC TRACES THAT MIGHT EVENTUALLY LEAD HIM TO US.
THE FARM WON'T BE SAFE FOR LONG.

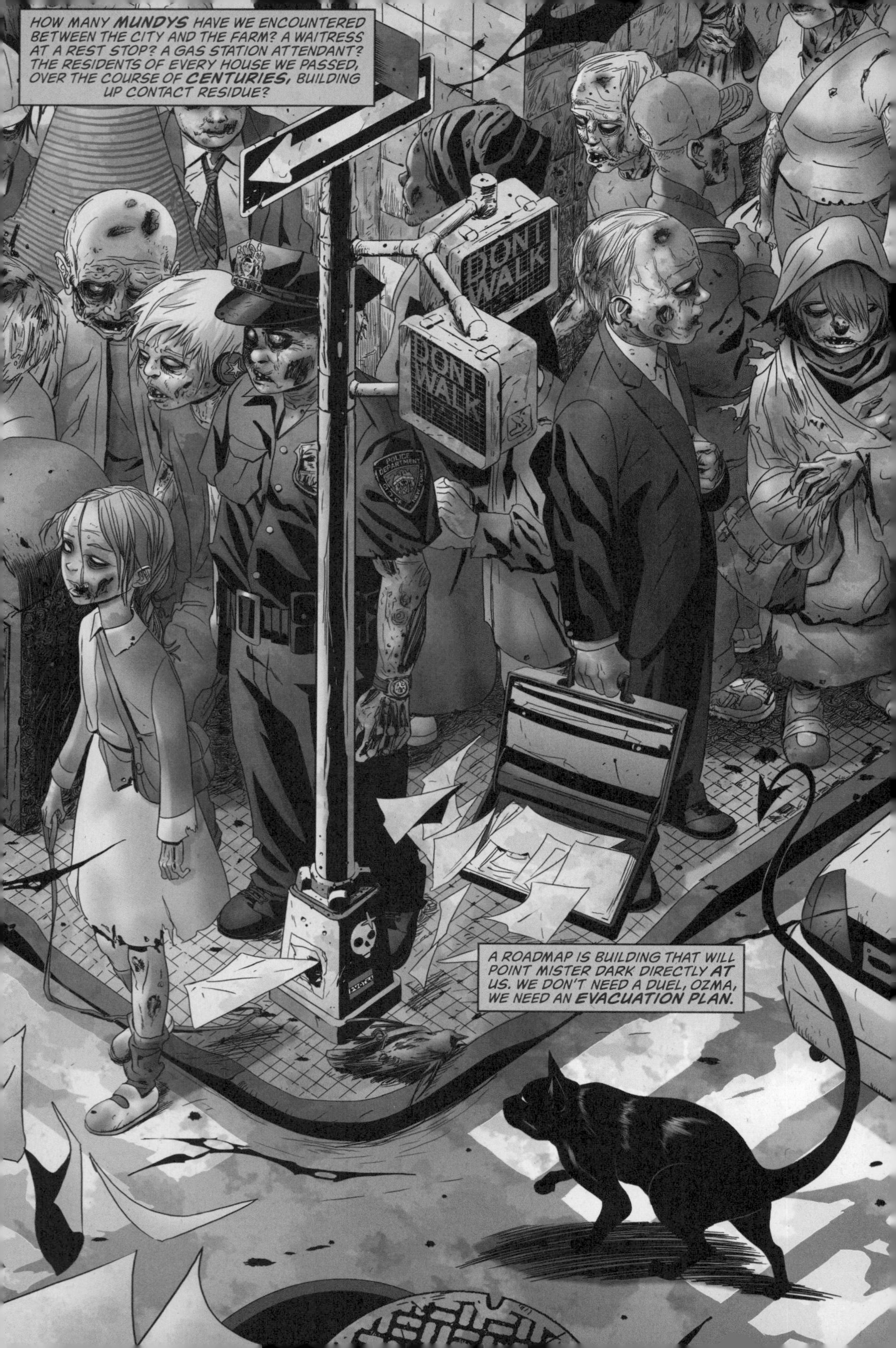
HOW MANY MUNDYS HAVE WE ENCOUNTERED BETWEEN THE CITY AND THE FARM? A WAITRESS AT A REST STOP? A GAS STATION ATTENDANT? THE RESIDENTS OF EVERY HOUSE WE PASSED, OVER THE COURSE OF CENTURIES, BUILDING UP CONTACT RESIDUE?
DONT WALK
DONT WALK
POLICE DEPARTMENT
A ROADMAP IS BUILDING THAT WILL POINT MISTER DARK DIRECTLY AT US. WE DON'T NEED A DUEL, OZMA, WE NEED AN EVACUATION PLAN.

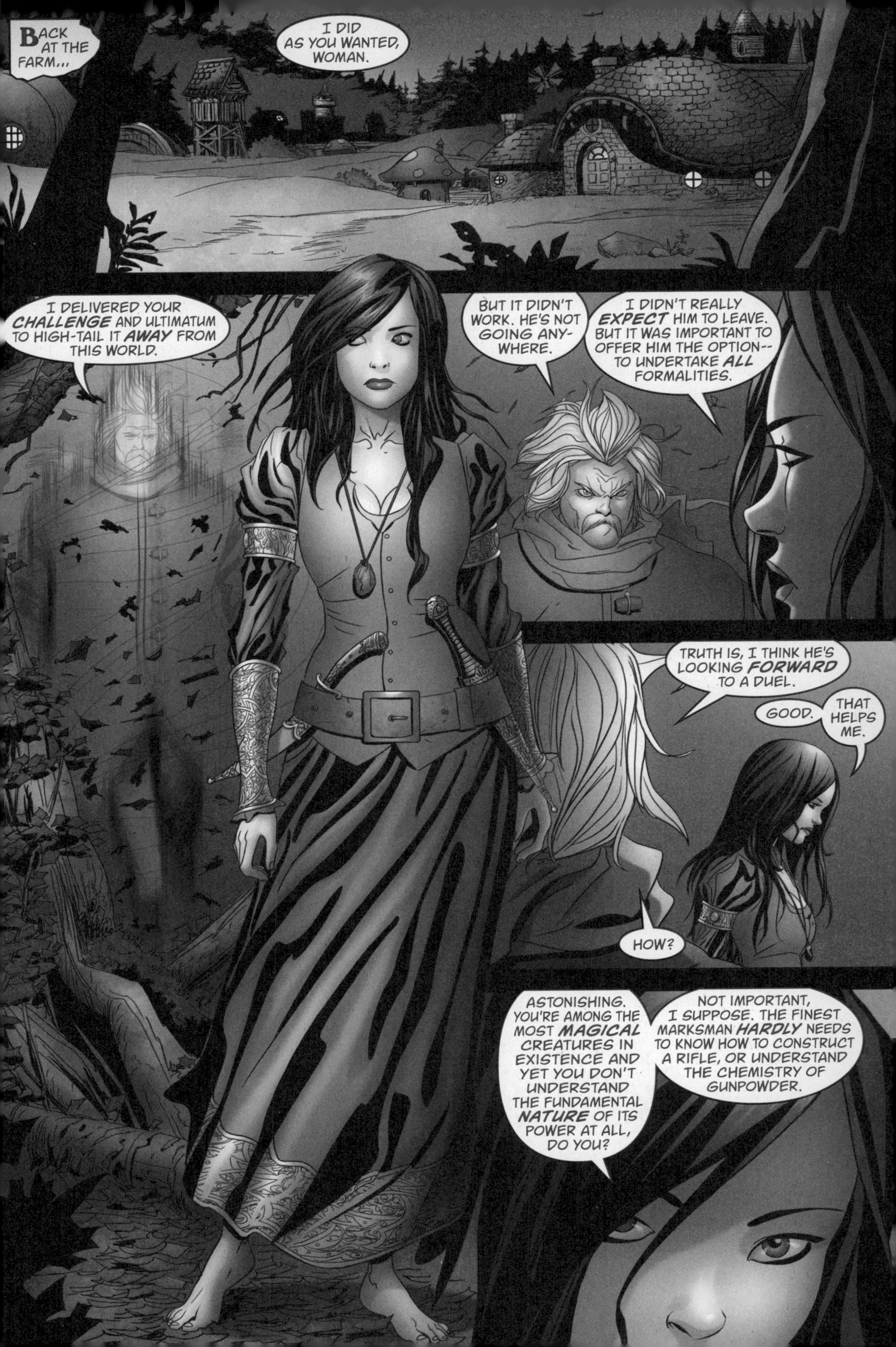
BACK AT THE FARM...
I DID AS YOU WANTED, WOMAN.
I DELIVERED YOUR CHALLENGE AND ULTIMATUM TO HIGH-TAIL IT AWAY FROM THIS WORLD.
BUT IT DIDN'T WORK. HE'S NOT GOING ANY-WHERE.
I DIDN'T REALLY EXPECT HIM TO LEAVE. BUT IT WAS IMPORTANT TO OFFER HIM THE OPTION-- TO UNDERTAKE ALL FORMALITIES.
TRUTH IS, I THINK HE'S LOOKING FORWARD TO A DUEL.
GOOD.
THAT HELPS ME.
HOW?
ASTONISHING. YOU'RE AMONG THE MOST MAGICAL CREATURES IN EXISTENCE AND YET YOU DON'T UNDERSTAND THE FUNDAMENTAL NATURE OF ITS POWER AT ALL, DO YOU?
NOT IMPORTANT, I SUPPOSE. THE FINEST MARKSMAN HARDLY NEEDS TO KNOW HOW TO CONSTRUCT A RIFLE, OR UNDERSTAND THE CHEMISTRY OF GUNPOWDER.

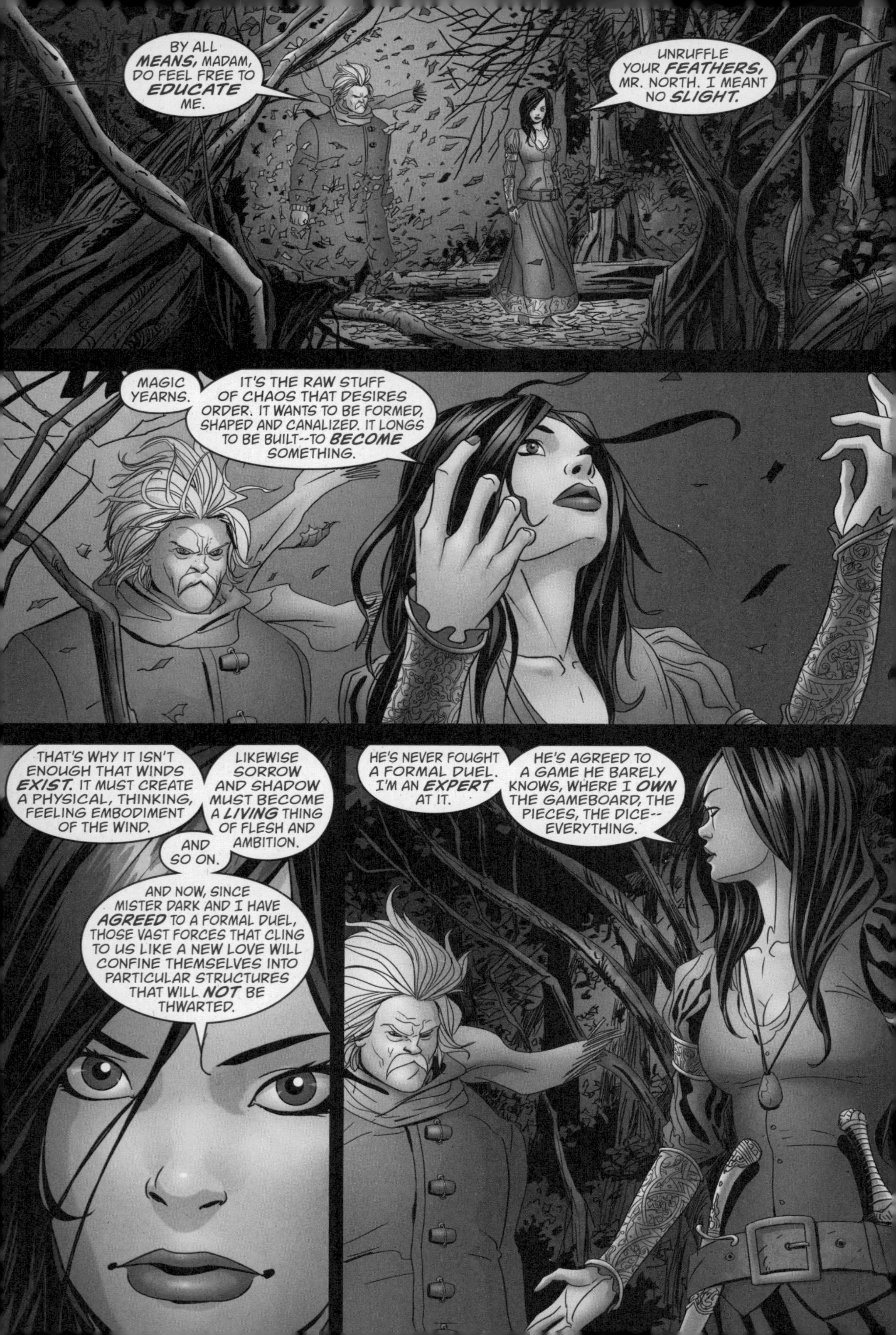
BY ALL MEANS, MADAM, DO FEEL FREE TO EDUCATE ME.
UNRUFFLE YOUR FEATHERS, MR. NORTH. I MEANT NO SLIGHT.
MAGIC YEARNS.
IT'S THE RAW STUFF OF CHAOS THAT DESIRES ORDER. IT WANTS TO BE FORMED, SHAPED AND CANALIZED. IT LONGS TO BE BUILT--TO BECOME SOMETHING.
THAT'S WHY IT ISN'T ENOUGH THAT WINDS EXIST. IT MUST CREATE A PHYSICAL, THINKING, FEELING EMBODIMENT OF THE WIND.
LIKEWISE SORROW AND SHADOW MUST BECOME A LIVING THING OF FLESH AND AMBITION.
AND SO ON.
AND NOW, SINCE MISTER DARK AND I HAVE AGREED TO A FORMAL DUEL, THOSE VAST FORCES THAT CLING TO US LIKE A NEW LOVE WILL CONFINE THEMSELVES INTO PARTICULAR STRUCTURES THAT WILL NOT BE THWARTED.
HE'S NEVER FOUGHT A FORMAL DUEL. I'M AN EXPERT AT IT.
HE'S AGREED TO A GAME HE BARELY KNOWS, WHERE I OWN THE GAMEBOARD, THE PIECES, THE DICE--EVERYTHING.

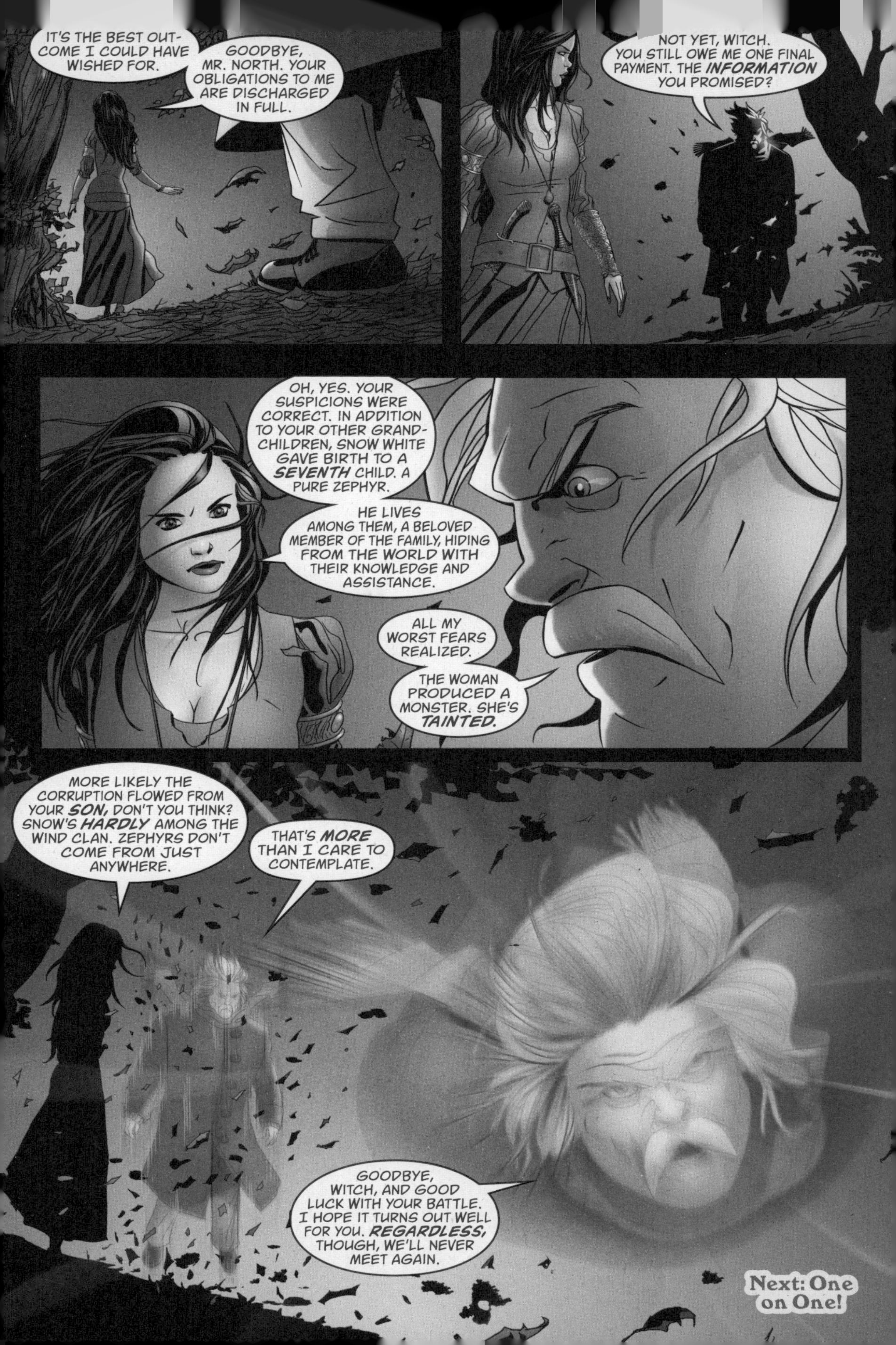
IT'S THE BEST OUT-COME I COULD HAVE WISHED FOR.
GOODBYE, MR. NORTH. YOUR OBLIGATIONS TO ME ARE DISCHARGED IN FULL.
NOT YET, WITCH. YOU STILL OWE ME ONE FINAL PAYMENT. THE INFORMATION YOU PROMISED?
OH, YES. YOUR SUSPICIONS WERE CORRECT. IN ADDITION TO YOUR OTHER GRAND-CHILDREN, SNOW WHITE GAVE BIRTH TO A SEVENTH CHILD. A PURE ZEPHYR.
HE LIVES AMONG THEM, A BELOVED MEMBER OF THE FAMILY, HIDING FROM THE WORLD WITH THEIR KNOWLEDGE AND ASSISTANCE.
ALL MY WORST FEARS REALIZED.
THE WOMAN PRODUCED A MONSTER. SHE'S TAINTED.
MORE LIKELY THE CORRUPTION FLOWED FROM YOUR SON, DON'T YOU THINK? SNOW'S HARDLY AMONG THE WIND CLAN. ZEPHYRS DON'T COME FROM JUST ANYWHERE.
THAT'S MORE THAN I CARE TO CONTEMPLATE.
GOODBYE, WITCH, AND GOOD LUCK WITH YOUR BATTLE. I HOPE IT TURNS OUT WELL FOR YOU. REGARDLESS, THOUGH, WE'LL NEVER MEET AGAIN.
Next: One on One!

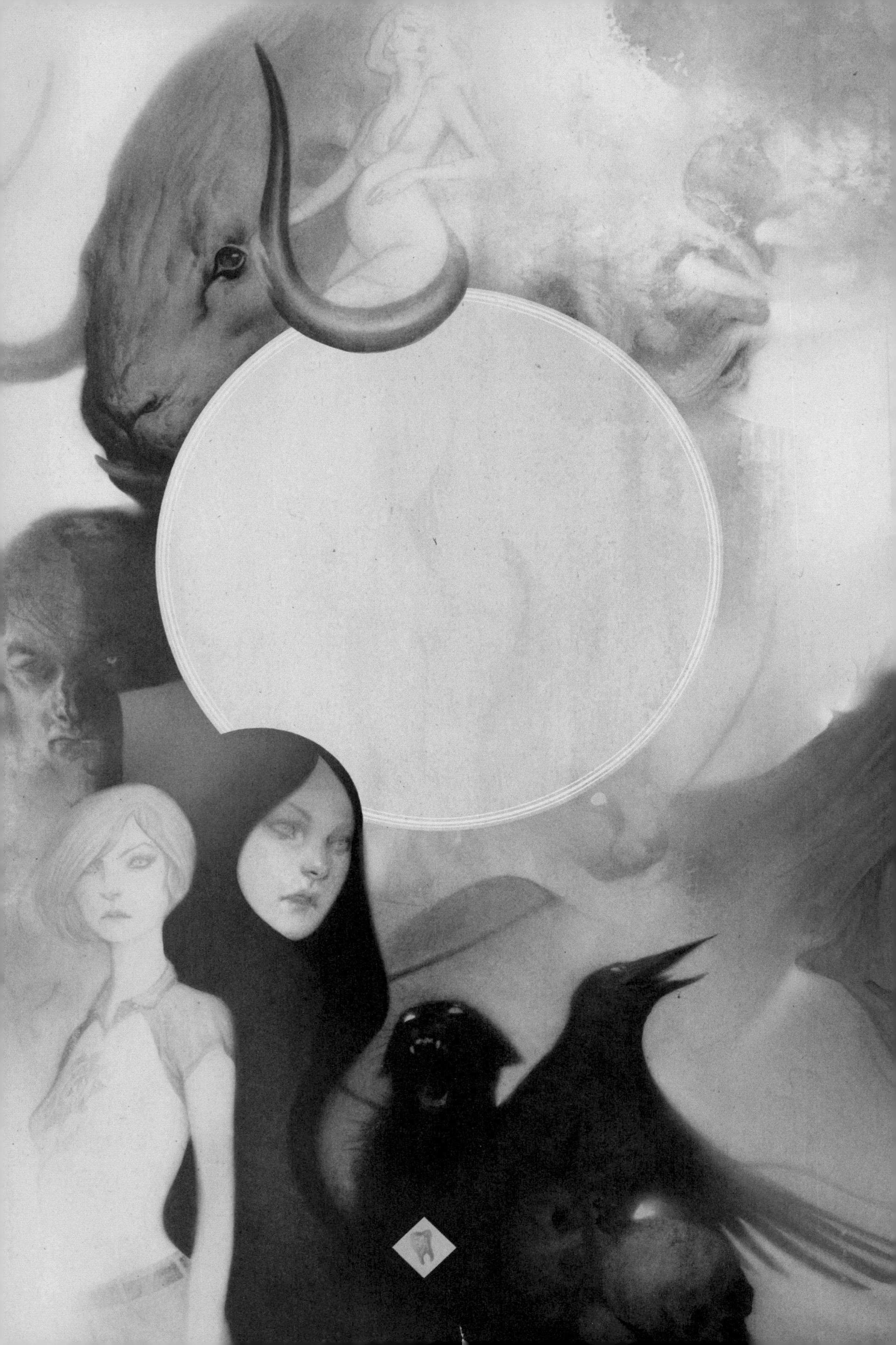

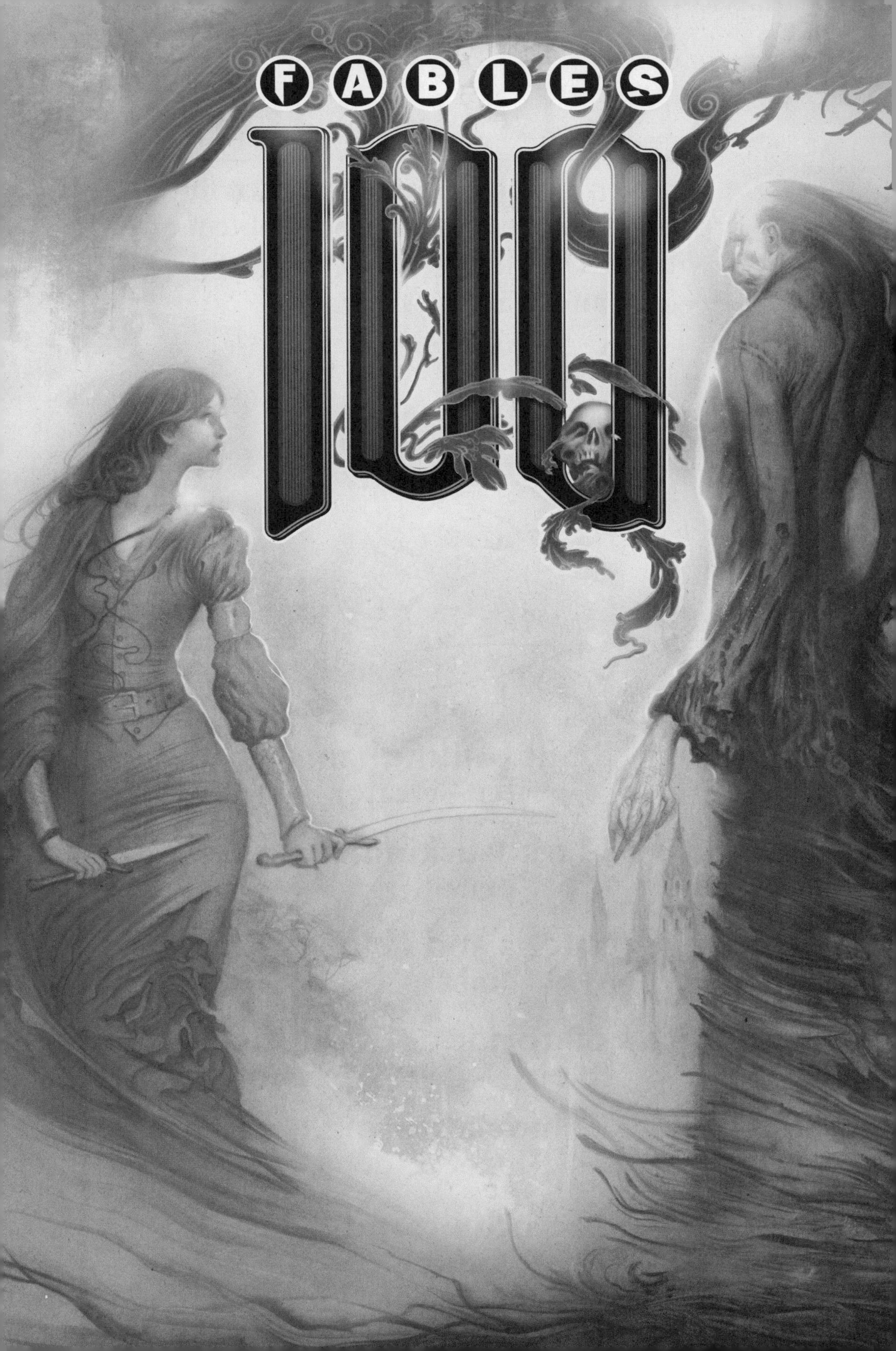
FABLES
100

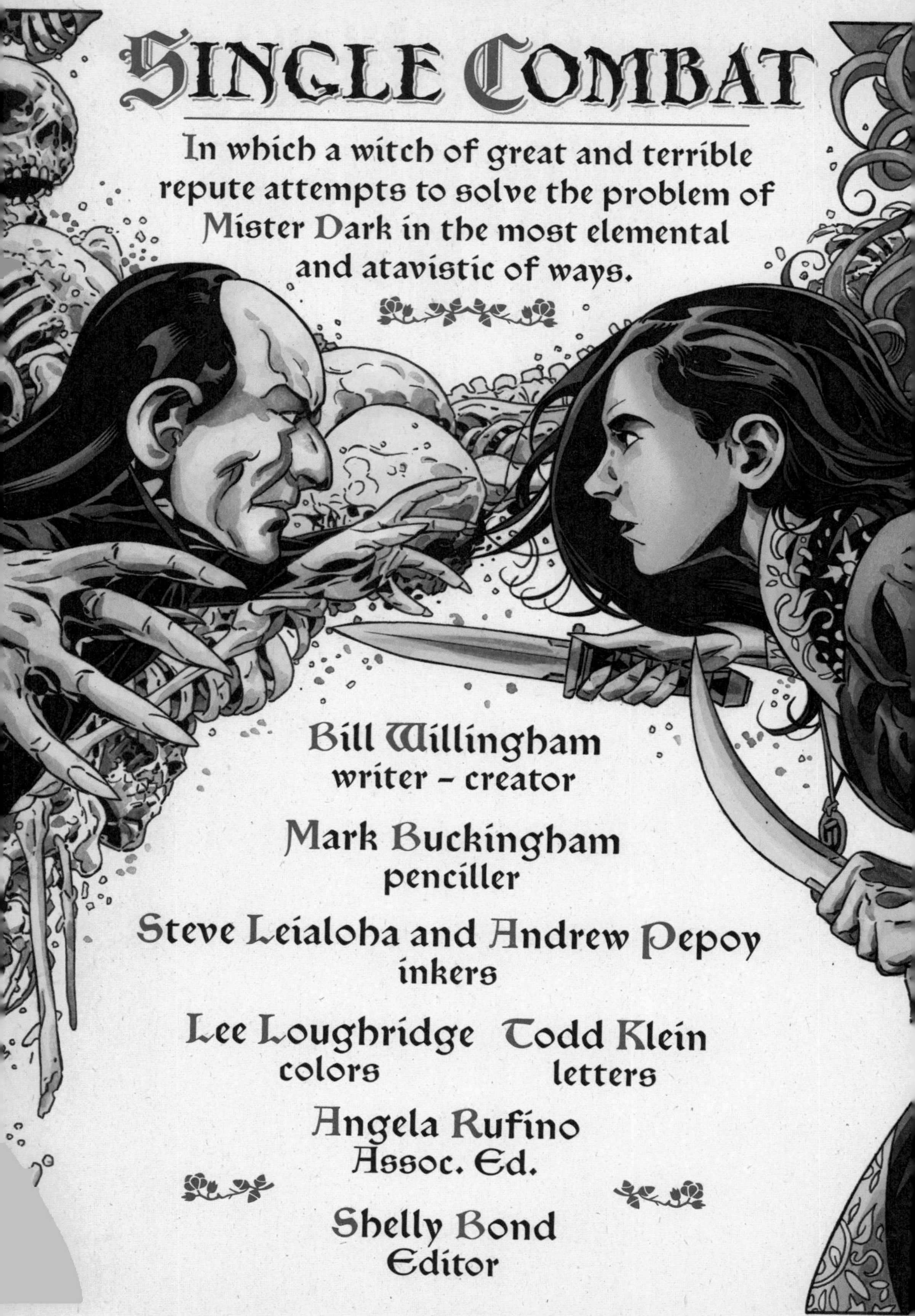

SINGLE COMBAT
In which a witch of great and terrible repute attempts to solve the problem of Mister Dark in the most elemental and atavistic of ways.
Bill Willingham
writer – creator
Mark Buckingham
penciller
Steve Leialoha and Andrew Pepoy
inkers
Lee Loughridge
colors
Todd Klein
letters
Angela Rufino
Assoc. Ed.
Shelly Bond
Editor

Chapter One: Dust in the Wind

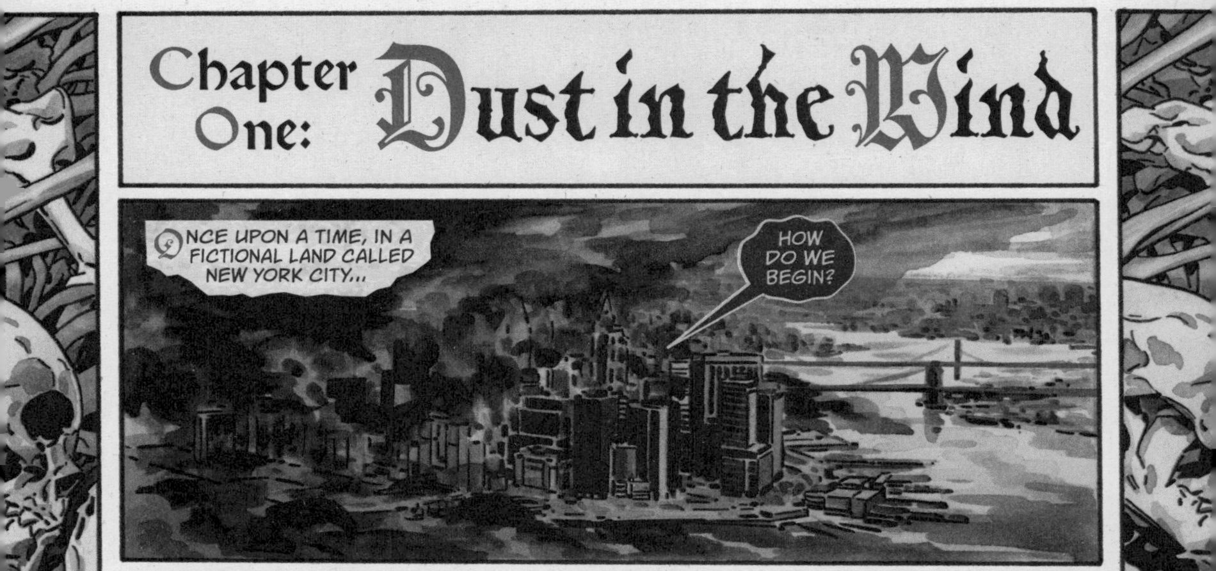
ONCE UPON A TIME, IN A FICTIONAL LAND CALLED NEW YORK CITY...
HOW DO WE BEGIN?

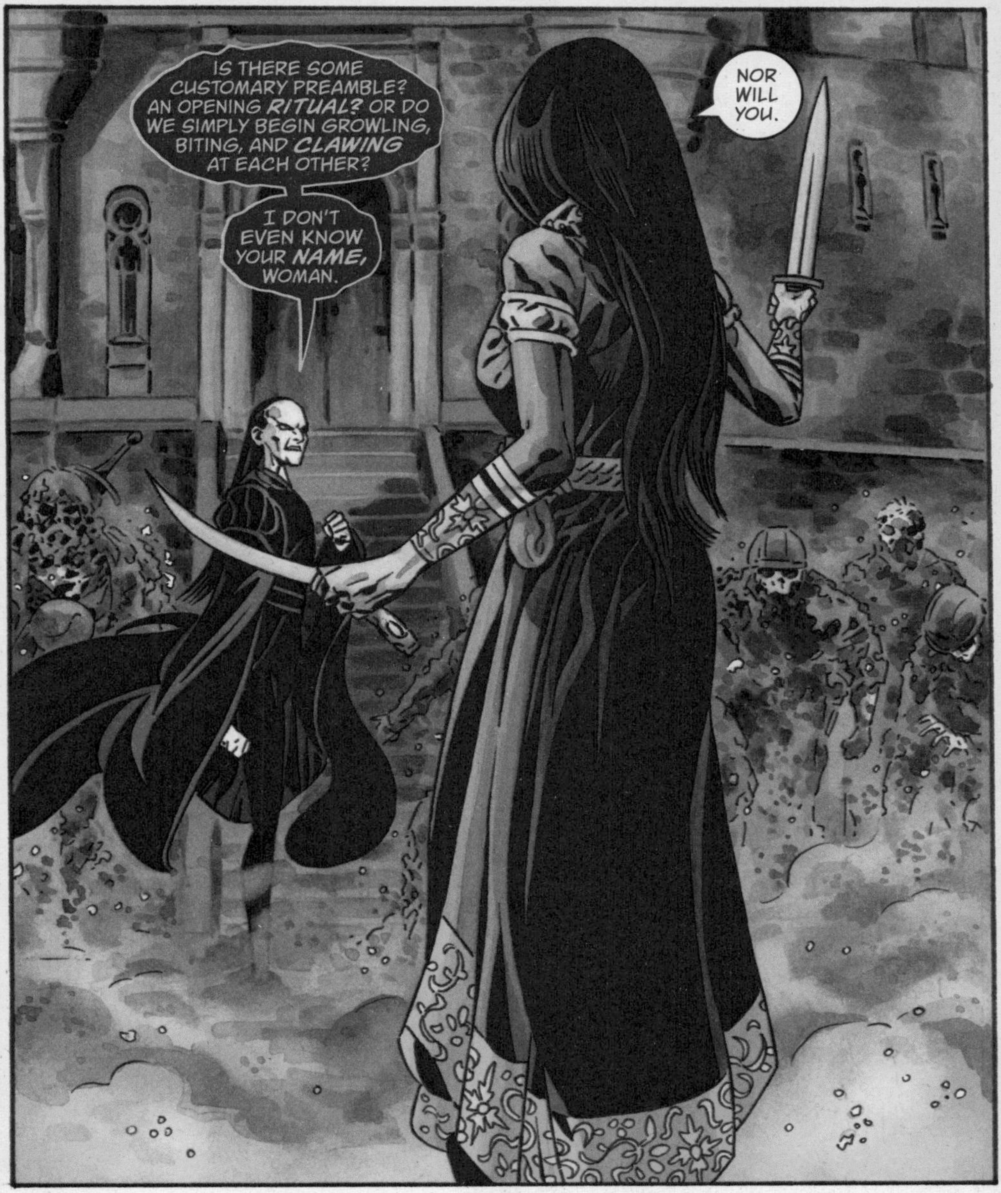
IS THERE SOME CUSTOMARY PREAMBLE? AN OPENING RITUAL? OR DO WE SIMPLY BEGIN GROWLING, BITING, AND CLAWING AT EACH OTHER?
I DON'T EVEN KNOW YOUR NAME, WOMAN.
NOR WILL YOU.

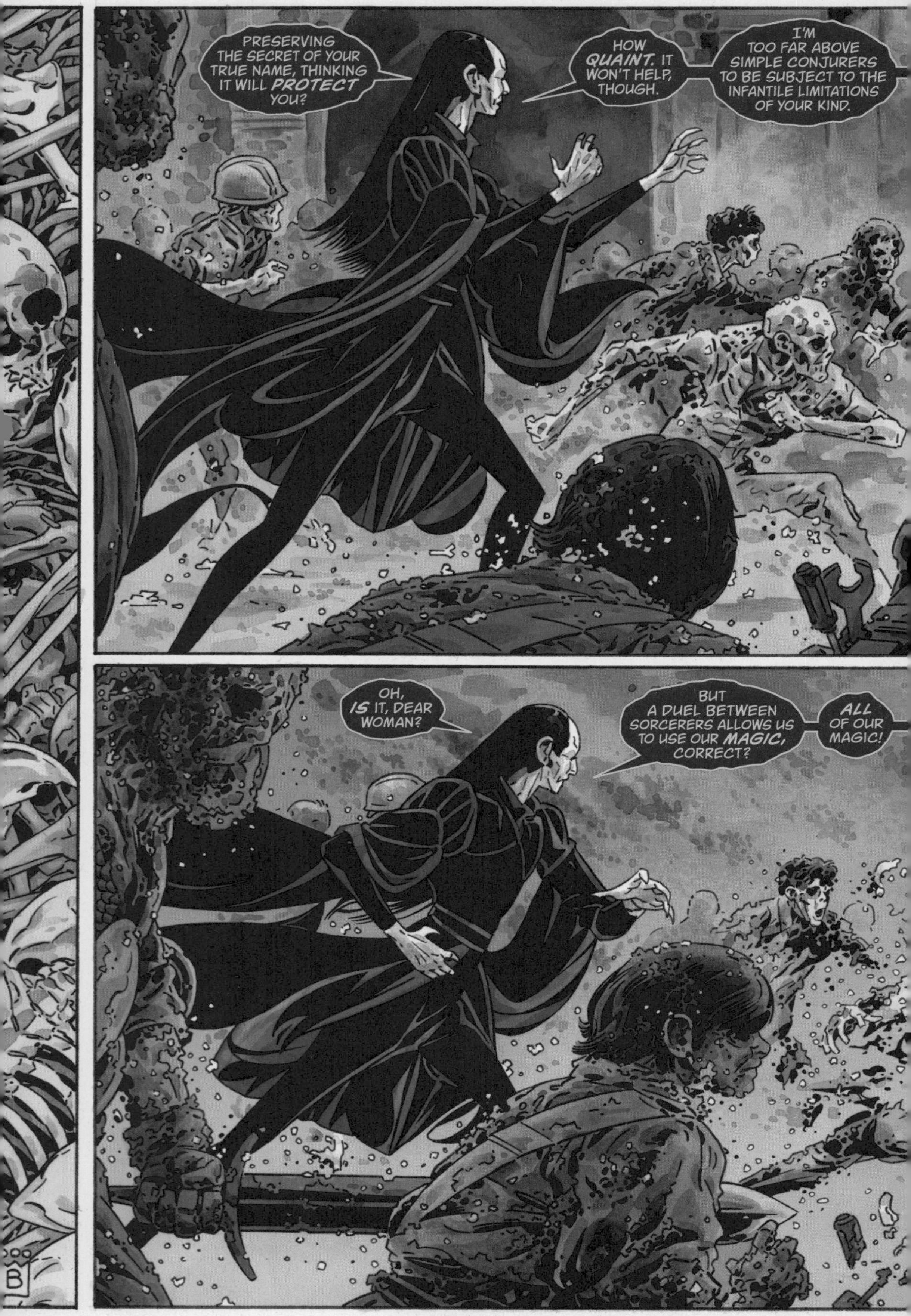
PRESERVING THE SECRET OF YOUR TRUE NAME, THINKING IT WILL PROTECT YOU?
HOW QUAINT. IT WON'T HELP, THOUGH.
I'M TOO FAR ABOVE SIMPLE CONJURERS TO BE SUBJECT TO THE INFANTILE LIMITATIONS OF YOUR KIND.
OH, IS IT, DEAR WOMAN?
BUT A DUEL BETWEEN SORCERERS ALLOWS US TO USE OUR MAGIC, CORRECT?
ALL OF OUR MAGIC!

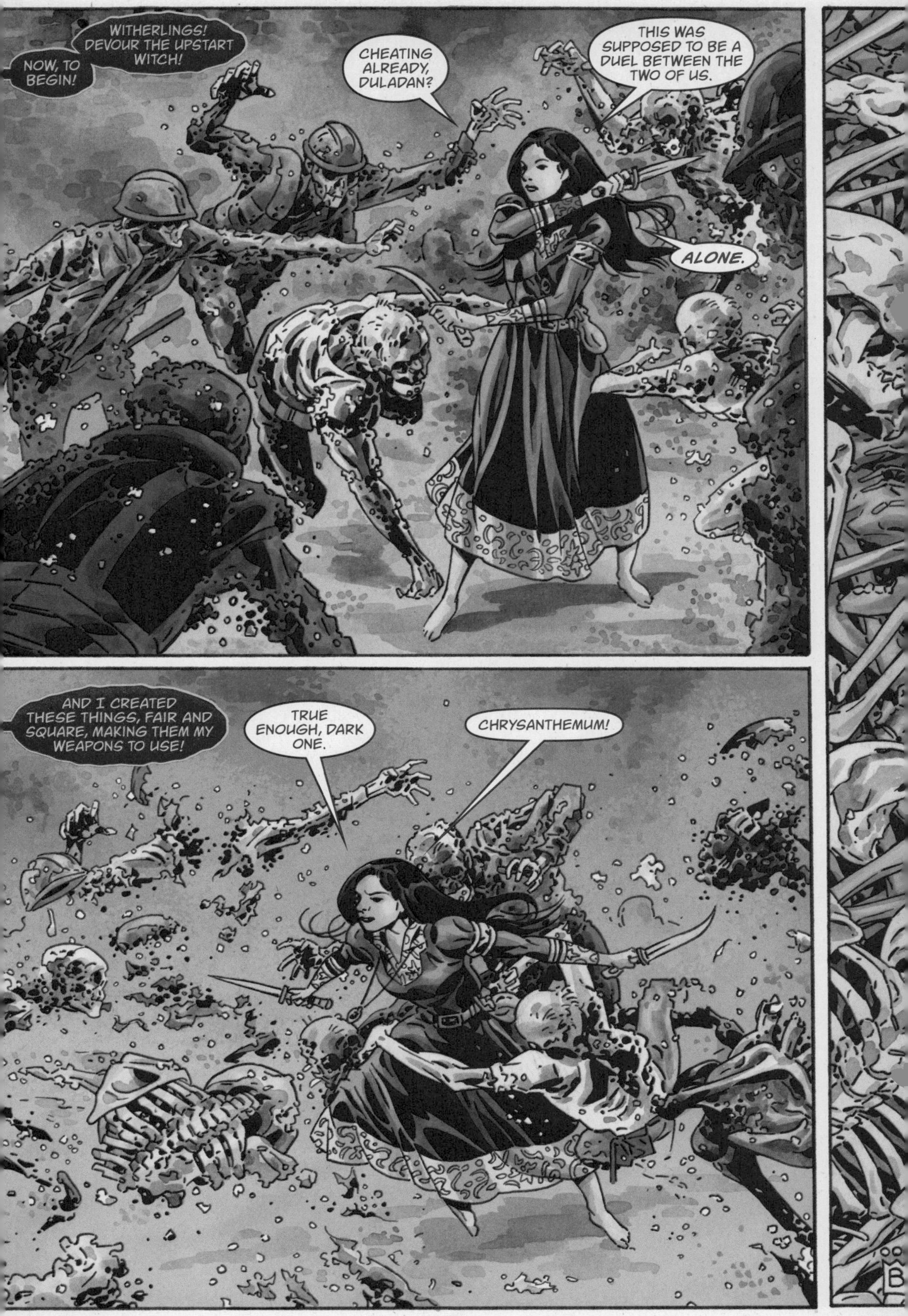
NOW, TO BEGIN!
WITHERLINGS! DEVOUR THE UPSTART WITCH!
CHEATING ALREADY, DULADAN?
THIS WAS SUPPOSED TO BE A DUEL BETWEEN THE TWO OF US.
ALONE.
AND I CREATED THESE THINGS, FAIR AND SQUARE, MAKING THEM MY WEAPONS TO USE!
TRUE ENOUGH, DARK ONE.
CHRYSANTHEMUM!

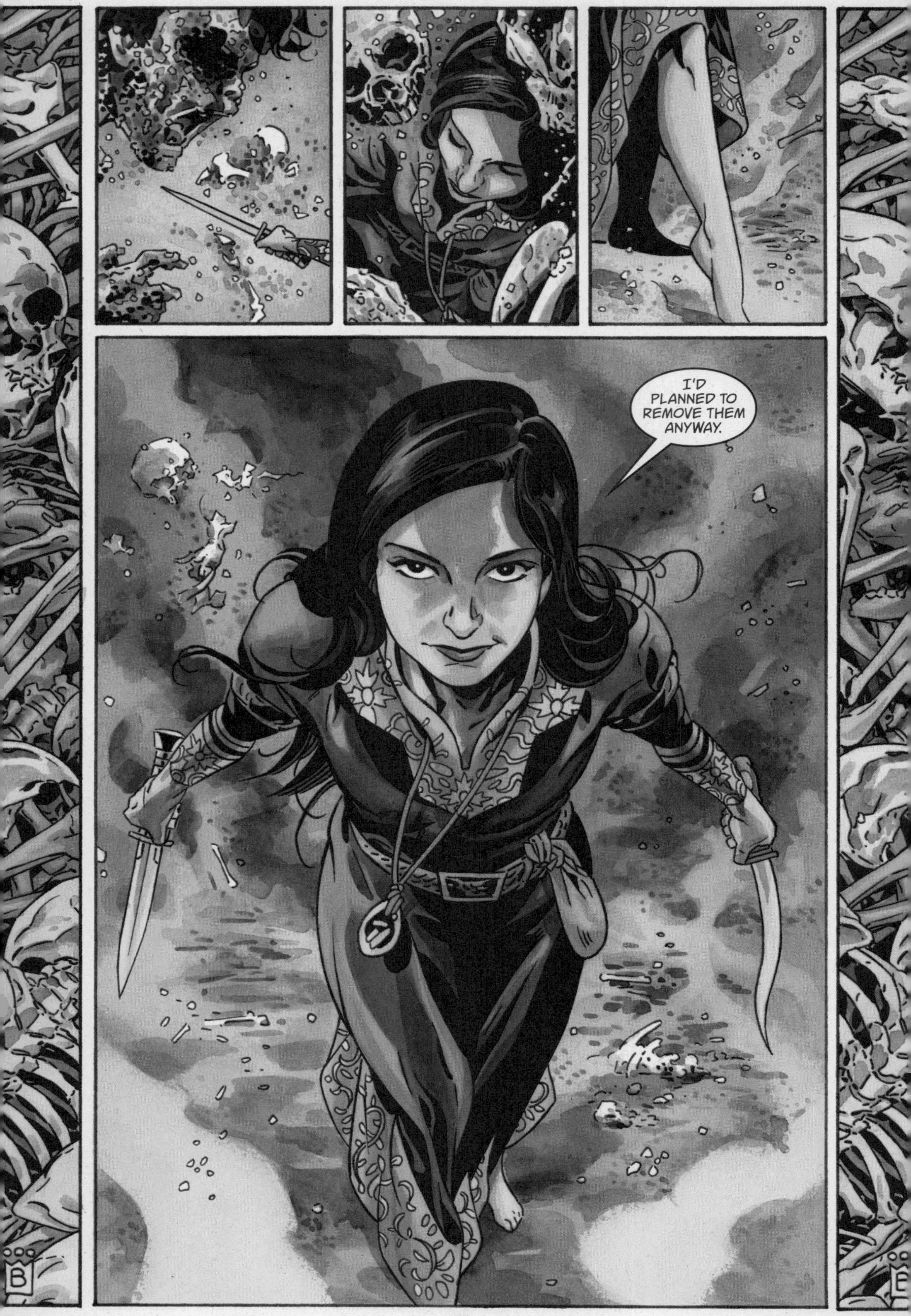
I'D PLANNED TO REMOVE THEM ANYWAY.

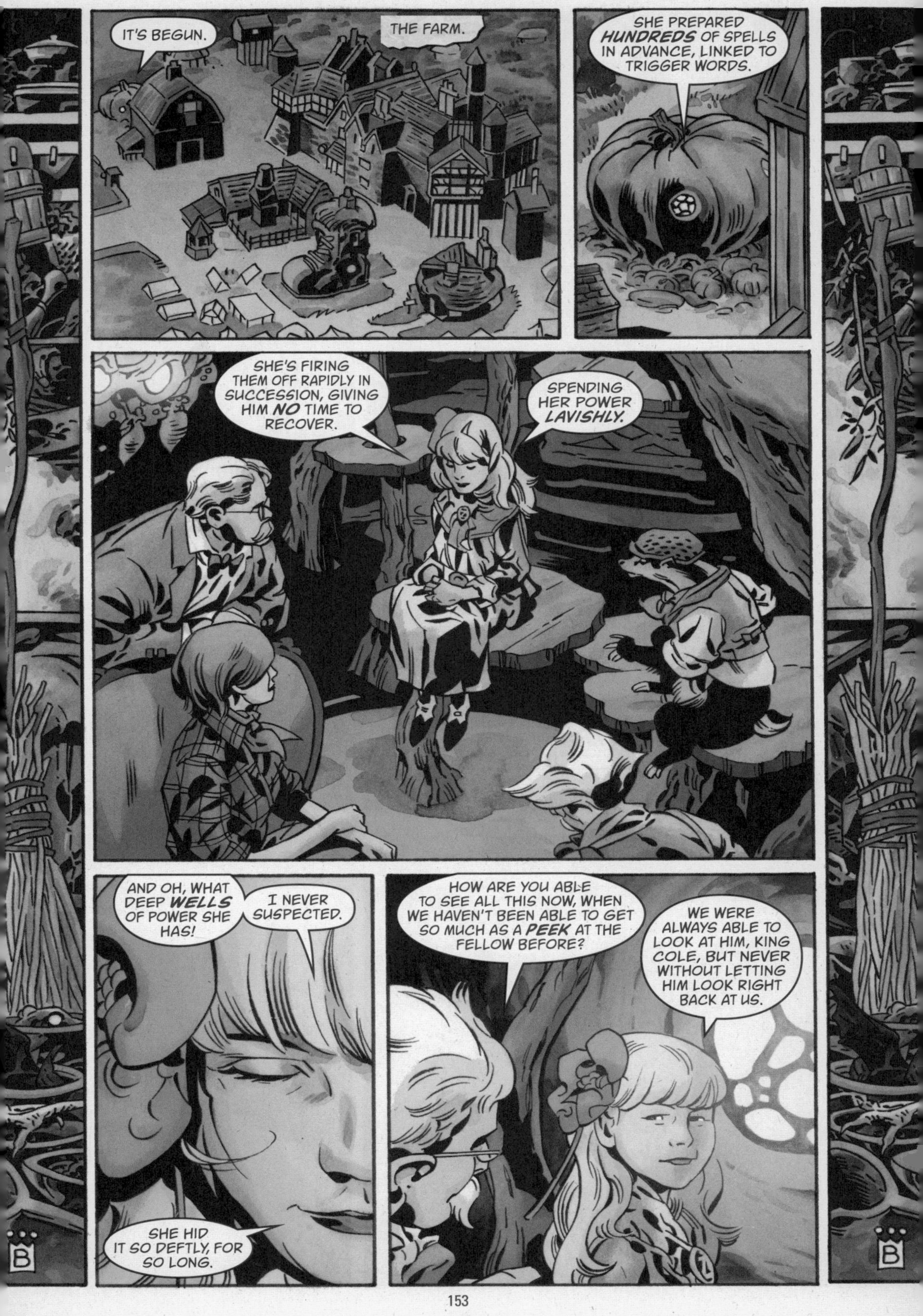
IT'S BEGUN.
THE FARM.
SHE PREPARED HUNDREDS OF SPELLS IN ADVANCE, LINKED TO TRIGGER WORDS.
SHE'S FIRING THEM OFF RAPIDLY IN SUCCESSION, GIVING HIM NO TIME TO RECOVER.
SPENDING HER POWER LAVISHLY.
AND OH, WHAT DEEP WELLS OF POWER SHE HAS!
I NEVER SUSPECTED.
SHE HID IT SO DEFTLY, FOR SO LONG.
HOW ARE YOU ABLE TO SEE ALL THIS NOW, WHEN WE HAVEN'T BEEN ABLE TO GET SO MUCH AS A PEEK AT THE FELLOW BEFORE?
WE WERE ALWAYS ABLE TO LOOK AT HIM, KING COLE, BUT NEVER WITHOUT LETTING HIM LOOK RIGHT BACK AT US.

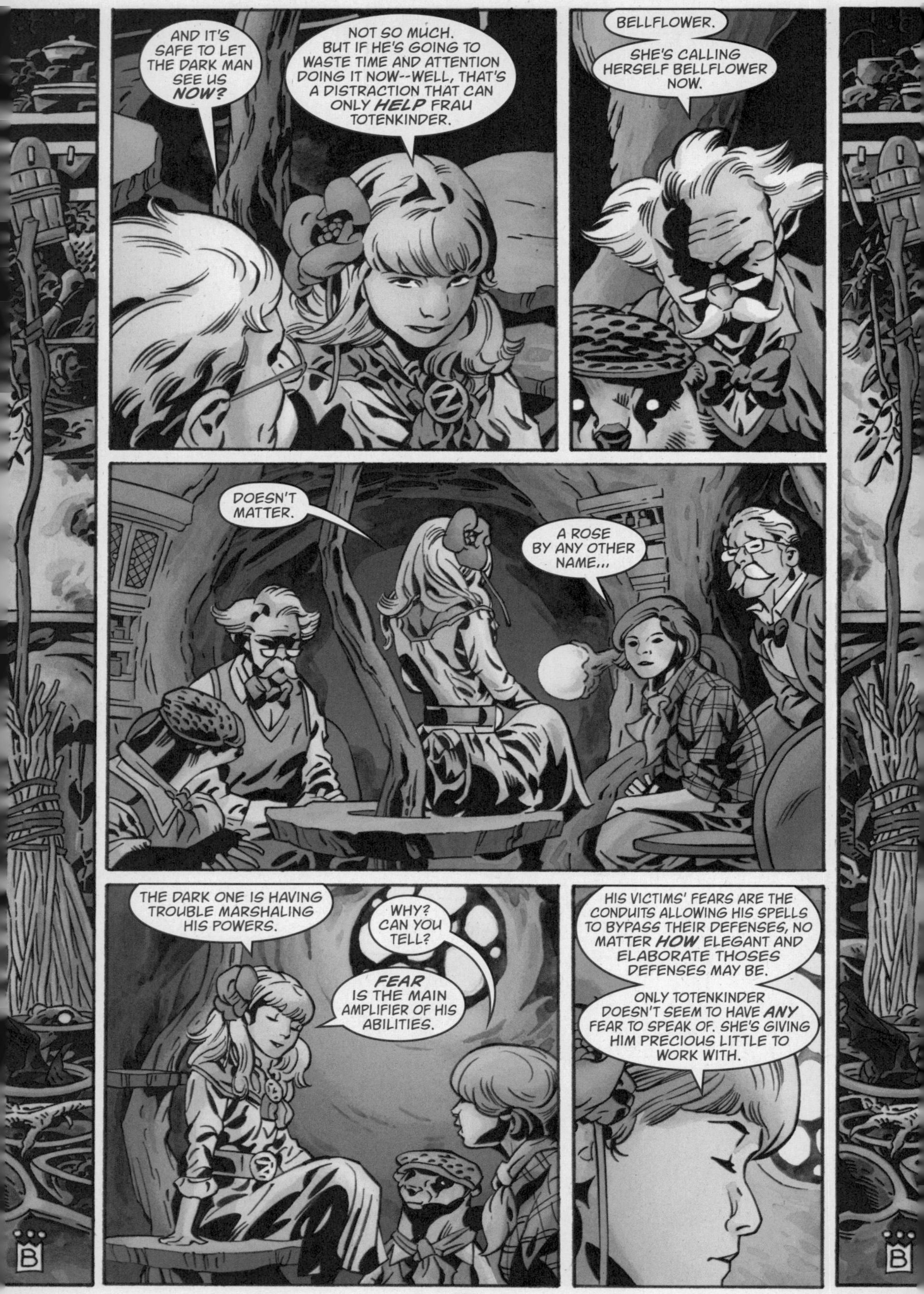
AND IT'S SAFE TO LET THE DARK MAN SEE US NOW?
NOT SO MUCH. BUT IF HE'S GOING TO WASTE TIME AND ATTENTION DOING IT NOW--WELL, THAT'S A DISTRACTION THAT CAN ONLY HELP FRAU TOTENKINDER.
BELLFLOWER.
SHE'S CALLING HERSELF BELLFLOWER NOW.
DOESN'T MATTER.
A ROSE BY ANY OTHER NAME...
THE DARK ONE IS HAVING TROUBLE MARSHALING HIS POWERS.
WHY? CAN YOU TELL?
FEAR IS THE MAIN AMPLIFIER OF HIS ABILITIES.
HIS VICTIMS' FEARS ARE THE CONDUITS ALLOWING HIS SPELLS TO BYPASS THEIR DEFENSES, NO MATTER HOW ELEGANT AND ELABORATE THOSES DEFENSES MAY BE.
ONLY TOTENKINDER DOESN'T SEEM TO HAVE ANY FEAR TO SPEAK OF. SHE'S GIVING HIM PRECIOUS LITTLE TO WORK WITH.

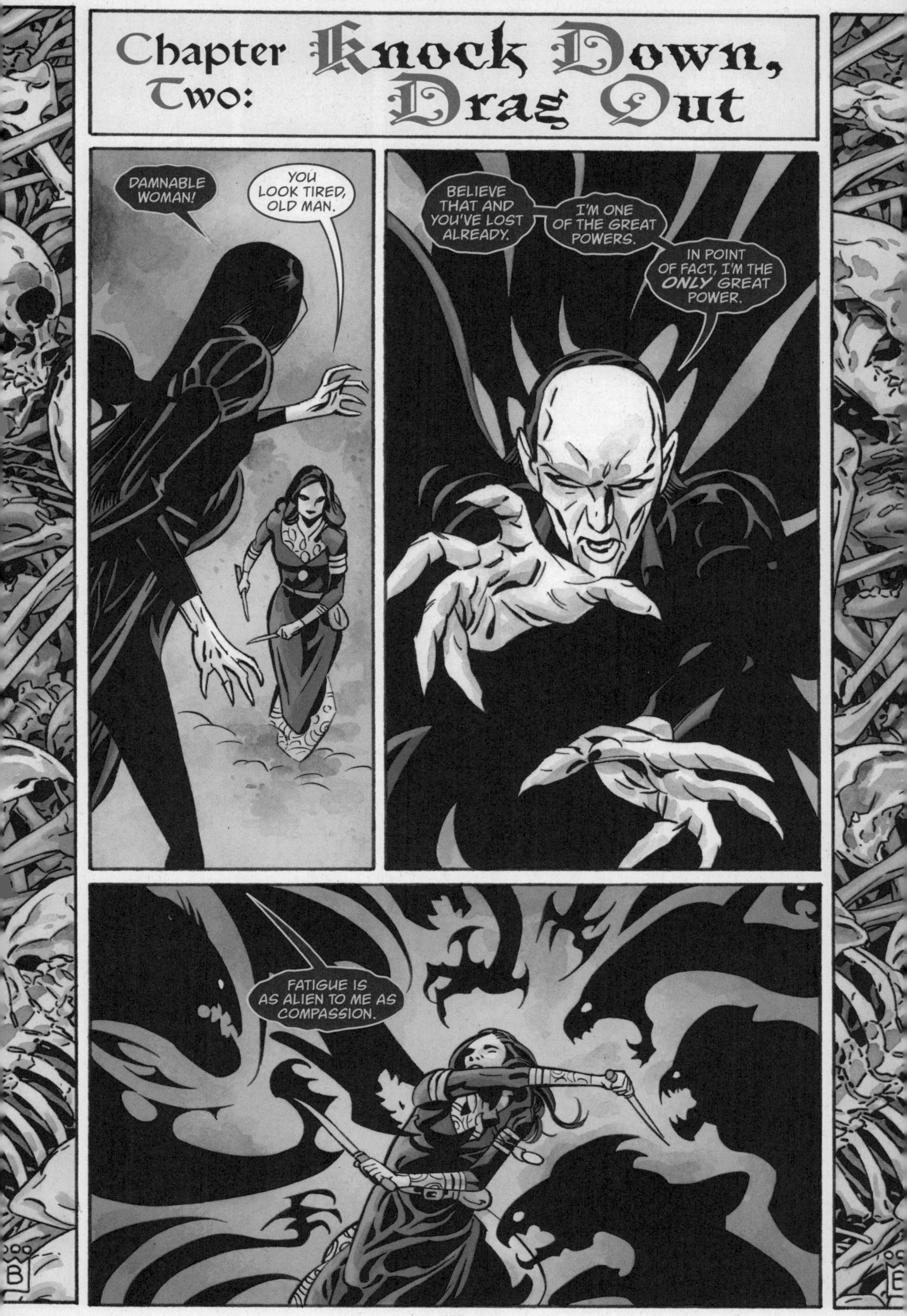
Chapter Two: Knock Down, Drag Out
DAMNABLE WOMAN!
YOU LOOK TIRED, OLD MAN.
BELIEVE THAT AND YOU'VE LOST ALREADY.
I'M ONE OF THE GREAT POWERS.
IN POINT OF FACT, I'M THE ONLY GREAT POWER.
FATIGUE IS AS ALIEN TO ME AS COMPASSION.

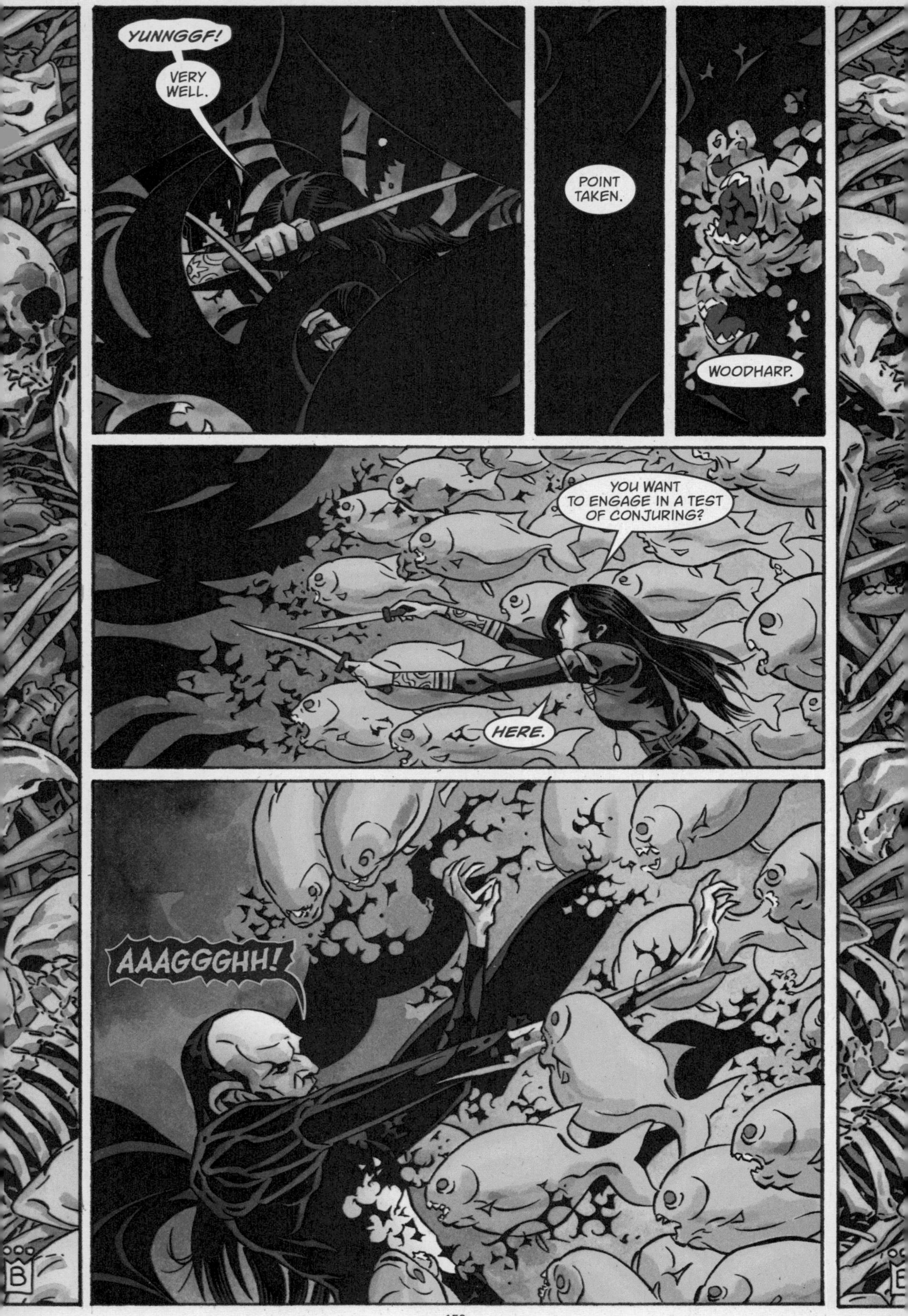
YUNNGGF!
VERY WELL.
POINT TAKEN.
WOODHARP.
YOU WANT TO ENGAGE IN A TEST OF CONJURING?
HERE.
AAAGGGHH!

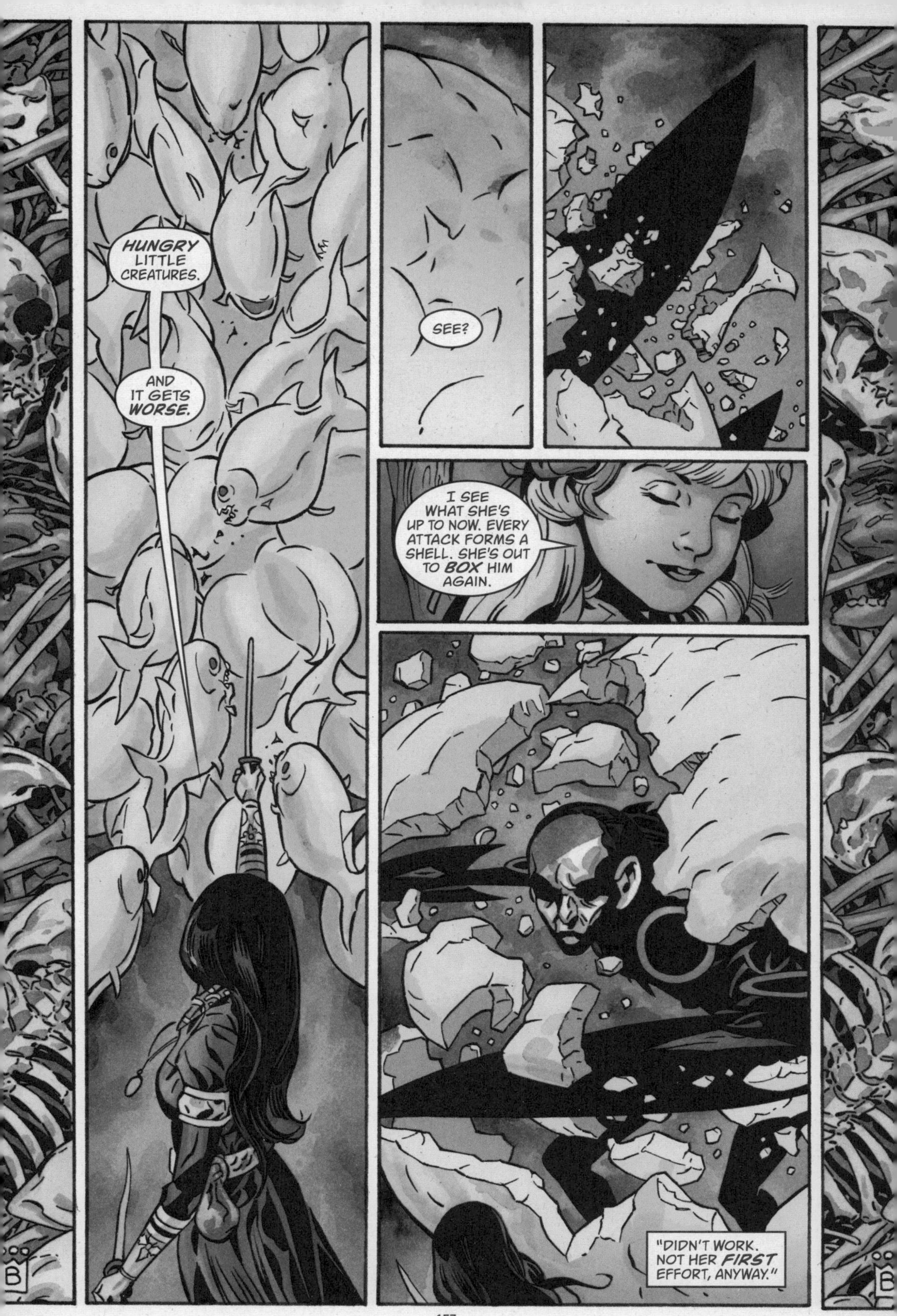

HUNGRY LITTLE CREATURES.
AND IT GETS WORSE.
SEE?
I SEE WHAT SHE'S UP TO NOW. EVERY ATTACK FORMS A SHELL. SHE'S OUT TO BOX HIM AGAIN.
"DIDN'T WORK. NOT HER FIRST EFFORT, ANYWAY."

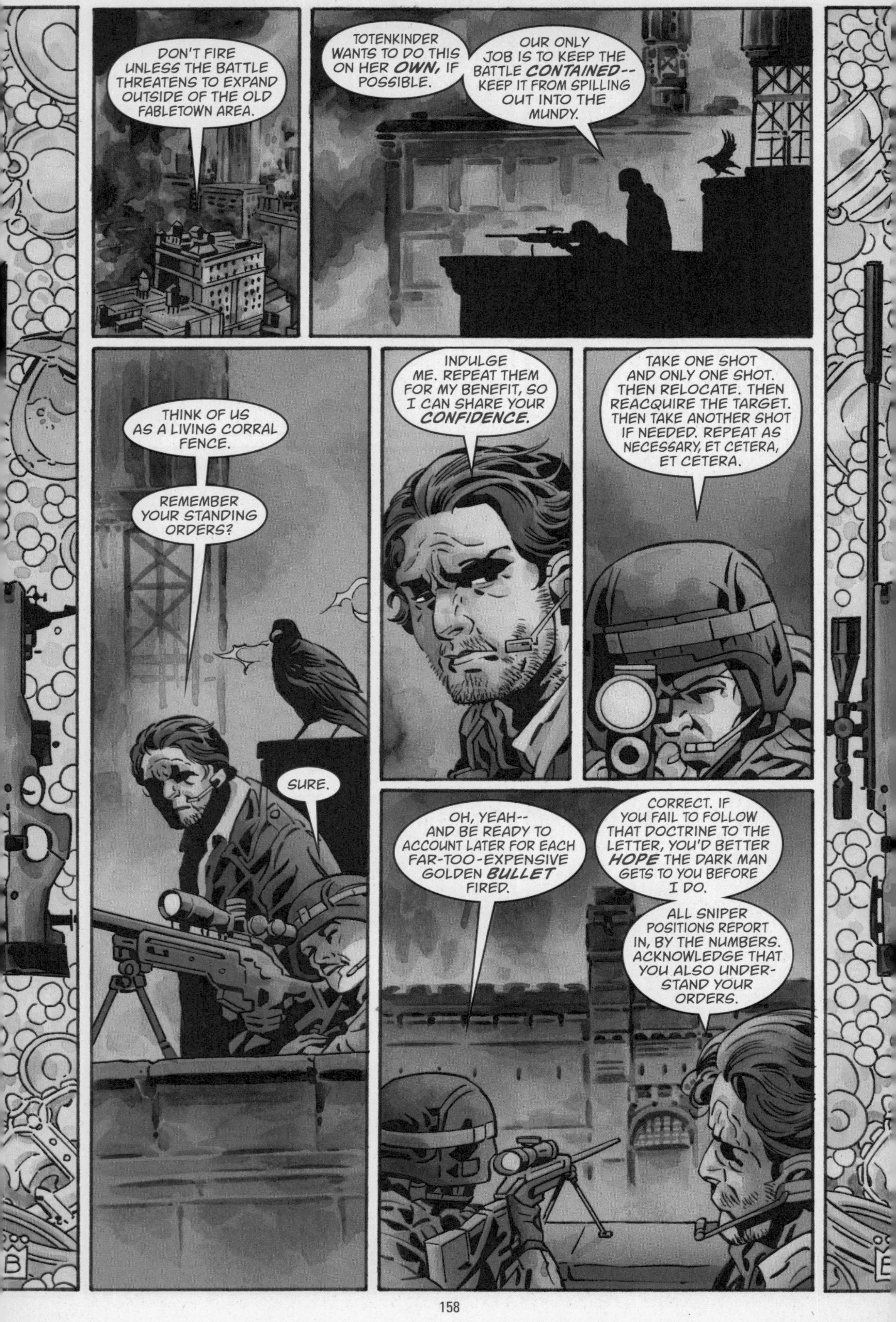
DON'T FIRE UNLESS THE BATTLE THREATENS TO EXPAND OUTSIDE OF THE OLD FABLETOWN AREA.
TOTENKINDER WANTS TO DO THIS ON HER OWN, IF POSSIBLE.
OUR ONLY JOB IS TO KEEP THE BATTLE CONTAINED-- KEEP IT FROM SPILLING OUT INTO THE MUNDY.
THINK OF US AS A LIVING CORRAL FENCE.
REMEMBER YOUR STANDING ORDERS?
SURE.
INDULGE ME. REPEAT THEM FOR MY BENEFIT, SO I CAN SHARE YOUR CONFIDENCE.
TAKE ONE SHOT AND ONLY ONE SHOT. THEN RELOCATE. THEN REACQUIRE THE TARGET. THEN TAKE ANOTHER SHOT IF NEEDED. REPEAT AS NECESSARY, ET CETERA, ET CETERA.
OH, YEAH-- AND BE READY TO ACCOUNT LATER FOR EACH FAR-TOO-EXPENSIVE GOLDEN BULLET FIRED.
CORRECT. IF YOU FAIL TO FOLLOW THAT DOCTRINE TO THE LETTER, YOU'D BETTER HOPE THE DARK MAN GETS TO YOU BEFORE I DO.
ALL SNIPER POSITIONS REPORT IN, BY THE NUMBERS. ACKNOWLEDGE THAT YOU ALSO UNDERSTAND YOUR ORDERS.

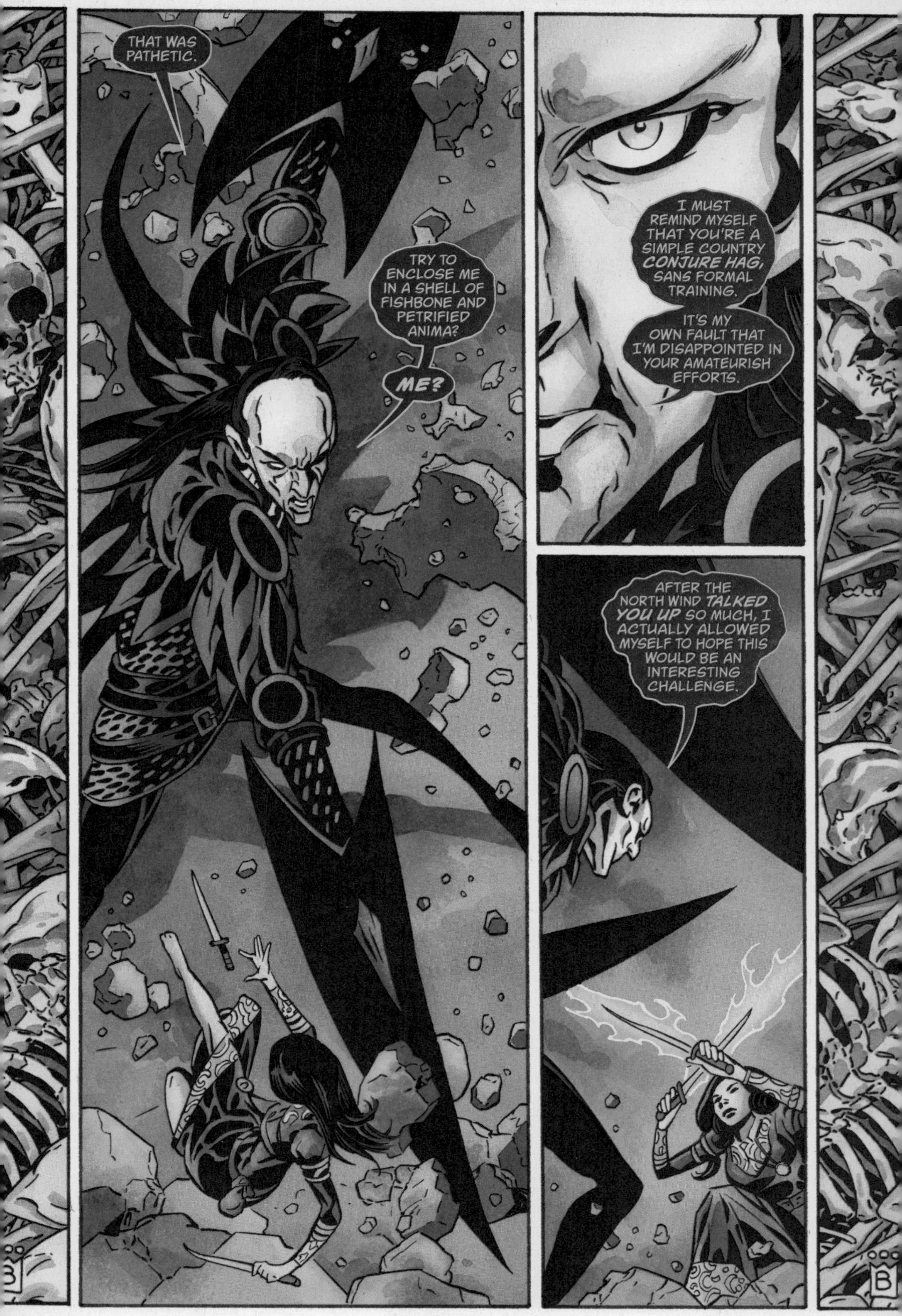
THAT WAS PATHETIC.
TRY TO ENCLOSE ME IN A SHELL OF FISHBONE AND PETRIFIED ANIMA?
ME?
I MUST REMIND MYSELF THAT YOU'RE A SIMPLE COUNTRY CONJURE HAG, SANS FORMAL TRAINING.
IT'S MY OWN FAULT THAT I'M DISAPPOINTED IN YOUR AMATEURISH EFFORTS.
AFTER THE NORTH WIND TALKED YOU UP SO MUCH, I ACTUALLY ALLOWED MYSELF TO HOPE THIS WOULD BE AN INTERESTING CHALLENGE.

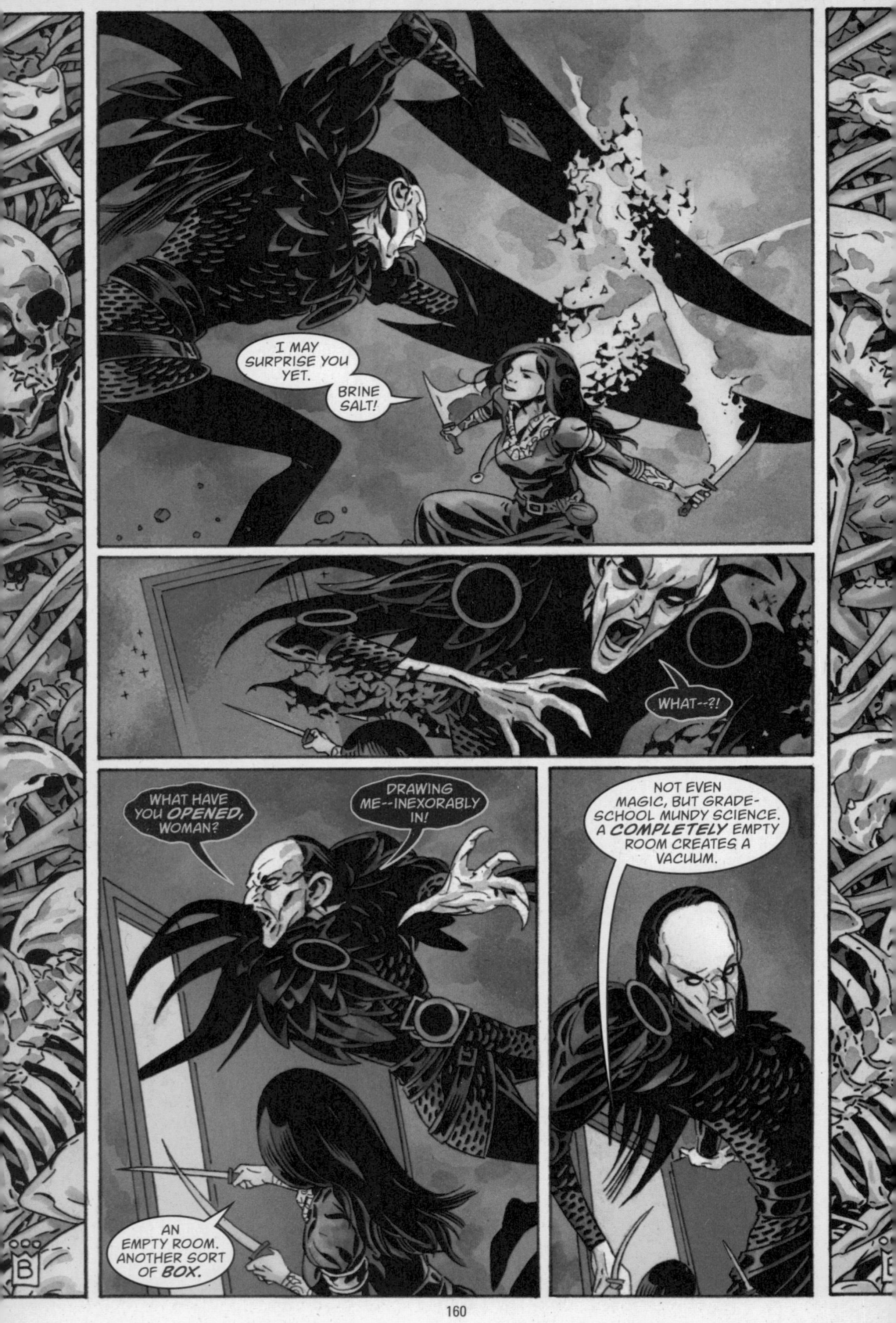
I MAY SURPRISE YOU YET.
BRINE SALT!
WHAT--?!
WHAT HAVE YOU OPENED, WOMAN?
DRAWING ME--INEXORABLY IN!
AN EMPTY ROOM. ANOTHER SORT OF BOX.
NOT EVEN MAGIC, BUT GRADE-SCHOOL MUNDY SCIENCE. A COMPLETELY EMPTY ROOM CREATES A VACUUM.

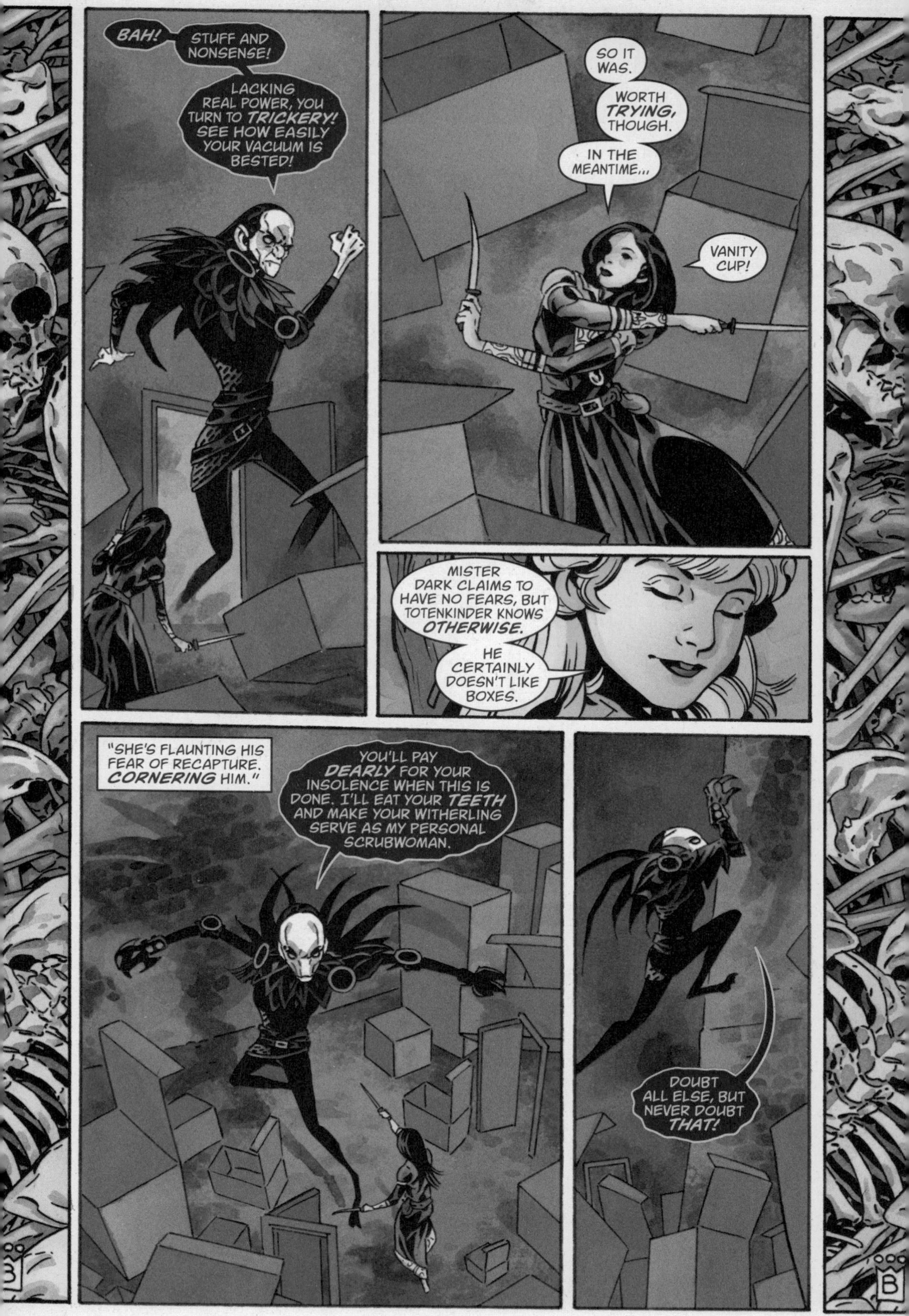
BAH!
STUFF AND NONSENSE!
LACKING REAL POWER, YOU TURN TO TRICKERY! SEE HOW EASILY YOUR VACUUM IS BESTED!
SO IT WAS.
WORTH TRYING, THOUGH.
IN THE MEANTIME...
VANITY CUP!
MISTER DARK CLAIMS TO HAVE NO FEARS, BUT TOTENKINDER KNOWS OTHERWISE.
HE CERTAINLY DOESN'T LIKE BOXES.
"SHE'S FLAUNTING HIS FEAR OF RECAPTURE. CORNERING HIM."
YOU'LL PAY DEARLY FOR YOUR INSOLENCE WHEN THIS IS DONE. I'LL EAT YOUR TEETH AND MAKE YOUR WITHERLING SERVE AS MY PERSONAL SCRUBWOMAN.
DOUBT ALL ELSE, BUT NEVER DOUBT THAT!

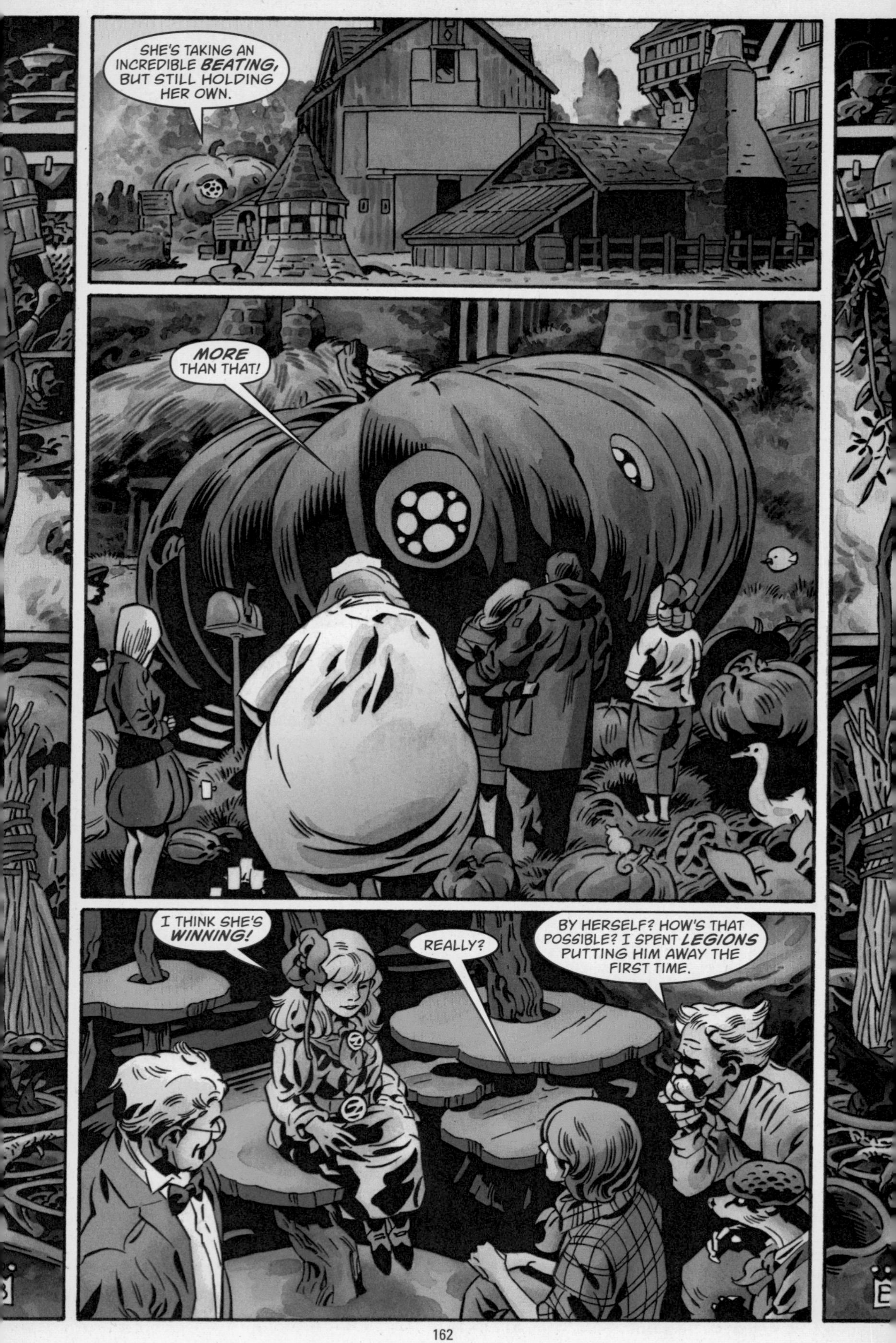
SHE'S TAKING AN INCREDIBLE BEATING, BUT STILL HOLDING HER OWN.
MORE THAN THAT!
I THINK SHE'S WINNING!
REALLY?
BY HERSELF? HOW'S THAT POSSIBLE? I SPENT LEGIONS PUTTING HIM AWAY THE FIRST TIME.

Chapter Three: The Labor Party

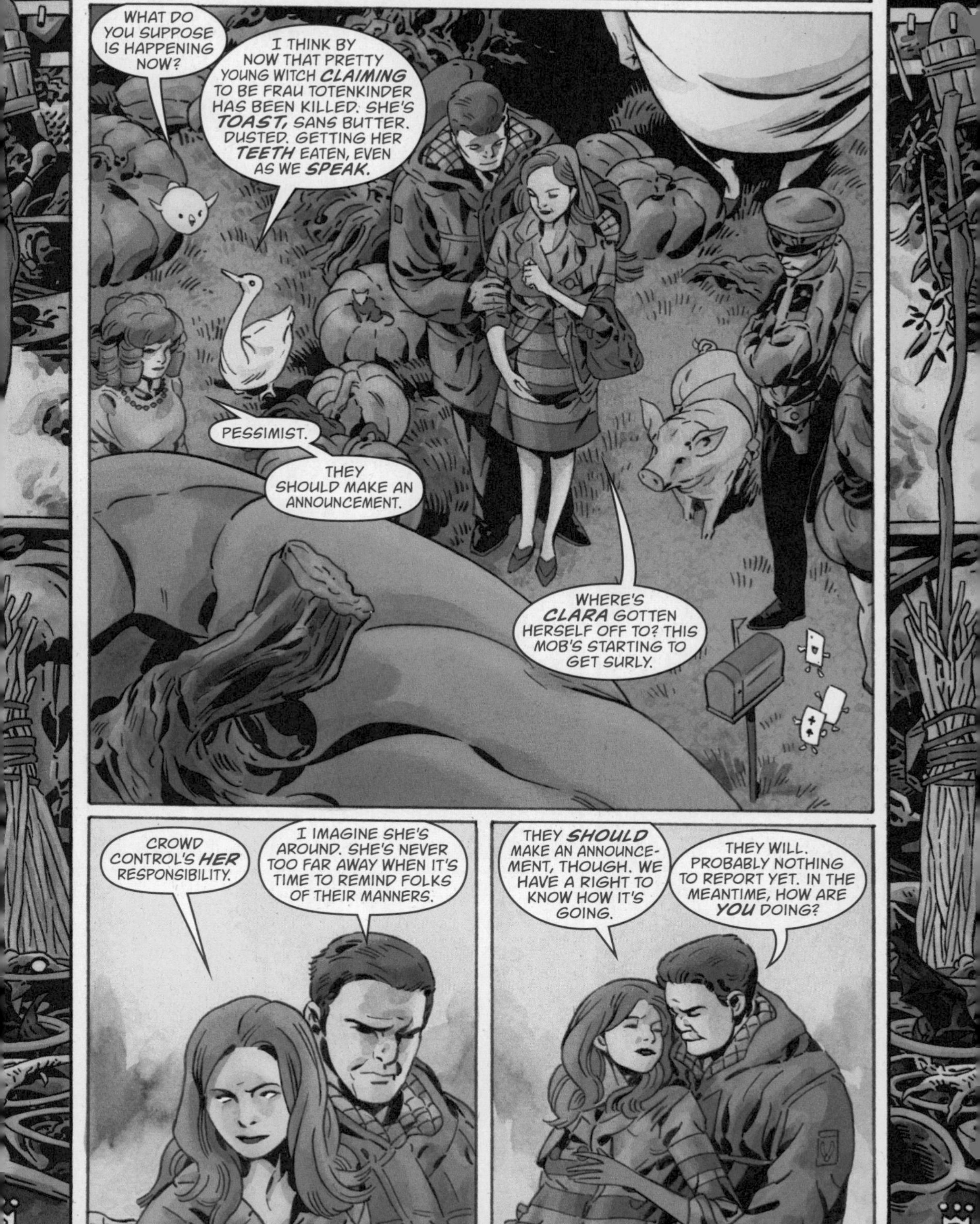
WHAT DO YOU SUPPOSE IS HAPPENING NOW?
I THINK BY NOW THAT PRETTY YOUNG WITCH CLAIMING TO BE FRAU TOTENKINDER HAS BEEN KILLED. SHE'S TOAST, SANS BUTTER. DUSTED. GETTING HER TEETH EATEN, EVEN AS WE SPEAK.
PESSIMIST.
THEY SHOULD MAKE AN ANNOUNCEMENT.
WHERE'S CLARA GOTTEN HERSELF OFF TO? THIS MOB'S STARTING TO GET SURLY.
CROWD CONTROL'S HER RESPONSIBILITY.
I IMAGINE SHE'S AROUND. SHE'S NEVER TOO FAR AWAY WHEN IT'S TIME TO REMIND FOLKS OF THEIR MANNERS.
THEY SHOULD MAKE AN ANNOUNCEMENT, THOUGH. WE HAVE A RIGHT TO KNOW HOW IT'S GOING.
THEY WILL. PROBABLY NOTHING TO REPORT YET. IN THE MEANTIME, HOW ARE YOU DOING?

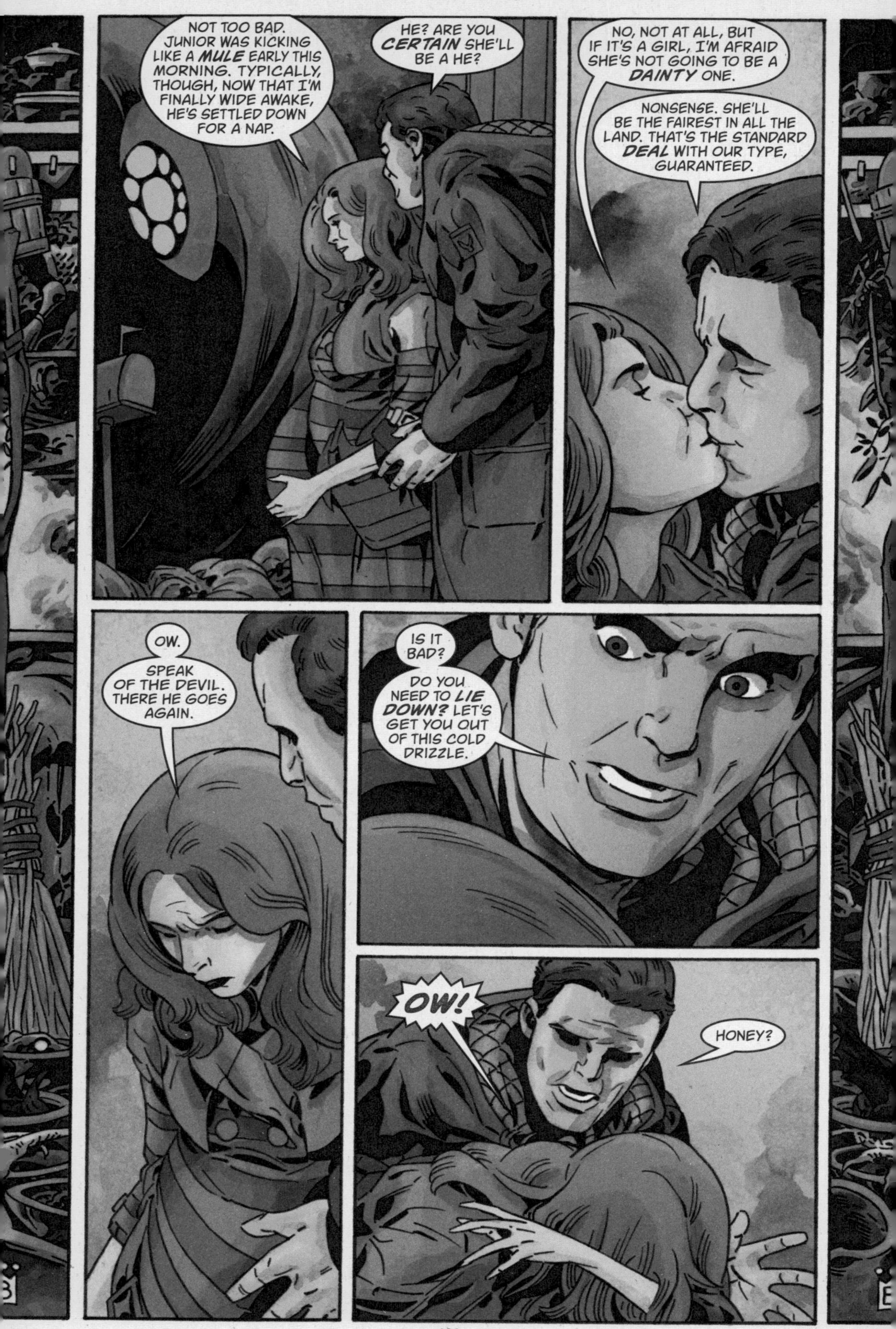
NOT TOO BAD. JUNIOR WAS KICKING LIKE A MULE EARLY THIS MORNING. TYPICALLY, THOUGH, NOW THAT I'M FINALLY WIDE AWAKE, HE'S SETTLED DOWN FOR A NAP.
HE? ARE YOU CERTAIN SHE'LL BE A HE?
NO, NOT AT ALL, BUT IF IT'S A GIRL, I'M AFRAID SHE'S NOT GOING TO BE A DAINTY ONE.
NONSENSE. SHE'LL BE THE FAIREST IN ALL THE LAND. THAT'S THE STANDARD DEAL WITH OUR TYPE, GUARANTEED.
OW.
SPEAK OF THE DEVIL. THERE HE GOES AGAIN.
IS IT BAD?
DO YOU NEED TO LIE DOWN? LET'S GET YOU OUT OF THIS COLD DRIZZLE.
OW!
HONEY?

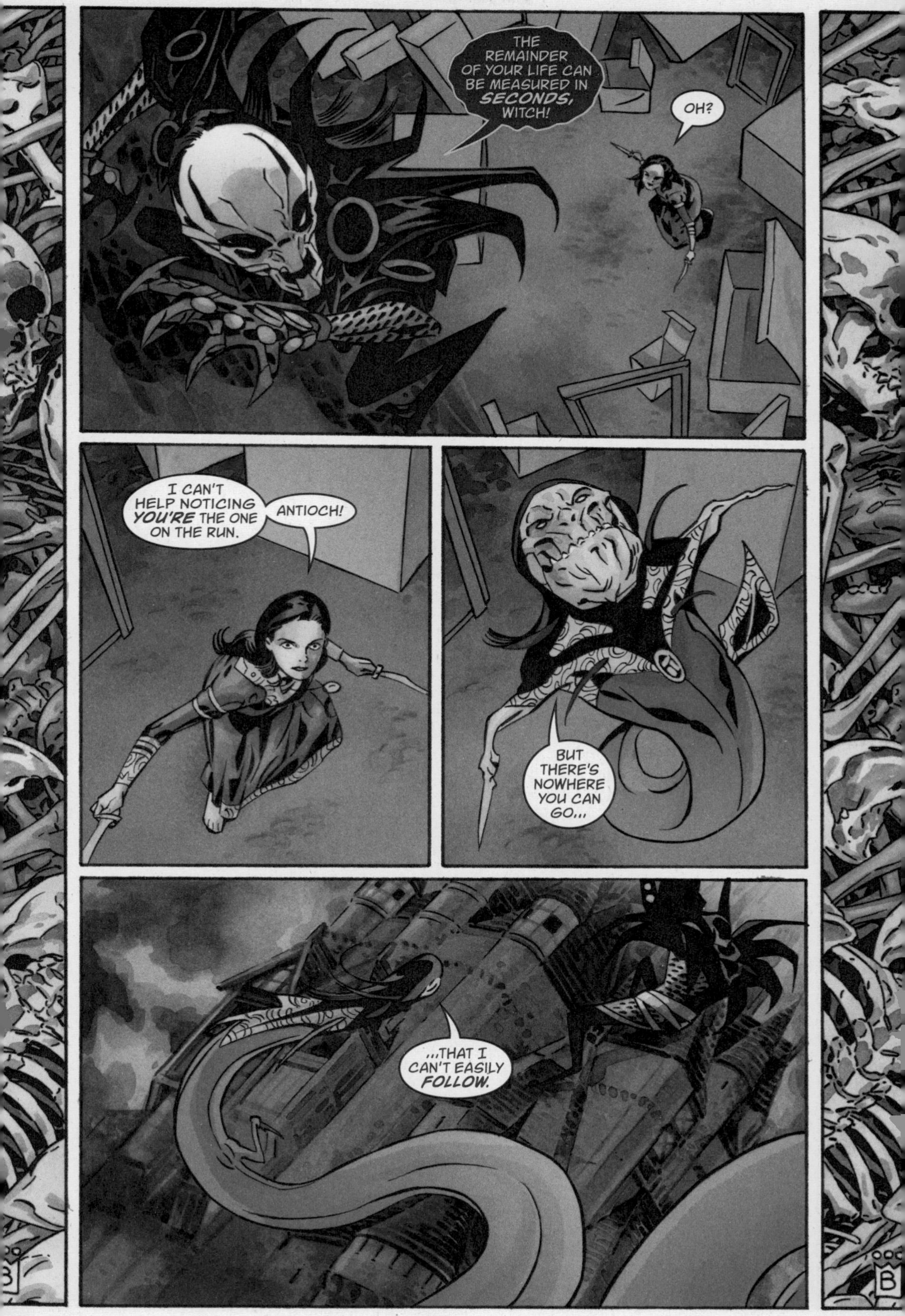
THE REMAINDER OF YOUR LIFE CAN BE MEASURED IN SECONDS, WITCH!
OH?
I CAN'T HELP NOTICING YOU'RE THE ONE ON THE RUN.
ANTIOCH!
BUT THERE'S NOWHERE YOU CAN GO...
...THAT I CAN'T EASILY FOLLOW.

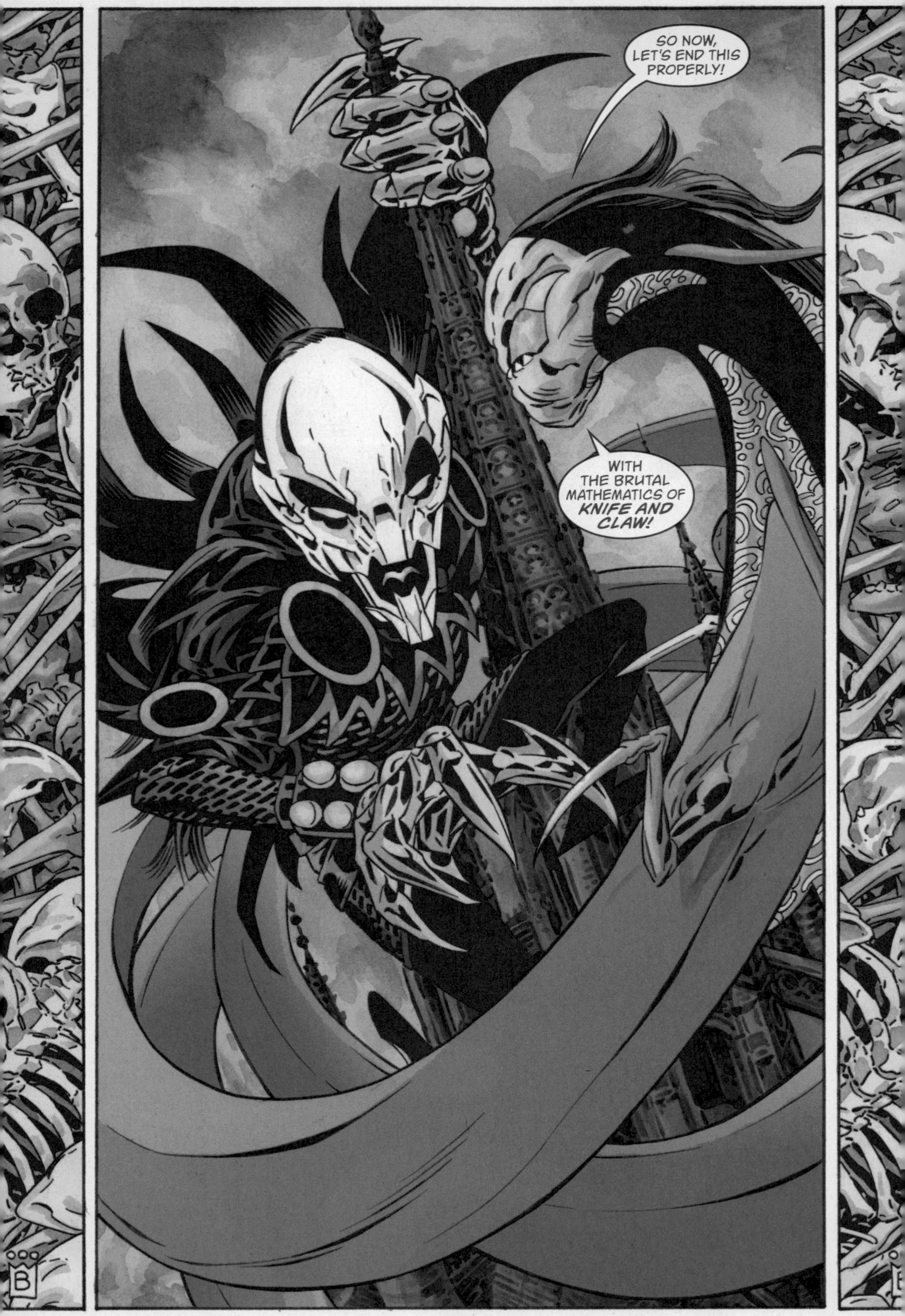
SO NOW, LET'S END THIS PROPERLY!
WITH THE BRUTAL MATHEMATICS OF KNIFE AND CLAW!

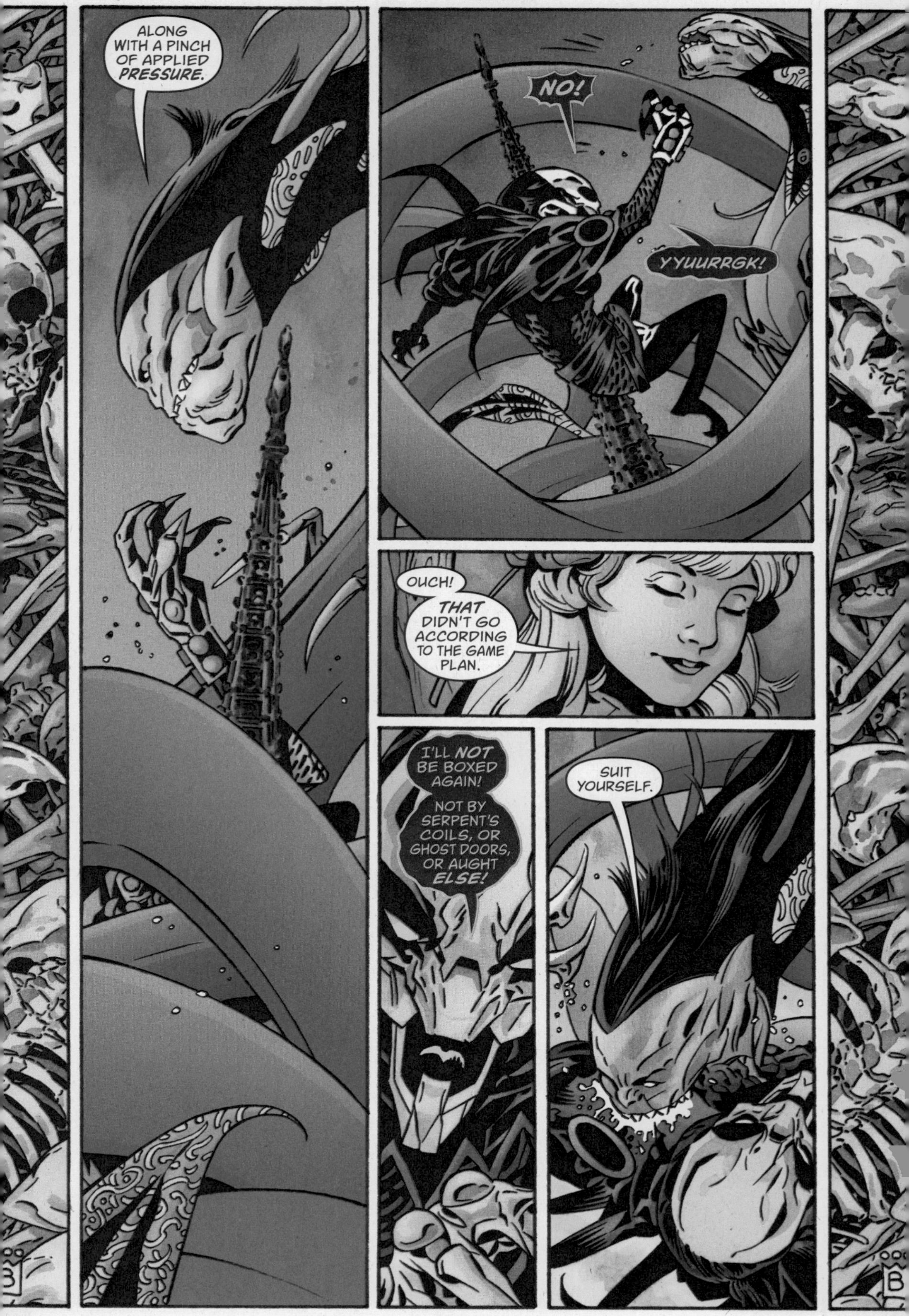
ALONG WITH A PINCH OF APPLIED PRESSURE.
NO!
YYUURRGK!
OUCH!
THAT DIDN'T GO ACCORDING TO THE GAME PLAN.
I'LL NOT BE BOXED AGAIN!
NOT BY SERPENT'S COILS, OR GHOST DOORS, OR AUGHT ELSE!
SUIT YOURSELF.

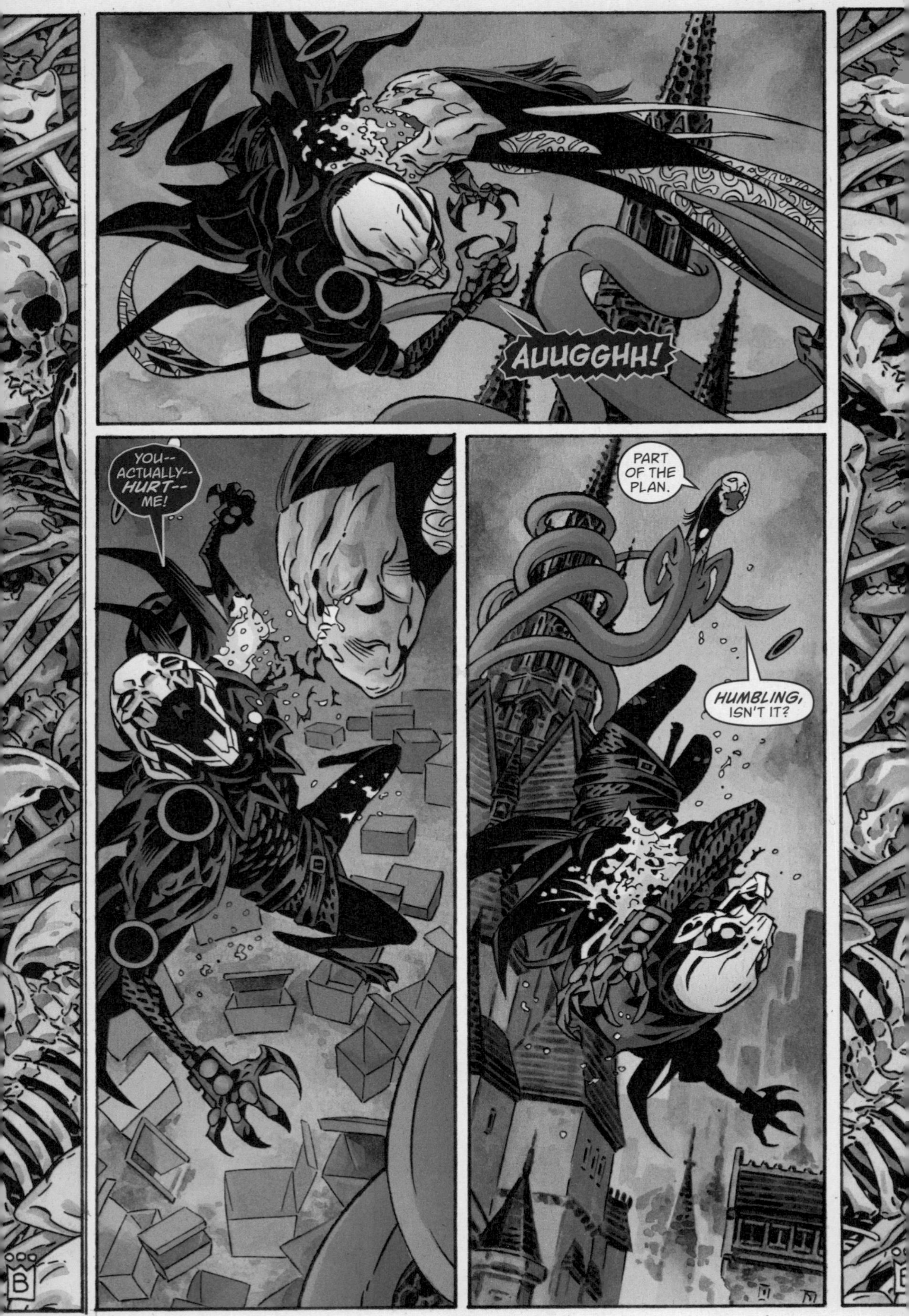
AUUGGHH!
YOU--
ACTUALLY--
HURT--
ME!
PART
OF THE
PLAN.
HUMBLING,
ISN'T IT?

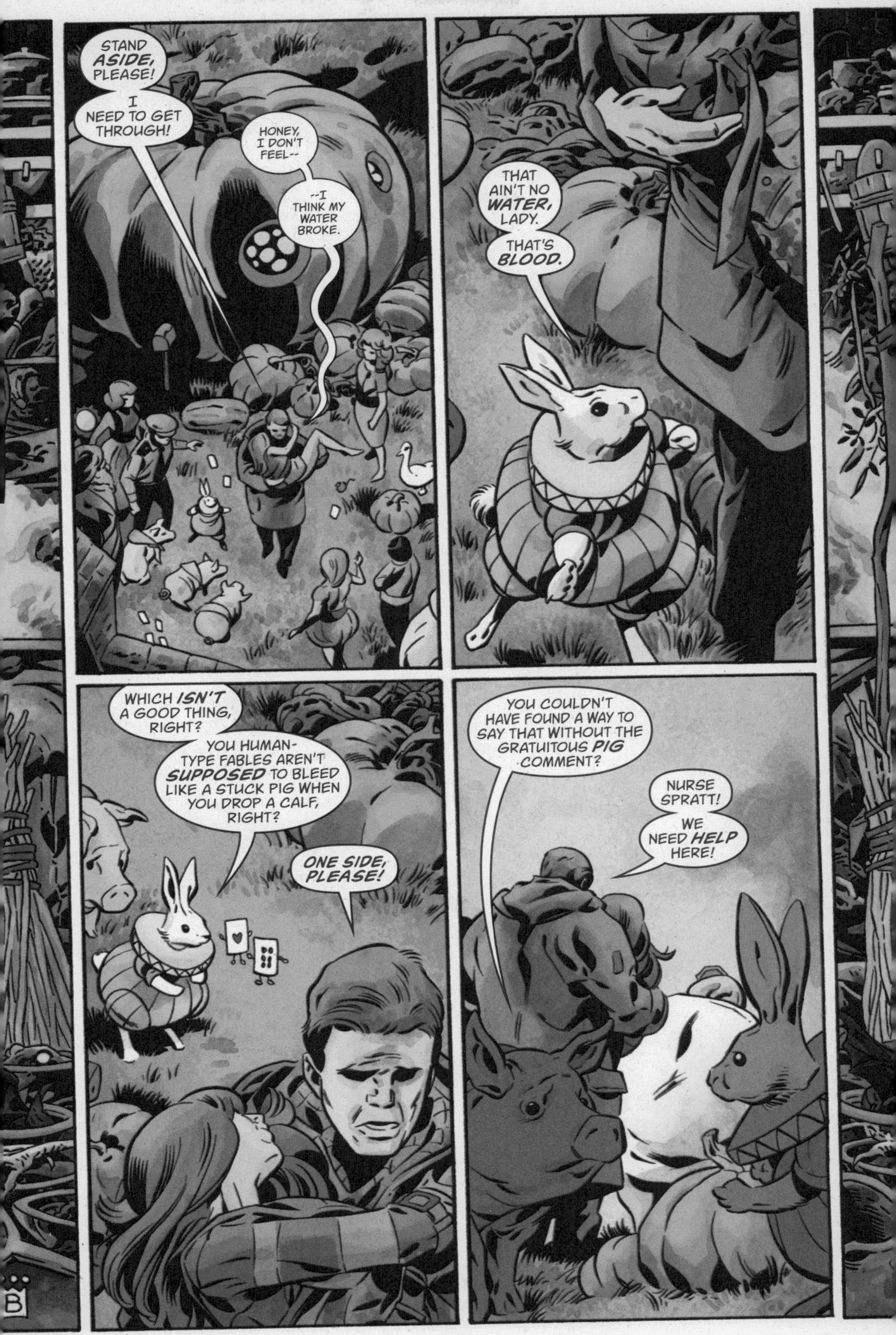
STAND ASIDE, PLEASE!
I NEED TO GET THROUGH!
HONEY, I DON'T FEEL--
--I THINK MY WATER BROKE.
THAT AIN'T NO WATER, LADY.
THAT'S BLOOD.
WHICH ISN'T A GOOD THING, RIGHT?
YOU HUMAN-TYPE FABLES AREN'T SUPPOSED TO BLEED LIKE A STUCK PIG WHEN YOU DROP A CALF, RIGHT?
ONE SIDE, PLEASE!
YOU COULDN'T HAVE FOUND A WAY TO SAY THAT WITHOUT THE GRATUITOUS PIG COMMENT?
NURSE SPRATT!
WE NEED HELP HERE!

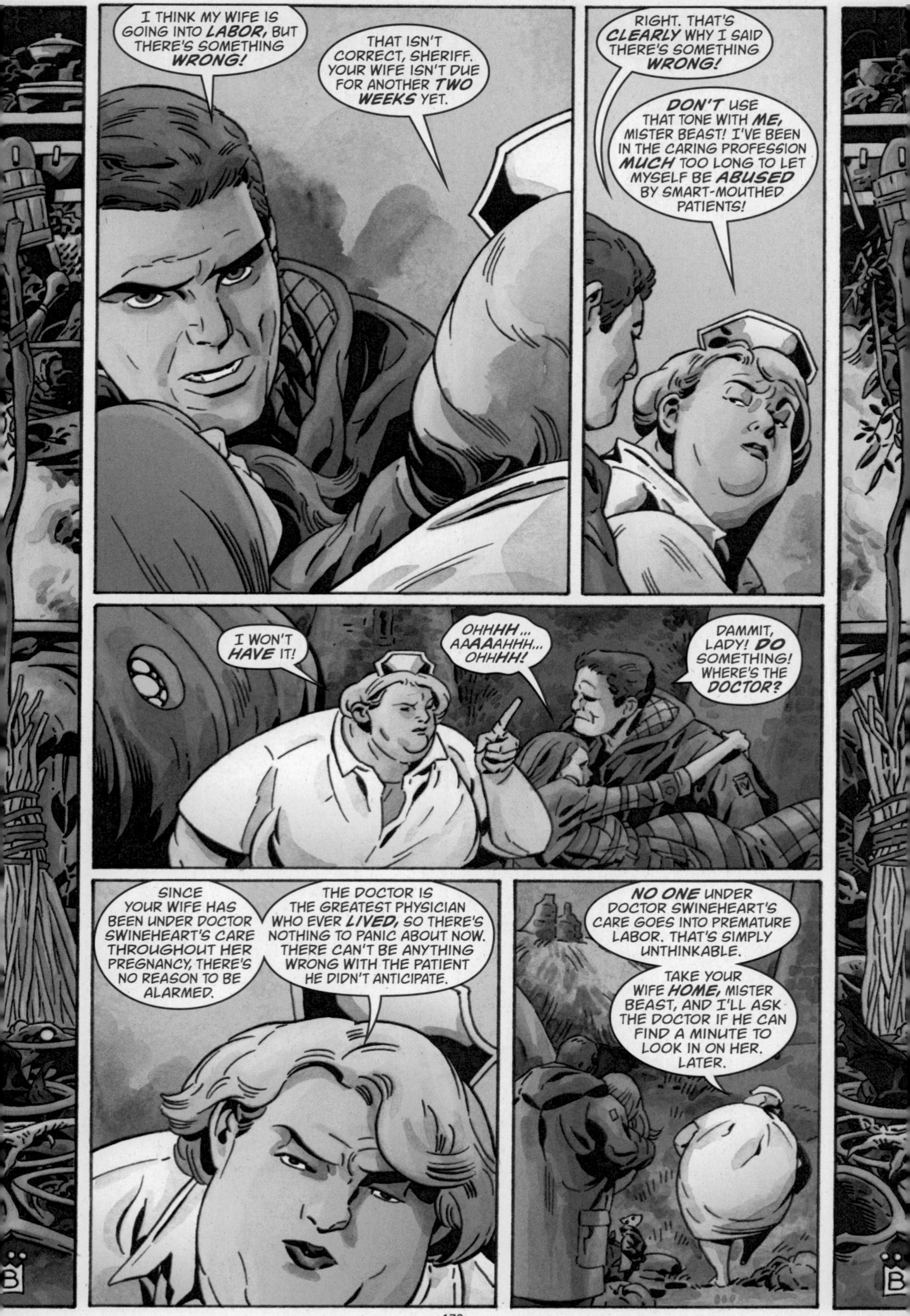
I THINK MY WIFE IS GOING INTO LABOR, BUT THERE'S SOMETHING WRONG!
THAT ISN'T CORRECT, SHERIFF. YOUR WIFE ISN'T DUE FOR ANOTHER TWO WEEKS YET.
RIGHT. THAT'S CLEARLY WHY I SAID THERE'S SOMETHING WRONG!
DON'T USE THAT TONE WITH ME, MISTER BEAST! I'VE BEEN IN THE CARING PROFESSION MUCH TOO LONG TO LET MYSELF BE ABUSED BY SMART-MOUTHED PATIENTS!
I WON'T HAVE IT!
OHHHH... AAAAAHHH... OHHHH!
DAMMIT, LADY! DO SOMETHING! WHERE'S THE DOCTOR?
SINCE YOUR WIFE HAS BEEN UNDER DOCTOR SWINEHEART'S CARE THROUGHOUT HER PREGNANCY, THERE'S NO REASON TO BE ALARMED.
THE DOCTOR IS THE GREATEST PHYSICIAN WHO EVER LIVED, SO THERE'S NOTHING TO PANIC ABOUT NOW. THERE CAN'T BE ANYTHING WRONG WITH THE PATIENT HE DIDN'T ANTICIPATE.
NO ONE UNDER DOCTOR SWINEHEART'S CARE GOES INTO PREMATURE LABOR. THAT'S SIMPLY UNTHINKABLE.
TAKE YOUR WIFE HOME, MISTER BEAST, AND I'LL ASK THE DOCTOR IF HE CAN FIND A MINUTE TO LOOK IN ON HER. LATER.

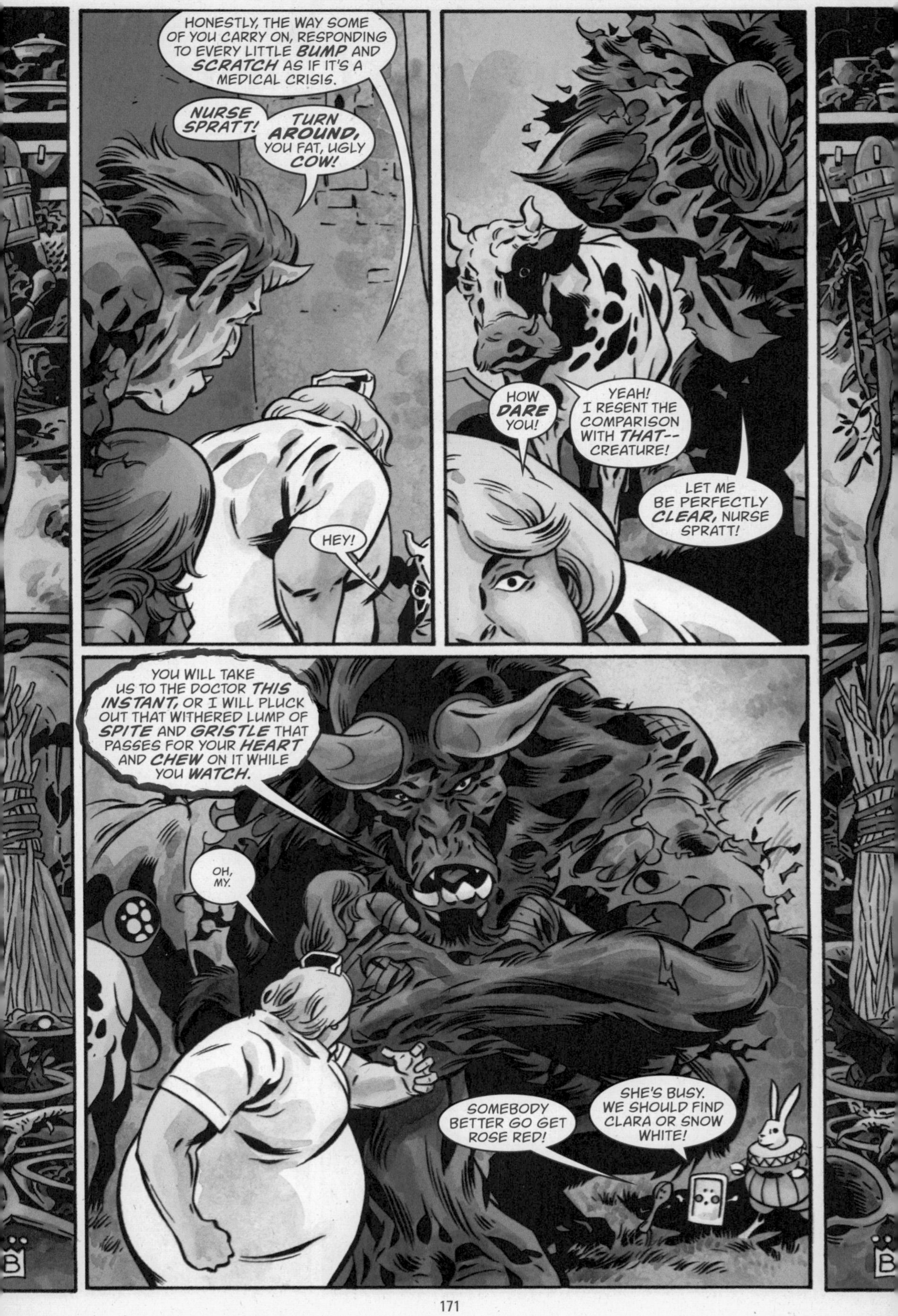
HONESTLY, THE WAY SOME OF YOU CARRY ON, RESPONDING TO EVERY LITTLE BUMP AND SCRATCH AS IF IT'S A MEDICAL CRISIS.
NURSE SPRATT!
TURN AROUND, YOU FAT, UGLY COW!
HEY!
HOW DARE YOU!
YEAH! I RESENT THE COMPARISON WITH THAT-- CREATURE!
LET ME BE PERFECTLY CLEAR, NURSE SPRATT!
YOU WILL TAKE US TO THE DOCTOR THIS INSTANT, OR I WILL PLUCK OUT THAT WITHERED LUMP OF SPITE AND GRISTLE THAT PASSES FOR YOUR HEART AND CHEW ON IT WHILE YOU WATCH.
OH, MY.
SOMEBODY BETTER GO GET ROSE RED!
SHE'S BUSY. WE SHOULD FIND CLARA OR SNOW WHITE!

Chapter Four: The Sweet Science

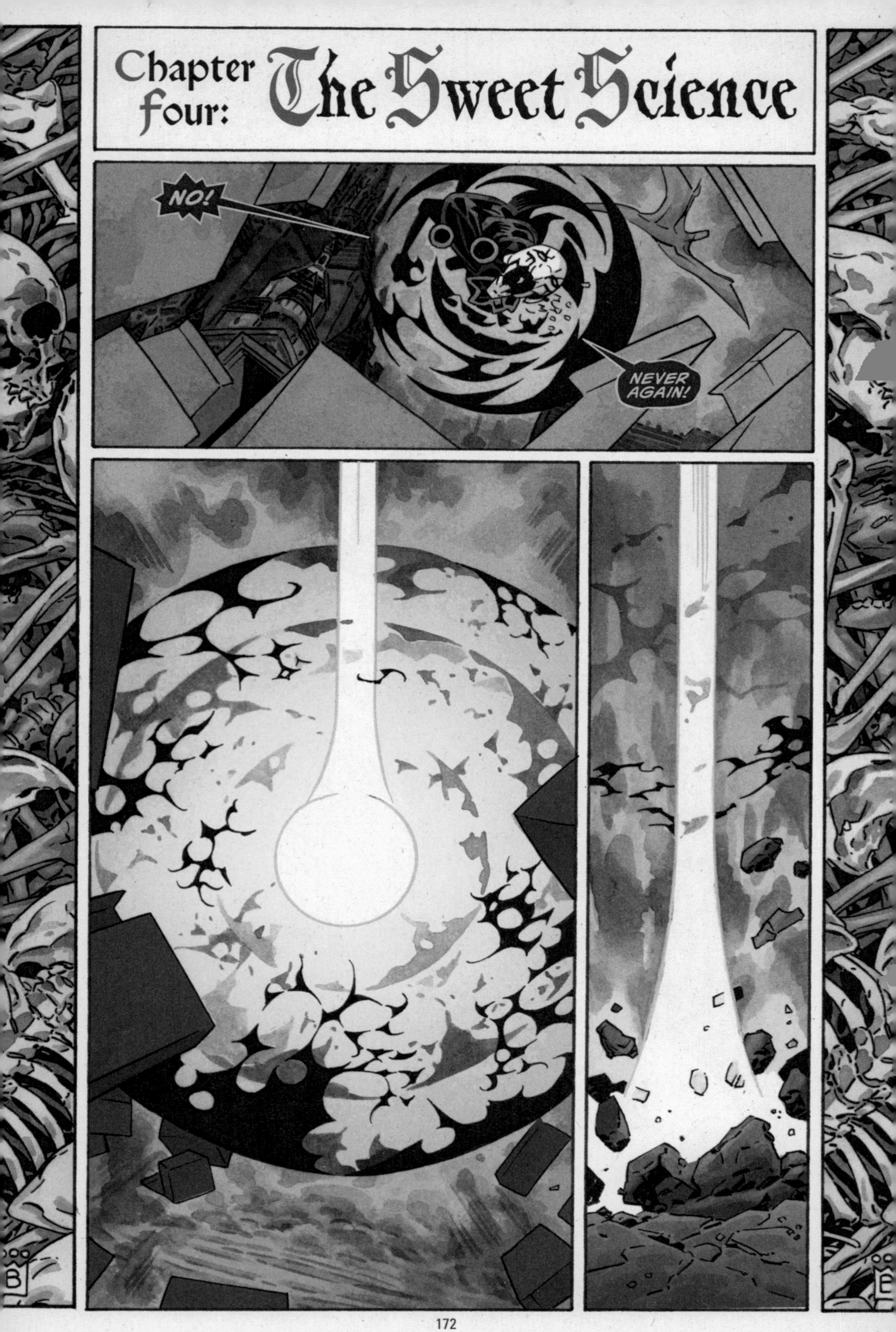
NO!
NEVER AGAIN!

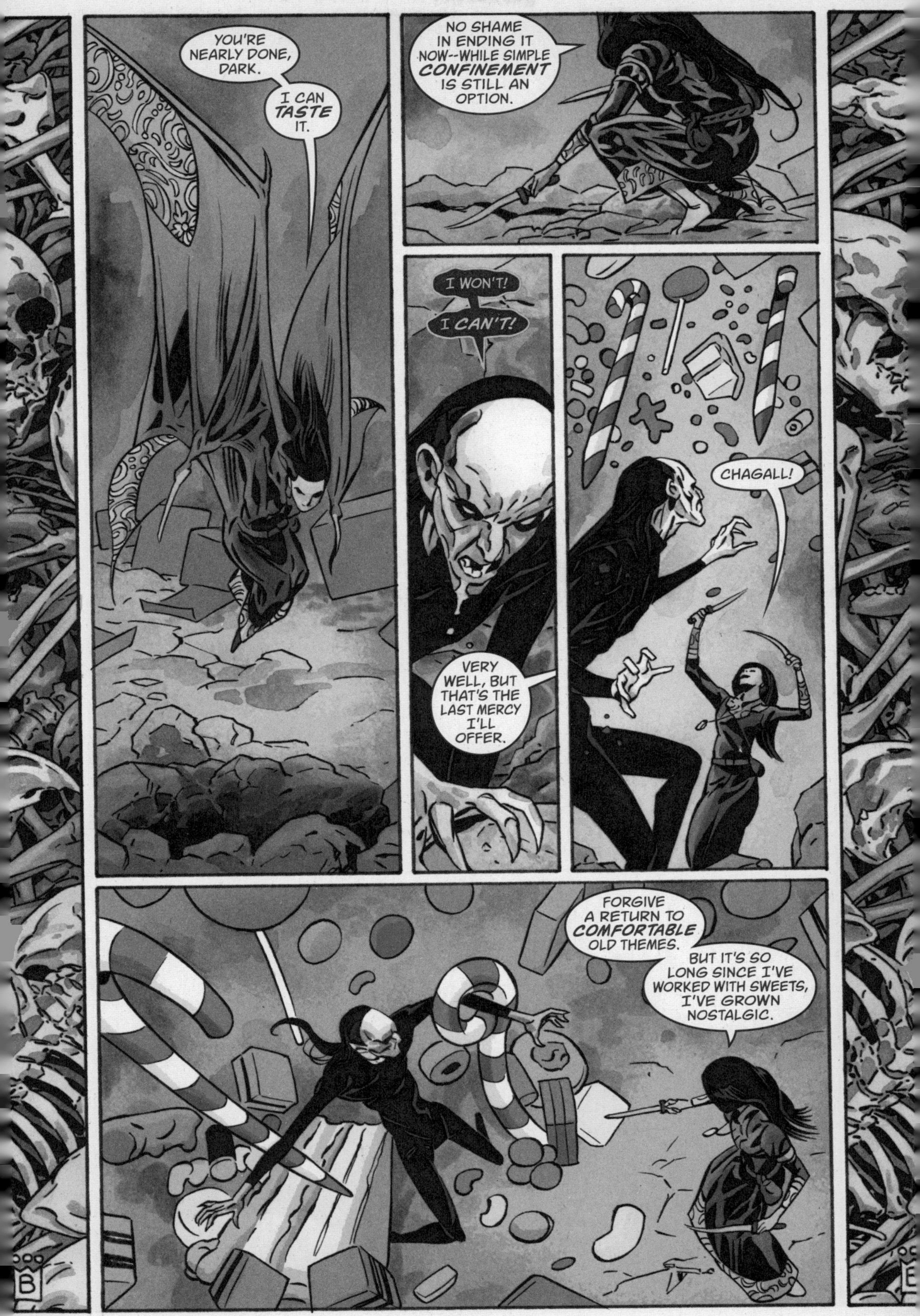
YOU'RE NEARLY DONE, DARK.
I CAN TASTE IT.
NO SHAME IN ENDING IT NOW--WHILE SIMPLE CONFINEMENT IS STILL AN OPTION.
I WON'T!
I CAN'T!
VERY WELL, BUT THAT'S THE LAST MERCY I'LL OFFER.
CHAGALL!
FORGIVE A RETURN TO COMFORTABLE OLD THEMES.
BUT IT'S SO LONG SINCE I'VE WORKED WITH SWEETS, I'VE GROWN NOSTALGIC.

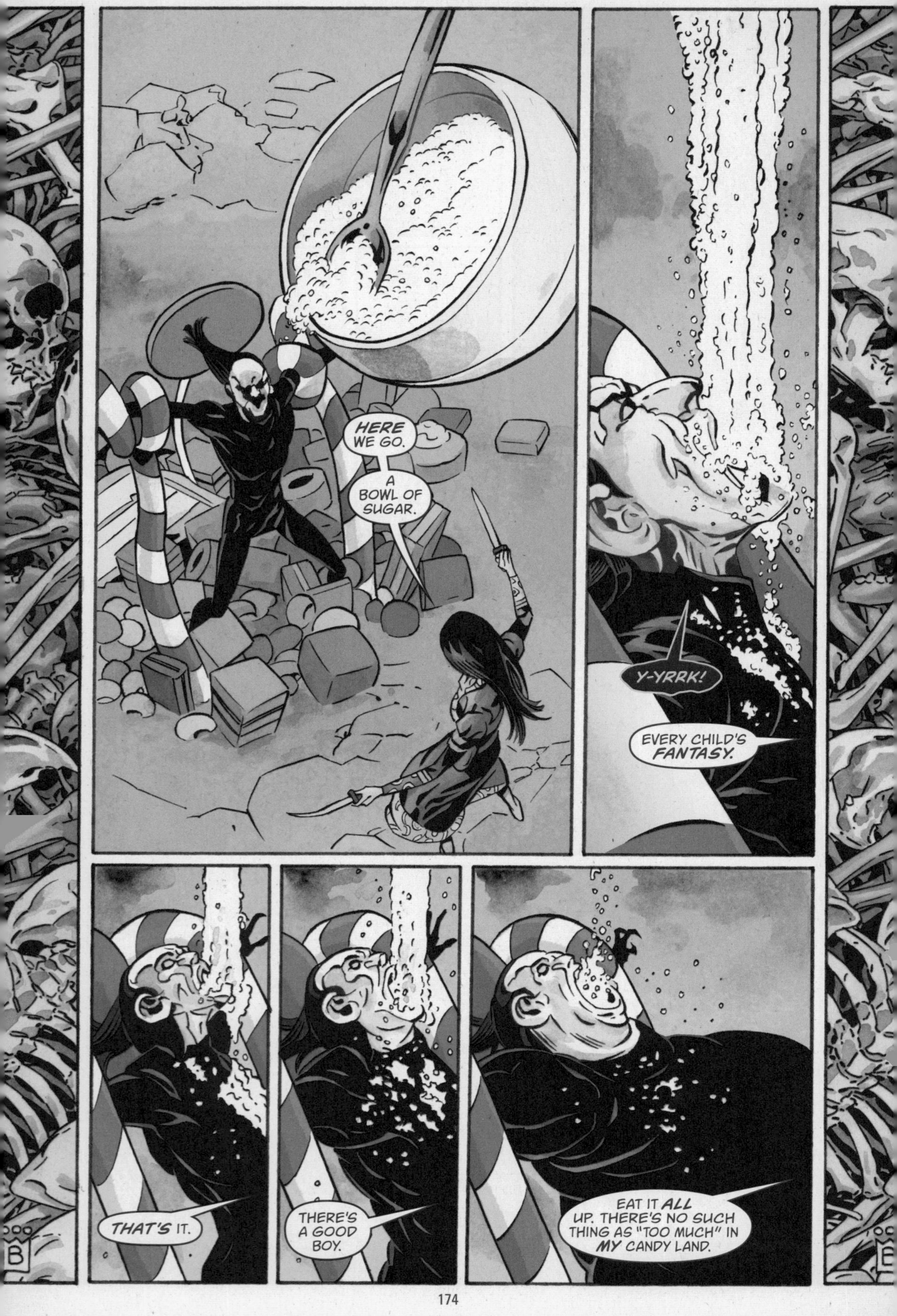
HERE WE GO.
A BOWL OF SUGAR.
Y-YRRK!
EVERY CHILD'S FANTASY.
THAT'S IT.
THERE'S A GOOD BOY.
EAT IT ALL UP. THERE'S NO SUCH THING AS "TOO MUCH" IN MY CANDY LAND.

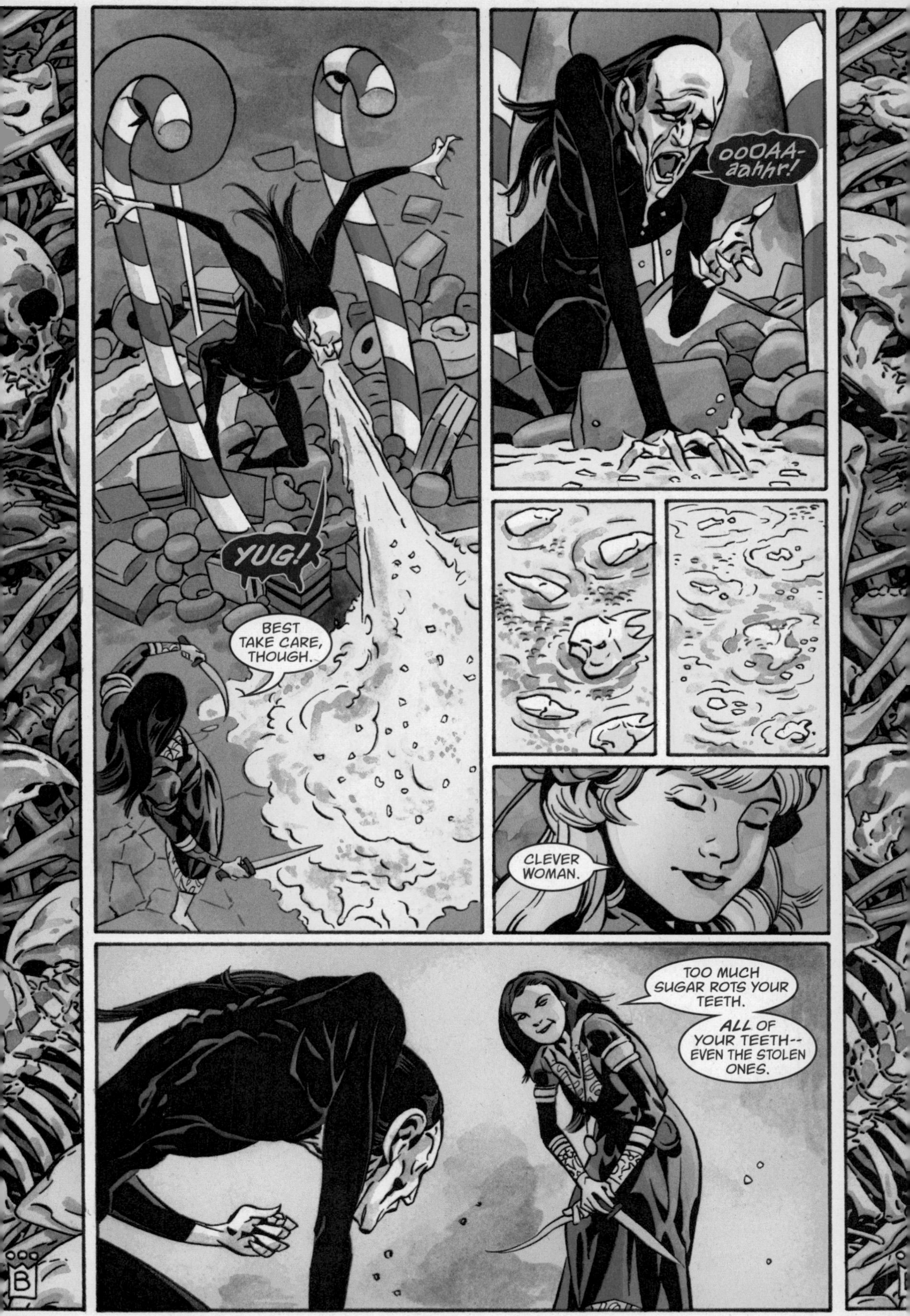

OOOAA-aahhr!
YUG!
BEST TAKE CARE, THOUGH.
CLEVER WOMAN.
TOO MUCH SUGAR ROTS YOUR TEETH.
ALL OF YOUR TEETH--EVEN THE STOLEN ONES.

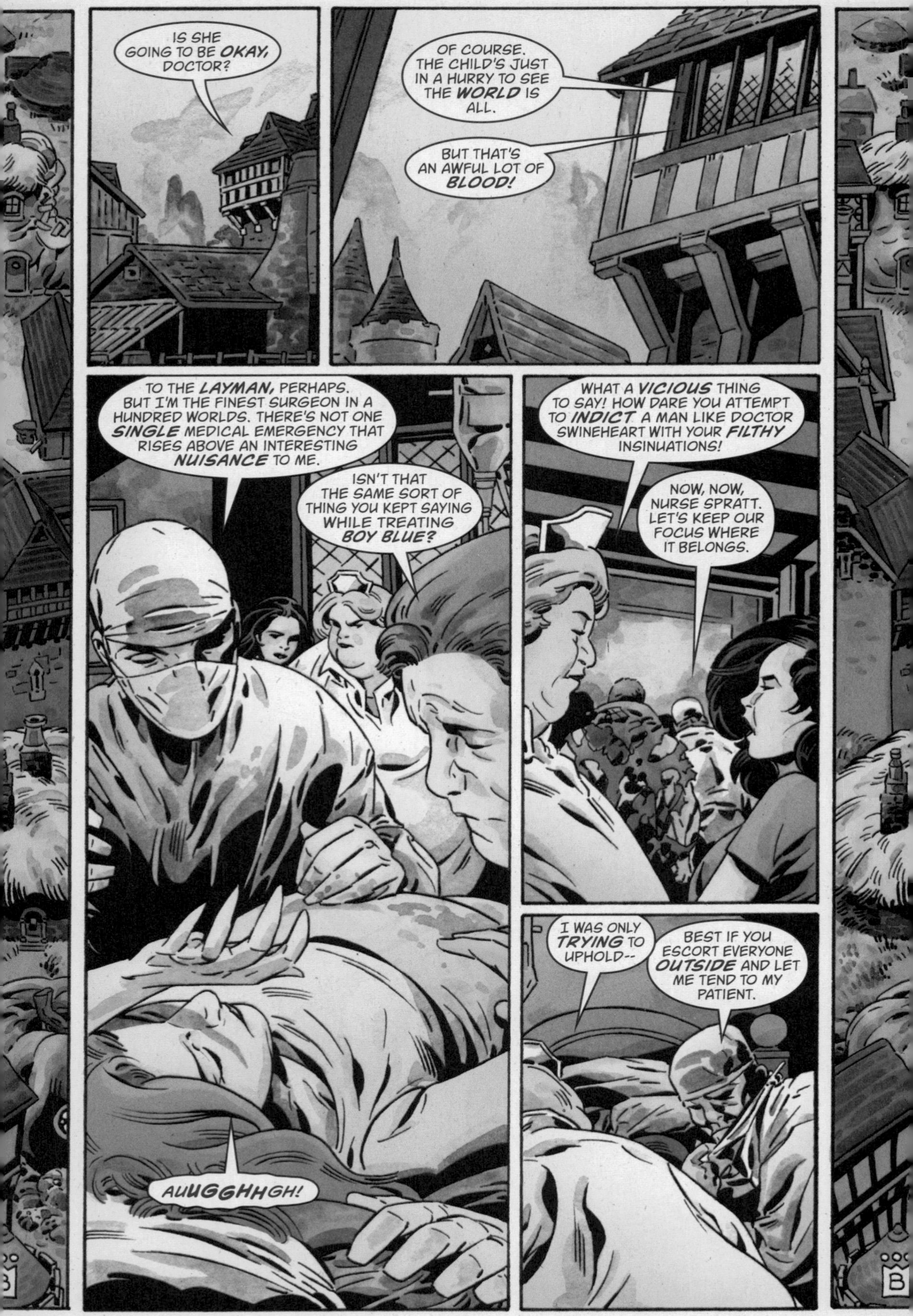
IS SHE GOING TO BE OKAY, DOCTOR?
OF COURSE. THE CHILD'S JUST IN A HURRY TO SEE THE WORLD IS ALL.
BUT THAT'S AN AWFUL LOT OF BLOOD!
TO THE LAYMAN, PERHAPS. BUT I'M THE FINEST SURGEON IN A HUNDRED WORLDS. THERE'S NOT ONE SINGLE MEDICAL EMERGENCY THAT RISES ABOVE AN INTERESTING NUISANCE TO ME.
ISN'T THAT THE SAME SORT OF THING YOU KEPT SAYING WHILE TREATING BOY BLUE?
AUUGGHHGH!
WHAT A VICIOUS THING TO SAY! HOW DARE YOU ATTEMPT TO INDICT A MAN LIKE DOCTOR SWINEHEART WITH YOUR FILTHY INSINUATIONS!
NOW, NOW, NURSE SPRATT. LET'S KEEP OUR FOCUS WHERE IT BELONGS.
I WAS ONLY TRYING TO UPHOLD--
BEST IF YOU ESCORT EVERYONE OUTSIDE AND LET ME TEND TO MY PATIENT.

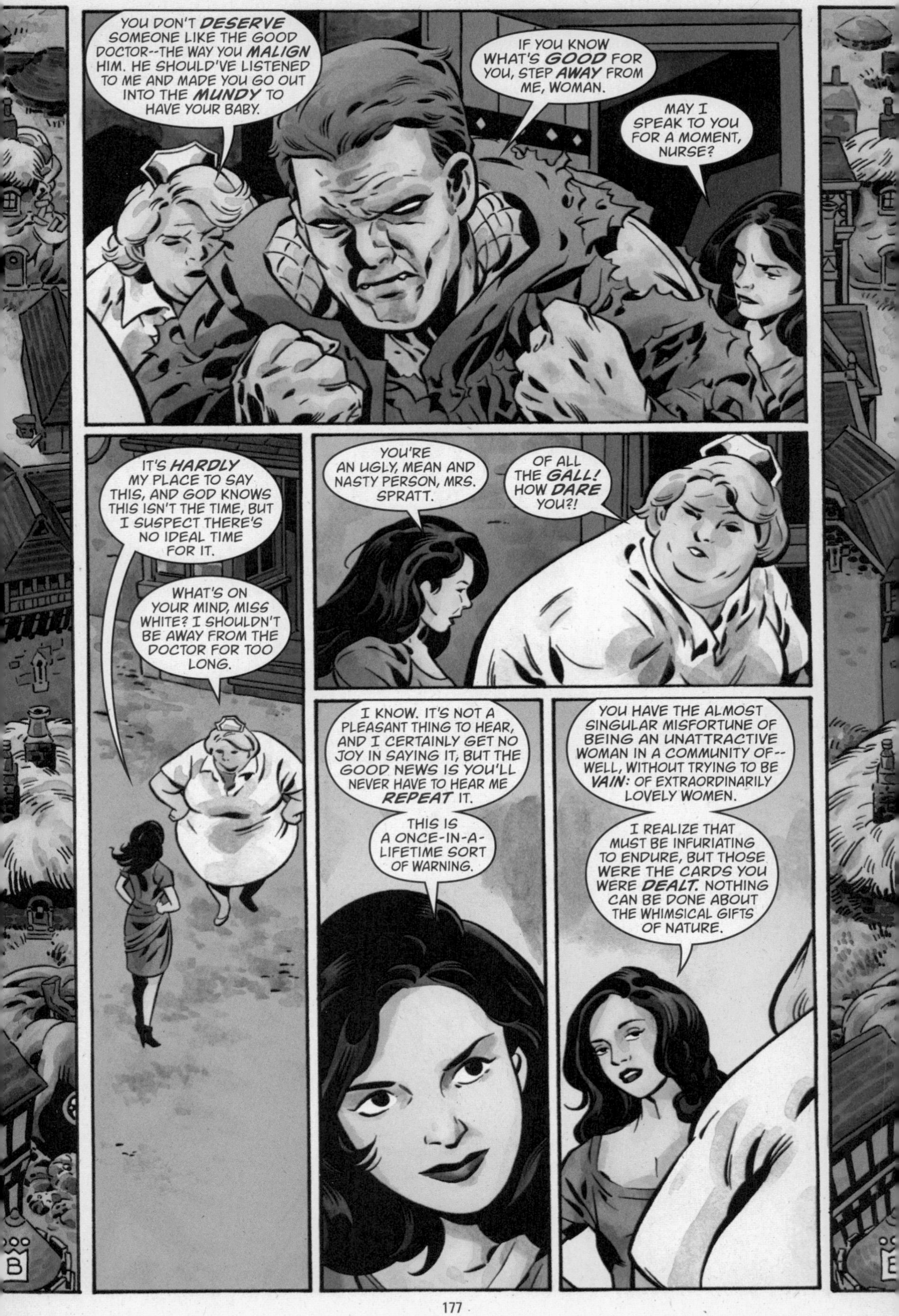
YOU DON'T DESERVE SOMEONE LIKE THE GOOD DOCTOR--THE WAY YOU MALIGN HIM. HE SHOULD'VE LISTENED TO ME AND MADE YOU GO OUT INTO THE MUNDY TO HAVE YOUR BABY.
IF YOU KNOW WHAT'S GOOD FOR YOU, STEP AWAY FROM ME, WOMAN.
MAY I SPEAK TO YOU FOR A MOMENT, NURSE?
IT'S HARDLY MY PLACE TO SAY THIS, AND GOD KNOWS THIS ISN'T THE TIME, BUT I SUSPECT THERE'S NO IDEAL TIME FOR IT.
WHAT'S ON YOUR MIND, MISS WHITE? I SHOULDN'T BE AWAY FROM THE DOCTOR FOR TOO LONG.
YOU'RE AN UGLY, MEAN AND NASTY PERSON, MRS. SPRATT.
OF ALL THE GALL! HOW DARE YOU?!
I KNOW. IT'S NOT A PLEASANT THING TO HEAR, AND I CERTAINLY GET NO JOY IN SAYING IT, BUT THE GOOD NEWS IS YOU'LL NEVER HAVE TO HEAR ME REPEAT IT.
THIS IS A ONCE-IN-A-LIFETIME SORT OF WARNING.
YOU HAVE THE ALMOST SINGULAR MISFORTUNE OF BEING AN UNATTRACTIVE WOMAN IN A COMMUNITY OF--WELL, WITHOUT TRYING TO BE VAIN: OF EXTRAORDINARILY LOVELY WOMEN.
I REALIZE THAT MUST BE INFURIATING TO ENDURE, BUT THOSE WERE THE CARDS YOU WERE DEALT. NOTHING CAN BE DONE ABOUT THE WHIMSICAL GIFTS OF NATURE.

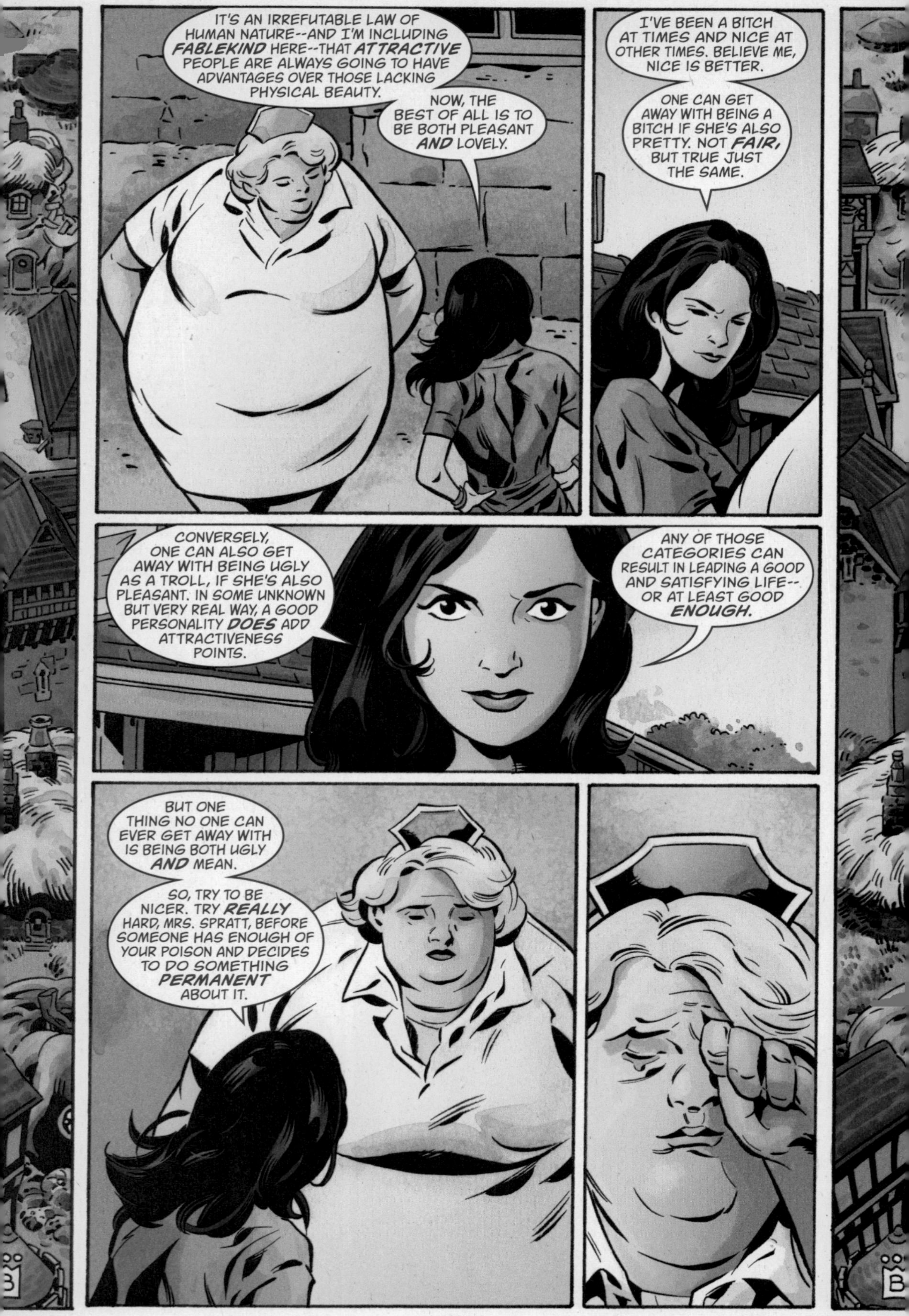
IT'S AN IRREFUTABLE LAW OF HUMAN NATURE--AND I'M INCLUDING FABLEKIND HERE--THAT ATTRACTIVE PEOPLE ARE ALWAYS GOING TO HAVE ADVANTAGES OVER THOSE LACKING PHYSICAL BEAUTY.
NOW, THE BEST OF ALL IS TO BE BOTH PLEASANT AND LOVELY.
I'VE BEEN A BITCH AT TIMES AND NICE AT OTHER TIMES. BELIEVE ME, NICE IS BETTER.
ONE CAN GET AWAY WITH BEING A BITCH IF SHE'S ALSO PRETTY. NOT FAIR, BUT TRUE JUST THE SAME.
CONVERSELY, ONE CAN ALSO GET AWAY WITH BEING UGLY AS A TROLL, IF SHE'S ALSO PLEASANT. IN SOME UNKNOWN BUT VERY REAL WAY, A GOOD PERSONALITY DOES ADD ATTRACTIVENESS POINTS.
ANY OF THOSE CATEGORIES CAN RESULT IN LEADING A GOOD AND SATISFYING LIFE--OR AT LEAST GOOD ENOUGH.
BUT ONE THING NO ONE CAN EVER GET AWAY WITH IS BEING BOTH UGLY AND MEAN.
SO, TRY TO BE NICER. TRY REALLY HARD, MRS. SPRATT, BEFORE SOMEONE HAS ENOUGH OF YOUR POISON AND DECIDES TO DO SOMETHING PERMANENT ABOUT IT.

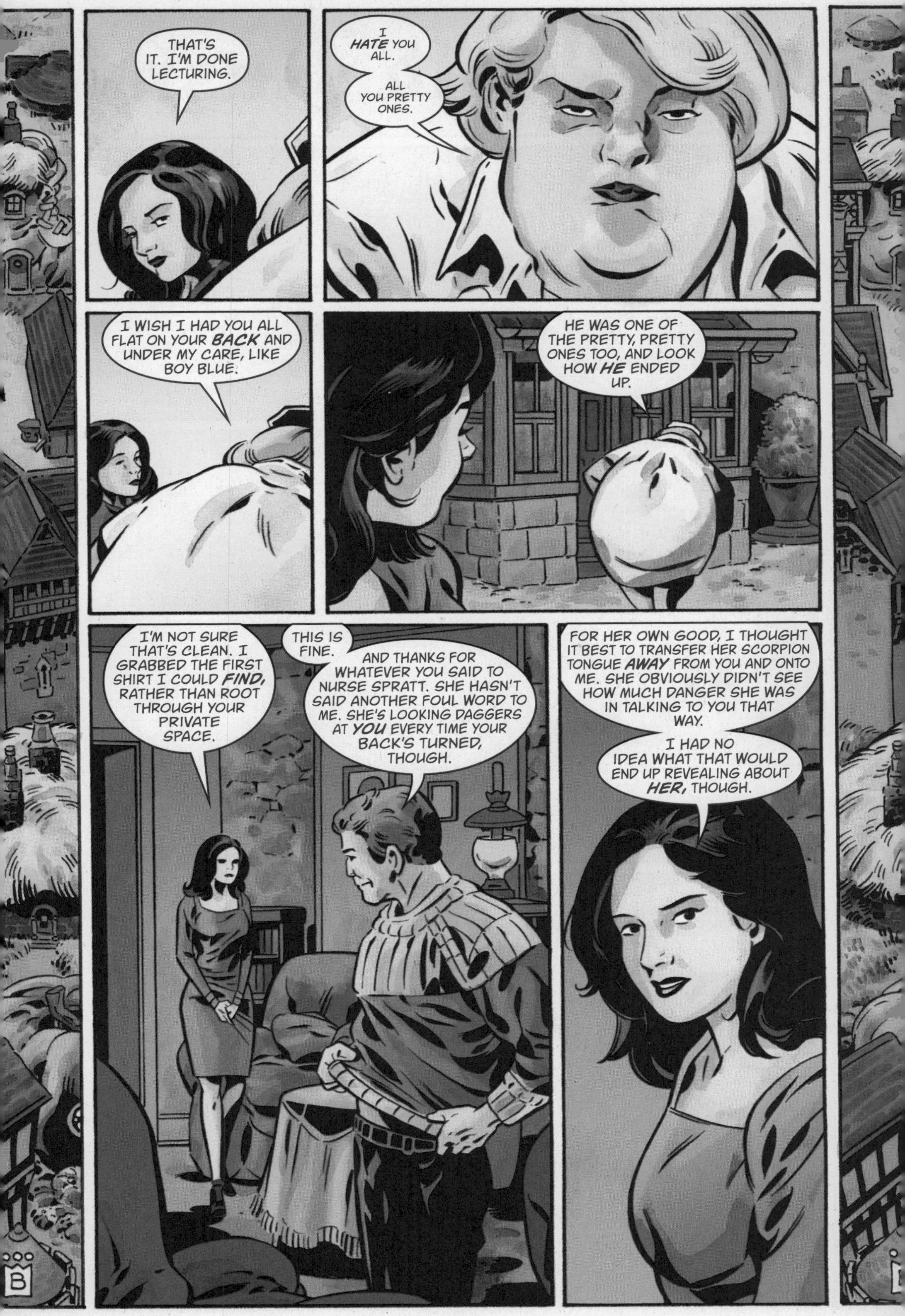
THAT'S IT. I'M DONE LECTURING.
I HATE YOU ALL.
ALL YOU PRETTY ONES.
I WISH I HAD YOU ALL FLAT ON YOUR BACK AND UNDER MY CARE, LIKE BOY BLUE.
HE WAS ONE OF THE PRETTY, PRETTY ONES TOO, AND LOOK HOW HE ENDED UP.
I'M NOT SURE THAT'S CLEAN. I GRABBED THE FIRST SHIRT I COULD FIND, RATHER THAN ROOT THROUGH YOUR PRIVATE SPACE.
THIS IS FINE.
AND THANKS FOR WHATEVER YOU SAID TO NURSE SPRATT. SHE HASN'T SAID ANOTHER FOUL WORD TO ME. SHE'S LOOKING DAGGERS AT YOU EVERY TIME YOUR BACK'S TURNED, THOUGH.
FOR HER OWN GOOD, I THOUGHT IT BEST TO TRANSFER HER SCORPION TONGUE AWAY FROM YOU AND ONTO ME. SHE OBVIOUSLY DIDN'T SEE HOW MUCH DANGER SHE WAS IN TALKING TO YOU THAT WAY.
I HAD NO IDEA WHAT THAT WOULD END UP REVEALING ABOUT HER, THOUGH.

Chapter five: Gold Rush

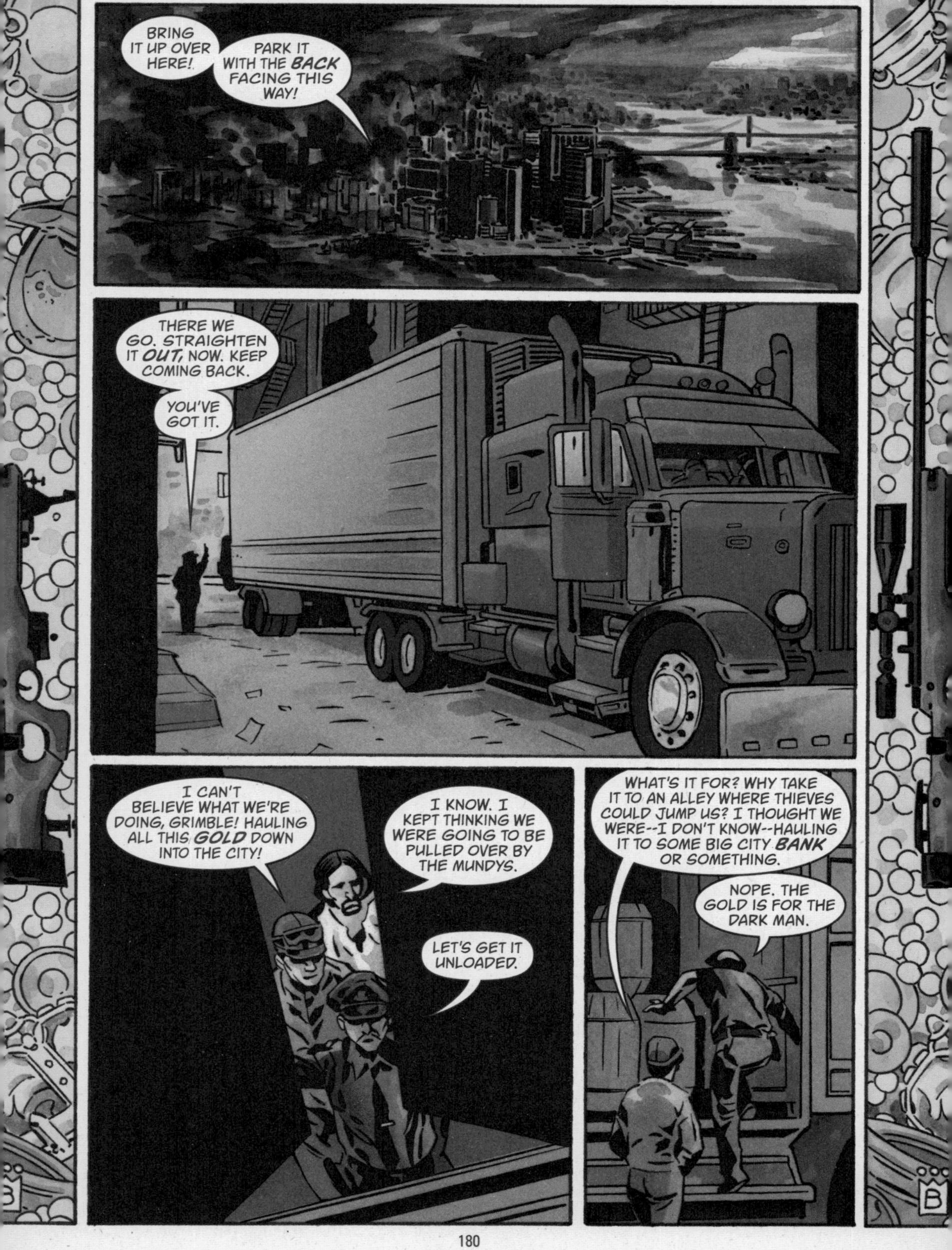
BRING IT UP OVER HERE!
PARK IT WITH THE BACK FACING THIS WAY!
THERE WE GO. STRAIGHTEN IT OUT, NOW. KEEP COMING BACK.
YOU'VE GOT IT.
I CAN'T BELIEVE WHAT WE'RE DOING, GRIMBLE! HAULING ALL THIS GOLD DOWN INTO THE CITY!
I KNOW. I KEPT THINKING WE WERE GOING TO BE PULLED OVER BY THE MUNDYS.
LET'S GET IT UNLOADED.
WHAT'S IT FOR? WHY TAKE IT TO AN ALLEY WHERE THIEVES COULD JUMP US? I THOUGHT WE WERE--I DON'T KNOW--HAULING IT TO SOME BIG CITY BANK OR SOMETHING.
NOPE. THE GOLD IS FOR THE DARK MAN.

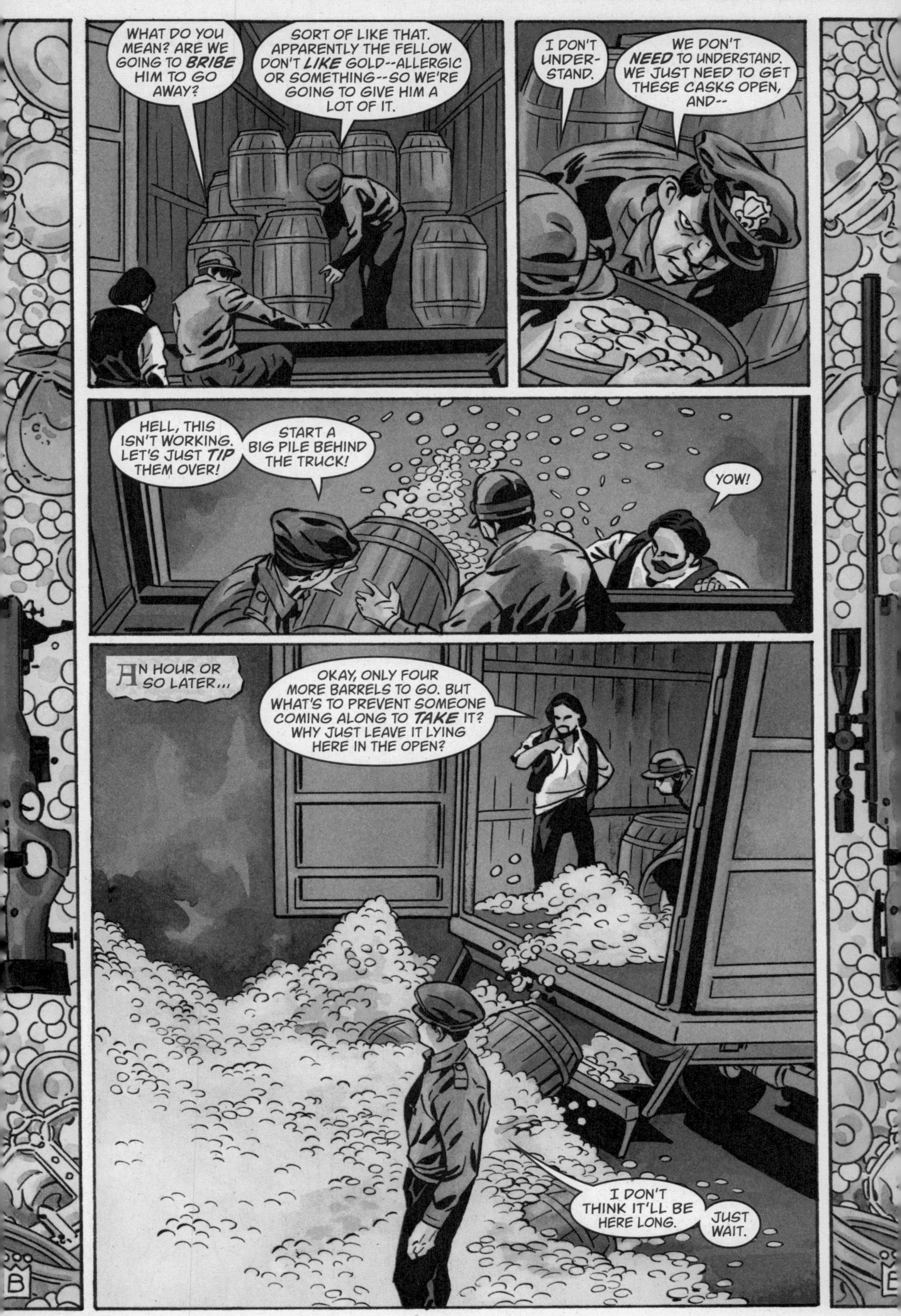
WHAT DO YOU MEAN? ARE WE GOING TO BRIBE HIM TO GO AWAY?
SORT OF LIKE THAT. APPARENTLY THE FELLOW DON'T LIKE GOLD--ALLERGIC OR SOMETHING--SO WE'RE GOING TO GIVE HIM A LOT OF IT.
I DON'T UNDER-STAND.
WE DON'T NEED TO UNDERSTAND. WE JUST NEED TO GET THESE CASKS OPEN, AND--
HELL, THIS ISN'T WORKING. LET'S JUST TIP THEM OVER!
START A BIG PILE BEHIND THE TRUCK!
YOW!
AN HOUR OR SO LATER...
OKAY, ONLY FOUR MORE BARRELS TO GO. BUT WHAT'S TO PREVENT SOMEONE COMING ALONG TO TAKE IT? WHY JUST LEAVE IT LYING HERE IN THE OPEN?
I DON'T THINK IT'LL BE HERE LONG.
JUST WAIT.

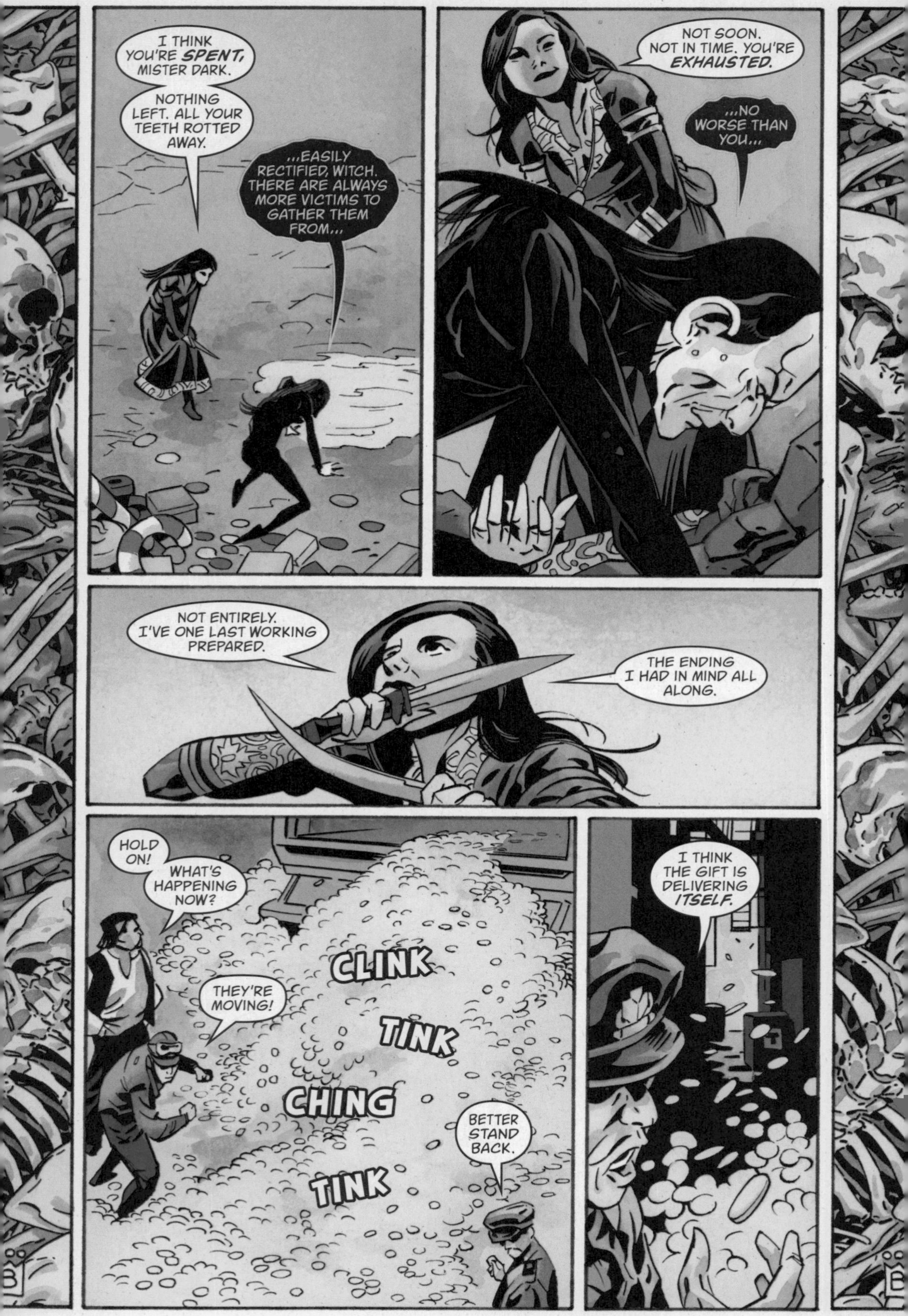

I THINK YOU'RE SPENT, MISTER DARK.
NOTHING LEFT. ALL YOUR TEETH ROTTED AWAY.
...EASILY RECTIFIED, WITCH. THERE ARE ALWAYS MORE VICTIMS TO GATHER THEM FROM...
NOT SOON. NOT IN TIME. YOU'RE EXHAUSTED.
...NO WORSE THAN YOU...
NOT ENTIRELY. I'VE ONE LAST WORKING PREPARED.
THE ENDING I HAD IN MIND ALL ALONG.
HOLD ON!
WHAT'S HAPPENING NOW?
THEY'RE MOVING!
CLINK
TINK
CHING
TINK
BETTER STAND BACK.
I THINK THE GIFT IS DELIVERING ITSELF.

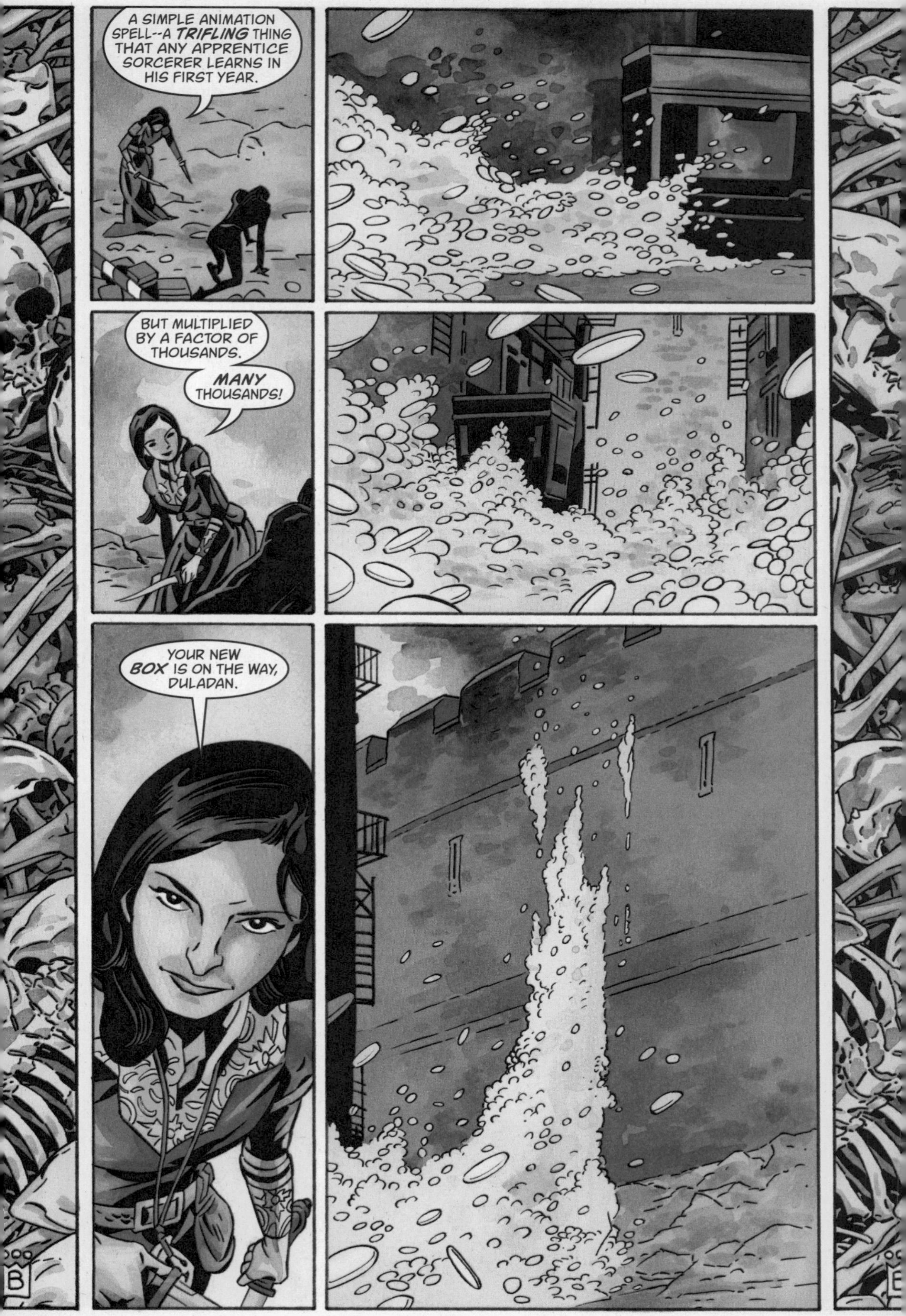
A SIMPLE ANIMATION SPELL--A TRIFLING THING THAT ANY APPRENTICE SORCERER LEARNS IN HIS FIRST YEAR.
BUT MULTIPLIED BY A FACTOR OF THOUSANDS.
MANY THOUSANDS!
YOUR NEW BOX IS ON THE WAY, DULADAN.

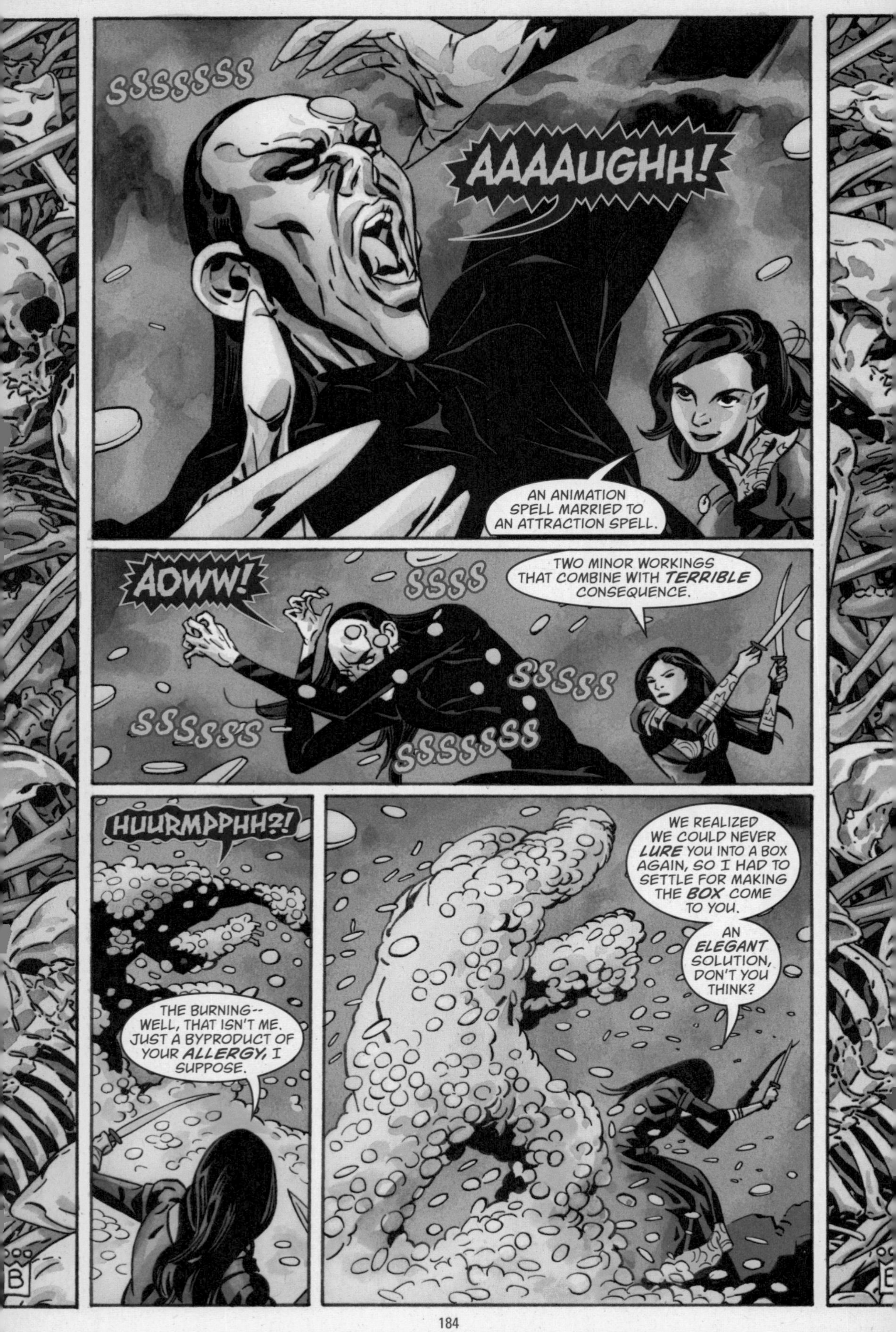
SSSSSSS
AAAAUGHH!
AN ANIMATION SPELL MARRIED TO AN ATTRACTION SPELL.
AOWW!
SSSS
TWO MINOR WORKINGS THAT COMBINE WITH TERRIBLE CONSEQUENCE.
SSSSS
SSSSSS
SSSSSSS
HUURMPPHH?!
THE BURNING-- WELL, THAT ISN'T ME. JUST A BYPRODUCT OF YOUR ALLERGY, I SUPPOSE.
WE REALIZED WE COULD NEVER LURE YOU INTO A BOX AGAIN, SO I HAD TO SETTLE FOR MAKING THE BOX COME TO YOU.
AN ELEGANT SOLUTION, DON'T YOU THINK?

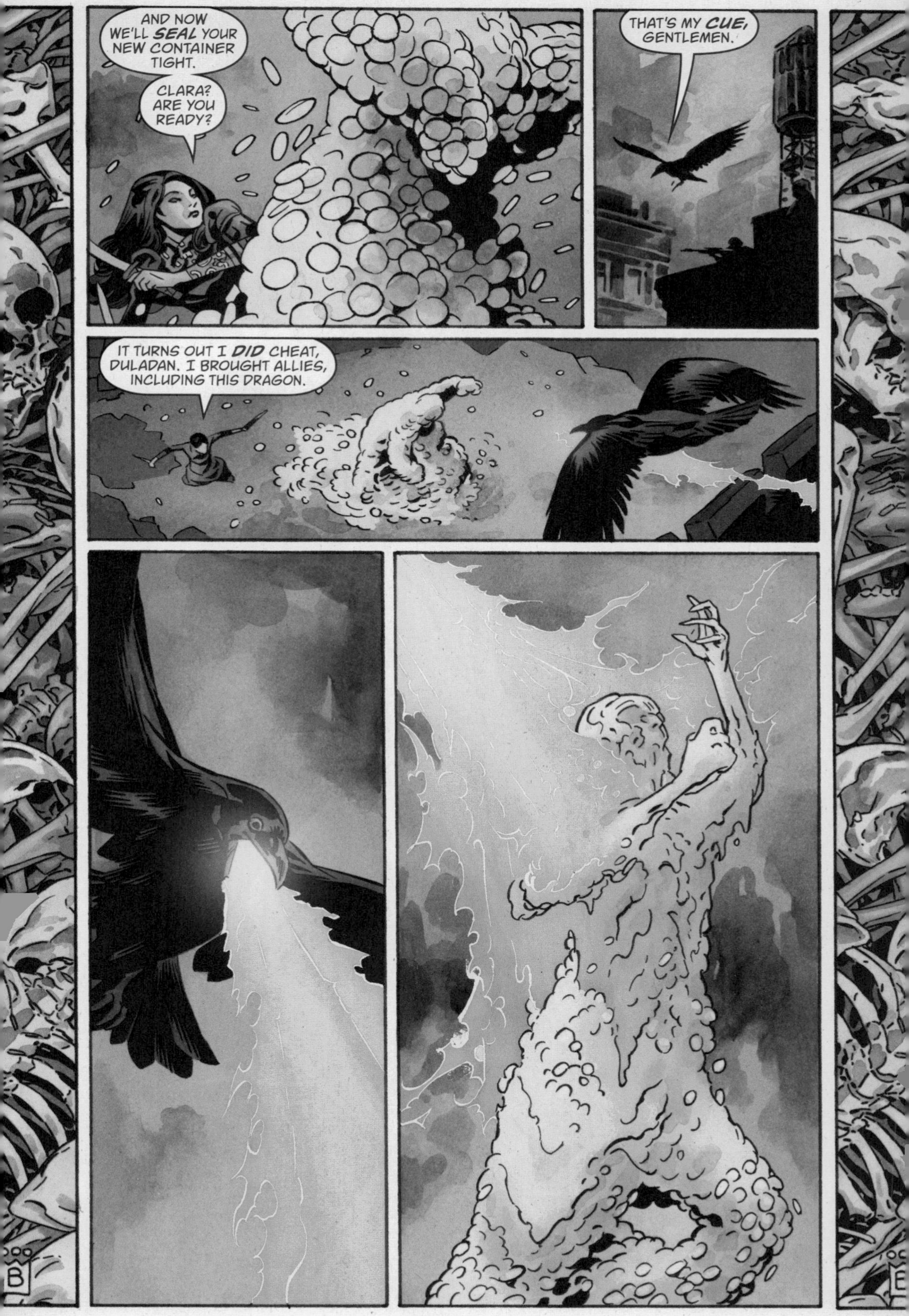
AND NOW WE'LL SEAL YOUR NEW CONTAINER TIGHT.
CLARA? ARE YOU READY?
THAT'S MY CUE, GENTLEMEN.
IT TURNS OUT I DID CHEAT, DULADAN. I BROUGHT ALLIES, INCLUDING THIS DRAGON.

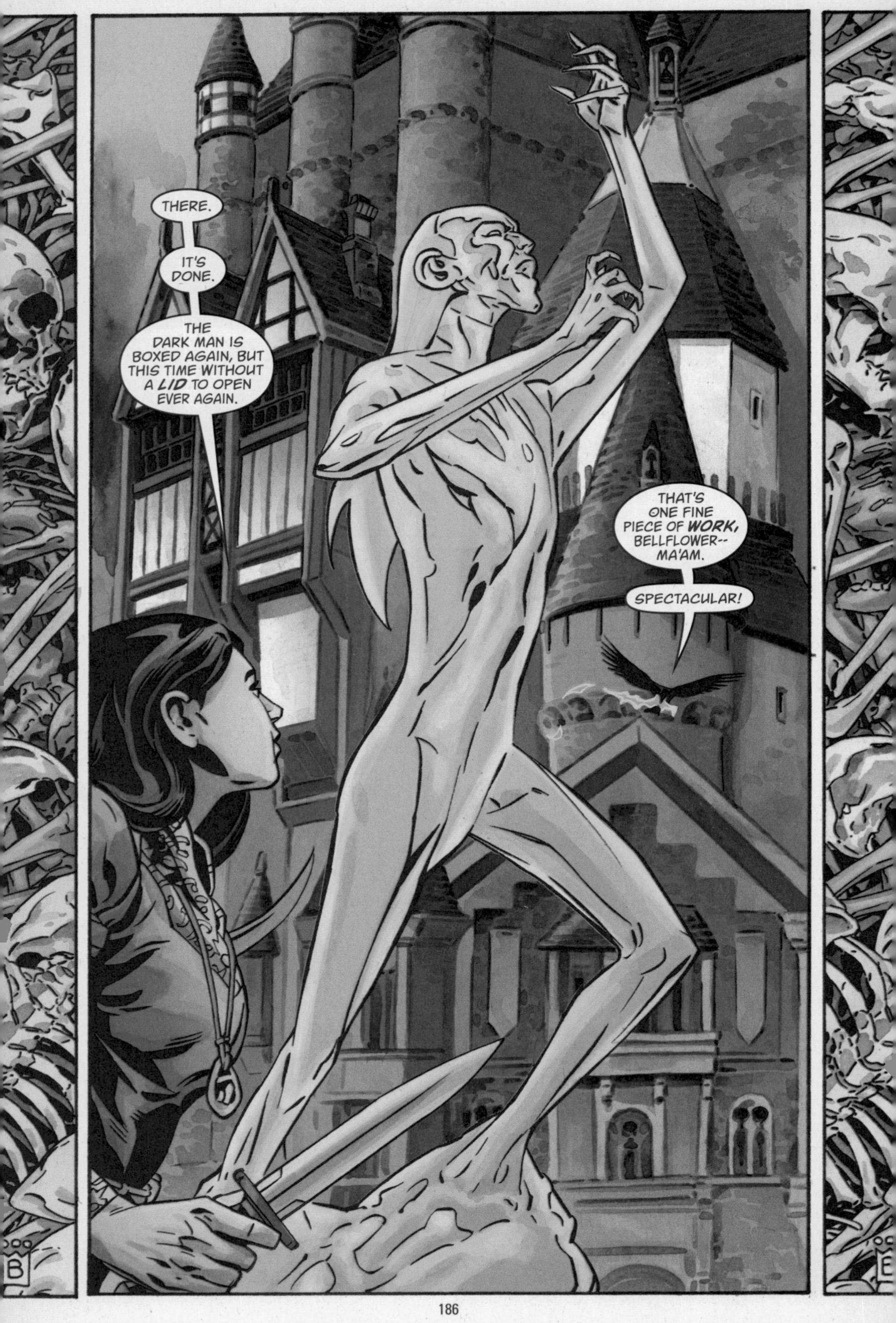
THERE.
IT'S DONE.
THE DARK MAN IS BOXED AGAIN, BUT THIS TIME WITHOUT A LID TO OPEN EVER AGAIN.
THAT'S ONE FINE PIECE OF WORK, BELLFLOWER--MA'AM.
SPECTACULAR!

Chapter Six: The Murpleblost Situation

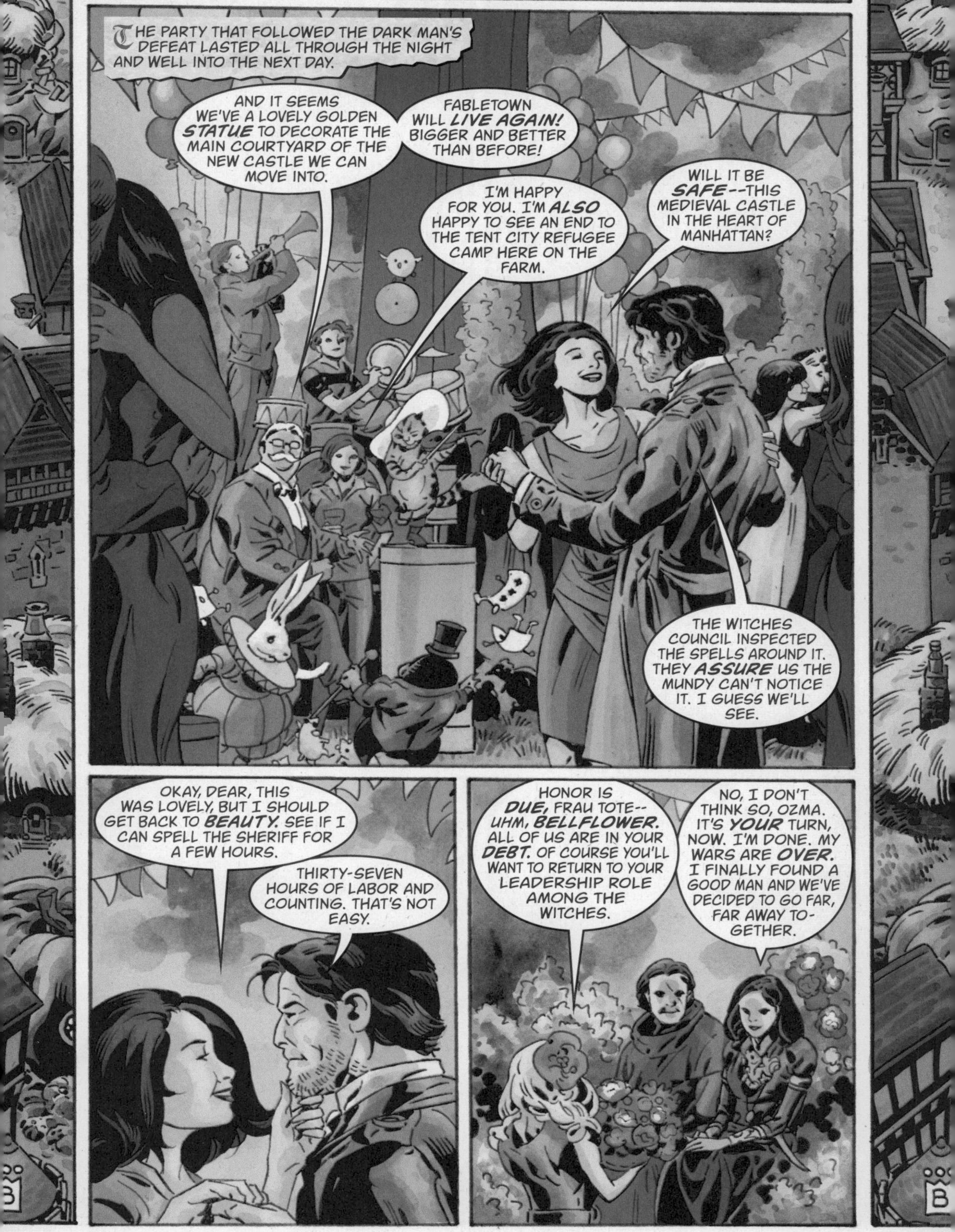

THE PARTY THAT FOLLOWED THE DARK MAN'S DEFEAT LASTED ALL THROUGH THE NIGHT AND WELL INTO THE NEXT DAY.
AND IT SEEMS WE'VE A LOVELY GOLDEN STATUE TO DECORATE THE MAIN COURTYARD OF THE NEW CASTLE WE CAN MOVE INTO.
FABLETOWN WILL LIVE AGAIN! BIGGER AND BETTER THAN BEFORE!
I'M HAPPY FOR YOU. I'M ALSO HAPPY TO SEE AN END TO THE TENT CITY REFUGEE CAMP HERE ON THE FARM.
WILL IT BE SAFE--THIS MEDIEVAL CASTLE IN THE HEART OF MANHATTAN?
THE WITCHES COUNCIL INSPECTED THE SPELLS AROUND IT. THEY ASSURE US THE MUNDY CAN'T NOTICE IT. I GUESS WE'LL SEE.
OKAY, DEAR, THIS WAS LOVELY, BUT I SHOULD GET BACK TO BEAUTY. SEE IF I CAN SPELL THE SHERIFF FOR A FEW HOURS.
THIRTY-SEVEN HOURS OF LABOR AND COUNTING. THAT'S NOT EASY.
HONOR IS DUE, FRAU TOTE--UHM, BELLFLOWER. ALL OF US ARE IN YOUR DEBT. OF COURSE YOU'LL WANT TO RETURN TO YOUR LEADERSHIP ROLE AMONG THE WITCHES.
NO, I DON'T THINK SO, OZMA. IT'S YOUR TURN, NOW. I'M DONE. MY WARS ARE OVER. I FINALLY FOUND A GOOD MAN AND WE'VE DECIDED TO GO FAR, FAR AWAY TO-GETHER.

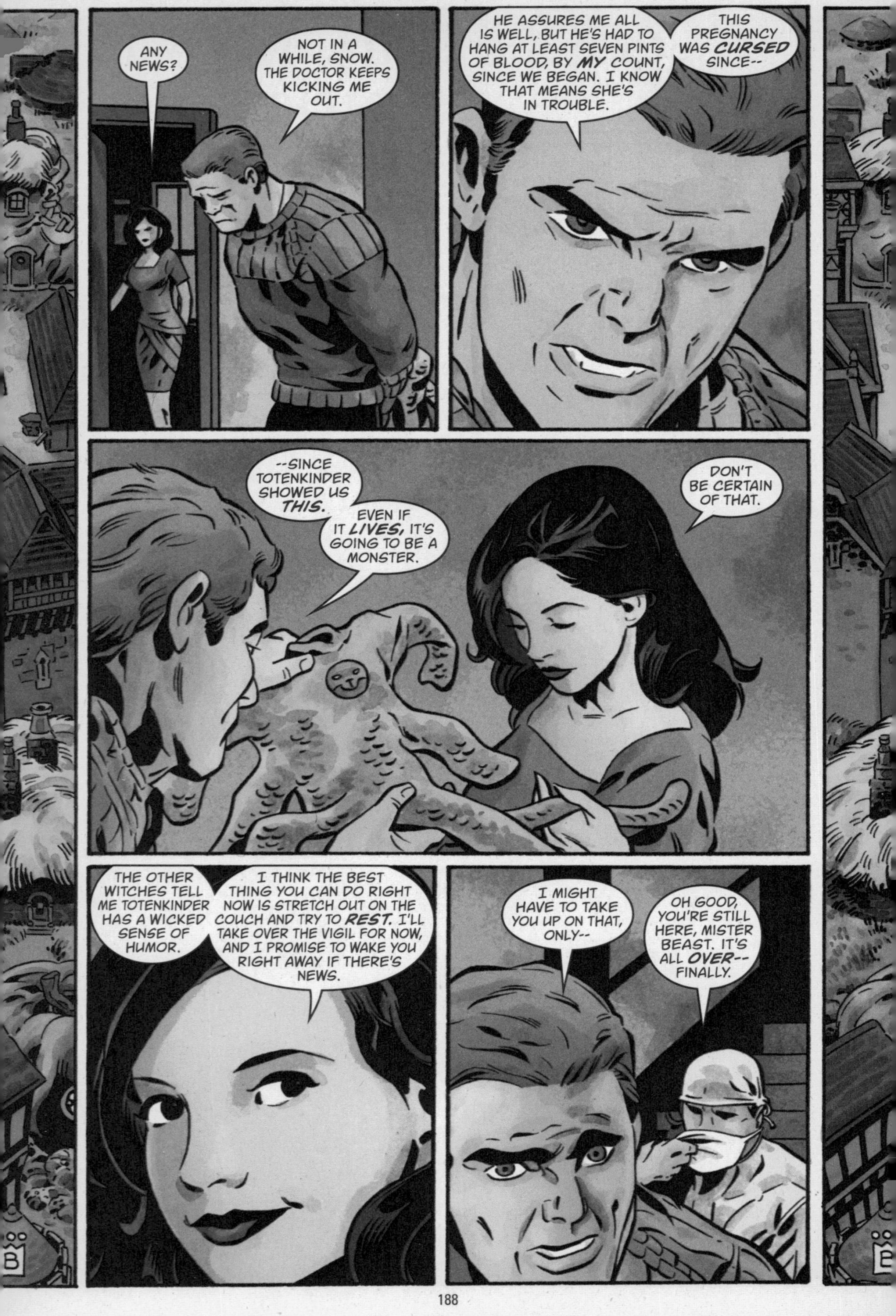
ANY NEWS?
NOT IN A WHILE, SNOW. THE DOCTOR KEEPS KICKING ME OUT.
HE ASSURES ME ALL IS WELL, BUT HE'S HAD TO HANG AT LEAST SEVEN PINTS OF BLOOD, BY MY COUNT, SINCE WE BEGAN. I KNOW THAT MEANS SHE'S IN TROUBLE.
THIS PREGNANCY WAS CURSED SINCE--
--SINCE TOTENKINDER SHOWED US THIS.
EVEN IF IT LIVES, IT'S GOING TO BE A MONSTER.
DON'T BE CERTAIN OF THAT.
THE OTHER WITCHES TELL ME TOTENKINDER HAS A WICKED SENSE OF HUMOR.
I THINK THE BEST THING YOU CAN DO RIGHT NOW IS STRETCH OUT ON THE COUCH AND TRY TO REST. I'LL TAKE OVER THE VIGIL FOR NOW, AND I PROMISE TO WAKE YOU RIGHT AWAY IF THERE'S NEWS.
I MIGHT HAVE TO TAKE YOU UP ON THAT, ONLY--
OH GOOD, YOU'RE STILL HERE, MISTER BEAST. IT'S ALL OVER-- FINALLY.

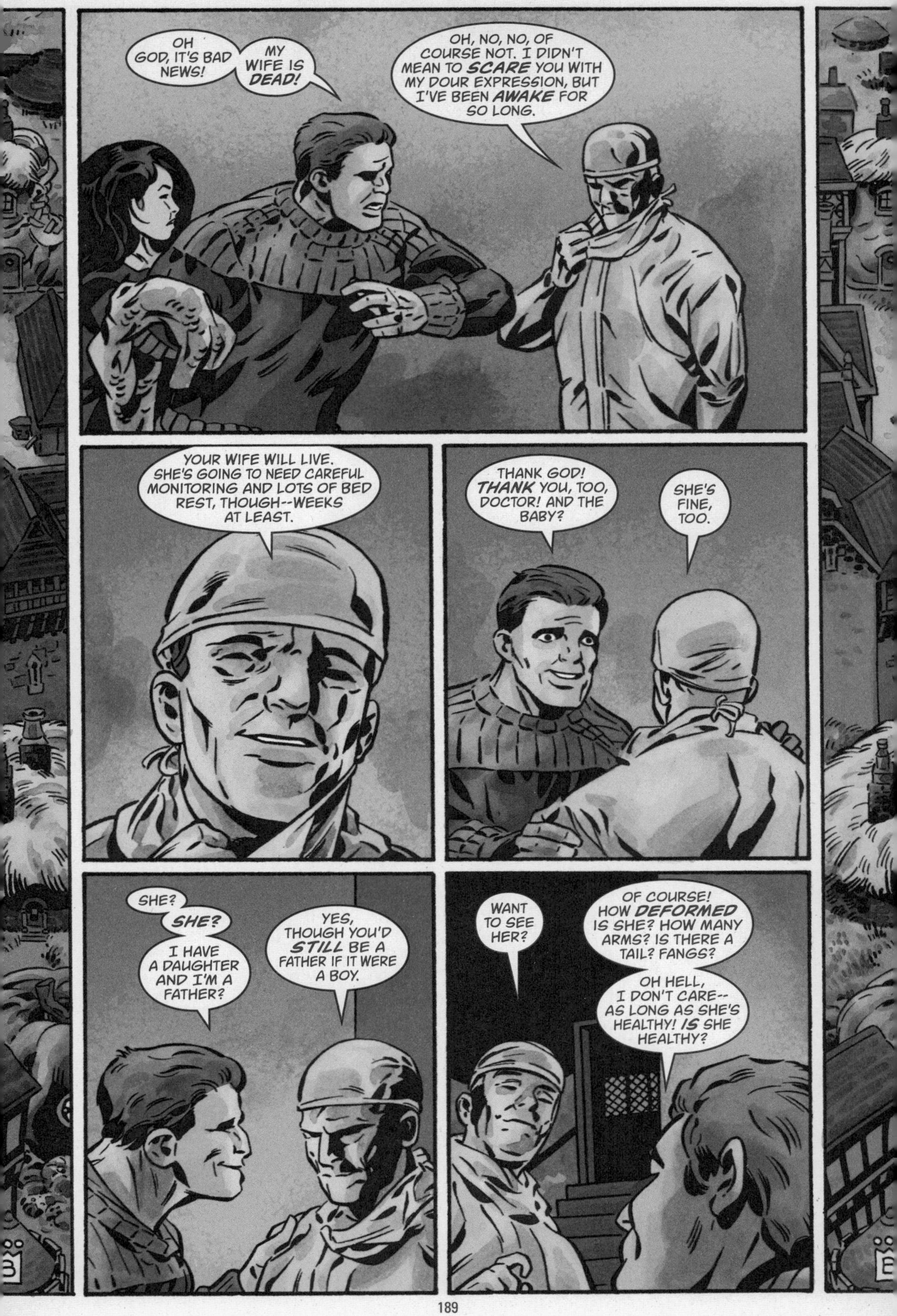
OH GOD, IT'S BAD NEWS!
MY WIFE IS DEAD!
OH, NO, NO, OF COURSE NOT. I DIDN'T MEAN TO SCARE YOU WITH MY DOUR EXPRESSION, BUT I'VE BEEN AWAKE FOR SO LONG.
YOUR WIFE WILL LIVE. SHE'S GOING TO NEED CAREFUL MONITORING AND LOTS OF BED REST, THOUGH--WEEKS AT LEAST.
THANK GOD! THANK YOU, TOO, DOCTOR! AND THE BABY?
SHE'S FINE, TOO.
SHE? SHE?
I HAVE A DAUGHTER AND I'M A FATHER?
YES, THOUGH YOU'D STILL BE A FATHER IF IT WERE A BOY.
WANT TO SEE HER?
OF COURSE! HOW DEFORMED IS SHE? HOW MANY ARMS? IS THERE A TAIL? FANGS?
OH HELL, I DON'T CARE-- AS LONG AS SHE'S HEALTHY! IS SHE HEALTHY?

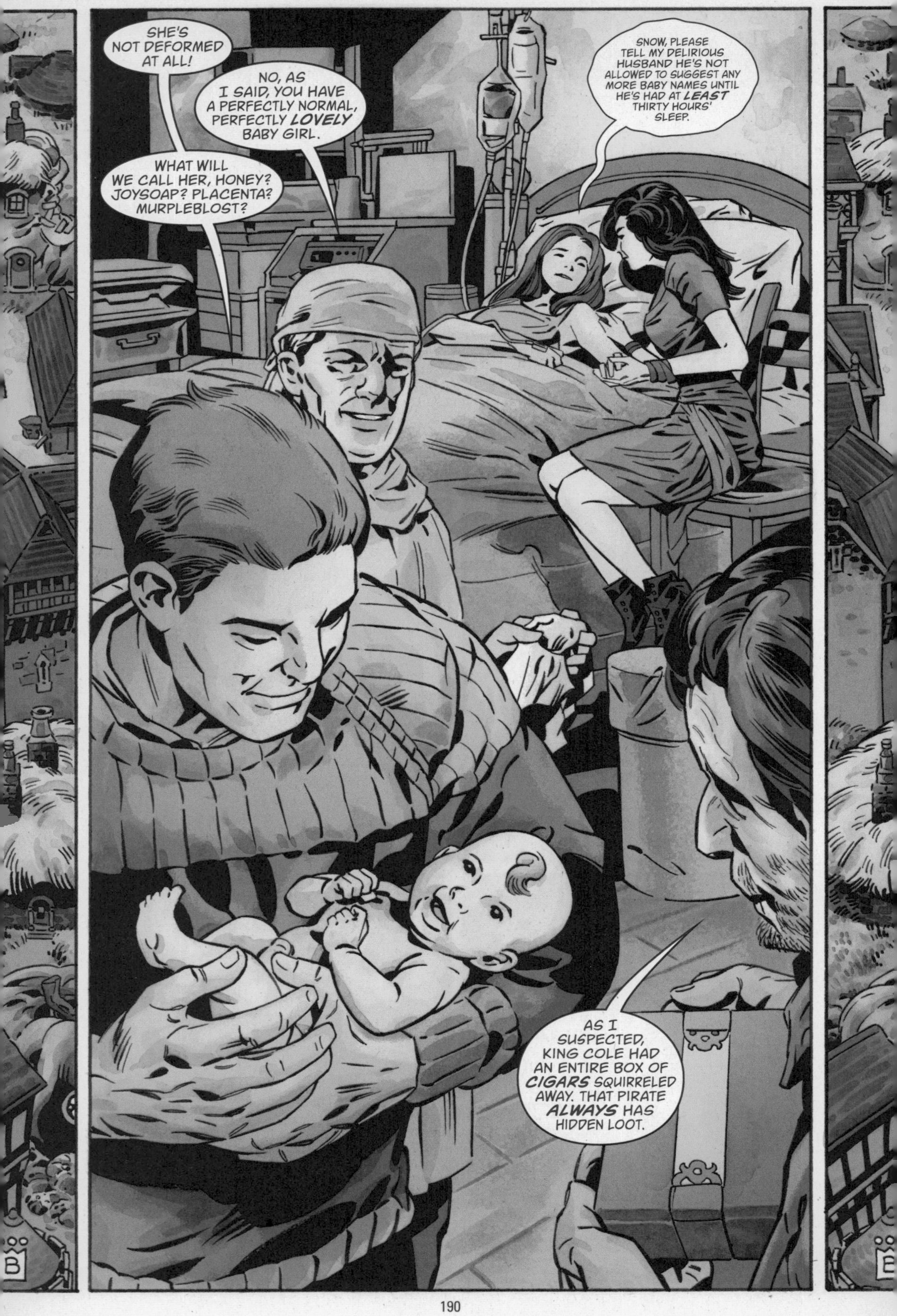

SHE'S NOT DEFORMED AT ALL!
NO, AS I SAID, YOU HAVE A PERFECTLY NORMAL, PERFECTLY LOVELY BABY GIRL.
WHAT WILL WE CALL HER, HONEY? JOYSOAP? PLACENTA? MURPLEBLOST?
SNOW, PLEASE TELL MY DELIRIOUS HUSBAND HE'S NOT ALLOWED TO SUGGEST ANY MORE BABY NAMES UNTIL HE'S HAD AT LEAST THIRTY HOURS' SLEEP.
AS I SUSPECTED, KING COLE HAD AN ENTIRE BOX OF CIGARS SQUIRRELED AWAY. THAT PIRATE ALWAYS HAS HIDDEN LOOT.

Chapter Seven: Or a Fortress Strong

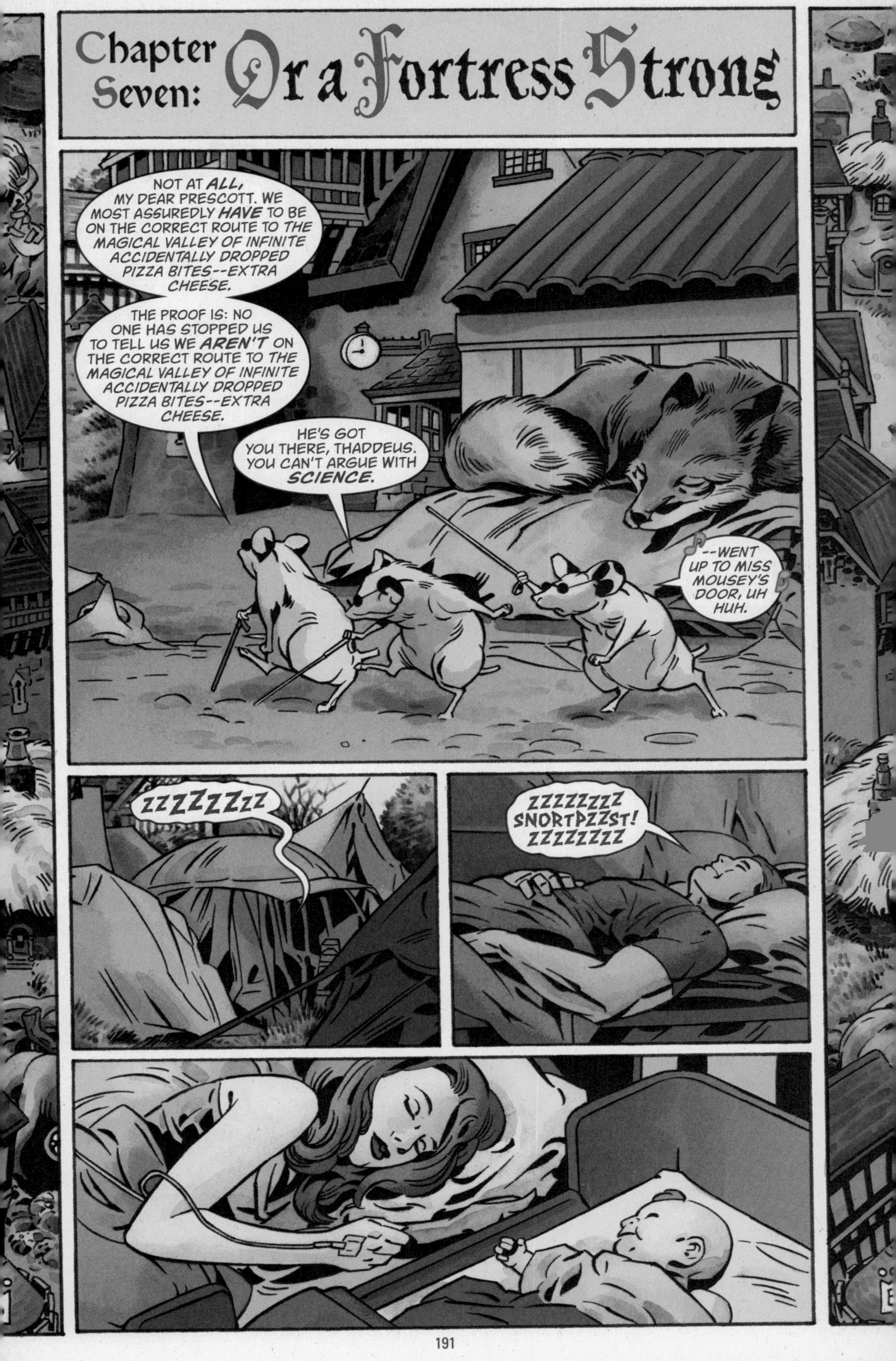
NOT AT ALL, MY DEAR PRESCOTT. WE MOST ASSUREDLY HAVE TO BE ON THE CORRECT ROUTE TO THE MAGICAL VALLEY OF INFINITE ACCIDENTALLY DROPPED PIZZA BITES--EXTRA CHEESE.
THE PROOF IS: NO ONE HAS STOPPED US TO TELL US WE AREN'T ON THE CORRECT ROUTE TO THE MAGICAL VALLEY OF INFINITE ACCIDENTALLY DROPPED PIZZA BITES--EXTRA CHEESE.
HE'S GOT YOU THERE, THADDEUS. YOU CAN'T ARGUE WITH SCIENCE.
--WENT UP TO MISS MOUSEY'S DOOR, UH HUH.
ZZZZZZzz
ZZZZZZZZ SNORTPZZST! ZZZZZZZ

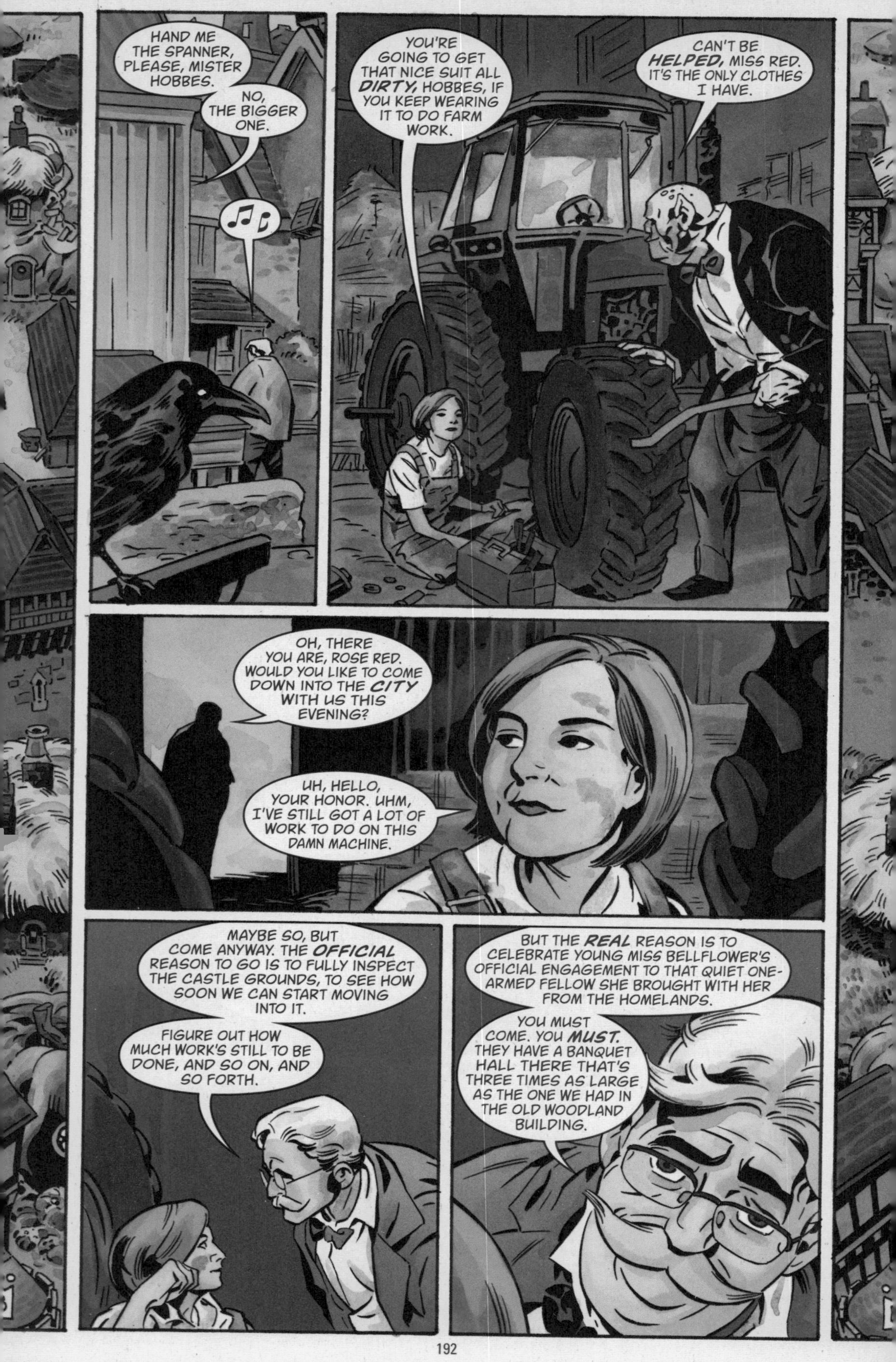
HAND ME THE SPANNER, PLEASE, MISTER HOBBES.
NO, THE BIGGER ONE.
YOU'RE GOING TO GET THAT NICE SUIT ALL DIRTY, HOBBES, IF YOU KEEP WEARING IT TO DO FARM WORK.
CAN'T BE HELPED, MISS RED. IT'S THE ONLY CLOTHES I HAVE.
OH, THERE YOU ARE, ROSE RED. WOULD YOU LIKE TO COME DOWN INTO THE CITY WITH US THIS EVENING?
UH, HELLO, YOUR HONOR. UHM, I'VE STILL GOT A LOT OF WORK TO DO ON THIS DAMN MACHINE.
MAYBE SO, BUT COME ANYWAY. THE OFFICIAL REASON TO GO IS TO FULLY INSPECT THE CASTLE GROUNDS, TO SEE HOW SOON WE CAN START MOVING INTO IT.
FIGURE OUT HOW MUCH WORK'S STILL TO BE DONE, AND SO ON, AND SO FORTH.
BUT THE REAL REASON IS TO CELEBRATE YOUNG MISS BELLFLOWER'S OFFICIAL ENGAGEMENT TO THAT QUIET ONE-ARMED FELLOW SHE BROUGHT WITH HER FROM THE HOMELANDS.
YOU MUST COME. YOU MUST. THEY HAVE A BANQUET HALL THERE THAT'S THREE TIMES AS LARGE AS THE ONE WE HAD IN THE OLD WOODLAND BUILDING.

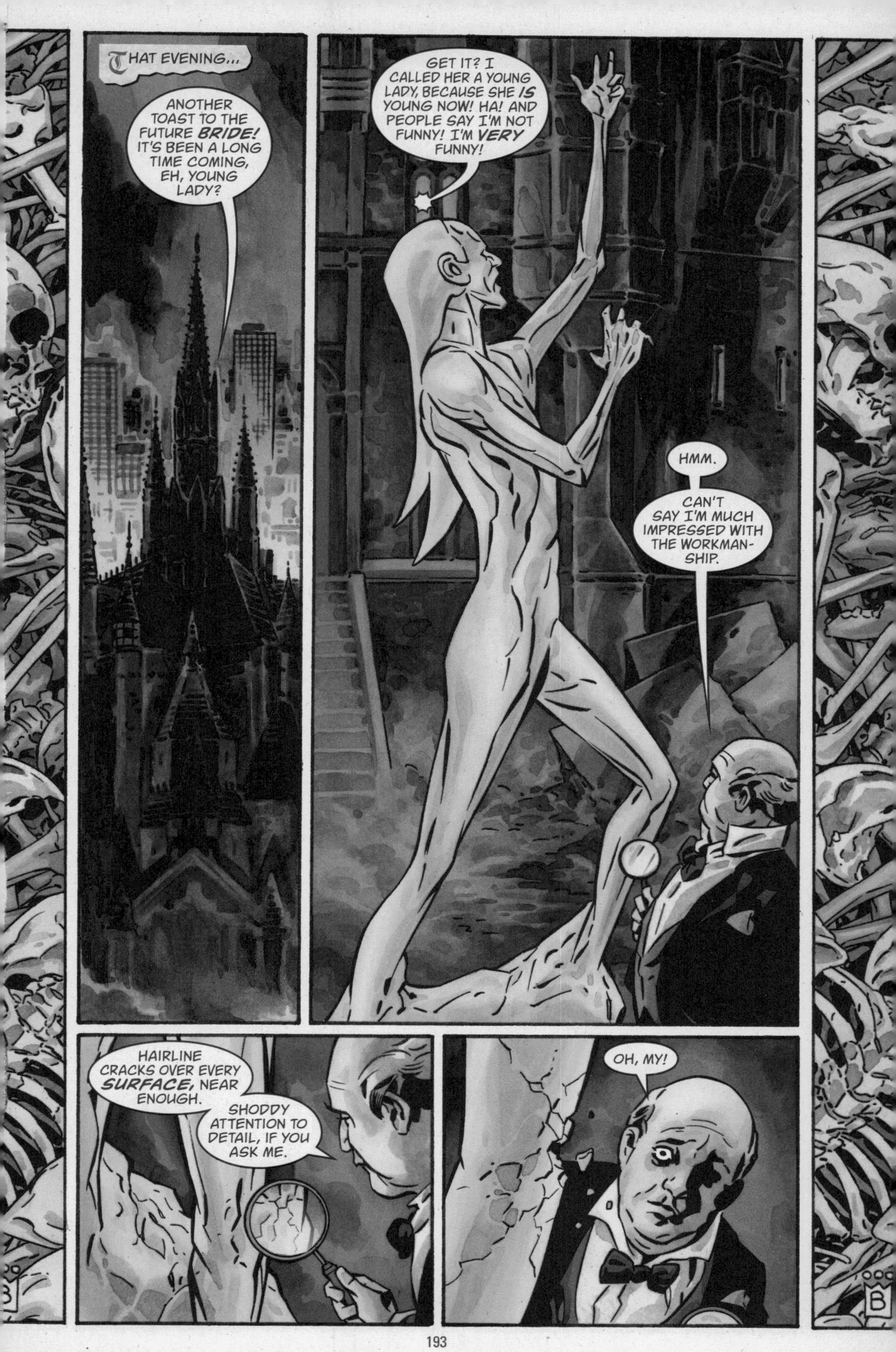
THAT EVENING...
ANOTHER TOAST TO THE FUTURE BRIDE! IT'S BEEN A LONG TIME COMING, EH, YOUNG LADY?
GET IT? I CALLED HER A YOUNG LADY, BECAUSE SHE IS YOUNG NOW! HA! AND PEOPLE SAY I'M NOT FUNNY! I'M VERY FUNNY!
HMM.
CAN'T SAY I'M MUCH IMPRESSED WITH THE WORKMAN-SHIP.
HAIRLINE CRACKS OVER EVERY SURFACE, NEAR ENOUGH.
SHODDY ATTENTION TO DETAIL, IF YOU ASK ME.
OH, MY!

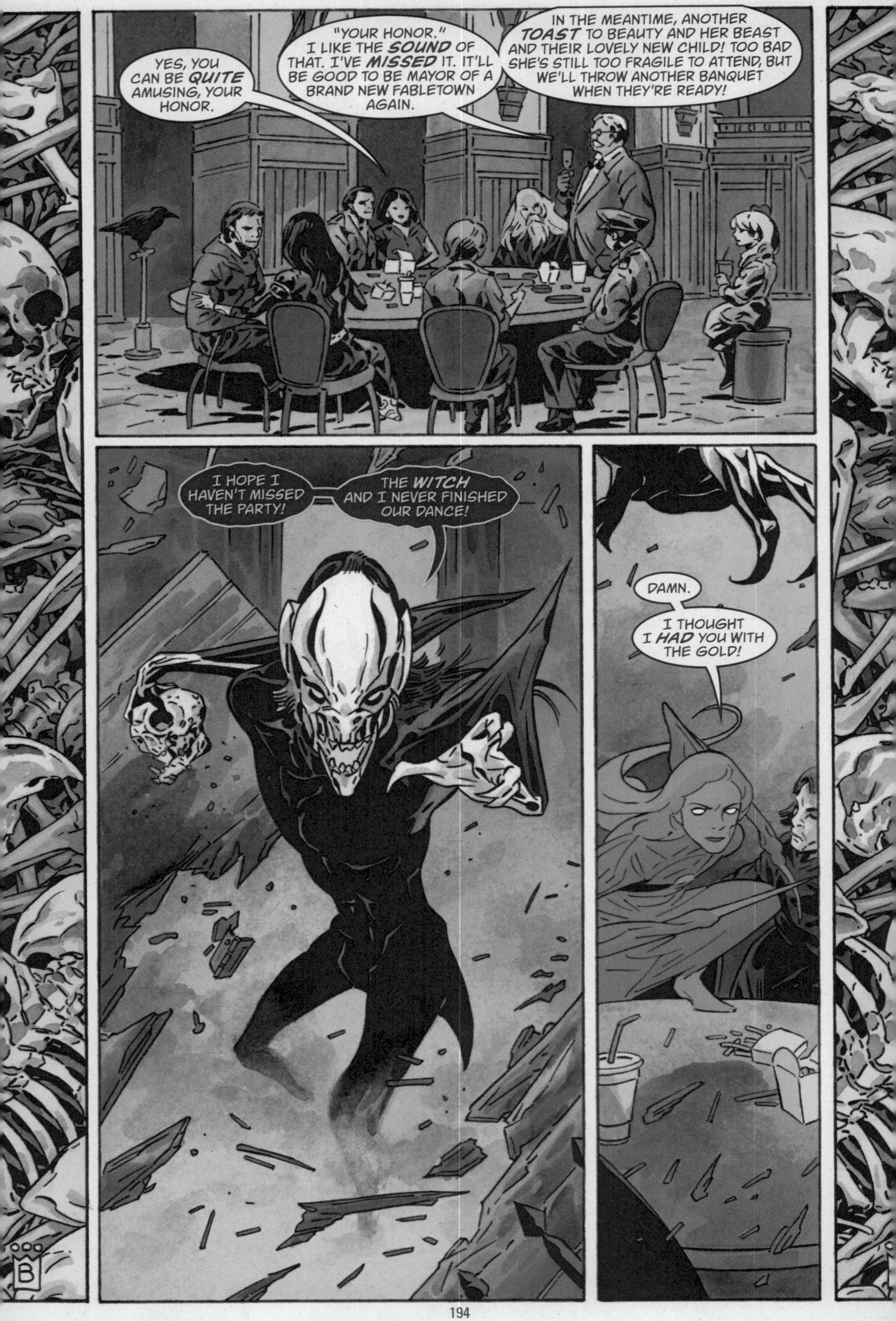
YES, YOU CAN BE QUITE AMUSING, YOUR HONOR.
"YOUR HONOR." I LIKE THE SOUND OF THAT. I'VE MISSED IT. IT'LL BE GOOD TO BE MAYOR OF A BRAND NEW FABLETOWN AGAIN.
IN THE MEANTIME, ANOTHER TOAST TO BEAUTY AND HER BEAST AND THEIR LOVELY NEW CHILD! TOO BAD SHE'S STILL TOO FRAGILE TO ATTEND, BUT WE'LL THROW ANOTHER BANQUET WHEN THEY'RE READY!
I HOPE I HAVEN'T MISSED THE PARTY!
THE WITCH AND I NEVER FINISHED OUR DANCE!
DAMN.
I THOUGHT I HAD YOU WITH THE GOLD!

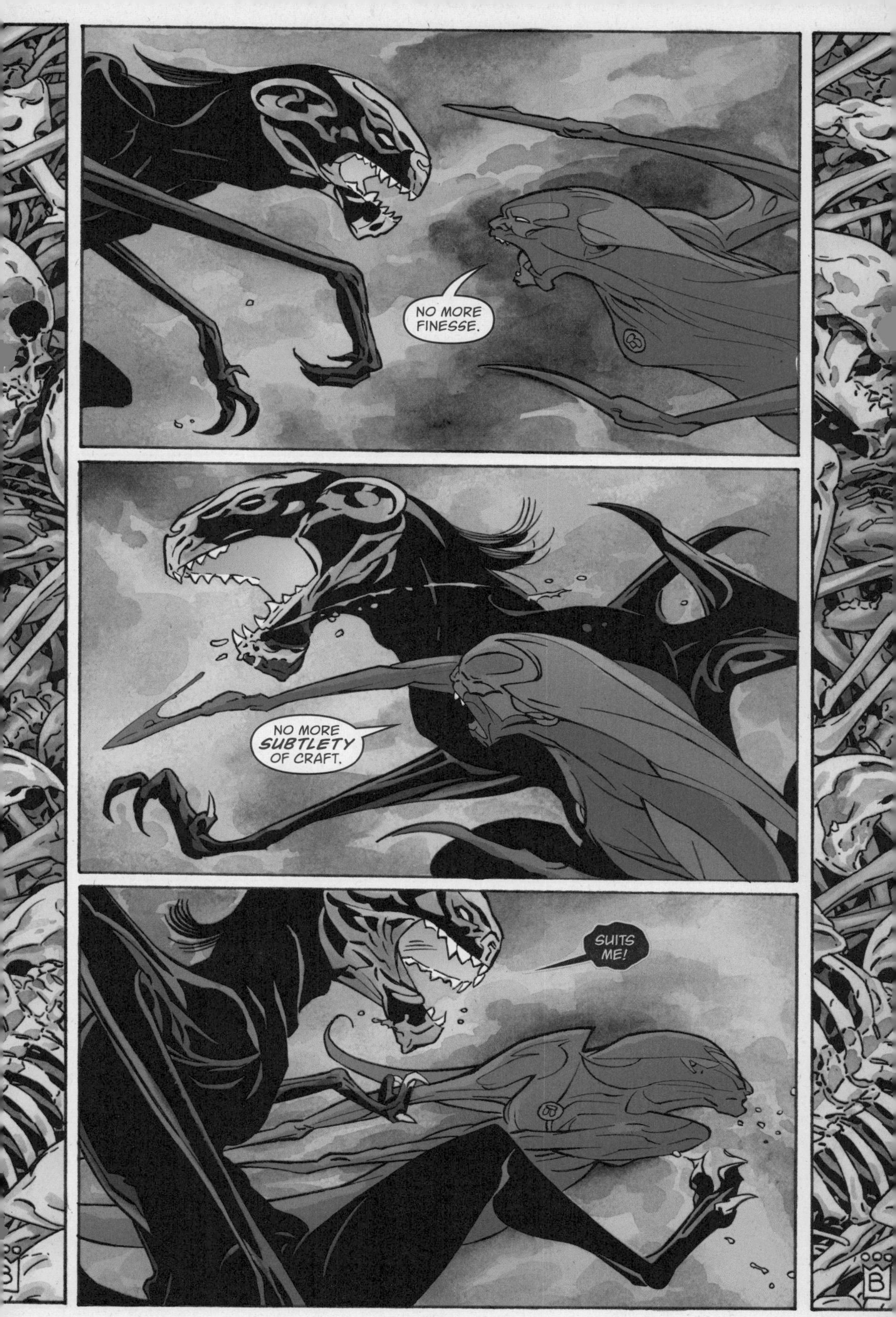
NO MORE FINESSE.
NO MORE SUBTLETY OF CRAFT.
SUITS ME!

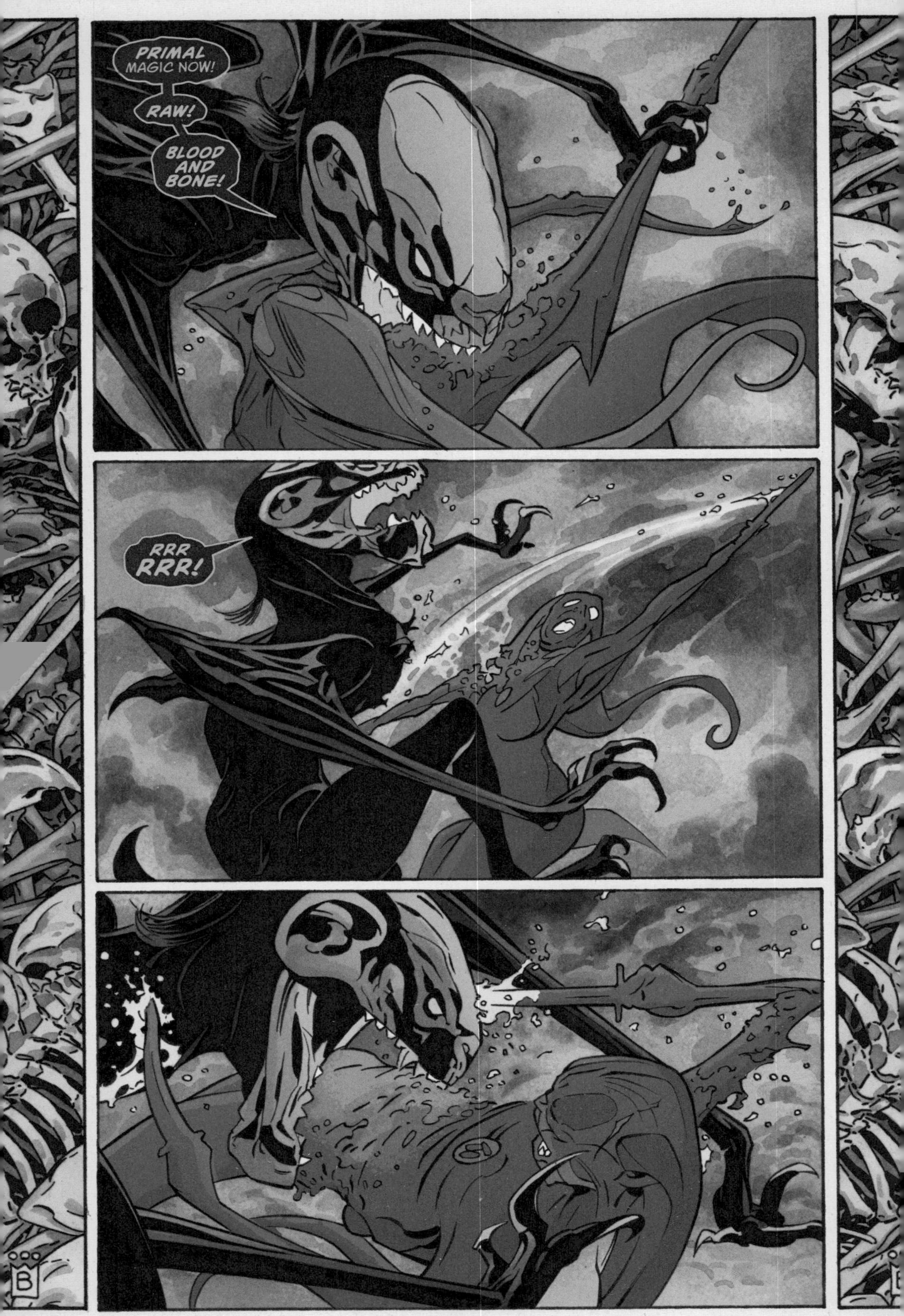
PRIMAL MAGIC NOW!
RAW!
BLOOD AND BONE!
RRR RRR!

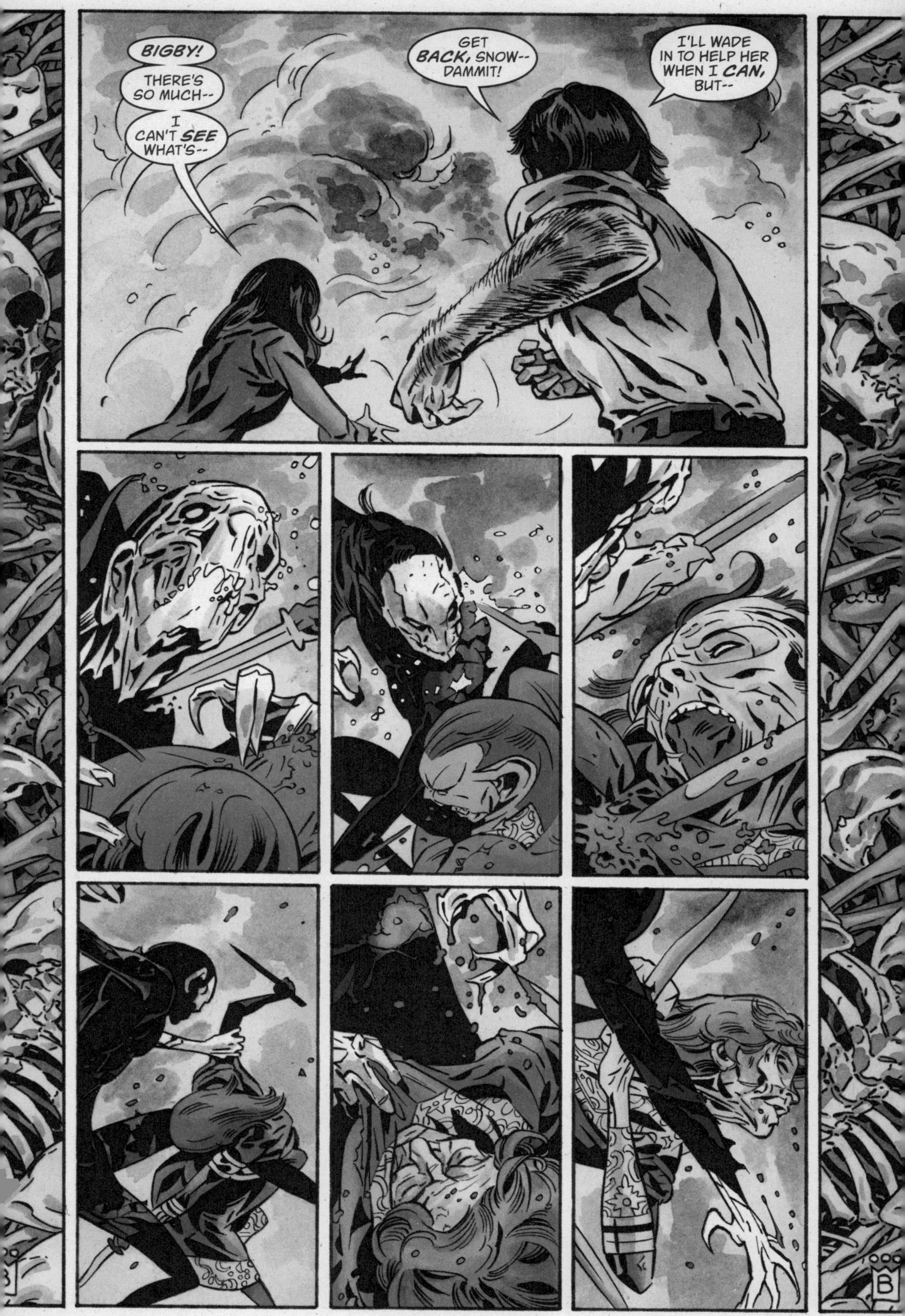
BIGBY!
THERE'S SO MUCH--
I CAN'T SEE WHAT'S--
GET BACK, SNOW-- DAMMIT!
I'LL WADE IN TO HELP HER WHEN I CAN, BUT--

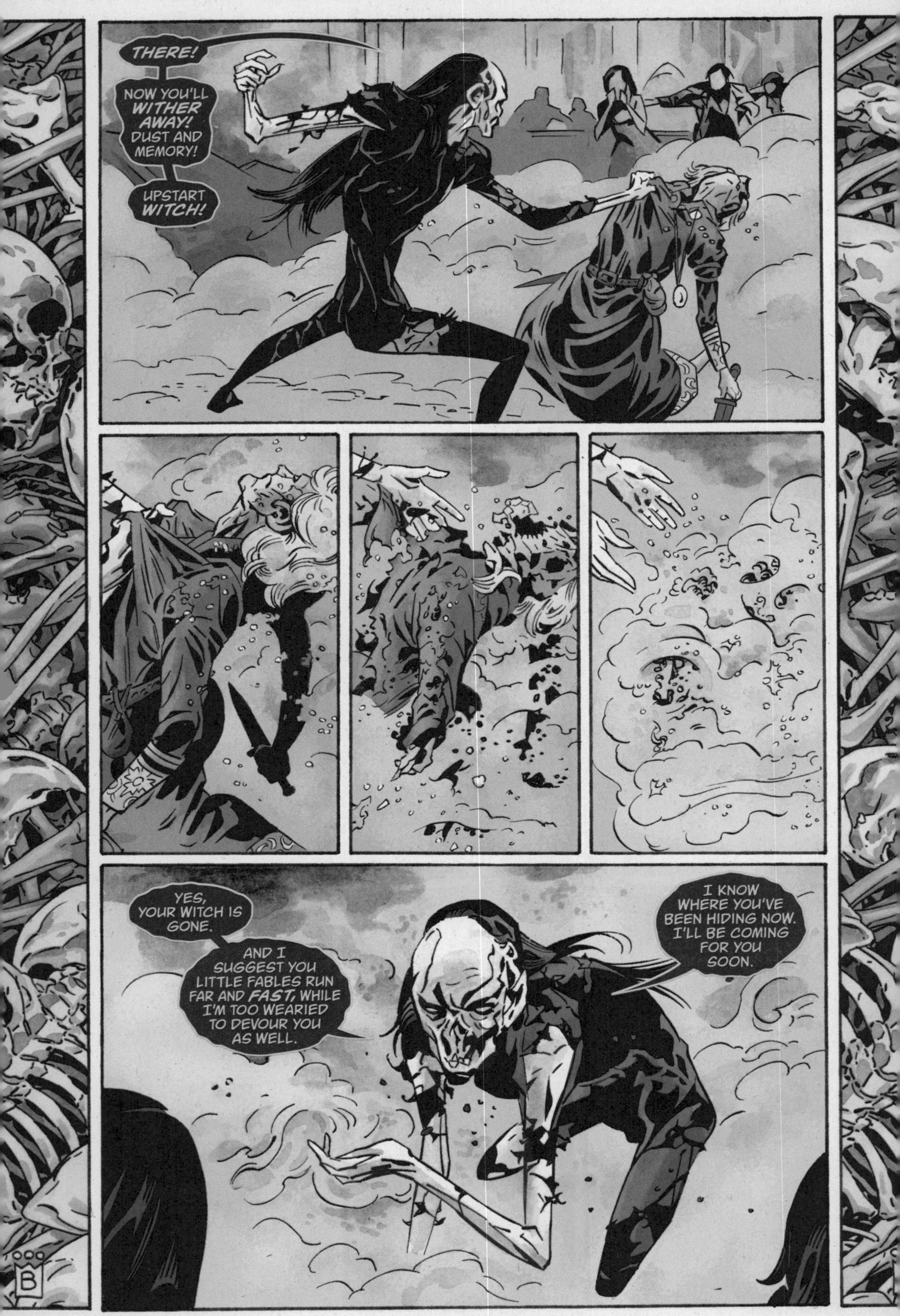
THERE!
NOW YOU'LL WITHER AWAY! DUST AND MEMORY!
UPSTART WITCH!
YES, YOUR WITCH IS GONE.
AND I SUGGEST YOU LITTLE FABLES RUN FAR AND FAST, WHILE I'M TOO WEARIED TO DEVOUR YOU AS WELL.
I KNOW WHERE YOU'VE BEEN HIDING NOW. I'LL BE COMING FOR YOU SOON.

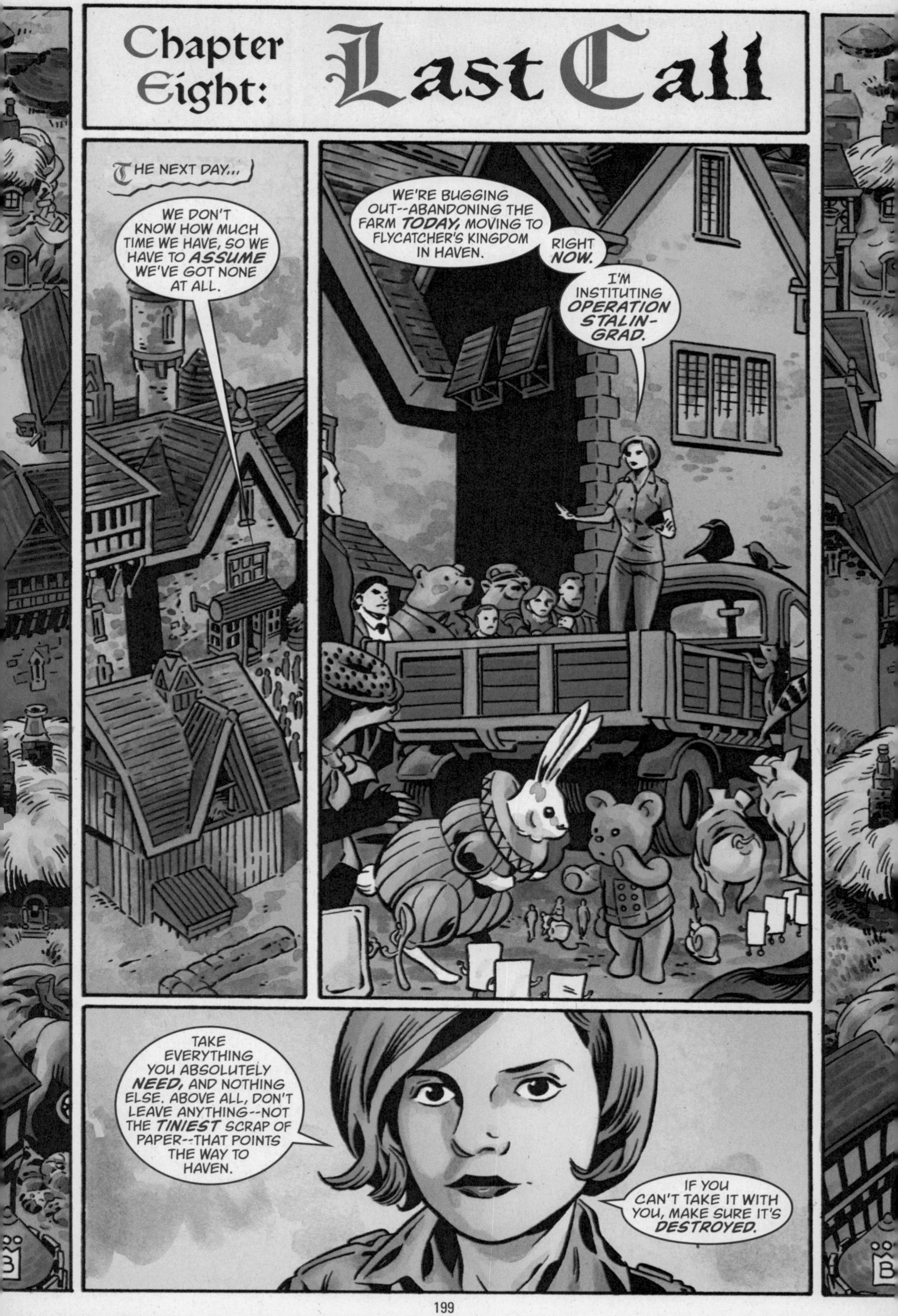

Chapter Eight: Last Call
THE NEXT DAY...
WE DON'T KNOW HOW MUCH TIME WE HAVE, SO WE HAVE TO ASSUME WE'VE GOT NONE AT ALL.
WE'RE BUGGING OUT--ABANDONING THE FARM TODAY, MOVING TO FLYCATCHER'S KINGDOM IN HAVEN.
RIGHT NOW.
I'M INSTITUTING OPERATION STALIN-GRAD.
TAKE EVERYTHING YOU ABSOLUTELY NEED, AND NOTHING ELSE. ABOVE ALL, DON'T LEAVE ANYTHING--NOT THE TINIEST SCRAP OF PAPER--THAT POINTS THE WAY TO HAVEN.
IF YOU CAN'T TAKE IT WITH YOU, MAKE SURE IT'S DESTROYED.

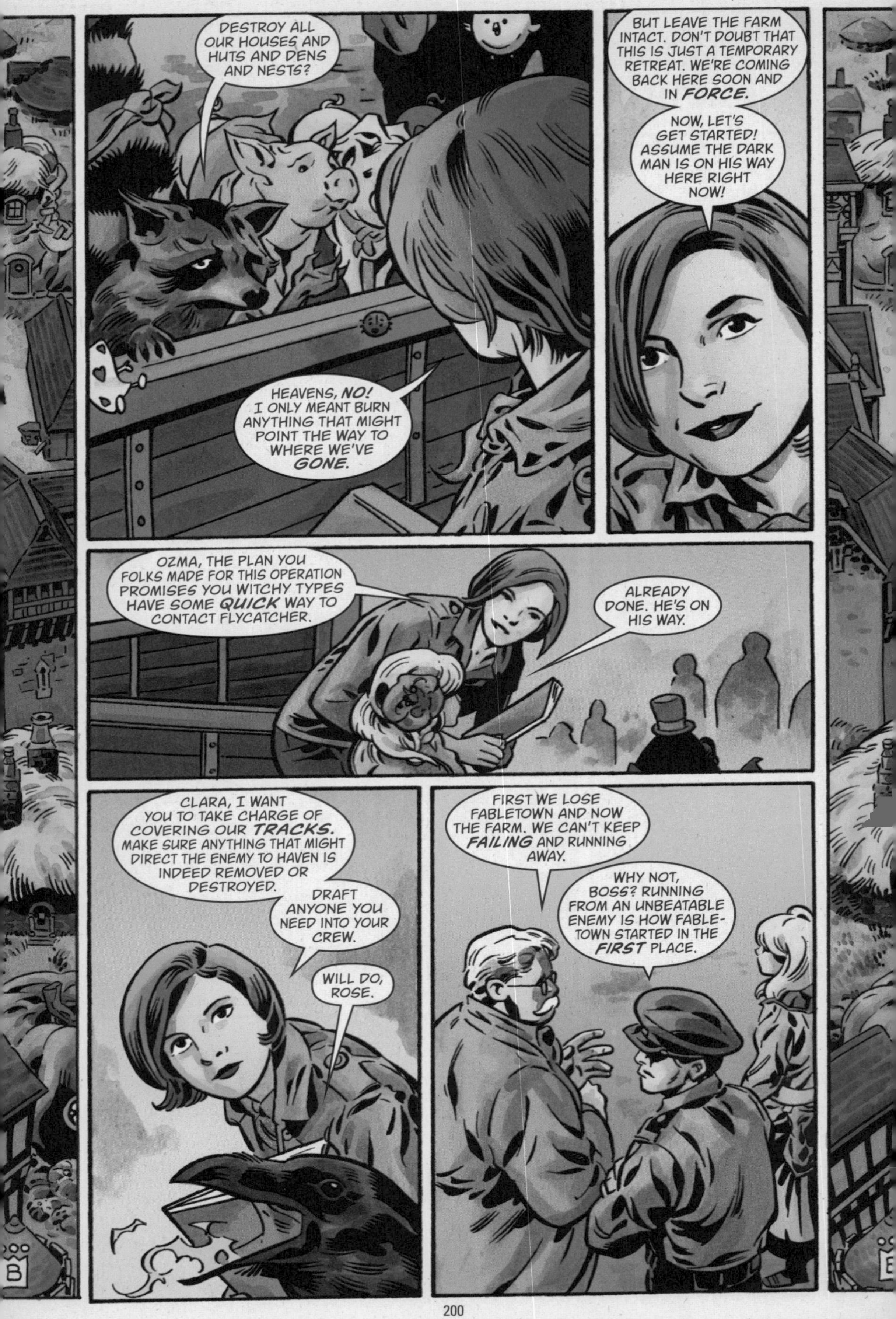

DESTROY ALL OUR HOUSES AND HUTS AND DENS AND NESTS?
HEAVENS, NO! I ONLY MEANT BURN ANYTHING THAT MIGHT POINT THE WAY TO WHERE WE'VE GONE.
BUT LEAVE THE FARM INTACT. DON'T DOUBT THAT THIS IS JUST A TEMPORARY RETREAT. WE'RE COMING BACK HERE SOON AND IN FORCE.
NOW, LET'S GET STARTED! ASSUME THE DARK MAN IS ON HIS WAY HERE RIGHT NOW!
OZMA, THE PLAN YOU FOLKS MADE FOR THIS OPERATION PROMISES YOU WITCHY TYPES HAVE SOME QUICK WAY TO CONTACT FLYCATCHER.
ALREADY DONE. HE'S ON HIS WAY.
CLARA, I WANT YOU TO TAKE CHARGE OF COVERING OUR TRACKS. MAKE SURE ANYTHING THAT MIGHT DIRECT THE ENEMY TO HAVEN IS INDEED REMOVED OR DESTROYED.
DRAFT ANYONE YOU NEED INTO YOUR CREW.
WILL DO, ROSE.
FIRST WE LOSE FABLETOWN AND NOW THE FARM. WE CAN'T KEEP FAILING AND RUNNING AWAY.
WHY NOT, BOSS? RUNNING FROM AN UNBEATABLE ENEMY IS HOW FABLETOWN STARTED IN THE FIRST PLACE.

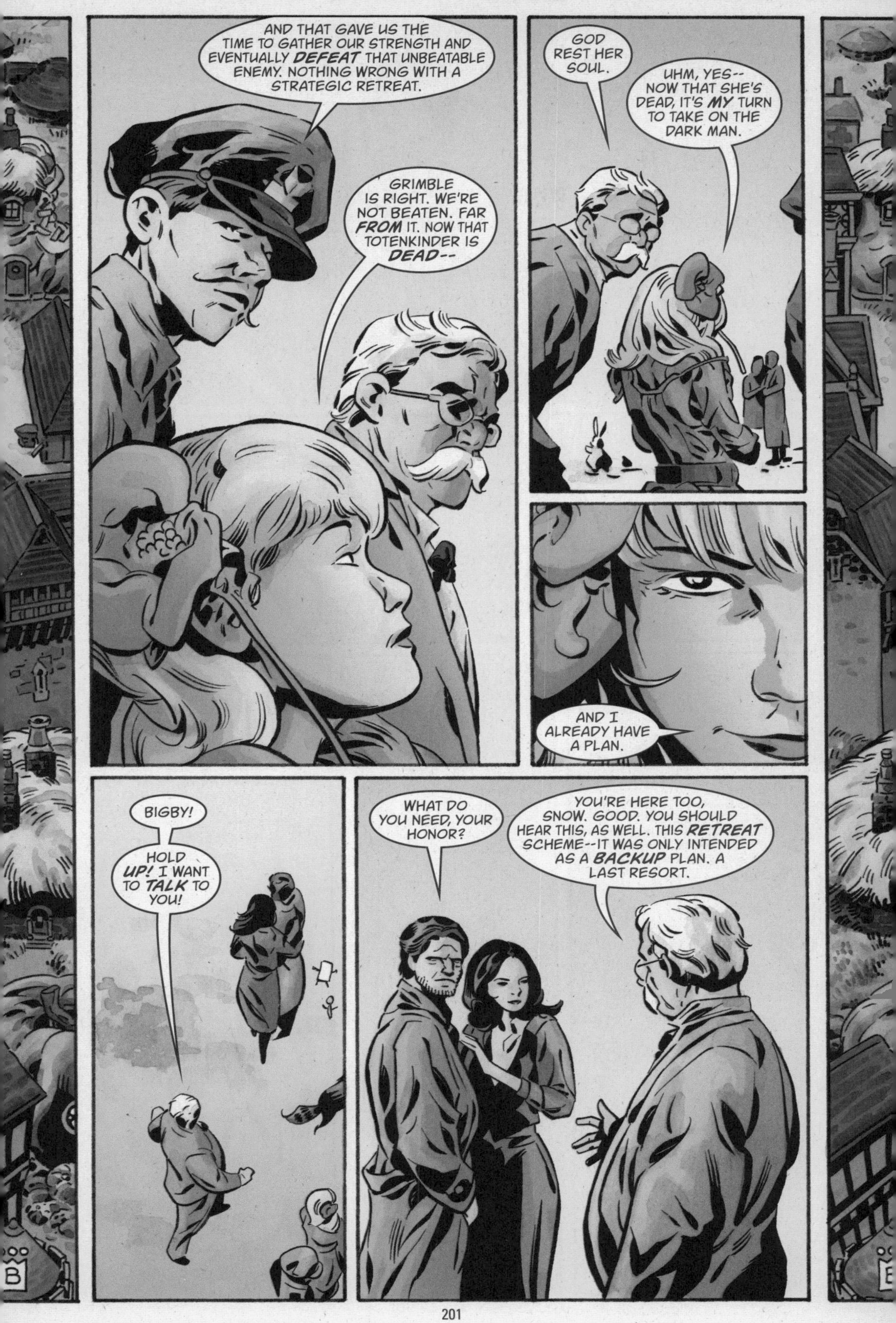
AND THAT GAVE US THE TIME TO GATHER OUR STRENGTH AND EVENTUALLY DEFEAT THAT UNBEATABLE ENEMY. NOTHING WRONG WITH A STRATEGIC RETREAT.
GRIMBLE IS RIGHT. WE'RE NOT BEATEN. FAR FROM IT. NOW THAT TOTENKINDER IS DEAD--
GOD REST HER SOUL.
UHM, YES-- NOW THAT SHE'S DEAD, IT'S MY TURN TO TAKE ON THE DARK MAN.
AND I ALREADY HAVE A PLAN.
BIGBY!
HOLD UP! I WANT TO TALK TO YOU!
WHAT DO YOU NEED, YOUR HONOR?
YOU'RE HERE TOO, SNOW. GOOD. YOU SHOULD HEAR THIS, AS WELL. THIS RETREAT SCHEME--IT WAS ONLY INTENDED AS A BACKUP PLAN. A LAST RESORT.

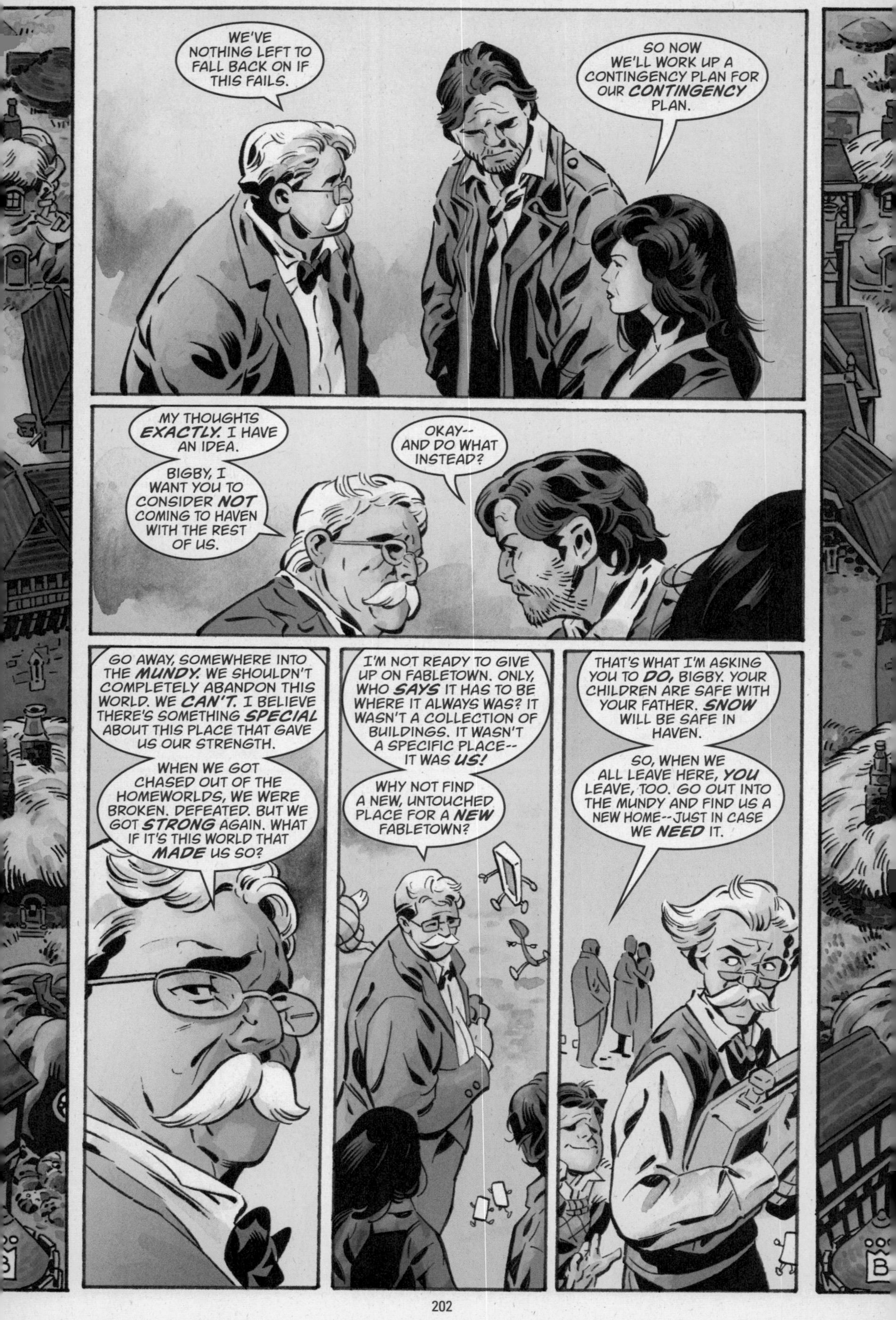

WE'VE NOTHING LEFT TO FALL BACK ON IF THIS FAILS.
SO NOW WE'LL WORK UP A CONTINGENCY PLAN FOR OUR CONTINGENCY PLAN.
MY THOUGHTS EXACTLY. I HAVE AN IDEA.
BIGBY, I WANT YOU TO CONSIDER NOT COMING TO HAVEN WITH THE REST OF US.
OKAY-- AND DO WHAT INSTEAD?
GO AWAY, SOMEWHERE INTO THE MUNDY. WE SHOULDN'T COMPLETELY ABANDON THIS WORLD. WE CAN'T. I BELIEVE THERE'S SOMETHING SPECIAL ABOUT THIS PLACE THAT GAVE US OUR STRENGTH.
WHEN WE GOT CHASED OUT OF THE HOMEWORLDS, WE WERE BROKEN. DEFEATED. BUT WE GOT STRONG AGAIN. WHAT IF IT'S THIS WORLD THAT MADE US SO?
I'M NOT READY TO GIVE UP ON FABLETOWN. ONLY, WHO SAYS IT HAS TO BE WHERE IT ALWAYS WAS? IT WASN'T A COLLECTION OF BUILDINGS. IT WASN'T A SPECIFIC PLACE-- IT WAS US!
WHY NOT FIND A NEW, UNTOUCHED PLACE FOR A NEW FABLETOWN?
THAT'S WHAT I'M ASKING YOU TO DO, BIGBY. YOUR CHILDREN ARE SAFE WITH YOUR FATHER. SNOW WILL BE SAFE IN HAVEN.
SO, WHEN WE ALL LEAVE HERE, YOU LEAVE, TOO. GO OUT INTO THE MUNDY AND FIND US A NEW HOME--JUST IN CASE WE NEED IT.

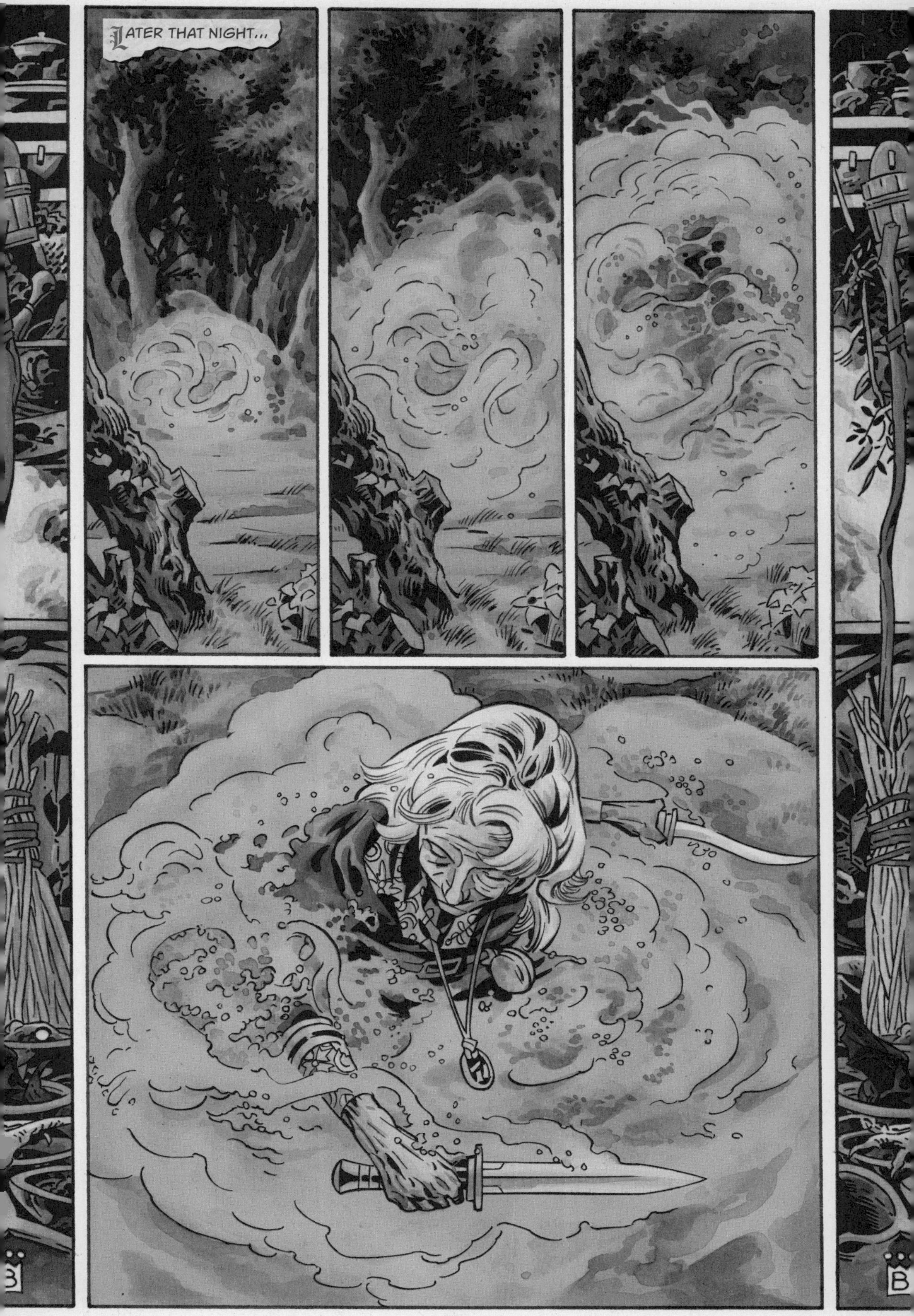
LATER THAT NIGHT...

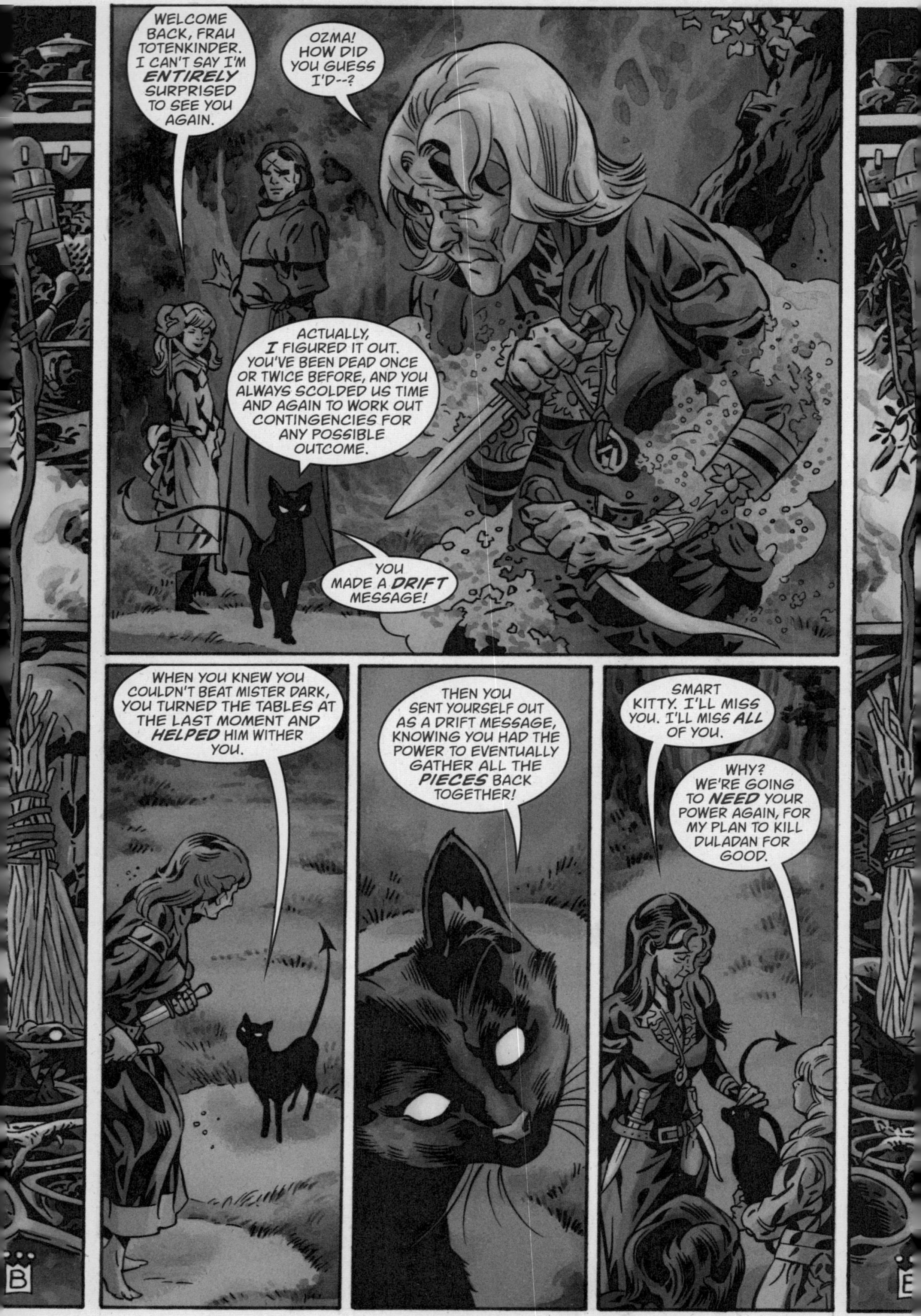

WELCOME BACK, FRAU TOTENKINDER. I CAN'T SAY I'M ENTIRELY SURPRISED TO SEE YOU AGAIN.
OZMA! HOW DID YOU GUESS I'D--?
ACTUALLY, I FIGURED IT OUT. YOU'VE BEEN DEAD ONCE OR TWICE BEFORE, AND YOU ALWAYS SCOLDED US TIME AND AGAIN TO WORK OUT CONTINGENCIES FOR ANY POSSIBLE OUTCOME.
YOU MADE A DRIFT MESSAGE!
WHEN YOU KNEW YOU COULDN'T BEAT MISTER DARK, YOU TURNED THE TABLES AT THE LAST MOMENT AND HELPED HIM WITHER YOU.
THEN YOU SENT YOURSELF OUT AS A DRIFT MESSAGE, KNOWING YOU HAD THE POWER TO EVENTUALLY GATHER ALL THE PIECES BACK TOGETHER!
SMART KITTY. I'LL MISS YOU. I'LL MISS ALL OF YOU.
WHY? WE'RE GOING TO NEED YOUR POWER AGAIN, FOR MY PLAN TO KILL DULADAN FOR GOOD.

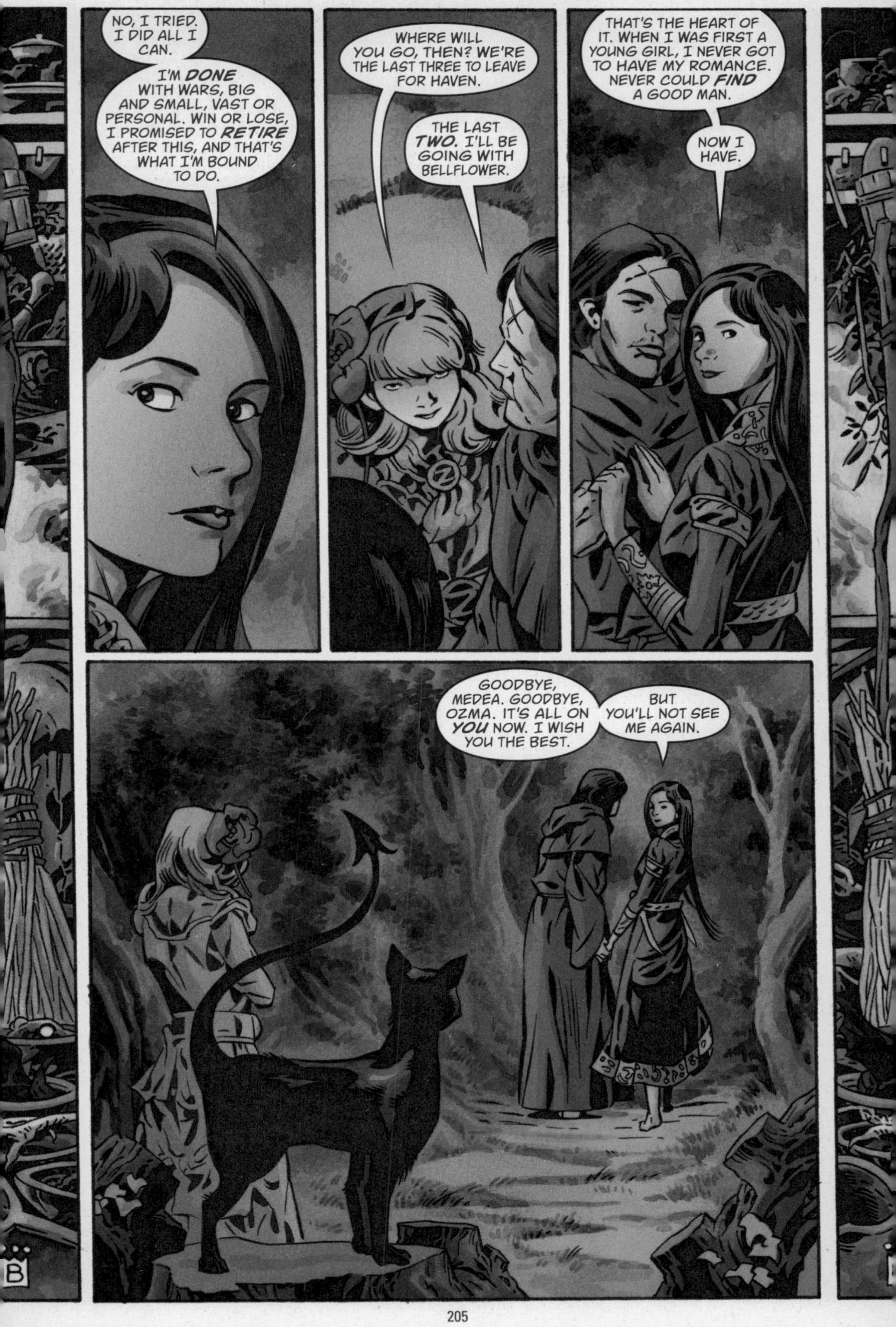
NO, I TRIED. I DID ALL I CAN.
I'M DONE WITH WARS, BIG AND SMALL, VAST OR PERSONAL. WIN OR LOSE, I PROMISED TO RETIRE AFTER THIS, AND THAT'S WHAT I'M BOUND TO DO.
WHERE WILL YOU GO, THEN? WE'RE THE LAST THREE TO LEAVE FOR HAVEN.
THE LAST TWO. I'LL BE GOING WITH BELLFLOWER.
THAT'S THE HEART OF IT. WHEN I WAS FIRST A YOUNG GIRL, I NEVER GOT TO HAVE MY ROMANCE. NEVER COULD FIND A GOOD MAN.
NOW I HAVE.
GOODBYE, MEDEA. GOODBYE, OZMA. IT'S ALL ON YOU NOW. I WISH YOU THE BEST.
BUT YOU'LL NOT SEE ME AGAIN.

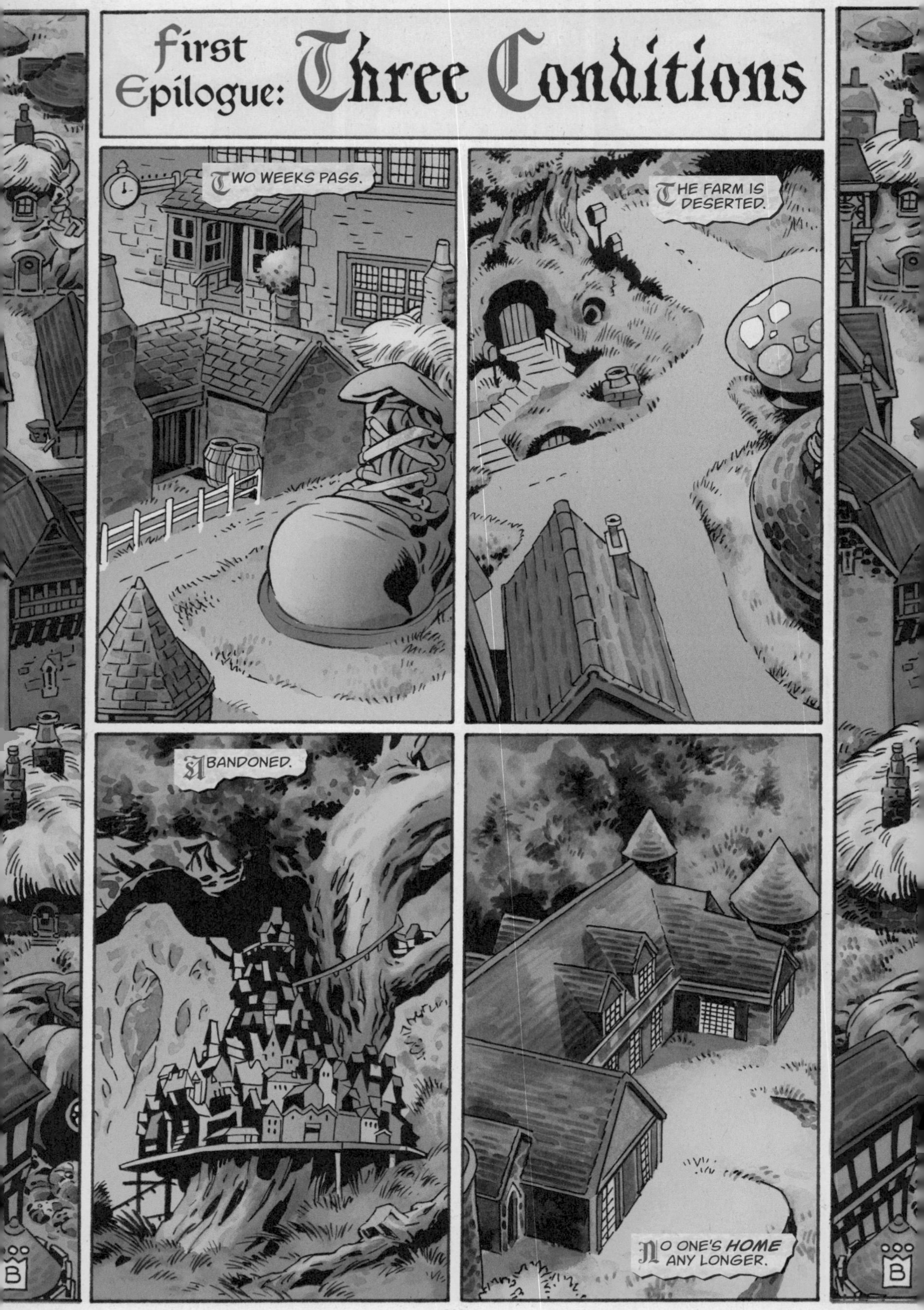

First Epilogue: Three Conditions
TWO WEEKS PASS.
THE FARM IS DESERTED.
ABANDONED.
NO ONE'S HOME ANY LONGER.

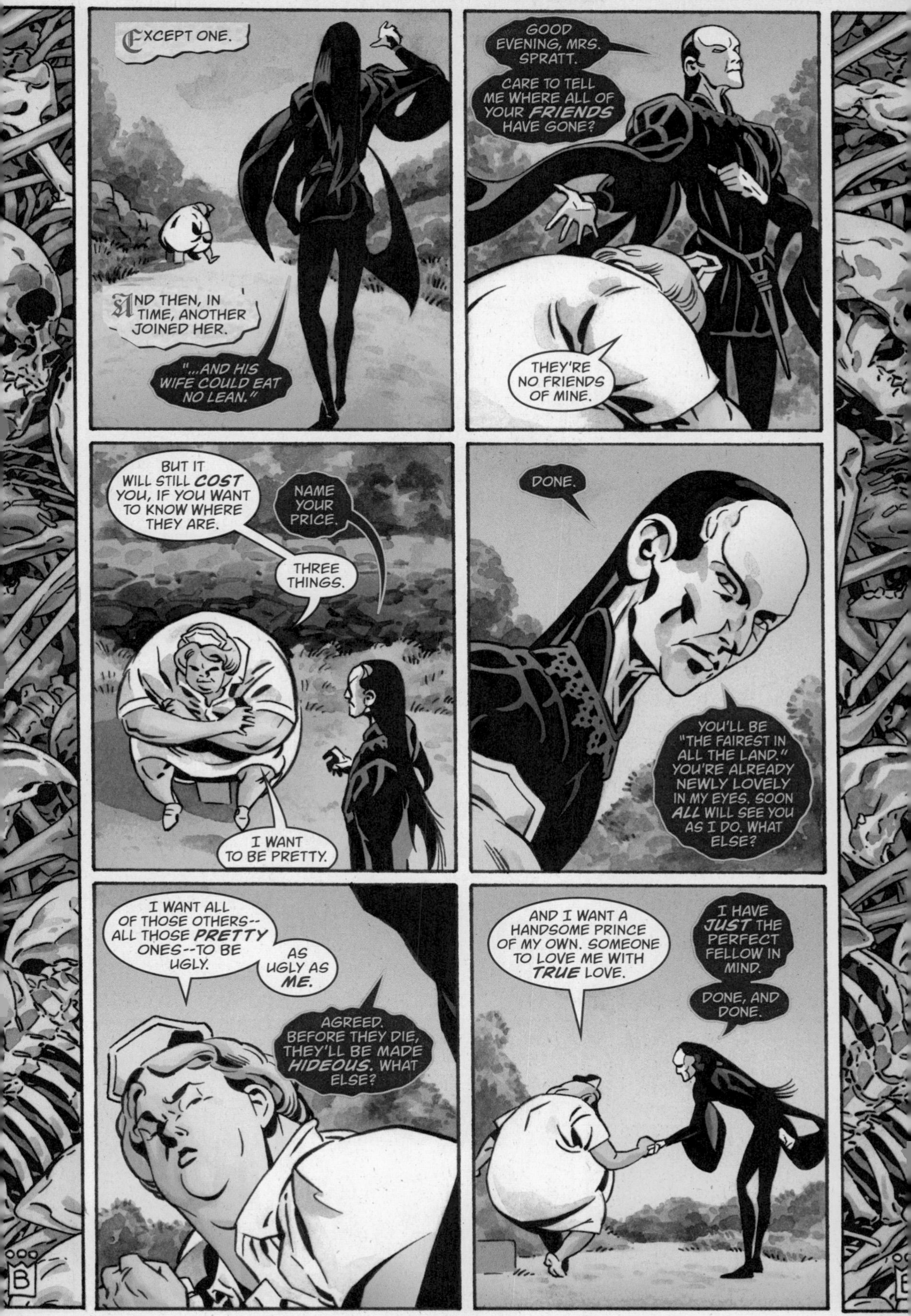
EXCEPT ONE.
AND THEN, IN TIME, ANOTHER JOINED HER.
"...AND HIS WIFE COULD EAT NO LEAN."
GOOD EVENING, MRS. SPRATT.
CARE TO TELL ME WHERE ALL OF YOUR FRIENDS HAVE GONE?
THEY'RE NO FRIENDS OF MINE.
BUT IT WILL STILL COST YOU, IF YOU WANT TO KNOW WHERE THEY ARE.
NAME YOUR PRICE.
THREE THINGS.
I WANT TO BE PRETTY.
DONE.
YOU'LL BE "THE FAIREST IN ALL THE LAND." YOU'RE ALREADY NEWLY LOVELY IN MY EYES. SOON ALL WILL SEE YOU AS I DO. WHAT ELSE?
I WANT ALL OF THOSE OTHERS--ALL THOSE PRETTY ONES--TO BE UGLY.
AS UGLY AS ME.
AGREED. BEFORE THEY DIE, THEY'LL BE MADE HIDEOUS. WHAT ELSE?
AND I WANT A HANDSOME PRINCE OF MY OWN. SOMEONE TO LOVE ME WITH TRUE LOVE.
I HAVE JUST THE PERFECT FELLOW IN MIND.
DONE, AND DONE.

Second Epilogue: Such a Lovely Little Darling

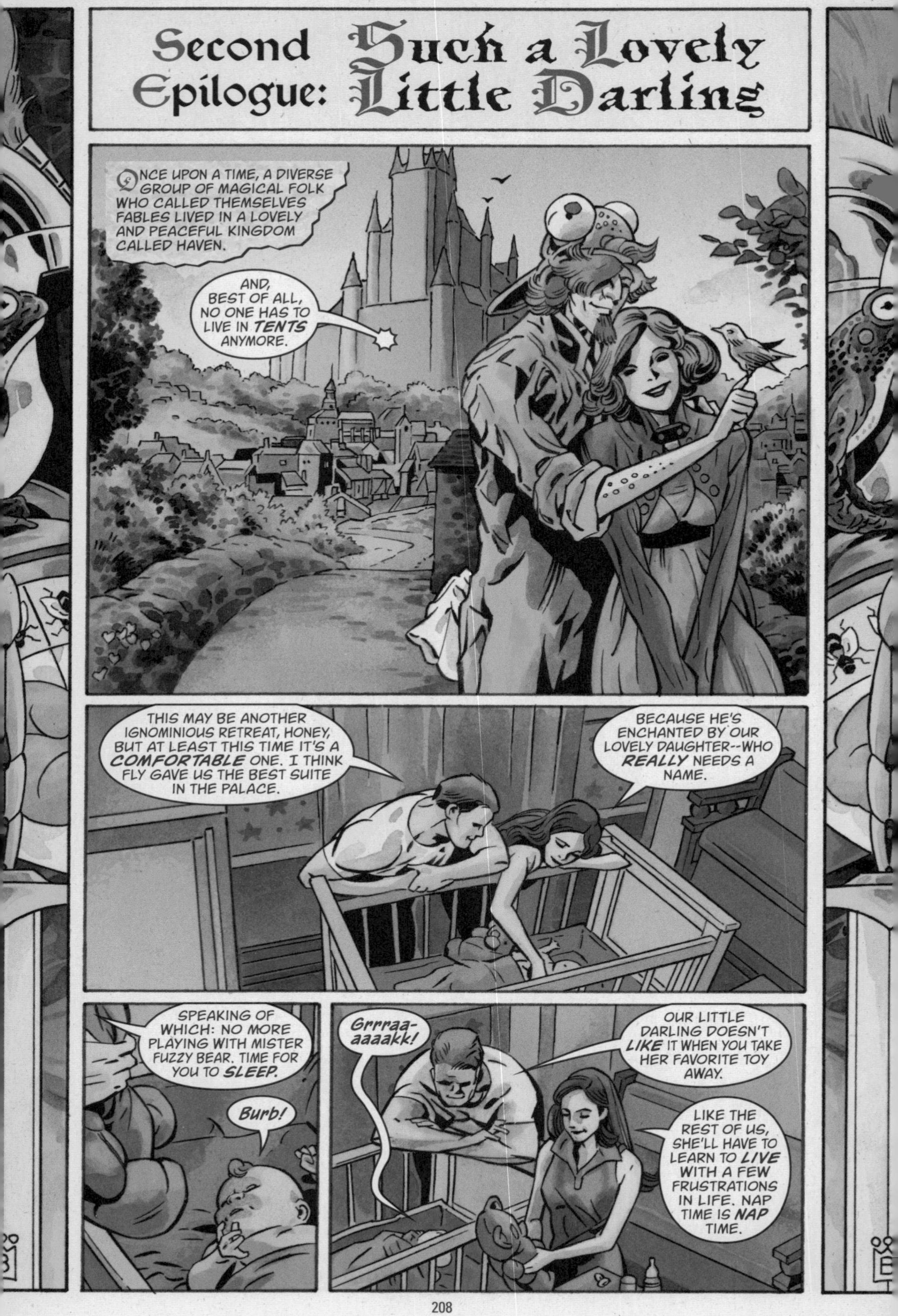
ONCE UPON A TIME, A DIVERSE GROUP OF MAGICAL FOLK WHO CALLED THEMSELVES FABLES LIVED IN A LOVELY AND PEACEFUL KINGDOM CALLED HAVEN.
AND, BEST OF ALL, NO ONE HAS TO LIVE IN TENTS ANYMORE.
THIS MAY BE ANOTHER IGNOMINIOUS RETREAT, HONEY, BUT AT LEAST THIS TIME IT'S A COMFORTABLE ONE. I THINK FLY GAVE US THE BEST SUITE IN THE PALACE.
BECAUSE HE'S ENCHANTED BY OUR LOVELY DAUGHTER--WHO REALLY NEEDS A NAME.
SPEAKING OF WHICH: NO MORE PLAYING WITH MISTER FUZZY BEAR. TIME FOR YOU TO SLEEP.
Burb!
Grrraa-aaaakk!
OUR LITTLE DARLING DOESN'T LIKE IT WHEN YOU TAKE HER FAVORITE TOY AWAY.
LIKE THE REST OF US, SHE'LL HAVE TO LEARN TO LIVE WITH A FEW FRUSTRATIONS IN LIFE. NAP TIME IS NAP TIME.

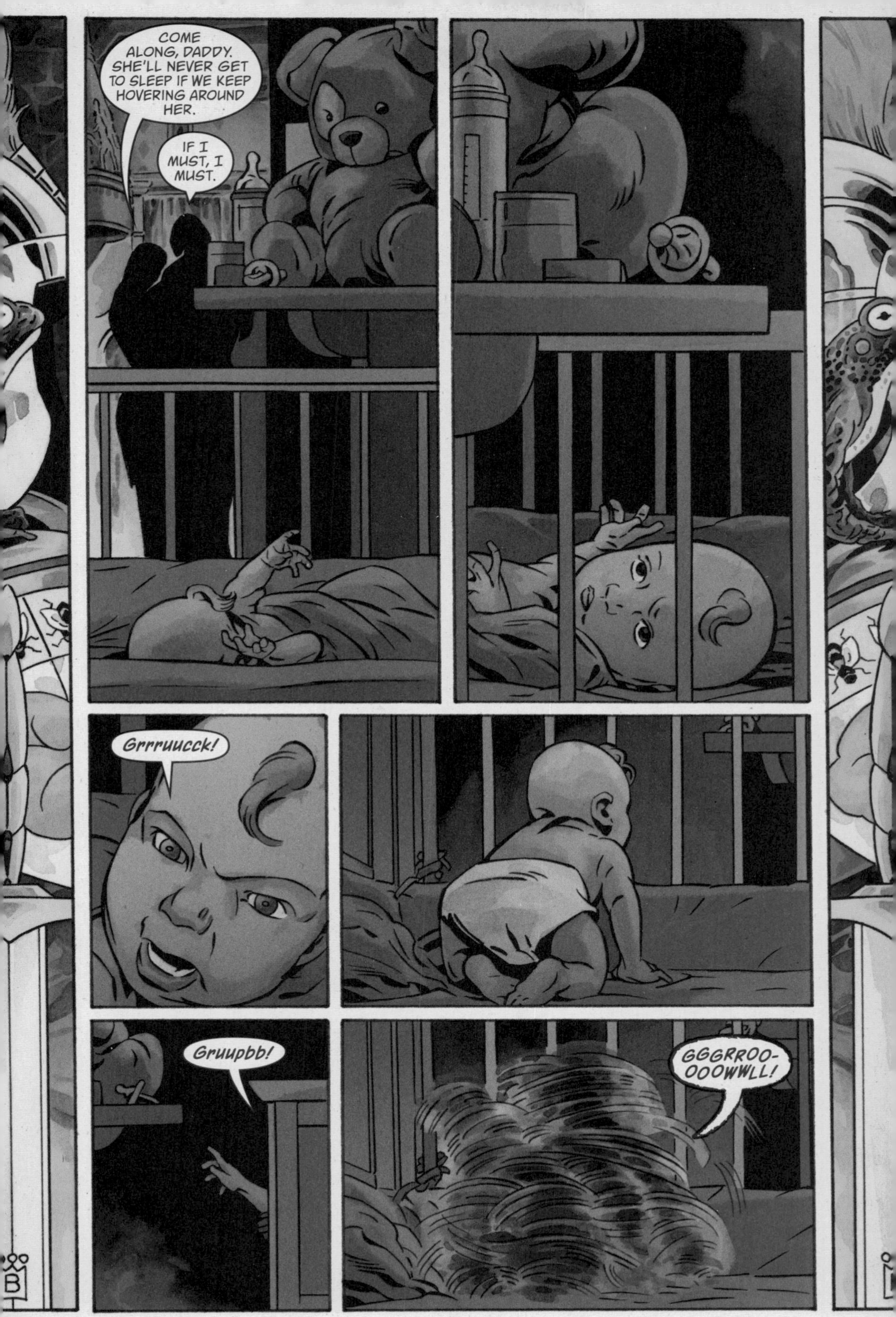
COME ALONG, DADDY. SHE'LL NEVER GET TO SLEEP IF WE KEEP HOVERING AROUND HER.
IF I MUST, I MUST.
Grrruucck!
Gruupbb!
GGGRROO-OOOWLL!

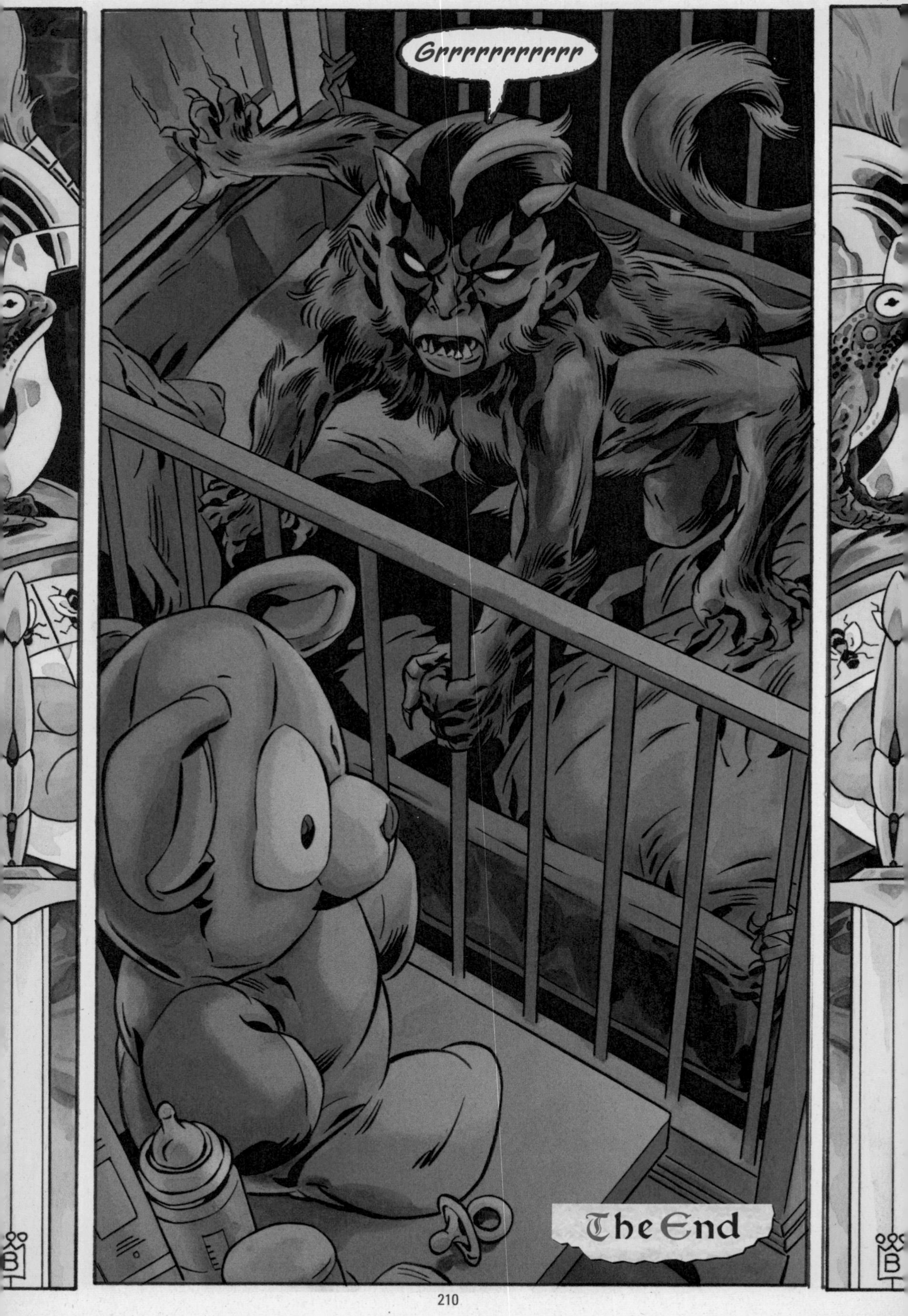
Grrrrrrrrrrr
The End

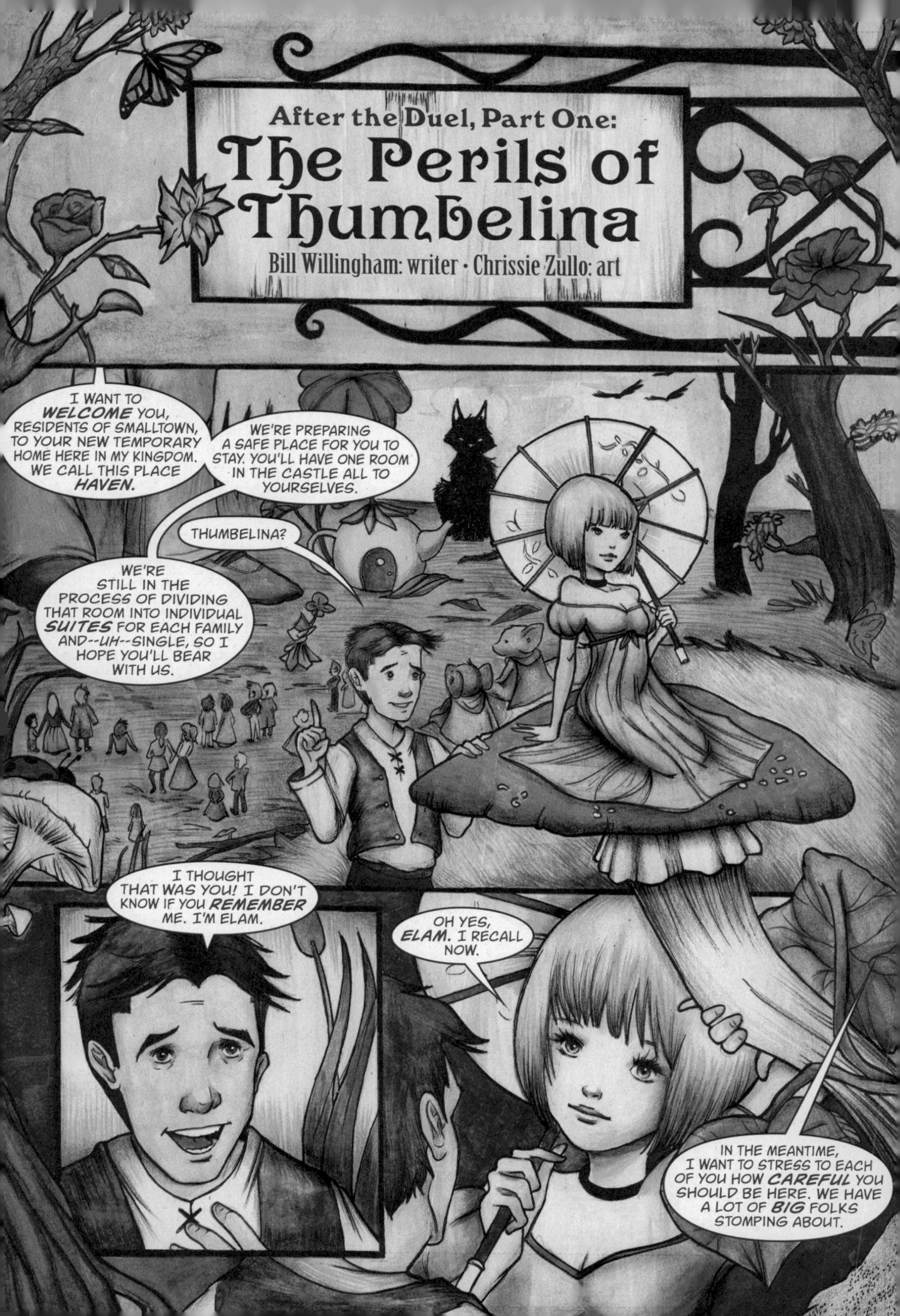
After the Duel, Part One:
The Perils of Thumbelina
Bill Willingham: writer • Chrissie Zullo: art
I WANT TO WELCOME YOU, RESIDENTS OF SMALLTOWN, TO YOUR NEW TEMPORARY HOME HERE IN MY KINGDOM. WE CALL THIS PLACE HAVEN.
WE'RE PREPARING A SAFE PLACE FOR YOU TO STAY. YOU'LL HAVE ONE ROOM IN THE CASTLE ALL TO YOURSELVES.
WE'RE STILL IN THE PROCESS OF DIVIDING THAT ROOM INTO INDIVIDUAL SUITES FOR EACH FAMILY AND--UH--SINGLE, SO I HOPE YOU'LL BEAR WITH US.
THUMBELINA?
I THOUGHT THAT WAS YOU! I DON'T KNOW IF YOU REMEMBER ME. I'M ELAM.
OH YES, ELAM. I RECALL NOW.
IN THE MEANTIME, I WANT TO STRESS TO EACH OF YOU HOW CAREFUL YOU SHOULD BE HERE. WE HAVE A LOT OF BIG FOLKS STOMPING ABOUT.

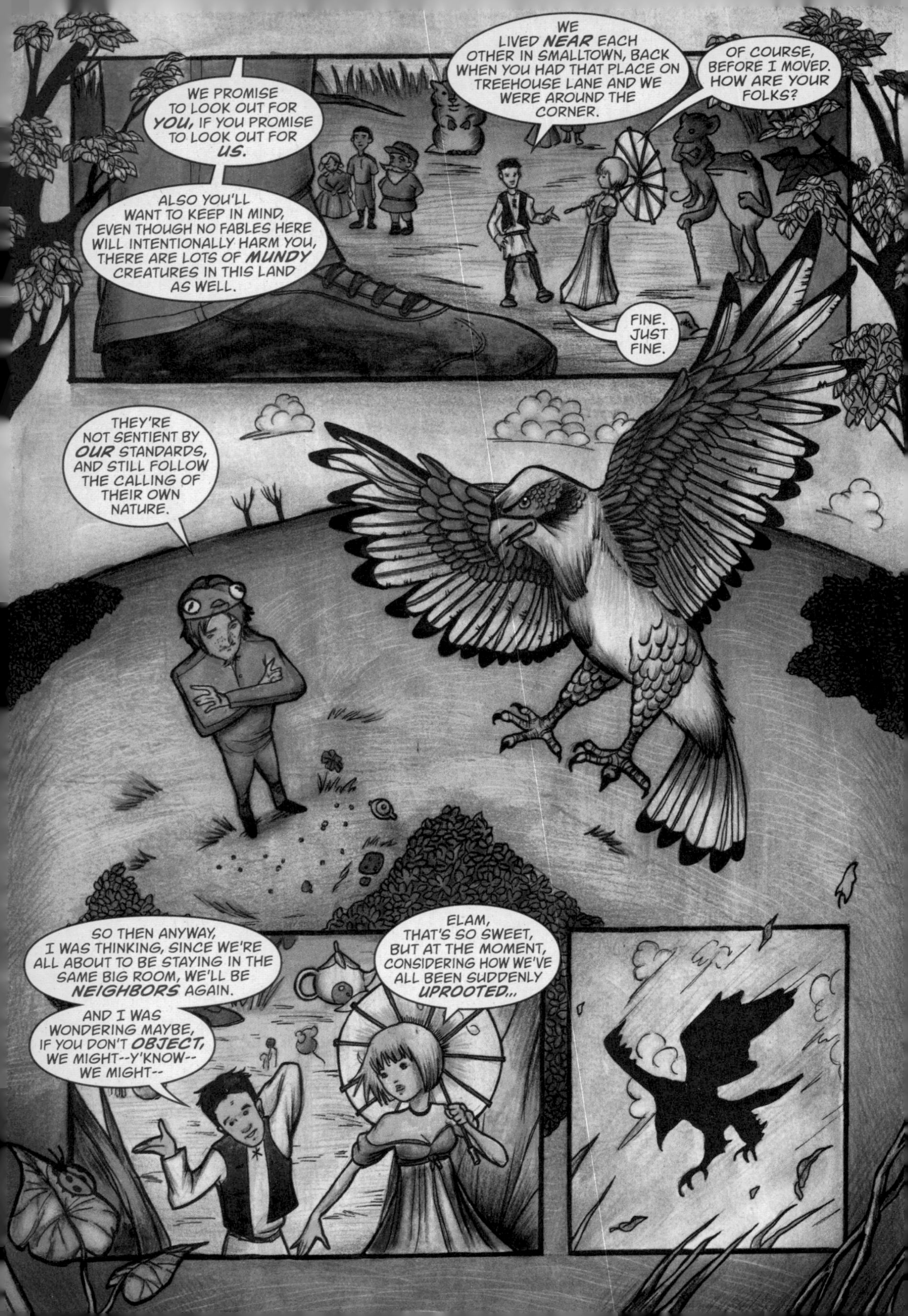
WE PROMISE TO LOOK OUT FOR YOU, IF YOU PROMISE TO LOOK OUT FOR US.
ALSO YOU'LL WANT TO KEEP IN MIND, EVEN THOUGH NO FABLES HERE WILL INTENTIONALLY HARM YOU, THERE ARE LOTS OF MUNDY CREATURES IN THIS LAND AS WELL.
WE LIVED NEAR EACH OTHER IN SMALLTOWN, BACK WHEN YOU HAD THAT PLACE ON TREEHOUSE LANE AND WE WERE AROUND THE CORNER.
OF COURSE, BEFORE I MOVED. HOW ARE YOUR FOLKS?
FINE. JUST FINE.
THEY'RE NOT SENTIENT BY OUR STANDARDS, AND STILL FOLLOW THE CALLING OF THEIR OWN NATURE.
SO THEN ANYWAY, I WAS THINKING, SINCE WE'RE ALL ABOUT TO BE STAYING IN THE SAME BIG ROOM, WE'LL BE NEIGHBORS AGAIN.
AND I WAS WONDERING MAYBE, IF YOU DON'T OBJECT, WE MIGHT--Y'KNOW-- WE MIGHT--
ELAM, THAT'S SO SWEET, BUT AT THE MOMENT, CONSIDERING HOW WE'VE ALL BEEN SUDDENLY UPROOTED...

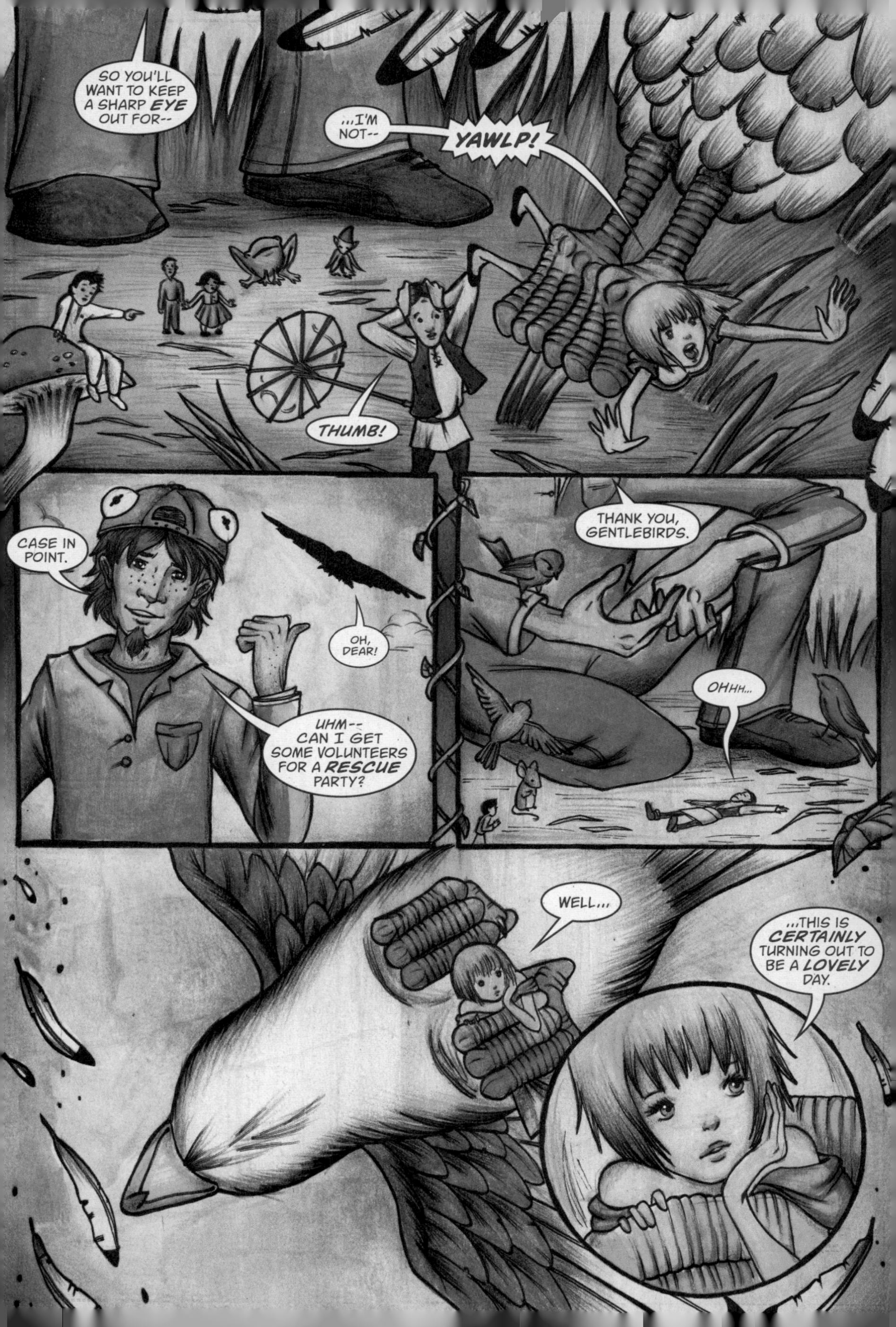
SO YOU'LL WANT TO KEEP A SHARP EYE OUT FOR--
...I'M NOT--
YAWLP!
THUMB!
CASE IN POINT.
OH, DEAR!
UHM-- CAN I GET SOME VOLUNTEERS FOR A RESCUE PARTY?
THANK YOU, GENTLEBIRDS.
OHHH...
WELL...
...THIS IS CERTAINLY TURNING OUT TO BE A LOVELY DAY.

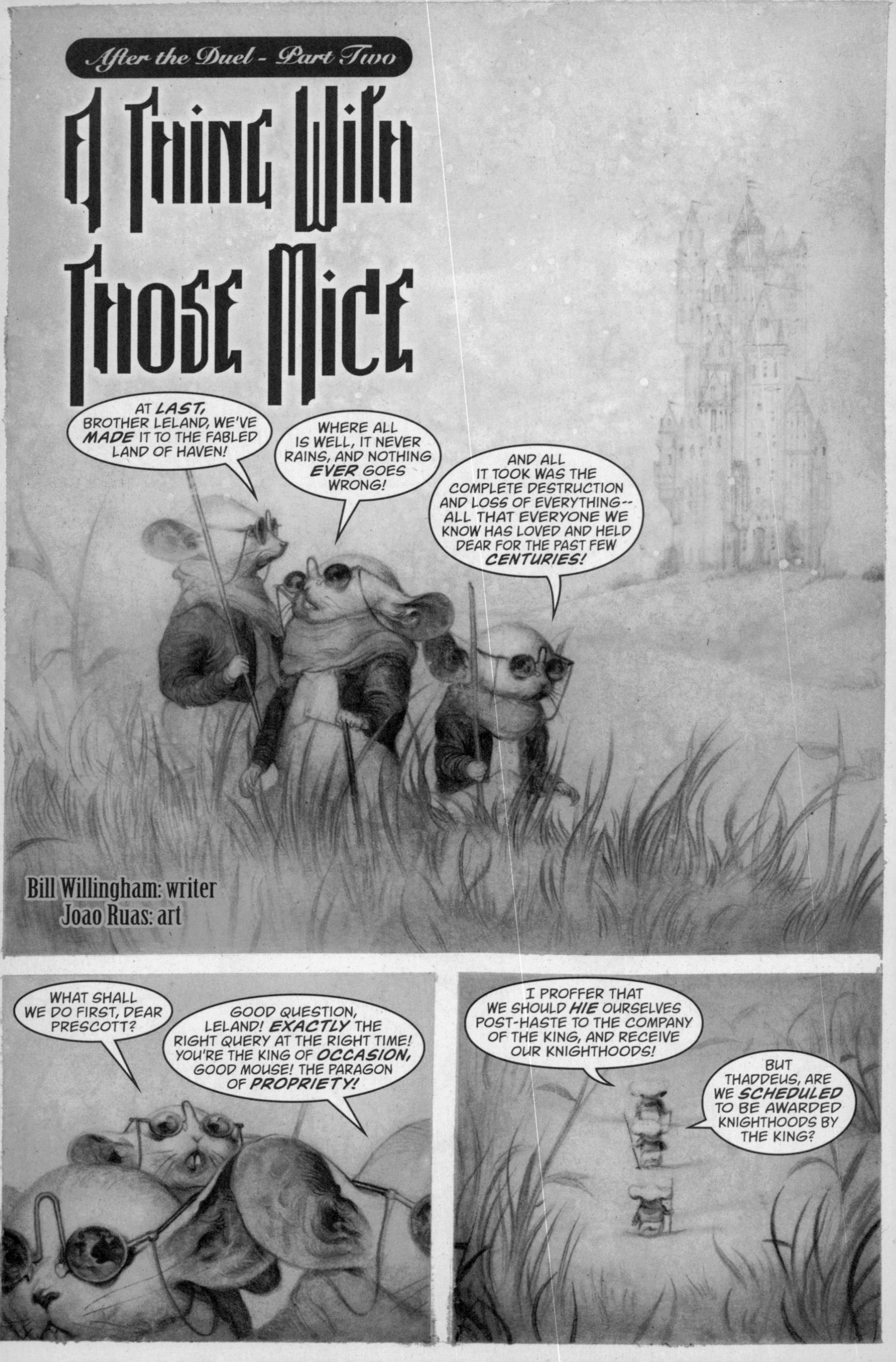
After the Duel - Part Two
A Thing With Those Mice
AT LAST, BROTHER LELAND, WE'VE MADE IT TO THE FABLED LAND OF HAVEN!
WHERE ALL IS WELL, IT NEVER RAINS, AND NOTHING EVER GOES WRONG!
AND ALL IT TOOK WAS THE COMPLETE DESTRUCTION AND LOSS OF EVERYTHING-- ALL THAT EVERYONE WE KNOW HAS LOVED AND HELD DEAR FOR THE PAST FEW CENTURIES!
Bill Willingham: writer
Joao Ruas: art
WHAT SHALL WE DO FIRST, DEAR PRESCOTT?
GOOD QUESTION, LELAND! EXACTLY THE RIGHT QUERY AT THE RIGHT TIME! YOU'RE THE KING OF OCCASION, GOOD MOUSE! THE PARAGON OF PROPRIETY!
I PROFFER THAT WE SHOULD HIE OURSELVES POST-HASTE TO THE COMPANY OF THE KING, AND RECEIVE OUR KNIGHTHOODS!
BUT THADDEUS, ARE WE SCHEDULED TO BE AWARDED KNIGHTHOODS BY THE KING?

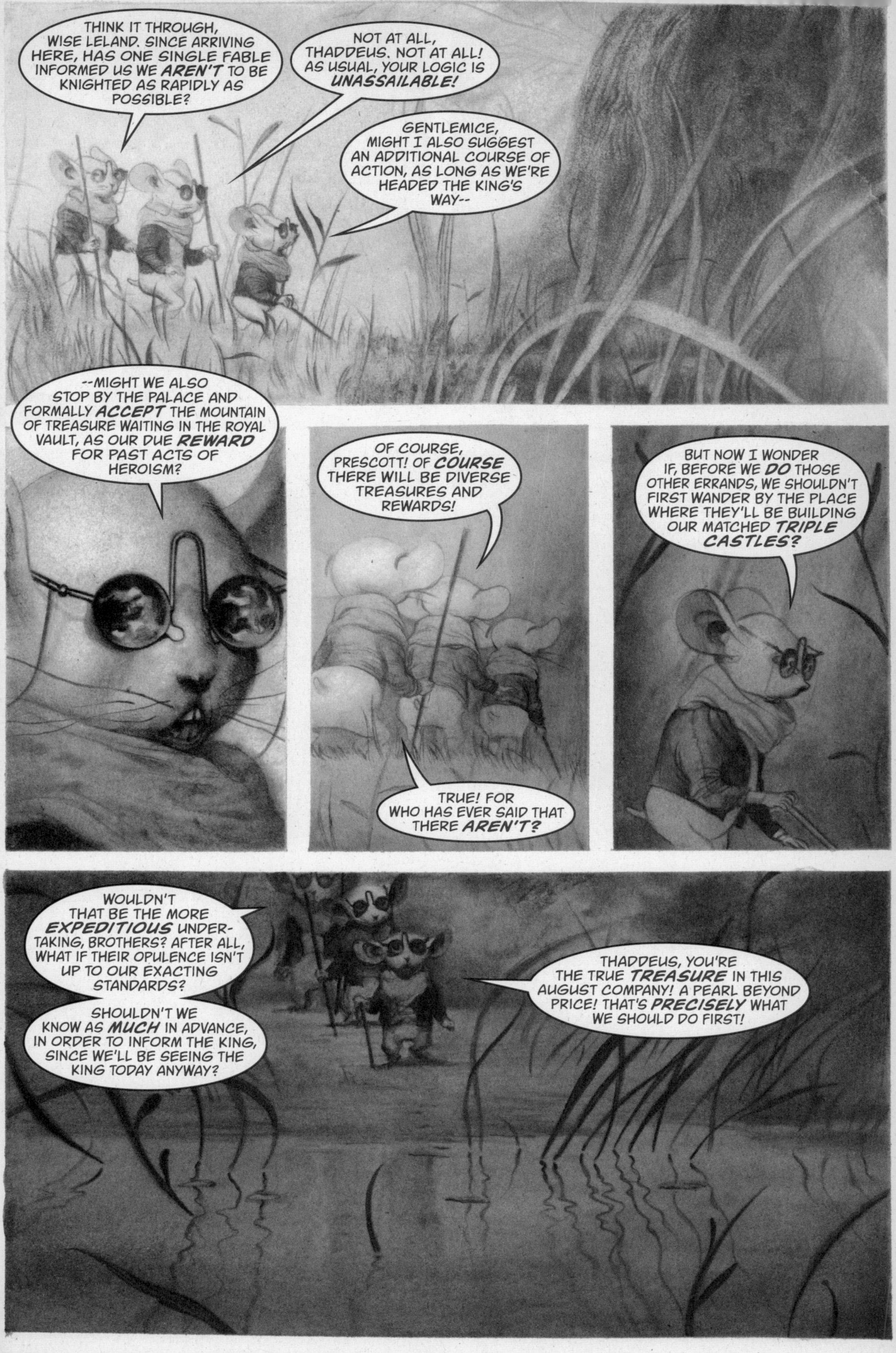
THINK IT THROUGH, WISE LELAND. SINCE ARRIVING HERE, HAS ONE SINGLE FABLE INFORMED US WE AREN'T TO BE KNIGHTED AS RAPIDLY AS POSSIBLE?
NOT AT ALL, THADDEUS. NOT AT ALL! AS USUAL, YOUR LOGIC IS UNASSAILABLE!
GENTLEMICE, MIGHT I ALSO SUGGEST AN ADDITIONAL COURSE OF ACTION, AS LONG AS WE'RE HEADED THE KING'S WAY--
--MIGHT WE ALSO STOP BY THE PALACE AND FORMALLY ACCEPT THE MOUNTAIN OF TREASURE WAITING IN THE ROYAL VAULT, AS OUR DUE REWARD FOR PAST ACTS OF HEROISM?
OF COURSE, PRESCOTT! OF COURSE THERE WILL BE DIVERSE TREASURES AND REWARDS!
TRUE! FOR WHO HAS EVER SAID THAT THERE AREN'T?
BUT NOW I WONDER IF, BEFORE WE DO THOSE OTHER ERRANDS, WE SHOULDN'T FIRST WANDER BY THE PLACE WHERE THEY'LL BE BUILDING OUR MATCHED TRIPLE CASTLES?
WOULDN'T THAT BE THE MORE EXPEDITIOUS UNDER-TAKING, BROTHERS? AFTER ALL, WHAT IF THEIR OPULENCE ISN'T UP TO OUR EXACTING STANDARDS?
SHOULDN'T WE KNOW AS MUCH IN ADVANCE, IN ORDER TO INFORM THE KING, SINCE WE'LL BE SEEING THE KING TODAY ANYWAY?
THADDEUS, YOU'RE THE TRUE TREASURE IN THIS AUGUST COMPANY! A PEARL BEYOND PRICE! THAT'S PRECISELY WHAT WE SHOULD DO FIRST!

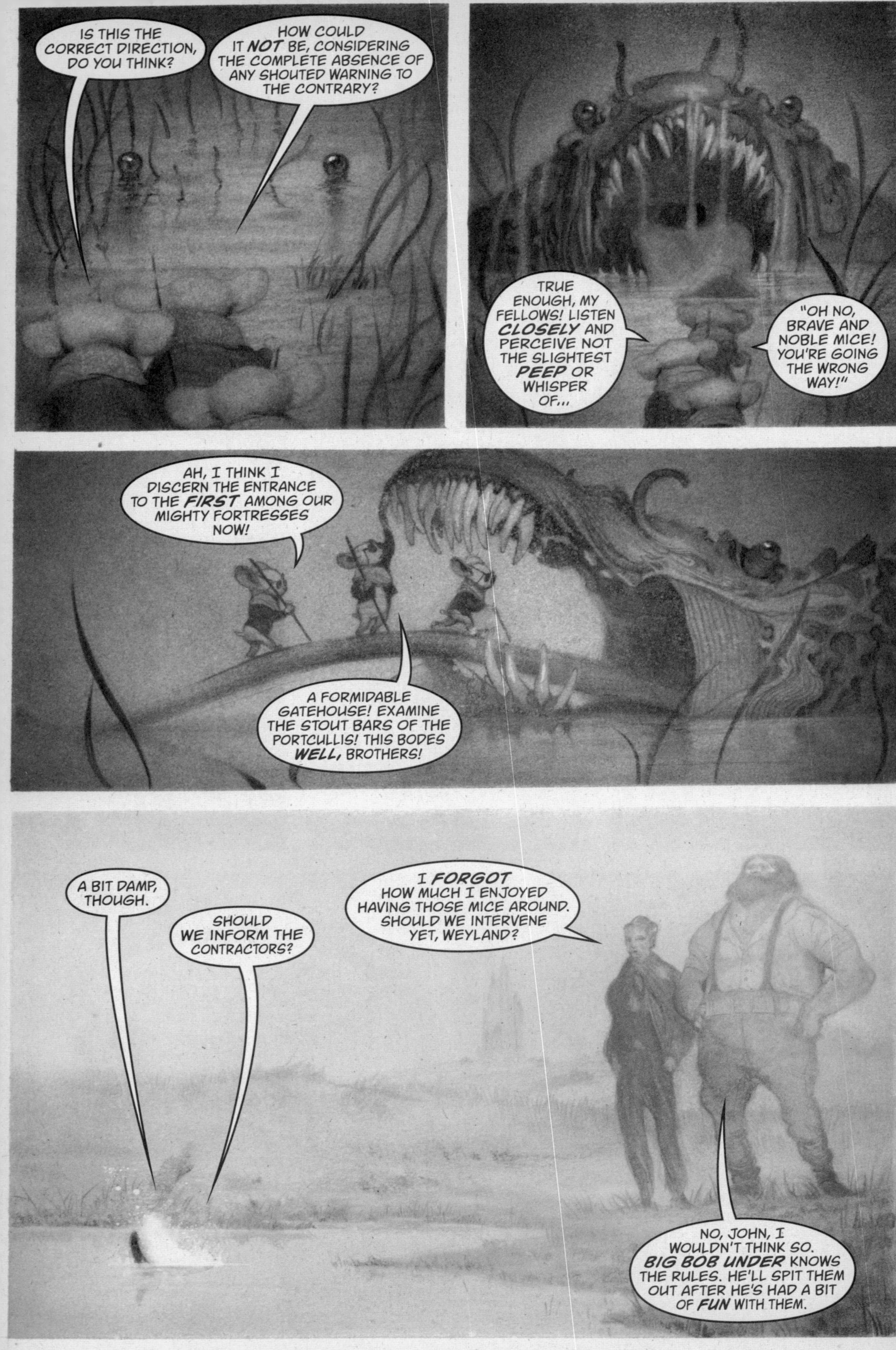
IS THIS THE CORRECT DIRECTION, DO YOU THINK?
HOW COULD IT NOT BE, CONSIDERING THE COMPLETE ABSENCE OF ANY SHOUTED WARNING TO THE CONTRARY?
TRUE ENOUGH, MY FELLOWS! LISTEN CLOSELY AND PERCEIVE NOT THE SLIGHTEST PEEP OR WHISPER OF...
"OH NO, BRAVE AND NOBLE MICE! YOU'RE GOING THE WRONG WAY!"
AH, I THINK I DISCERN THE ENTRANCE TO THE FIRST AMONG OUR MIGHTY FORTRESSES NOW!
A FORMIDABLE GATEHOUSE! EXAMINE THE STOUT BARS OF THE PORTCULLIS! THIS BODES WELL, BROTHERS!
A BIT DAMP, THOUGH.
SHOULD WE INFORM THE CONTRACTORS?
I FORGOT HOW MUCH I ENJOYED HAVING THOSE MICE AROUND. SHOULD WE INTERVENE YET, WEYLAND?
NO, JOHN, I WOULDN'T THINK SO. BIG BOB UNDER KNOWS THE RULES. HE'LL SPIT THEM OUT AFTER HE'S HAD A BIT OF FUN WITH THEM.

Pinocchio's Army

Written by **Mark Buckingham**
Illustrated by **Bill Willingham**

Chapter One

A VERY NAUGHTY BOY

Pinocchio grinned as he ran along the cobbled paths and grassy lanes that circled the farm. He had started his day of mischief by putting dish-washing liquid in the farm's fountain and laughing as the pond it sat in disappeared under a blanket of foam. He then stopped briefly by the Three Little Pigs' house where he wafted a hot bacon sandwich under their window. Then Pinocchio had followed this up by hiding a rotten fish in Nurse Spratt's tent in the bottom of her panty drawer. She had been perpetually mean to his best friend Boy Blue all through Blue's terrible illness, and Pinocchio believed she was due some payback.

Now Pinocchio was looking forward to a treat of a more adult nature. With the Farm now home not only to its usual animal residents but also to the hundreds of human refugees from the ruins of Fabletown, it had soon become apparent that extra facilities were desperately required to meet their hygienic needs. Two washrooms had been built, one for the men and, more important to Pinocchio, one just for the ladies. In a community made up of women who were among the fairest of them all, Pinocchio knew he could be guaranteed his own private strip club. Glancing around to make sure he was alone, the boy crept up to the women's washroom and searched the timbers for a gap or a hole. Finding one, Pinocchio leaned forward, pushing his face hard against the wooden cabin, and peered inside. "It's showtime," he whispered with a lascivious grin.

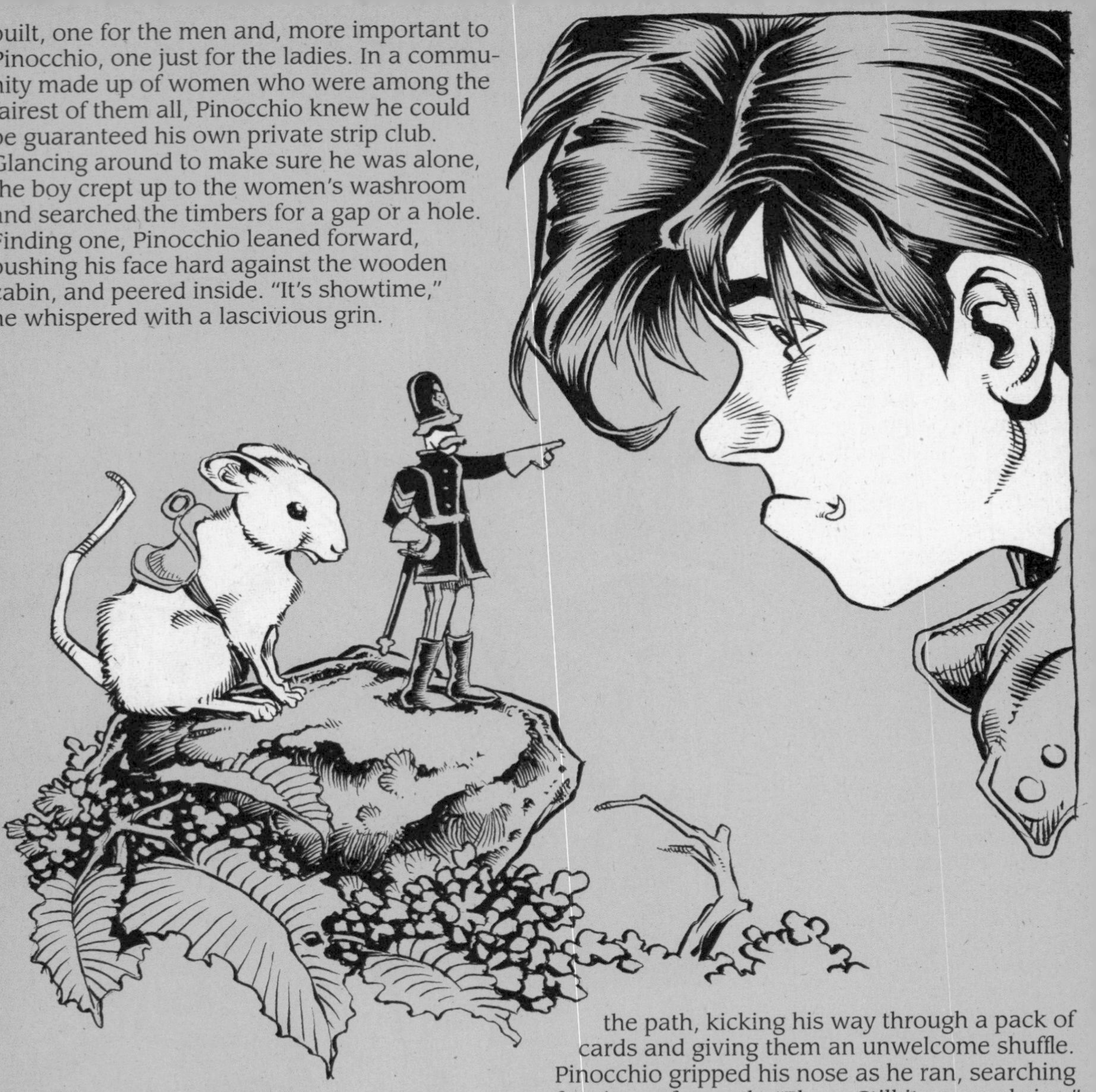

Suddenly a tiny voice from behind him called out, "Hello, hello, hello. What do we have here, then?"

Pinocchio spun around, his face flushed with embarrassment. Below him he saw the diminutive form of Sergeant Wilfred, the bravest and most esteemed member of Smalltown's Mouse Police, riding out from the grass verge astride his little rodent steed.

"Up to no good, no doubt!" said Wilfred.

"What? No, not at all," exclaimed Pinocchio. "I'm checking this property for wear and tear. Just doing my civic duty, Sergeant."

Wilfred regarded him with skepticism. "Move along, Pinocchio," he said.

Pinocchio turned tail and sprinted off down the path, kicking his way through a pack of cards and giving them an unwelcome shuffle. Pinocchio gripped his nose as he ran, searching for signs of growth. "Phew. Still its normal size," he said. "Mind you, it was only a little lie."

Chapter Two

A FAMILY DISCUSSION

The Farm bustled with more life than it had at any time in its centuries of existence. With the destruction of The Woodland, their New York City home, the human refugees, and those who by way of curse or glamour had passed as such, now found themselves bunkmates with their upstate animal cousins.With space in the main house already nonexistent, most had found themselves utilizing the various tents left over from the great military campaign that had finally beheaded the Empire. While many grabbed any available cubbyhole in and around the main farm building, most of the human ex-residents of Fabletown had formed a higgledy-piggledy canvas community. It was here, just beyond the brick home of the Three Little Pigs, that the Greenwood family had set down roots. Rodney and June Greenwood were originally a wooden son and daughter of Geppetto who had dared to love each other and craved humanity. They now lived as flesh and blood in the mundane world, where they raised their own little girl named Junebug, but remained forever in debt to Geppetto. The spells that originally gave them life included bonds of loyalty, and they must always do what is best for their father.

"Hello, little brother, " said Pinocchio as he rounded the path beside the Greenwoods' tent in search of Rodney. "I'd say good morning, but, you know, it isn't easy to be chipper when you share your home with a perpetual grouch."

"You shouldn't joke about Father Geppetto," said Rodney as he emerged from his family's three-berth tent. "I'm really worried about him," Rodney added, the concern etched across his brow.

"It's serious," concurred June, popping into view from behind her husband. "You know how mad he got after that animal mob buried him in the woods!"

"No, really?" said Pinocchio, with more than a hint of sarcasm. Nonetheless June continued.

"Since Rose Red canceled the election and sent his dryad protectors, Prince Aspen and Princess Alder, running back to the shade of Grandfather Oak, he's descended into an even darker place."

Rodney looked to Pinoccchio with increasing desperation. "You are his beloved, first-carved son. Surely he will take some comfort in your words?"

"Please, Pinocchio," pleaded June. "It's our sworn duty to do what's best for our honored father."

With a heavy sigh and a pout that was more pronounced than usual, Pinocchio succumbed to sibling pressure. He had planned on swinging by the women's shower room for another peek, but reluctantly admitted to himself that family issues would have to come first.

"Okay. You're right. I'll go talk to Pops," said Pinocchio. "But you guys *so* owe me! "

Chapter Three

THE DEPTHS

On their first arrival at the Farm, Pinocchio and Geppetto had, like the Greenwoods, been immediately billeted in the impromptu tent village that grew up overnight across the east field. To Geppetto, for whom power rather than the finer things in life had always taken precedence,

such humble surroundings were perfectly adequate. However, he never hid his displeasure in living at such close quarters with all the nasty exiles who had betrayed him.

Pinocchio, on the other hand, craved the home comforts he had been used to in The Woodland, Fabletown's apartment building in Manhattan. He knew that Internet porn and an espresso machine were things he would have to live without for now, but hot running water and a sofa would be a start. Also, being a loyal son, he wanted a more fitting residence for the Father of the Empire. A proper bed for a one-thousand-year-old man seemed the least he could do for his dear old dad. When Geppetto's mayoral campaign had been at its height, Pinocchio had been quick to capitalize on their rising prominence in the community by securing a more substantial property. Weyland Smith's workshop, the blacksmith's forge, had lain abandoned for most of the years since his untimely death in the battle of Fabletown. Flycatcher, also known as Ambrose the frog prince, had returned once or twice to fetch tools for Weyland since he, and the others whose remains had been committed to the Witching Well, had been restored to physical form in Haven, Ambrose's kingdom. But as Weyland could only remain solid in Haven, this presented no barrier to a change of occupant. In addition to the main workshop, the building possessed a modest living space, with a single leaded window, a bedroom and an outside toilet. Not the most desirable property, but under the prevailing circumstances it had looked like luxury to Pinocchio. Using both Geppetto's mayoral bid combined with his insistence that the workshop environment might encourage his father to undertake much needed repair work around the Farm, Pinocchio and Geppetto took possession of their new home. However, in a few short weeks, much had changed for the father of the one-time little wooden boy.

Pinocchio opened the gate to the workshop's rear yard and poked his head nervously around the back door. Despite the warm glow emanating from the fireplace, the blacksmith's cottage felt cold. "Pops?"

At first Pinocchio thought the room was empty, until finally a shape shifted in the shadows of its darkest corner. A chair squeaked and a gruff voice mumbled, "What do you want, boy?"

"Well, um, you see..." Pinocchio began.

"Spit it out!" the old man hollered.

"I was just talking with my brother and sister...and...we're worried about you, Pops."

The shadow moved once more and let out a huff. "Bah! Worrying doesn't build empires," scoffed the woodcarver. "If you were really my loyal children you'd put that Rose girl and her meddlesome ilk to the sword, and then we could run the rest of this riffraff properly." His voice turned more forceful and bitter in tone.

Pinocchio tried his best to be positive. "It's not all bad, Pops. You're one of Rose Red's inner council of advisors. That's more than the old Fabletown bosses got. You should'a seen the look on Beast's horns when he found out!" said Pinocchio with a grin.

Geppetto leaned forward from the shadows, but his face remained as ebony as the void he had inhabited moments earlier. "Bah! I was simply thrown a bone, as a way to keep me removed from any real leadership."

Geppetto pointed to the fireplace. Half a dozen broken placards burned in the grate, the last vestiges of the painted slogan *Geppetto for Mayor* licked away by the flames that rose around them. "Those damned ruffians put a torch to everything I do," Geppetto said. "I've no power here now. They've left me with nothing but ashes."

Geppetto turned away and disappeared once more into the darkest recesses of the room. Pinocchio lowered his head. With a heavy heart he walked the few short steps from Geppetto's armchair to the wooden rear door. Without looking back he turned the iron handle, stepped outside and quietly closed the door behind him.

Chapter Four

SONS (AND DAUGHTERS) OF EMPIRE

"I'm all out of ideas," sighed a deflated Pinocchio as he slumped into an incongruously colorful deck chair in front of the Greenwoods' tent. At his feet a giggling Junebug had arranged a dozen toy animals in the grass. Beside them, Rodney dutifully held out a bag of clothes pins and a basket of wet laundry which June hung out on a line to dry. June's delight turned to dismay when she noticed Junebug carefully tearing and folding little shapes out of a pile of blue paper napkins. One by one Junebug fashioned a little neckerchief for each stuffed beast.

"Poor father. Did we do wrong to bring him here?" sighed Rodney.

"No regrets, husband," June replied firmly, returning her attention to more adult matters. "We made a choice. Pinocchio was right. He should never have been the Emperor. As his loyal children we must help him find a new path."

Pinocchio lifted his furrowed brow from where it was buried in his hand and glanced hopefully at the sky. "Someone send us a bloody sign!"

Suddenly, with much whooping and hollering, came Red Cap the Troll, bursting out of the bushes. He was wrapped in a war-surplus blackout cloth, and was being chased by little bear Boo. Brandishing a wooden sword and wearing a paper crown pulled down hard over his ears, Boo came running and jumping through the ramshackle campsite, ducking under wash lines and leaping over fences crying, "I am Sir Boo of the Bear Kingdom and I will vanquish you, Dark Man!" Before the Greenwoods could react, the two came hurtling past their tent, missing little Junebug by a whisker.

"Bloody little vandals!" screamed Rodney as he pulled his daughter close to his side. "Watch where you're going!" Her parents' relief that she was unharmed swiftly turned to alarm as Junebug looked down and burst into tears. Before her the toy animals were strewn about, trampled into the mud beneath iron boots and bear hindpaws.

With the child still in a flood of tears, June quickly picked up Junebug into a comforting embrace. Leaning in close to Rodney, June whispered, "Fetch Mister Snuggles."

Rodney dived into the tent while June met Pinocchio's curious glance and explained. "When you persuaded us to surrender ourselves over to the Fabletown Authorities, we only had the briefest opportunity to collect a few things from our old apartment."

Rodney reappeared clutching a bright pink, flower-patterned comfort blanket. "It's the one thing our 'little weed' insisted on bringing with her. Whenever she's sad it's the only thing that soothes her, bringing back happy memories of her first home."

"Of course!"cried Pinocchio. "Curse my woodworm-riddled plank of a mind! I know what to do!" And with that he ran as fast as his little legs could carry him to the main farmhouse.

Chapter Five

THE SUITCASE

Pinocchio bounded through the Farm's porch entrance, down the short corridor and then climbed the main staircase, which he cleared two steps at a time. "Yes, yes, yes!" he gleefully exclaimed. On reaching the second landing he came to an abrupt halt, coming face-to-face with a solemn Brock Blueheart. The loyal badger, duster and polish in his paws, moved to block Pinocchio's path.

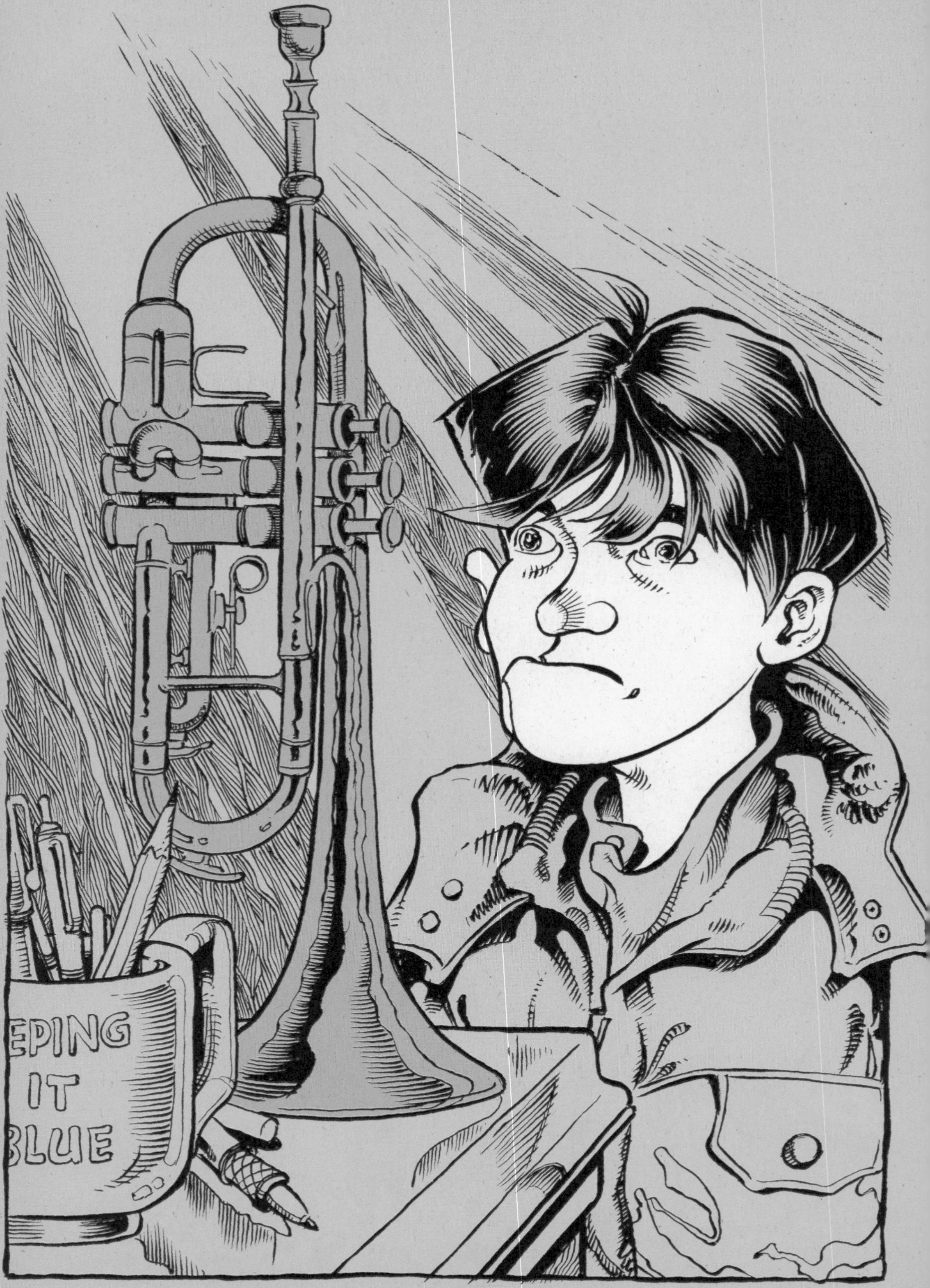
EPING
IT
BLUE

"Show some respect," said the Badger in the sternest of tones, "and keep your voice down. You know this is a sacred place." With that, Brock Blueheart stepped past the boy and slowly made his way down the stairs.

"Sorry, 'Stinky,'" muttered Pinocchio with a smirk upon his face.

Two doors down was the entrance to Boy Blue's Room. Not the VIP room where he had ended his days in pain, riddled with decay, but the little attic room he had made his home during his years of community service at the Farm. All around the doorway and spilling out into the corridor were a sea of little tributes left by the devoted followers of the Cult of Blue. Flowers in tiny vases, little messages, sweets and trinkets. This space was now a shrine to a fallen hero, kept exactly as Blue had left it, in the heartfelt belief that he might one day return to save them all. Despite the fight for space on the Farm, Brock Blueheart would brook no requests to reassign the room.

Pinocchio tiptoed between the little offerings, careful not to disturb a single one, until he reached the door and slowly turned the handle. He paused for a moment, took a deep breath, and then stepped inside. He surveyed the room. Everything was exactly as he remembered, and it was spotless. Blue was always the most fastidious of Fables when it came to order and cleanliness. "A place for everything and everything in its place," he would say. Brock had taken this to heart and had made the meticulous cleaning of Blue's room a personal priority. On the bedside table Blue's trumpet gleamed, reflecting its light in the table's polished surface. But the trumpet wasn't the boy's objective.

Kneeling down beside the mattress, Pinocchio lifted up the edge of the blanket and reached deep into the dark recesses under the bed. He shuddered for a moment as a large spider ran across his hand and scurried out of the room. Looking under the bed this time, what Pinocchio saw next replaced a moment of trepidation with a combination of nostalgia and deep sadness. Covered in a fine layer of dust was a bundle of comic books and a long forgotten box of sweets. Pinocchio longed for those happier times when he, Blue and Fly made their weekly assault on Nod's Comic Book Nook and Edward Bear's Candies. Sitting on The Woodland steps together, the three amigos were lost in four-color thrills and sugar rushes.

Pinocchio fought back a tear. Blue was dead, now. Fly lived far away in Haven, his Homelands kingdom, and Fabletown had been reduced to rubble. There was nothing he could do to bring them back. Pinocchio did, however, have a new family now and a father who needed his help. Lying on his stomach and pushing his arm deeper in, a determined look upon his face, he eventually caught sight of a sliver of metal and cream. His fingers found their target, and Pinocchio slid the object he sought from beneath the bed.

He smiled as he looked down at his prize. In his hands he held a small cream-colored suitcase with brown trim and a squared metal handle. It was the one thing he had saved when The Woodland building collapsed. In turn its contents had been the only possession he was able to bring with him out of the Homelands centuries earlier. Clutching it close to his chest, a broad smile replaced Pinocchio's perpetual frown. Once clear of Blue's room, he dashed down the stairs and ran straight across the main square towards home, almost tripping from the excitement.

Chapter Six

PINOCCHIO'S GIFT

"Pops! Pops! Where are you?" Running through the workshop, the suitcase handle gripped tightly in his hand, Pinocchio could barely contain himself. He entered the living room as Geppetto grumbled from his shadowy corner, "Leave me alone, boy."

Pinocchio, refusing to be dismissed by his father, grabbed him by the hand and tugged hard. "I'm in no mood for childish games or tittle-tattle," said Geppetto.

Undeterred, the little boy dragged him up from his seat and out of the shadows. "Please, Pops! I've got something for you! Pleeaaassse!"

"Well, it seems you'll give me no peace until you've shown me whatever it is that has you so unbearably giddy," Geppetto replied tersely.

"Come into the workshop!" Pinocchio said as he dragged his father from the room. "The light's better in here!"

Compared to the dark and restricted living space from which they had emerged, the workshop seemed vast. Above them the ceiling was open to sturdy oak rafters supporting slate tiles. The roof was held by huge beams down its entire length, anchored at each end in the thick, dry stone wall from which the whole blacksmith's cottage had been constructed. At the far end was a bin for coal, as well as an array of raw materials and timber. Next to this stood a white ceramic sink on an elegant iron stand. Beside it a row of equally elaborate coat hooks held a hand towel, a pair of thick leather gloves and a heavy leather apron liberally patterned with scorch marks. In the center of the room stood the forge above which rose a huge stone chimney breast, both thick with soot from centuries of use. In front of it, a giant anvil gleamed in the sunlight from the open doorway which led directly onto the Farm's main square. All around the forge every inch of wall space was crammed with shelves, hooks and little cupboards. These, in turn, were home to a vast array of tongs, hammers, brushes, brass rules, stamps, fullers, files, pritchels and all manner of other metalwork essentials.

Pinocchio and Geppetto stood with the door to the living quarters behind them. This was the area Weyland had specifically set aside for woodwork. In the corner was a small lathe, next to it ran a long workbench adorned with clamps and vises. Above this was a large leaded window, on either side of which were shelves covered in little jars of screws, nails and tacks.

Settling down upon a stool next to the woodwork bench, Geppetto fixed his son with an inquisitive glare. "Well?" he demanded.

Suddenly anxious that his great idea might fail to achieve its desired effect, Pinocchio nervously lifted up the little cream-colored suitcase in front of his father. Geppetto raised an eyebrow. "You make this much fuss over a piece of luggage?"

Realizing his mistake, Pinocchio fumbled frantically for the lock. "No! Wait! Inside… " With a click he released the clasp and slowly, offering it up once more to his father, opened the lid of the case.

For a moment Geppetto froze. Within the suitcase lay forty or more little toy soldiers. Each one consisted of a circular base on which stood a tiny knight. Some held swords. Most carried a spear. The one thing they shared was their construction. They were all made of wood.

"I … I recognize these…!" A look of wonder illuminated the old man's face for the first time in many, many days. "I carved them!"

Regaining confidence, Pinocchio spoke up. "Yes, Pops. When I made it to this mundane world, not knowing if you were dead or not, these were all I had to remember you by. My irreplaceable keepsakes down through the centuries."

With the most delicate care, Geppetto lifted each tiny soldier from within the case and lined them up along the workbench. Filled with joy at the sight of each new toy, Geppetto's eyes sparkled and his smile grew wider. Scrutinizing each figure with considerable intensity, he glanced back at his son and, for a moment, his scowl returned. "Some of these are broken!"

Pinocchio shrank in shame, nervously shuffling his feet on the woodshaving-covered floor. He recalled the many times Fly had snuck into his room to play with the figures. And with a wince, Pinocchio remembered the scolding Blue gave him, and his bitter rebuff, that time he jumped out of bed and actually stood on one of the toys.

"Hrrummm," said Geppetto. Then, suddenly, the glare was gone and a gentle smile took its place. "Well, at least you kept all the pieces! I see nothing here a man of my skills can't repair."

With the last of the soldiers in position, Geppetto took the suitcase from Pinocchio's outstretched hands, clicked it shut and put it down on the stool next to him. With a grin broader than his son had ever thought possible, Geppetto leaned down and patted Pinocchio's head. "You are a good boy, a clever boy, to have kept them safe all this time."

Pinocchio beamed. "I wanted you to think back to happier times. Before the Empire. When you were my Dad, the woodcarver. I know we can be happy again. You have a family here. Maybe you could even carve again?"

Geppetto rubbed his chin and contemplated for a moment. "You know, my boy, I think I will. Be good to your father and go back to the main house for me. I seem to be missing some of…"

"Who used to live here?"

"Weyland." replied a desperate-to-be-helpful Pinocchio. "Weyland Smith."

"Yes, go see if you can find out where they stored his more refined tools. I'll make a start by fixing our little treasures!"

"Anything for you, Pops!" cried Pinocchio, elated to the bursting point. They had turned a corner. He had made a connection with his father. Everything would be better from now on.

Geppetto's gaze followed his son until he was quite sure Pinocchio had left the workshop. Then Geppetto's smile slipped away in favor of a far more sinister expression. Turning his attention back to the workbench, he surveyed the row of wooden toy soldiers once more before leaning forward to speak. "Welome home, my smallest children."

"What are our first orders, Honored Father?" replied the leader of the knights.

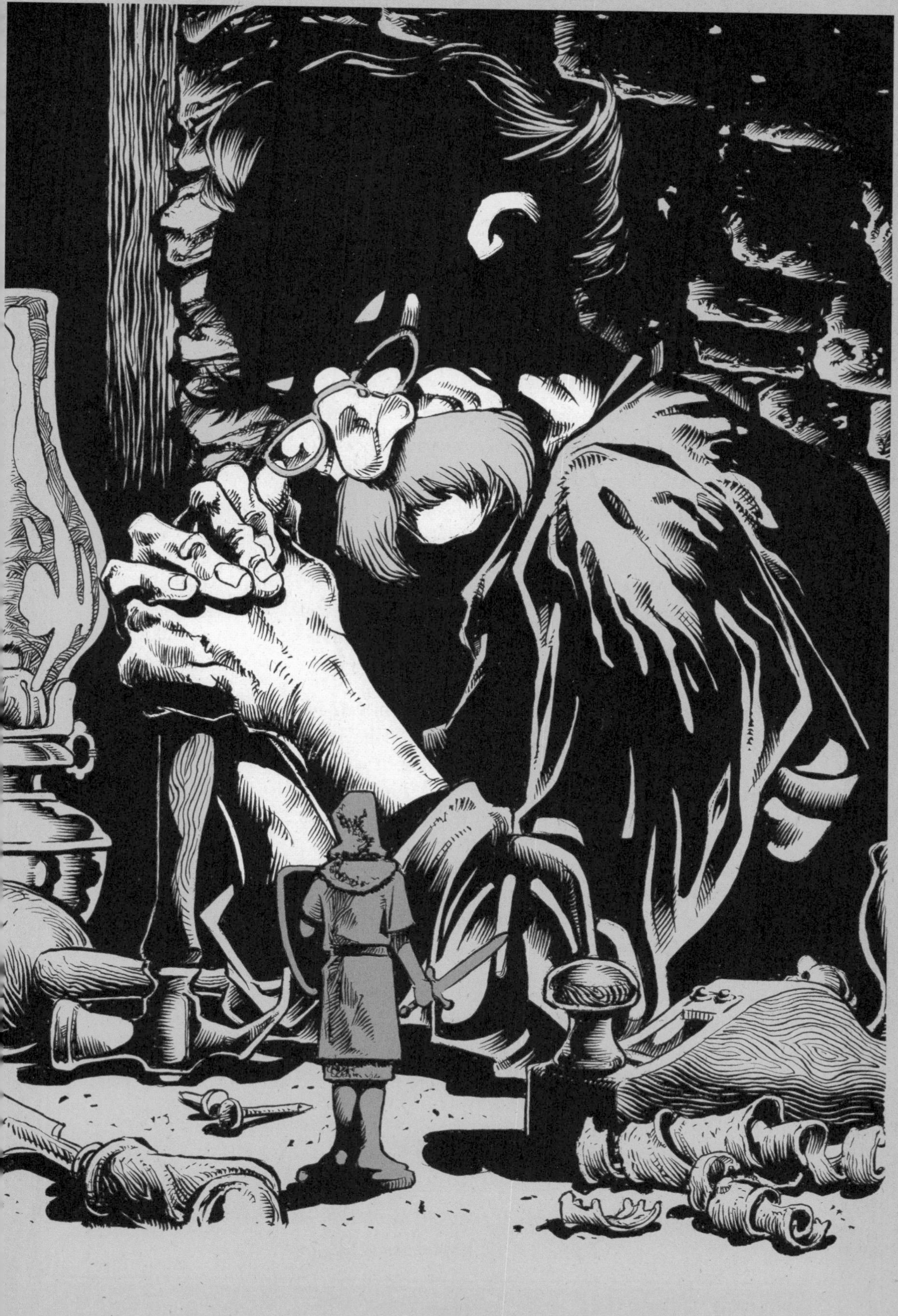

Celebrity Burning Questions

In which we return to reveal just a few more of the great and not-so-great heretofore unanswered mysteries of the Fables saga so far.

Not so long ago, at least as continents and glaciers measure time, we took an issue (59) to address the specific questions of some of our Fables readers. Now, since we have a bit of room in this very special issue, we're going to take a few more questions from some of our readers, but this time with a twist. Over the years we've found out that some of the most loyal Fables readers are celebrities. We here at Fables Central (an office somewhere in the deep woods) think that's pretty cool and set out to draft a few of those readers of note into service. So here, simply because it's a fun thing to do, are four Burning Questions written by Bill Willingham at the command of four readers whose names you might recognize. They are:

1: Phil LaMarr, who was a longtime series regular (performer and writer) on *Mad TV*, a big bloody mess in the car in *Pulp Fiction*, and one of my favorite (and most obscure) of his many roles, a really bad fellow named Anthony in the short-lived drama called *Philly*. His question is illustrated by Dave Johnson.

2: Eddie Cahill, one of the series regulars on *CSI New York*, played hockey phenom Jim Craig in *Miracle* (my friend Mike's favorite movie ever), and (since Nicole would kill me if I didn't mention it) he was also **Tag from Friends!** (You have to scream that and jump up and down.) His question is illustrated by Adam Hughes.

3: Cobie Smulders, who plays terminally hot Robin Scherbatsky in *How I Met Your Mother*, was credited (no argument here) as "Exotic Beauty" in 2004's version of *Walking Tall*, and was a recurring character in *The L Word*. Her question is illustrated by Kate McElroy.

4: Last but not least, Michael McMillian, who played my all-time favorite character in *True Blood* (the anti-vampire evangelist, don't you know), and keeps showing up in some of my favorite series, such as *Firefly*, *Veronica Mars*, and *The Mentalist*, to name a few. His question is illustrated by J.H. Williams III.

We're deeply indebted to these fine folks for their willingness to play along, and in return I think we should make an effort to seek out and support anything they happen to show up in. Thanks, lady and gentlemen. We literally couldn't have done this without you.

Phil LaMarr from "Mad TV" asks:

Who makes the Fabletown comic books?

ILLUSTRATED BY DAVE JOHNSON

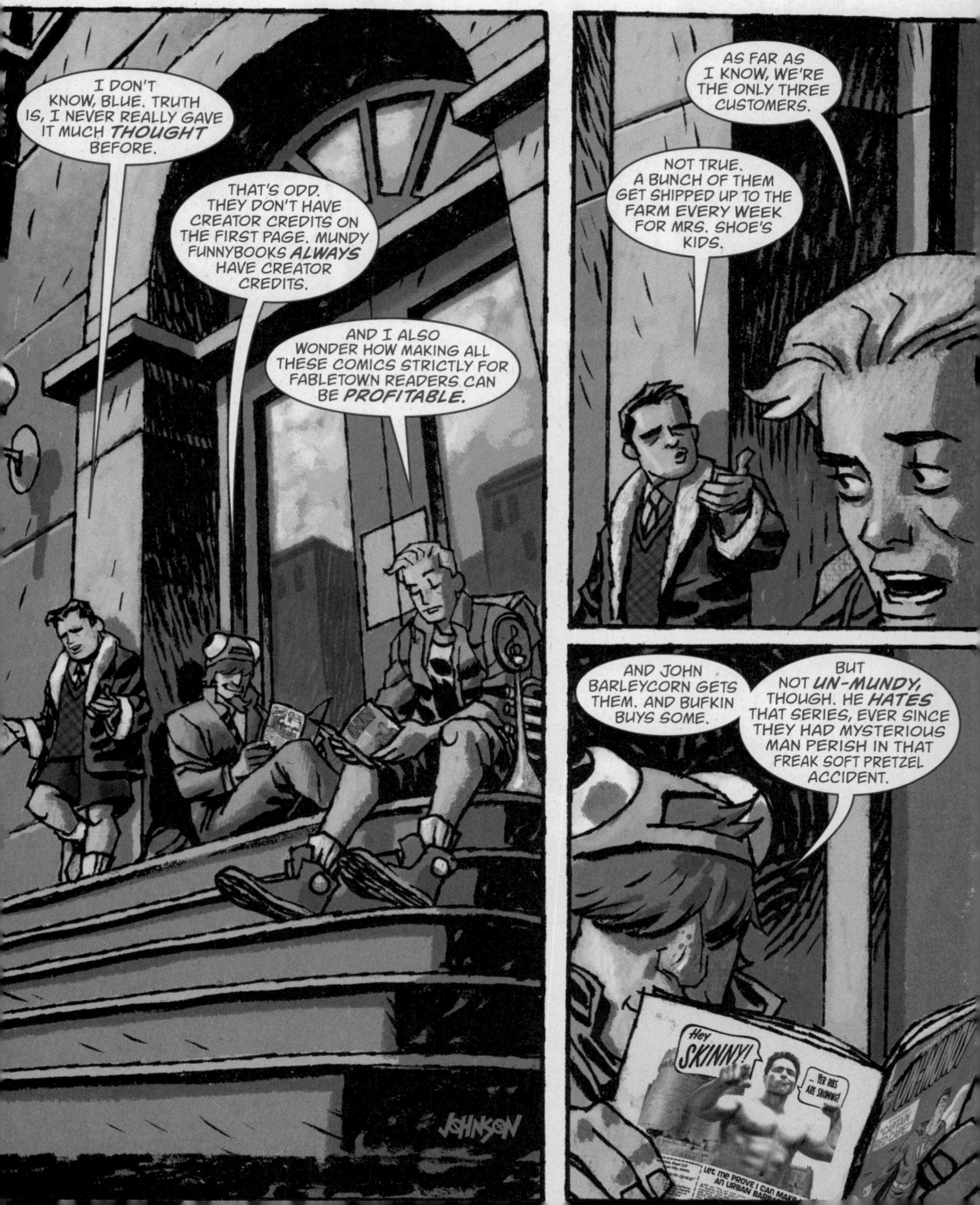

I DON'T KNOW, BLUE. TRUTH IS, I NEVER REALLY GAVE IT MUCH *THOUGHT* BEFORE.
THAT'S ODD. THEY DON'T HAVE CREATOR CREDITS ON THE FIRST PAGE. MUNDY FUNNYBOOKS *ALWAYS* HAVE CREATOR CREDITS.
AND I ALSO WONDER HOW MAKING ALL THESE COMICS STRICTLY FOR FABLETOWN READERS CAN BE *PROFITABLE.*
JOHNSON
AS FAR AS I KNOW, WE'RE THE ONLY THREE CUSTOMERS.
NOT TRUE. A BUNCH OF THEM GET SHIPPED UP TO THE FARM EVERY WEEK FOR MRS. SHOE'S KIDS.
AND JOHN BARLEYCORN GETS THEM. AND BUFKIN BUYS SOME.
BUT NOT *UN-MUNDY,* THOUGH. HE *HATES* THAT SERIES, EVER SINCE THEY HAD MYSTERIOUS MAN PERISH IN THAT FREAK SOFT PRETZEL ACCIDENT.
Hey SKINNY!
...YER RIBS ARE SHOWING!

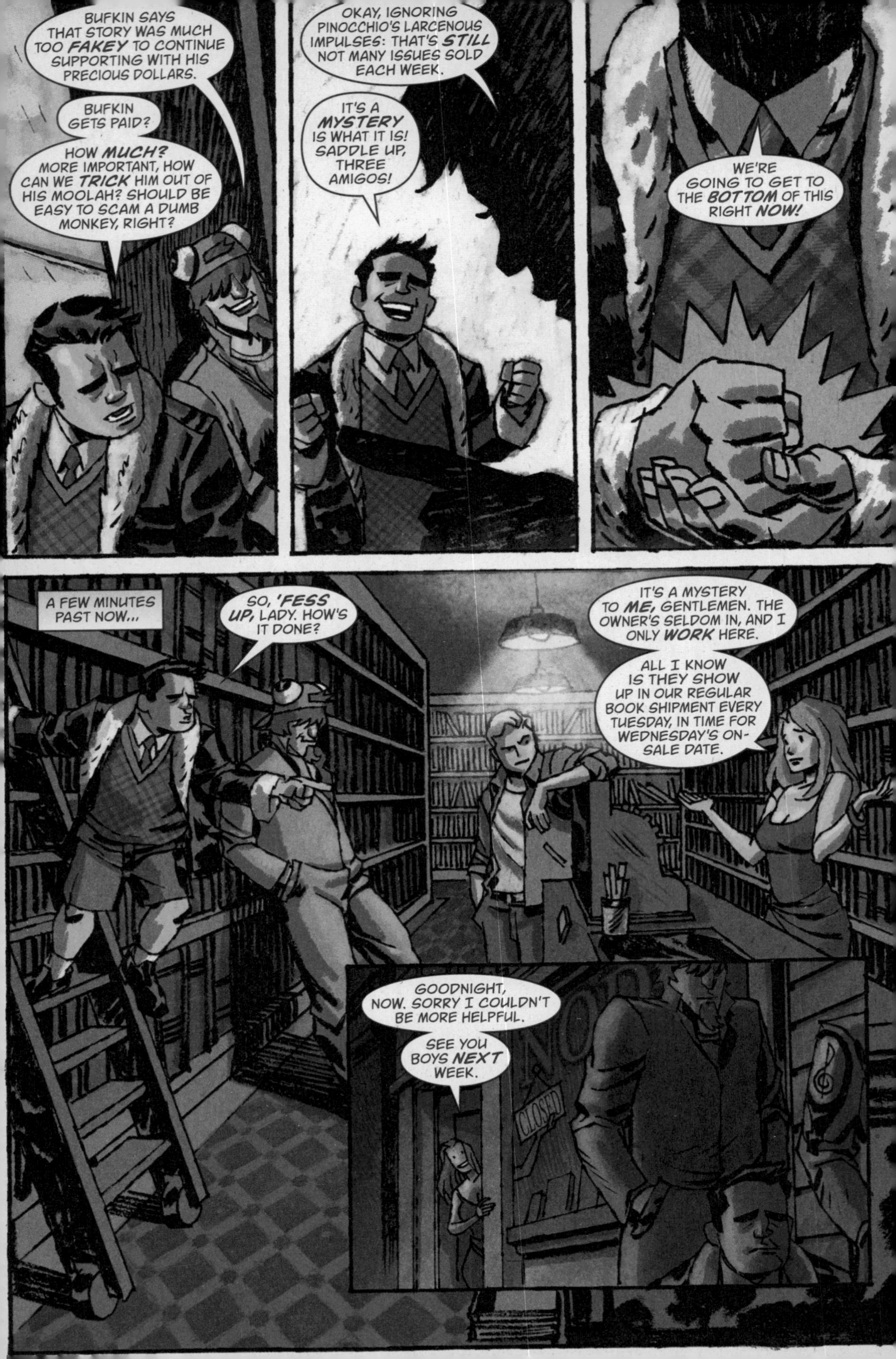

BUFKIN SAYS THAT STORY WAS MUCH TOO FAKEY TO CONTINUE SUPPORTING WITH HIS PRECIOUS DOLLARS.
BUFKIN GETS PAID?
HOW MUCH? MORE IMPORTANT, HOW CAN WE TRICK HIM OUT OF HIS MOOLAH? SHOULD BE EASY TO SCAM A DUMB MONKEY, RIGHT?
OKAY, IGNORING PINOCCHIO'S LARCENOUS IMPULSES: THAT'S STILL NOT MANY ISSUES SOLD EACH WEEK.
IT'S A MYSTERY IS WHAT IT IS! SADDLE UP, THREE AMIGOS!
WE'RE GOING TO GET TO THE BOTTOM OF THIS RIGHT NOW!
A FEW MINUTES PAST NOW...
SO, 'FESS UP, LADY. HOW'S IT DONE?
IT'S A MYSTERY TO ME, GENTLEMEN. THE OWNER'S SELDOM IN, AND I ONLY WORK HERE.
ALL I KNOW IS THEY SHOW UP IN OUR REGULAR BOOK SHIPMENT EVERY TUESDAY, IN TIME FOR WEDNESDAY'S ON-SALE DATE.
GOODNIGHT, NOW. SORRY I COULDN'T BE MORE HELPFUL.
SEE YOU BOYS NEXT WEEK.
CLOSED

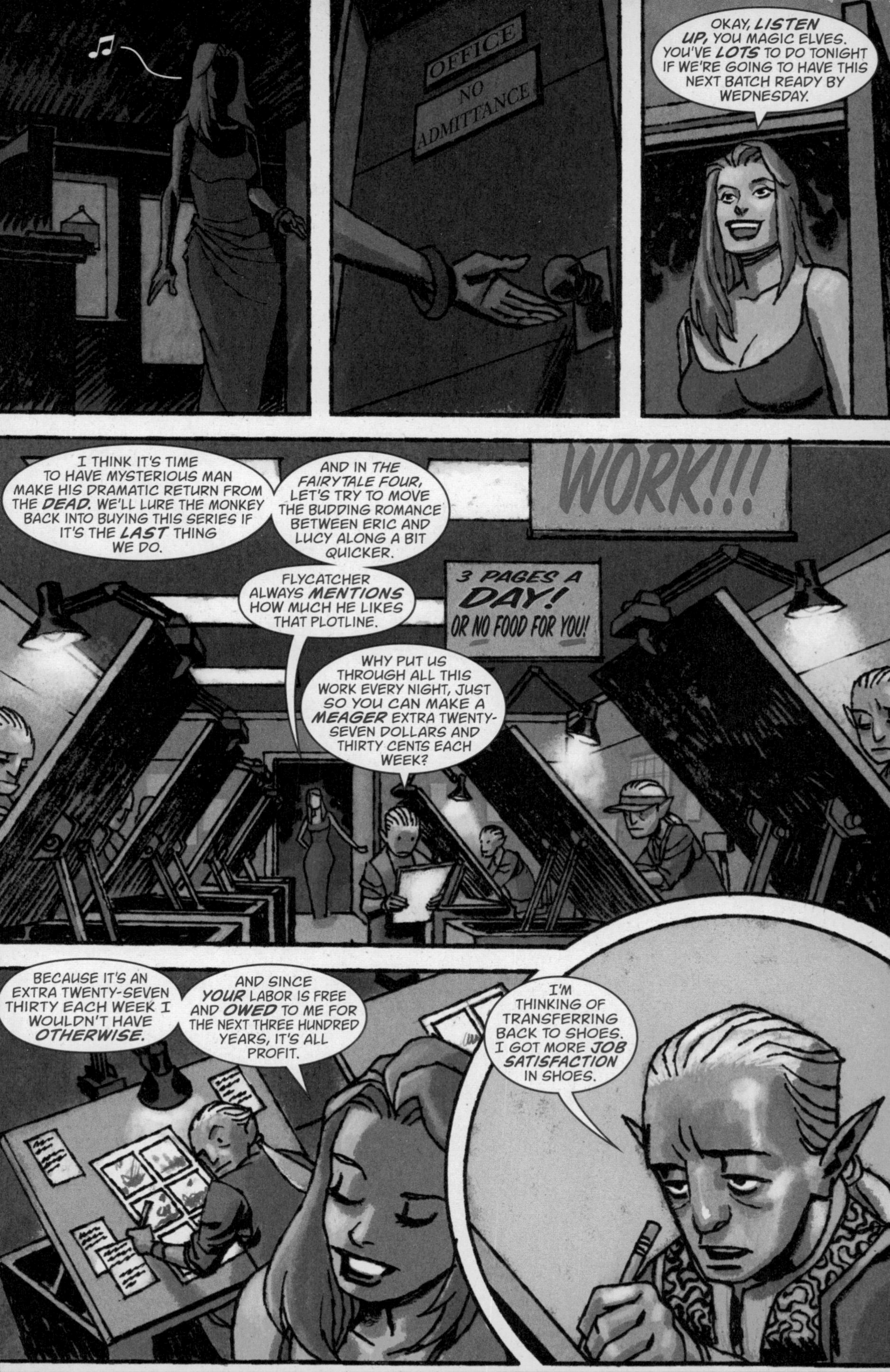
OFFICE
NO ADMITTANCE
OKAY, LISTEN UP, YOU MAGIC ELVES. YOU'VE LOTS TO DO TONIGHT IF WE'RE GOING TO HAVE THIS NEXT BATCH READY BY WEDNESDAY.
I THINK IT'S TIME TO HAVE MYSTERIOUS MAN MAKE HIS DRAMATIC RETURN FROM THE DEAD. WE'LL LURE THE MONKEY BACK INTO BUYING THIS SERIES IF IT'S THE LAST THING WE DO.
AND IN THE FAIRYTALE FOUR, LET'S TRY TO MOVE THE BUDDING ROMANCE BETWEEN ERIC AND LUCY ALONG A BIT QUICKER.
WORK!!!
FLYCATCHER ALWAYS MENTIONS HOW MUCH HE LIKES THAT PLOTLINE.
3 PAGES A DAY! OR NO FOOD FOR YOU!
WHY PUT US THROUGH ALL THIS WORK EVERY NIGHT, JUST SO YOU CAN MAKE A MEAGER EXTRA TWENTY-SEVEN DOLLARS AND THIRTY CENTS EACH WEEK?
BECAUSE IT'S AN EXTRA TWENTY-SEVEN THIRTY EACH WEEK I WOULDN'T HAVE OTHERWISE.
AND SINCE YOUR LABOR IS FREE AND OWED TO ME FOR THE NEXT THREE HUNDRED YEARS, IT'S ALL PROFIT.
I'M THINKING OF TRANSFERRING BACK TO SHOES. I GOT MORE JOB SATISFACTION IN SHOES.

Eddie Cahill from "CSI New York" asks:

Can I have Snow White's phone number?

ILLUSTRATED BY ADAM HUGHES

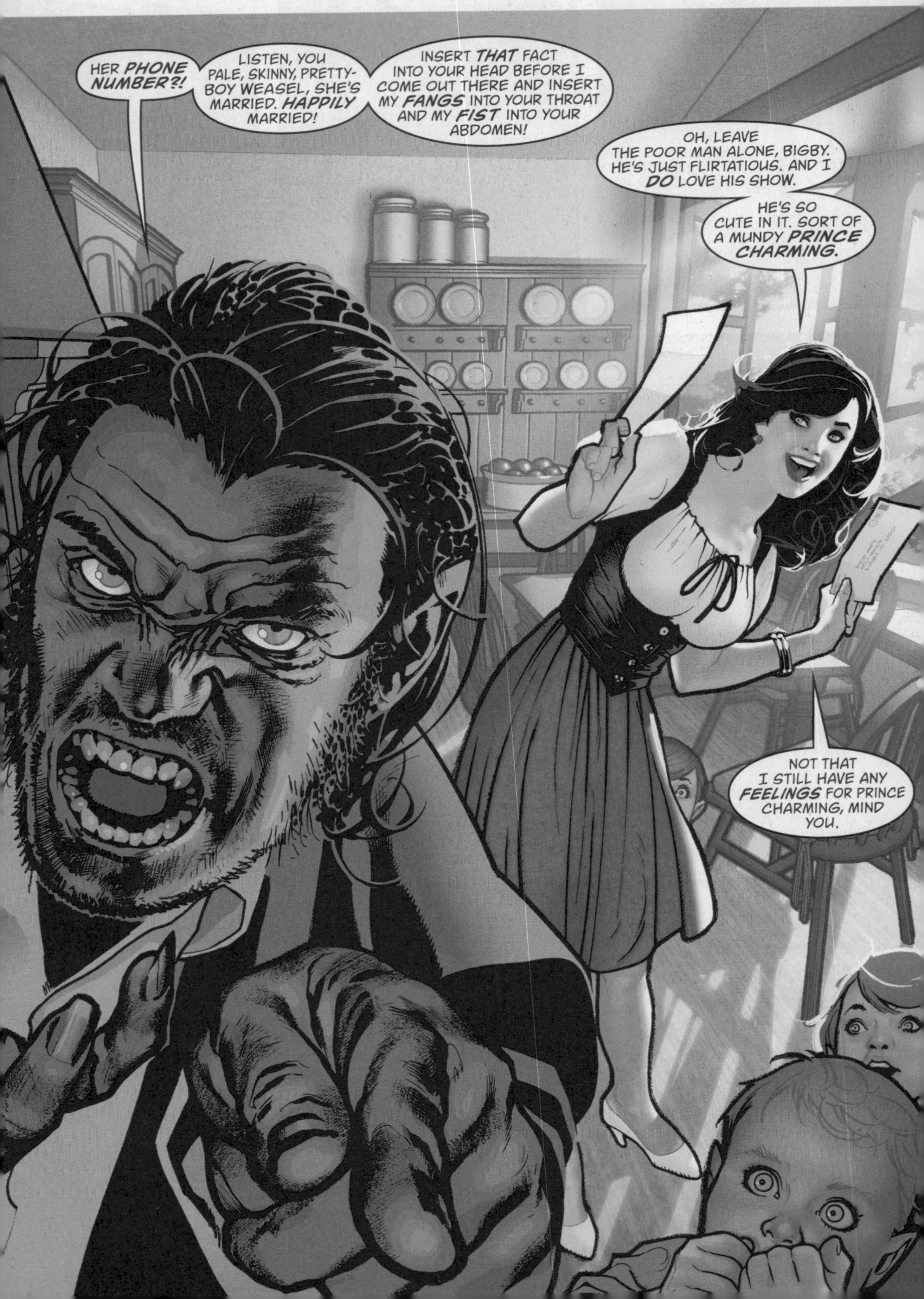

HER PHONE NUMBER?!
LISTEN, YOU PALE, SKINNY, PRETTY-BOY WEASEL, SHE'S MARRIED. HAPPILY MARRIED!
INSERT THAT FACT INTO YOUR HEAD BEFORE I COME OUT THERE AND INSERT MY FANGS INTO YOUR THROAT AND MY FIST INTO YOUR ABDOMEN!
OH, LEAVE THE POOR MAN ALONE, BIGBY. HE'S JUST FLIRTATIOUS. AND I DO LOVE HIS SHOW.
HE'S SO CUTE IN IT. SORT OF A MUNDY PRINCE CHARMING.
NOT THAT I STILL HAVE ANY FEELINGS FOR PRINCE CHARMING, MIND YOU.

Cobie Smulders from "How I Met Your Mother" asks: Now that Baba Yaga is dead, how is Bufkin passing the time?

ILLUSTRATED BY KATE McELROY

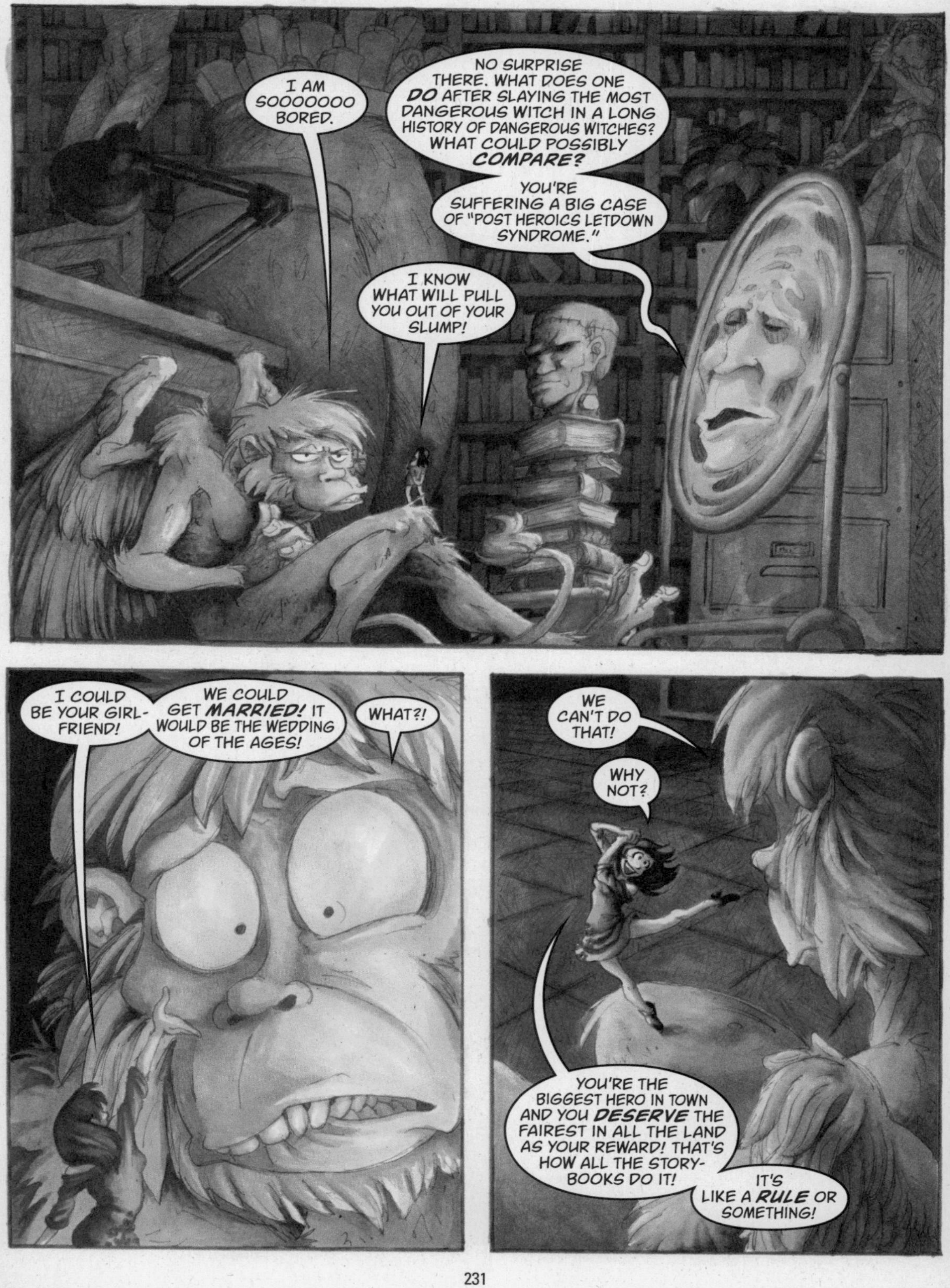
I AM SOOOOOOO BORED.
NO SURPRISE THERE. WHAT DOES ONE *DO* AFTER SLAYING THE MOST DANGEROUS WITCH IN A LONG HISTORY OF DANGEROUS WITCHES? WHAT COULD POSSIBLY *COMPARE?*
YOU'RE SUFFERING A BIG CASE OF "POST HEROICS LETDOWN SYNDROME."
I KNOW WHAT WILL PULL YOU OUT OF YOUR SLUMP!
I COULD BE YOUR GIRL-FRIEND!
WE COULD GET *MARRIED!* IT WOULD BE THE WEDDING OF THE AGES!
WHAT?!
WE CAN'T DO THAT!
WHY NOT?
YOU'RE THE BIGGEST HERO IN TOWN AND YOU *DESERVE* THE FAIREST IN ALL THE LAND AS YOUR REWARD! THAT'S HOW ALL THE STORY-BOOKS DO IT!
IT'S LIKE A *RULE* OR SOMETHING!

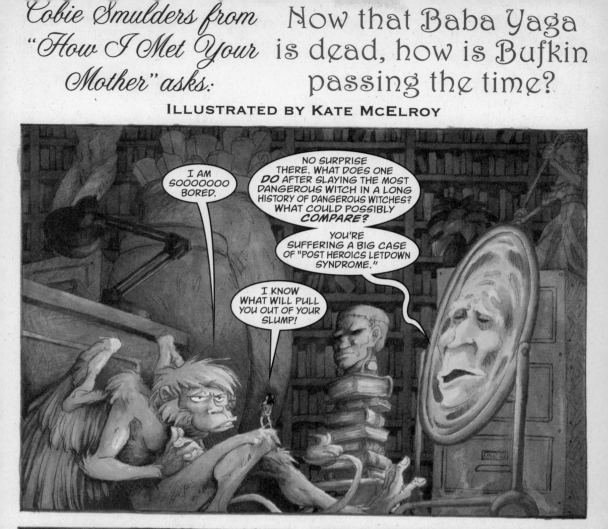

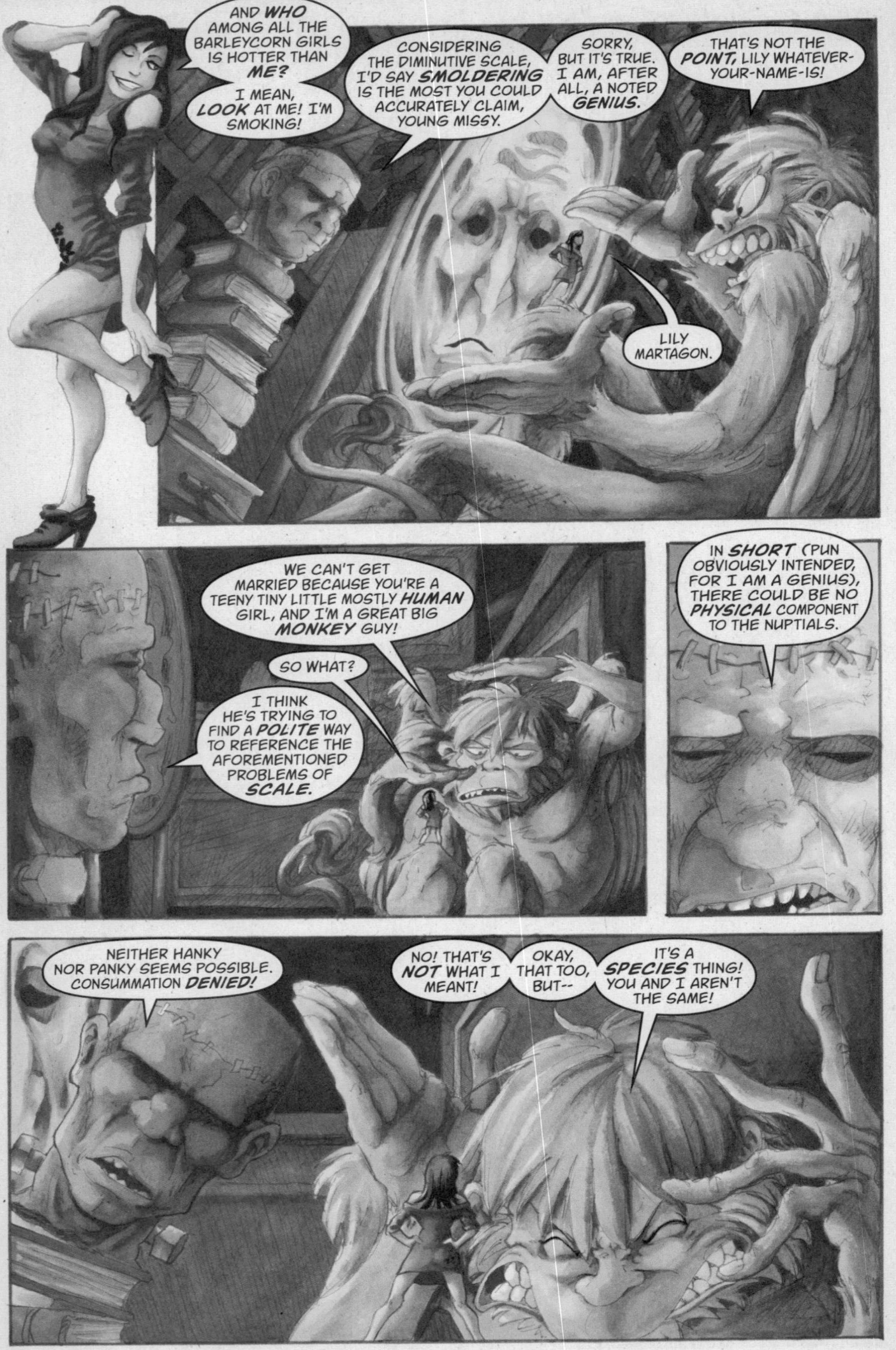
AND WHO AMONG ALL THE BARLEYCORN GIRLS IS HOTTER THAN ME?
I MEAN, LOOK AT ME! I'M SMOKING!
CONSIDERING THE DIMINUTIVE SCALE, I'D SAY SMOLDERING IS THE MOST YOU COULD ACCURATELY CLAIM, YOUNG MISSY.
SORRY, BUT IT'S TRUE. I AM, AFTER ALL, A NOTED GENIUS.
THAT'S NOT THE POINT, LILY WHATEVER-YOUR-NAME-IS!
LILY MARTAGON.
WE CAN'T GET MARRIED BECAUSE YOU'RE A TEENY TINY LITTLE MOSTLY HUMAN GIRL, AND I'M A GREAT BIG MONKEY GUY!
SO WHAT?
I THINK HE'S TRYING TO FIND A POLITE WAY TO REFERENCE THE AFOREMENTIONED PROBLEMS OF SCALE.
IN SHORT (PUN OBVIOUSLY INTENDED, FOR I AM A GENIUS), THERE COULD BE NO PHYSICAL COMPONENT TO THE NUPTIALS.
NEITHER HANKY NOR PANKY SEEMS POSSIBLE. CONSUMMATION DENIED!
NO! THAT'S NOT WHAT I MEANT!
OKAY, THAT TOO, BUT--
IT'S A SPECIES THING! YOU AND I AREN'T THE SAME!

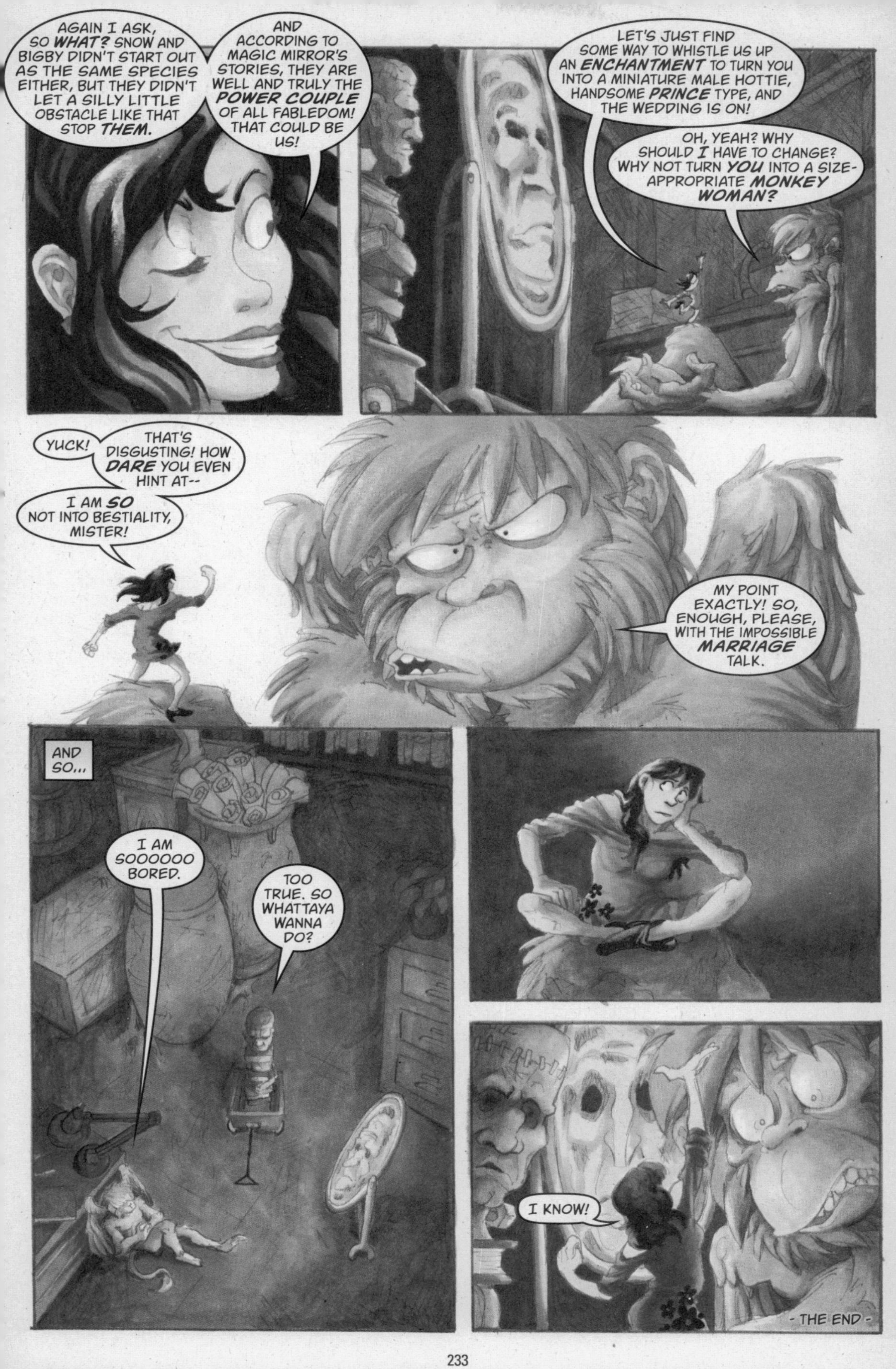
AGAIN I ASK, SO WHAT? SNOW AND BIGBY DIDN'T START OUT AS THE SAME SPECIES EITHER, BUT THEY DIDN'T LET A SILLY LITTLE OBSTACLE LIKE THAT STOP THEM.
AND ACCORDING TO MAGIC MIRROR'S STORIES, THEY ARE WELL AND TRULY THE POWER COUPLE OF ALL FABLEDOM! THAT COULD BE US!
LET'S JUST FIND SOME WAY TO WHISTLE US UP AN ENCHANTMENT TO TURN YOU INTO A MINIATURE MALE HOTTIE, HANDSOME PRINCE TYPE, AND THE WEDDING IS ON!
OH, YEAH? WHY SHOULD I HAVE TO CHANGE? WHY NOT TURN YOU INTO A SIZE-APPROPRIATE MONKEY WOMAN?
YUCK!
THAT'S DISGUSTING! HOW DARE YOU EVEN HINT AT--
I AM SO NOT INTO BESTIALITY, MISTER!
MY POINT EXACTLY! SO, ENOUGH, PLEASE, WITH THE IMPOSSIBLE MARRIAGE TALK.
AND SO...
I AM SOOOOOO BORED.
TOO TRUE. SO WHATTAYA WANNA DO?
I KNOW!
- THE END -

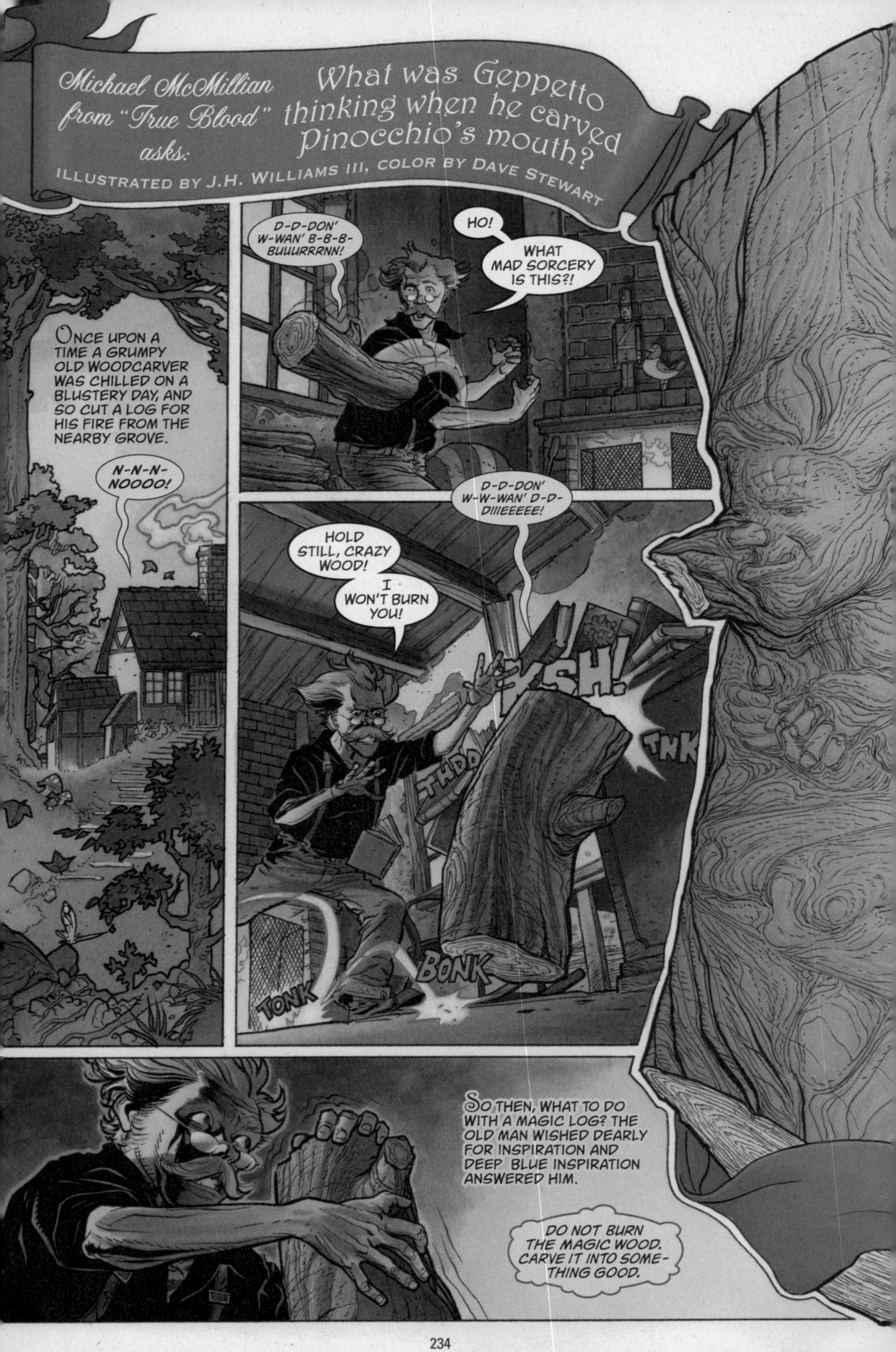
Michael McMillian from "True Blood" asks:
What was Geppetto thinking when he carved Pinocchio's mouth?
ILLUSTRATED BY J.H. WILLIAMS III, COLOR BY DAVE STEWART
ONCE UPON A TIME A GRUMPY OLD WOODCARVER WAS CHILLED ON A BLUSTERY DAY, AND SO CUT A LOG FOR HIS FIRE FROM THE NEARBY GROVE.
N-N-N-NOOOO!
D-D-DON' W-WAN' B-B-B-BUUURRRNN!
HO!
WHAT MAD SORCERY IS THIS?!
D-D-DON' W-W-WAN' D-D-DIIIEEEEE!
HOLD STILL, CRAZY WOOD!
I WON'T BURN YOU!
TNK
THDD
BONK
TONK
SO THEN, WHAT TO DO WITH A MAGIC LOG? THE OLD MAN WISHED DEARLY FOR INSPIRATION AND DEEP BLUE INSPIRATION ANSWERED HIM.
DO NOT BURN THE MAGIC WOOD. CARVE IT INTO SOME-THING GOOD.

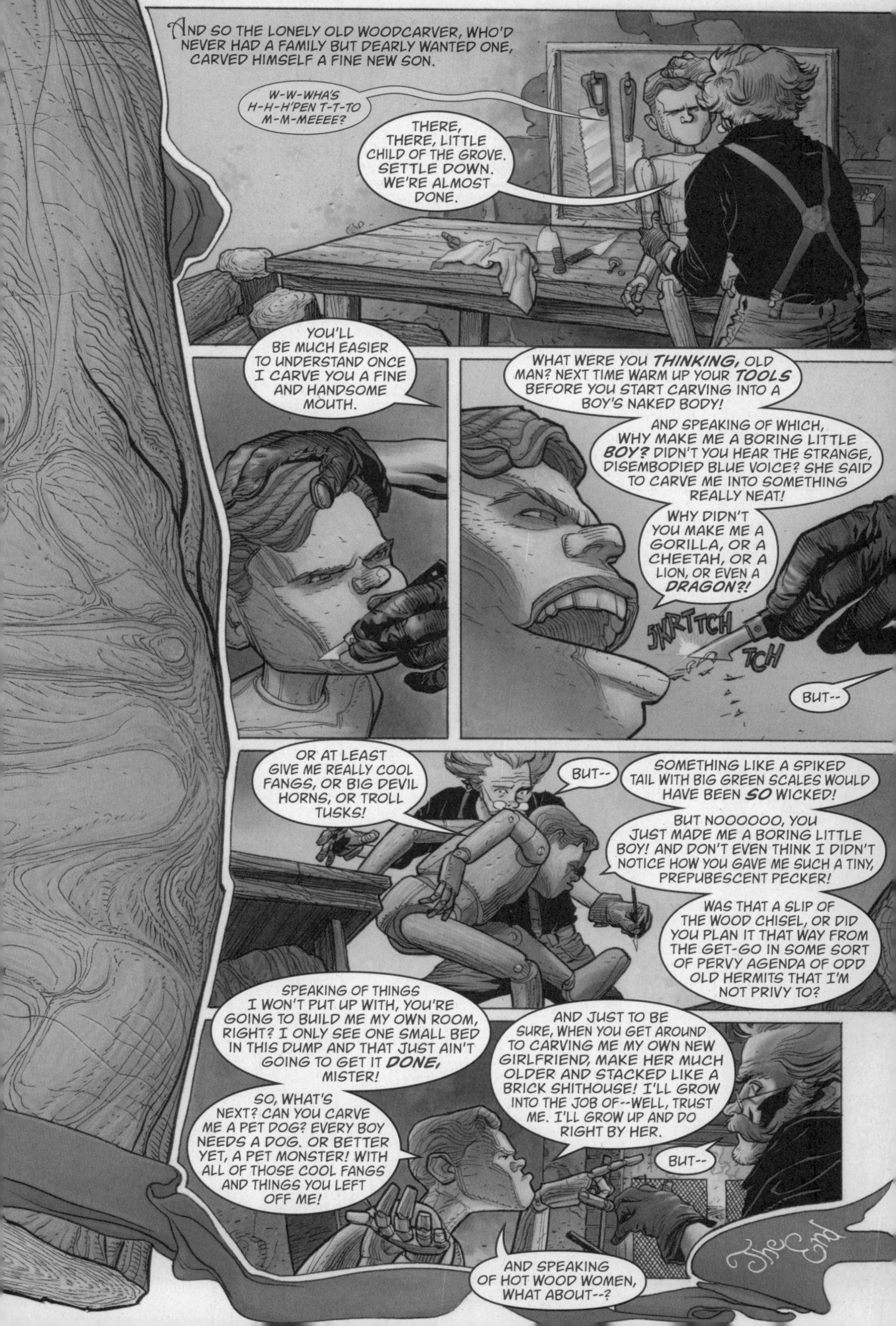
AND SO THE LONELY OLD WOODCARVER, WHO'D NEVER HAD A FAMILY BUT DEARLY WANTED ONE, CARVED HIMSELF A FINE NEW SON.
W-W-WHA'S H-H-H'PEN T-T-TO M-M-MEEEE?
THERE, THERE, LITTLE CHILD OF THE GROVE. SETTLE DOWN. WE'RE ALMOST DONE.
YOU'LL BE MUCH EASIER TO UNDERSTAND ONCE I CARVE YOU A FINE AND HANDSOME MOUTH.
WHAT WERE YOU THINKING, OLD MAN? NEXT TIME WARM UP YOUR TOOLS BEFORE YOU START CARVING INTO A BOY'S NAKED BODY!
AND SPEAKING OF WHICH, WHY MAKE ME A BORING LITTLE BOY? DIDN'T YOU HEAR THE STRANGE, DISEMBODIED BLUE VOICE? SHE SAID TO CARVE ME INTO SOMETHING REALLY NEAT!
WHY DIDN'T YOU MAKE ME A GORILLA, OR A CHEETAH, OR A LION, OR EVEN A DRAGON?!
SKRTTCH
TCH
BUT--
OR AT LEAST GIVE ME REALLY COOL FANGS, OR BIG DEVIL HORNS, OR TROLL TUSKS!
BUT--
SOMETHING LIKE A SPIKED TAIL WITH BIG GREEN SCALES WOULD HAVE BEEN SO WICKED!
BUT NOOOOOO, YOU JUST MADE ME A BORING LITTLE BOY! AND DON'T EVEN THINK I DIDN'T NOTICE HOW YOU GAVE ME SUCH A TINY, PREPUBESCENT PECKER!
WAS THAT A SLIP OF THE WOOD CHISEL, OR DID YOU PLAN IT THAT WAY FROM THE GET-GO IN SOME SORT OF PERVY AGENDA OF ODD OLD HERMITS THAT I'M NOT PRIVY TO?
SPEAKING OF THINGS I WON'T PUT UP WITH, YOU'RE GOING TO BUILD ME MY OWN ROOM, RIGHT? I ONLY SEE ONE SMALL BED IN THIS DUMP AND THAT JUST AIN'T GOING TO GET IT DONE, MISTER!
SO, WHAT'S NEXT? CAN YOU CARVE ME A PET DOG? EVERY BOY NEEDS A DOG. OR BETTER YET, A PET MONSTER! WITH ALL OF THOSE COOL FANGS AND THINGS YOU LEFT OFF ME!
AND JUST TO BE SURE, WHEN YOU GET AROUND TO CARVING ME MY OWN NEW GIRLFRIEND, MAKE HER MUCH OLDER AND STACKED LIKE A BRICK SHITHOUSE! I'LL GROW INTO THE JOB OF--WELL, TRUST ME. I'LL GROW UP AND DO RIGHT BY HER.
BUT--
AND SPEAKING OF HOT WOOD WOMEN, WHAT ABOUT--?
The End

THE FABLES PAPER PUPPET THEATRE

CONCEIVED, WRITTEN AND DRAWN BY
MARK BUCKINGHAM
WITH
DAN GREEN: INKS
LEE LOUGHRIDGE: COLORS
TODD KLEIN: LETTERS
ANGELA RUFINO: ASSOC. EDITOR
SHELLY BOND: EDITOR

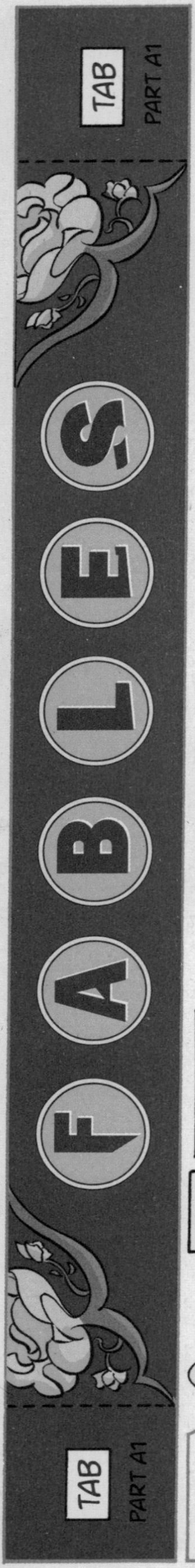
TAB
PART A1
FABLES
TAB
PART A1

REENACT YOUR FAVORITE STORIES OR CREATE BRAND NEW ONES WITH THE *FABLES PAPER PUPPET THEATRE.*

ASSEMBLY INSTRUCTIONS

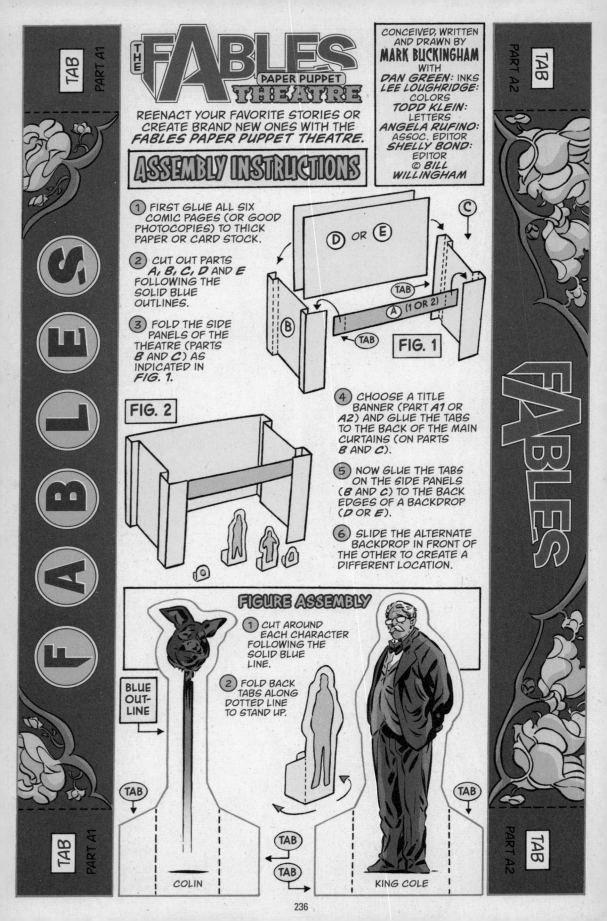

1. FIRST GLUE ALL SIX COMIC PAGES (OR GOOD PHOTOCOPIES) TO THICK PAPER OR CARD STOCK.
2. CUT OUT PARTS *A, B, C, D* AND *E* FOLLOWING THE SOLID BLUE OUTLINES.
3. FOLD THE SIDE PANELS OF THE THEATRE (PARTS *B* AND *C*) AS INDICATED IN *FIG. 1*.

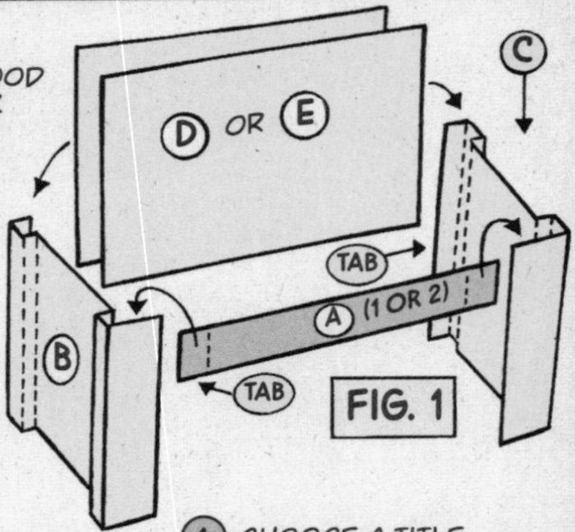
D OR E
C
TAB
A (1 OR 2)
B
TAB

FIG. 1

FIG. 2

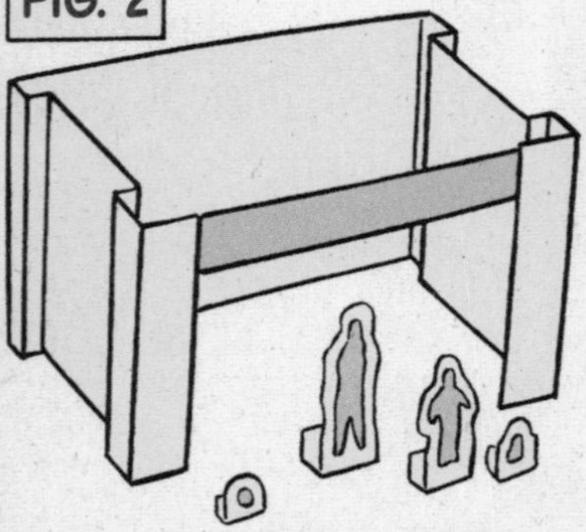

4. CHOOSE A TITLE BANNER (PART *A1* OR *A2*) AND GLUE THE TABS TO THE BACK OF THE MAIN CURTAINS (ON PARTS *B* AND *C*).
5. NOW GLUE THE TABS ON THE SIDE PANELS (*B* AND *C*) TO THE BACK EDGES OF A BACKDROP (*D* OR *E*).
6. SLIDE THE ALTERNATE BACKDROP IN FRONT OF THE OTHER TO CREATE A DIFFERENT LOCATION.

FIGURE ASSEMBLY

1. CUT AROUND EACH CHARACTER FOLLOWING THE SOLID BLUE LINE.
2. FOLD BACK TABS ALONG DOTTED LINE TO STAND UP.

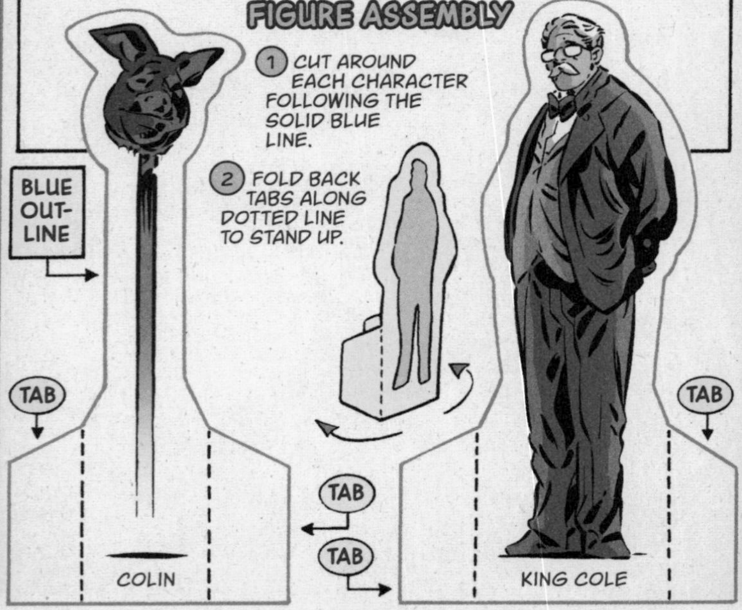
BLUE OUT-LINE
TAB
TAB
TAB
TAB
COLIN
KING COLE

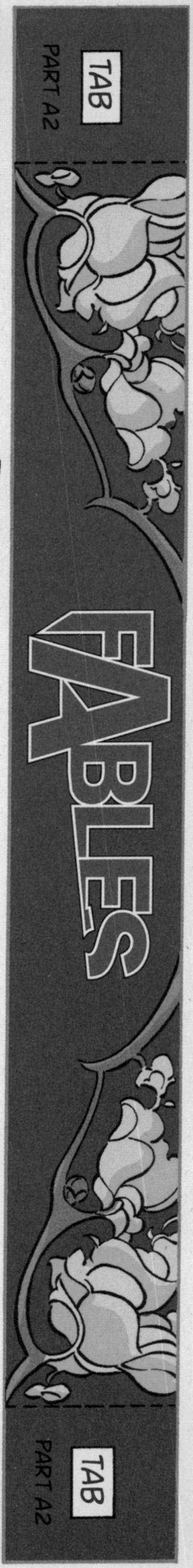
TAB
PART A2
FABLES
PART A2
TAB

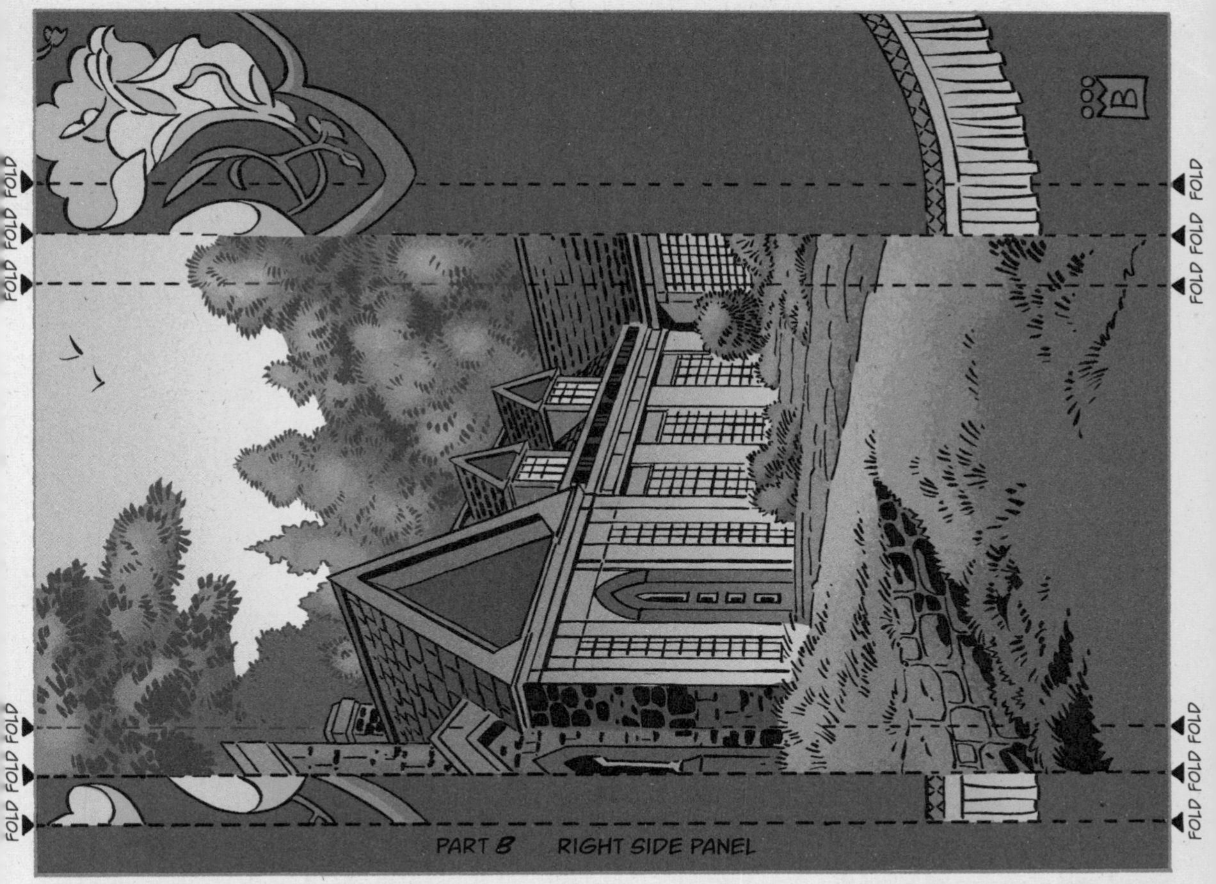
FOLD FOLD FOLD
FOLD FOLD FOLD
FOLD FOLD FOLD
FOLD FOLD FOLD
PART B RIGHT SIDE PANEL

PART C LEFT SIDE PANEL
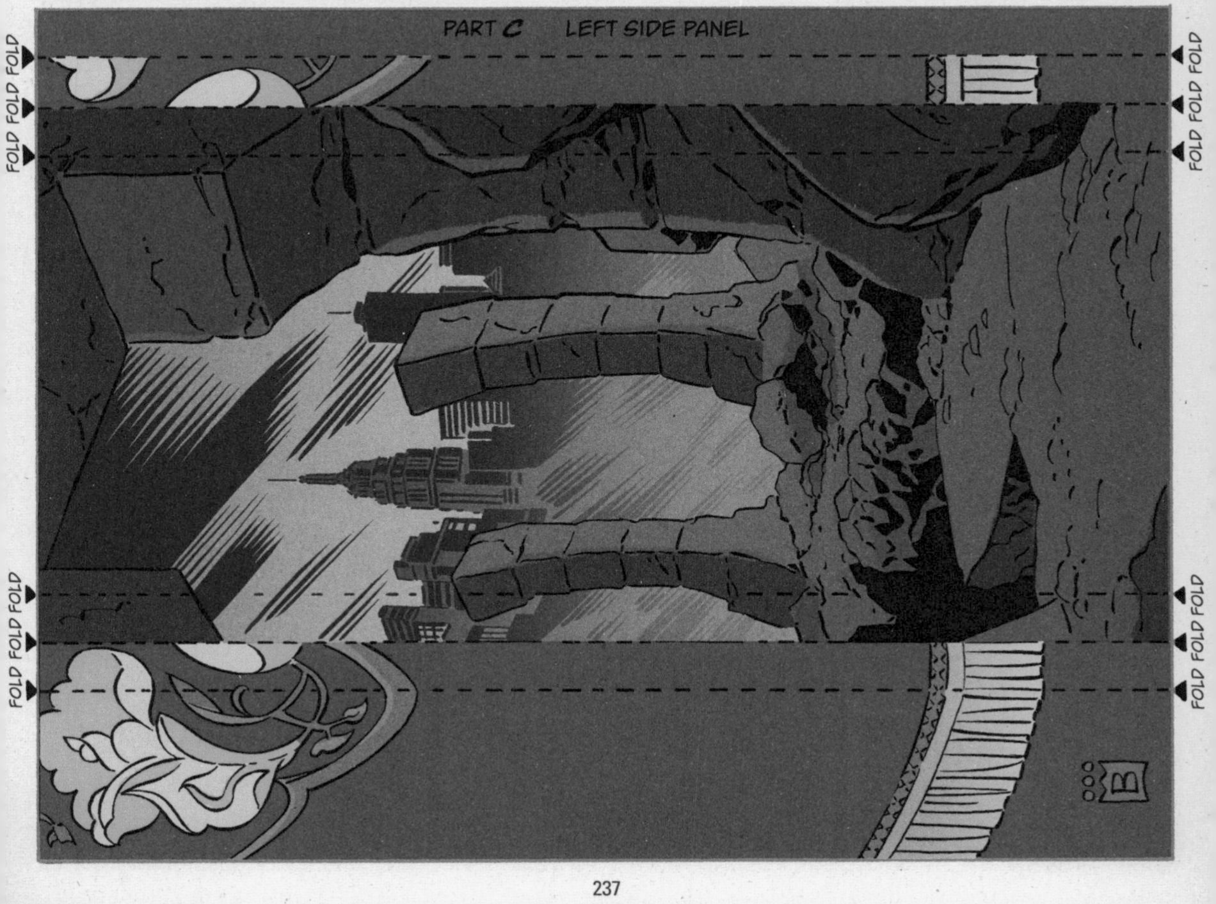
FOLD FOLD FOLD
FOLD FOLD FOLD
FOLD FOLD FOLD
FOLD FOLD FOLD

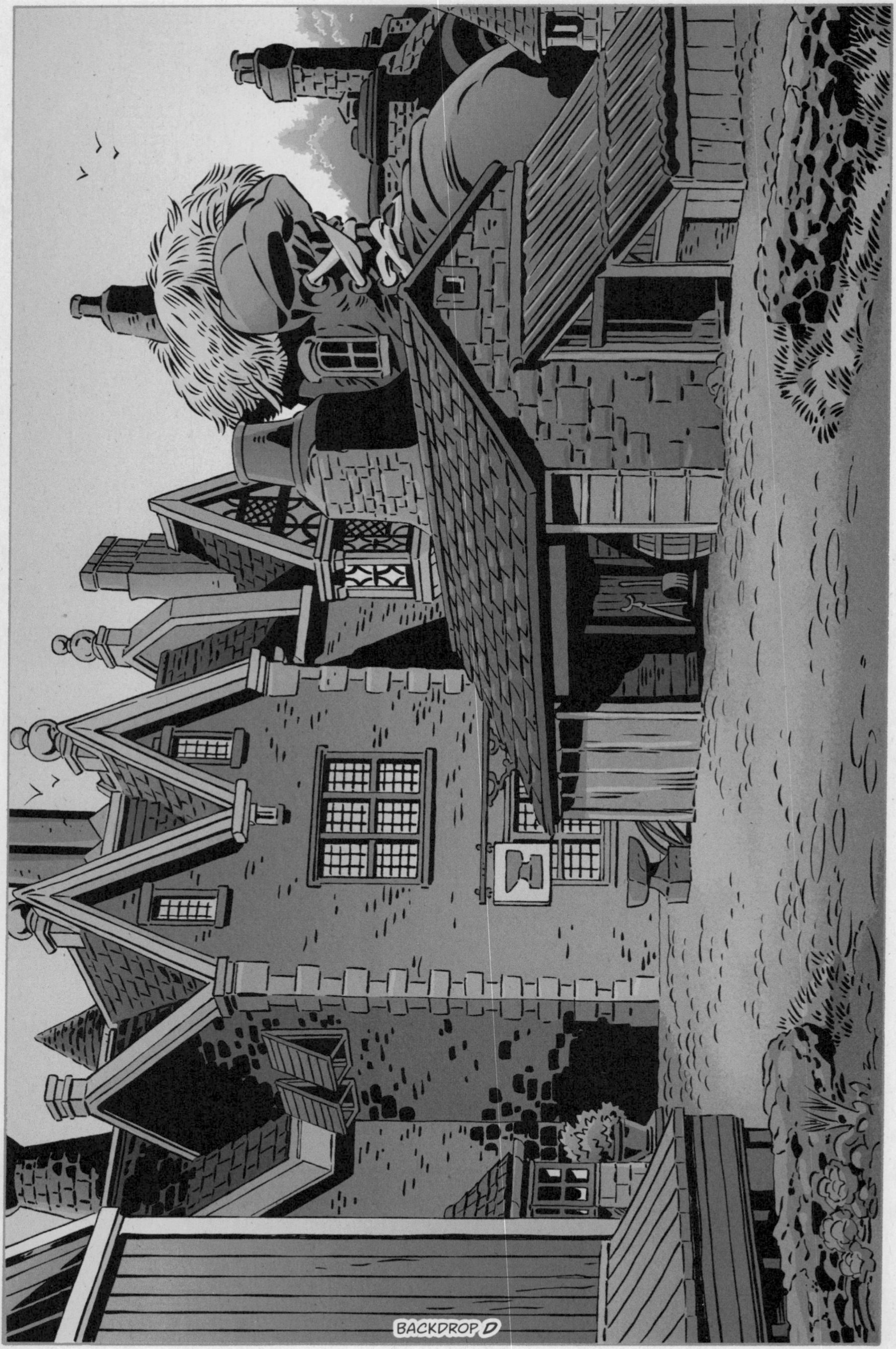
BACKDROP D

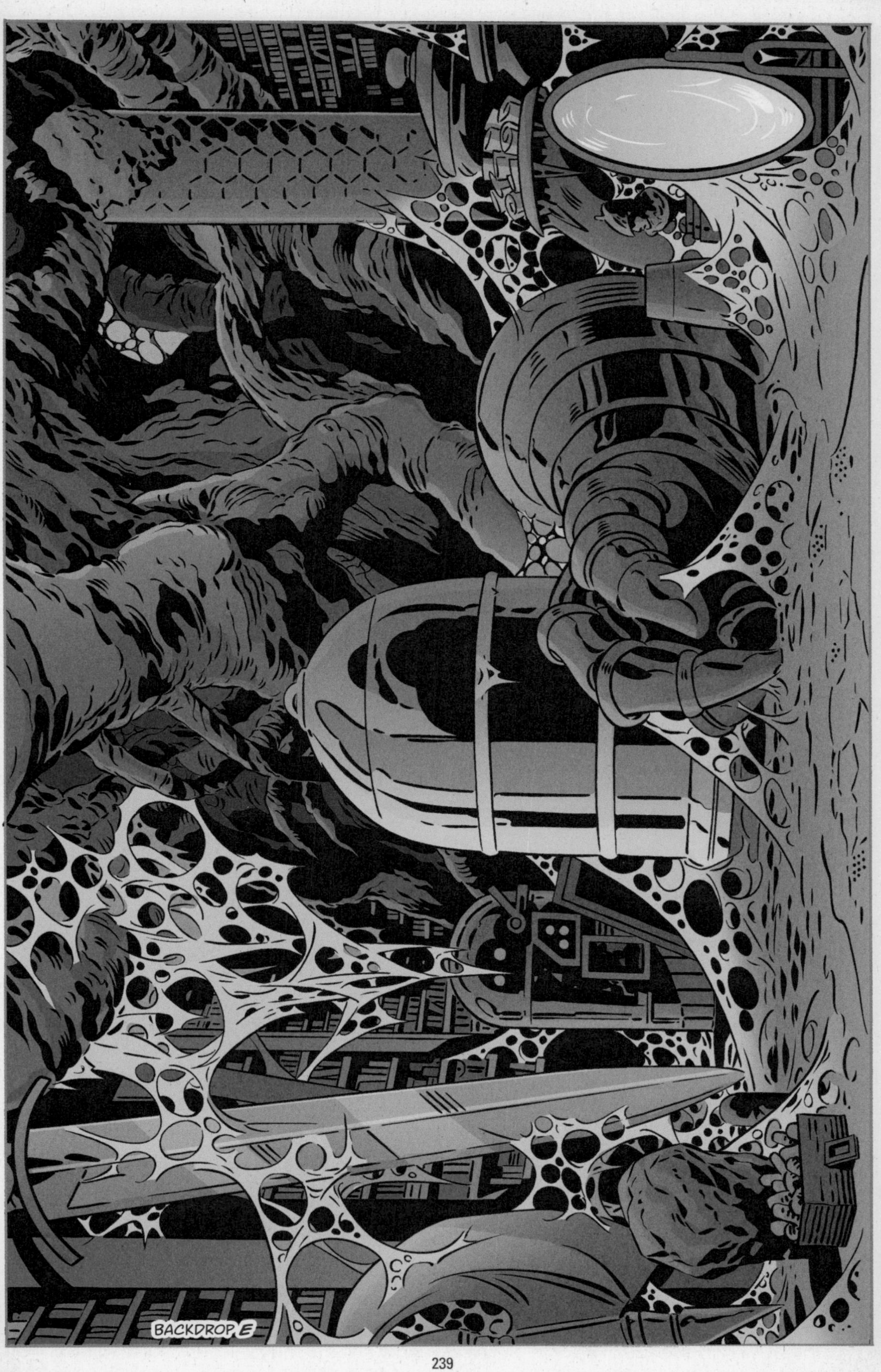
BACKDROP E

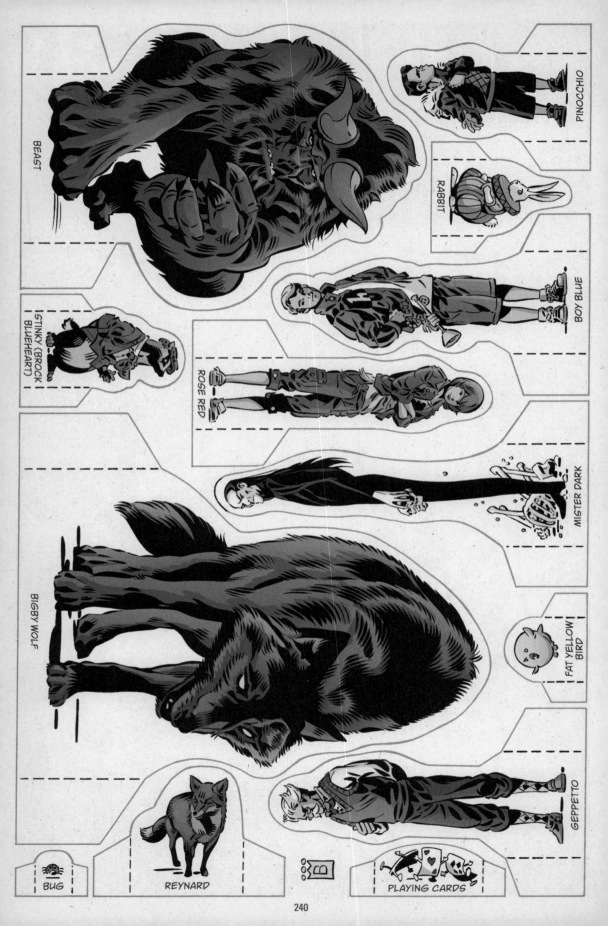

BEAST

PINOCCHIO

RABBIT

STINKY (BROCK BLUEHEART)

BOY BLUE

ROSE RED

MISTER DARK

BIGBY WOLF

FAT YELLOW BIRD

BUG

REYNARD

PLAYING CARDS

GEPPETTO

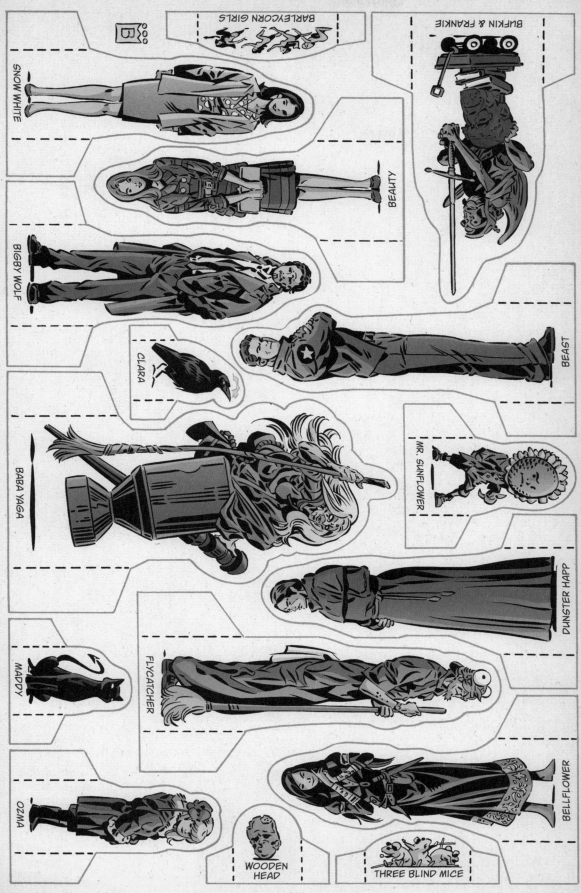

SNOW WHITE

BARLEYCORN GIRLS

BUFKIN & FRANKIE

BEAUTY

BIGBY WOLF

BEAST

CLARA

MR. SUNFLOWER

BABA YAGA

DUNSTER HAPP

MADDY

FLYCATCHER

BELLFLOWER

OZMA

WOODEN HEAD

THREE BLIND MICE

241

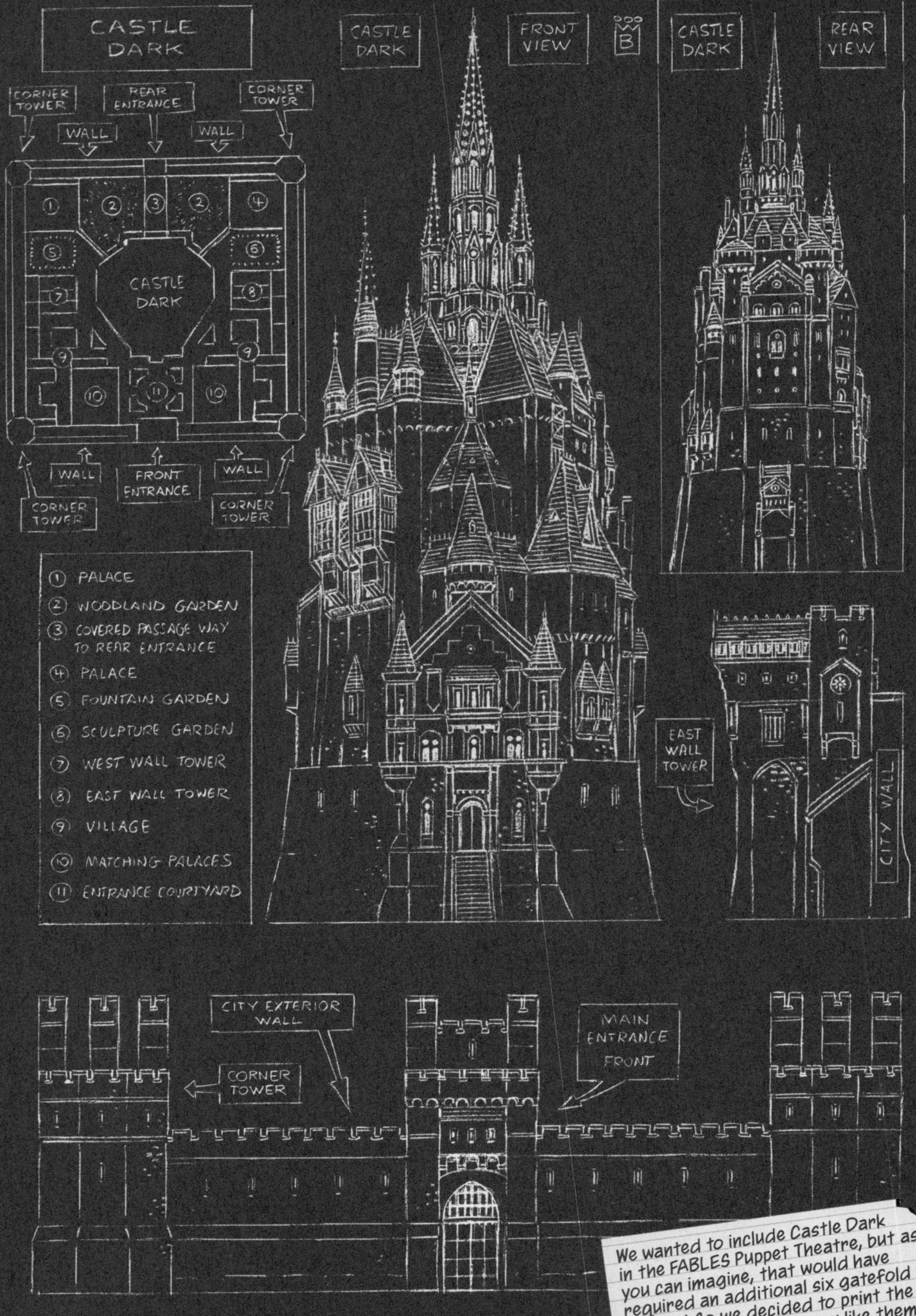
CASTLE DARK
CORNER TOWER
REAR ENTRANCE
CORNER TOWER
WALL
WALL
CASTLE DARK
WALL
FRONT ENTRANCE
WALL
CORNER TOWER
CORNER TOWER
① PALACE
② WOODLAND GARDEN
③ COVERED PASSAGE WAY TO REAR ENTRANCE
④ PALACE
⑤ FOUNTAIN GARDEN
⑥ SCULPTURE GARDEN
⑦ WEST WALL TOWER
⑧ EAST WALL TOWER
⑨ VILLAGE
⑩ MATCHING PALACES
⑪ ENTRANCE COURTYARD
CASTLE DARK
FRONT VIEW
B
CASTLE DARK
REAR VIEW
EAST WALL TOWER
CITY WALL
CITY EXTERIOR WALL
CORNER TOWER
MAIN ENTRANCE FRONT

We wanted to include Castle Dark in the FABLES Puppet Theatre, but as you can imagine, that would have required an additional six gatefold inserts! So we decided to print the designs instead. Hope you like them.
— Bucky

FABLES

ESCAPE TO WOLF MANOR
For two to ten players

Rules: Bill Willingham. Game Board Art: Mark Buckingham. Game Board Lettering: Todd Klein.

Oh no! Not only did the duel to kill Mister Dark fail, but now he knows the way to The Farm. He and his army of witherlings may be on the way here right now! You, along with all the rest of the Farm Fables, have to evacuate to the Kingdom of Haven right away! You need to escape to Wolf Manor where King Flycatcher is waiting to transport you to safety. But be careful! Your opponents might be some of Mister Dark's witherlings in disguise! You need to get to Wolf Manor before they do!

The Objective: To win the game, all you have to do is be the first player to make it safely to Wolf Manor.

The Rules

1) Each player takes turns rolling one six-sided die. Then you advance that many spaces on the game board.

2) If you land on a shortcut space, which are the spaces with the arrows, you can choose, if you want, to take that shortcut. But you must land on the space to have this option. You might try to take one of these shortcuts, through the haunted woods, or across the bridge over the river, or through the hidden pass through the hills, but beware of the dangers lurking near these places.

3) There are three DEADLY SPACES on the board. They're marked with the skulls. In the first one you're attacked in the deep woods by Grandfather Oak. In the second you're ambushed by a horde of Mister Dark's witherlings. In the third you're caught in an avalanche in the hills surrounding Wolf Valley. In each case, if you land on one of these DEADLY SPACES you have to go back to the beginning and start over on your next turn.

4) There are six TREASURE BOX spaces on the board. If you land on one of them, roll the die once again and consult the following list of results:
   a) Roll die again and advance that many spaces.
   b) Roll die again and send any single opponent back that many spaces.
   c) Advance to share a space with any opponent who's ahead of you. If no opponent is currently ahead of you, you have to stay put.
   d) Roll the die twice on your next turn and advance the total number of spaces.
   e) Pick any single opponent and make him lose his next turn.
   f) Switch spaces with any one opponent. Note that your opponent will now be on your TREASURE BOX space, but he doesn't get to roll for rewards.

5) There are five Geppetto MISFORTUNE spaces. If you land on any of these, roll the die again and go back that many spaces.

6) There are six Emperor Puppet MISFORTUNE spaces. If you land on any of these, you lose your next turn.

That's it. You're nearly ready to play. We've provided the game board and the rules. You need to provide your own six-sided die and one player piece pawn for each player in the game. Use anything you like, but make sure they're items you can easily tell apart from each other.

If you want some fun, and funny, advanced rules for FABLES: ESCAPE TO WOLF MANOR, go to Graphic Content, the official Vertigo Blog at: vertigoblog.com where we've posted a few additions to the game.

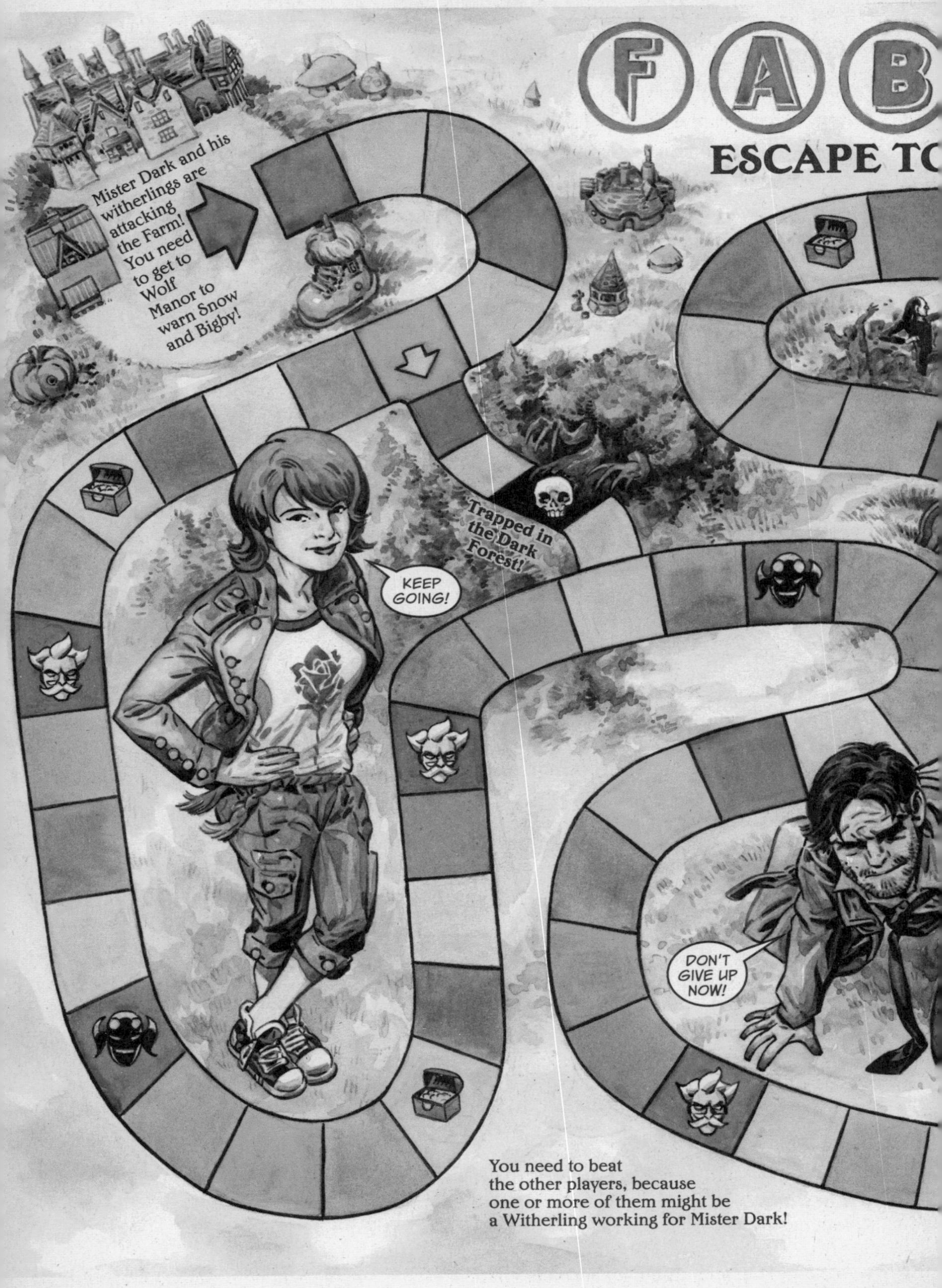

FAB
ESCAPE TO
Mister Dark and his witherlings are attacking the Farm! You need to get to Wolf Manor to warn Snow and Bigby!
Trapped in the Dark Forest!
KEEP GOING!
DON'T GIVE UP NOW!
You need to beat the other players, because one or more of them might be a Witherling working for Mister Dark!

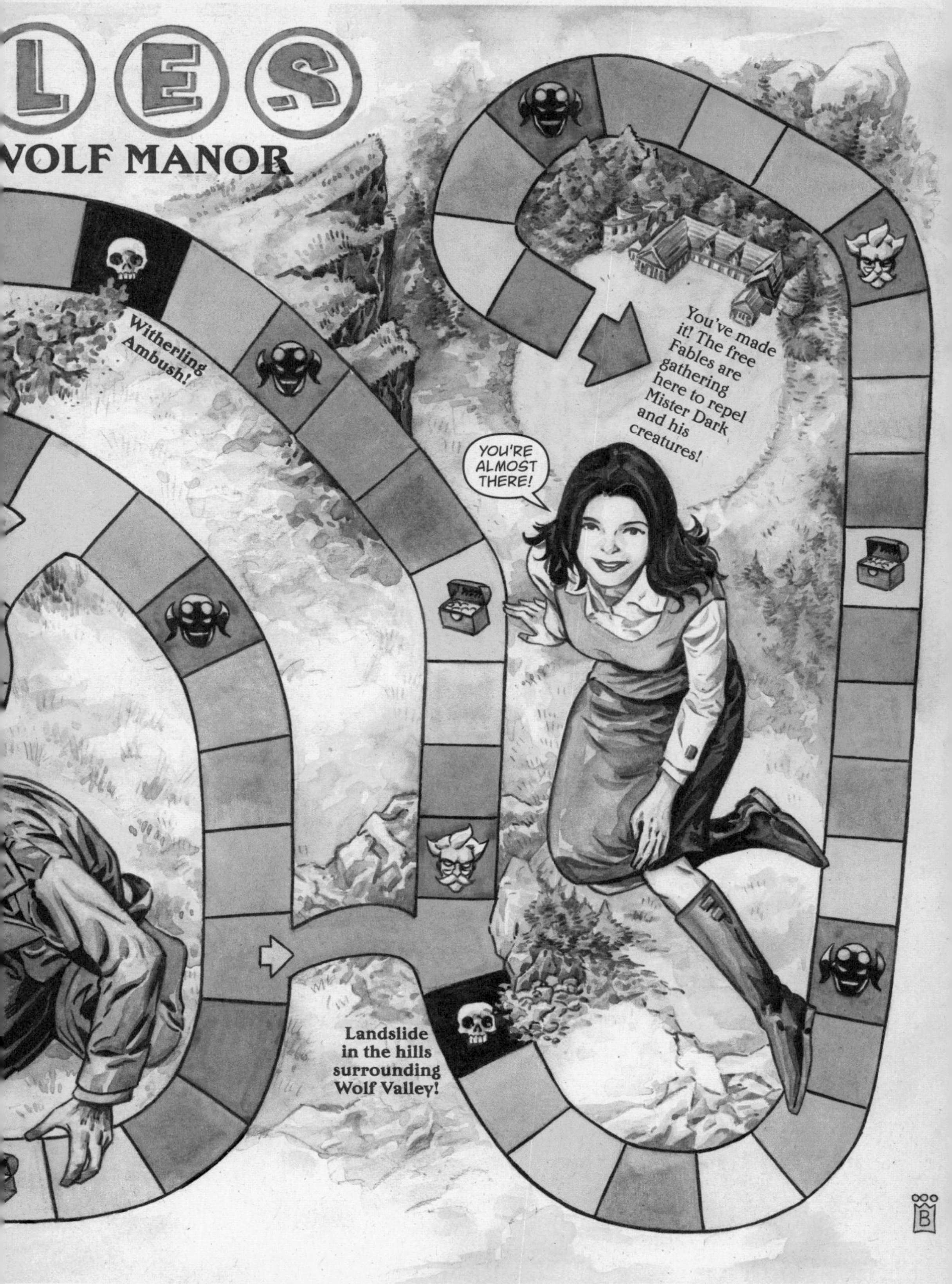

LES
WOLF MANOR
Witherling Ambush!
You've made it! The free Fables are gathering here to repel Mister Dark and his creatures!
YOU'RE ALMOST THERE!
Landslide in the hills surrounding Wolf Valley!

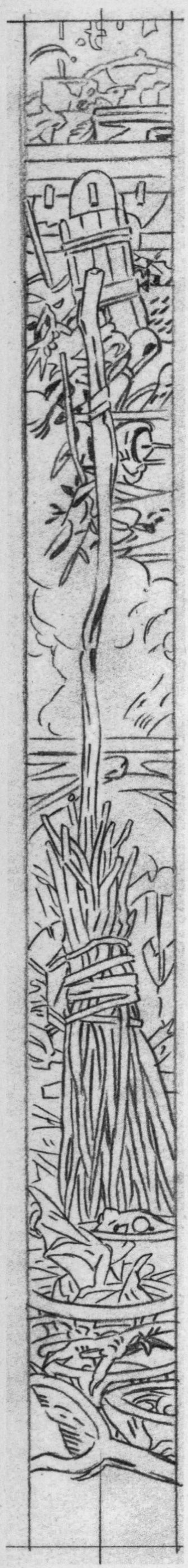

A Rose By Any Other Name

Designs and Sketches by Mark Buckingham

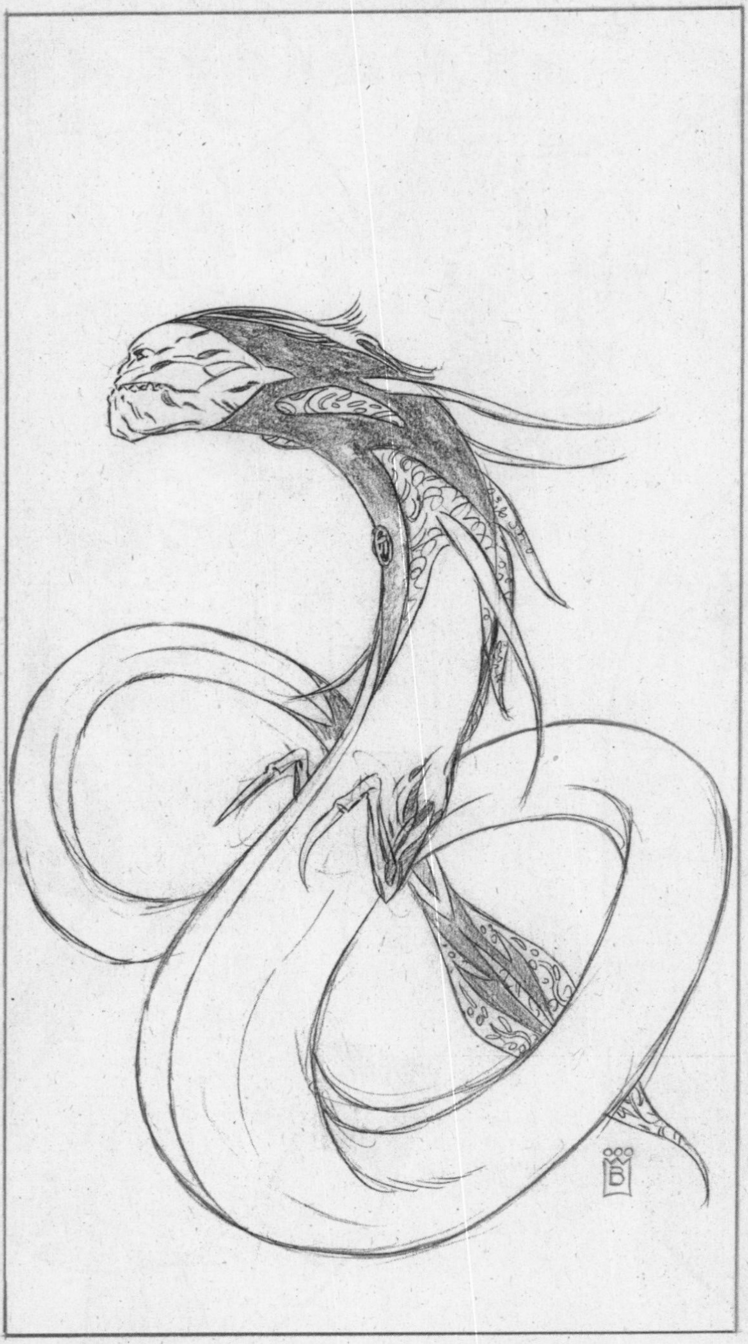

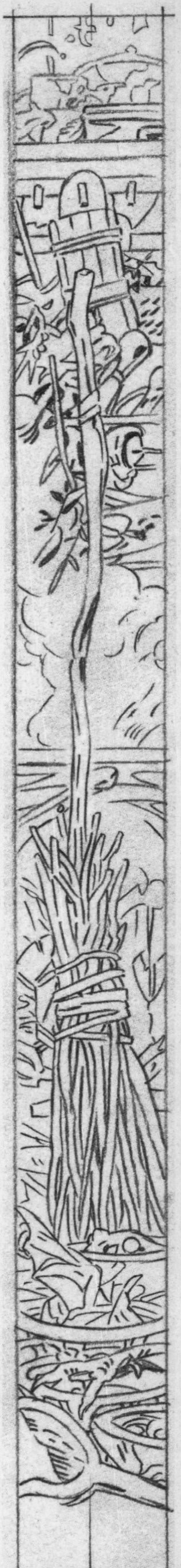

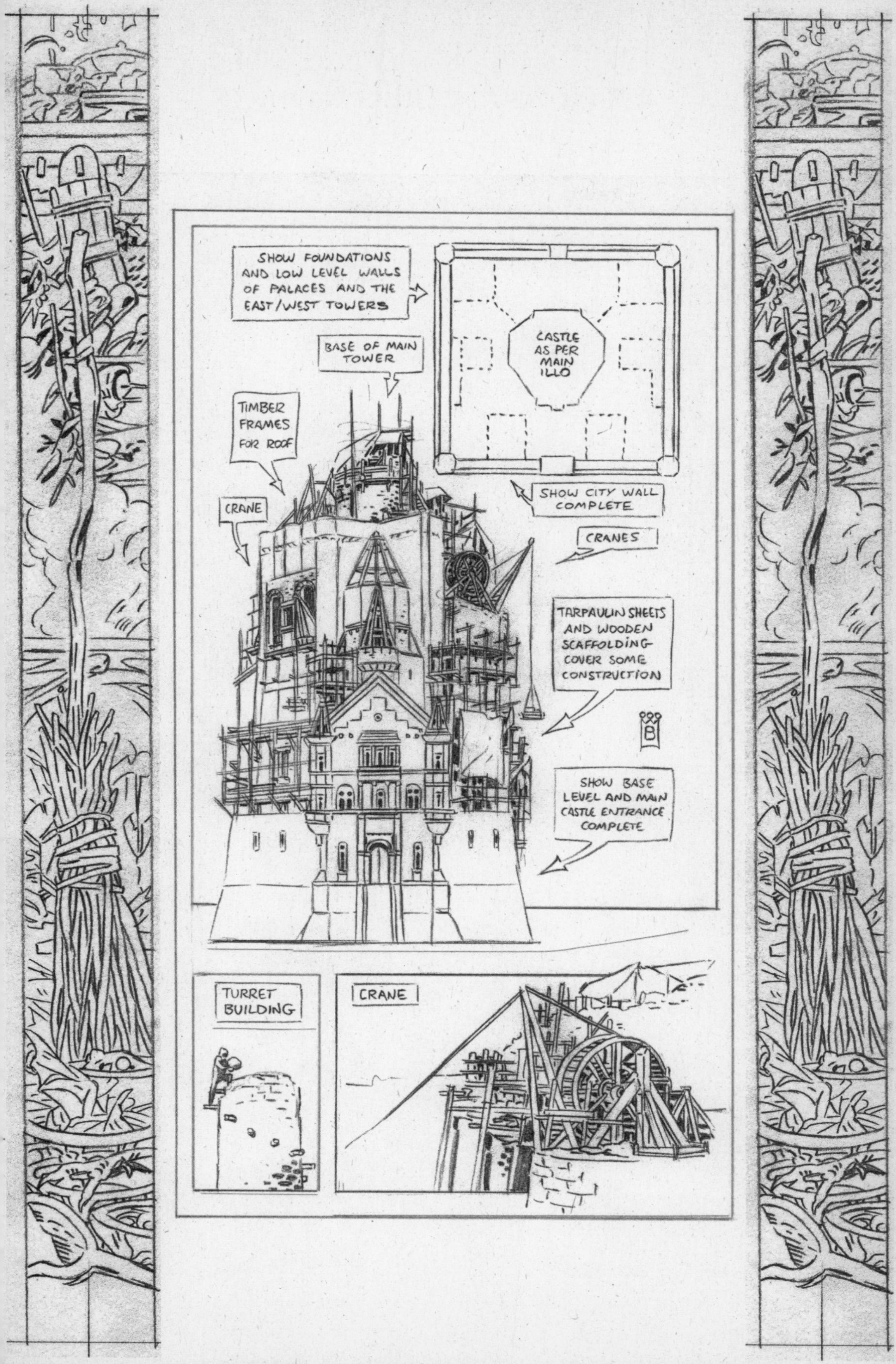
SHOW FOUNDATIONS AND LOW LEVEL WALLS OF PALACES AND THE EAST/WEST TOWERS
CASTLE AS PER MAIN ILLO
BASE OF MAIN TOWER
TIMBER FRAMES FOR ROOF
SHOW CITY WALL COMPLETE
CRANE
CRANES
TARPAULIN SHEETS AND WOODEN SCAFFOLDING COVER SOME CONSTRUCTION
B
SHOW BASE LEVEL AND MAIN CASTLE ENTRANCE COMPLETE
TURRET BUILDING
CRANE

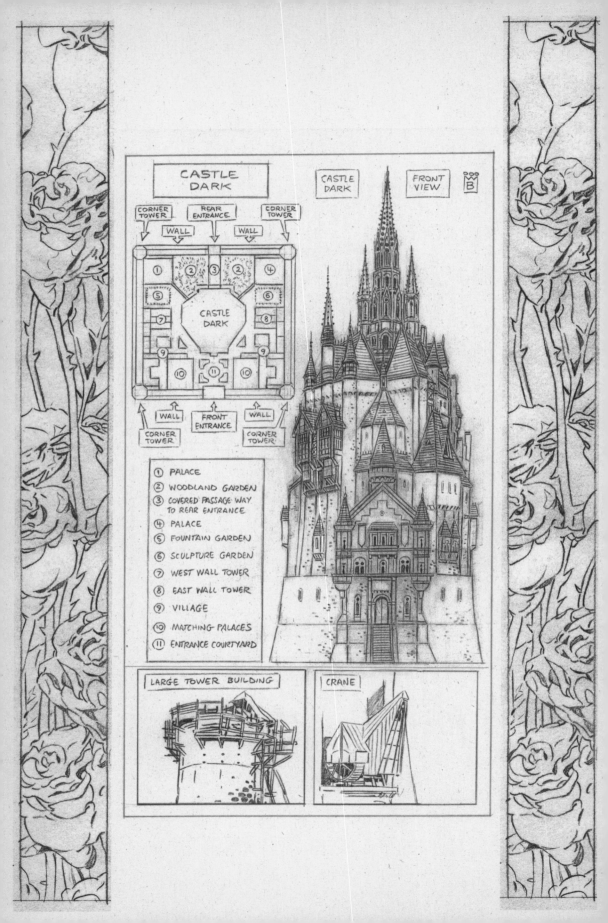

CASTLE
DARK

CASTLE
DARK

FRONT
VIEW

CORNER
TOWER

REAR
ENTRANCE

CORNER
TOWER

WALL

WALL

① ② ③ ② ④
⑤ ⑥
⑦ ⑧

CASTLE
DARK

⑨ ⑨
⑩ ⑪ ⑩

WALL

FRONT
ENTRANCE

WALL

CORNER
TOWER

CORNER
TOWER

① PALACE
② WOODLAND GARDEN
③ COVERED PASSAGE WAY
TO REAR ENTRANCE
④ PALACE
⑤ FOUNTAIN GARDEN
⑥ SCULPTURE GARDEN
⑦ WEST WALL TOWER
⑧ EAST WALL TOWER
⑨ VILLAGE
⑩ MATCHING PALACES
⑪ ENTRANCE COURTYARD

LARGE TOWER BUILDING

CRANE

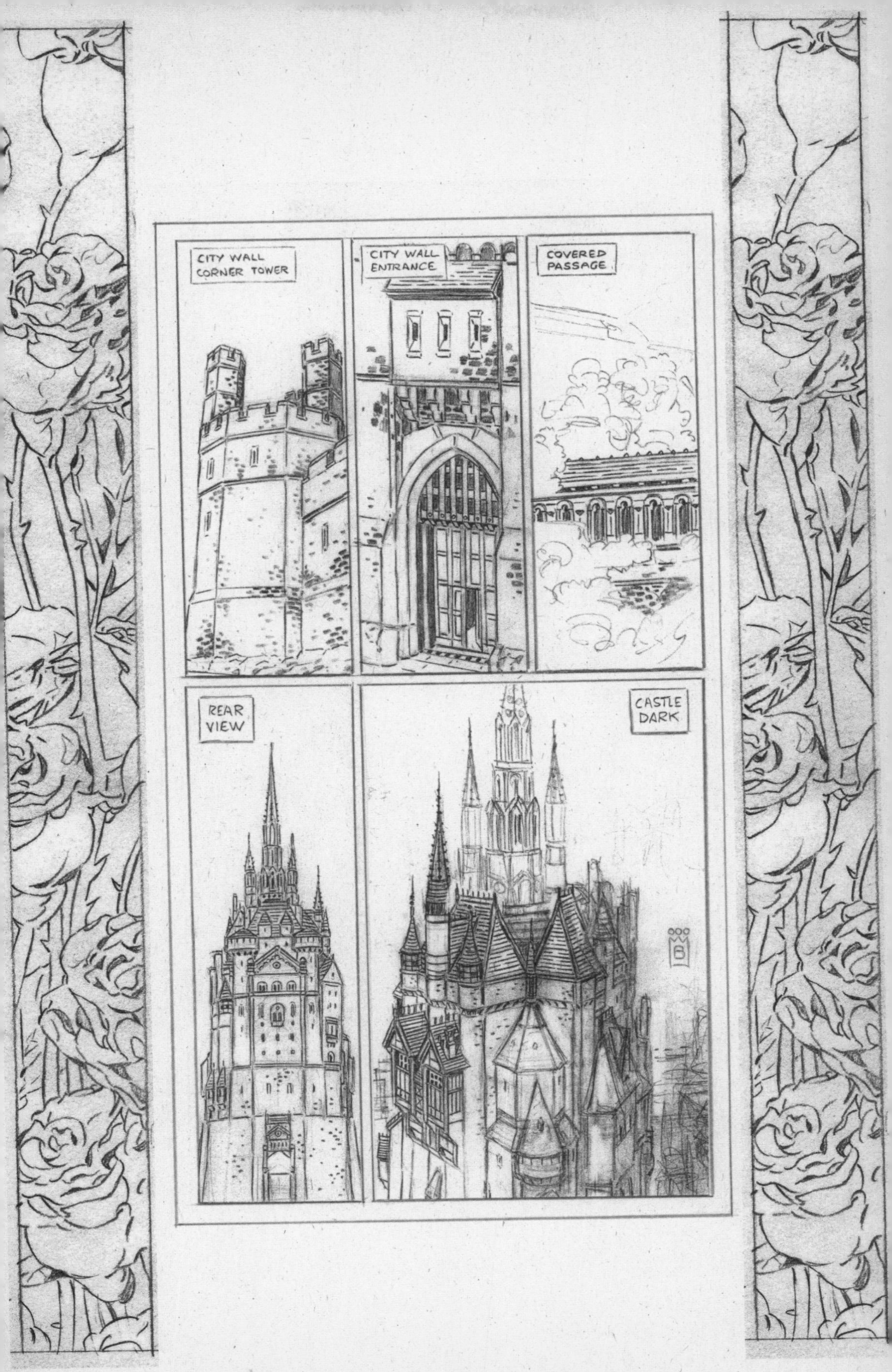

CITY WALL CORNER TOWER
CITY WALL ENTRANCE
COVERED PASSAGE
REAR VIEW
CASTLE DARK

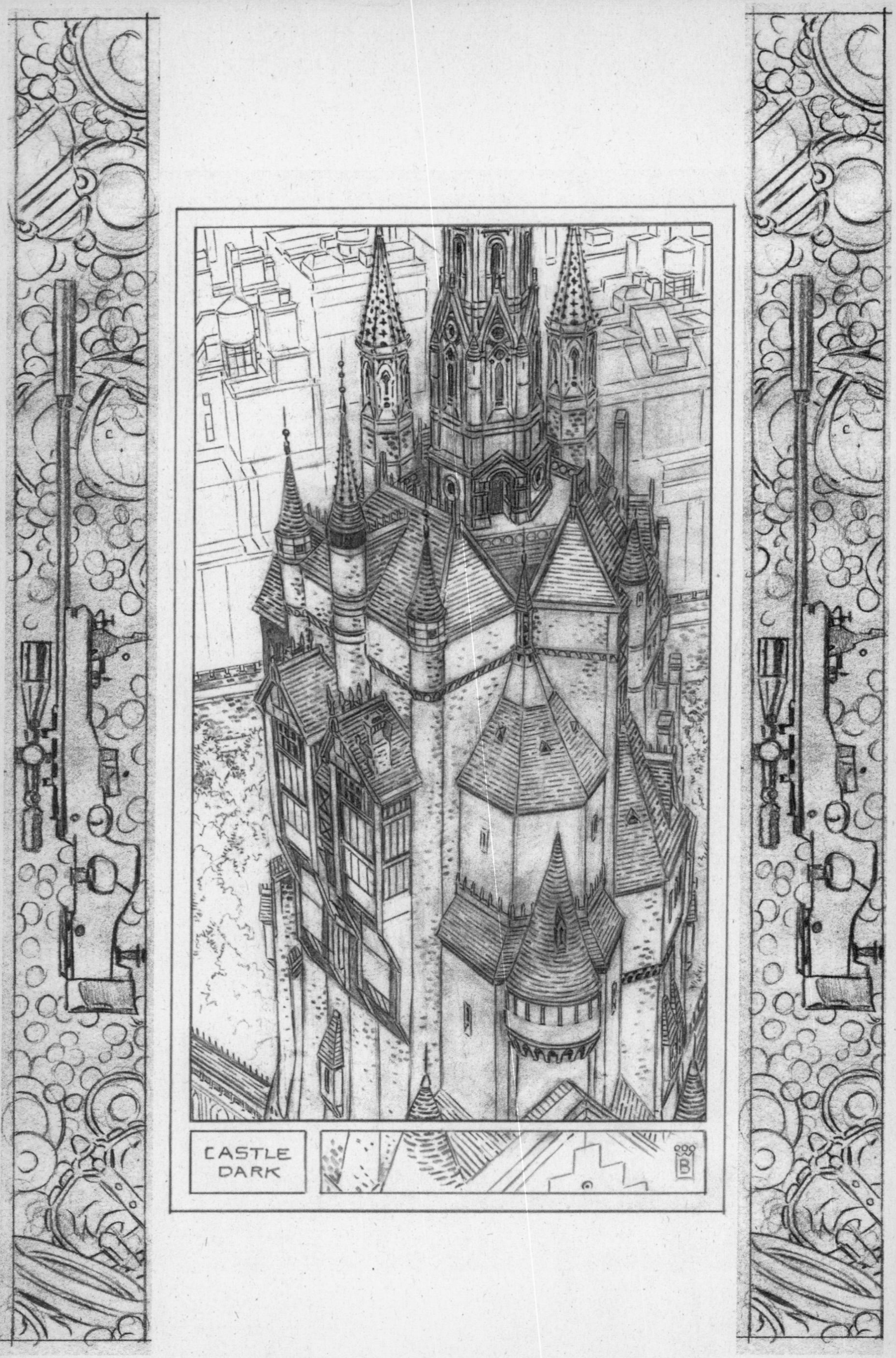
CASTLE
DARK

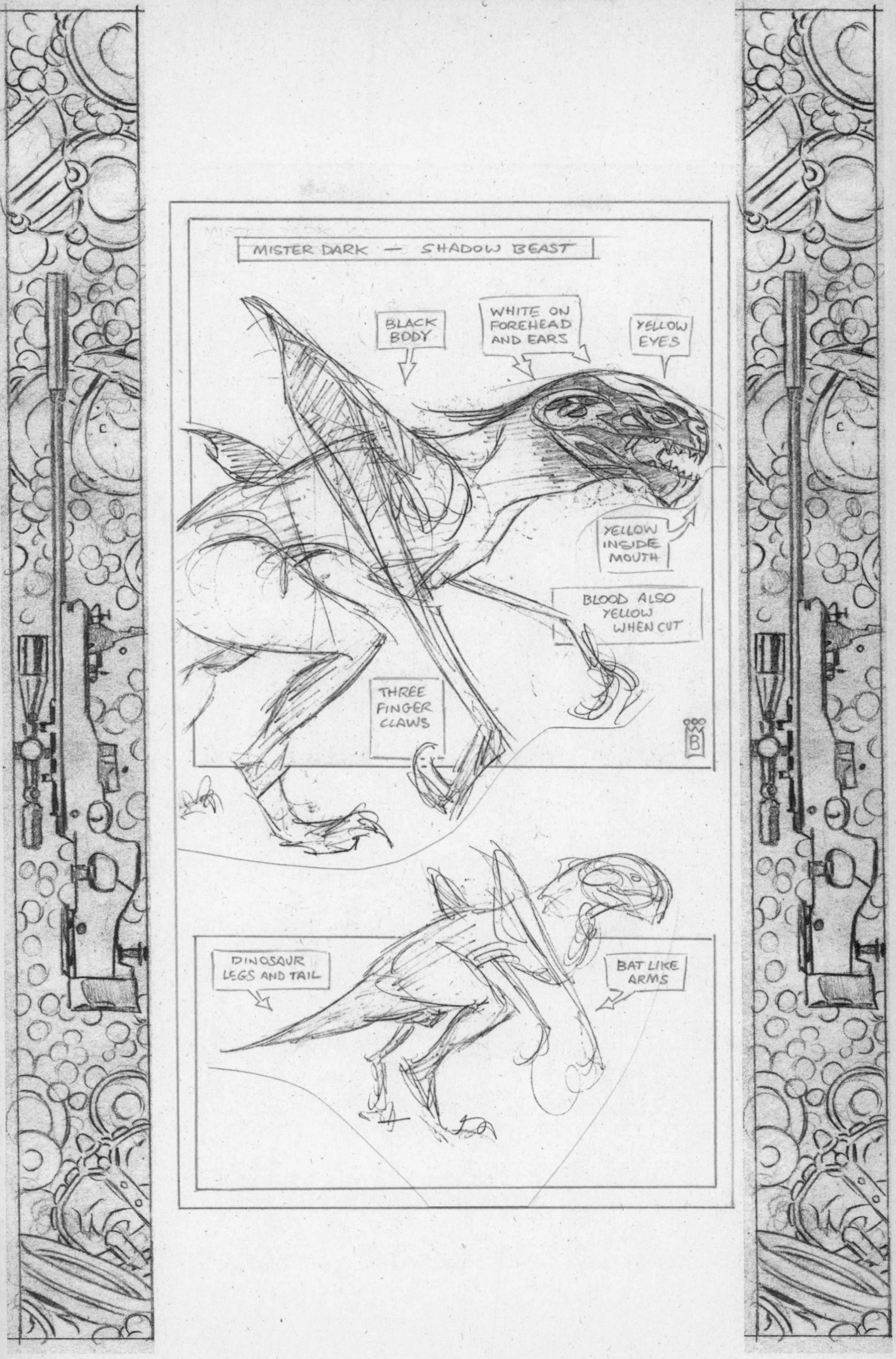

MISTER DARK — SHADOW BEAST
BLACK BODY
WHITE ON FOREHEAD AND EARS
YELLOW EYES
YELLOW INSIDE MOUTH
BLOOD ALSO YELLOW WHEN CUT
THREE FINGER CLAWS
DINOSAUR LEGS AND TAIL
BAT LIKE ARMS

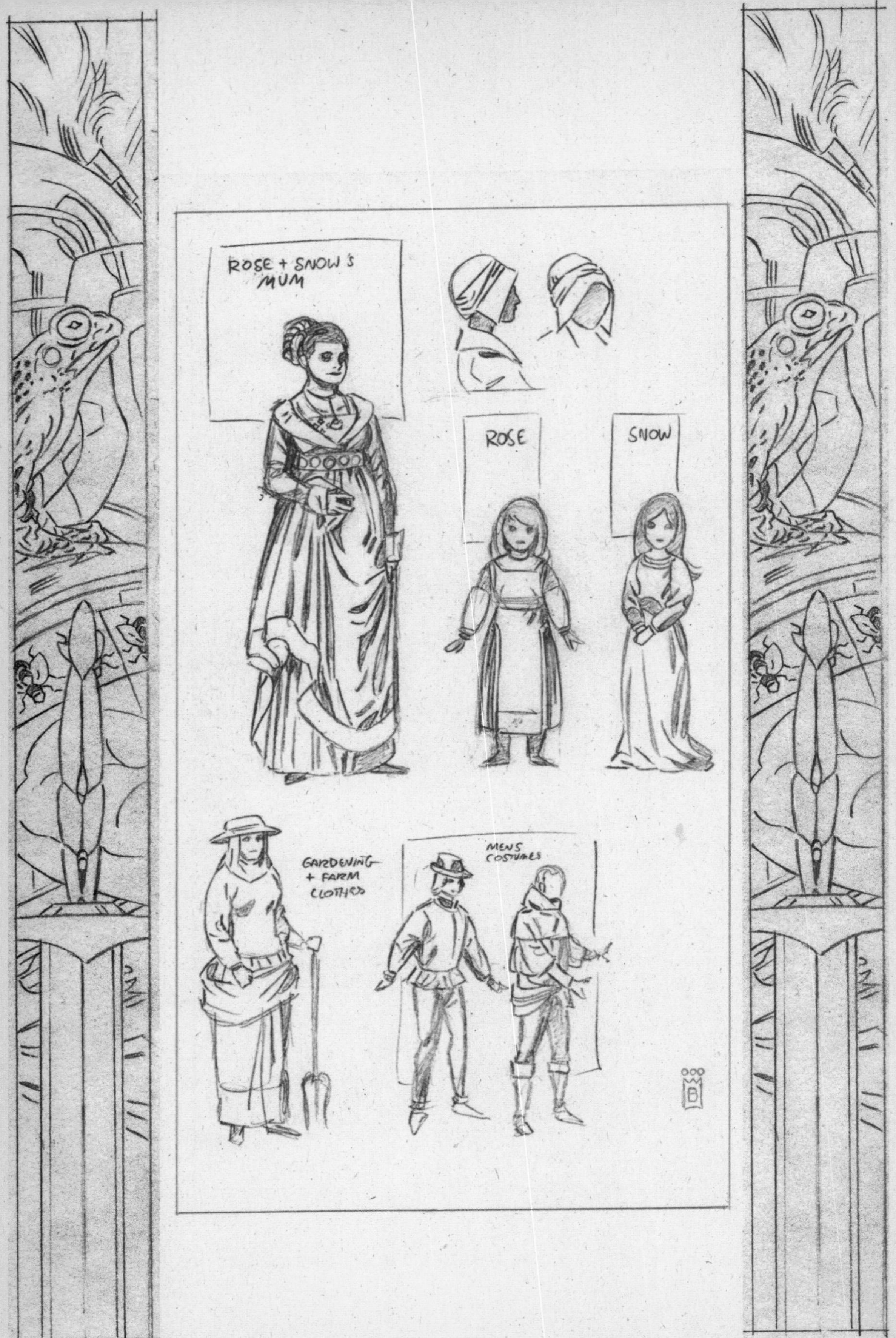
ROSE + SNOW'S MUM
ROSE
SNOW
GARDENING + FARM CLOTHES
MENS COSTUMES

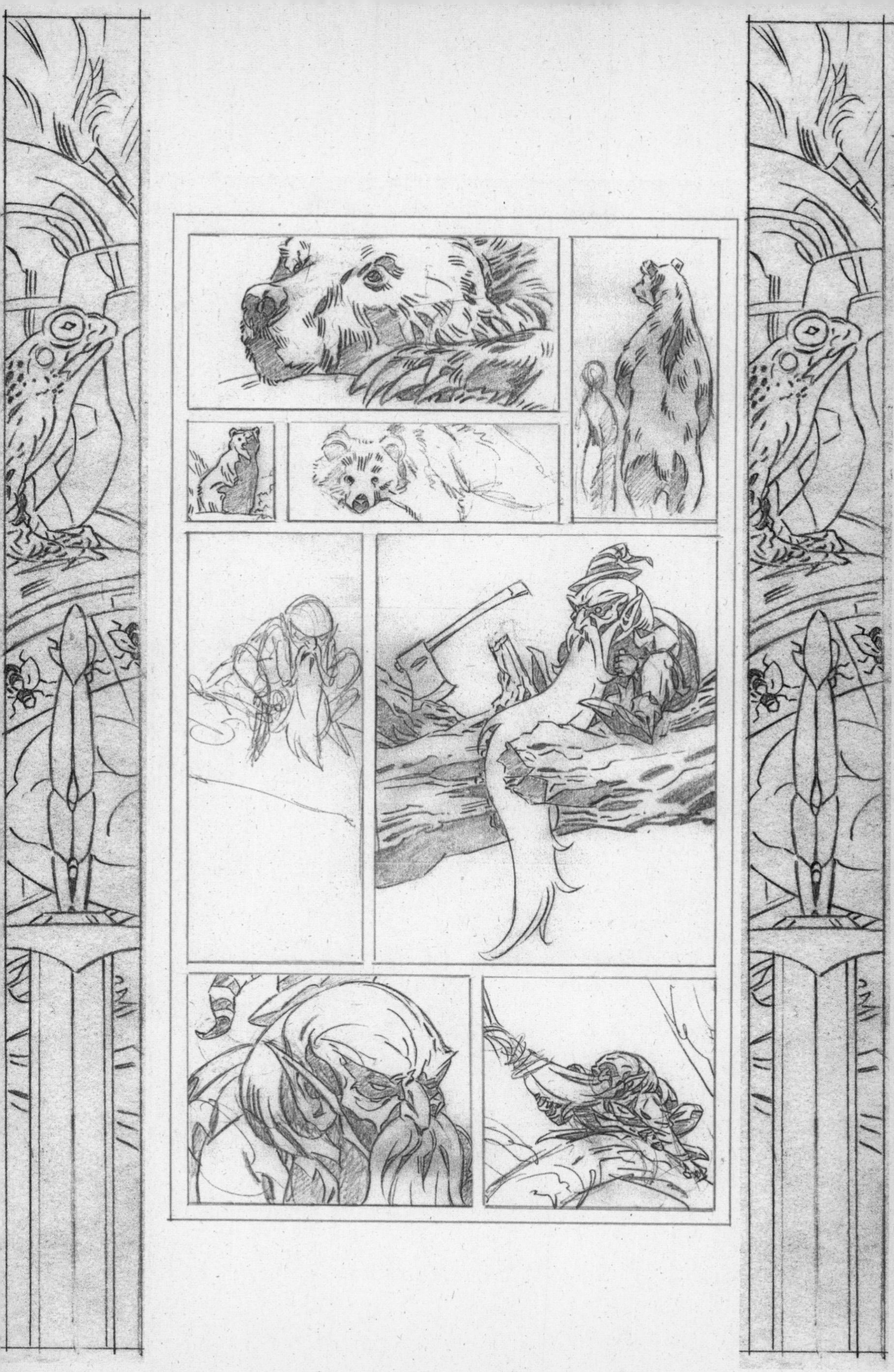

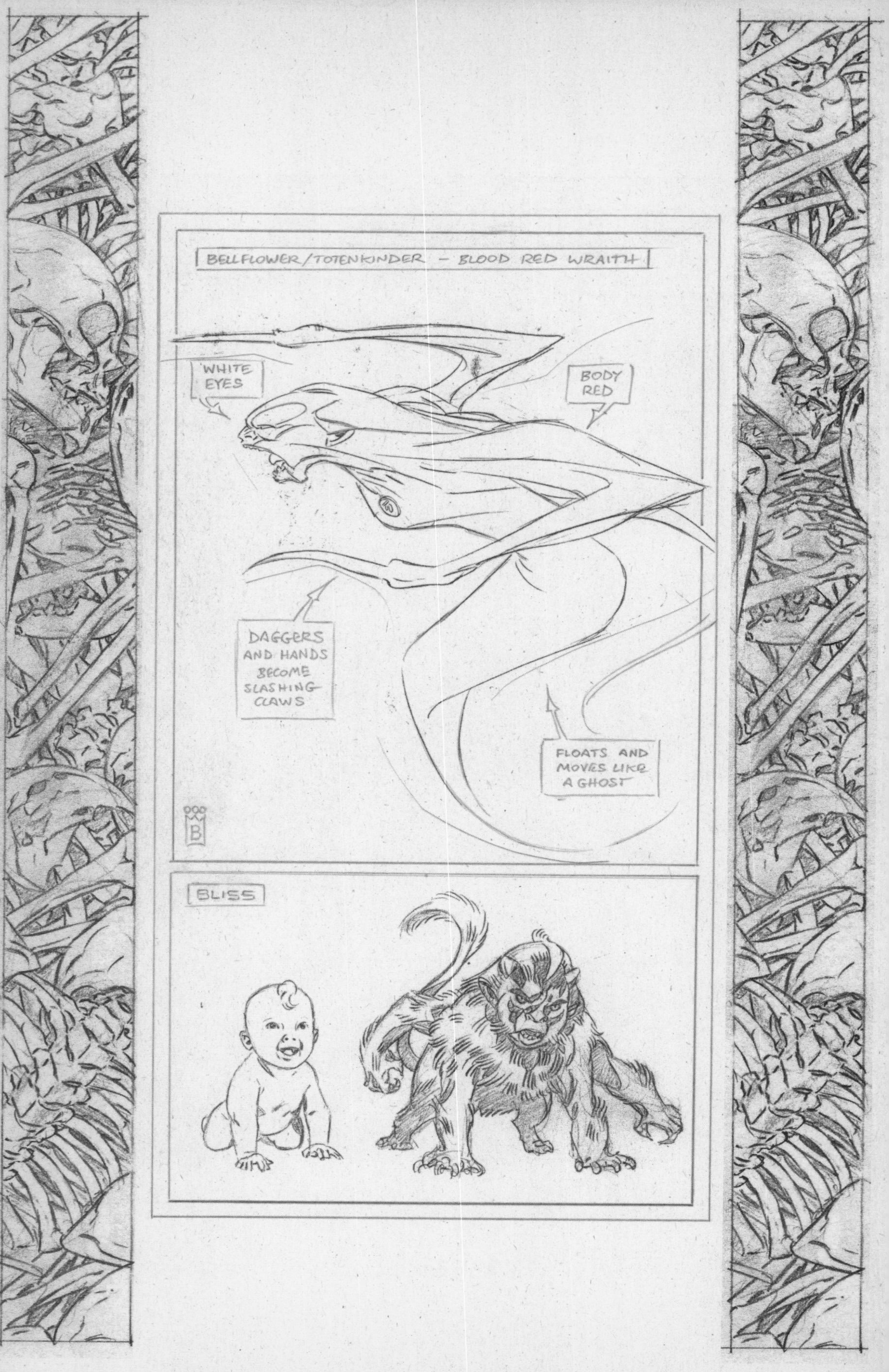
BELLFLOWER/TOTENKINDER – BLOOD RED WRAITH
WHITE EYES
BODY RED
DAGGERS AND HANDS BECOME SLASHING CLAWS
FLOATS AND MOVES LIKE A GHOST
BLISS